MED. LIT.

R.W. Collier,
Dept. of English Language,
Glasgow University.
July 1974

# A CATALOGUE OF PERSONS NAMED IN GERMAN HEROIC LITERATURE

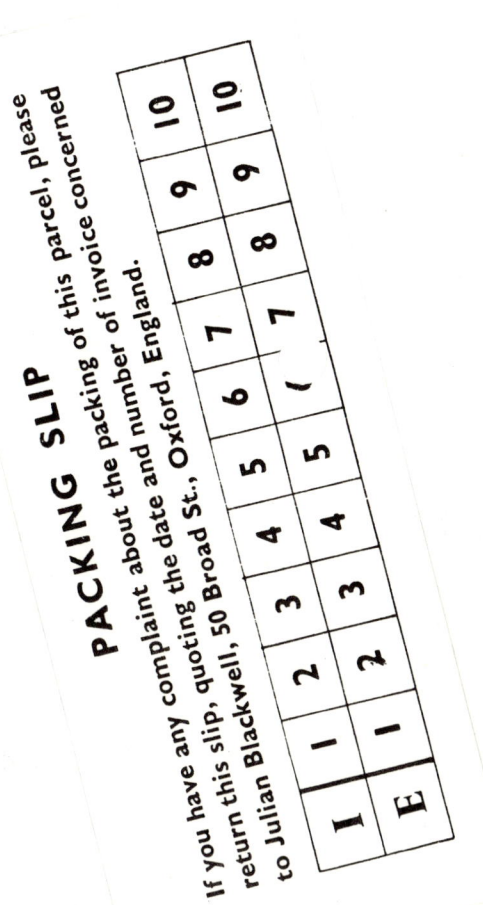

# A CATALOGUE
# OF PERSONS NAMED IN
# GERMAN HEROIC
# LITERATURE

## (700–1600)

### INCLUDING NAMED ANIMALS
### AND OBJECTS
### AND ETHNIC NAMES

BY

GEORGE T. GILLESPIE

OXFORD
AT THE CLARENDON PRESS
1973

Oxford University Press, Ely House, London W. 1

GLASGOW NEW YORK TORONTO MELBOURNE WELLINGTON
CAPE TOWN IBADAN NAIROBI DAR ES SALAAM LUSAKA ADDIS ABABA
DELHI BOMBAY CALCUTTA MADRAS KARACHI LAHORE DACCA
KUALA LUMPUR SINGAPORE HONG KONG TOKYO

© Oxford University Press 1973

*All rights reserved. No part of this publication may be reproduced, stored in a retrieval system, or transmitted, in any form or by any means, electronic, mechanical, photocopying, recording, or otherwise, without the prior permission of Oxford University Press*

Printed in Great Britain
at the University Press, Oxford
by Vivian Ridler
Printer to the University

TO
HERBERT APPELTSHAUSER

# ACKNOWLEDGEMENTS

THIS work has grown out of my studies for the doctor's degree of the University of London, and I am sad that Professor Frederick Norman, who encouraged me in this somewhat arduous task, did not live to see its completion, for it was by him that my interest in the field of Germanic and German heroic literature was kindled in my student days at King's College, London. I owe an even greater debt to my tutor at King's, Dr. H. H. K. Thoma, from whom I acquired what knowledge of Middle High German I may possess.

I wish to thank Mr. John L. Flood, also of King's, who devoted much time to reading this work at an earlier stage and prevented several errors, and Professor P. B. Salmon of the University of Edinburgh, who kindly put his Middle Dutch material at my disposal. My thanks are also due to my colleagues at University College, Cardiff, for much encouragement and many useful suggestions, especially to Mr. William B. Sullivan of the Department of French, who helped me with the Anglo-Norman *Romance of Horn*, and to Professor Henry Loyn of the Department of History for reading the manuscript. I am grateful to the staff of the library at University College, Cardiff, for their unfailing help and courtesy in obtaining the various books I required.

Through the patience of the Clarendon Press editorial staff and the helpful suggestions of its advisers the book has been greatly improved for the reader and the bibliography made more manageable.

My task would never have been completed without the constant encouragement and support of my wife, who has, indeed, shown the devotion of Kûdrûn.

G. T. G.

*Cardiff 1971*

## CONTENTS

GENERAL ABBREVIATIONS — xi

INTRODUCTION
§ 1. General Remarks — xiii
§ 2. Arrangement of the Catalogue — xiv

BIBLIOGRAPHY
§ 1. Survey of the Sources
    i. German — xv
    ii. Old English — xix
    iii. Scandinavian — xx
§ 2. The Sources — xxii
§ 3. Abbreviations — xxvi
§ 4. Books, Articles, and Editions — xxviii

THE CATALOGUE — 1

INDEX — 155

# GENERAL ABBREVIATIONS

For further abbreviations used throughout the Catalogue see the Introduction and the Bibliography, pp. xiv and xxii–xxviii.

| | |
|---|---|
| ch.d.g. | *chanson*(s) *de geste* |
| Du | Dutch |
| f. | female |
| Gmc. | Germanic |
| Goth. | Gothic |
| IE | Indo-European |
| Lat. | Latin |
| Lb | Langobardic |
| LFr | Low Franconian |
| LG | Low German |
| m. | male |
| MDu | Middle Dutch |
| ME | Middle English |
| MG | Middle German |
| MHG | Middle High German |
| MLat. | Medieval Latin |
| MLG | Middle Low German |
| NHG | New High German |
| OE | Old English |
| OFr | Old French |
| OFris. | Old Frisian |
| OHG | Old High German |
| ON | Old Norse |
| OS | Old Saxon |
| OSlav. | Old Slavonic |
| pl. | plural |
| pn | personal name(s) |
| ref | reference(s) |
| sg. | singular |
| Slav. | Slavonic |
| UG | Upper German |
| WFr | West Frankish |
| WGmc. | West Germanic |

# INTRODUCTION

## §1. GENERAL REMARKS

HEROIC literature derives largely from traditional native sources, in which history and myth have been blended and plots altered and expanded during centuries of oral transmission. The relative stability of role-names in this literature is the basis for the arrangement of this Catalogue, in which information about the characters in German heroic literature between c. 700 and 1600, as it has been preserved in manuscripts and prints, is set out under their names in alphabetical order. Additional information is also given from the English and Scandinavian analogues as well as from other European literatures (see p. xiv).

A modern reader cannot easily associate the role of a character in one epic with the activities of that character in other stories: he is, therefore, deprived of an extra dimension characteristic of oral tradition and frequently used by poets as an artistic device. This Catalogue is designed to fill the gap: the study of the available information about any given character in the epics reveals the interplay between the traditional knowledge of audiences and the imagination of individual poets and story-tellers over many generations.

The poems and prose works containing the information set out in the Catalogue have been edited on diverse principles during the past century and a half: thus some editors have based their editions on one manuscript or print, whilst others have produced reconstructed texts, in which the orthography is standardized and allegedly interpolated passages are excluded. Hence certain inconsistencies have been unavoidable: for instance, vowel-length signs are not usually shown in names deriving from the diplomatic editions of the Middle High German *König Rother* and *Dukus Horant* and the Old Norse *Þiðriks saga*; and both editions of the later *Wolfdietrich* epics are referred to, the first by Holtzmann (1865) and the second by Amelung and Jänicke (1871–3), since the former is comprehensive, though defective by modern standards, while the latter offers somewhat truncated texts (see p. xxvi).

This Catalogue is an onomasticon only in a restricted sense, for the names contained in it were used for a specific genre of literature. Reference is made to the records of these names in Continental Germanic and Old English contained in the standard onomastica, some of which are idiosyncratic or in need of revision; nevertheless, they remain the chief source of information about the occurrence and distribution of personal names, which can be supplemented or modified by the monographs on the subject appearing from time to time.

The occurrence of names in non-literary records, however, by no means proves the existence of a knowledge of heroic traditions at any given time or place, since most of these names were in common use; for this reason the

# INTRODUCTION

origin, etymology, and significance of a name are discussed only where this contributes to the understanding of a character and his or her roles in heroic literature.

Abbreviations for the sources, that is to say the German sources, on which the Catalogue is based, together with the primary Old English and Scandinavian sources, are set out in the Bibliography on pp. xxii–xxvi. Abbreviations for collections, works of reference, and periodicals will be found on pp. xxvi–xxviii. Section 4 of the Bibliography, pp. xxviii ff., comprises those works frequently referred to in the Catalogue, usually by the author's name alone or together with an easily identifiable short title. Full details are given in the Catalogue for all other works cited.

## §2. THE ARRANGEMENT OF THE CATALOGUE

The personal names are arranged alphabetically. They are given in Middle High German, except where the only record is in Old High German, Early New High German, or in a latinized form. Under each name the following information may be found:

(a) (i) An account of the activities of the character in German heroic literature. Entries are usually brief, being intended for reference rather than as synopses of plots. To avoid repetition, detailed cross-references are used.

(ii) References to the character in German heroic literature, for which the following abbreviations are used:
m first mentioned ⎫ only when unnamed or when the name appears
n first named ⎭ at a much later point in the text.
Note: Variants from edited texts are given in brackets; these are in italics where they represent the spellings of manuscripts or early prints. Where a text is based on a single manuscript this is referred to as 'MS.'; otherwise the appropriate sigla are employed.

(b) References in other German sources up to c. 1600.
(c) References in English, Scandinavian, and other European literatures, and in histories and chronicles of Late Antiquity and the Middle Ages.
(d) Records of the personal name.
(e) Historical information.

# BIBLIOGRAPHY

## §1. SURVEY OF THE SOURCES

(i) *German*

The names in the Catalogue are the personal names found in the German vernacular poems dealing with heroic material. The exceptions to this principle are discussed below: they are *Waltharius* (**W**) and *Ruodlieb* (**Ru**) in Latin hexameters, and *Das Volksbuch vom gehörnten Siegfried* (**gS**) and *Der Anhang des Heldenbuches* (**AHb**) in German prose.

Monuments of German heroic literature survive from the eighth to the fifteenth century in manuscript and from then on in print.[1] In the fifteenth and sixteenth centuries many of the poems were collected in the so-called 'Heldenbücher' (1472–1590).[2] A brief review of these sources reveals the vast gaps in the recorded German tradition, which can only be partly made good by reference to other literatures, to histories, and to chronicles.

The earliest recorded German heroic poem is *Das Hildebrandslied* (**äH**), which concerns the fight between a father and son; it was composed possibly as early as the seventh century, and derives ultimately from a lay transmitted from Langobardic Italy to Bavaria. The manuscript in which it has been preserved (*c.* 810) represents an attempt by an Upper German speaker, probably at Fulda, to transcribe it into Low German.[3] These sixty-eight lines are the sole remnant of heroic alliterative poetry preserved in German. *Das jüngere Hildebrandslied* (**jH**) on the same theme exists in numerous rhymed strophic versions dating from the fifteenth to the seventeenth century;[4] there are also Low German, Dutch, Yiddish, and Danish translations. Between *Das Hildebrandslied* (**äH**) and the written record of another undoubtedly heroic poem on a native theme in German there is a gap of about four centuries. The following two poems in Latin only partly fill the gap.

*Waltharius* (**W**) is in Latin hexameters, but its names and themes have secured it a place in German heroic literature.[5] Its date and authorship are

[1] K. C. King, 'The Early Printed Versions of Mediaeval German Heroic Literature', *Bulletin of the John Rylands Library*, XXXIX (1956), 97–131, and John L. Flood, 'Some Notes on German Heroic Poems in Print', *The Transactions of the Bibliographical Society* (Sept. 1967), 228–42.

[2] There are three 'Heldenbücher': *Das Dresdner Heldenbuch* (1472), copied by Kaspar von der Rhön of Münnerstadt for Duke Balthasar of Mecklenburg; *Das Straßburger Heldenbuch*, printed *c.* 1483, 1491, 1509, 1545, 1560, and 1590, also in manuscript *c.* 1480; *Das Ambraser Heldenbuch*, contained in a codex compiled between 1504 and 1515 by Hans Ried for the Emperor Maximilian.

[3] Schneider, *GHS* I. 58; de Boor, *GDL* I. 66 f.

[4] These probably derive from a 13th-cent. original: the *Þiðriks saga* (*c.* 1250–60) includes an episode based on it (Þs II. 345 ff.), and Wolfram von Eschenbach (*c.* 1210–20) refers to it (*Willehalm*, 439, 16).

[5] E. Schröder, *DNK* 88, considers that the names derive from a German poetic source. Topoi such as Mars for 'war', Bacchus for 'wine', Aeolus for 'wind', etc., have been omitted from the Catalogue.

still under discussion.[1] Dates between *c*. 880 and 990 have been put forward:[2] if one accepts the authorship of Eckehard I of St. Gall, the date of composition would be *c*. 930, his aged teacher Geraldus having dedicated the poem to Bishop Erckambald of Straßburg (965–93);[3] if the author is Geraldus, the composer of the Dedication, and the recipient of the Dedication Bishop Erckambald of Eichstätt (884–916), composition *c*. 880–90 must be assumed;[4] if the recipient is in this case Erckambald, Bishop of Straßburg, a date of composition between 965 and 990 may be assumed.[5] The poem describes the escape of hostages, Waltharius and Hiltgunt, from the land of the Huns and Waltharius's fight against the men of Guntharius. Only fragments of an Austrian epic on the same subject, *Walther und Hildegunde* (**WuH**), have survived; this dates from *c*. 1220.[6]

*Ruodlieb* (**Ru**), a romance in rhymed Latin hexameters, was written *c*. 1050 at Tegernsee.[7] It is fragmentary and is perhaps less justifiably included in heroic material, but Section XVIII includes an episode in which the hero encounters certain persons who feature elsewhere in heroic literature; their names have therefore been included in the Catalogue.

The first medieval epic in German based on native material is *König Rother* (**R**), written in a Middle Franconian dialect *c*. 1160.[8] Its theme is a bridal quest of the type found in similar 'Spielmannsepen'. The question as to whether the native material worked into this framework derives ultimately from Langobardic tradition or from contemporary events is still under discussion.[9]

The composition of *Das Nibelungenlied* (**N**) in the Austrian Danube region *c*. 1200,[10] with its various editions, represented today by texts A, B, and C, constitutes a major literary event of the Hohenstaufen epoch. This epic is concerned with Sîfrit's winning of Brünhilt for Gunther, Hagen's murder of Sîfrit, and the destruction of the Burgundians in the land of the Huns. Its strophic form, its heroic themes, its accommodation of those themes to contemporary problems, its remodelling of the material under the influence of the OFr *chansons de geste*, and its scenic technique give this epic a central position in any study of German heroic literature. It stimulated the creation of similar works which used variations of the Nibelungen-strophe to retell and remodel other themes from native heroic tradition. *Die Klage* (**Kl**), a commentary in

---

[1] O. Schumann, 'Waltharius-Literatur seit 1926', *AfdA* LXV (1951), 13–41, provides a useful survey of the literature. The most important articles to do with *Waltharius* research have been reprinted in *Waltharius und Walthersage*, hrsg. von E. E. Ploß (Hildesheim, 1969); see also Erckambaldus in the Catalogue.

[2] See Karl Langosch, 'Ekkehard I', *VfL* V (1955), 822 ff.; Wisniewski, *DHS* (1964), 133 f.

[3] Schneider, *GHS* I. 59; Karl Langosch, 'Der Verfasser des "Waltharius"', *ZfdPh* LXV (1940), 117–42.

[4] Karl Hauck, 'Das Walthariusepos des Bruders Gerald von Eichstätt', *GRM* XXXV (1954), 1–27.

[5] R. Reeh, 'Zur Frage nach dem Verfasser des Waltharilides', *ZfdPh* LI (1926), 413–31.

[6] Schneider, loc. cit.

[7] K. H. Halbach, 'Epik des Mittelalters', *Aufriß* II (1960²), 476.

[8] De Boor, *GDL* I. 255.

[9] W. J. Schröder, *Spielmannsepik* (Stuttgart, 1962), 24 ff.      [10] De Boor, *GDL* II. 157.

rhyming couplets on the events of *Das Nibelungenlied* (**N**), is preserved in all the main manuscripts of that epic; it was probably written soon after, certainly by 1230.[1]

Two poems in Middle Dutch have been included in the Catalogue: *Van Bere Wisselauwe* (**BW**), which probably originated in the thirteenth century,[2] recounts the activities of a bear among cooks, and contains certain names known to *Das Nibelungenlied* (**N**) and related poems;[3] *De vier heeren wenschen* (**Vhw**), a poem of the late fourteenth century,[4] in which four leading characters from *Das Nibelungenlied* (**N**), Gunther, Hagen, Gêrnôt, Rüedegêr, express the wishes they would like fulfilled if they could live for ever.

*Kudrun* (**Ku**), written in the Bavarian-Austrian region between 1230 and 1240,[5] is dependent formally on *Das Nibelungenlied* (**N**), but it deals with the bridal-quest and abduction themes of the 'Spielmannsepen', and in many respects it is close to the courtly romances;[6] the characters involved originate ultimately in the North Sea region. The only manuscript of this poem is contained in the codex of *Das Ambraser Heldenbuch*.[7] *Dukus Horant* (**DH**), a poem written in Hebrew characters in a Middle German dialect[8] and probably originating in the thirteenth century, is preserved in a codex dated 1382, which was discovered in the Cairo Genizah; it is apparently a conflation of bridal-quest themes from *Kudrun* (**Ku**) and *König Rother* (**R**); persons from both these epics appear in it.

Numerous epics dealing with the exploits of Dietrich von Berne originate in the thirteenth century: *Dietrichs Flucht* (**DF**) and *Die Rabenschlacht* (**Rs**) tell of Dietrich's exile among the Huns at Etzel's court, and of his battles to win back his kingdom in Italy from Ermenrîch; these epics were written in Austria *c.* 1290, but they may well derive from poems of the first decades of the thirteenth century, or even earlier.[9] *Alpharts Tod* (**A**), written *c.* 1250,[10] concerns a single episode during Dietrich's defence of Berne (= Verona) against Ermenrîch. The garbled version of a Low German poem about the death of Ermenrîch is preserved in a Lübeck broadsheet of *c.* 1540;[11] it has been entitled *Koninc Ermenrîkes Dôt* (**ED**) by its editors.

The earliest extant versions of *Der Rosengarten zu Worms* (**Rg**) derive from the fifteenth century,[12] although the original poem may have been written *c.* 1250 in Austria:[13] this epic describes the combats at Kriemhilt's rose-garden

---

[1] De Boor, *GDL* II. 167, dates it between 1220 and 1230.
[2] Martin, *Wisselauwe*, 71.
[3] The episode has some similarities to Vildiver's exploit in bear-disguise (Ps I. 261 ff.).
[4] Wilhelm Grimm, *DHS*, 309.
[5] De Boor, *GDL* II. 205; Stackmann, *Kudrun*, viii–xi.
[6] Ibid. xxxvii ff.        [7] See p. xv n. 2.
[8] Regarding the language of the manuscript see *Dukus Horant*, hrsg. von P. F. Ganz, F. Norman, W. Schwarz, mit einem Exkurs von S. A. Birnbaum (Tübingen, 1964), 15–74.
[9] De Boor, *GDL* III. i. 149.        [10] Ibid. 155.
[11] John L. Flood, op. cit. 231.
[12] The fragments of a Low German version are contained in a Pommersfelden manuscript dated 1470; there are also fragments of a Czech version of the 14th cent. See Holz, *Rosengarten*, lxx–lxxiii.
[13] De Boor, op. cit. 170.

between her Burgundian champions and the heroes brought against them by Dietrich; interest is centred on the combat between Dietrich and Sîfrit, Kriemhilt's betrothed. This situation is used for the climax of *Biterolf und Dietleib* (**B**), an epic dating from *c.* 1260,[1] in which the combined forces of Etzel, Dietrich, and Ermenrîch meet the Burgundians in combat at Worms; the earlier part of this poem concerns the adventures of Biterolf and his son Dietleip, and Dietrich's battles against east European peoples. In the fragment *Dietrich und Wenezlan* (**DuW**), dated *c.* 1300,[2] Dietrich's combat with a Slavonic leader is described.

Dietrich's adventures with a dwarf, the owner of another rose-garden, are related in *Laurin* (**L**), the earliest version of which was probably written *c.* 1250 in the Tyrol;[3] there are several late printed versions of the poem.[4] *Walberan* (**L(K)II**), a sequel to *Laurin* (**L**), was written in the early fourteenth century.[5] *Virginal* (**V**), an epic originating in the Tyrol *c.* 1300,[6] and preserved in three later variant versions, describes Dietrich's youthful adventures with dragons and giants and his marriage to the elf-queen Virginâl. The fragment *Goldemar* (**G**) begins the story of Dietrich's rescue of a maiden from a dwarf.

The most famous poem about Dietrich as a giant-fighter, *Das Eckenlied* (**E**), the original version of which was probably written in the Tyrol *c.* 1250,[7] is preserved in redactions of the early fourteenth century (one fragment from the thirteenth century, **E(B)**, is preserved in the manuscript of the *Carmina Burana*); it was often printed between 1491 and 1590. *Sigenot* (**Sn**), which deals with Dietrich's capture by a giant and his rescue by Hildebrant, was even more frequently printed, being published also in Low German and Yiddish;[8] it was probably written soon after *Das Eckenlied* (**E**);[9] the earlier version of this poem, *Der ältere Sigenot* (**äSn**), *c.* 1250, has survived only in the redaction of the fourteenth-century manuscript L; the version represented by six manuscripts from the fifteenth century and prints published between 1487 and 1661 is termed *Der jüngere Sigenot* (**jSn**).[10] *Der Wunderer* (**Wu**), written *c.* 1350 or even later,[11] describes Dietrich's encounter with a cannibal giant.

In *Ortnit* (**O**), composed before 1250,[12] the hero abducts a heathen princess, but he is killed by a dragon introduced into his kingdom of Lombardy by her father. *Wolfdietrich* (**Wd**) is a sequel to *Ortnit* (**O**), in which Wolfdietrich kills the dragon, marries Ortnît's widow, wins back his own kingdom of Greece from his hostile brothers, and frees his faithful vassals, whom his brothers have imprisoned. There are four variant versions: A, composed before 1250,[13] B and C between 1250 and 1300, the main manuscripts dating

---

[1] De Boor, op. cit. 173.  [2] Ibid. 177.  [3] Ibid. 166.
[4] See Karl Schorbach, *Laurin* (Halle, 1904), regarding the early printed versions, and Torsten Dahlberg, *Zum dänischen Lavrin und dem niederdeutschen Lorin* (Lund, 1950), regarding the translations into Low German, Danish, and Czech.
[5] O. Jänicke, *DHB* I. lv; Holz, *Laurin*, xviii.  [6] De Boor, op. cit. 162.
[7] Ibid. 159.  [8] John L. Flood, op. cit. 229.  [9] De Boor, op. cit. 161 f.
[10] John L. Flood, op. cit. 228 ff.  [11] Zink, *Wunderer*, 35.
[12] De Boor, *GDL* II. 206; A. Amelung, *DHB* III. xxviii ff., dates it *c.* 1226.
[13] De Boor, loc. cit.; Schneider, *Wolfdietrich* (1931), v ff., considers strs. 1–503 to have been

from the fifteenth century or later;¹ in the early fourteenth century a compiler combined versions close to B and C to produce *Der Große Wolfdietrich* (**Wd(D); Wd(Gr)**),² the version found in *Das Straßburger Heldenbuch*, *c.* 1480.³

Apart from brief references in *Das Nibelungenlied* (**N**) and *Der Rosengarten A* (**Rg(A)**), accounts of the youthful adventures of Siegfried (MHG Sîfrit) are relatively late in German sources. *Das Lied vom hürnen Seyfrid* (**hS**) exists in prints between *c.* 1530 and 1642 and must be considered a work of the sixteenth century, although the material on which it is based is considerably older.⁴ This poem was dramatized by Hans Sachs in his *Der hürnen Seufrid* (**hS(Sachs)**) of 1557, in which he includes the fight between Sîfrit and Dietrich from *Der Rosengarten* (**Rg**). It was also expanded into a prose version in the seventeenth century, *Das Volksbuch vom gehörnten Siegfried* (**gS**).⁵

Included in *Das Straßburger Heldenbuch* (*c.* 1480–1590) is a prose summary of the epics contained in it; this summary, sometimes termed *Der Anhang des Heldenbuches* (**AHb**), also includes material not found elsewhere in German sources. It may, therefore, be regarded as a source in its own right.

(ii) *Old English*

The bulk of Old English material is to be found in a few alliterative poems considerably older than most of the German sources on which the Catalogue is based; they are:

*Widsith*, a poem containing many names from German heroic tradition. The major part was probably composed in the late seventh century;⁶ it is preserved in the Exeter Book, a manuscript of the late tenth century.⁷

*Beowulf*, in which figures from German heroic tradition are mentioned. The date of composition of this epic is still the subject of controversy;⁸ the

---

composed in the second decade of the 13th cent., and the remainder, strs. 504–606 (= **Wd(A²)**) based on a B-version, some time before 1250 (see p. xxvi).

¹ Ibid. vi f.; de Boor, *GDL* III. i. 178.
² Ibid.
³ The trilogy *Von Hueg Diterichen*, *Von dem Keiser Ottnit*, and *Vom Wolff Dieterichen*, published at Nürnberg in 1618 in the *Opus Theatricum* of Jakob Ayrer (1543–1605), follows faithfully the printed version of this 'Heldenbuch', and has not been used for this Catalogue (see A. von Keller, *Ayrers Dramen*, Bd. II (Stuttgart, 1865, *LVSt* LXXVII), 943–1205).
⁴ See Golther, *Hürnen Seyfrid*, xxix–xlii, and King, *Hürnen Seyfrid*, 40–90, regarding this material. A Czech version was published in Prague in 1615 (see John L. Flood, op. cit. 238).
⁵ The first print of the 'Volksbuch' was probably made in Hamburg in 1637, the original for the existing prints dating from 1657. A sequel about Siegfried's son Löwhardus appeared shortly afterwards (see Harold Jantz, 'The Last Branch of the Nibelungen Tree', *MLN* LXXX (1965), 433–40).
⁶ Malone, *Widsith* (1962), 116.
⁷ N. R. Ker, *Catalogue of Manuscripts Containing Anglo-Saxon* (Oxford, 1957), 153 (no. 116).
⁸ Dates for composition ranging from the 7th cent. (Ritchie Girvan, *Beowulf and the Seventh Century* (London, 1935)) to the close of the 8th cent. (Dorothy Whitelock, *The Audience in Beowulf* (Oxford, 1952), 22 ff.) have been put forward. See C. L. Wrenn's Supplement to R. W. Chambers, *Beowulf* (Cambridge, 1963³), 531 ff.

manuscript in which it is preserved (Cotton Vitellius A. xv) dates from *c.* 1000.¹

*Finnsburg*, a fragment, in which certain names and situations recall those of German tradition. It was composed at about the same period as *Beowulf*, but is only preserved in a transcript of 1705.²

*Deor*, a strophic lay containing several allusions to German heroic tradition. It was probably composed *c.* 900³ and is preserved in the same late tenth-century manuscript as *Widsith*.

*Waldere*, dealing with the same subject-matter as *Waltharius* (see pp. xv f.). Dates ranging from the eighth to the late tenth century have been proposed for the composition of this poem;⁴ the manuscript fragments have been dated *c.* 1000.⁵

(iii) *Scandinavian*

The most important sources of analogous material are:

*Gesta Danorum*, by Saxo Grammaticus (Saxo): a history of Denmark, written in Latin and completed in the first decade of the thirteenth century;⁶ it depends on heroic tradition for the early period covered by the first nine books.

The following three bodies of material, often referred to in the Catalogue by the collective term 'Eddic tradition':

*Snorra Edda* or *Prose Edda* (*Sn E*): this compilation of poetic lore, in which stories from heroic tradition are recounted in prose, was completed between 1220 and 1230 by the Icelander Snorri Sturluson (†1241).⁷

*Sæmundar Edda* or *Poetic Edda* (*Edda*): this collection was made in Iceland *c.* 1250;⁸ the oldest manuscript, that of the Codex Regius, can be dated *c.* 1270. It contains many heroic lays, which were composed mainly between *c.* 800 and 1200 in Norway and Iceland:⁹ of these lays the *Völundarkviða* (Vkv), *Atlakviða* (Akv), and *Hamðismál* (Hm) were probably composed as early as the ninth century;¹⁰ the bulk of the Eddic poems on heroic themes originated in the eleventh and twelfth centuries: *Grottasöngr* (Grt), the Helgi lays (HHu I, HHu II, HHv), *Brot af Sigurðarkviða* (Br), the two Guðrun lays (Gðr I, Gðr II), *Oddrúnargrátr* (Od), *Atlamál* (Am), *Reginsmál* (Rm), *Fáfnismál* (Fm), *Sigrdrífomál* (Sd), and *Helreið Brynhildar* (Hlr); on the other hand, *Grípisspá* (Grp), *Guðrúnarkviða in Þriðja* (Gðr III), *Guðrúnarhvöt* (Ghv), and probably *Sigurðarkviða in Skamma* (Sg)

---

[1] Ker, op. cit. 281 ff. (no. 216).  [2] Klaeber, *Beowulf*, cxiii.
[3] Malone, *Deor*, 1 ff., 22.
[4] Schneider, *GHS* I. 64; Panzer, *Wasichenstein*, 74 ff.; K. Stackmann, 'Antike Elemente im Waltharius', *Euphorion* XL (1950), 236 f.; F. Genzmer, 'Wie der Waltharius entstanden ist', *GRM* XXXV (1954), 161–74.
[5] Ker, op. cit. 141 ff. (no. 101).
[6] Schneider, *GHS* I. 66; Stefán Einarsson, *A History of Icelandic Literature* (New York, 1957), 158.
[7] Ibid. 14 f.  [8] Ibid. 15.  [9] Ibid. 20.
[10] Ibid. 22, 33; Jan de Vries, *Altnordische Literaturgeschichte*, Bd. I (Berlin, 1941), 46 f., 54.

## BIBLIOGRAPHY

may be assigned to the thirteenth century.[1] Apart from verse of Eddic type contained in manuscripts other than the Codex Regius, passages from very early heroic lays are quoted in the sagas, two of the most important being the *Hlöðskviða* (Hlöð), the so-called 'Battle of the Goths and Huns', in the *Hervarar saga ok Heiðreks* (late 13th cent.),[2] and the 'Lost Lay of Hildebrand' (Hild) in the *Ásmundar saga kappabana* (14th cent.).[3] In the satiric *Skíða ríma* (Skr) of the fifteenth century,[4] which contains Eddic material as well as names also found in the *Þiðriks saga* (see below), the tramp Skíði encounters ancient heroes in his dream. Certain skaldic poems also refer to heroic tradition, e.g. the *Ragnarsdrápa* (Rdr) of Bragi the Old (early ninth century)[5] and the *Eiríksmál* (Em) of the tenth century.[6]

*Völsunga saga* (Völss): this saga, preserved as a prologue to the thirteenth-century *Ragnars saga loðbrókar*,[7] is based largely on lays closely related to those of the *Sæmundar Edda* (*Edda*), and includes prose versions of material otherwise lost through the gap in the Codex Regius. The oldest manuscript dates from *c.* 1400, but the saga itself was probably composed between 1260 and 1270 in Iceland or possibly Norway.[8]

*Þiðriks saga af Bern* (Þs): this saga, the contents of which derive mainly from German written and oral sources, was probably compiled for the royal court of Norway at Bergen between 1250 and 1260;[9] the oldest manuscript stems from the end of the thirteenth century. There is also a mid-fifteenth-century Swedish version.

Danish ballads,[10] collected and written down since the sixteenth century.[11] Closely related to them is the Danish translation of the *Hven Chronicle*[12] made in 1603.[13]

Faroese ballads,[14] certain of which were still being sung in the nineteenth century and were first collected then;[15] they are concerned with heroic tradition and, like the Danish ballads, show certain affinities with the *Þiðriks saga*; other features recall Eddic tradition.[16]

---

[1] De Vries, ibid. II. 148, 150, 211 f.
[2] Einarsson, 33, 159.
[3] Ibid. 166.
[4] Ibid. 90.
[5] De Vries, op. cit. I. 91; Einarsson, 44.
[6] De Vries, op. cit. I. 112 f.
[7] *FAS* I. 219–85. The *Norna-Gests þáttr* (*FAS* I. 305–35), which retells material based on that of the *Völsunga saga* and the *Sæmundar Edda*, is not referred to in the Catalogue.
[8] R. Finch, *Völsunga Saga* (London, 1965), ix.
[9] Schneider, op. cit. I. 67 ff.
[10] Ed. Svend Grundtvig and others, in *Danmarks gamle Folkeviser* (Copenhagen, 1853–1948).
[11] Schneider, op. cit. I. 70 f.; Einarsson, 91.
[12] Ed. O. L. Jiriczek, *Die Hvenische Chronik in diplomatischem Abdruck*, Acta Germanica, III. ii (Berlin, 1892).
[13] Schneider, op. cit. I. 70.
[14] Ed. Chr. Matras, *Corpus Carminum Faeroensium*, vol. I: *Föroya Kvæði* (Copenhagen, 1951–4).
[15] Schneider, loc. cit.
[16] See H. de Boor, *Die färöischen Lieder des Nibelungenzyklus* (Heidelberg, 1918).

# BIBLIOGRAPHY

## §2. THE SOURCES

### *Editions, with their Abbreviations and Short Titles*

The German sources on which the Catalogue is based are shown in bold type. Abbreviations for collections will be found on pp. xxvi–xxviii.

| | |
|---|---|
| **A** | *Alpharts Tod*, Ernst Martin, *DHB* II (1866), 3–54. |
| **äH** | *Das Hildebrandslied*, in W. Braune and E. A. Ebbinghaus, *Althochdeutsches Lesebuch* (Tübingen, 1962¹⁴), 81–3. |
| **AHb** | *Anhang des Heldenbuches*, in A. von Keller, *Das Heldenbuch* (Stuttgart, 1867), *LVSt* LXXXVII. 1–11 (based on the earliest printed edition of *Das Straßburger Heldenbuch* (*c.* 1483). W. Grimm, *DHS*, 325–38, gives extracts from the print of 1509). |
| Akv | *Atlakviða in grönlenzka*, *Edda*, 240–7. |
| Am | *Atlamál in grönlenzko*, *Edda*, 248–63. |
| **äSn** | *Sigenot*, Julius Zupitza, *DHB* V (1870), 207–15. |
| **B** | *Biterolf und Dietleib*, Oskar Jänicke, *DHB* I (1866), 1–197. |
| Beowulf | *Beowulf and the Fight at Finnsburg*, Fr. Klaeber (Boston, New York, etc., 1941³), 1–120. |
| Br | *Brot af Sigurðakviða*, *Edda*, 198–201. |
| **BW** | *Van Bere Wisselauwe*, Ernst Martin (Straßburg), *QF* LV (1889), 40–63. |
| Deor | *Deor*, Kemp Malone (London, 1949²), 23–7. |
| **DF** | *Dietrichs Flucht*, Ernst Martin, *DHB* II (1866), 57–215 (based on MS. R (*c.* 1300), with readings from MSS. A and W. The poem is sometimes termed 'Das Buch von Bern'). |
| **DH** | *Dukus Horant*, P. F. Ganz, F. Norman, W. Schwarz (Tübingen, 1964), 132–219. |
| Dr | *Dráp Niflunga*, *Edda*, 223 (Preface to Gðr II). |
| **DuW** | *Dietrich und Wenezlan*, Julius Zupitza, *DHB* V (1870), 267–74. |
| **E(a)** | *Ecken außfart*, Karl Schorbach (Leipzig, 1897. Facsimile of the print of 1491. Only variant spellings or additions are given from this edition, which is almost identical with **E(s)**). |
| **E(B)** | *Carmina Burana*, J. A. Schmeller (Breslau, 1883), 71 (Stück CLXXX a). |
| **E(d)** | *Ecken Ausfahrt*, *HPHB* II (1825), 74–116 (based on the version of the *Dresdner Heldenbuch* of 1472). |
| **E(L)** | *Ecken Liet*, Julius Zupitza, *DHB* V (1870), 219–64. |
| **E(s)** | *Ecken Auszfart*, Oskar Schade (Hannover, 1854. This Straßburg print of 1559 is usually termed 's¹' to distinguish it from the almost identical 's²' printed in 1577). |
| **ED** | *Koninc Ermenrîkes Dôt*, K. Gödeke (Hannover, 1851). |
| Em | *Eiríksmál*, *CPB* I, 260 f. |
| Finnsburg | *Beowulf and the Fight at Finnsburg*, Fr. Klaeber (Boston, New York, etc., 1941³), 245–9. |

# BIBLIOGRAPHY

| | |
|---|---|
| Fm | *Fáfnismál, Edda*, 180–8. |
| Form | *Formáli, Sn E*, 1–8. |
| G | *Goldemar*, Julius Zupitza, *DHB* v (1870), 203 f. |
| Gðr I | *Guðrúnarkviða in fyrsta, Edda*, 202–6. |
| Gðr II | *Guðrúnarkviða önnor, Edda*, 224–31. |
| Gðr III | *Guðrúnarkviða in Þriðja, Edda*, 232–3. |
| Ghv | *Guðrúnarhvöt, Edda*, 264–8. |
| Grm | *Grímnismál, Edda*, 57–68. |
| Grp | *Grípisspá, Edda*, 164–72. |
| Grt | *Grottasöngr, Edda*, 297–301. |
| gS | *Das Volksbuch vom gehörnten Siegfried* (1726), appendix to *Das Lied vom Hürnen Seyfrid*, W. Golther (Halle, 1911$^2$), 61–99. (The Introduction to this chap-book (p. 63) and the passage containing references to romances of chivalry (p. 69, 1–26) have not been used for the Catalogue.) |
| Gylf | *Gylfaginning, Sn E*, 9–96. |
| Hátt | *Háttatal, Sn E*, 247–304. |
| Háv | *Hávamál, Edda*, 17–44. |
| Hdl | *Hyndloljóð, Edda*, 288–96. |
| HHu I | *Helgakviða Hundingsbana in fyrri, Edda*, 130–9. |
| HHu II | *Helgakviða Hundingsbana önnor, Edda*, 150–61. |
| HHv | *Helgakviða Hjörvarðszsonar, Edda*, 140–9. |
| Hild | 'The Lost Lay of Hildebrand', in *Ásmundar saga kappabana, Edda*, 313 f. |
| Hlöð | *Hlöðskviða* ('The Battle of the Goths and Huns'), in *Hervarar saga ok Heiðreks, Edda*, 303–12. |
| Hlr | *Helreið Brynhildar, Edda*, 219–22. |
| Hm | *Hamðismál, Edda*, 269–74. |
| hS | *Das Lied vom Hürnen Seyfrid*, W. Golther (Halle, 1911$^2$), 1–59. (This edition gives full details of prints; for additional material see K. C. King, 'Das Lied vom hürnen Seyfrid', *Bulletin of the John Rylands Library*, xxxv (1952), 61–87, and *Das Lied vom hürnen Seyfrid*, critical ed., with Introduction and notes (Manchester, 1958).) |
| hS(Sachs) | *Der hürnen Seufrid: Tragoedie in 7 Acten von Hans Sachs* (1557), Edmund Goetze (Halle, 1880; repr. Tübingen, 1967). |
| jH | *Das jüngere Hildebrandslied* in *Denkmäler deutscher Poesie und Prosa aus dem VIII.-XII. Jh.*, E. Steinmeyer (Berlin, 1892$^3$), II. 26–30. |
| jSn | *Der jüngere Sigenot*, A. C. Schoener (Heidelberg, 1928). (The Introduction to this work gives details of MSS. and prints; for additional information see John L. Flood, 'Studien zur Überlieferung des jüngeren Sigenot', *ZfdA* xcv (1966), 42–79.) |
| Kl | *Die Klage*, A. Edzardi (Hannover, 1875). (Variants from texts A and |

# BIBLIOGRAPHY

    C are given in parallel columns in this edition of the B-text, which is also the basis of the edition of Karl Bartsch, *Diu Klage* (Leipzig, 1875; repr. Darmstadt, 1964).)

**Ku**    *Kudrun*, B. Symons and Bruno Boesch (Tübingen, 1954³). (The first edition by B. Symons (Halle, 1883) and those by Ernst Martin (Halle, 1872) and Karl Bartsch, revised by Karl Stackmann (Wiesbaden, 1965⁵), are referred to in the Catalogue.)

**L(A)**    *Laurin A* and *Fortsetzung in K*, in *Laurin und der Kleine Rosengarten*, G. Holz (Halle, 1897), 1–59. (O. Jänicke prints this text as one poem in *DHB* I (1866), 201–37. See E. Klaass, 'König Laurin', *VfL* (1936), 841 f., H. Rosenfeld, 'König Laurin', *VfL* V (1955), 530, and Torsten Dahlberg, *Zwei unberücksichtigte Laurinversionen* (Lund, 1948), 9–12, for information about the various versions of *Laurin*; see also p. xviii).

**L(D)**    *Laurin D*, in *Laurin und der Kleine Rosengarten*, G. Holz (Halle, 1897), 96–182.

**L(DrHb)**    *Zwerg Laurin*, *HPHB* II (1825), 160–87 (based on the version of the *Dresdner Heldenbuch* of 1472: a late abbreviated version with some divergences, especially additional giants' names).

**L(K)II**    *Laurin K II*, in *Laurin und der Kleine Rosengarten*, G. Holz (Halle, 1897), 59–95. (O. Jänicke prints this poem under the title *Walberan* in *DHB* I (1866), 238–57. It is complete only in the 14th-cent. MS. K.)

**N**    *Das Nibelungenlied*, Karl Bartsch and H. de Boor (Wiesbaden, 1956¹³). (This edition is based on the B-text. The C-text is referred to in cases of divergence.)

**N(C)**    *Das Nibelungenlied*, Fr. Zarncke (Leipzig, 1876²).

**N(k)**    *Das Nibelungenlied nach der Piaristenhandschrift*, A. von Keller (Tübingen, 1879), *LVSt* CXLVII. (A 'modernized' C-text of the 15th cent.; it is only referred to in cases of divergence.)

**N(m)**    *Der Nibelunge Nôt*, Bd. I, Karl Bartsch (Leipzig, 1870), xxv–xxvii (only the âventiure-headings of this 15th-cent. version are preserved).

**N(T)**    *Het Nevelingenlied*, in *Middelnederlandsche epische fragmenten*, G. Kalff (Leiden, 1885), 1–8.

**O**    *Ortnit*, Arthur Amelung, *DHB* III (1871), 3–77.

**O(C)**    *Ortnit C*, Oskar Jänicke, *DHB* IV (1873), 3–10 (fragmentary).

**O(k)**    *Ortnit*, *HPHB* I (1820), 1–26 (based on the version of *Das Dresdner Heldenbuch* of 1472; reference is only made to this shortened version in cases of divergence).

**O(w)**    *Ortneit*, J. Lunzer (Stuttgart, 1906), *LVSt* CCXXXIX. 1–57 (from the 15th-cent. Piarist MS. in Vienna; only variants are given).

**Od**    *Oddrúnargrátr*, *Edda*, 234–9.

**R**    *König Rother*, Th. Frings and Joachim Kuhnt (Bonn, 1922, based on the late 12th-cent. MS. H). (The edition by Jan de Vries (Heidelberg, 1922) has also been referred to. See W. J. Schröder, 'Zur Textgestaltung des "König Rothers"', *PBB* LXXIX (Halle, 1957), 204–33.)

**Rdr**    *Ragnarsdrápa*, *CPB* II. 6–9.

# BIBLIOGRAPHY

**Rg(ADF)**  *Die Gedichte vom Rosengarten zu Worms*, G. Holz (Halle, 1893). (See the Introduction to this edition for a description of the manuscripts.)

**Rg(C)**  *Der Rosengarte*, Wilhelm Grimm (Göttingen, 1836, based on a 14th-cent. MS., referred to in Holz's edition above as *f*).

**Rg(P)**  'Der Rosengarte', Karl Bartsch, *Germania* IV (1859), 8–33 (based on the main MS. of the P-redaction (14th cent.), termed *p* in Holz's edition above).

**Rg(V)**  'Ain Vasnach spill von den Risn oder Reckhn', J. G. Obrist, *Germania* XXII (1877), 420–9 (a paper MS. of the early 16th cent.).

Rm  *Reginsmál, Edda*, 173–9.

**Rs**  *Die Rabenschlacht*, Ernst Martin, *DHB* II (1866), 219–326 (based on MS. R (*c.* 1300) with readings from MSS. A and W).

**Ru**  *Ruodlieb*, Fr. Seiler (Halle, 1882. A new edition by Edwin H. Zeydel, *Ruodlieb* (Capel Hill, 1959), includes an English translation).

Saxo  *Saxonis Grammatici Gesta Danorum*, J. Olrik and H. Ræder, (2 vols., Copenhagen, 1931–57).
*The First Nine Books of the Danish History of Saxo*, trans. Oliver Elton (London, 1893).

Sd  *Sigrdrífomál, Edda*, 189–97.
Sf  *Frá dauða Sinfjötla, Edda*, 162 f.
Sg  *Sigurðarkviða in Skamma, Edda*, 207–18.
Sk  *Skáldskaparmál, Sn E*, 97–246.
Skm  *Skírnismál (For Skírnis), Edda*, 69–77.
Skr  *Skíða ríma, CPB* II. 398–407.
**Sn**  see **äSn** and **jSn**.
Þrk  *Þrymskviða, Edda*, 11–15.
Þs  *Þiðriks saga af Bern*, Henrik Bertelsen (2 vols., Copenhagen, 1905–11).
*Die Geschichte Thidreks von Bern*, übertragen von Fine Erichsen (Jena, 1924; Sammlung Thule 22).

**V(d)**  *Dietrich und seine Gesellen*, *HPHB* II (1825), 143–59 (based on the version of the *Dresdner Heldenbuch* of 1472).

**V(h)**  *Virginal*, Julius Zupitza, *DHB* V (1870), 1–200 (based on the 15th-cent. Heidelberg MS.).

**V(w)**  *Dietrichs erste Ausfahrt*, Franz Stark (Stuttgart, 1860), *LVSt* LII (based on the 15th-cent. Piarist MS. in Vienna).

**Vhw**  *De vier heeren wenschen*, in *Oudvlaemsche Gedichten* II, Ph. Blommaert (Ghent, 1841), 114 ff.

Vkv  *Völundarkviða, Edda*, 116–23.
Völss  *Völsunga Saga*, R. Finch (London, 1965).
*Die Geschichte von den Völsungen*, in *Isländische Heldenromane*, übertragen von Paul Hermann (Jena, 1923; Sammlung Thule 21), 39–136.

Vsp  *Völuspá, Edda*, 1–15.
Vspsk  *Voluspá in skamma, Edda* (Jónsson), 499–505.

# BIBLIOGRAPHY

| | |
|---|---|
| **W** | *Waltharius*, hrsg. von Karl Strecker; deutsche Übersetzung von Peter Vossen (Berlin, 1947³). |
| *Waldere* | *Waldere*, F. Norman (London, 1933). |
| **Wd(A)** | *Wolfdietrich A*, Hermann Schneider (Halle, 1931; strophes 1–503: see p. xviii n. 13 above). |
| **Wd(A²)** | *Wolfdietrich A*, Arthur Amelung, *DHB* III (1871), 139–52 (strophes 504–606, which are probably by a different author from **Wd(A)**: see Amelung's Introduction, *DHB* III. xlvi, and that of Schneider in his above-mentioned edition, vi and xx). |
| **Wd(B)** | *Wolfdietrich B*, Oskar Jänicke, *DHB* III (1871), 167–301. |
| **Wd(CD)** | *Wolfdietrich C und D*, Oskar Jänicke, *DHB* IV (1873), 13–236 (C is fragmentary, and D (*Der Große Wolfdietrich*) is incomplete in this edition). |
| **Wd(Gr)** | *Der Große Wolfdietrich*, A. Holtzmann (Heidelberg, 1865, the only comprehensive edition). |
| **Wd(k)** | *Studies in the Dresdner Heldenbuch: an Edition of Wolfdietrich k*, E. A. H. Fuchs (Chicago, 1935). |
| **Wd(w)** | *Wolfdietrich*, J. Lunzer (Stuttgart, 1906), *LVSt* ccxxxix. (Variants only are given from this edition based on the 15th-cent. Piarist MS. in Vienna.) |
| *Widsith* | *Widsith*, Kemp Malone (London, 1936, Copenhagen, 1962²) (Reference is also made to the edition by R. W. Chambers, *Widsith: a Study in Old English Heroic Legend* (Cambridge, 1912).) |
| **Wu(B)** | *Le Wunderer*, Georges Zink (Paris, 1949, a facsimile edition of the print of 1503 published at Grüneck, near Straßburg). |
| **Wu(H)** | *Etzels Hofhaltung*, *HPHB* II (1825), 55–73 (based on the version of the *Dresdner Heldenbuch* of 1472; this version is only referred to in rare cases of divergence from **Wu(B)**). |
| **Wu(k)** | *Ain spruch von aim konig mit namen Ezell*, A. von Keller (Stuttgart, 1855), *LVSt* xxxv. 1–9 (fragment from a Bavarian MS. dated *c.* 1400). |
| **WuH** | *Walther und Hildegunde*, in *Das Waltharilied*, W. Eckerth (Halle, 1902²), 70–83. |

## §3. ABBREVIATIONS

Date and place of publication are given for collections and works of reference, but for periodicals only where confusion is possible.

| | |
|---|---|
| *AfdA* | *Anzeiger der Zeitschrift für deutsches Altertum und deutsche Literatur*. |
| *Aufriß* | *Die deutsche Philologie im Aufriß*, hrsg. von Wolfgang Stammler (3 Bde., Berlin, 1957; 1959–62²). |
| *BzNf* | *Beiträge zur Namenforschung*. |
| *CCF* | *Corpus Carminum Faeroensium*, vol. I: *Föroya Kvæði*, ed. Chr. Matras (Copenhagen, 1951–4). |
| *CMH* | *The Cambridge Mediaeval History*, planned by J. B. Bury, ed. H. M. Gwatkin and others (8 vols., Cambridge, 1911–36). |

## BIBLIOGRAPHY

| | |
|---|---|
| *CPB* | *Corpus Poeticum Boreale*, ed. Gudbrand Vigfusson and F. York Powell (2 vols., Oxford, 1883). |
| *DgF* | *Danmarks gamle Folkeviser*, ed. S. Grundtvig, A. Olrik, and H. Grüner Nielsen (Copenhagen, 1853–1948). |
| *DHB* | *Deutsches Heldenbuch*, hrsg. von K. Müllenhoff, E. Martin, A. Amelung, O. Jänicke und J. Zupitza (5 Bde., Berlin, 1866–73; repr. Berlin and Zürich, 1963–8). |
| *DVjs* | *Deutsche Vierteljahresschrift für Literaturwissenschaft und Geistesgeschichte*. |
| *DWb* | *Deutsches Wörterbuch*, hrsg. von Jacob und Wilhelm Grimm und anderen (Leipzig, 1854–1959). |
| *Edda* | *Edda: Die Lieder des Codex Regius nebst verwandten Denkmälern*, hrsg. von Gustav Neckel (2 Bde., Heidelberg, 1927²); Bd. I: *Text*, 4 Auflage von Hans Kuhn (Heidelberg, 1962).[1] |
| | *Eddukvæði* (*Sæmundar-Edda*), ed. Guðni Jónsson (2 vols., Reykjavík, 1949). |
| | *The Poetic Edda*, ed. and trans. Ursula Dronke, vol. 1: *Heroic Poems* (Oxford, 1969). |
| | *Die Edda*, übertragen von Felix Genzmer (Jena, 1928; Sammlung Thule 1–2). |
| *FAS* | *Fornaldar Sögur Nordurlanda*, ed. Guðni Jónsson (4 vols., Reykjavík, 1950). |
| *FF* | *Forschungen und Fortschritte*. |
| *FFC* | *Folklore Fellows Communications*. |
| *GDHS* | *Zur germanisch-deutschen Heldensage*, hrsg. von Karl Hauck (Darmstadt, 1961). |
| *Germania* | *Germania*: Vierteljahrsschrift für deutsche Altertumskunde, begr. von Franz Pfeiffer (Stuttgart und Wien, 1856–92). |
| *Germania* (von der Hagens) | *Germania*: Jahrbuch der Berlinischen Gesellschaft für deutsche Sprache und Altertumskunde, hrsg. von Fr. H. von der Hagen (Berlin, 1836–53). |
| *GRM* | *Germanisch-Romanische Monatsschrift*. |
| *HPHB* | *Der Helden Buch in der Ursprache*, 2 Tle., hrsg. von Fr. H. von der Hagen und A. Primisser (Berlin, 1820–5 Bd. II: *Deutsche Gedichte des Mittelalters*, hrsg. von Fr. H. von der Hagen und J. Büsching). |
| *KHM* | *Kinder- und Hausmärchen*, gesammelt durch die Brüder Grimm (München, 1856³). |
| *KLD* | *Deutsche Liederdichter des 13. Jahrhunderts*, Bd. I: *Text*, hrsg. von Carl von Kraus (Tübingen, 1952). |
| *LVSt* | *Bibliothek des Litterarischen Vereins in Stuttgart*. |
| *MED* | *Middle English Dictionary*, ed. H. Kurath, S. M. Kuhn, and others (University of Michigan Press, 1954– ). |

[1] Prose passages are referred to by the page number of this edition; the verse is shown by the number of the strophe in the poem concerned.

## BIBLIOGRAPHY

*MF*      *Des Minnesangs Frühling*, hrsg. von Karl Lachmann, neu bearbeitet von Fr. Vogt (Leipzig, 1930$^5$).

*MGH ss*    *Monumenta Germaniae Historica*, ed. G. H. Pertz, etc. (Berlin, 1826– ).
  *MGH auct. ant.*      *MGH, auctores antiquissimi* (1887– ).
  *MGH leges*      *MGH, leges nationum Germanicarum* (1888– ).
  *MGH script. rer. Lang.*    *MGH, scriptorum rerum Langobardicarum et Italicarum saec. VI–IX* (1878– ).
  *MGH script. rer. Merov.*    *MGH, scriptorum rerum Merovingicarum* (1885– ).

*MLN*      *Modern Language Notes.*

*MLR*      *Modern Language Review.*

*OGS*      *Oxford German Studies.*

*PBB*      *Beiträge zur Geschichte der deutschen Sprache und Literatur* (Halle, 1874– , and Tübingen, 1955– ).

*QF*      *Quellen und Forschungen.*

*Sn E*      *Edda Snorra Sturlusonar, Nafnaþulur og Skáldatal*, ed. Guðni Jónsson (Reykjavík, 1949).
       *Die jüngere Edda mit dem sogenannten grammatischen Traktat*, übertragen von Gustav Neckel und Felix Genzmer (1942$^2$; Sammlung Thule 20).

*VfL*      *Die deutsche Literatur des Mittelalters: Verfasserlexikon*, hrsg. von Wolfgang Stammler und Karl Langosch (5 Bde., Berlin und Leipzig, 1933–55).

*ZfdA*      *Zeitschrift für deutsches Altertum und deutsche Literatur.*

*ZfdPh*      *Zeitschrift für deutsche Philologie.*

*ZfdWf*      *Zeitschrift für deutsche Wortforschung.*

*ZffrSL*      *Zeitschrift für französische Sprache und Literatur.*

### §4. BOOKS, ARTICLES, AND EDITIONS

Works listed here are often referred to in the Catalogue either by the authors' names alone or by abbreviated titles as well (preceded by the sign '=' in this list). Full bibliographical details are given in the Catalogue for all other works referred to.

Medieval authors before 1400 are listed under their first names. The titles of anonymous works are arranged alphabetically.

Albrecht von Scharfenberg, *Merlin und Seifrid de Ardemont von Albrecht von Scharfenberg in der Bearbeitung Ulrich Füetrers*, hrsg. von Fr. Panzer (Stuttgart, 1909), *LVSt* CCXXVII. 39–169. ( = *Seifrid de Ardemont*.)

Altheim, Franz, *Geschichte der Hunnen* (2 Bde., Berlin, 1959–60).

Amelung, Arthur, *Deutsches Heldenbuch*, Bd. III (Berlin, 1871). ( = Amelung, *DHB*.)

Ammianus Marcellinus, *Ammianus Marcellinus, with an English Translation*, ed. John C. Rolfe (Loeb Classical Library, 3 vols., London and Cambridge, Mass., 1950–2).

*Annales Quedlinburgenses*, ed. G. H. Pertz (Hannover, 1839; *MGH ss* III. 22–90). ( = *Ann. Quedl.*)

# BIBLIOGRAPHY

Bach, Adolf, *Deutsche Namenkunde* (3 Bde., Heidelberg, 1952–6).

Baesecke, Georg, *Das Hildebrandlied* (Halle, 1945). ( = Baesecke, *Hildebrandlied*.)

—— *Vor- und Frühgeschichte des deutschen Schrifttums*, Bd. I: *Vorgeschichte des deutschen Schrifttums* (Halle, 1940). ( = Baesecke, *Vorgeschichte*.) See *Oswald*.

Bede, *Historia Ecclesiastica Gentis Anglorum*, in *Venerabilis Baedae Opera Historica*, ed. C. Plummer (Oxford, 1896). ( = Bede, *History*.)

—— *Bede: a History of the English Church and People*, trans. Leo Sherley-Price (Penguin Books), Harmondsworth, 1955.

Bédier, Joseph. See *La Chanson de Roland*.

Benary, Walther, *Die germanische Ermanarichsage und die französische Heldensage* (Halle, 1912; Beiheft zur *Zeitschrift für romanische Philologie* XL).

Berger, A. E. See *Orendel*.

Betz, Werner, 'Die deutsche Heldensage', *Aufriß* III (1957), 1459–1547; (1962²), 1871–1970. ( = Betz, *Aufriß* III.)

Bickel, Ernst, 'Römisch-Germanischer Namen-Nimbus im deutschen Mittelalter', *Rheinisches Museum für Philologie*, Neue Folge (Frankfurt, 1955), 193–258.

Binz, G., 'Zeugnisse zur germanischen Sage in England', *PPB* XX (1895), 141–223.

Björkman, Erik, *Studien über die Eigennamen im Beowulf* (Halle, 1920).

Bleyer, Jacob, 'Die germanischen Elemente der ungarischen Hunnensage', *PBB* XXXI (1906), 429–599.

Boer, R. C., *Die Sagen von Ermanarich und Dietrich von Bern* (Halle, 1910). ( = Boer, *Sagen*.)

Boesch, Bruno, *Kudrun*, hrsg. von B. Symons: dritte Auflage von Bruno Boesch (Tübingen, 1954).

Bolte, J., and Polívka, C., *Anmerkungen zu den Kinder- und Hausmärchen der Brüder Grimm* (5 Bde., Leipzig, 1913–32).

Boor, Helmut de, *Geschichte der deutschen Literatur*, H. de Boor und R. Newald (München), vols. I–III by H. de Boor: Bd. I (1960⁴), *Die deutsche Literatur von Karl dem Großen bis zum Beginn der höfischen Dichtung 770–1170*; Bd. II (1955²), *Die höfische Literatur: Vorbereitung, Blüte, Ausklang 1170–1250*; Bd. III, i (1962), *Die deutsche Literatur im späten Mittelalter*. ( = de Boor, *GDL*.)

—— *Kleine Schriften* (2 Bde., Berlin, 1964–6). ( = de Boor, *Kl. Schr*.)

Bosworth, J. See Toller, T. Northcote.

Brady, Caroline, *The Legends of Ermanaric* (Berkeley and Los Angeles, Calif., 1945).

Bruckner, Wilhelm, *Die Sprache der Langobarden* (Straßburg, 1895).

Cassiodorus, *Variae*, ed. Th. Mommsen (Berlin, 1894; *MGH auct. ant.* XII).

Chambers, R. W., *Beowulf: an Introduction to the Study of the Poem: Supplement* by C. L. Wrenn (Cambridge, 1963³). ( = Chambers, *Beowulf*.)
*Widsith: a Study in Old English Heroic Legend* (Cambridge, 1912). ( = Chambers, *Widsith*.)

*La Chanson de Roland*, commentée par Joseph Bédier (Paris, 1927²).

# BIBLIOGRAPHY

Chaucer, Geoffrey, *The Complete Works*, ed. F. N. Robinson (Oxford University Press, London, 1957[2]).

Davidson, H. R. Ellis, *The Sword in Anglo-Saxon England* (Oxford, 1962).

Drescher, C., 'Studien zu Hans Sachs, II: Hans Sachs und die Heldensage', *Acta Germanica* II. ii (Berlin, 1891).

Düwel, Klaus, *Runenkunde* (Stuttgart, 1968).

Einarsson, Stéfan, *A History of Icelandic Literature* (New York, 1957).

Ekwall, Eilert, *The Concise Oxford Dictionary of English Place-Names* (Oxford, 1960[4]).

Elliot, Ralph W., *Runes* (Manchester, 1959).

Feilitzen, C. O. von, *The Pre-Conquest Personal Names of Domesday Book* (Uppsala, 1937).

Feist, Sigmund, *Vergleichendes Wörterbuch der gotischen Sprache* (Leiden, 1939[3]).

Flasdieck, Hermann M., 'Harlekin: "Germanischer Mythos in romanischer Wandlung"', *Anglia* LXI (1937), 225–340.

Flutre, Louis-Fernand, *Table des noms propres avec toutes leurs variantes figurant dans les romans du Moyen Âge écrits en français ou en provençal et actuellement publiés ou analysés* (Poitiers, 1962).

Förstemann, Ernst, *Altdeutsches Namenbuch* (2 Bde., Bonn), Bd. I: *Personennamen* (1900[2]); Bd. II: *Orts- und sonstige geographische Namen*, 2 Tle., hrsg. von Hermann Jellinghaus (1913–16[3]).

*Friedrich von Schwaben*, hrsg. von M. H. Jellinek (Berlin, 1904).

Frings, Th., and Kuhnt, J., *König Rother* (Bonn, 1922). ( = Frings–Kuhnt, *Rother*.)

Frings, Th., and Schieb, G. See Heinrich von Veldeke.

Füetrer, Ulrich. See Albrecht von Scharfenberg.

Gamillscheg, Ernst, *Romania Germanica* (3 Bde., Berlin und Leipzig, 1934).

Genzmer, Felix, *Edda, Skalden, Saga: Festschrift zum 70. Geburtstage von Felix Genzmer*, hrsg. von Hermann Schneider (Heidelberg, 1952). See under *Edda*, p. xxvii.

Golther, Wolfgang, *Deutsche Heldensage* (Dresden, 1894). ( = Golther, *DHS*.)

—— *Das Lied vom Hürnen Seyfrid* (Halle, 1911[2]). ( = Golther, *Hürnen Seyfrid*.)

Gottfried von Straßburg, *Tristan und Isold*, hrsg. von Fr. Ranke (Berlin, 1959[4]).

Gregory of Tours, *Gregorii Turonensis opera*, ed. W. Arndt et B. Krusch (Berlin, 1883; *MGH script. rer. Merov.* I. i). ( = Greg. Tur.)

—— *The History of the Franks*, trans. O. M. Dalton (2 vols., Oxford, 1927).

Grimm, Jacob, *Geschichte der deutschen Sprache* (Leipzig, 1868[3]). ( = J. Grimm, *GDS*.)

Grimm, Wilhelm, *Die deutsche Heldensage* (Gütersloh, 1889[3]; repr. Darmstadt, 1957). ( = W. Grimm, *DHS*.)

Grundtvig, Svend. See under *DgF*, p. xxvii.

Hagen, Fr. H. von der, *Gesamtabenteuer* (3 Bde., Stuttgart und Tübingen, 1850; repr. Darmstadt, 1961).

# BIBLIOGRAPHY

Harvey, Ruth, *Moriz von Craûn and the Chivalric World* (Oxford, 1961).

Hauck, Karl, 'Brieflicher Hinweis auf eine kleine ostnordische Bilder-Edda', *PBB* LXXXII (Sonderband, Halle, 1961), 47–67. ( = Hauck, *Bilder-Edda*.)

—— 'Germanische Bilderdenkmäler des früheren Mittelalters', *DVjs* XXXI (1957), 349–79. ( = Hauck, *Bilderdenkmäler*.)

Heinrich der Glîchesære, *Das mittelhochdeutsche Gedicht vom Fuchs Reinhart*, hrsg. von G. Baesecke, 2. Aufl. besorgt von Ingeborg Schröbler (Halle, 1952).

Heinrich von Veldeke, *Eneide*, hrsg. von Gabriele Schieb und Theodor Frings (3 Bde., Berlin, 1964–70). (References are to the text on the left-hand pages based on MS.G.)

—— *Servatius*, hrsg. von Theodor Frings und Gabriele Schieb (Halle, 1956).

Heinzel, Richard, 'Über die Nibelungensage', *Sitzungsberichte: Phil-hist. Cl. Kais. Akd. d. Wiss*. Bd. CIX, Abh. II (Wien, 1885). ( = Heinzel, *Nibelungensage*.)

—— 'Über die ostgotische Heldensage', *Sitzungsberichte: Phil-hist. Cl. Kais. Akd. d. Wiss*. Bd. CXIX, Abh. II (Wien, 1889). ( = Heinzel, *Ostgotische Heldensage*.)

—— 'Über die Walthersage', *Sitzungsberichte: Phil.-hist. Cl. Kais. Akd. d. Wiss*. Bd. CXVII, Abh. II (Wien, 1888). ( = Heinzel, *Walthersage*.)

Helm, Karl, *Erbe der Vergangenheit: Festgabe für Karl Helm* (Tübingen, 1951).

Hempel, Heinrich, *Nibelungenstudien I* (Heidelberg, 1926; no further volumes).

Henzen, Walter, *Deutsche Wortbildung* (Tübingen, 1957$^2$).

Heusler, Andreas, 'Heldennamen in mehrfacher Lautgestalt', *ZfdA* LII (1910), 97–107. ( = Heusler, *Heldennamen*.)

—— *Nibelungensage und Nibelungenlied* (Dortmund, 1955$^5$). ( = Heusler, *Nibelungensage*.)

Hodgkin, T., *Italy and her Invaders*, vol. III: *The Ostrogothic Invasion* (Oxford, 1896$^2$).

Höfler, Otto, *Germanisches Sakralkönigtum*, Bd. I: *Der Runenstein von Rök und die germanische Individualweihe* (Tübingen, Münster, Köln, 1952). ( = Höfler, *Sakralkönigtum*.)

—— 'Siegfried, Arminius und die Symbolik', *Festschrift für Franz Rolf Schröder* (Heidelberg, 1959), 11–121. ( = Höfler, *Siegfried*.)

Holthausen, F., *Gotisches etymologisches Wörterbuch* (Heidelberg, 1934). ( = Holthausen, *GEWb*.)

—— 'Studien zur Thidrekssaga', *PBB* IX (1884), 451–503. ( = Holthausen.)

Holz, Georg, *Die Gedichte vom Rosengarten zu Worms* (Halle, 1893). ( = Holz, *Rosengarten*.)

—— *Laurin und der Kleine Rosengarten* (Halle, 1897). ( = Holz, *Laurin*.)

—— *Der Sagenkreis der Nibelungen* (Leipzig, 1920$^3$). ( = Holz, *Sagenkreis*.)

*Hven Chronicle*, *Die Hvenische Chronik in diplomatischem Abdruck*, hrsg. von O. L. Jiriczek, *Acta Germanica* III. ii (Berlin, 1892). ( = *Hven. Chron*.)

Jänicke, Oskar, *Deutsches Heldenbuch*, Bde. I, III, IV (Berlin, 1866–73). ( = Jänicke, *DHB*.)

—— 'Zeugnisse und Excurse zur deutschen Heldensage', *ZfdA* XV (1872), 310–32. ( = Jänicke, *ZE*.)

# BIBLIOGRAPHY

Jiriczek, Otto L., *Deutsche Heldensagen*, Bd. I (Straßburg, 1898; no further volumes). ( = Jiriczek, *DHS* (1898).)
*Die deutsche Heldensage* (Leipzig, 1911³). ( = Jiriczek, *DHS* (1911).) See *Hven Chronicle* above.

Jóhannesson, Alexander, *Isländisches etymologisches Wörterbuch* (Bern, 1956).

Johannes von Tepl (Johannes von Saaz), *Der Ackermann aus Böhmen*, ed. M. O'C. Walshe (London, 1951).

Johannes von Würzburg, *Wilhelm von Österriech*, hrsg. von Ernst Regel (Berlin, 1906).

Jónsson, Guðni. See under *Edda*, p. xxvii, and *Sn E*, p. xxviii.

Jordanes, *Jordanis Romana et Getica*, ed. Th. Mommsen (Berlin, 1882; *MGH auct. ant.* v. i).

—— *The Gothic History of Jordanes in English Version*, C. C. Mierow (Princeton, 1915).

Jungandreas, Wolfgang, *Die Gudrunsage in den Ober- und Niederlanden* (Göttingen, 1948). ( = Jungandreas, *Gudrunsage*.)

Kahle, B., 'Altwestnordische Namenstudien', *Indogermanische Forschungen* XIV (1903), 133–224.

*Kaiserchronik*, hrsg. von Eduard Schröder (Hannover, 1892; *MGH ss, qui vernacula lingua usi sunt* I; repr. Berlin, 1964).

Kalbow, Werner, *Die germanischen Personennamen des altfranzösischen Heldenepos und ihre lautliche Entwicklung* (Halle, 1913).

Karsten, T. E., *Die Germanen* (Berlin und Leipzig, 1928).

Kaufmann, Henning, *Ergänzungsband zu Ernst Förstemann: Altdeutsche Personennamen* (München, 1968).

Keller, M. L., *The Anglo-Saxon Weapon Names* (Heidelberg, 1906).

Ker, N. R., *Catalogue of Manuscripts Containing Anglo-Saxon* (Oxford, 1957).

King, K. C., *Das Lied vom hürnen Seyfrid*: critical edition, with Introduction and notes (Manchester, 1958). ( = King, *Hürnen Seyfrid*.)

Klaeber, Fr., *Beowulf and the Fight at Finnsburg* (Boston, New York, etc., 1941³). ( = Klaeber, *Beowulf*.)

Kluge, Fr., *Etymologisches Wörterbuch der deutschen Sprache*, 17. Auflage bearbeitet von W. Mitzka (1957). ( = Kluge, *EWb*.)

Kögel, Rudolf, *Geschichte der deutschen Litteratur bis zum Ausgang des Mittelalters*, Bd. I, 2 Tle. (Straßburg, 1894–7).

Konrad (Pfaffe Konrad), *Das Rolandslied*, hrsg. von Carl Wesle, 2. Auflage besorgt von Peter Wapnewski (Tübingen, 1967).

Kralik, Dietrich von, *Das Nibelungenlied*, übersetzt von Karl Simrock mit einer Einleitung von Dietrich von Kralik (Stuttgart, 1954), vii–xlviii. ( = Kralik, *Nibelungenlied*.)

—— *Die Sigfridtrilogie im Nibelungenlied und in der Thidrekssaga*, Tl. I (Halle, 1941; no further volumes). ( = Kralik, *Trilogie*.)

Krappe, A. H., *Études de mythologie et de folklore germaniques* (Paris, 1927). ( = Krappe, *Mythologie*.)

## BIBLIOGRAPHY

Kromp, Justina, 'Die Personennamen der mittelhochdeutschen Heldenepen in den Urkunden vor deren Entstehungszeit', dissertation in typescript (Wien, 1943).

Kuhn, Hugo, 'Brunhild und das Kriemhildlied', in *Frühe Epik Westeuropas und die Vorgeschichte des Nibelungenliedes* (Tübingen, 1953), 9–21 (see Wais, Kurt).

Lamprecht (Pfaffe Lamprecht), *Lamprechts Alexander*, hrsg. von Karl Kinzel (Halle, 1884).

Langlois, Ernst, *Table des noms propres de toute nature compris dans les chansons de geste imprimées* (Paris, 1904).

Lexer, Matthias, *Mittelhochdeutsches Handwörterbuch* (3 Bde., Leipzig, 1872–8).

Leyen, Fr. von der, *Deutsches Sagenbuch* (2 Tle., München), I: *Die Götter und Göttersagen der Germanen* ($1924^3$); II: *Die deutsche Heldensage* ($1923^2$). (= von der Leyen, *Sagenbuch*.)

Lunzer, Justus, 'Elegast', *PBB* LI (1927), 149–95. (= Lunzer, *Elegast*.)

Malone, Kemp, *Deor* (London, $1949^2$). (= Malone, *Deor*.)

—— *Studies in Heroic Legend and Current Speech* (Copenhagen, 1959). (= Malone, *Studies*.)

—— *Widsith* (London, 1936; Copenhagen, $1962^2$). (= Malone, *Widsith*.)

*Der Marner*, hrsg. von Philip Strauch (Straßburg, 1876; *QF* XIV).

Martin, Ernst, *Van Bere Wisselauwe* (Straßburg, 1889; *QF* LV). (= Martin, *Wisselauwe*.)

—— *Deutsches Heldenbuch*, Bd. II (Berlin, 1866). (= Martin, *DHB*.)

—— *Kudrun* (Halle, 1872). (= Martin, *Kudrun*.)

—— *Wolframs von Eschenbach Parzival und Titurel* (2 Bde., Halle, 1903). (= Martin, *Parzival*.)

Matras, Chr. See under *CCF*, p. xxvi.

Meier, John, *Balladen* (*Deutsche Literatur in Entwicklungsreihen*, 2 Bde., Leipzig, 1935). (= Meier, *Balladen*.)

Mone, Franz Joseph, *Untersuchungen zur Geschichte der teutschen Heldensage* (Quedlinburg und Leipzig, 1836).

Moravcsik, Gyula, *Byzantinoturcica* (2 Tle., Budapest, 1942–3), I: *Die byzantinischen Quellen der Geschichte der Türkvölker*; II: *Sprachreste der Türkvölker in den byzantinischen Quellen*.

Much, Rudolf, *Deutsche Stammeskunde* (Berlin und Leipzig, $1920^3$).

—— *Die Germania des Tacitus* (Heidelberg, 1937; Darmstadt, $1959^2$). (= Much, *Germania*.)

Müllenhoff, Karl, 'Zeugnisse und Excurse zur deutschen Heldensage', *ZfdA* XII (1865), 253–386, 413–36. (= Müllenhoff, *ZE*.)

Naumann, Hans, 'Altnordische Namenstudien', *Acta Germanica*, Neue Reihe I (Berlin, 1912).

Neckel, Gustav, *Edda* (2 Bde. Heidelberg, $1927^2$). (= Neckel, *Edda*.)

—— *Deutsche Sagen*, Bd. I: *Sagen aus dem germanischen Altertum* (Leipzig, 1935). (= Neckel, *Deutsche Sagen*.) See under *Sn E*, p. xxviii.

# BIBLIOGRAPHY

Neidhart von Reuental, *Neidharts Lieder*, hrsg. von Moriz Haupt, neu bearbeitet von Edmund Wießner (Leipzig, 1923²).

Norman, Frederick, *Dukus Horant*, hrsg. von P. F. Ganz, F. Norman und W. Schwarz (Tübingen, 1964), 'Die Sagen- und literargeschichtlichen Probleme', 75–131.

—— *Waldere* (London, 1933).

Ohly, Ernst Friedrich, *Sage und Legende in der Kaiserchronik* (Münster, 1940).

*Orendel*, hrsg. von A. E. Berger (Bonn, 1880).

*Oswald, Der Münchener Oswald*, hrsg. von Georg Baesecke (Breslau, 1907).

Paff, William J., *The Geographic and Ethnic Names in the Þiðriks saga* (Harvard Germanic Studies II, 's-Gravenhage, 1959).

Panzer, Friedrich, *Deutsche Heldensage im Breisgau* (Heidelberg, 1904). ( = Panzer *Heldensage im Breisgau*.)

—— *Hilde-Gudrun* (Halle, 1901).

—— *Italische Normannen in deutscher Heldensage* (Frankfurt am Main, 1925). ( = Panzer, *Italische Normannen*.)

—— *Der Kampf am Wasichenstein* (Speyer, 1948). ( = Panzer, *Wasichenstein*.)

—— *Das Nibelungenlied* (Stuttgart, 1955). ( = Panzer, *Nibelungenlied*.)

—— *Studien zur germanischen Sagengeschichte*, Bd. II: *Sigfrid* (München, 1912). ( = Panzer, *Sigfrid*.)

Paulus Diaconus, *Pauli Diaconi Historia Langobardorum*, ed. H. Droysen (Berlin, 1878; MGH script. rer. Lang. II). ( = Paul. Diac.)

—— *The History of the Langobards by Paul the Deacon*, trans. W. D. Foulke (New York, 1907).

Ploß, E. E., 'Die Nibelungenüberlieferung im Spiegel der langobardischen Namen', *FF* XXXIV (1960), 53–60.

Plötzeneder, Gisela, *Die Teufelssage von Dietrich von Bern* (Germanistiche Abhandlungen VI, Innsbruck, 1959).

Priscus, *Historici graeci minores*, vol. I, ed. L. Dindorf (Leipzig, 1870). (Priscus' report of the East Roman embassy to Attila is translated in Gustav Freytag, *Bilder aus der deutschen Vergangenheit*, Bd. I: *Aus dem Mittelalter* (Leipzig, 1922⁴²), 143–72.)

Procopius, *Procopius, with an English Translation*, by H. B. Dewing (Loeb Classical Library, 6 vols., London and New York), II: *The Vandalic War* (1916) ( = *Vand*.); III–V: *The Gothic War* (1919–28) ( = *Goth*.).

Raßmann, August, *Die deutsche Heldensage* (2 Bde., Hannover, 1857–8). ( = Raßmann, *DHS*.)

Redin, M., *Studies on Uncompounded Personal Names in Old English* (Uppsala, 1919).

Röhrich, Lutz, *Erzählungen des späten Mittelalters* (2 Bde., Bern und München, 1962, 1967). ( = Röhrich, *Erzählungen*.)

Rosenfeld, Hellmut, 'Die Namen der Heldendichtung, insbesondere Nibelung, Hagen, Wate, Hetel, Horand, Gudrun', *BzNf*, Neue Folge I (1966), 231–65. ( = Rosenfeld, *Namen*.)

## BIBLIOGRAPHY

Rudolf von Ems, *Willehalm von Orlens*, hrsg. von Victor Junk (Berlin, 1905).

*Salman und Morolf*, hrsg. von Fr. Vogt (Halle, 1880. *Die deutschen Dichtungen von Salomon und Markolf*, Bd. I).

Schieb, Gabriele. See Heinrich von Veldeke.

Schlaug, Wilhelm, *Die altsächsischen Personennamen vor dem Jahre 1000* (Kopenhagen und Lund, 1962). (= Schlaug I.)

—— *Studien zu den altsächsischen Personennamen des 11. und 12. Jahrhunderts* (Kopenhagen und Lund, 1955). (= Schlaug II.)

Schneider, Hermann, *Deutsche Heldensage* (Berlin und Leipzig, 1930). (= Schneider, *DHS*.)

—— *Die Gedichte und die Sage von Wolfdietrich* (München, 1913). (= Schneider, *Wolfdietrich* (1913).)

—— *Germanische Heldensage* (3 Bde., Berlin und Leipzig, 1928–34); Bd. I (Berlin, 1962²). (= Schneider, *GHS*.)

—— *Kleine Schriften zur Heldensage und Literatur des Mittelalters* (Berlin, 1962). (= Schneider, *Kl. Schr.*)

—— *Wolfdietrich A* (Halle, 1931). (= Schneider, *Wolfdietrich* (1931).)

Schoener, A. C., *Der jüngere Sigenot* (Heidelberg, 1928). (= Schoener, *Sigenot*.)

Schönfeld, M., *Wörterbuch der altgermanischen Personen- und Völkernamen nach der Überlieferung des klassischen Altertums bearbeitet* (Heidelberg, 1911).

Schramm, Gottfried, *Namenschatz und Dichtersprache* (Göttingen, 1957).

Schröder, Eduard, *Deutsche Namenkunde* (Göttingen, 1944²). (= E. Schröder, *DNK*.) See *Kaiserchronik* above.

Schütte, Gudmund, *Gotthiod und Utgard* (2 Bde., Kopenhagen und Jena, 1935–6). (= Schütte, *Gotthiod*.)

Schwarz, Ernst, *Deutsche Namenforschung*, Bd. I: *Ruf- und Familiennamen* (Göttingen, 1949).

Searle, W. G., *Anglo-Saxon Bishops, Kings and Nobles* (Cambridge, 1894). (= Searle II.)

—— *Onomasticon Anglo-Saxonicum* (Cambridge, 1897). (= Searle.)

See, Klaus von, *Germanische Heldensage* (Frankfurt am Main, 1971). (= von See, *GHS*.)

*Seifrid de Ardemont*. See Albrecht von Scharfenberg.

Smith, William, *A Smaller Classical Dictionary*, ed. E. H. Blakeney (London, 1910).

Socin, Adolf, *Mittelhochdeutsches Namenbuch nach oberrheinischen Quellen des zwölften und dreizehnten Jahrhunderts* (Basel, 1903).

Splett, J., *Rüdiger von Bechelaren* (Heidelberg, 1968).

Stackmann, K., *Kudrun*, hrsg. von Karl Bartsch, überarbeitet und neu eingeleitet von Karl Stackmann (Wiesbaden, 1965⁵).

Strecker, Karl, *Waltharius* (Berlin, 1947³).

Stroheker, K. F., 'Studien zu den historisch-geographischen Grundlagen der Nibelungendichtung', *DVjs* XXXII (1958), 216–40.

# BIBLIOGRAPHY

Sweet, Henry, *The Oldest English Texts* (*EETS*, London, 1885).

Symons, B., *Germanische Heldensage* (Straßburg, 1892²). ( = Symons, *Heldensage*.)

—— *Kudrun* (Halle, 1883).

Tacitus, P. Cornelius, *De Origine et situ Germanorum*, ed. J. G. C. Anderson (Oxford, 1938). ( = Tacitus, *Germania*.)

Thompson, E. A., *A History of Attila and the Huns* (Oxford, 1948).

Toller, T. Northcote, *An Anglo-Saxon Dictionary*, based on the manuscript collections of Joseph Bosworth (Oxford, 1882–7). ( = Bosworth–Toller.)

Tonnelat, Ernst, *La Chanson des Nibelungen* (Paris, 1926).

Ulrich von Zazikhoven, *Lanzelet*, hrsg. von K. A. Hahn (Frankfurt am Main, 1845).

Voretzsch, Carl, *Epische Studien I: Die Composition des Huon von Bordeaux* (Halle, 1900).

Vries, Jan de, *Altnordische Literaturgeschichte* (2 Bde., Berlin, 1941–2). ( = de Vries, *Altn. Litg.*)

—— *Heldenlied und Heldenepos* (Bern und München, 1961). ( = de Vries, *Heldenlied*.)

—— *Kelten und Germanen* (Bern und München, 1960).

—— *König Rother* (Heidelberg, 1922). ( = de Vries, *Rother*.)

Wackernagel, W., 'Die deutschen Appellativnamen', *Germania* IV (1859), 129–59.

Wais, Kurt, *Frühe Epik Westeuropas und die Vorgeschichte des Nibelungenliedes*, Bd. I, mit einem Beitrag von Hugo Kuhn (Tübingen, 1953; no further volumes). ( = Wais, *Frühe Epik*.)

Walther von der Vogelweide, *Die Gedichte Walthers von der Vogelweide*, hrsg. von Karl Lachmann, 9. Auflage besorgt von Carl von Kraus (1930).

Wartmann, H., *Urkundenbuch der Abtei Sanct Gallen* (Zürich und St. Gallen, 1863).

Werle, Georg, *Die ältesten germanischen Personennamen* (Straßburg, 1910).

Wernher der Gartenære, *Meier Helmbrecht*, hrsg. von Fr. Panzer (Tübingen, 1953⁵).

Widukind, *Widukindi rerum gestarum Saxonicarum*, ed. P. Hirsen et H.-E. Lohmann (Hannover, 1935); trans. Ernst Metelmann in *Chroniken des Mittelalters* (Winkler-Verlag, München, 1964), 20–118.

*Wigamur*, hrsg. von Carl von Kraus (Heidelberg, 1926²).

Wirnt von Grafenberg, *Wigalois*, hrsg. von J. M. N. Kapteyn (Bonn, 1926).

Wisniewski, Roswitha, *Die Darstellung des Niflungenuntergangs in der Thidrekssaga* (Tübingen, 1961). ( = Wisniewski, *Thidrekssaga*.)

—— *Deutsche Heldensage*, von Hermann Schneider, 2. Auflage besorgt von Roswitha Wisniewski (1964). ( = Wisniewski, *DHS* (1964).)

Wittenwiler, Heinrich, *Heinrich Wittenwilers Ring*, hrsg. von E. Wiessner (*Deutsche Literatur in Entwicklungsreihen*, Leipzig, 1931).

Wolff, K. F., *König Laurin und sein Rosengarten* (Bozen, 1947³). ( = Wolff, *Laurin*.)

Wolfram von Eschenbach, *Wolfram von Eschenbach*, hrsg. von Karl Lachmann (Berlin und Leipzig, 1930⁶): *Parzival*, 13–388; *Titurel*, 389–420; *Willehalm*, 423–640 (7th ed., revised by E. Hartl (Berlin, 1952), contains an index of personal names). See Martin, Ernst.

# BIBLIOGRAPHY

Woolf, H. B., *The Old Germanic Principles of Name-Giving* (Baltimore, 1939).

Wrenn, C. L., *Supplement* to R. W. Chambers, *Beowulf* (Cambridge, 1963³). ( = Wrenn, *Supplement*.)

Wyatt, A. J., *An Anglo-Saxon Reader* (Cambridge, 1930⁴).

Zeuß, Kaspar, *Die Deutschen und die Nachbarstämme* (München, 1837; repr. Heidelberg, 1925).

Zingerle, I. V., 'Zu den Bildern in Runkelstein', *Germania* XXIII (1878), 28–30.

Zink, Georges, *Les Légendes héroïques de Dietrich et d'Ermrich dans des littératures germaniques* (Lyon et Paris, 1950). ( = Zink, *Légendes*.)

—— *Le Wunderer* (Paris, 1949). ( = Zink, *Wunderer*.)

Zupitza, Julius, *Deutsches Heldenbuch*, Bd. V (Berlin, 1870). ( = Zupitza, *DHB*.)

# THE CATALOGUE

# ERRATA

p. 3, note 4. *Delete* 'glow'

p. 4, note 3. *For* p. 157 *read* p. 57

p. 11, right column, line 10. *For* p. 101 *read* p. 10

p. 16, note 8, line 5. *For* n. 7 *read* n. 1

p. 24, left column, line 40. *For* reader *read* leader

p. 25, left column, l. 8. *For* 'Vildimælrik' *read* 'Vildimælrikr'
    right column, add to references under DIETMAR (1): **Wd (B)** 99, 6

p. 28, left column, line 28. *For* Erdman *read* Erdmann

p. 29, note 7. *For* Falke *read* Valke

p. 30, left column, line 43. *For* p. 114 *read* p. 113 ff.

p. 48, right column, line 42. *For* Froute *read* Fruote

p. 53, right column, line 3. *For* Hildur *read* Hilldur

p. 57, right column, line 43. *For* p. 4 *read* p. 9

p. 121, right column, line 32. *For* Seinild *read* Sienild

p. 139, right column, line 31. *For* Hrimniir *read* Hrimnir
               line 53. *For* Bern *read* Berne

p. 146, note 6, line 4. *For* Diderick *read* Diderik

p. 151, note 7, line 6. *For* pp. 103 ff. *read* pp. 102 ff.

p. 155, right column, line 9. *For* Andvaranaulr *read* Andvaranautr

p. 158, left column, line 13. *For* Fruote (A) *read* Fruote (1)

p. 163, right column, line 1. *Add* , 113.

# A

ÂBEL
Dietwart's companion.
ref: **DF** 401
pn: biblical.

ABELON, ABELUNG, see AMELUNC (2)

ABENTROT, see EBENRÔT

ABILA, see SEBEL

ABRAHEMISCH, adj.
The messenger of Machorel, who brings dragons' eggs to Ortnît, states that one of them contains 'ûz dem garten ein abrahemschiu krote', which, when full-grown, will produce a marvellous jewel.
ref: **O** 510, 4
The reference to the jewel found in a toad's head is a well-known superstition, but whether the toad is thought to come from the Garden of Abraham near Jerusalem or the Giardino d'Abraham near Merano in Italy is uncertain (A. Amelung, *DHB* IV. 260; Bach II, § 740).

ACHIVI, pl.
ref: **W** 729
The Greeks.

ADÂM
ref: **R** 374; **jSn** 5, 6; **V(w)** 108, 3
The first man of biblical tradition.

ADEL
Reproaches Orgeis for harming women.
ref: **V(w)** 189, 4
pn: descriptive, cf. MHG *adel*, 'nobility'.

ADELGÊR, see MADELGÊR
pn: from 8th-cent. German, especially LG (Förstemann I. 166 f.; Schlaug I. 49 f.; II. 65), 9th-cent. OE (Searle, 37 f.) and Lb (Bruckner, 216). In the *Kaiserchronik* a Bavarian duke named Adelgêr defeats the Roman army of Severus (6623 ff.).[1] The name also occurs for a peasant in *Neidharts Lieder* 62, 8.

ADELGUNDA, see SIGELINT (1)

ADELHART
Dietrich's man.
ref: **B** 10380
pn: from 8th-cent. German (Förstemann I. 170 f.; Schlaug I. 50; II. 66), from *c.* 700 OE (Searle, 39 f.; Feilitzen, 184).

ADELLINT
Sintram's daughter, attendant on Helche.
ref: **Kl** 2469
pn: 8th-cent. German (Förstemann I. 174; Schlaug I. 51; II. 66).

ADELRANT
A giant in the service of Nîtgêr, killed by Îmîân (see Wîcram).
ref: **V(h)** 716, 1; **V(w)** 647, 1

ADELREICH, see AMELRÎCH

ADRÎÂN, see ALDRÎÂN

AFFIGANT, see TERFÎANT

ALBERÎCH
In **N**, a dwarf with the strength of twelve. Sîfrit defeats him in a wrestling bout and wins the cloak of invisibility (MHG *tarnkappe*) from him as well as control of the Nibelunge treasure.[2] Thenceforth he acts as Sîfrit's treasurer. Later Sîfrit pulls his beard in mock combat (see Eugel, p. 43).
In **O**, a five-hundred-year-old dwarf ruler of an underground realm in Lombardy, who is only visible to the possessor of a magic ring. He appears in the form of a small child or angel to his son Ortnît, to whose mother he has given the magic ring now in Ortnît's possession;[3] after defeating his son in a wrestling bout, Alberîch gives him the sword Rôse.[4] He helps Ortnît win the daughter of the heathen king, Machorel, on whom he plays tricks: unseen, he casts down the heathen's idols, strikes him in the face, and impersonates his god Mahmet. Alberîch takes back the ring from Ortnît and warns him against the fatal encounter with the dragon.

---

[1] See Ohly, 144 ff., regarding the 'Adelgersage'.
[2] In ON Eddic tradition (Rm prose; Sk ch. 46), the dwarf Andvari is the original owner of the treasure won by Sigurðr from the dragon (see Eugel, p. 43, Nibelunc (1), p. 98, and Sîfrit, p. 120 and n. 4).
[3] Alberîch has ravished Ortnît's mother (see Hempel, *Nibelungenstudien*, 150 ff., regarding this incubus motif).
[4] In **O(k)** he fetches it from Almarî in Göikelsas, probably the same place as Gloggensachsen, where he has his smithy in **AHb**, possibly Armenia (?) in the Caucasus, though the **AHb** form shows folk-etymology to MHG, *glogge, glocke*, 'glow' 'bell' (Kluge, *EWb*, 261).

## ALBERÎCH

ref: **AHb** p. 3, 18 (*Elberich*); **B** 7839; **L(DrHb)** 69, 7 (Riche); **L(K)II** 13; **N** 96, 2; **O** m 92, 4 n 119, 2; **O(C)** 237, 2 (Elberîch); **O(k)** 65, 8 (*Albreich*); **O(w)** 113, 3; **jSn** 47, 5 (MSS. *elbrich*, prints *albrecht*); **Wd(A)** m 418, 1; **Wd(k)** 317, 1 (*Albreich*)

Outside the epics rare references to the dwarf Alberîch occur in German literature from the late 13th cent. (W. Grimm, *DHS*, 187, 309; Jänicke, *ZE*, 330).[1] He is depicted on the 14th-cent. frescoes at Runkelstein in the South Tyrol (Zingerle, 28).

In the Þs the dwarf Alfrikr (I. 34, 21; B *Alpris*) has made the swords Ekkisax and Naglringr; he obtains the latter for Þiðrekr (see Eckesahs, p. 34, Grîme, p. 53, and Nagelrinc, p. 96).

pn: 5th-cent. WFr (Baesecke, *Vorgeschichte*, 41); 8th-cent. German (Förstemann I. 71; Socin, 566, 572; Schlaug I. 43; II. 70); from *c.* 600 OE (Searle, 16 ff., 533; Feilitzen, 176 ff.).

The OFr equivalent, *Auberi*, of which *Auberon* is the hypocoristic form, occurs in the *ch.d.g.* (Langlois, 52 f.).

Although the name Alberîch (MHG *alp*, 'elf', *rîche*, 'powerful', cf. Goth. *reiks*, 'ruler') can be appropriately interpreted as 'ruler of supernatural beings',[2] it is probably brought into **N** from outside;[2] in **O** his name and role may well derive from French sources, for his activities on Ortnît's bridal quest closely parallel those of Auberon in the 12th-cent. OFr epic *Huon de Bordeaux* (see Voretzsch, 250 ff.; Schneider, *Wolfdietrich* (1913), 387).

## ALBRANT, see ALEBRANT

## ALBRECHT von Kemenâten
Reputed author of *Goldemar* (**G**).

ref: **G** 2, 2

He is referred to by Rudolf von Ems in his *Willehalm von Orlens*, 2244 f., and his *Alexander*, 3252 f., and in records between 1230 and 1240 in Thurgau and the Tyrol (E. Klaass, 'Goldemar', *VfL* II (1936), 55–7).

## ALBRIAN
Father of Albrianus.

ref: **E(s)** 187, 1

Alberîch is probably intended.

## ALBRIANUS
A dwarf, the son of Albrianus, who warns Dietrich against Fasolt.

ref: **E(a)** 186, 3 (*elbrians* gen.); **E(s)** 186, 3

---

[1] In the 12th-cent. 'Spielmannsepik' *Orendel*, a dwarf named Alban (2414) attempts to ravish the Amazonian heroine, Brîde, who tramples on him, after which he submits and aids her and the hero, Orendel: thus he plays the roles of Alberîch in **N** and **O**.
[2] Kralik, *Trilogie*, 213, takes him to be the original guardian of the treasure.
[3] In **W** Hagano's father is named Hagathio (see p. 157).

## ALPHART

ALDEBRANT, see ALEBRANT (3)

## ALDRÎAN
Father of Hagen (1),[3] and once a distinguished vassal of Etzel (**N** 1755); in **N** his name is first used by the water-sprite Sigelint to address Hagen as 'Aldrîânes kint' (1539). In **Rg** he is killed by Ilsân in the combats at Worms.

ref: **N** 1539, 2 (*C-text always Adrîân); **Rg(D)** 44, 3; **Rg(F)** v. 2, 1 (MS. *Adrian*); **Rg(P)** 65 (MS. *allorianis* gen.)

In the Þs Aldrian (I. 319, 6; Mb[2] *Irungr*), a king in Niflungaland, and Oda are the parents of Gunnarr, Gisler, and Gernoz, but Oda bears Högni by a demon.[4] This name is also used for Högni's son (II. 323, 5) and for the son of Attila and Grimilldr (II. 281, 10).[5] (See pp. 60, 100.)

pn: no record found.[6]

## ALEBRANT (1) Hildebrant's son, see HADUBRANT

pn: 8th-cent. Lb (Bruckner, 220); German from 11th cent. (Förstemann I. 81; Schlaug II. 68; Holthausen, 499; Müllenhoff, *ZE*, 357 f.).

## ALEBRANT (2) Dietrich's man
Fights Uolrîch von Tegelingen at Rabene (Ravenna).

ref: **Rs** 736, 1 (Albrant)

## ALEBRANT (3) Berhtunc's son
Receives Brâbant from Wolfdietrich; he is killed at Tischcâl.

ref: **Wd(D)** IX. 100, 1 (Albrant); **Wd(Gr)** 1988, 1; **Wd(w)** 1903, 3 (Aldebrant)

## ALEXANDER
In **R** he is said to have brought back the jewel Claugustian from the Orient.

ref: **E(d)** 35, 9; **R** 4951; **V(h)** 868, 10; **V(w)** 715, 10

Alexander the Great, the Macedonian conqueror (†323 B.C.), is celebrated in medieval epic, e.g. the 12th-cent. *Alexanderlied* of Pfaffe Lamprecht.

## ALPHART
Dietrich's man, nephew of Hildebrant and brother of Wolfhart; in **AHb** and **V(w)** his father is Amelolt, in **A** Sigehêr (see the genealogy under Hildebrant, p. 65 n. 3). In **DF** and **Rs** his death in battle against Ermenrîch's forces at Bôlonje (Bologna) is

---

[4] Gibeche (ON Gjúki) is the traditional father of the Burgundians as in **hS**, but Dancrât replaces him in **N** (see Gibeche (1), p. 51 and n. 1.).
[5] The name Aldrias occurs for Högni's son in the Faroese ballad *Aldrias táttur* (*Sjúrðar kvæði* IV, version Bb and D: *CCF* I, 84 ff., 137 ff.).
[6] See Panzer, *Nibelungenlied*, 313, and S. Gutenbrunner, 'Über einige Namen in der Nibelungendichtung', *ZfdA* LXXXV (1954–5), 53 ff., for discussion of this name.

## ALPHART

bitterly lamented by Dietrich.[1] In **A** the young hero, with covered shield, rides alone against the army of Ermenrîch besieging Berne (Verona) and routs 80 men; he is then attacked by Witege and Heime, and Witege kills him with a blow from behind.[2] His death increases Dietrich's resolve to defend Berne.

ref: **A** 15, 4; **AHb** p. 3, 6; **DF** 3010 (MS. A *Hibart*); **Rg(D)** 53, 1; **Rg(F)** II. 15, 1; **Rg(P)** 261; **Rs** 10, 5; **V(w)** 843, 4

pn: 8th-cent. German (Förstemann I. 68 f.; Schlaug I. 42; II. 69); the OFr equivalent, *Aufart*, occurs in the *ch.d.g.* for Saracens (Langlois, 56).

## ALPHERE (ALPKÊR)

Father of Walther: in **W** he rules Aquitania and gives his son as a hostage to Attila. In **WuH** he waits for Walther and Hildegunde at Lengers (Langres). In **Rs** he is one of Dietrich's men.

ref: **B** 9904 (Alpkêr); **Rs** 265, 1 (W *Alpher*, R *Apher*); **W** 77 (Alphere); **WuH** (Wien) I. 9, 1 (Alpkêr)

In the 14th-cent. German poem *Diu Heidin* (Hagen, *Gesamtabenteuer* I. 409), Alpharius woos a princess Dêmuot (745 ff.).

In the OE *Waldere*, Waldere is termed 'Ælfheres sunu' (I. 11), cf. 'Alpharides' (**W** 839, etc.).

pn: originally in front variation to *Walther*; the second component *-here* (OHG *heri*, 'army') sometimes is replaced by *-kêr* (OHG *kêr*, *gêr*, 'spear') (see Volker): 8th-cent. German (Förstemann I. 67, 69; Schlaug I. 41 f.; II. 69; Kögel I. ii. 285) and Lb (Bruckner, 220), and 9th-cent. OE (Searle, 12 f., 532; Binz, 160).

## AMBOLT, see AMELUNC (2)

## AME
Related to Astolt.[3]

ref: **B** 5500

pn: masc. *Amo* and fem. *Ama* 8th- and 9th-cent. German (Förstemann I. 87; Schlaug I. 45).

## AMELGART (1) von der Normandîe (Normandy)
Daughter of Ballus, wife of Sigehêr (4), and mother of Ortnît (1).

ref: **DF** 1944 (A *Amergalt*); **O** m 70, 1; **O(C)** 179, 2

pn: *Amel-* suggests connection with Dietrich's kin (see Amelunc (1)): 8th-cent. German (Förstemann I. 93).

## AMELGART (2) von Swêden (Sweden)
Betrothed to Alphart.

ref: **A** 108, 1

---

[1] By an oversight of the author he is killed twice: by Biterunc von Engellant and by Reinhêr von Pârîse (**DF** 952 6 ff., 969 3 ff.).
[2] Courtly etiquette forbids him to reveal his identity (see G. Ehrismann, 'Zum Hildebrandsliede', *PBB* XXXIV (1907), 276): his device, which

## AMELGÊR (1) von Tengelingen
Father of Wolfrât and regent of Italy during Rother's absence. Rebellion breaks out on his death. Formerly he has been driven from his kingdom by Elvewine, and Berhter (1) has restored him to it.

ref: **R** 736

pn: 7th-cent. WFr, 8th-cent. German (Förstemann I. 92 f.; II. i. 121; Schlaug I. 44). This figure may represent the Bavarian counts of Tegelingen, with possessions extending from Salzburg to Friuli in the 12th cent. (Panzer, *Italische Normannen*, 63 ff.).

## AMELGÊR (2) von Brisen[4]
Dietrich's man.

ref: **A** 74, 3

## AMELHERE, see RÛMELHER

pn: 9th-cent. German (Förstemann I. 94).

## AMELO(L)T, see AMELUNC (2)

## AMELRÎCH
The brother of Else's ferryman at the Danube crossing, who has been exiled because of a feud: at the suggestion of the water-sprite, Sigelint, Hagen pretends to be 'Amelrîch', but the ferryman realizes the imposture and strikes Hagen with an oar; Hagen kills him (see Else m. (1), pp. 35 f.).

ref: **N** 1548, 2; **N(k)** 1554, 2 (*Adelreiche*)

In the Þs Þetleifr calls himself 'Vildimælrikr' at Sigurðr's castle (I. 225, 5: A *Hilldimel*) and 'Elminrikr' when he joins Þiðrek's company (I. 236, 6: A *Æmelrik*, B *Enielrik*) (see p. 25).

pn: 5th cent. for the son of the Visigothic King Alaric; 8th-cent. German (Förstemann I. 94 f.; II. i. 121; Schlaug I. 45; II. 71). It occurs for a peasant in *Neidharts Lieder*, 59, 31.

## AMELUNC (1) family name (pl. AMELUNGE)

The name applies to Dietrich's relatives and to his heroes; his kingdom, with its capitals at Berne (Verona) and Rabene (Ravenna), is 'Amelunge lant', and Dietrich himself is the 'vogt von Amelungen'. Unlike **N**, in which all Dietrich's men are termed 'Amelunge' (1981, 3, etc.), **DF** and **Rs** make a distinction between 'Amelunge' and 'Wülfinge', the latter being related to Hildebrant (see Wülfinge, p. 153). The term 'Amelunc' is also used for Dietrich himself (**B** 8098; **DF** 3382, etc.).

ref: **A** 77, 3; **B** 5174; **DF** 7228; **Kl** 3476; **N** 1721, 2; **Rs** 611, 6; **jSn** 102, 10; **V(w)** 299, 6

The Þs, like the MHG epics, refers to

---

is Dietrich's, a golden lion and eagle on a white ground, would have saved him.
[3] Either wife (W. Grimm, *DHS*, 154) or brother (Müllenhoff, *ZE*, 237).
[4] The manuscript has 'Brysen': this may represent MHG Brissen, Brescia in N. Italy.

## AMELUNC (1)

Þiðrekr's people as 'Aumlungar' (II. 180, 11, etc.) and to his kingdom in North Italy as 'Amlungaland (Aumlungaland)' (I. 134 (4), etc.).

pn: 7th-cent. Lb (Paul. Diac. ch. v, 10), 8th-cent. German (Förstemann I. 90; Socin, 566, 572; Schlaug I. 45; II. 71); see also *Neidharts Lieder*, 64, 28, where the name is used for a peasant.

The component *Amel-* is frequent in Bavarian and Alemannic place-names, cf. the 12th-cent. Regensburg gloss 'Amelunge' for 'Baier' (Müllenhoff, *ZE*, 415).
This name, which probably signified 'bravery' and 'vigour' (Goth. *amals, ON *aml*: see J. Grimm, *GDS*, 313; Holthausen, *GEWb*, 6), originally belonged to the royal family of the Ostrogoths, whose early ruler Ermanarîc (see Ermenrîch) is termed 'nobilissimus Amalorum' by Jordanes in the 6th cent. (ch. xxiii); Theodoric the Great (see Dietrich (1)) was also of this family, cf. 'Þēodrīc wæs Amulinga' in King Alfred's OE translation of Boethius (Wyatt, VIII. 21 f.). Jordanes calls the Ostrogoths 'Amalae' (ch. v), although, in fact, their tribal name was 'Greutingi' (Zeuß, 420 f.). Jordanes makes 'Amalus' the eponymous hero of the Goths (loc. cit.), whereas in Cassiodorus he is named 'Amala' (XI. 1).[1]

## AMELUNC (2) (ABELON, ABELUNG, AMELO(L)T, AMBOLT, AMELON, AMEROLD, LUMMERT, etc.) von Garten (Garda in N. Italy)

Dietrich's man, Hildebrant's brother-in-law —he marries Hildebrant's sister, Mergart— and father of Wolfhart, Sigestap, and Alphart: in **jH** he warns Hildebrant against the latter's son, Alebrant (see Hadebrant (1), pp. 56 f.). In the epics he plays minor roles: in **DF** he remains at Garte; in **Rg(D)** he stays at Berne (Verona), whereas in **Rg(A)** he goes with Dietrich's men to Worms and defeats Gunther in the combats. In **ED** a 'Lummert ût dem Garten' accompanies Dirik's expedition against the 'köninck van Armentriken' (= Ermenrîch).[2]

ref: **A** 44, 2 (MS. *amelot*); **AHb** p. 3, 4 (*Amlung*; p. 6, 4 *amelolt*, etc.); **DF** 3633 (Amelolt: MS. A *amlot*; 3700 MS. A *Arnolt*); **ED** 17, 3 (*her Lummert vth dem garden*); **jH** 2, 1 (eir *Abelon*, l *Amelon*, a *awelung*, bedfgmop *Abelung*, knq *Amelung*, D *Abelan*, N *Abeloen*, W *Ambelung*, V *Amalunc*); **Rg(A)** 102, 3 (Amelolt: f *amelung*, etc.); **Rg(C)** 389 (*Amelolt*, also *Amerold*); **Rg(D)** 81, 1 (*Amelolt*); **Rg(P)** 234 (*Amesiges kint* = Wolfhart); **jSn** 93, 7 (prints *amellung*); **V(w)** 843, 7 (*Ambolt*)

In the Þs the pn Amlungr (Aumlungr) is used for two persons: (1) The son of Hornbogi (I. 249, 15), who joins Þiðrekr's company. In Bertangaland Þiðrekr sends Amelung's horse and shield as gifts to King Isungr, whose messenger, Sigurðr, has demanded tribute; Amlungr rides after him, and Sigurðr, who is a relative, allows Amlungr to bind him to a tree and returns him his property; Viðga, disbelieving Amlungr's assertion that he has forced Sigurðr to return it, is convinced when he sees the broken fetters left by Sigurðr (II. 6–14); in the combats he defeats the sixth son of Isungr (II. 20–2).[3] (2) The nephew of the younger Elsungr (II. 337, 20). Hildibrandr defeats him when he returns to Bern—in Þs a certain Konrádur (II. 343, 9) takes the role of Amelunc (2), and warns Hildibrandr against his son, Alibrandr.

pn: considerable variation in transmission; late forms show a replacement of the suffix *-unc* by *-olt* (from OHG *waltan*). The form *Amelolt* occurs frequently in *Neidharts Lieder*, 89, 15, etc.

## AMELUNC (3) von Rœmisch lant (Italy)
The son of Hugdietrich and the father of Diethêr, Ermenrîch, and Dietmâr in **DF** (see the genealogy under Dietrich, p. 26 n. 1).

ref: **DF** 2379

AMEROLD, see AMELUNC (2)

## ÂMÎE
Daughter of Wernhêr von Wernhêres marke. Wolfdietrich wins a tournament for her hand, but arranges for his vassal Herbrant (1) to marry her: their children are Hildebrant, Nêre, Elsân, and Mergart (see the genealogy under Hildebrant, p. 75 n. 3).

ref: **AHb** p. 6, 2; **Wd(D)** VII. 143, 1; **Wd(Gr)** 1451, 1

pn: MHG *amîe*, 'beloved', is possibly the origin.

## ANASTASIUS
In **E(s)** Dietrich is said to have ruled in his time.

ref: **E(s)** 284, 6

Anastasius II was Pope from 492 to 497, during the reign of Theodoric the Great in Italy.

## ANTFUHS von Gabelîn
Etzel's power is greater than his.

ref: **B** 314

## ANTZÎUS von Kriechenlande (ANZIGUS)
Father of Hugdietrich.

---

[1] Possibly this family name is preserved in the ON Hlöð ('Battle of the Goths and Huns'), where Hlöðr, the son of the Goth, Heiðrekr, by the daughter of Humli, the King of the Huns, is termed 'Humlungr' (10, 9). See Baesecke, *Vorgeschichte*, 178.

[2] It is possible that there is influence from the Danish ballads here (de Boor, *Kl. Schr.* I. 46; see also n. 3 below)

[3] This figure is reflected in the youthful hero Humblum (Humerlumer, Hommerlom, etc.) of the Danish ballads *Kong Diderik og hans Kæmper*, in which his father's name is Abelon, and *Kong Diderik i Birtingsland* (*DgF* I. 94 ff., 124 ff.).

## ANTZÎUS

ref: **AHb** p. 6, 15 (*anzigus*); **Wd(B)** 3, 1 (ef *antzius*, K *anccius*, B *anczrvs*, a *atzius*, c *a(n)tzerus*, z *attenus*, *atnus*, *anzins*, *anzigus*, H *artus*); **Wd(Gr)** 9, 1; **Wd(w)** 5, 1 (*Artus*)

pn: borne by the father of Pepin II, the ancestor of Charlemagne (Paul. Diac. VI. 23), later accommodated to *Anchises*, thus linking the Carolingian dynasty with Troy (Bach I, §496); 8th-cent. German (Förstemann I. 126); the form in **Wd** and **AHb** probably derives from OFr *Anseis*, which occurs frequently in the *ch.d.g.* (Langlois, 34).[1]

The first component probably corresponds to Goth *ans*, ON *áss*, 'god' (see A. H. Krappe, 'Anses', *PBB* LVI (1932), 1–10).

## AP(P)OLLE (AP(P)OLLO)
A Saracen god.

ref: **O** 271, 2; **V(d)** 17, 9; **V(h)** 63, 4; **V(w)** 93, 11; **Wd(D)** v. 4, 3; **Wd(Gr)** 842, 3; **Wd(k)** 260, 5

pn: frequent in OFr epic (Langlois, 38 f., under *Apollin*; Flutre, 17, under *Apolan*).[2]

## AQUITANUS
= Waltharius (see Walther); pl. the people of Aquitaine.

ref: sg. **W** 972 (= Waltharius); pl. **W** 77

## ARABAN, see ORKÎSE
pn: Arabian, cf. MHG *Arâbîn*.

## ARMENTRIKEN, see ERMENRÎCH

## ARNALD, see ÎRINC

## ARNOLT (1) Rother's helper
An exiled count at the court of Constantin at Constantinople: he intervenes with 5,000 men to rescue Rother from being hanged by the men of Ymelot von Babilonie. He possesses the sword Mâl (see Wolfhart).

ref: **R** 1387

In the ME epic of *Horn*,[3] a certain Arnoldin helps Horn free the princess Rimenhild.

pn: 6th-cent. WFr, 8th-cent. German (Förstemann I. 140; Socin, 3; Schlaug I. 46; II. 72; Bach I, §301).

## ARNOLT (2) Dietwart's man
Dietwart sends him as messenger for the hand of Minne.

ref: **DF** 422

This figure probably derives from Arnolt (1)

[1] He is one of Charlemagne's warriors in the *Chanson de Roland*; the name *Anseis* for this person is retained in Pfaffe Konrad's *Rolandslied*, 113.
[2] See also Pfaffe Konrad's *Rolandslied*, 806.
[3] *King Horn*, ed. J. Hall (Oxford, 1901).
[4] One other giant is named: Grimme (see p. 53).
[5] In 1101 a Lombard crusader is reported to have killed the tame lion of the Byzantine Emperor

above (E. Martin, *DHB* II. lxvi; de Vries *Rother*, lxxiii).

## ARTELAẎ, see BETLÎ

## ARTÛS
Etzel's court is compared to that of Artûs (King Arthur) in the later Dietrich-epics.

ref: **DF** 106; **V(w)** 482, 5; **Wu(B)** 3, 1; **Wu(k)** p. 2, 12

In Þs, Iron and Apollonius, the sons of Artus, take refuge with Attila. Þiðrekr sends Herburt as his messenger to the court of Artus in Bertangaland (II. 47, 16) for the hand of his daughter Hilldr (see Herbort, p. 68).

## ASPRÎÂN
In **R** he leads twelve giants, who accompany King Rother on his bridal quest to Constantinople, he keeps the giant Witolt on a chain.[4] At the court of Constantin he kills a tame lion by hurling it against the wall (see Witolt, p. 147).[5] In **DH** he and his brothers, Witolt and Wate, accompany Horant on a bridal quest to the Greeks (zu den krichen F 48, 3, 1).

In **Rg(AD)** he is one of Kriemhilt's champions at the rose-garden in Worms, and, although he wields two swords, he is defeated by Witege (killed by him in **Rg(D)**); in **Rg(P)** he has a brother named Strûtân.

In **V(hw)** he is one of Nîtgêr's giants at Mûter and is killed by Blœdelîn (see Wîcram).

In **BW** a giant fighting the bear Wisselau calls for his help.

ref: **AHb** p. 2, 40 (*Asperian*); **BW** 11 (*espriaen*); **DH** F 41, 5, 3 (*Asprion*, later *Asprian*); **R** 626 (704 H *aspriant*, 764 Ha *aspriam*); **Rg(A)** 8, 1; **Rg(C)** 31; **Rg(D)** 46, 1; **Rg(P)** 71 (*asspan*); **Rg(V)** 224; **V(h)** 740, 4; **V(w)** 671, 4

This giant is frequently referred to in late MHG and early NHG monuments (W. Grimm, *DHS*, 173, 195, 308, 343, 353; Müllenhoff, *ZE*, 366 f.; Jänicke, *ZE*, 327; 330).

In Þs Asplian (I. 48, etc.; II. 65, etc.), the giant son of Nordian, has three brothers: Ædgæir,[6] Avæntroð, and Viðolfr (see Ebenrôt, p. 32, and Witolt, p. 148); they accompany Osanctrix on his bridal quest for Oda, the daughter of Milias (see Ôserîch, p. 103, and Rother, p. 109, n. 4).[7] Asplian is finally killed by Heimir, when he threatens the monastery to which Heimir has retired as a monk (see Heime, p. 65).

pn: mid-13th-cent. German (Mone, 95 f.; Alexius (Panzer, *Italische Normannen*, 57 n. 2).

[6] This name is cognate with that of Ogier, the warrior of Charlemagne in the *Chanson de Roland* (also in Pfaffe Konrad's *Rolandslied*, 1178), familiar in the *Karlmagnussaga* (see Paff, 53). He also appears together with Viðolfr and Avæntroð in the Skr 76 (see also p. 138 n. 6).
[7] In version I Asplian sends his three brothers, but does not go himself.

ASPRÎAN              BALÎN

Müllenhoff, *ZE*, 362); possible OFr origin, cf. *Asperant* in the *ch.d.g.* (Langlois, 50).

## ASTOLT
In **N**, the ruler of Medelicke (Melk in Austria): he gives wine to Kriemhilt and her company and directs them to Mûtâren (Mautern);[1] in **B**, he and his brother Wolfrât fight Biterolf; later they aid Biterolf and Dietleip against Gunther at Worms; in **Rs** Astolt aids Dietrich against Ermenrîch.

ref: **B** 1051; **N** 1329, 1; **Rs** 59, 1

pn: 7th-cent. Visigothic (Gamillscheg I. 356); 9th-cent. Lb (Förstemann I. 151; Ploß, 56); no record in German, but OFr equivalent *Estout* (*Estolt*) occurs in *ch.d.g.* (Langlois, 207 f.).

The first component possibly represents Goth. *asts*, 'branch', cf. Goth. *astaþ*, 'safety'.

ATTILA, see ETZEL(E)

## AUGUSTULUS
In **E(s)** it is known that Octaher von Lampart expelled him from Rome (see Ôtacher).

ref: **E(s)** 283, 5

Romulus Augustulus, the last Roman Emperor in the West, was deposed by Odoacer in 476.

## AVARES pl.
= the Huns (see Hiunen).

ref: **W** 40

The notorious Hunnish greed for gold (Lat. *avarus*, 'greedy') probably contributed to this identification of the Huns of the 5th cent. with the Avars of the 6th to 8th.

# B (see also under P)

## BÂBEHILT
A water-nymph (MHG *merwîp*): she tends Dietrich's wounds after his fight with Ecke, and prophesies that 'vrô Sælde' (Fortuna) will henceforth protect him (see Sælde, p. 114).

ref: **E(L)** m 151, 6 n 158, 4

pn: possibly based on MHG *bâbe*, *bôbe*, 'old woman', cf. Slav. *baba* (Lexer I. 107).

BALDEGRÎN (1) a giant: see VIDELNSTÔZ

pn: probably a phrase-name, based on MHG *balt*, 'quick to', and *grînen*, 'bellow, yell'.

BALDEGRÎN (2) a robber: see WIDERGRÎN

## BALDEMAR
A giant; he is killed by Wolfdietrich in Ceciljenlant (Sicily).

ref: **Wd(D)** VII. 33, 2; **Wd(Gr)** 1354, 3; **Wd(w)** 1269, 2 (1288, 4 *Waldemare*)

pn: 7th-cent. WFr, 9th-cent. German and Lb (Förstemann I. 240; Schlaug II. 73).

BALDEWÎN (1) Dietwart's man
Dietwart sends him as a messenger for the hand of Minne.

ref: **DF** 431

pn: 7th-cent. German (Förstemann I. 242; Schlaug II. 73; Bach I, § 456).

BALDEWÎN (2) a robber: see BETEWÎN

BALDUNC (1) a dwarf
Descended from Alberîch: Dietrich rescues him from a 'wilder man', and he gives Dietrich a jewel to protect him in his encounter with the giant Sigenôt; it is also effective against fatigue, hunger, thirst, and snakes (55 ff.).

ref: **jSn** m 31, 4 n 47, 4 (v *ballunt*, d *waldung*)

pn: 8th-cent. German (Förstemann I. 236 f.; Schlaug I. 56; Bach I, § 106).

BALDUNC (2) von Parîse (Paris)
Ermenrîch's man: he fights Helferîch von Lunders at Rabene (Ravenna).

ref: **Rs** 707, 2

BALDUNC (3) von Tirol (Tyrol)
Nephew of Îmîân and husband of Valentrin.

ref: **V(h)** 302, 10; **V(w)** 496, 12

BALIGÂN von Lybîâ (Libya)
Etzel's magnificence is greater than his.

ref: **B** 315

pn: probably derives from Konrad's *Rolandslied*, where Baligan von Persia (7150) comes to the aid of the Saracen king, Marsilie (in the OFr original, *La Chanson de Roland*, Baligant is King of Babylon); *Baligan(t)* is a common name for Saracens in OFr epic (Langlois, 66).

BALÎN
Brother of Baldewîn (1): companion of Dietwart.

ref: **DF** 432

---

[1] See Fr. Panzer, 'Der Weg der Nibelungen', *Helm Festgabe* (Tübingen, 1951), 94 ff., for an interpretation of this figure.

**BALMUNC (1)** Sîfrit's sword
In **N** Schilbunc and Nibelunc give it to Sîfrit when he agrees to share their father's treasure between them (see Nibelunge, p. 97). Hagen acquires it after murdering Sîfrit, and displays it across his knees to provoke Sîfrit's widow, Kriemhilt; she finally beheads him with it.
In **Rg(A)** Sîfrit is known to have found it 'ûf dem steine' after killing the dragon; in **Rg(D)** and **E(L)** it is termed 'der zwelf swert einez' (**Rg(D)** 47; **E(L)** 209) (see also Hertrîch, p. 71, and Mîme, p. 94).
In **hS** the giant Kuperan shows Seyfrid a sword hanging in the cave on the 'Trachenstain'; Seyfrid kills the dragon with it.

ref: **B** 7226; **E(L)** m 209, 4; **N** 95, 1; **Rg(A)** 330, 4; **Rg(C)** 38 (*phalmungen*); **Rg(D)** 47, 4; **Rg(P)** 78; **Rs** 683, 1; **hS** m 107, 4 (?); **hS(Sachs)** m 656 (?)

Outside the epics there are no references to Balmunc, but Sîfrit is depicted holding it on one of the 14th-cent. frescoes at Runkelstein in the South Tyrol (W. Grimm, *DHS*, 372; Müllenhoff, *ZE*, 386).
In ON Eddic tradition Sigurðr possesses three swords: Gramr (Rm prose, p. 177; Fm 25, 3; Sd prose, p. 189; Sg 22, 6; Sk ch. 47; Völss ch. 12;[1] Þs I. 314, 9)[2] and Riðill (Fm prose, p. 185; Völss ch. 19; Refill in Sk ch. 47), made by the smith Reginn, the first to kill the dragon Fáfnir, the second to cut the dragon's heart out; Sigurðr finds the third sword, Hrotti (Fm prose, p. 188; Völss ch. 19)[3] among the treasure of the dead Fáfnir, together with the Ægishjálmr ('terror helmet') and the Gullbrynja ('golden byrnie').[4]
In the Danish ballads Syfred's sword is named Adelryng (see Nagelrinc, p. 96).

pn: based on MHG *balme*, 'rock, rocky cave' (MLat *palma*), to designate a sword found in a cave (Gamillscheg I. 280; see also E. Schröder, *DNK*, 59; Kralik, *Trilogie*, 225).

**BALMUNC (2)** von Gâlaber (Calabria) Dietwart's companion.

ref: **DF** 499

**BALTHÊR (1)** Etzel's man
He aids Dietrich against Ermenrîch.

ref: **DF** 5153

pn: 8th-cent. German (Förstemann I. 238 f.).

**BALTHÊR (2)** von Etzelingen
Ermenrîch's man.

ref: **Rs** 719, 5

**BALTRAM (1)** Etzel's man
Aids Dietrich against Ermenrîch and fights Volkêr at Rabene (Ravenna).

ref: **DF** 5153; **Rs** 57, 2

In Þs Boltram af Fenedi (Venice) is the brother of Reginballdr, father of Hildibrandr (I. 32, 21); Hildibrandr assumes this name when he encounters Viðga (I. 144, 4).

pn: 8th-cent. German (Förstemann I. 239; Schlaug II. 73).

See also Rentwîn, p. 107, and Sintram (1), pp. 127 f.

**BALTRAM (2)** ûz Alexandrîn (Alexandria in Egypt)
künec ze Pülle (Apulia): he supports Gunther in the combats at Worms, where he is defeated by Dietleip.

ref: **B** 2559

**BALTRAM (3)** von Bulgerîe (Bulgaria)
Brother-in-law of Berhtunc (1), whom he defends at his trial for the alleged murder of the infant Wolfdietrich.

ref: **Wd(A)** 166, 3; **Wd(k)** 61, 6

**BÂRUC** von Palacker (Baghdad?)
Brother of Limhêr: aids the heathen Tarîas against Wolfdietrich at Tischcâl.

ref: **Wd(D)** x. 39, 2; **Wd(Gr)** 2151, 2

pn: possibly based on Wolfram von Eschenbach's 'bâruc ze Baldac' (*Parzival*, 13, 16; *Willehalm*, 73, 21), cf. Arabic *barūk*, 'the blessed'.

**BASILISTIUM**
The son of Ymelot von Babilônie: Constantin, King at Constantinople, betroths his daughter to him, although she is already the wife of Rother. He is hanged after Rother's defeat of Ymelot.

ref: **R** 3839

pn: based on *Basilius*, a term for the Byzantine Emperor (Panzer, *Italische Normannen*, 51; *Hilde-Gudrun*, 269 n. 1).

**BECHELER**, see BERHTER (2)

**BECHTUNG**, see BERHTUNC (1)

**BÊHEIM, BÊHEIMLANT**
Bohemian, Bohemia:[5] in **B** the Bohemians

---

[1] The ancestral sword of the Völsungar in Völss (see Sigemunt (1), pp. 125 f.).

[2] In the Þs Sigurðr obtains Gramr from Mimir; after his death Gunnarr gives it to Roðingeirr, who gives it to Gisler. Gisler kills Roðingeirr with it in the fight at Susat, but, after Gisler's death, Hildibrandr is in possession of it and finally leaves it to his son, Alibrandr.

[3] Cf. Hrunting, the sword lent to Bēowulf by Unferð (*Beowulf*, 1457), the name of which may be based on OE *hrindan*, 'thrust' (see Davidson, 167 n. 1).

[4] The dragon which kills Bēowulf guards treasure including ancient helmets (*Beowulf*, 2762). In **Wd**, Wolfdietrich uses the sword, helmet, and golden byrnie of the dead Ortnît, which he finds in the cave, to kill the dragon (see Rôse, p. 109, and Nagelrinc, p. 96). In **hS**, Kuperan also keeps a flashing helmet and a golden byrnie in the cave on the 'Trachenstain'.

[5] See Much, *Deutsche Stammeskunde*, 53 f.; Karsten, 16, regarding this originally Celtic name.

BÊHEIM

fight with flails, and a linden-branch is depicted on their banner.

ref: **B** 1722; **R** 4865

BEIER, BEIER(N)LANT
Bavarian, Bavaria:[1] they have a reputation for robbery and boastfulness (**N** 1302; **B** 3145, etc.).

ref: **B** 843; **DF** 2437; **E(L)** 66, 11; **Kl** 3596; **N** 1174, 3; **R** 3571; **Rg(F)** I. 1, 2; **Rs** 65, 1; **Wd(D)** I. 2, 1; **Wd(Gr)** 2, 1

BEIERLANT[2]
The sword of Treferîs.

ref: **Wd(D)** v. 171, 2; **Wd(Gr)** 1010, 3

BELCHE
Dietleip's horse, which is from the same stud as Dietrich's.

ref: **B** 2275

pn: refers to the blaze (Gmc. *balaz-, Goth. bals, 'white') on the horse's forehead, cf. MHG belche, 'coot' (DWb I. 1439; Lexer I. 171; E. Schröder, DNK, 54 ff.).

BELDELÎN
A dwarf sent by Îbelîn to Virginâl and Hildebrant with the news of Dietrich's capture by Nîtgêr's giants.

ref: **V(h)** m 437, 5 n 462, 5

pn: possibly based on MHG balt, 'brave, quick'.

BELERANT, see BITTERKRÛT

BELÎÂN
A heathen, the son of Grippîân von Riuzen and the father of Marpaly (see p. 93): he displays the heads of Christians on the battlements of his castle of Falkenîs at Büden (Vidin in Bulgaria). Wolfdietrich kills him in a knife-fight.

ref: **Wd(B)** m 265, 2 n 266, 35; **Wd(D)** VI. 8, 1; **Wd(Gr)** 344, 3; **Wd(k)** m 352, 4

pn: a typical Saracen name: Belîân von Babilonîe appears in the 12th-cent. 'Spielmannsepen' (Orendel, 411; Salman und Morolf, 748, 3); cf. Beliant (Belians), the Saracen king of Cordova in OFr epic (Langlois, 83; see also Baligân above).

BELMUNT
A heathen giant, brother of Olfân (1) and ruler of Troimunt. Wolfdietrich kills him and wins from him the 'sant Jörgen hemt' (shirt of St. George), which thenceforth preserves the hero's life.

ref: **Wd(D)** IV. 6, 3; **Wd(Gr)** 396, 3

BENIG, see BLANKE

[1] Much, op. cit. 107 f.; Bach I, § 173, 1.
[2] In the mid-12th-cent. Kaiserchronik the excellence of Bavarian swords is mentioned (313 ff.), quoting the late 11th-cent. Annolied: 'Da lisit man Noricus ensis, / Das diudit ein suert

BERHTRAM (1)

BERHTER (1) von Mêrân (Maronia) (cf. BERHTUNC (1))
'grâve' (**R** 467, also 'herzoge' **R** 541): he educates the young Rother. Seven of his twelve sons are imprisoned when they are sent by Rother on a bridal quest for King Constantin's daughter. Berhter accompanies Rother on his expedition to Constantinople, in the course of which his sons are freed and Rother wins the princess. He later leads Rother's army against the heathen Ymelot von Babilonie. He retires to a monastery, but reappears when Rother's son, Pippin, becomes a knight. Berhter's device is a chameleon, and he wears the jewel Claugestian on his helmet.

Three of his sons are named: Erewîn, Luppolt, and Helferîch.

ref: **R** 452 (MS. spellings also Berker, Berther, Berter, Bercher, etc.)[3]

pn: 6th-cent. WFr, 7th-cent. German and Lb (Förstemann I. 288 f.; Schlaug I. 60; II. 74; Bruckner, 234; Ploß, 59); it is recorded in Domesday in OE (Feilitzen, 194).

The first component, Gmc. *berhta, 'bright, shining', is almost exclusively WGmc. and typically Frankish (Malone, Studies, 120; see the index to MGH script. rer. Merov. II. 530; cf. Berhtunc (1)).

Berhter's title may refer to the Bavarian counts of Dachau, who held the ducal title of Maronia between 1153 and 1178; it was later held by Berhtold IV of Andechs (see p. 28 n. 4).

BERHTER (2) son of Berhtunc (1) von Mêrân
He is killed at Tischcâl, aiding Wolfdietrich against Tarîas.

ref: **AHb** p. 6, 5 (Becheler); **Wd(D)** IX. 100, 1; **Wd(Gr)** 1988, 1

BERHTER (3) Dietrich's man

ref: **A** 73, 2; **DF** 5731

BERHTOLT
'grâve von Elsâzen' (**B** 5079; 7736 B. von der Swâbe lande), supports Gunther in the combats at Worms.

ref: **B** 5079

pn: 7th-cent. WFr, Lb, and OE; 8th-cent. German (Förstemann I. 295 f.; Schlaug I. 60; II. 74; Bach I, § 216, 2; Searle, 95, 540).

BERHTRAM (1) Dietwart's companion

ref: **DF** 425

pn: frequent in WFr and German, being first recorded for the Bishop of Bordeaux (566–86) (Förstemann I. 290 f.; Schlaug II. 75; Socin, 4). Bertram is frequent in the OFr

Beierisch' (Das Anno-Lied, hrsg. von Martin Opitz. MDCXXXIX, besorgt von W. Bulst (Heidelberg, 1961²), 24).
[3] See Frings-Kuhnt, Rother, 187.

BERHTRAM (1)

*ch.d.g.* (Langlois, 93 ff.). See also *Neidharts Lieder*, 98, 1.

BERHTRAM (2) von Tuscân (Tuscany), also 'von dem Berge'
Ermenrîch's man; he is killed by Hildebrant.

ref: **A** 200, 2

BERHTRAM (3) von Bôle (Pola)
Dietrich's man: killed by Reinhêr von Parîse at Bôlonje (Bologna), in **DF**; in **Rs** he fights Witegîsen at Rabene (Ravenna).

ref. **DF** 3017; **Rs** 114, 4

BERHTRAM (4) von Salnicke (Salonika)[1]
Etzel's man; he supports Dietrich against Ermenrîch at Rabene (Ravenna), where he fights Sigehêr von Zæringen.

ref: **Rs** 71, 2

BERHTUNC (1) von Mêrân (cf. BERHTER (1))
In **Wd(A)** herzoc Berhtunc preserves the life of the infant Wolfdietrich against the machinations of Sabene, the evil counsellor of Wolfdietrich's father, Hugdietrich. On Hugdietrich's death he supports Wolfdietrich and his mother against Wolfdietrich's hostile brothers, and six of his sixteen sons are killed in battle against them at Constantinople. Wolfdietrich and his mother take refuge at his castle of Lilienporte (Durazzo?). Wolfdietrich sets out for Lombardy to obtain help for his eleven vassals from Ortnît (see Wolfdietrich).
In **Wd(BD)** herzoc Berhtunc, Hugdietich's loyal major-domo, educates the young Wolfdietrich, especially in knife-throwing,[2] and supports him against his hostile brothers. Six of his sons are killed in battle; he and the remaining ten are imprisoned. Wolfdietrich, after many adventures, returns to Constantinople and frees Berhtunc's sons. Berhtunc has died meanwhile, but speaks to Wolfdietrich from the grave (in 'sant Jörgen münster' **(Wd(B)** 900); at 'sant Jôhans alter' **(Wd(D)** IX. 150 f.)).
The following nine sons of Berhtunc are named in the epics: Alebrant, Berhter (2), Berhtunc (2), Berhtwîn, Hâche, Herebrant (1), Schiltbrant (2), Schiltwîn, and Hildebrant (2). Six of them are killed at Tischâl, aiding the aged Wolfdietrich in the defence of his monastery against the giant Tarîâs **(Wd(D)** x): Berhter (2), Berhtwîn, Schiltwîn, Alebrant, Schiltbrant (2), and Berhtunc (2).

ref: **AHb** p. 3, 5 (*Bechtung*); **Wd(A)** 5, 3; **Wd(B)** 4, 1; **Wd(C)** II. 10, 2; **Wd(D)** IV. 98, 1; **Wd(Gr)** 10, 1; **Wd(k)** 3, 5 (*Puntvnge*)

[1] His title is thought to derive from **Wd**: it is Wolfdietrich's birth-place in **Wd(A)** 532, 4 and **Wd(D)** VIII. 119, 1; in **Wd(B)** it is ruled by Wolfdietrich's father-in-law, Walgunt (15, 2): see O. Jänicke, *DHB* III. lxix.
[2] Fischart in his translation of *Gargantua* (1590) refers to 'das Baderisch und Bechtungisch

pn: 9th-cent. German (Förstemann I. 283).
Such stories about loyal vassals abound in OFr *ch.d.g.*: *Parise la Duchesse* offers close parallels: the major-domo Clarembaut[3] and his sons protect their mistress and her youngest son, Huguet, against her estranged husband and his evil counsellors (see Wolfdietrich, pp. 150 f.).
It is possible that the name and role of Berhtunc (see also Berhter (1), p. 101.) derive ultimately from a vassal story stemming from Merovingian dynastic troubles (see Hugdietrich and Wolfdietrich, pp. 82 f., 150 f.). The title 'von Mêrân' was probably introduced by the author of **R**, whence it comes into **Wd**, where the rescue of vassals is an integral part of the plot, in which Berhter-Berhtunc plays a leading role (see Schneider, *DHS* (1930), 129).

BERHTUNC (2) son of Berhtunc (1) von Mêrân
Killed at Tischcâl.

ref: **AHb** p. 6, 5 (*Bechtung*); **Wd(D)** IX. 213, 4; **Wd(Gr)** 2101, 4

BERHTUNC (3) son of Witzlân (2) von Kriechenlant
Nephew of Herman (8).

ref: **DF** 470

pn: probably derives from **Wd** (see Berhtunc (1)).

BERHTUNC (4) von Rabene (Ravenna)
An Amelunc related to Biterolf (1), he leads Ermenrîch's men at Worms, fights Ortwîn, and is struck down by Sîfrit.

ref: **B** 4757

BERHTUNC (5) Etzel's man
Related to Herrât: aids Dietrich against Ermenrîch.

ref: **Rs** 73, 2

BERHTWÎN
Son of Berhtunc (1): killed at Tischcâl.

ref: **Wd(D)** IX. 100, 1; **Wd(Gr)** 1988, 1

pn: 7th-cent. German (Förstemann I. 297; Schlaug I. 60 f.), rare before 1000 in OE (Searle, 97 f.).

BERILLE
Sister of Drasîân: killed by Wolfdietrich.

ref: **Wd(B)** 454, 57 (*DHB* IV. 306); **Wd(Gr)** 735, 1; **Wd(w)** 691, 3 (*Parilla*)

pn: 8th-cent. WFr (Förstemann I. 261).

BERKÊR
Father of Rienolt and Randolt.

messerwerfen' (Jänicke, *ZE*, 331). See Beliân, p. 10.
[3] This pn (Langlois, 148) contains the Romance element *clar-*, Lat. *clarus*, equivalent to Gmc. *\*berhta*, 'bright, shining' (Kaufmann, 59: cf. Berhter (1)).

## BERKÊR

ref: **B** 4601

pn: 10th-cent. German (Förstemann I. 261).

## BERNÆRE (BERNER)
Refers to Dietrich, whose capital is Berne (Verona), and occasionally to Dietrich's men; 'Berners marke' and 'Bernerlant' refer to Dietrich's realm in North Italy.

ref: sg. = Dietrich: **A** 13, 4; **AHb** p. 3, 32; **B** 8359; **DF** 2484; **DuW** 45; **E(a)** 5, 1; **E(d)** 2, 10; **E(L)** 3, 2; **E(s)** 5, 1; **ED** 1, 2; **G** 2, 12; **Kl** 768 (C), 1141; **L(A)** 20; **L(D)** 258; **L(DrHb)** 5, 1; **L(K)II** 21; **N** 1903, 1; **Rg(A)** 4, 1; **Rg(C)** 89; **Rg(D)** 19, 3; **Rg(F)** II. 4, 1; **Rg(P)** 17; **Rg(V)** 20; **Rs** 17, 6; **hS(Sachs)** 838; **äSn** 3, 3; **jSn** 4, 1; **V(d)** 4, 5; **V(h)** 2, 5; **V(w)** 25, 5; **Wu(B)** 146, 3; Bernerlant: **V(h)** 1073, 4; Berners marke: **jH** 5, 1

pl. = Dietrich's men: **B** 5233; **Kl** 4209

## BERSÂBE
herzoginne: betrothed to Sabîn.

ref: **Rg(A)** 16, 1; **Rg(C)** 49 (*Versâbe*)

pn: corrupt; probably represents 'vro Sabîn'.

## BERTE
Wife of Pippin and mother of Carl in **R**.

ref: **R** 4782

In **Ps**, Berta (I. 49, 17; II. 97, 11) is the daughter of Osanctrix; she is abducted by Roðolfr (see Helche, p. 66).

pn: the mother, sister, and daughter of Charlemagne are so named: 8th-cent. German (Förstemann I. 281 f.; Schlaug II. 176); it occurs in the OFr *ch.d.g.* (Langlois, 92).

## BERTÛNE
Accompanies Walther at Worms.

ref: **B** 6635

## BETEWÎN
A robber killed by Wolfdietrich (see Rûmelher).

ref: **Wd(D)** v. 7, 1; **Wd(Gr)** 845, 1; **Wd(w)** 787, 1 (*Baldewin*)

pn: recorded at Trier in 698 (Förstemann I. 230); possibly a corrupt form of OFr *Beduin*, a Saracen people in OFr epic (Langlois, 81).

## BETLÎ
A robber killed by Wolfdietrich (see Rûmelher).

ref: **Wd(D)** v. 14, 2; **Wd(Gr)** 851, 2; **Wd(w)** 794, 2 (*Artelaÿ*)

## BÎBUNC (1) Virginâl's dwarf messenger
Brother of Sigram: he shows great terror at the numerous slaughtered giants and dragons he sees during his search for Dietrich and Hildebrant.

ref: **V(d)** 24, 11 (*Wiwurgk*; 69, 10 *Wiburg*; 118, 2 *Willung*); **V(h)** 141, 2; **V(w)** 264, 2

pn: possibly based on MHG *biben*, 'tremble', although the editors print the name with long *i* (see J. Lunzer, 'Drei Namen der deutschen Heldensage', *PBB* XLIX (1925), 461 f.).

## BÎBUNC (2) Wolfdietrich's dwarf helper
Helps Wolfdietrich against Belmunt.

ref: **Wd(D)** m IV. 40, 3 n IV. 51, 3; **Wd(Gr)** m 432, 3 n 441, 3

## BILLUNC (1) a dwarf
Seizes Wolfdietrich's wife Liebgart; Wolfdietrich kills him.

ref: **Wd(B)** 800, 3; **Wd(Gr)** 853, 1

pn: 8th-cent. German (Förstemann I. 304; Schlaug I. 62; II. 77); 9th-cent. Lb and OE (Bruckner, 234; Searle, 107; Binz, 221). In ON the pn *Billungr* is used for a dwarf (Vsp 13, 5 (variant in MS. H); Sk ch. 58) and for a giant (Háv 97, 1). The name occurs in OE *Widsith*, 25 for *Billing*, ruler of the Werne, and in the 12th MHG *Rolandslied* of Pfaffe Konrad a *Pillunc* appears among the Christian warriors (4952),[1] his name probably deriving from the Saxon ducal family founded by Hermann Billung in the 10th cent.

The name here has appellative force, being based on Gmc. *\*bil-*, 'miraculous power' (cf. *Bilwis*: Kluge, *EWb*, 77). MHG *billunc*, 'spite, spiteful person', probably derives from the reputed character of dwarfs.

## BILLUNC (2) a robber
Killed by Wolfdietrich (see Rûmelher).

ref: **Wd(D)** v. 16, 1; **Wd(Gr)** 853, 1

## BINÔSE
Wife of Jubart.

ref: **DF** 9984

## BIRKHILT
A giantess, wife of Nettinger (**AHb** Mentiger) and mother of Ecke, Vâsolt, Ebenrôt, and Uodelgart: Dietrich kills her.

ref: **AHb** p. 3, 39 (*gudengart*); **E(L)** 228, 13

pn: probably based on MHG *birke*, 'birchtree'.

## BITEROLF (1) von Stîre (Styria)
Father of Dietleip: in **B** he leaves his wife Dietlint at his capital of Tôlêt (Toledo) in order to take service with Etzel, King of the Huns (399 ff.); in a campaign against the Prussians he and Rüedegêr are taken prisoner at Gamalî, but Biterolf escapes and captures the Prussian king, Bodeslau (1376 ff.). He then assumes the byname 'Fruote' (1912 ff.; later 'Diete', 3408 ff.). On a subsequent campaign against the Poles he fights his own

---

[1] The name does not appear in the OFr *Chanson de Roland*.

## BITEROLF (1)

son Dietleip in the confusion of battle, but Rüedegêr stops the combat (3633 ff.). In the final combats at Worms against Gunther's men he fights Gêrnôt (7635 ff.) and Sîfrit (9745 ff.), but refuses to fight his own nephew Walther (9928 ff). Etzel grants him Styria for twelve years (13278 ff.). His device is a unicorn (10814),[1] and he possesses three swords: Schrit (123), Welsunc (561), and Hornbîle (12262).
In **DF** he aids Dietrich against Ermenrîch. In **V(h)** he is one of Dietrich's men and kills the giant Hôhermuot (see Wîcram).

ref: **AHb** p. 3, 36; **B** m 12 n 39; **DF** 5151; **L(D)** 2322; **Rg(A)** 110, 3; **Rg(C)** 429; **Rs** 42, 1; **V(h)** 378, 6; **V(w)** 564, 6

In Þs Biturulfr (I. 209, 6), father of Þetleifr and husband of Oda, rules at Skane (Scania, Denmark, for MHG Spanje, Spain?).[2]

pn: 12th-cent. German (W. Grimm, *DHS*, 461; Mone, 76; Müllenhoff, *ZE*, 337, 414; Jänicke, *ZE*, 311; Socin, 566); it is used for a singer in the *Wartburgkrieg* (Müllenhoff, *ZE*, 337) and for a peasant in *Neidharts Lieder*, 66, 22 in the 13th cent. It is originally a byname, cf. MHG *biterolf*, 'tyrant, choleric person' (Lexer I. 287).

## BITEROLF (2) a robber
Killed by Wolfdietrich (see Rûmelher).

ref: **Wd(D)** v. 8, 1; **Wd(Gr)** 846, 1

## BITERUNC (1) von Heste (Este, near Padua?)
Dietwart's companion.

ref: **DF** 459

## BITERUNC (2) von Engellant (England)
Ermenrîch's man: kills Alphart and is killed by Dietrich von Berne at Bôlonje (Bologna).

ref: **DF** 9431

## BITERUNC (3) von Môrlande[3]
Ermenrîch's man: fights Dietrich von Kriechen at Rabene (Ravenna).

ref: **Rs** 714, 1

## BITTERBÛCH (FELSENSTRAUCH)
A giant killed by Schiltwîn (see Wîcram).

ref: **V(h)** 879, 4; **V(w)** 726, 2 (*Felsenstrauch*)
pn: probably appellative with the meaning 'sour guts'.

## BITTERKRÛT (BELERANT)
A giant killed by Sigestap (see Wîcram).

ref: **V(h)** 885, 2; **V(w)** 732, 2 (*Belerant*)
pn: is recorded as a byname in the 13th cent. (Socin, 410), cf. MHG *bitterkrût*, 'bitter lettuce' (Lexer I. 287).

[1] Also the device of the 13th-cent. Styrian noble, Otto von Mîssowe (O. Jänicke, *DHB* I. 273).
[2] Scania is now a Swedish province.
[3] See Sîfrit (3) von Môrlant, p. 123, and Mœre, p. 95.

## BLANKE (BENIG)
Ilsân's horse.

ref: **Rs** 362, 1; **Rg(D)** 114, 3 (MS. h only, *Benig*)[4]

In Þs Alibrandr gives Þiðrekr a horse named Blanka (II. 391, 10).

pn: based on OHG *blanc*, 'white' (cf. ON *blankr*); OE *blanca*, *blonca*, is used for a 'white horse', and also for a horse generally (Bosworth–Toller, 108); it continues in ME in the latter sense (*MED* B IV. 953); ON *blakkr*, 'pale, dun', has a similar extension of meaning (Jóhannesson, 645; Kahle, 156), cf. the horse-name Blakkr in Sk ch. 72.
In the OFr *ch.d.g.*, *Blanchart* (*Blancart*) is the name of a white horse (Langlois, 99; see Schneider, *Kl. Schr.* 74).

## BLŒDEL(ÎN)
Etzel's brother: in **N**, Kriemhilt promises him the hand of Nuodunc's widow and Nuodunc's estates if he will agree to attack the Burgundians. He and his men kill the Burgundian squires, but Blœdel himself is beheaded by Dancwart in the fighting.

In other epics he is among Dietrich's men: in **DF** and **Rs** he aids Dietrich against Ermenrîch and fights Sturmholt at Rabene (Ravenna); in **B**, where he is said to rule Vlâchenlant (Rumania), he fights Witzlân and Poytân at Worms; in **V(hw)** he kills the giants Asprîân and Rûmedenwalt (Ösenwalt) at Mûter (see Wîcram).

ref: **B** 4716; **DF** 5145; **Kl** 375; **N** 1346, 2; **Rs** 45, 1; **V(h)** 610, 11; **V(w)** 671, 1

Outside the epics Blœdel is not mentioned in MHG literature, apart from the mid-12th-cent. *Kaiserchronik*, 1386 f., where he appears as Etzel's son.

In Þs Bloðlin (Blodlenn) is one of Attila's leaders (II. 302, 2); he is killed by Gernoz in the fighting against the Niflungar—in Þs it is Irungr who kills the squires (see Îrinc, p. 85).

pn: *Bleda* of the Latin chronicles (Bede has *Blæda*) is probably of Hunnish origin (Moravcsik II. 90); the form *Bletla* (*Blêdla*) of the *Ann. Quedl.* (*MGH* ss III. 31) shows OE *-la* suffix,[5] cf. the OE pn *Blædla* (Sweet, 133, 159).
The historical Bleda, son of Mundzucus, was murdered by his younger brother, Attila, *c.* 445 (Jordanes, ch. xxxv) and probably had shared the kingship of the Huns with him till then (see Etzel, p. 42).[6] It is possible that this figure is represented by the unnamed brother of Atli who is killed by Guðrún in the ON Am (Panzer, *Nibelungenlied*, 408).

## BLŒDELINCK
'köninck in Frankrîken', son of a proud

[4] The form of **Rg(D)** is probably corrupt, but could be based on MHG *baneken*, 'cavort, sport, play' (Lexer I. 119).
[5] See p. 62 n. 6.
[6] Attila's brother is named Buda in Hungarian tradition (see p. 41).

## BLŒDELINCK

widow:[1] he accompanies Dirik (MHG Dietrich) on an expedition against the 'köninck van Armentrîken' (MHG Ermenrîch). He is of giant stature and kills 350 men. He is found in the cellars after the fight.

ref: **ED** m 1, 1 n 9, 1

A similar character named Kanselin (Genselin), cf. NHG *Gänslein*, 'little goose, fool' (?), appears in the Danish ballads, *Grimilds Hævn* and *Greve Genselin* (*DgF* I. 44 ff., 223 ff.), and probably derives likewise from Blœdelîn.

## BODISLAU
King of the Priuzen (Prussians), captured by Etzel's forces (see Biterolf, p. 12).

ref: **B** 1473

## BŒMRÎÂN (MOREAN)
A giant killed by Dietleip at Mûter (see Wîcram).

ref: **V(h)** 736, 11; **V(w)** 667, 11 (*Morean*)

pn: probably derogatory, cf. NHG *Böhmer*, 'waxwing', i.e. 'Bohemian chatterer', a bird of ill omen (*DWb* II. 224).

## BOGE, see BOUGE

## BÔLÆRE pl.
Men of Bôle (Pola) who support Dietrich against Ermenrîch.

ref: **DF** 8116

## BÔLÂN, see PÔLÂN

## BÔNÎSE
A lady at the court of Virginâl.

ref: **V(h)** 473, 1

## BOPPE ûz Tenelant (Denmark)
Nephew of Herbort: aids Gunther at Worms and defeats Eckehart in the combats.

ref: **B** 6512

In Johannes von Tepl's *Der Ackermann aus Böhmen* (*c.* 1400), Death refers to the trouble he has had with 'der starke Boppe' (ch. xxx).[2]

pn: *Bobo, Bopo*, etc., occur from 8th cent. in German records (Förstemann I. 317).

## BOTELUNC
Etzel's father: in **Wd(A)** he is Hugdietrich's brother-in-law.

ref: **B** 366; **DF** 5352; **Kl** 76 (C); 93 (B); **N** 1251, 4 (C); 1314, 2; **Wd(A)** 3, 1; **Wd(k)** 2, 1

Heinrich von Veldeke in *Servatius* (*c.* 1170) refers to Attila as 'Bodelinghes son' (3369).

In ON Eddic tradition the father of Atli and Brynhildr is named Buðli (Am 38, 4; Grp 27, 5; Br 8, 2; Sg 15, 3; Hlr 4, 2; Gðr I 23, 2; Gðr II 26, 6; Gðr III 1, 2; Völs ch. 25; also in the Faroese ballad *Brynhildur táttur* (*CCF* I. 8 ff.)), and pl. Buðlungar refers to the race to which they belong (Akv 42, 7; Sk ch. 80). In the fragments about Hildibrand's death contained in *Ásmundar saga kappabana*, ch. 8 (*FAS* I. 399 ff.), Buðli is the grandfather of Hildibrandr and Ásmundr; he formerly owned the swords, 'Buðlanautar', with which they fight each other (Hild. 2, 3). In Saxo's history Buthlus is the name given to the uncle of Iarmericus (MHG Ermenrîch) and regent of Denmark (Saxo VIII. ix. 1–x. 5).

pn: 8th-cent. German (Förstemann I. 322; Mone, 71 f.; Socin, 572; see G. Schramm, 'Etzels Vater Botelung', *BzNf* N. F. I (1966), 266–90): the name may well stem from, or be an accommodation to, the equivalent of OHG *boto*, 'messenger', and the ON *Buðlungr* has been related to ON *bjóða*, 'offer', cf. Gmc. root *\*buð-* (Jóhanneson, 607 f.). In ON *buðlungr* acquires the meaning 'prince' (Neckel, Edda II. 19). However, it is possible that this name derives ultimately from that of the Visigothic dynasty of the *Balthae*, to which Brunihildis, wife of Sigebert of Metz, belonged (S. Singer, 'Brünhild', *PBB* XLII (1917), 541).

The historical name of Attila's father was Mundiucos (Priscus) or Mundzucus (Jordanes) (see Etzel, p. 42).

## BOTTEL, see GOTELE (1)

## BOTZOLDE
Takes part in the jousting at Virginâl's court at Jeraspunt.

ref: **V(h)** 1043, 8

pn: probably based on MHG *bôzen*, 'strike, knock'; *bôzolt* is also a term for 'dance' or 'love-play' (*DWb* II. 271; Lexer I. 336 f.).

## BOUGE (1) Wolfdietrich's brother (cf. DIETRICH (4), (5), and (6), p. 31)
Bouge and Wahsmuot usurp the kingdom of Constantinople from their brother Wolfdietrich, who ultimately defeats them (see Hugdietrich, p. 82, and Wolfdietrich, pp. 148 ff.).

ref: **AHb** p. 6, 8 (*Bogen*); **Wd(B)** 258, 3; **Wd(D)** III. 6, 1; **Wd(Gr)** 261, 3; **Wd(w)** 308, 3 (*Boder*)

pn: 7th-cent. WFr, 9th-cent. German (Förstemann I. 252), 8th-cent. OE (Searle, 82).

## BOUGE (2) Dietrich's man

ref: **A** 73, 1 (omitted from the index to *DHB* II)

this name is depicted in the illustrated MSS. as a bearded giant (W. Grimm, *DHS*, 315 f.; A. Wallner, 'Herren und Spielleute im Heidelberger Liedercodex', *PBB* XXXIII (1908), 510 f.).

---

[1] 'ein Wedewe stolt' (**ED** 5, 1). Cf. Kriemhilt, 'diu stolze witewe' (**N** 1143, 4), who incites Blœdelîn to attack the Burgundians in N.

[2] The late 13th-cent. 'Minnesänger' who bears

## BOUMGART
A giant relative of Velle: killed by Ortnît.

ref: **Wd(B)** 488, 3; **Wd(Gr)** 789, 3 (Brumfart); **Wd(w)** 738, 3 (*Brünwart*)

## BOYMUNT
Rüedegêr's horse.

ref: **Kl** 3141 (Db *Roymunt*, A *poimunt*)

pn: well known through the descendants of Robert Guiscard, the Norman rulers of Sicily and famous crusaders named Bohemund (Panzer, *Nibelungenlied*, 80). It is recorded for a Bavarian duke in the 12th-cent. *Kaiserchronik* (300) and in documents from the 12th cent. on (Müllenhoff, *ZE*, 355; Jänicke, *ZE*, 312).

## BRAMKÊR
Dietrich's man.

ref: **A** 74, 3 (W. Grimm, *DHS*, 263, reads *Branker*)

## BRIGIDA
The wife of Ernthelle.

ref: **AHb** p. 1, 11

pn: the name, of which the contracted form, *Brîde*, is used in the 'Spielmannsepos' *Orendel* (c. 1190?), derives from that of the 5th-cent. Irish St. Brigid; it is recorded from the 8th cent. in German (Förstemann 1. 335).

## BRINNIC
Hildebrant's sword.

ref: **A** 350, 2

pn: cf. MHG *brinnec*, 'burning' (*DWb* 11. 392; Lexer 1. 354).
Hildebrant's sword is named Freise in **V**, Freissan in **jSn**, and Lagulfr in Þs (see p. 74 n. 11).

## BRUGIGAL
A master cook: the bear Wisselau boils and eats him.

ref: **BW** 442

pn: possibly appellative and connected with MDu *broeyen*, 'boil'.

## BRUMFART, see BOUMGART

## BRÜNHILT
Queen of Îslant (Iceland): in **N**, Sîfrit, acting for Gunther and unseen in the *tarnkappe* (cloak of invisibility), defeats Brünhilt in athletic contests at her castle of Îsenstein; she therefore agrees to wed Gunther and returns to Burgundy with him. Sîfrit, again invisible, is required by Gunther to subdue his new queen in the bridal chamber (see Gunther, p. 54), and he takes a ring and girdle from her in the process. Brünhilt objects to the marriage of Gunther's sister, Kriemhilt, to Sîfrit, whom she assumes to be Gunther's vassal; the two queens compare their husbands while watching jousting, and a quarrel ensues, in the course of which Kriemhilt produces the ring and girdle and accuses Brünhilt of having been Sîfrit's mistress. From this public humiliation of Gunther's queen stems Hagen's plan to murder Sîfrit, to which Brünhilt agrees (see Sîfrit (1), pp. 118 f.).

In **B** and **Rg(D)** Brünhilt watches the combats at Worms.

ref: **B** 6840; **Kl** 2890; **N** 329, 2; **Rg(D)** 414, 3

In ON Eddic tradition Sigurðr wins the love of Brynhildr (Hlr prose, p. 219; 4, 1; Grp 27, 3; Br 3, 1; Gðr I 22, 5; Gðr II 27, 3; Sg 3, 1; Dr prose, p. 223; Od 16, 1; Sk ch. 48; Völss ch. 19; Faroese ballads *Brynhildar táttur* and *Høgna táttur* (*CCF* 1. 8 ff., 22 ff.)), a valkyrie sleeping in armour,[1] on the mountain of Hindarfjall—she is also named 'Sigrdrífa' (Fm 44, 5; Sd prose, p. 190)—by riding through the wall of flame (ON *vafrlogi*) and passing through the stockade of shields surrounding her: she wakes, when he removes her helmet and cuts her armour from her.[2] Sigurðr then marries Guðrún (MHG Kriemhilt), the sister of Gunnarr. In order to win Brynhildr for Gunnarr, Sigurðr changes shapes with him and rides once more through the flames to Brynhildr: they sleep on the mountain for three nights with a drawn sword between them, and exchange rings. Brynhildr weds Gunnarr; she and Guðrún quarrel about precedence when bathing in the river—in Sk ch. 49 when washing their hair—and Guðrún displays the ring Sigurðr originally received from Brynhildr. Brynhildr contrives Sigurðr's murder, since he has betrayed their love; she kills herself, and orders her body to be burnt beside his.[3]

In Þs Sigurðr kicks open the iron gates of Brynilldr's castle at Segarðr in Svava (Swabia, South Germany), fights her retainers, and catches the wild horse Grani from her stud. Later he persuades Gunnarr to wed her, but, as in **N**, he has to master her for Gunnarr—in Þs he deflowers her—and they exchange rings; Sigurðr gives his ring to his wife Grimilldr, who displays it during a quarrel with Brynilldr, after Grimilldr

---

[1] The composition of Brünhilt's name is based on the equivalents of OHG *brunia*, 'byrnie'. and *hiltia*, 'conflict', the latter occurring as an appellative for 'valkyrie', *hildr* in ON; this gives the possible meaning 'valkyrie in the byrnie' and may well have inspired the creation of the figure of the warrior-maiden, whom Óðinn has pricked with the sleep-thorn (ON *svefnþorn*), in late ON tradition.

[2] Grp and Völss ch. 24 tell of another meeting: Sigurðr, following his hawk which has flown through her window, finds Brynhildr in the house of Heimir weaving a tapestry, on which his deeds are depicted (see Heime, p. 65).

[3] In Sg. she orders her servants to be killed after her death (see p. 16 n. 4).

has omitted to stand up before her. Brynilldr incites Gunnarr, Högni, and Gernoz to murder Sigurðr, and, after Högni has killed him out hunting, she congratulates the hunters on their kill (see Sîfrit (1), p. 121).

In the Danish ballad *Sivard og Brynild* (*DgF* I. 16 ff.), Sivard rescues Bryneld from a glass mountain¹ and gives her to Hagenn. While they are washing their clothes at the river she sees Sivard's ring worn by Sienild, Sivard's wife; she urges Hagenn to kill Sivard, and Hagenn brings her Sivard's head; he then cuts her to pieces and kills himself.

pn: for the 6th-cent. Visigothic Queen *Brunihildis* (see below); 7th-cent. WFr, 8th-cent. German (Förstemann I. 340; Socin, 572; Jänicke, *ZE*, 312; Schlaug I. 65; II. 78), rare in South-East German records (Kromp I. 22). In OFr epic the name *Brunehaut* occurs for the daughter of Judas Maccabaeus, and also for the mother of Julius Caesar (Langlois, 120).

The name and role of Brünhilt have often been connected with the historical Brunihildis, daughter of Athanagild, the Visigothic King of Spain (see Botelunc, p. 14).² She married Sigebert of Metz, son of Chlotar I, in 567, and she was for many years in conflict with Fredegunda, the concubine of her brother-in-law Chilperic, who instigated the murder of Sigebert in 575 (see Sîfrit (1), p. 122). Chilperic himself was murdered out hunting in 584; Brunihildis was blamed for this and other murders (Fredegar IV. 42).³ She ruled Burgundy after the death of another brother of Sigebert, named Gunthram (see Gunther, p. 56),⁴ from 599 to 613, when her enemies had her trampled to death by horses.

All evidence points to the Rhine-Frankish area for the origins of Brünhilt and her story: the quarrel of the queens is indeed the kernel of the plot,⁵ although, according to some critics, the roles of the two women have been reversed in narrative tradition, Kriemhilt taking the role of Brunihildis and Brünhilt that of Fredegunda.⁶

Brünhilt's role in **N** and **Þs**, the warrior-maiden who can only be won by physical tests, is thought by Fr. Panzer to derive from a folk-tale type current in North-West Russia,⁷ which has replaced a 'Dornröschen' type of bridal quest apparent in the ON Eddic versions.⁸

BUOZOLT von Norwæge (Norway)
Ermenrîch's man: he fights Wolfhart at Rabene (Ravenna).⁹

ref: **Rs** 718, 1 (A *Pawsolt*)

pn: 8th-cent. German (Förstemann I. 332).

BURGONDE (BURGONDÆRE, BURGONJE, BURGENTRÎCHE, BURGUN, BURGUNDIA)
Ethnic name, also for the country in such terms as 'ze Burgonden, Burgondenlant', etc.: in **W**, Heriricus, the father of Hiltgunt, rules Burgundia; his capital is at Châlons.

In **N** the Burgundians are ruled by Gunther, Gêrnôt, and Gîselhêr, with their capital at Worms. They are first referred to as 'Nibelunge' (**N** 1523, 1, etc.) on reaching the Danube in the course of their journey to Hungary (see Nibelunge pl., pp. 97 f.). In the later epics the Burgundians are always the followers of Gunther.

ref: Burgonde sg.: **N** 2215, 3 (= Gêrnôt)
pl.: **B** 2374 (MS. *Burgundi lant*, 2380 MS. *Burgonie lant*, 6643 MS. *Burgonde lant*, 7267 MS. *Burgundilannt*, etc.); **Kl** 22 (A always *Burgonde*, D *Burgunden*); **N** 2, 1 (C *Buregonden*, D *burigunden*, d always *burgenden*, I *burgonde*);
**WuH** (Wien) I. 7, 1 (*Bvrgonde*); II. 18, 4 (*Bvrgŏnde lant*)
Burgondære pl.: **B** 4703
Burgônis man: **DF** 9117 (A *Burgunis*);
Burgonje: **B** 811 (MS. *Burgone*); **Rs** 224, 2 (A *Burgundie*)
Burgentrîche: **Rg(D)** 8, 1; **Rg(F)** I. 3, 1
Burgun: **AHb** p. 1, 23; **E(L)** 22, 6
Burgundia: **W** 34

In OE tradition Gifica is the ruler of the

---

¹ For this folk-tale motif see *Die Rabe* (*KHM* no. 93; Bolte–Polívka II. 335 f.).
² The designations *lectulus Brunihildae*, recorded in 1043 for the Feldberg in the Taunus, *Brunehildenstein* in the 16th cent. for the Hohe Kanzel, also in the Taunus, and *chaussées Brunehaut* in Picardy and Artois for certain roads refer to this historic queen (W. Braune, 'Brünhildenbett', *PBB* XXIII (1898), 252 f.; Kralik, *Trilogie*, 825; H. Grégoire, 'La patrie des Nibelungen', *Byzantion* IX (1934), 75). Baesecke, *Vorgeschichte*, 37, refers to the place-name *Brunildeberg* in an English document of *c*. 1220–50.
³ Ed. B. Krusch (Berlin, 1877; *MGH script. rer. Merov.* II).
⁴ In 580 Gunthram's queen, Austrechild, ordered her two Italian doctors to be killed after her death (Greg. Tur. v. 35).
⁵ Such a quarrel between two Ostrogothic noblewomen in the public baths in Italy *c*. 540, because one did not rise before the other, resulted in the murder of Urajas, one of their husbands (Procopius, *Goth.* III. i, 37 ff.).
⁶ A. Giesebrecht, 'Über den Ursprung der Siegfriedsage', *Germania* (von der Hagens) II (1837), 208, and more recently Hugo Kuhn, 'Brünhild und das Kriemhildlied', *Frühe Epik*, 12 f.
⁷ Fr. Panzer, 'Nibelungische Ketzereien: das russische Brautwerbermärchen im Nibelungenlied', *PBB* LXXII (1950), 465–98. Heusler, *Nibelungensage*, 9, and Kralik, *Trilogie*, 810 ff., consider it to be her original role; see also von See, *GHS*, 29 f.
⁸ It is uncertain whether a German 'awakening' story is reflected in Seyfrid's rescue of Krimhilt from the 'Trachenstain' in **hS** or in the winning of Mundirosa by Seyfrid de Ardemont (see Sîfrit (1), pp. 119 n. 8, 122 n. 8, 123 n. 7). It seems likely that the mythical element is a Scandinavian innovation (see von See, *GHS*, 24 f., 34).
⁹ In **Rg(A)** the giant Pûsolt is killed by Wolfhart (see p. 106).

# BURGONDE

Burgundians (*Widsith*, 19) and Gūðhere is associated with them (*Widsith*, 65 f.), being termed 'wine Burgenda' (*Waldere* II. 14); in ON Eddic tradition, however, Gunnarr and his brothers are referred to as 'Niflungar' (see Nibelunge pl., p. 98); only once is the archaic term 'vín Borgunda' applied to Gunnarr (Akv 18, 3) (see Gunther, p. 55).

The earliest recorded forms of this ethnic name are as follows (Schönfeld, 55 ff.; Bach I, § 179, 5): *Burgundiones*, Pliny (1st cent. A.D.); *Burgiones*, Ptolemy (2nd cent.); *Burgundii*, Ammianus Marcellinus (4th cent.). Originally the name must have meant 'dwellers in the high places (forts)' (J. Grimm, *GDS*, 486), cf. OHG *burg*, 'fortress', and Celtic \**brig*-, 'hill'. This tribe probably gave its name to the island of Bornholm (ON *Borgundarhólmr*); Alfred in his *Orosius* refers to its inhabitants as '*Burgendas*' (Wyatt II. 1, 44). In OHG *Burguntare* refers to the inhabitants of Burgundy in the South of France; the form *Burgonde* with *-o-* first appears in N and probably shows Romance influence (Förstemann I. 350; E. Schröder *DNK*, 102 ff.; Bach I, § 22)—the form of the *Kaiserchronik* (mid 12th cent.) is *Burgundêre* (15270): it seems probable, therefore, that the form in N, applied to Gunther and his people, is a learned reintroduction.

This tribe moved from Scandinavia in the 2nd cent. B.C. (Karsten, 78 f., 222 f.), and were neighbours of the Goths on the Baltic in the 3rd cent. (see Jordanes ch. xvii). In the 4th cent. they appeared on the Main and became allies of the Romans against the Alemanni. About the year 406 they crossed the Rhine, and in 413, for their support of the Emperor Honorius, they received territory, probably on the Lower Rhine.[1] In 423 they invaded Upper Belgium, and in 435 Gundaharius, their king, was defeated by Aetius, the Governor of Gaul, at whose instigation a Hun force destroyed 20,000 Burgundians, including Gundaharius and his family, in 437. Aetius moved the survivors to Sapaudia (Savoy). These Burgundians of South Gaul took part in the Battle of Châlons in 451, when they were allied with Aetius against the Huns led by Attila.[2] From this new Burgundian kingdom in 516 King Gundobad issued his code of laws (*Lex Burgundionum*),[3] in the preamble to which the names of Gundaharius and other 'ancestors' appear: 'Si quos apud regiae memoriae auctores nostros, id est: *Gibicam, Gundomarem,*[4] *Gislaharium, Gundaharium,* patrem quoque nostrum et patruum liberos liberasve fuisse constiterit, in eadem libertate permaneant.' This Burgundian kingdom was incorporated into the realm of the Merovingian Franks between 532 and 534 (see Sigemunt, p. 126), but the Burgundian nobility retained its language and identity till the 7th cent. (Stroheker, 229 ff.).

# C (K)

## KALLECH
A giantess at the castle of Zere.

ref: **E(d)** 274, 2

pn: probably appellative, based on MHG *kallec*, 'chattering' (Lexer I. 1497).

## CAMALO
Ruler of Metz: Guntharius sends him to demand the treasure from Waltharius; Waltharius kills him.

ref: **W** 581

pn: 6th-cent. WFr and German (Förstemann I. 592); possibly the hypocoristic form to OHG *gamal*, 'old, experienced' (Kögel I. ii. 303).

## CANDUNC
Dietwart's companion.

ref: **DF** 402

pn: the simplex *Cando* is recorded in German in the 7th cent. (Förstemann I. 594); cf. ON *gandr*, 'magic wand' (Kaufmann, 136).

## KARINAS, see TARÎAS

## KARL(E) (1)
the Frankish emperor Charlemagne († 814) is mentioned very rarely (see Rother, p. 109, and Wisselau, pp. 144 f.).

ref: **BW** 156 (Karel); **DF** 8651; **R** 3477

pn: 7th-cent. WFr and German (Förstemann I. 359).

---

[1] It is not certain whether this territory was in Germania Secunda or Germania Prima (see H. Grégoire, 'La patrie des Nibelungen', *Byzantion* IX (1934), 2 f., 7 ff., and Stroheker, 217 ff. Probability rests with the area round Worms (Stroheker, 223; von See, *GHS*, 65). Worms is first mentioned as Gunther's capital in **W**, although he is a Frank in that poem.

[2] The battle is described in epic fashion by Jordanes: the streams ran with blood and the wounded drank it (ch. xl); cf. the scene in **N** where the Burgundians drink blood (str. 2078) (see also p. 42).

[3] *Leges Burgundionum, Liber Constitutionum* III, ed. L. R. de Salis (Hannover, 1892; *MGH Legum* I, *leges* ii. 1, 43).

[4] A variant reading is *Godomarem*.

## KARL(E) (2)

**KARL(E) (2)** Ermenrîch's man
Brother of Môrolt von Arle.
ref: **DF** 8650

## CELTICUS adj.
Waltharius mocks Ekivrid's Saxon speech, terming it 'Celtica lingua'.
ref: **W** 765
This probably suggests 'elaborate' speech (Strecker, *Waltharius*, 156).

## KERLINGEN
France (see also Frankrîche under Franke, p. 46): it refers in particular to Walther's realm.
ref: **A** 77, 2; **AHb** p. 2, 36; **B** 2105; **DF** 2401; **E(d)** 317, 12; **O** 253, 1; **R** 4882; **Rg(D)** 44, 4; **Rg(P)** 66; **WuH** (Wien) II. 15, 3
This name, originally a d. pl. of *Kerlinc*, i.e. 'the people of Karl', stems from the royal dynasty founded by Charlemagne (see Karle (1) above).

## KIMO
Kamalo's nephew: killed by Waltharius. His byname is Scaramundus.
ref: **W** 687
pn: *Gimmo (Gimo)* recorded in the 10th cent. in German (Kögel I. ii. 306 f.).

## CLAUGESTIAN
The light-giving jewel in the helmet of Berhter (1) (see Hildegrîn, p. 78); it has been brought back from a foreign land by Alexander.
ref: **R** 4955

## KLINGELBOLT (AMEROLT)
A giant killed by Heime (see Wîcram).
ref: **V(h)** 870, 7; **V(w)** 717, 7 (*Amerolt*)
pn: probably appellative, based on MHG *klingelen*, 'make a noise, chatter'.

## KOBER (KNABER)
A messenger sent by the Saracen Janapas to lure Dietrich and Hildebrant to his castle at Ortneck.
ref: **V(d)** 90, 2 (Knaber); **V(w)** 420, 2
pn: possibly based on Hebrew *gober*, 'burying', a derogatory term for demons or enemies (Lunzer, *Elegast*, 152).

## CONSTANTIN (1) father of Rother's bride
The ruler of Greece, with his capital at Constantinople: he imprisons the messengers sent by Rother for the hand of his daughter. Rother visits Constantinople and abducts her. Constantin sends a minstrel to bring her back from Italy, and is about to give her in marriage to Basilistium, son of the heathen Ymelot, when Rother arrives to rescue her. Throughout **R**, Constantin is shown as cowardly and henpecked.
ref: **R** 69
In Þs Milias plays a similarly faint-hearted role when Osanctrix woos his daughter Oda (see Ôserîch, p. 103).
pn: the name derives from that of Constantine the Great (†337), founder of Byzantium; it occurs in OFr epic (Langlois, 157).
This figure symbolizes the contempt of Western crusaders for the rulers of the East Roman Empire, in particular for Alexius Comnenus (1081–1118) (Panzer, *Italische Normannen*, 74; Frings-Kuhnt, *Rother*, 213 f.; de Vries, *Rother*, xcv).

## CONSTANTIN (2) son of Helena
= Constantine the Great (see above).
ref: **R** 4394

## KRIECHE (KRIECHEN(LANT), GRECIA; KRIECHISCH adj.)
An ethnic name, also used for the country of Greece, especially the East Roman Empire, in such terms as 'ze Kriechen, Kriechenlant', etc. The following persons are connected with Greece: Alebrant (**jH**), Antzîus (**AHb**), Arnolt (**R**), Berhtunc (1) (**Wd(A)**), Dietrich (2) (**DF**; **Rg(D)**; **Rs**), Hildeburc (2) (**Kl**), Hugdietrich (**Wd(A)**), Sintram (1) (**B**), Wate (**DH**), Witzlân (**DF**), and Wolfdietrich (**E**; **Wd(ABD)**).
ref: Krieche sg.: **B** 1109 (= Sintram); 3648, etc.; **Wd(A)** 3, 4 (= Hugdietrich); 84, 4 (= Berhtunc); 324, 1 (= Wolfdietrich); **Wd(C)** VIII. 3, 4 (= Wolfdietrich); **Wd(D)** IV. 22, 2 (= Wolfdietrich); **Wd(Gr)** 892, 4 (= Wolfdietrich)
Kriechen pl. (people, country—von den Kriechen, (der) Kriechen lant, etc.): **AHb** p. 6, 14; **B** 1107; **DF** 472; **DH** F 42, 1, 1; **E(d)** 22, 2; **jH** 14, 2; **Kl** 403; **N** 1339, 1; **O(k)** 158, 5; **R** 200; **Rg(D)** 74, 3; **Rg(P)** 123; **Wd(A)** 1, 1; **Wd(B)** 65, 4; **Wd(C)** II. 10, 3; **Wd(D)** III. 7, 1; **Wd(Gr)** 97, 2; **Wd(k)** 1, 5
Kriechinne f. pl.: **Wd(D)** IX. 32, 3
kriechisch adj.: **Kl** 398 (kr. lant); **V(w)** 20, 2 (kr. feür); 787, 2 (kr. wein); **Wd(A)** 2, 3 (kr. rîche); **Wd(D)** III. 13, 1 (kr. rîche)
Grecia: **R** 4714

## KRIEMHILT
Sister of the Burgundian kings, Gunther, Gêrnôt, and Gîselhêr. In **N** she dreams that two eagles kill her tame falcon, which her mother Uote interprets as presaging the death of her future husband (see Sîfrit, (1), p. 118).[1] Gunther agrees to the marriage between Sîfrit and Kriemhilt after Sîfrit has helped him win the hand of Brünhilt. Sifrit rashly gives Kriemhilt the ring and girdle he has taken from Brünhilt when subduing her

---
[1] Regarding the falcon dream, see E. Ploß, 'Byzantinische Traumsymbolik und Kriemhilds Falkentraum', *GRM* XXXIX (1958), 218–26. See also Hagen (1), p. 59 and n. 10.

for Gunther in the bridal chamber (see Gunther (1), p. 54); in the course of a quarrel Kriemhilt accuses Brünhilt of being Sîfrit's mistress and displays the ring and girdle. Although Sîfrit's denial is publicly accepted by Gunther, Hagen, Gunther's leading vassal, plans his murder and learns from Kriemhilt the secret of his vulnerable spot between the shoulder-blades (see Sîfrit (1), p. 118 and n. 4). Before Sîfrit's murder by Hagen out hunting, Kriemhilt dreams that two wild boars kill him and that two mountains crush him (see Sîfrit (1), p. 118 and n. 5). Although she becomes reconciled with her brothers after the murder, Kriemhilt swears vengeance on Hagen, who has had the treasure left her by Sîfrit sunk in the Rhine. After thirteen years of widowhood Kriemhilt marries Etzel, the powerful ruler of Hiunenlant (Hungary), whom she persuades to invite her brothers to visit the Hunnish court: on their arrival she realizes that they have been warned, since Hagen refuses to allow the Burgundians to hand over their weapons on entering the palace (1745 ff.); Kriemhilt then incites Blœdel, Etzel's brother, to kill the Burgundian squires; in retaliation Hagen beheads Ortliep, the son of Kriemhilt and Etzel, and the child's severed head falls in Kriemhilt's lap. Kriemhilt now urges various warriors to attack the Burgundians, and even has the hall in which they are defending themselves set on fire. Finally, Dietrich von Berne binds the two surviving Burgundians, Gunther and Hagen, and hands them over to Kriemhilt. She has them imprisoned separately, then demands that Hagen should reveal the hiding-place of the treasure;[1] as he maintains that he cannot divulge it while his lord still lives, Kriemhilt has her brother executed and shows his head to Hagen. Hagen now declares that the treasure is safe for ever; at this she beheads him with the sword Balmunc, recalling her beloved Sîfrit, to whom it once belonged (N 2371 f.). For this deed Hildebrant, Dietrich's major-domo, cuts her down.

In the **Kl**, Kriemhilt's actions in **N** are justified by her loyalty to Sîfrit, since her vengeance is directed at his murderer, Hagen; this view is also shown in **N(C) (Kl(B)** 309 ff.; **N(C)** 2086, 5 ff.).

In **Rg**, Kriemhilt wishes to see Sîfrit, her betrothed, matched against Dietrich von Berne: a challenge is sent to Dietrich and his warriors to win a rose wreath from her rose-garden[2] and a kiss, as the prize for victory in combats against twelve Burgundian champions at Worms. In the final combat between Dietrich and Sîfrit she intervenes to save Sîfrit's life. In **B** she also intervenes between Dietrich and Sîfrit in a similar combat at Worms (**B** 12532 ff.).

In **AHb** it is thought that Crimhilt marries Etzel after Seifrit has been killed by Dietrich at the rose-garden, and that she summons the heroes to Ofen in Hungary in order to take revenge. She provokes Hagen by urging her son to strike him on the cheek: as in **N**, Hagen beheads the boy, and the conflict breaks out (p. 10, 22 ff.); finally Dietrich binds Gunther and Hagen, both of whom he beheads, for which deed Dietrich cuts her in half (p. 11, 8 ff.).

In **hS** Seyfrid rescues Krimhilt from a dragon which has imprisoned her on the 'Trachenstain'. They return to her father Gybich at Worms.[3] **gS**, in which she is named Florigunda, follows **hS**.[4]

ref: **AHb** p. 1, 24; **B** m 5102 n 6211; **ED** m 5, 1 (?);[5] **Kl** 45 (C); 105 (B); **N** 2, 3; **N(k)** 2, 2; **N(m)** Av. 5 (*Krenhilt*); **N(T)** 1037, 4 (*Crimelden*); **Rg(A)** 2, 4; **Rg(C)** 16; **Rg(D)** 6, 4; **Rg(F)** 1. 7, 4; **Rg(P)** 35; **Rg(V)** 11; **gS** p. 66, 22 (*Florigunda*); **hS** m 12, 2 n 51, 3 (FBa *Grimhild*, *Grymhild*, other prints *Krimhilt*); **hS(Sachs)** 21 (*Crimhilt*)

Outside the epics, few references to Kriemhilt occur in German literature, and these show a pejorative view of her character: although the view that her actions were motivated by avarice is opposed in a Latin sermon of Berthold von Regensburg († 1272) (Jänicke, ZE, 316), in a late-13th-cent. poem a disobedient girl is termed 'diu übliu Chriemhilt' (W. Grimm, *DHS*, 187), and in a poem of the 14th cent. Herodias is compared with Kriemhilt (Müllenhoff, ZE 360 f.); in 1388 a Nürnberg cannon is named after her (Bach 1, § 496, 1, 4); Wilwolt von Schaumburg in the 15th cent. refers to her pleasure at the fighting in the rose-garden (Müllenhoff, ZE, 430).

In ON Eddic tradition Gjúki's daughter is named Guðrún (Grp 34, 3; Br 3, 5; Gðr I 1, 1; Sg 2, 3; Hlr 13, 1; Dr prose, p. 223; Gðr II 10, 5; Gðr III 2, 1; Od 27, 1; Akv 29, 1; Am 46, 1; Ghv 1, 8; Hm 2, 7; Hdl 27, 3; Sk chs. 13; 48; Völss ch. 24): she weds Sigurðr after his first visit to Brynhildr,[6] and bears him a son, Sigmundr, and a daughter, Svanhildr. Sigurðr gives Guðrún the ring he received from Brynhildr when he won her for

---

[1] In ON Eddic tradition (Akv, Am) Atli demands this from Gunnarr, who later knows the secret is safe, when he has seen Högni's heart, which has been cut out and brought to him (see Gunther (1), p. 55, and Hagen (1), p. 59.
[2] See p. 88 n. 1, regarding the silken thread encircling the rose-garden.
[3] In **N(m)**, of which only the âventiure-headings are preserved, the seizure of Kriemhilt by the dragon is placed before Gunther's bridal quest for Brünhilt.

[4] See Sîfrit (1), p. 119 n. 8, regarding the winning of Mundirosa by Seyfrid de Ardemont.
[5] See Blœdelinck (p. 14 n. 1).
[6] Völss ch. 25 prefaces Guðrún's story with her dreams that presage her marriage to Sigurðr, his murder, and the deaths of her brothers at the hands of her second husband, Atli: she dreams of a hawk with feathers of gold (see **N** 13 ff.) and of a golden stag she catches, which is shot dead by Brynhildr (cf. **N** above).

Gunnarr (see Brünhilt, p. 15). Guðrún and Brynhildr quarrel, whilst bathing in a river (Sk ch. 49 whilst washing their hair), about whose husband is the better man, and Guðrún reveals that it is Sigurðr who has passed through the flames, in Gunnarr's semblance, to win Brynhildr.[1] Brynhildr urges Gunnarr to have Sigurðr murdered and laughs at Guðrun's lamentations.[2]

Gunnarr and his brothers give Guðrún in marriage to Atli, who invites them to visit his kingdom. In spite of Guðrún's warning,[3] her brothers journey to Atli's hall, where Atli has them killed when they refuse to divulge the hiding-place of the Niflungar treasure (see Nibelunge pl., p. 98).[4] After the funeral feast Guðrún kills her two sons by Atli, Erpr and Eitill, and serves their roasted hearts for him to eat (Akv),[5] kills him with a sword while he sleeps, and then burns the hall over the heads of the drunken Huns.[6]

According to Hm, Ghv, and Völss, Guðrún bears Sörli and Hamðir by a third husband, Jónakr (in Ghv, Sk ch. 50, and Völss ch. 39, she has a third son, Erpr):[7] she urges them to avenge their half-sister, Svanhildr, whom Jörmunrekr has had trampled to death by horses (see Ermenrîch, p. 38), and gives them weapons and armour (in Völss ch. 42 and Sk ch. 50 the armour is proof against metal).[8] Her sons are killed when they enter Jörmunrekr's hall (see Erpfe, p. 40).

In Gðr III Herkja, Atli's concubine (see Helche, p. 66), tells Atli that Þjóðrekr and Guðrún are lovers. Guðrún proves her innocence by plucking a jewel from a boiling cauldron: Herkja scalds her hands and is led to her death in a bog (see Dietrich (1), 29).

In Þs, Grimilld (1. 322, 5) is the daughter of Aldrian af Niflungaland. Her husband Sigurðr, at their marriage feast, urges her brother, Gunnarr, to seek the hand of Brynilldr, although he has previously sworn oaths of loyalty to her himself (II. 37-43) (see Gunther (1), p. 55). The two queens quarrel when Grimilldr refuses to stand up before Brynilldr (see pp. 15 and 16 n. 5); Grimilldr reveals to Brynilldr the deception on her wedding-night, when Sigurðr has deflowered Brynilldr in the guise of Gunnarr (see Gunther (1), p. 55), and displays the ring Sigurðr took from her. Brynilldr demands Sigurðr's death, and Högni kills him out hunting (see Sîfrit (1), p. 121). Guðrún realizes that Högni is the 'wild boar' which, he claims, killed Sigurðr (II. 258-68).

She marries Attila for the sake of his power, and persuades him to invite her brothers, the Niflungar, to visit Húnaland. She then bribes Irungr to kill the young knights (see Blœdelîn, p. 13) and her son Aldrian to slap Högni's face: thus the conflict breaks out. She prevents the Niflungar escaping from a walled orchard by having fresh oxhides spread before the gate, so that they fall and are killed by Irungr and his men; she urges Attila to have the captive Gunnarr cast into a snake-pit; finally, Þiðrekr cuts her in half when he finds her pushing lighted firebrands into the mouths of her brothers, Gernoz and Gisler, to see if they are dead.

In the Danish ballads Kriemhilt appears under various name-forms: in *Sivard og Brynild* (*DgF* 1. 16-23), Sienild (A 3, 1; B Signelille) quarrels with Bryneld with the result that her husband, Sivard, is killed (see Brünhilt, p. 16). In *Frændehævn* (*DgF* 1. 26-32), Ellind (A 3, 1; B Sinnelille; C Senild) is married to Her Loumer, her father's murderer, who also kills her brothers: she takes revenge by killing him, his brothers, and her own sons by him. In *Grimilds Hævn* (*DgF* 1. 44-50), Kremold (A 1, 1; B Kremoldt; C Grimild) invites her brothers, Hagenn and Falquor (MHG Volkêr), to a feast,[9] and urges Kanselin (see Blœdelîn and Blœdelinck, pp. 13 f.)[10] to kill them. In version C she has fresh oxhides spread on the floor to make Hagenn fall, as in Þs, and Rancke, Hagenn's son by Hvenild, locks Grimold in a cave with '*Nidings Skat*' (the Nibelungen treasure) to starve to death (see Hagen (1), p. 60, and Nibelunge, p. 98).[11]

In the Faroese ballad *Høgna táttur* (*CCF* I. 23-32), Guðrún is hostile to her brothers and loyal to Atli, as in N and Þs; she is also referred to in *Brynhildur táttur* (ibid. 8-22).

pn: 8th-cent. German, with spellings *Grim-*, *Crem-*, etc. (Förstemann 1. 672; Schlaug II. 102; Mone, 67 f.; Müllenhoff, *ZE*, 299);[12]

---

[1] In Völss ch. 28 she displays the ring on her finger. In Sk ch. 49 she recognizes the ring on Brynhildr's finger.
[2] In Gðr II and Völss ch. 32 Guðrún then departs for Denmark.
[3] She send runes with Atli's messenger and a ring with a wolf's hair twisted into it; in Am and Völss ch. 33 the messenger purposely confuses the runes (see Wärbel, p. 137).
[4] In Völss ch. 36 the treasure has been bequeathed to Guðrún by Sigurðr (in N it is Sîfrit's wedding gift to her).
[5] In Am and Völss ch. 38 she offers him beer mixed with their blood in goblets fashioned from their skulls (cf. Wielant, p. 142). Alboin, the 6th-cent. Langobard conqueror of N. Italy, is said to have forced his wife Rosamunda to drink from her father's skull (Paul Diac. 1. 27).
[6] In Am, Sk ch. 50, and Völss ch. 38, Högni's son (by Guðrún in Am), (H)niflungr, helps her kill Atli (cf. Sigmundr and Signý: see p. 125).
[7] In Hm, Erpr is Jónakr's son by another wife.
[8] Cf. Saxo VIII. x. 14, where a sorceress named Guthruna blinds the men of Jarmericus (see Ermenrîch, p. 36).
[9] In version A she welcomes all save Hagen (cf. N 1737 ff.); in version B she asks her brothers to hand over their swords, as in N (see p. 19).
[10] In *Greve Genselin* (*DgF* I. 223-30) she attends his wedding.
[11] This is repeated in the *Hven. Chron.*
[12] The problems connected with the first component of this pn have been thoroughly investigated in K. Bohnenberger, 'Kriemhilt', *PBB* XXIV (1899), 221-31: \*Grim- (OHG *grim*, 'terrible') has apparently replaced \*Grîm- (OE

only four records of the pn occur in the South-East between 700 and 1250 (Kromp III. 34); place-names from the 9th cent. (W. Grimm, *DHS*, 169; Müllenhoff, *ZE*, 301; Jänicke, *ZE*, 313).

The earliest record of Attila's death in 453 is that of the 6th-cent. Gothic historian, Jordanes (ch. xlix), who used the report of Priscus (5th-cent.), in which it is stated that Attila died from bleeding of the nose when drunk, at the side of his newly wed Germanic bride, Ildico (\**Hildiko*). Jordanes's contemporary, Marcellinus Comes, reports that Attila was killed by a woman (*MGH auct. ant.* XI. 86; W. Grimm, *DHS*, 9). In the 9th cent. the *Poeta Saxo* records that Attila was murdered by his wife in revenge for her father's death (*MGH ss* I. 247; W. Grimm, *DHS*, 10). The *Ann. Quedl.* (*c.* 1000) record that Attila was killed by a girl whose father he had killed when abducting her (*MGH ss* III. 32; W. Grimm, ibid.).¹ Already in the 8th cent., Attila was thought to have been responsible for the destruction of the Burgundians and the death of their king, Gundaharius, in 437 (Paul. Diac. XIV. 5: see Gunther); it is not surprising, therefore, that in Germanic tradition Attila's last wife becomes the sister of the Burgundian kings, whose death she avenges by killing him. The name \**Grimhild* (or \**Krēmhild*), which probably derives from South-East Germanic traditions about this \**Hildiko*, is retained in **N** and subsequent MHG monuments: *Kriemhilt* (cf. also *Grimilldr* of Þs and *Kremold*, etc., of the Danish ballads).²

It is very probable that the quarrel between the wife of Siegfried (MHG Sîfrit, ON Sigurðr) and her brother's wife, which leads to Siegfried's murder, stems from the conflict between Brunihildis and Fredegunda after the murder of Brunihildis's husband, the Merovingian Sigebert, in 575, but the historical roles of the women have been reversed in epic tradition (see Brünhilt, p. 16., and Sîfrit (1), p. 122); if this is so,

*grīma*, 'mask'). E. Schröder, 'Codex Laurishamensis', *AfdA* (1937), 56 ff., postulates an otherwise unknown Gmc. root \**Krēm-* as a basis. See also G. Schramm, 'Der Name Kriemhilt', *ZfdA* XCIV (1965), 39–57, and Kaufmann, 154 f.

¹ 16th-cent. German references to Gunther as King of Thuringia and father of Grimylda, Attila's last wife (W. Grimm, *DHS*, 340 f.; 344), are learned attempts to reconcile epic tradition with Jordanes's account.

² In his *Chronica Hungarorum* (1282–90), Simon Kéza follows Jordanes's account of Attila's death (W. Grimm, *DHS*, 181–4), but apparently uses such South-East German traditions to deal with subsequent events (Bleyer, 429 ff.): Attila's son by the German Crimild is said to have been supported by Detricus de Verona (see Dietrich (1), p. 28) against Chaba (or Kewe), Attila's son by the daughter of the Greek Emperor (see Helche, p. 67); the ensuing conflict is termed 'praelium Crumhelt' in an addition to the chronicle printed in 1781 (W. Grimm, *DHS*, 184). Stroheker, 237 ff., surmises that this conflict reflects traditions about the battle of Nedao

the original name of Attila's last wife has apparently been transferred to her mother ON Grímhildr: see Uote(1), pp. 132 f.), when the wife of the murdered Siegfried becomes identified with the sister of the Burgundian kings, whose original name, \**Gunprūn* (ON *Guðrún*),³ alliterates with theirs, in the versions of 'Siegfried's Death' (Br, Sg, Völss chs. 13–32) and the 'Destruction of the Burgundians' (Akv, Am, Völss chs. 33–8) which reached Scandinavia.

Kriemhilt's role of avenger of her husband Sîfrit on her brothers (**N**, Þs) is first recorded with certainty in **N** (*c.* 1200);⁴ the reference by the Marner (*c.* 1250) to 'wen Kriemhilt verriet' (W. Grimm, *DHS*, 179) confirms the popularity of **N**. Her role as a maiden rescued from a dragon (**hS**) is unlikely to be earlier than the 13th cent.⁵ Guðrún's role as the wife of Jónakr and mother of Hamðir and Sörli (Hm, Ghv), linking her with the story of 'Ermanaric's Death' (see Ermenrîch, p. 38), is a specifically Scandinavian innovation, and her involvement with Herkja and Þjóðrekr in Gðr III suggests direct influence from the Dietrich-epics of 13th-cent. Germany.

C(H)RIST, KRIST
Occurs in formulas of exclamation and supplication.
ref: **A** 105, 2; **B** 2475; **DF** 902; **E(d)** 100, 2; **E(s)** 48, 8; **jH** 9, 2; **Kl** 3257; **Ku** III, 4; **L(A)** 1776; **L(D)** 1792; **N** 103, 3; **O** 396, 2; **R** 64; **Rg(A)** 164, 3; **Rg(C)** 619; **Rg(D)** 322, 2; **Rg(P)** 840; **Rs** 314, 2; **Ru** IV. 81; **hS** 29, 2; **jSn** 58, 12; **V(d)** 27, 9; **V(h)** 40, 1; **V(w)** 77, 3; **Wd(A)** 110, 2; **Wd(B)** 599, 3; **Wd(D)** III. 20, 4; **Wu(B)** 126, 5

KÛDRÛN
Kûdrûn is kept in strict seclusion by her father, Hetele von Tenelant (Denmark); she is betrothed to Herwîc von Sêlant, but a rejected suitor, Hartmuot von Ormanîe (Normandy), who is aided by his father

between the rebellious Germanic peoples led by Ardaric and their Hunnish rulers in 454; the name and role would reach the Burgundians, he suggests, in the 6th cent., when Bavarians settled in the Burgundian kingdom in South Gaul (see Burgonde, p. 17).

³ See Kûdrûn, p. 22, regarding this pn.
⁴ Saxo, in his *Gesta Danorum*, XIII. vi. 5–9, records for the year 1131 that a Saxon singer, sent by King Magnus of Denmark to lure Cnut Lavard of Slesvig into an ambush, tried in vain to warn him by reciting the well-known story of the treachery of Grimilda against her brothers. It seems likely, however, that Saxo, who wrote the relevant part of the history after 1204, obtained this motif from German sources, not necessarily earlier than **N** (see Tonnelat, 187), for, according to extracts from a life of Cnut dedicated to the Danish King Erik Edmund (†1157), a singer named Siaward warned Cnut three times by the recital of lays about parricide (Müllenhoff, *ZE*, 335 f.).
⁵ King, *Hürnen Seyfrid*, 76, dates it between 1280 and 1400.

## KÛDRÛN

Ludewîc, abducts her, and Hetele loses his life in a battle with Hartmuot and his men at Wülpensant.[1] Kûdrûn suffers great hardship at the hands of Hartmuot's mother, Gêrlint; Hartmuot, on the other hand, treats her courteously during her thirteen years' captivity in Ormanîe. While Kûdrûn and her faithful handmaiden, Hildeburc,[2] are washing clothes for Gêrlint on the seashore, an angel in the form of a sea-bird informs them of the approach of a rescuing fleet sent by Hilde, Kûdrûn's mother. The next day Kûdrûn's brother, Ortwîn, and her betrothed, Herwîc, approach the shore in a small boat: the pair recognize each other from their betrothal rings, and Herwîc promises to return the next day with the rescuing army, which is concealed in a wood.[3] Kûdrûn hurls Gêrlint's washing into the sea and laughs for the first time since her capture. On the following day Hartmuot prevents Gêrlint having Kûdrûn murdered during the battle between the Normans and the rescuing army. The Normans are defeated, Kûdrûn returns to Denmark, weds Herwîc, and arranges the marriages of Hartmuot to Hildeburc and of Ortwîn to Ortrûn, Hartmuot's sister; she then departs with Herwîc for Sêlant.

ref: **Ku** 575, 2 (normally *Chaudrun*; *Chautrun* 18 times; other spellings are *Chutrum*, *Chuttrun*, *Chautrum*, etc.)

pn: this form with loss of nasal before dental spirant is rare in UG records (Mone, 68; Förstemann I. 662; Müllenhoff, *ZE*, 315; Kaufmann, 150),[4] and, as far as **Ku** is concerned, probably originates in the Low Franconian region (Stackmann, *Kudrun*, lxxix), being ultimately of Norse provenance, cf. ON *Guðrún* (< Gmc. *Gunprūn*).

Such stories of abducted women were current in Scandinavia of the Viking Age: Áslaug in the *Ragnars saga* (*FAS* I. 219–85), Herborg in Góðr I,[5] and Syrith (Sigred) in Saxo, VII. iv. 1–7, endure hardships similar to those of Kûdrûn.

Kûdrûn's story is of the 'Aschenputtel' folk-tale type (*KHM* no. 21) represented by the so-called 'Sudeli' and 'Die schöne Meererin' ballads (Meier, *Balladen* I. 52–4; II. 16–24); it is possible, however, that the latter derive from **Ku** itself (Stackmann, *Kudrun*, lxxxv ff.). The story of Olimpia in Book IX of the third version of Ariosto's *Orlando Furioso* (ed. 1532) bears striking similarities to Kûdrûn's story, but it is arguable that it, too, derives directly from **Ku** (H. Frenzel, 'Von der Olimpia-Episode der Parerga des Orlando Furioso', *GRM* XXXVI (1955), 166, but see Fr. Neumann, 'Kudrun', *VfL* II (1936), 961–83; v (1955), 572–80; Stackmann, *Kudrun*, lxxx ff.).

## KÜNHILT (SÎMILTE)

Dietleip's sister: in **L** she is abducted by the dwarf, Laurîn; later she helps Dietrich and his men escape from imprisonment in Laurîn's subterranean kingdom. When Laurîn is captured, Künhilt, nevertheless, intercedes for him, and Dietrich spares his life. Dietleip arranges for her marriage to a worthy man.

ref: **B** m 4204; **L(A)** m 574 n 747 ('Künhilt' is a conjecture;[6] various MS. spellings are *Krimhilt* (*Kreimhilt*), *Krinhilt*, *Bronhilt*, etc.); **L(D)** m 21 n 1146 (Sîmilte); **L(DrHb)** m 132, 4

pn: 7th-cent. German (Förstemann I. 381; Schlaug I. 70); in the 15th cent. it occurs in error for *Kriemhilt* (W. Grimm, *DHS*, 320).

## KUONRÂT

In the **Kl**, Bishop Pilgerîn von Pazzouwe (Passau) has the story of **N** written down in 'latînischen buochstaben' (4679),[7] and

    daz mære brieven dô began
    sîn schrîbære meister Kuonrât.
    getihtet man ez sît hât
    dicke in tiuscher zungen.
                    (4694–7)

ref: **Kl** 4695

It has sometimes been thought that this refers to the author of **N**, but it is now generally accepted that the author of **N** has remained anonymous.[8]

The Þs uses the name Konrádur (see Amelunc (2), p. 6).

pn: extremely common; 7th-cent. German (Förstemann I. 373 f.).

## KUPERAN

A giant who rules a thousand dwarfs and is presumably in the service of the dragon who has imprisoned Krimhilt in a cave on the 'Trachenstain'. Seyfrid, guided by the dwarf Eugel, arrives at the 'Trachenstain', defeats Kuperan, and forces him to unlock Krimhilt's prison. Inside the cave Kuperan shows Seyfrid the sword with which the dragon can be killed (see Balmunc (1), p. 9). Kuperan again attacks Seyfrid, who hurls him from the mountain.

ref: **gS** p. 71, 42 (*Wulffgrambåhr*); **hS** 59, 2 (prints N, H, and F *Kuperan*; other prints

---

[1] This battle belonged originally to the Hildestory (see Hegelinge, p. 64).
[2] A foil to Hildeburc is the unfaithful Heregart (see p. 69).
[3] Cf. Rother and Wolfdietrich, pp. 109, 149.
[4] The full form is equally rare (Förstemann I. 708 f.; Kaufmann, 158 f.).
[5] Compare the names in Góðr I and **Ku**: Guðrún and Herborg; Kûdrûn, *Here*gart, and Hilde*burc*.

[6] See Holz, *Laurin*, xxxiii, 190 f., and O. Jänicke, *DHB* I. 282, regarding the spelling of the name in MSS. and prints.
[7] This may refer to the script (K. Schiffmann, 'Die "latînischen buochstabe" der Klage v. 2145 ff.', *PBB* LV (1931), 309).
[8] O. Höfler, 'Die Anonymität des Nibelungenliedes', *DVjs* XXIX (1955), 170 ff.; Panzer, *Nibelungenlied*, 89 f., refers to the similar formula of 'pfaffe Chunrat' in the *Rolandslied* (9079–83).

also have *Ruperan*); **hS(Sachs)** m 26 n 456 (*Kuperon*)

The name may well represent a corrupt form of Cypriân,[1] the name of the heathen father of Salmân's wife in *Salman und Morolf*, 3, 1 (12th cent.); a giant of this name is referred to in *Reinfried von Braunschweig* (*c.* 1300), and by Ulrich von Türheim (*c.* 1240) (W. Grimm, *DHS*, 195). Fischart in his *Gargantua* (ed. 1594) refers to 'Riss Rupran' (W. Grimm, *DHS*, 352), and Jacob Ayrer (†1605) consigns Kuperan to hell (Müllenhoff, *ZE*, 379 f.).

It should be noted that in ON Eddic tradition, Fáfnir, the dragon killed by Sigurðr, is also thought of as a giant, and his death is planned by his brother, the dwarf Reginn; in **N**, Sîfrit kills the twelve giants in the service of the Nibelunge before he wins the treasure.

# D (see also under T)

DANCRÂT
Father of the Burgundians, Gunther and his brethren, in **N**, **Kl**, and **B**.[2]

ref: **B** 2617; **Kl** 35; **N** 7, 2

In **W**, **Rg**, **hS**, and **AHb**, Gibeche is the father of Gunther and his brothers (see Gibeche (1), p. 51).

In Þs, Aldrian is the father of Gunnarr, Gisler, Gernoz, and Grimilldr (see Aldrîân, p. 4).

pn; 9th-cent. German (Förstemann I. 1404; Schlaug I. 159; II. 82); place-names in 8th cent. (Bach II, § 105). The name, obviously from a German source, appears in ON Vkv for Níðuðr's man, Þakkráðr (see Wielant, p. 142).

DANCWART
Hagen's younger brother: in **N** he kills Blœdel, when the latter leads the attack on the Burgundian squires. He is killed by Helferich (1); in the **Kl** he is also known to have killed Wolfbrant and Hâwart in the fighting against the men of Etzel and Dietrich.

In **DF** he is with Hagen supporting Dietrich at the battle of Bôlonje (Bologna). In **Rg(F)** he is the beloved of Sêburc and thought to be Hildebrant's brother.

ref: **DF** 8599; **KL** 473; **N** 9, 2; **Rg(F)** I. 3, 3

pn: 9th-cent. German (Förstemann I. 1405; Schlaug I. 159; II. 82).

DANÎÊL
Wolfdietrich in distress recalls God's help to Daniel.

ref: **Wd(D)** VIII. 123, 1; **Wd(Gr)** 1659, 1

In OFr epic Daniel is frequently invoked (Langlois, 171; Flutre, 57).

DELFÎÂN
Nephew of Merzîân: killed by Wolfdietrich.

ref: **Wd(D)** V. 147, 1; **Wd(Gr)** 983, 1

(DÊMUOT)
Sister of Biterolf and mother of Alphere.

ref: **B** m 671; **WuH** m II (Wien), 3, 1

pn: 9th-cent. German (Förstemann I. 1460; Schlaug I. 71; II. 186).

DENEMARCKE, etc., see TENE

DIEPOLT (1) von Franken (Franconia)
Dietwart's companion.

ref: **DF** 538

pn: 6th-cent. WFr (*Theudobald*), 8th-cent. German (Förstemann I. 1417 ff., 1460); the form *Diepolt* appears in UG first in 1098 (cf. Tîbalt (1), p. 131).

In Pfaffe Konrad's *Rolandslied* (*c.* 1170) a Diepolt appears among the Christian warriors (846).

DIEPOLT (2) von Gruonlande (Greenland)
Ermenrîch's man.

ref: **DF** 8636

DIEPOLT (3) von Beiern (Bavaria)
Etzel's man: he aids Dietrich against Ermenrîch.

ref: **Rs** 65, 1

DIEROLT
A heathen killed by Wolfdietrich.

ref: **Wd(D)** V. 157, 1; **Wd(Gr)** 993, 1

pn: 7th-cent. WFr (Förstemann I. 408 f.).

DIETE
Biterolf's incognito at Etzel's court.

ref: **B** 3408

pn: hypocoristic form for compound names with first component *Diet-*, usually for Dietrich.

---

[1] J. Lunzer, 'Drei Namen der deutschen Heldensage', *PBB* XLIX (1925), 468 f., suggests MHG *cyprîan*, 'cypress' as a basis for the name.
[2] Panzer, *Nibelungenlied*, 80, considers that the pn came from the **Kl**, which named Gunther's father after the famous Tancred of Lecce, a South Italian Norman (†1194); the name *Tangré* is popular in the OFr *ch.d.g.* (Langlois, 630).

## DIETHÊR (1)

**DIETHÊR (1)** son of Dietmâr (1)
Dietrich's younger brother: in **DF** and **Rg(D)** he takes no part in the fighting, but in **Rs** Dietrich puts him, together with Scharpfe and Orte, the sons of Etzel and Helche, in the care of Elsân at Berne (Verona). The youths persuade their guardian to let them follow Dietrich's army in the campaign against Ermenrîch; they lose their way and are killed by the traitor Witege at Rabene (Ravenna). Before he dies Diethêr grasps earth in lieu of the sacrament.

ref: **AHb** p. 6, 35; **DF** 2517; **E(L)** 198, 2; **ED** m 15, 3 (?);[1] **Rg(C)** 665; **Rg(D)** 63, 4; **Rs** 293, 4; **äSn** 32, 12; **jSn** 20, 13; **V(d)** 31, 3; **V(h)** 74, 7; **V(w)** 192, 7 (*Dithman*)

In Wernher der Gartenære's *Meier Helmbrecht* (c. 1250-80) it is known that Witege killed Diethêr and Helche's sons (76 ff.), but it is the hero, Helmbrecht, who receives the earth-sacrament (1902 ff.).

In Þs, Þether, Þiðrekr's brother (II. 176, 10), kills Runga at the battle of Gronsport (Ravenna?); he then attacks Viðga, who has already killed Attila's sons, Erpr and Ortvin. Viðga kills him after he has killed Viðga's horse, Skemmingr (see Witege, p. 146).

pn: 6th-cent. WFr and German; frequent in 8th-cent. German records, also occurs in place-names (Förstemann I. 1433 f.; II. ii. 1045; Schlaug I. 161); recorded for a 6th-cent. prince in OE (Searle, 444).

Theodoric's brother Theodemund was nearly captured in an ambush of Theodoric's baggage-train in the Balkans in 479 by the Roman general Sabinianus (see Dietrich (1), p. 30, and Sabene (1), pp. 113 f), but the fate of Diethêr in **Rs** may well reflect that of Theodahad, Theodoric's nephew, killed on the orders of Vitigis, a later reader of the Goths in Italy, in 536 (Schütte, *Gotthiod* II. 189: see Witege, p. 147).

**DIETHÊR (2)** father of the Harlunge
In **DF** he is the brother of Ermenrîch and Dietmâr, and he rules at Breisach and in Bavaria; his three sons are hanged by Ermenrîch.

ref: **DF** 2409

Heinrich von München follows **DF** (W. Grimm, **DHS**, 225), but the father of the Harlunge is variously named elsewhere (see Harlung, p. 62).

**DIETHÊR (3)** father of Dietlint (1)
ref: **B** 4146

## DIETLEIP

**DIETLEIP von Stîre (Styria)**
Son of Biterolf and Dietlint: in **B** he leaves his home in Spain to seek his father, who is serving Etzel. 'Der kindische degen' (2109), mounted on Belche, and bearing his father's sword Welsunc, is attacked by Gunther and his men when he reaches the Rhine: he wounds Gunther, Gêrnôt, and Hagen.[2] At Etzel's court Dietleip's good looks impress Queen Helche and her ladies. He joins Etzel's army and captures the leader of the Poles, winning Pomerania for Etzel; in the confusion of battle he fights his own father, Biterolf, but the two are reconciled by Rüedegêr. Etzel supplies Dietleip with an army to exact vengeance on Gunther; Ermenrîch, Dietrich, Rüedegêr, and others join the campaign. In the ensuing combats at Worms Dietleip fights a drawn combat with Gunther. Finally the gates of the city are stormed and the opponents reconciled. Biterolf receives the fief of Styria from Etzel; hence Dietleip's designation in subsequent epics: 'von Stîre', 'der Stîrehelt', etc.

In **DF** and **Rs** he aids Dietrich against Ermenrîch: he kills Wate (2) at Meilân (Milan), fights Heime at Bôlonje (Bologna), and Marke at Rabene (Ravenna).

In **Rg(A)** he has been wounded by a sea-monster (MHG *merwunder*) in Sibenbürgen (Transylvania) (119), but joins Dietrich's champions at Kriemhilt's rose-garden, where he fights a drawn combat with Walther; in **Rg(D)** he kills his opponent, Stüefinc (**Rg(F)** Schrûtan).

In **L** Dietleip's sister Künhilt has been abducted by the dwarf Laurîn, whom he defends when Dietrich is about to kill him. Later he aids Dietrich and his men against Laurîn's dwarfs and giants. After Künhilt's rescue he arranges a marriage for her (see Laurîn, p. 89).

In **V(h)** he kills the giants Bœmrîan (**V(w)** Morean) and Videlnstôz (**V(w)** Baldegrein) on the expedition to free Dietrich from Nîtgêr's giants at Mûter (see Wîcram).

In **hS(Sachs)** his name is used for a counsellor of Sigmunt.

Dietleip's device varies: a unicorn (**Rg(F)**: see Biterolf (1), p. 13);[3] a panther (**Rg(P)**); and a sea-monster (**L(A)**).

ref: **AHb** p. 3, 36 (*Dietlieb*); **B** 193; **DF** 3635; **ED** m 15, 3 (?);[4] **L(A)** 421; **L(D)** 20; **L(DrHb)** 8, 7 (*Ditlaub*); **L(K)**II 522; **Rg(A)** 106, 2; **Rg(C)** 412; **Rg(D)** 75, 1; **Rg(F)** 111. 19, 2 (*dietlif*); **Rg(P)** 125; **Rg(V)** 109 (*Dietlieb*); **V(h)** 378, 8; **V(w)** 564, 6

Dietleip is rarely mentioned in German literature outside the epics: in *von dem üblen wîbe* (c. 1250) his fight with the 'merwîp' is described (Müllenhoff, *ZE*, 369), and he is among Dietrich's men opposing the giants in Wittenwiler's *Ring* (c. 1410).

In Þs, Þetleifr (1. 209), son of a Dane,

---

[1] See n. 4 below.
[2] Schneider, *GHS* I. 326 f., considers that the first five âventiure of **B** derive from the lost MHG Walter-epic see Walther, pp. 135, 137).
[3] Dietleip bears a shield with a unicorn depicted on it and the sword 'Belsung' in the late-14th-cent. frescoes at Runkelstein (Müllenhoff, *ZE*, 386). In **B** both Dietleip and his father, Biterolf, possess the sword Welsunc (see p. 139).
[4] 'sinen broder van der stœre' probably refers to Diethêr, but he has been confused with Dietleip 'von Stîre'.

## DIETLEIP

Biturulfr, and a Saxon woman, Oda, appears dull-witted in youth, but saves his father's life in a fight with the robber Ingram and his men. He leaves home to visit his Saxon grandfather and comes to the castle of Marsteinn in the Borgarskogr (I. 223),[1] which belongs to Sigurðr the Greek; under the incognito 'Vildimælrik' (see Amelrîch, p. 5) he fights Sigurðr till sunset. Sigurðr's daughter steals her father's victory-stone and sleeps with him: Þetleifr defeats Sigurðr the next day and wins her hand.

Þetleifr joins Þiðrekr's company under the incognito 'Elminrikr' and becomes involved in a dispute with Valtari (MHG Walther), who rebukes him for his greed and extravagance: he defeats Valtari in a weight-putting and shaft-throwing contest. On Þiðrekr's Bertangaland expedition he defeats the ninth son of Isungr. Later he weds the daughter of Drusian (see Drasîân, p. 32). He is killed by Ostacia in dragon-shape, when he is fighting her husband, Hertnið (see Hertnît (1), p. 70). In the Þs, Þetleifr's device is an elephant.[2]

In Version F of the Danish ballad *Kong Diderik og hans Kæmper* (*DgF* I. 108–10), Dettloff Danske is one of Dietrich's heroes.

pn: 8th-cent. Lb (Paul. Diac. IV. 16; VI. 58), 9th-cent. German (Förstemann I. 1438; Schlaug I. 162; II. 84).

From the brief reference in **Rg(A)** it is apparent that a story about a fight with a sea-monster was connected with Dietleip (see also Dietlint (1), Dietleip's mother, below): Þetleifr's death fighting Ostacia in Þs may reflect it.

## DIETLINT (1) mother of Dietleip
Wife of Biterolf.

ref: **B** 59

In Þs, Biturulfr's wife is named Oda (I. 209, 8).

pn: 5th-cent. inscription at Mainz (Förstemann I. 1440); 7th-cent. Lb (Bruckner, 310), 8th-cent. German (Förstemann I. 1439 f.; Schlaug I. 162; II. 84).

There were certainly traditions about the historical Theudolinda, daughter of Duke Garibald of Bavaria, who married the Langobard, King Authari (†590).[3] Hans Sachs, in his two poems about her, tells how she was ravished by a sea-monster.[4]

## DIETLINT (2) Rüedegêr's daughter
Betrothed to Gîselhêr in **N**. In the **Kl**, before she learns of her father's death, she dreams that his horse has drowned; her uncle, Dietrich, after she has learnt of the deaths of her betrothed, Gîselhêr, and of her father, Rüedegêr, promises to find her a husband.

ref: **Kl** 2974; **N** m 1163, 2

## DIETLINT (3) mother of Wolfdietrich
Wife of Trippel von Athenîs.

ref: **Wd(C)** II. 8, 2

See Hildeburc (2), p. 78.

## DIETMÂR (1) father of Dietrich (1) von Berne

In **DF** the son of Amelunc (3) von Rœmischlant (Italy), brother of Ermenrîch, and uncle of the Harlunge: he rules Lombardy, Rome, Istria, Friuli, and the Inn Valley; he builds Berne (Verona) and dies aged 346.

In **AHb** he is the son of Wolfdietrich and Sîdrât (a confusion: see the genealogical tree under Dietrich (1), p. 26 n. 1).

ref: **A** m 5, 3 n 85, 2; **AHb** p. 6, 29; **B** m 7988 n 8039; **DF** 2419; **E(d)** 82, 11; **E(L)** 73, 11; **E(s)** 173, 5; **ED** m 3, 4; **Kl** 2791 (C); **N(k)** 1387, 2; **Rg(C)** 1729; **Rg(D)** 484, 4; **Rg(P)** 709; **Rs** 52, 4; **V(h)** m 10, 2 n 74, 11; **V(w)** 192, 11

In German references to him outside the heroic epics he is the father of Dietrich von Berne (see p. 28.). In the mid-12th-cent. *Kaiserchronik* he is the son of 'der alte Dietrich': he wins back Mêrân after Etzel's death and defeats Etzel's sons (see Dietrich (1), p. 28).

In the late ON Eddic poem Gðr III, Þjóðrekr is referred to as 'Þjóðmars son' (3, 5), and in the Faroese ballad *Høgna táttur* (*CCF* I. 22–31), Tíðrikur is termed 'Tíðrikur Tatlarason' (137, 3).

In Þs, Þetmarr (I. 23, 6), son of Samson, is Þiðrekr's father; he is the brother of Erminrikr and half-brother of Áki Aurlungatrausti (see Hâche). He weds Odilia, daughter of Elsungr, from whom Samson originally conquered Bern (Verona). The name Þetmarr is also used in Þs for Samson's uncle (I. 18, 14).

This figure represents the historical father of Theodoric the Great, Theodemer the Ostrogoth, who, with his brothers Valamer and Vidimer, served Attila (†453). After Attila's death they revolted against the Huns in 454 (see Etzel, p. 43.). Theodemer succeeded Valamer as king and led the Ostrogoths into Moesia in 473. He was

---

[1] Possibly recalls MHG 'der Bulgerîe walt' (cf. **Wd(A)** 2, 1), 'Bulgaria', where lies Büden (Vidin), the town by which the castle of Falkenîs is situated; in this castle Wolfdietrich has similar experiences in **Wd(BD)** (see Marpaly, p. 93).

[2] Sigurðr the Greek rides one, but it may recall Ortnît's device (**Wd(B)** 512, 3).

[3] Paul. Diac. III. 30: Authari, disguised as his own messenger, takes part in an embassy to fetch his bride, only revealing his identity on the journey home.

[4] Hans Sach's sources are unknown (see Drescher, 436 ff.), but in a poem contained in the *Dresdner Heldenbuch* (1472), entitled '*Das Meerwunder*' (*HPHB* II (1825), 222–6), an unnamed queen of Lombardy is ravished by a sea-monster, which is subsequently killed, together with its offspring, by the king and his son. This story stems possibly from Merovingian tradition: the 5th-cent. Meroveus was reputed to be the offspring of the union of the wife of the Frankish king, Chlodio, with a sea-monster (Jiriczek, *DHS* (1898), 264; Baesecke, *Vorgeschichte*, 132).

## DIETMÂR (1)

succeeded by his son, Theodoric, in 475 (see Dietrich (1), p. 30).

pn: 8th-cent. German (Förstemann I. 1440 ff.; Schlaug I. 162; II. 840), 6th-cent. Gothic (Schönfeld, 231), and 8th-cent. Lb (Bruckner, 310).

## DIETMÂR (2) von Wienen (Vienna)

Etzel's man: he aids Dietrich against Ermenrîch.

ref: **Rs** 62, 1

## DIETRICH (1) von Berne (Verona)

In **äH**, Hiltibrant has accompanied Deotrîch into exile for sixty summers and winters, fleeing eastward from the hostility of Ôtacher (see Hildebrant, p. 74).

In **N**, Dietrich, an exile at Etzel's court, becomes involved in the fighting between the Burgundians and Huns through the death of Rüedegêr, and loses all his men, apart from Hildebrant (see p. 110); he binds the last surviving Burgundians, Gunther and Hagen (see pp. 54, 58).

In the **Kl** he organizes the burial of the dead, sends messengers to the bereaved, and departs with his wife Herrât and Hildebrant to his kingdom of Amelunge lant (see p. 5).

In **DF** Dietrich's uncle Ermenrîch[1] invades his kingdom, which comprises Lombardy, Istria, Friuli, and the Inn Valley: in spite of his victory at Meilân (Milan) Dietrich abandons his realm to Ermenrîch to save the lives of his men captured by Witege and Heime at Bôle (Pola) and takes refuge with King Etzel in Hiunenlant (Hungary); he twice returns to Italy and defeats Ermenrîch at Meilân, Rabene (Ravenna), and Bôlonje (Bologna), with armies supplied by Etzel, and then withdraws to Hiunenlant. In **Rs** Dietrich once more leads an army supplied by Etzel into Italy, and puts Ermenrîch to flight at the battle of Rabene, in the course of which his brother Diethêr and the sons of Etzel, Scharpfe and Orte, are killed by Witege. Dietrich beheads Elsân, in whose charge he has left the young princes (see Ilsân, pp. 84 f.), and, belching flame,[2] vainly pursues Witege, who escapes by riding into the sea. Etzel and his queen,

[1] Dietrich's genealogy in **DF**, followed by Heinrich von München in the 14th cent. (W. Grimm, *DHS*, 224; cf. that of Ps on p. 29), may be shown thus:

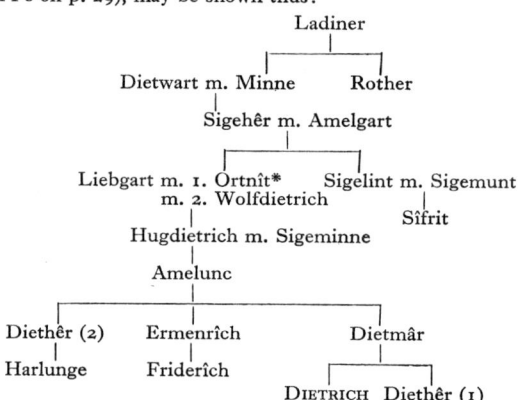

* Variations occur in **AHb** (pp. 6 f.), in which Wolfdietrich is likewise made the ancestor of Dietrich von Berne in an attempt to fit in the relationships of **Wd(D)**; however, Wolfdietrich's son is named Dietmâr, not Hugdietrich (see Wolfdietrich, p. 149):

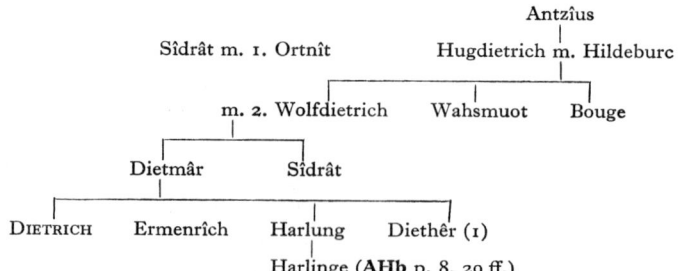

Harlinge (**AHb** p. 8, 29 ff.)

[2] Frequent reference is made to Dietrich's fiery breath when roused to anger, cf. **Rg** below, and Ps, p. 29 and n. 5. It may well derive from the fiery beam emanating from the mouth, symbolizing divine kingship, attributed to Germanic kings said to be descended from Woden (see S. R. T. O. d Ardenne, 'A Neglected Manuscript of British History', *English and Mediaeval Studies* presented to J. R. R. Tolkien (London, 1962), 92).

Helche, on Rüedegêr's intercession,[1] forgive Dietrich the loss of their sons, and he enters Etzelnburc triumphantly to kneel in homage to Etzel. In **A** Dietrich's defence of Berne and defeat of Ermenrîch become acts of vengeance for the death of the youthful Alphart at the hands of Witege and Heime. In **ED** Dirik van dem Berne leads his men against the 'koeninck van Armentriken' (= Ermenrîch) at Freysack and beheads him.[2]

In **Rg**, in the final combat between the champions of Worms and Berne at Kriemhilt's rose-garden at Worms, the reluctant Dietrich, urged on by Hildebrant and Wolfhart, defeats Sîfrit by melting his horn skin with his fiery breath;[3] in **B**, too, in the final battle against Gunther's men at Worms, Dietrich,[4] belching flames, forces Sîfrit to retreat (see Kriemhilt, p. 19).[5] In **DuW** Dietrich is pitted against Wenezlân, King of Poland, in a drawn combat.

Dietrich's encounters with giants[6] and dwarfs are also the subject of epics: in **E**, wearing his shining helmet Hildegrîn, he slays the young giant Ecke and takes his armour and sword (see Eckesahs, pp. 34 f.[7]); after rescuing a maiden from Ecke's brother Vâsolt, who is pursuing her with hounds, he kills Vâsolt and other relatives of Ecke (see Birkhilt, Eckenôt, Runze, and Uodelgart); finally he casts Ecke's head at the feet of the three queens of Jochgrîm, at whose behest Ecke has sought combat with Dietrich (**E(ds)** only). In **Sn**, Dietrich is seized by the giant Sigenôt, whose uncle Grîme he has killed (see Grîme, p. 53, Hilde (3), p. 74, and Hildegrîn, p. 78); the giant throws him into a pit full of serpents, from which Hildebrant ultimately rescues him (see Eckerîch (2), p. 34). In **Wu**, Dietrich kills a cannibal monster who has pursued Frau Sælde (= Fortuna); she prophesies Dietrich's future fame (see Sælde, p. 114, and Wunderer, pp. 153 f.).

In **L(AD)**, Dietrich and his men enter Laurîn's rose-garden, defeat the dwarf king's dwarf and giant warriors, and rescue Dietleip's sister, whom Laurîn has abducted.[8] In **L(K)II**, Walberân, Laurîn's uncle, defeats Dietrich in single combat before Berne, after which Laurîn arranges a truce (see Walberân, p. 134). The fragment **G** also treats of Dietrich's encounter with a maidenstealing dwarf (see Goldemâr, p. 52).

In **V** the youthful Dietrich, loath to leave the pleasures of court, is urged by Hildebrant to seek adventure in the Tyrol: they rescue a maiden, left as tribute by the elf-queen Virginâl, from the heathen Orkîse (see pp. 45 f., 100), and a knight, Rentwîn, from the jaws of a dragon.[9] Rentwîn's father, Helferîch (5), entertains the heroes in his castle of Ârône (Arona). Here in **V(dw)** Dietrich defeats the warrior Libertîn, who then aids him against Janapas, the son of Orkîse. On the way to Virginâl's court at Jeraspunt Dietrich is seized by the leader of Nîtgêr's giants, Wîcram, and imprisoned at Mûter, but his heroes kill the giants and free him (see Nîtger, p. 99, Wîcram, p. 140, and Ibelîn, p. 84). Finally he weds Virginâl.

In **AHb** Dietrich's mother is said to have been visited by a demon named Machmet,[10] who prophesies the future power and fiery breath of her son. When all Dietrich's men have died, a dwarf leads him to another world, since when he has not been seen again.[11]

ref: **A** 4, 4; **AHb** m p. 3, 32 n p. 5, 3; **B** 2279; **DF** m 2484 n 2517; **DuW** 23; **E(B)** 4; **E(d)** 2, 10; **E(L)** 2, 10; **E(s)** 2, 10; **ED** m 1, 2 n 4, 4 (*Dirik*; 21, 2 *diderik*); **G** 1, 3; **äH** 19 (MS. *theotrihhe*, 23 *detrihhe*, 26 *deotrichhe*); **jH** 4, 1

---

[1] Dietrich recalls Rüedegêr's help in this matter, in the **Kl** 2116 ff.

[2] In **AHb** Ermenrîch is killed by Eckehart.

[3] In **AHb** Dietrich is said to have killed Sîfrit in the battle in the rose-garden at Worms (see Sîfrit, p. 119).

[4] His coat of arms is a golden lion on a blue ground (**B** 9792 f.); in Þs a golden lion on a red ground; in **E** and **Rg(D)** a golden lion, in **A** a golden eagle, in **Sn** and **V** a lion and an eagle (see W. Grimm, *DHS*, 156 f., 261, 462; also Wolfdietrich, p. 151 n. 5). In the Danish ballads, too, a golden lion is depicted on his shield (see below).

[5] He also wears a magic shirt, which garment is mentioned in **Rs** when he defeats Sîfrit in the fighting at Rabene (see p. 149 n. 4).

[6] In the 14th-cent. MS. of the *Lambrecht Chronicle*, Dietrich and his men are themselves regarded as giants (W. Grimm, *DHS*, 313).

[7] In the Runkelstein frescoes (late 14th cent.) he is depicted holding 'Sachs' (W. Grimm, *DHS*, 372).

[8] Dietrich's fight with Laurîn is depicted in the frescoes at Lichtenberg in Vinstgau (15th cent.) (see Laurîn, pp. 88 ff.).

[9] The dragon is killed by Hildebrant, but in a bas-relief (early 12th cent.) in Basel Cathedral Dietrich is depicted performing this deed (see Rentwîn, p. 107).

[10] Such an incubus story is found also in **O** and **Wd(A)** (see Alberîch, p. 3, and Wolfdietrich, p. 148). Dietrich's daemonic nature is stressed in **E(L)**, where Ecke maintains that a devil fights together with Dietrich (123, 9), and in Þs, where Högni accuses Þiðrekr of being the Devil himself (II. 324, 20). His fire-breathing propensities are part of his daemonism (see p. 26 n. 2). In a 15th-cent. play Dietrich appears among Herod's soldiers (K. Bartsch, 'Über ein geistliches Schauspiel des XV. Jahrhunderts', *Germania* III (1858), 279 ff.).

[11] In the *Wartburgkrieg* (14th cent.) Laurîn leads him through a mountain to another kingdom in the East, where he will live a thousand years, though people will believe him to have vanished into a volcano (see Laurîn, p. 89 and n. 4). This touches on the ecclesiastical version of Theodoric's end, which has him cast into a volcano, first recorded in the *Dialogues* of Pope Gregory the Great (†601), and followed in the mid-12th-cent. *Kaiserchronik*, 14170 ff. (see p. 31), and by Hans Sachs in his *Boecii des christlichen philosophi und poeten history* (1558) (cit. Drescher, 428).

# DIETRICH (1)

(N *Diederick*); **Kl** 366; **L(A)** 3; **L(D)** m 226 n 241; **L(DrHb)** 3, 7; **L(K)II** 10; **N** 1347, 1; **O** 597, 3; **Rg(A)** m 4, 1 n 12, 3; **Rg(C)** m 85 n 103; **Rg(D)** m 5, 3 n 17, 1; **Rg(F)** m II. 4, 1 n 11. 24, 4; **Rg(P)** 19; **Rg(V)** 50; **Rs** m 1, 6 n 3, 3; **gS** p. 89, 7; **hS** 15, 7; **hS(Sachs)** 35; **äSn** 1, 4; **jSn** 2, 4; **V(d)** m 4, 5 n 10, 8; **V(h)** m 2, 5 n 10, 1; **V(w)** 27, 1; **Wd(D)** m VIII. 142, 4; IX. 211, 4; **Wd(Gr)** m 1678, 4; 2099, 4; **Wu(B)** m 86, 4 n 91, 3 (see also Bernære)

Traditions about Dietrich von Berne are recorded from the beginning of the 11th cent.: the *Ann. Quedl.* (c. 1000), in a late interpolation, refer to 'Thideric de Bern de quo cantabant rustici olim' (*MGH ss* III. 31; W. Grimm, *DHS*, 35 f.) and Odoacer is named as the evil counsellor who urges Ermanaric to banish Theodoric from Verona (see Ôtacher p. 104, and Sibeche, pp. 117 ff.), so that he takes refuge with Attila.[1] Eckehard in his *Chronica Urspergense* (up to 1126) finds it strange for Ermanaric and Theodoric, son of Dietmar, to be contemporaries (W. Grimm, *DHS*, 41 f.). In the year 1061 the cathedral schoolmaster Meinhard complains that Bishop Günther of Bamberg concerns himself with Attila and Amalung (= Dietrich (Karl Erdman, 'Fabulae curiales', *ZfdA*, LXXIII (1936), 87–98). In the mid-12th-cent. *Kaiserchronik* (see Ohly, 218 ff.), history and oral tradition appear to be combined (13840 ff.): 'der alte Dietrich' is said to have fled from Mêrân to Lancparten to avoid becoming Etzel's vassal;[2] his son Dietmâr retakes Mêrân, and sends his own son Dietrich as a hostage to the court of Zêne (Zeno) at Constantinople; Dietrich returns to Italy with an army comprising Russians, Pomeranians, Prussians, Poles, Patzinaks, Kumans, and Wends (see Riuzen, Pomerân, Priuzen, Pôlân, Petschenære, Valwen, Windisch) to defeat Ôtacher (Odoacer), who has usurped the crown of Rome; at the siege of Raben (Ravenna) Ôtacher taunts Dietrich with being the son of a concubine, and Dietrich kills him (see also p. 31 n. 1).

Dietrich's popularity is well attested (see W. Grimm, *DHS*, 175 f., 186, 188–93, 196, 307–11, 313 f., 316, 320–4): in Eilhart's *Tristrant* (late 12th cent.), Dietrich and Hildebrant are mentioned together (see p. 75 n. 5). The Marner (1230–70) knows of Dietrich's exile, 'wie Dietrich von Berne schiet' (xv. 14, 261 ff.). In Wernher der Gartenære's *Meier Helmbrecht* (c. 1260) the narrator refers to the death of Diethêr and of Helche's sons at the hands of Witege at Rabene (76 ff.). Death in Johannes von Tepl's *Der Ackermann aus Böhmen* (c. 1400) mentions Dietrich among heroes he has dealt with (ch. xxx). Wittenwiler's *Ring* (c. 1410), in which one of the villagers sings about Dietrich (5920 ff.), ends with a battle in which Dietrich and his heroes take part (8066 ff.). References continue in the 16th cent. (W. Grimm, *DHS*, 341–4, 348 f., 350, 352, 354 f., 358; Müllenhoff, *ZE*, 344, 363 f., 370–8), even assuming a proverbial character: 'Eck an den Berner kam' ('Greek met Greek') and 'so reden sie weit herumb von Dietherich von Bern, ee sie vff den puncten kumen' ('they are slow in getting to the point') (Müllenhoff, *ZE*, 430 f.; Jänicke, *ZE*, 327); preachers, including Luther, were not above referring to Dietrich in their sermons in order to keep the attention of their congregations (see John L. Flood, 'Theologi et Gigantes', *MLR* LXII (1967), 654–60).

A bronze statue of Theodoric cast in 1513 by Peter Vischer is among the mourning figures at the tomb of the Emperor Maximilian (†1519) in Innsbruck.

The account of Dietrich in Simon Kéza's *Chronica Hungarorum* (1282–90) appears to depend on German traditions as well as on historical sources (W. Grimm, *DHS*, 182): Detricus de Verona has an arrow lodged in his head (in **AHb** Hildebrant has such a wound), and is thought to be immortal; he also possesses a helmet that shines intensely (see Hildegrîn, pp. 78 f.); on the death of Ethele (= Attila) he successfully supports Aladarius, Ethele's son by the German Crimild, against Chaba, Ethele son by a Greek princess.

In OE there are two references to Þeodrīc:[3] 'Þeodrīc ahte þritig wintra / Mǣringa burg ...' (*Deor*, 18 f.).[4] In *Waldere* it is said that Þeodrīc has considered giving a sword (Mimming?) to Widia (MHG Witege) for his aid against giants (II. 4 ff.).[5]

---

[1] The phrase 'Dietrich von Berne von dem die geburen also vil singent und sagent' is first recorded in the *Elsassische Chronik* (c. 1388), continuing in almost proverbial use into the 16th cent. (W. Grimm, *DHS*, 313, 316, 321, 324, 341, 349; Jänicke, *ZE*, 320).

[2] Apparently an invention to substantiate Theodoric's claim to Italy (see also Wolfdietrich, p. 151 n. 7).

[3] In *Widsith*, 115, 'Seafola ond Þeodrīc' have been interpreted variously: as Dietrich von Berne and Sabene von Rabene (Chambers, *Widsith*, 40 f.), and as Wolfdietrich and the evil counsellor, Sabene (Malone, *Widsith*, 191 f.; *Studies*, 117 ff.).

[4] 'Mǣringa burg' may well be connected with MHG Mêrân (Maronia in Istria) (see Malone, *Deor*, 9; Schütte, *Gotthiod* 1. 74; Höfler, *Sakralkönigtum*, 25); in the 12th cent. a Regensburg gloss gives, 'Meranare' for 'Gothi' (Müllenhoff, *ZE*, 415). The Rök Stone in Östergötland, Sweden (c. 900), bears a runic inscription, according to which Theodoric (ÞiaurikR), prince of the Mærings (skati Mǣringa), is said to have ruled over the Gothic shore (strandu Hræiþmarar), but now sits on his horse with his shield on his shoulder (text in E. V. Gordon, *An Introduction to Old Norse*[2] (Oxford, 1957), 190); this possibly recalls an equestrian statue of Theodoric, originally in Ravenna, but taken to Aachen by Charlemagne, and described by Walafried Strabo in 829 (W. Grimm, *DHS*, 44): the Þs also refers to such an equestrian statue of Þiðrekr (see below).

[5] In fact Waldere possesses the sword Mimming (see Walther, p. 136). See p. 29 n. 4 regarding Þeodrīc's trouble with giants.

References to Þjóðrekr in the ON Eddic poems (Dr prose, p. 223; Gðr III 2, 5) are rare and late (13th cent.): he is said to have lost all his men in the fight with the Gjúkungar at Atli's court; in Gðr III, Guðrún and Þjóðrekr are accused of being lovers by Atli's concubine, Herkja (see Kriemhilt, p. 20, and Helche, p. 66).

In Þs, Þiðrekr (1. 1, 8),[1] who rules Amlungaland (see Amelunc (1), pp. 5 f.), with its capital at Bern (Verona), and has been brought up by Hildibrandr, wins in youth the sword Naglringr from the dwarf Alfrikr see Alberîch, p. 4, and Nagelrinc, p. 96, the helmet Hildigrímur from the giant pair Hilldur and Grímur (see Grîme, p. 53, and Hildegrîn, p. 78), and the sword Ekkisax from the giant Ekka (see Ecke, pp. 32 f., and Eckesahs, p. 34). Various heroes join his company: Heimir, Viðga, Fasold, Þetleifr, and Sintram (see Heime, Witege, Vâsolt, Dietleip, and Sintram (1)).[2]

Þiðrekr undertakes an expedition to Bertangaland (Britain or Brittany?), where his men fight combats against the champions of the King, Isungr:[3] in the final combat Þiðrekr defeats Sigurðr with Viðga's sword Mimungr (see Mimminc, pp. 94 f.).[4]

Erminrikr forces Þiðrekr to take refuge with Attila at Susat (Soest in Westphalia), and is entertained *en route* by Roðingeirr at Bakalar (see Rüedegêr, p. 114). In Attila's service he campaigns against Osanctrix (see Ôserîch, p. 103) and Valldemarr af Holmgarðr (Russia), in the course of which campaigning he beheads Valldemarr's son, Þiðrekr (see Helche, p. 66, and Dietrich (2), p. 31), and Valldemarr himself. After twenty years' exile Þiðrekr returns to Amlungaland with an army supplied by Attila: at the battle of Gronsport (Ravenna?) Viðga, now in Erminrikr's service, kills Þiðrekr's brother Þether and the sons of Attila, but escapes Þiðrekr's wrath by riding down the Moselle (see Witege, p. 146). Roðingeirr intercedes for Þiðrekr with Attila and Erka, and they forgive him the loss of their sons (see Helche, p. 66). Þiðrekr only takes part in the fighting at Susat against the Niflungar, the brothers of Grimilldr, Attila's second wife, and their men, when Roðingeirr is killed: he beheads Folker, forces Högni to surrender through his fiery breath,[5] and finally cuts Grimilldr in two when he finds her pushing firebrands into the mouths of her wounded brothers, Gisler and Gernoz, to see if they are dead (see Kriemhilt, p. 20).[6]

After serving Attila for thirty-two years, Þiðrekr returns to Amlungaland with his wife Herrað and Hildibrandr; they are opposed by Elsungr and his men *en route*, but defeat them (see Hildebrant, p. 76). Þiðrekr finally defeats Sifka, who has usurped the kingdom on Erminrikr's death, at the battle of Ran (Ravenna), and assumes control of his kingdom, in which he erects many fine buildings.[7] After the death of Attila he also rules Húnaland.

After the death of Herrað and Hildibrandr he kills a dragon to avenge King Hertnið, marries his widow, Isollde, and defeats robbers threatening her kingdom (see Ortnît, p. 101, and Wolfdietrich, p. 150).[8] Later he slays the giant, who has killed Heimir (see Heime).

Whilst bathing he sees a golden stag (see

[1] His genealogy in Þs may be shown thus (cf. those of **DF** and **AHb** on p. 26:

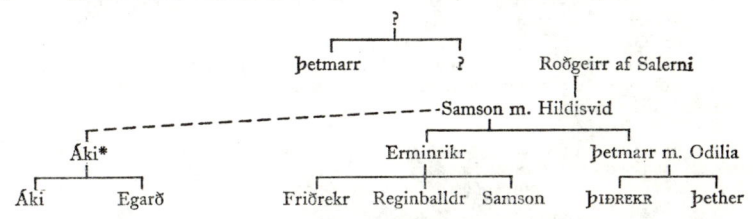

* See Hâche and Harlunge, pp. 56, 62 f.

[2] Þiðrekr saves Sintram from the jaws of a dragon (see Rentwîn, p. 107).

[3] Besides Sigurðr, these consist of Isungr and his eleven sons, who are also mentioned in the 15th-cent. ON Skr. 81.

[4] In the Danish ballads, *Kong Diderik og hans Kæmper* and *Kong Diderik í Birtingsland* (DgF I, 94–122, 124–6), Diderik leads his men to adventures in Byerting-byerig. Cf. the reference to Dietrich and his men killing two hundred giants in Britanje (Brittany?) in **V(h)** 377 (see Wîcram, p. 140).

[5] In the Faroese ballad *Høgna táttur* (CCF I. 22–31), Tíðrikur Tatlarason (137, 3) takes the form of a fire-spitting dragon when fighting Högni.

[6] In **AHb**, too, he cuts Kriemhilt in two (p. 11, 9), but in **N**, Hildebrant is her executioner (2376 f.).

[7] The sagaman mentions 'Þiðreks bað' (II. 357, 10: Bagnarea, north of Viterbo (?)), a copper statue of himself on Falka (MHG Falke) on the town wall at Rome, one at Bern (Verona), and others (see Müllenhoff, ZE, 324 f., 428 f.). In the medieval period public buildings in Italy are referred to as 'Theodorici domus' (MHG *Dietrîches hûs*), etc., including the amphitheatre at Verona (W. Grimm, DHS, 45). In the 14th cent. Heinrich von München refers to a 'wunderhûs' built by Dietmâr, Dietrich's father, at Berne (W. Grimm, DHS, 226); in the **AHb**, Machmet, the spirit which visits Dietrich's mother before his birth, is said to have built the city in three nights (p. 7, 4 f.).

[8] The Danish ballad *Kong Diderik og Löven* (DgF I. 132–40) reflects this episode confusedly (see Nagelrinc, p. 96).

Drasîan, p. 32 n. 1) and pursues it on a black horse he finds saddled near by; realizing too late that he is mounted on the Devil, he calls on God and the Virgin Mary to save him.¹

The 15th-cent. Swedish version of Þs (Sv) ends differently: Didrik, riding a black horse, seeks out and kills Wideke, but succumbs to his own wounds (see Witege, p. 146 n. 10).²

pn: this is an early type of name-composition (Schramm, 97), based on Gmc. \*þeudo- (Goth. *þiuda*, OHG *diota*, 'people') and \*rik- (Goth. *reiks*, 'ruler', cf. OHG *rîhhi*, 'powerful'): it is a frequent royal name among the Goths, Vandals, and Franks (Schönfeld, 232 ff.; Förstemann I. 1445 ff.), and became famous through two 6th-cent. bearers of it, Theodoric the Ostrogoth (†526)³ and Theodoric the Frank (†534);⁴ it is rare in OE, but less so after the Norman Conquest (Searle, 444; Binz, 200; Feilitzen, 382 f.); it is widespread and common in medieval German documents (Förstemann I. 1445 ff.; Socin, 11 f.; Schlaug I. 163; II. 85; Kromp I. 29); the byname 'Berner' or 'von Bern' is frequently added from the 14th cent. on (Socin, 566; Müllenhoff, *ZE*, 318 f., 415).

Dietrich von Berne may be identified with the Ostrogoth, Theodoric the Great (†526), son of King Theodemer by Erelieva, a Catholic. In youth he was sent as a hostage to the court of the Emperor Leo at Constantinople, where he remained from 461 to 472; he became the Emperor's 'son-in-arms' and was made consul in 478.⁵ In 475 he succeeded his father as King of the Ostrogoths, then in the Balkans, and led his people in many battles and wanderings: in the course of his Balkan campaigns Theodoric was opposed by his namesake, Theodoric Strabo, son of Triarius (see Dietrich (2), p. 31), and in 479 the East Roman general, Sabinianus (see Sabene (1), p. 114), ambushed a Gothic baggage-train and captured 5,000 men and 2,000 wagons, Theodoric's mother and younger brother, Theodemund, barely escaping (see Diethêr (1), p. 241).

In 488 Theodoric, as 'magister militum' of the Emperor Zeno, led the Ostrogoths into Italy in order to expel the usurper Odoacer (see Ôtacher, pp. 103 f.). In August 489 he defeated Odoacer on the Isonzo and again in September near Verona. Odoacer's general, Tufa, defected to Theodoric, but later handed over a large Gothic force to Odoacer at Faventia (see Witege, p. 147 ¹n. 3); because of this, Theodoric was forced to withdraw from the siege of Ravenna to Pavia, where he himself was besieged, being relieved by a Visigothic army. Theodoric's ally, Fridericus the Rugian, also acted treacherously in this campaign (see Friderîch (2), p. 47). In August 490 Odoacer was forced back on Ravenna and capitulated after three years' siege, when it was arranged that he and Theodoric should rule Italy jointly. On 15 March 493 Theodoric murdered Odoacer at a banquet in the palace at Ravenna, apparently as an act of private vengeance (Hodgkin, 212); Theodoric also had Odoacer's family and followers slaughtered. Theodoric now ruled Italy as a peaceful monarch,⁶ striving to extend his influence through marriage alliances, although his own marriage to Audefleda, sister of Clovis,⁷ failed to allay Frankish hostility. Religious difficulties troubled his reign and were aggravated by his being of the Arian faith; towards the end of his life he let Boethius and Symmachus be put to death, and was held responsible for the death of Pope John I. Theodoric died in 526, aged 72, and was buried at Ravenna in the austere mausoleum, which still stands; the church authorities removed the body of the King, held to be a heretical Arian, in the mid 6th cent.

Some thirty years after his death Justinian's generals, Belisarius and Narses, put an end to Gothic rule in Italy, the last fortress capitulating in the year 561 or 562.

---

¹ A similar story is told of a Roman king in the German text of the *Gesta Romanorum*, and a bas-relief to the right of the entrance to the basilica of St. Zeno at Verona (c. 1100) depicts a naked man with flying cloak, thought to be Theodoric, riding in pursuit of a stag: the inscription makes it clear that the horse and stag are of infernal origin (see Müllenhoff, *ZE*, 331 ff.). Otto von Freising (early 12th cent.) records that Pope John and Symmachus cast Theodoric into Etna, but also mentions German popular traditions about Theodoric's disappearance on a black horse (W. Grimm, *DHS*, 42 ff.), and Godefrid of Cologne in 1197 reports that Dietrich was seen on a black horse beside the Moselle, prophesying dire events (op. cit. 54), which suggests that Dietrich has assumed the role of 'der Wilde Jäger' (see Plötzeneder, 36 f.). In **Wu(B)** and *Die Mœrin* (15th cent.), Dietrich is said to have been carried off on an evil horse to 'die wûste rumanyag' (the Romagna, Rumania, or a desert region of Asia Minor?), where he fights dragons till doomsday (**Wu(B)** 131 ff.: see Zink, *Wunderer*, 81 f.).

² In the church at Floda in Södermanland, Sweden, a 15th-cent. fresco depicts Wideke next to Didrik, who is belching flame (W. Grimm, *DHS*, 477).

³ Theodoric the Great also used the name of his uncle, Valamer.

⁴ It should be noted that the pn *Tierri* (*Thierri*) is frequent in OFr epic (Langlois, 637 ff.).

⁵ See Ohly, 145 ff., regarding the Byzantine-Gothic story of Theodoric's youth at the Emperor's court and the loyalty of his friend Tolomeus, first recorded by Fredegar in the 7th cent.

⁶ An idealized portrait of him appears on a gold solidus stemming from Senigallia which was issued during his reign; it is remarkable in that no crown is depicted. The inscription reads: 'Rex Theodericus pius princis' (Museo delle Terme, Rome).

⁷ He had already married a wife in Moesia. Dietrich von Berne in German tradition is credited with the following wives: Herrât (**AHb, N, Kl, B, DF, Rs, Þs**), Hertlîn (**AHb**); Þs adds two: Gudelinda and Isollde. See Herrât, p. 70.

## DIETRICH (1)

Dietrich's traditional role as an exile at the court of Etzel—perhaps he once reflected the hopes of the scattered Gothic remnants—is recorded as early as the 8th cent. (**äH**), and probably derives from the period of his long sojourn as a hostage at the Byzantine court, and his struggle for power both in the Balkans and in Italy (461–93), as well as from the position of his father Theodemer as subject and ally of Attila (see Dietmâr (1), pp. 25 f.); in the 8th cent. (**äH**) Odoacer (†493) is still his enemy, but is later replaced in German tradition by Dietrich's hostile uncle Ermenrîch, i.e. Ermanaric (†375).

The legend of his daemonic nature and hellish end certainly stemmed from the hostility of the Roman Catholic Church and Theodoric's Italian subjects to this Arian ruler, the murderer of Boethius and Symmachus[1]

Dietrich's earliest companions are Hildebrant, Witege, and Heime (see also Ermenrîch, p. 39 n. 7 ); in the 12th and 13th cents. additional heroes appear among his company (see Zink, *Légendes*, 134 ff.), notably Rüedegêr, who acts as mediator between Dietrich and Etzel after the death of Etzel's sons at the battle of Rabene. Dietrich's campaigns in Etzel's service against the Slavs (**DuW**, **Þs**) reflect historical events of the 10th, 11th, and 12th cents. during the colonization of East Germany (see Ôserîch, Priuzen, Riuzen, Pôlân, and Wilzen), while the topography of his campaigns against Ermenrîch (**DF**, **Rs**) would be well known in 12th- and 13th-cent. Germany from the emperors' campaigns in Italy. Dietrich's universal fame brings him into **N** (*c*. 1200) as an ideal arbiter of the conflict.

Although his difficulties with giants are known as early as the 10th cent. (OE *Waldere*: see p. 28), the MHG epics of a fairytale nature cannot be dated earlier than *c*. 1250; in these tales, frequently set in the Tyrol (**E**, **V**, **L**, **Sn**, etc.), Dietrich becomes a conqueror of supernatural beings, such as giants, dwarfs, and dragons.

## DIETRICH (2) von Kriechen (Greece)

In **DF** and **Rs** he is Etzel's man: he aids Dietrich (1) von Berne against Ermenrîch and fights Biterunc (3) at Rabene (Ravenna). In **Rg(D)** ('der schœne' 74, 3, etc.):[2] one of Dietrich von Berne's champions; he kills Herbort in the combats at Worms.

ref: **DF** 5158; **Rg(D)** 74, 3; **Rg(P)** 123; **Rs** 53, 3

The Þiðrekr, son of Valldemarr, in Þs (II. 185, 7), who opposes Þiðrekr af Bern and is beheaded by him (see Helche, p. 66), has sometimes been identified with this figure. Less plausibly Theodoric Strabo (†481), Theodoric the Great's opponent in the Balkans (Jordanes, ch. lii), has been suggested as the historical model (see Schneider, *GHS* I. 236 ff.).

## DIETRICH (3) Rother's incognito

Rother, pretending to be outlawed by himself, assumes this name at the court of Constantin.

ref: **R** 813

In Þs, Osanctrix, in similar circumstances at the court of Milias, assumes the name 'Þiðrekr' (II. 78 ff.; Mb I has 'Friðrik', I. 53 ff.)[3] (see Ôserîch, p. 103).

## DIETRICH (4) = Wolfdietrich

In **Wd(A)** all three sons of Hugdietrich, including Wolfdietrich, are named Dietrich (cf. n 2. below).[4] In **Wd(B)** Wolfdietrich receives the name at baptism. In **Wd(D)** he uses this name when he is captured by Merzîân.

ref: **Wd(A)** 4, 2; 380, 1; **Wd(B)** 107, 4; **Wd(D)** v. 200, 4; **Wd(Gr)** 221, 4; **Wd(k)** 2, 8

It is just possible that 'der alte Dietrich' of the *Kaiserchronik* represents Wolfdietrich (see p. 28 and Dietrich von Berne's genealogy, p. 26 n. 1).

## DIETRICH (5) Wolfdietrich's first brother

See Dietrich (4).

ref: **Wd(A)** 4, 2

## DIETRICH (6) Wolfdietrich's second brother

See Dietrich (4).

ref: **Wd(A)** 4, 2

## DIETWART

The ruler of Rœmisch lant (Italy) and ancestor of Dietrich (1) von Berne (see genealogy, p. 26 n. 1): he weds Minne, daughter of Ladiner, having killed a dragon on the journey to fetch his bride from Westerner. He dies aged 400 and leaves a son, Sigehêr, as successor.

ref: **DF** 8

pn: 7th-cent. German (Förstemann I. 1451; Schlaug I. 164; II. 85). This ideal prince was probably introduced by Heinrich der Vogelære, the redactor of **DF** (de Boor, *GDL* III. i. 149).

## DIEZOLT von Tenemarke (Denmark)

Ermenrîch's man.

ref: **DF** 8634

and then maligns and persecutes her. E. Schröder, *Kaiserchronik*, 289 n. 1, connects the story with the *turris Crescentii* at Rome, also named *domus Theoderici* (see Ohly, 189 ff.).
[3] There is an official named Friderîch at Constantin's court in **R** (see Friderîch (4), p. 47.
[4] In **Wd(BD)** Wolfdietrich's brothers are named Bouge and Wahsmuot.

---

[1] In the mid-12th-cent. *Kaiserchronik*, 'Dietrich der ubel wuotgrimme' (14154) is cast by devils into 'den berch ze Vulkân' (14172) because of the deaths of Boethius, Seneca (= Symmachus), and Pope John (see Ohly, 221 ff.).
[2] In the mid-12th-cent. *Kaiserchronik* 'der scône Dieterîch' (11401) and 'der ungetâne Dieterîch' (11407) are the sons of the Emperor Narcissus; 'der scône Dieterîch' fails to seduce Crescentîâ,

DIEZOLT

pn: no record; first component *Diez-*, a variant of *Diet-*, from 11th-cent. German (Förstemann I. 1454).

DIRIK, see DIETRICH (1)

DITHMAN, see DIETHÊR (1)

DIUTSCH, see TIUTSCH

DOLOBER (LODOBER)
A dwarf: he jousts with Bîbunc during the festivities at the wedding of Dietrich and Virginâl.

ref: **V(d)** 118, 3; **V(w)** 803, 1 (*Lodober*, also *Lodaber*)

DRASÎAN
'der alte Drasîân' diverts Wolfdietrich's attention with a golden-antlered stag[1] and abducts his wife, Sigeminne; Wolfdietrich, disguised as a pilgrim, rescues Sigeminne, kills Drasîân, and burns his castle of Altenfels.[2]

ref: **Wd(B)** 390, 4; **Wd(Gr)** 619, 4; **Wd(w)** 626, 2 (*Trusian*, etc.)

In Þs the widow of Drusian af Drekanflis (I. 175, 4) is betrothed to Ekka (MHG Ecke). Þiðrekr marries one of her nine daughters.
pn: the ending *-îân* (< Latin *-ianus*: see Bach I, § 270) is frequently used in the names of heathens, giants, and dwarfs. Names with the first component *þrasa-* (cf. Goth. *þras*, 'quick', ON *þrasa*, 'threaten, quarrel') abound in WFr and Lb, the simplex *Thraso* being recorded for the Bishop of Ancona in the 5th cent. (Förstemann I. 1462; Kauf-mann, 358 f.); names such as *Druso* (*Drusio*), which occur in the 6th cent. in WFr (Förstemann I. 430), are apparently based on *þreut-*, 'cause trouble' (see Kaufmann, 99).
Somewhat bizarre origins for this character have been mooted: the Gepid Thrafstila, who was defeated by Theodoric the Great in 488 (S. Bugge, 'Die Heimat der altnordischen Lieder von den Welsungen II', *PBB* xxxv (1909), 266 ff.); the Roman general Drusus, who campaigned in Germany in 13–9 B.C. (Schütte, *Gotthiod* II. 14, 198; Bickel, 198).

DÜRINGEN(LANT)
The people and inhabitants of Thuringia: in **N**, Irnfrit is the representative hero; his men aid Etzel against the Burgundians (see also Îrinc). A 'Markîs von Düringen' appears among Ermenrîch's men in **Rs**.

ref: **B** 1237; **Kl** 442; **N** 1345, 3; **R** 4841; **Rs** 730, 5; **Wd(D)** VIII. 13, 1; **Wd(Gr)** 1549, 1
The origin of this ethnic name is uncertain: possibly *þuringoz*, 'the brave' (Schönfeld, 239). If the *Teuriohamæ* of Ptolemy (2nd cent. A.D.) represent the same people, then they are the 'inhabitants of the land of the Teurii', a Celtic tribe (Zeuß, 102, 353); it is also possible they are connected with the *Hermunduri* of Classical authors (Karsten, 93).
In the 6th cent. the Thuringian kingdom extended from Central Germany to the Danube; it was incorporated into the Frankish realm in 531 (see Irnfrit and Îrinc, pp. 85 f.).

# E

EBENRÔT (EBERROT)
Brother of Ecke and Vâsolt.

ref: **AHb** p. 3, 38 (*abentrot*); **E(d)** 2, 7; **E(L)** 2, 7; **E(s)** 2, 7 (*Eberrot*)

In Þs the name Avæntroð (I. 48, 17) is used for one of the giant sons of Nordian; his brothers are Ædgæir, Asplian, and Viðolfr.[3] He is killed by Vildiver (see Wisselau, p. 144).

pn: the variant of **E(s)** is recorded in the 8th cent. in German, *Eburrad* (Förstemann I. 444 f.).
It is possible that Ebenrôt is a corrupt form of the name Eckenôt, which is borne by another relative of Ecke (Jiriczek, *DHS* (1898), 197 f.); it has also been equated with MHG *âbentrôt*, 'sunset' (*DWb* I. 25; Kluge, *EWb*, 2).

ECKE
In **E**, Ecke, a young giant in the service of Sêburc, one of the queens on Jochgrîm, wishes to fight Dietrich von Berne; clad in the golden armour of Ortnît with which Sêburc has equipped him, he sets out on foot, since no horse can carry him. He finds Dietrich in a forest in the Tyrol, which is illuminated by Dietrich's helmet Hildegrîn.

[1] Diversion of the guardian's attention by this means occurs in the 'Spielmannsepos' *Oswald* (2335 ff.) and in a Danish ballad (*DgF* II. 68 ff.). It should be noted that Þiðrekr in Þs is lured to hell by a golden stag (see pp. 29 f.). See M. Curschmann, *Der Münchener Oswald und die deutsche spielmännische Epik* (München, 1964), 25 ff., regarding this motif.

[2] In Þs a knight named Loðvígr lives at Aldinflis (I. 201, 8), possibly identified there with Oldenfels in Westphalia.

[3] He appears with his giant brothers in the 15th-cent. ON *Skr* 76.

Dietrich, at first reluctant to fight, defeats Ecke and beheads him when he refuses to swear homage. Dietrich dons Ecke's armour and takes his sword; he rides off with Ecke's head tied to his saddle.

In **E(ds)** Dietrich casts the severed head at the feet of the queens on Jochgrîm.[1]

In **AHb** Ecke's father is named Mentiger and his aunt Runze.[2]

ref: **AHb** p. 3, 38; **E(B)** 4 (MS. *erekke*); **E(d)** 2, 6; **E(L)** 2, 6; **E(s)** 1, 9; **Rg(P)** 718; **hS(Sachs)** 830; **äSn** 1, 13; **V(h)** 745, 11; **V(w)** 675, 11

References to Ecke and his role in **E** occur in German literature from the mid 13th cent. on (W. Grimm, *DHS*, 176, 179, 185, 190 f., 352). In Wittenwiler's *Ring* (c. 1410) Herr Guggoch sings a parody of the opening lines of **E** (5929 ff.), and in the cosmic battle concluding the village conflict Dietrich cuts the giant Egge to pieces (9032 f.).

In Þs, Þiðrekr's encounter with the giant Ekka (I. 175, 7) follows **E**: here Ekka is equipped by the widow of Drusian af Drekanflis, who dies of grief at his death. Þiðrekr defeats Ekka after his horse, Falka, has broken the young giant's back (see Valke, p. 44, and Wolfdietrich, p. 149 n. 3). The sword Þiðrekr takes from Ecke is named Ekkisax (see Eckesahs, pp. 34 f.).

pn: widespread and common in German records, also occurring in Lb and OE, it frequently represents compound names with the first component Gmc. *\*agjō-*, '(sharp) blade' (Förstemann I. 15 f.; Schlaug I. 74 f.; II. 191; Ploß, 59; Searle, 217).

It is very likely that **E** has its starting-point in the name of Dietrich's sword, Eckesahs (de Boor, *GDL* III. 1, 160), and that it is a derivative of a story preserved in the 14th-cent. French *Le Chevalier du Papagau*, in which a young giant in the service of the Duchess d'Estrales sets out on foot to fight the Chevalier du Papagau: like Ecke, he is defeated, and his vanquisher dons his armour, has his wounds tended by a lady (see Bâbehilt, p. 8), and subsequently fights the giant's brother (cf. Vâsolt) (see Otto Freiberg, 'Die Quelle des Eckenliedes', *PBB* XXIX (1904), 1–79).

ECKEHART

Son of Hâche (**B**, **Wd(D)**): the protector of the Harlunge, associated with Breisach (**A**, **AHb**) and Alsace (**AHb**).[3] He possesses a horse named Rusche (**B**; Röschlîn in **A**) and a sword named Gleste (**A**).

In **A** he aids Dietrich against Ermenrîch: he kills Gêre and pursues Sibeche in the battle at Berne (Verona).

In **DF** at Bôlonje (Bologna) he kills Ribestein for inciting Ermenrîch against the Harlunge. In **Rs** at Rabene (Ravenna) he captures Sibeche, whom he binds naked across his saddle; then he declares his intention of hanging him for the death of the Harlunge.[4]

In **Rg(A)** he defeats Hagen; in **Rg(F)** he is matched against Herbort in the combats at Worms. In **B** he defeats Boppe in the combats at Worms.

In **AHb** 'der getruwe Eckart' (p. 3, 22 ff.) kills Ermentrich for hanging the Harlinger. He is thought to stand before the Venusberg till doomsday, warning those about to enter (p. 11, 25 ff.).

The 'Hardenacke mit dem barde', who accompanies Dirik on his expedition against the 'köninck van Armentriken' to Freysack in **ED**, may well represent Eckehart.[5]

ref: **A** 74, 1; **AHb** p. 3, 22 (*eckart*); **B** 4771; **DF** 4682; **ED** 17, 4 (*Hardenacke*); **Rg(A)** 100, 4; **Rg(C)** 578 (*Eckewart*); **Rg(D)** 63, 1; **Rg(F)** III. 13, 1; **Rs** 863, 4; **Wd(D)** IX. 212, 4; **Wd(Gr)** 2100, 4

German references to Eckehart begin in the 13th cent. (W. Grimm, *DHS*, 179, 190). In Wittenwiler's *Ring* (c. 1410) Egghart seeks vengeance for the death of his son (9245 ff.), and fights with the heroes against the heathen in the final battle. Hans Sachs makes 'Der trew Eckhart' the warner in his *Hoffgesindt Veneris* (1517) and the speaker of the moral epilogue in *Der Kampff mit fraw Armut und fraw Glück* (1554) (see Drescher, 405, 422). Fischart mentions him in his *Gargantua* (ed. 1594) (see W. Grimm, *DHS*, 352).

---

[1] See p. 66 regarding a similar episode in Þs, in which Þiðrekr beheads his namesake, the son of Valldemarr (II. 192 ff.).

[2] Ecke's genealogy is as follows:

```
        Velle (Helle) m. Runze (Rachin)        Mentiger (Nettinger) m. Gudengart (Birkhilt)
         |                                                    |
   Zere (Zorre)   Welderich                                   |
                                                              |
                                   ECKE   Vâsolt   Ebenrôt   Eckenôt (?)   Eckwit (?)   Uodelgart
```

[3] Goldast in the 16th cent. likewise associates him with Alsace (W. Grimm, *DHS*, 362, 489 f.).

[4] 'Der Wilde Jäger' of folklore behaves thus to his victims (see Neckel, *Deutsche Sagen* I. 22, and Harlunge, p. 63).

[5] Meier, *Balladen* I. 45, takes this to be Hertnît (I) von Riuzen, but Baesecke, *Vorgeschichte*, 458, accounts for the corruption by the probability that the name has been printed in two halves, one above the other, in the original from which the existing print derives: thus the form in **ED** represents a reversal of the components *Ecke-* and *-hart*.

## ECKEHART

In Þs the name Ækkiharð is used for a smith (see Eckerîch (1) below) and the role of Eckehart is taken by Fritila, who is the guardian of the sons of Áki Aurlungatrausti, Egarð and Áki, whom Erminrikr orders to be hanged (see Frîtele, p. 47, and Harlunge, p. 63).

pn: widespread and frequent from the 8th cent. in German records (Förstemann I. 20 ff.; Socin, 13; Schlaug I. 74; II. 88), also OE (Searle, 219; Binz, 210).

The St. Gall document of 12 December 786, with the names of *Saraleoz* and *Eghiart* as witnesses to the gift of *Heimo* and *Suanailta* (Wartmann I. 104 (no. 110); Müllenhoff, *ZE*, 302), is doubtful evidence for Eckehart's early connection with the story of Ermanaric (see Ermenrîch, p. 39). Various 'Eckartsberge' have been recorded from the 12th cent. on (W. Grimm, *DHS*, 50), but they do not necessarily indicate the existence of traditions about this figure at an early date (see Panzer, *Heldensage im Breisgau*, 9). Many topographical names incorporating this pn are recorded (Förstemann II. i, 19 f.).

The name Eckehart is not connected with the role of a warner before the 15th cent. (**AHb**), although Eckewart in **N** is a warner (c. 1200) (see Panzer, op. cit. 48 ff.; Baesecke, *Vorgeschichte*, 13).

## ECKELEIT

A sword found by Wolfdietrich in the dragon's cave; it was brought there by a giant.[1] Wolfdietrich breaks it on a stone; later he finds Ortnît's sword and kills the dragon with it.[2]

ref: **Wd(D)** VIII. 121, 4; **Wd(Gr)** 1657, 4

In Þs, Þiðrekr breaks his sword when defending a lion against a dragon. In the dragon's lair he finds Hertnið's sword and kills the dragon with it (Þs II. 361 ff.).

## ECKENÔT (1) a giant

A relative of Ecke and Vâsolt: Dietrich kills him.

ref: **AHb** p. 4, 7 (*Ecknad*); **E(d)** 306, 4; **E(L)** 210, 11; **E(s)** 220, 2

pn: *Eginot* is recorded at Fulda in the 8th cent. (Förstemann I. 23).

## ECKENÔT (2) Dietrich's man

Killed by Reinhêr von Parîse at Bôlonje (Bologna).

ref: **DF** 4155

## ECKERÎCH (1) a master smith

In **Rg(A)** he is known to have brought up Sîfrit in his smithy and to have made his byrnie. In **hS** Seyfrid takes service with a smith, who sends him into the forest, where he meets the dragon (see Sîfrit (1), p. 119).

ref: **Rg(A)** 331, 2; **gS** m p. 64, 25; **hS** m 4, 5

In ON Eddic tradition Sigurðr's fosterfather is named Reginn. In Þs it is Mimir, whose assistant is named Ækkiharð (I. 306, 4) (see Mîme, p. 94, Sîfrit (1), pp. 120 f.).

pn: 6th-cent. WFr, 8th-cent. German (Förstemann I. 24 f.; Schlaug II. 88), 7th-cent. OE (Searle, 220).

## ECKERÎCH (2) a dwarf

Hildebrant forces him to reveal where Grîn's leather ladder is hidden and then rescues Dietrich from Sigenôt's snake-pit with it.

ref: **äSn** 33, 4 (Eggerîch); **jSn** 194, 5

## (ECKESAHS)

In **E(L)** Ecke tells Dietrich that his sword was made by dwarfs and then hidden in a mountain; a thief brought it to Ruotliep, who passed it on to his son, Herbort, whence it came to Ecke (80 ff.). In **E(d)** Ecke states that it was stolen by two dwarfs who gave it to Weigant, whose son Gabein killed the giant Greim and then gave the sword to the queens of Gochereim (=Jochgrîm). Dietrich takes the sword from Ecke after he has killed him;[3] it is referred to in **B** and **Rg(P)**.[4]

ref: **B** m 9269 (daz alte sahs); 12269 (daz alte sahs); **E(d)** m 58, 4 (den Sachß), etc.; 205, 2 (her Ecken Sachs); **E(L)** m 80, 2 (ein sahs); 91, 13 (der sahs); **Rg(P)** m 691 (Sachsen), etc.

Heinrich von Veldeke in his *Eneide* (c. 1180) relates how Vulcan made Aeneas a sword sharper than Ecke sachs, Mynning, Nagelring, or Durendart (5726 ff.); the first (5728) must refer to Dietrich's sword, since the second two belong to his heroes, Witege and Heime (see pp. 94, 96).

In Þs, Ekka tells Þiðrekr that Alfrikr has fashioned Ekkisax (I. 179, 4), which was later hidden; Alfrikr has stolen it from its hiding-place and given it to Rozeleif, and finally it has come into Ekka's possession; Þiðrekr takes it after killing Ekka. The serpentine design makes this sword seem alive.[5]

---

[1] In the context the name may belong to the giant.

[2] See Schneider, *Wolfdietrich* (1913), 253, regarding the formula by which the hero finds the sword, with which the dragon can be killed, at the scene of the encounter (cf. Balmunc, p. 9).

[3] Dietrich is shown with it on the frescoes at Runkelstein (14th cent.): the inscription reads 'Ditterich von Pern treit sachs' (W. Grimm, *DHS*, 372).

[4] In **Rg(P)** it is not certain whether the sword Dietrich is using belonged originally to Ecke or to Wolfdietrich: 'mit Wolfdietriches Sachsen sluoc her im einen slac / ader mit Ecken swerte' (717 f.). In **Rg(CD)**, on the other hand, Dietrich bears Rôse, the sword that was originally given to Ortnît by Alberîch and later belonged to Wolfdietrich.

[5] This phenomenon is explained by the pattern-welding on the blade (see Davidson, 166 f.).

(ECKESAHS)

pn: the sword-name[1] in German tradition is the starting-point for a story to explain it; de Boor, *GDL* II. 1, 160: '"Das Schwert mit der scharfen Schneide" . . . wird zum "Schwert des Riesen Ecke", der zu diesem Zweck erfunden ist' (see Ecke, p. 33). The pn is recorded at Königshofen near Straßburg in 1294 (Socin, 566).

EKIVRID
The fourth of Guntharius's men killed by Waltharius. He is known to have killed a man in Saxony, and is, therefore, an outlaw (see Hadawardus, p. 56).

ref: **W** 756

pn: 8th-cent. German (Förstemann I. 20; II. i. 19), 7th-cent. OE (Searle, 219).

ECKEWART
marcgrâve: in **N** he is closely associated with Kriemhilt: on her marriage to Sîfrit he accompanies her to Santen (Xanten); later he goes with her to Hungary when she becomes Etzel's queen. On their journey to Etzel's court the Burgundians find Eckewart asleep on the border of Rüedegêr's march. Hagen takes his sword, but returns it to him with a gift of six gold rings. Eckewart then warns the Burgundians of Kriemhilt's unrelenting hostility.

In **DF** he reports to Dietrich that Witege has treacherously surrendered Rabene (Ravenna) to Ermenrîch; he is later killed by Reinhêr von Pârîse at Bôlonje (Bologna). In **Rs** he fights Gêrnôt at Rabene.

ref: **DF** 3009; **N** 9, 3 (MS. A has forms with *-hart*: 700, 4; 765, 2; MS. a likewise: 1633); **N(k)** 10, 1 (*Eckart*, otherwise *Eckwart*); **Rs** 723, 2

The **Ps** account of the meeting between Ekkivorðr (II. 290, 12: MS. A *Ekkihard*, B *Ekevard*) and the Niflungar follows that of **N**.

pn: rare; 11th-cent. German (Förstemann I. 26; Socin, 13; Schlaug I. 74; II. 88).

This figure has been thought to derive from the historical margrave of Meißen, Eckehard I († 1002), or from his son, Eckehard II († 1046) (*CMH* III. 216; see Panzer, *Nibelungenlied*, 394 f.). Gêre, with whom Eckewart is associated in **N**, is thought to have similar historical origins (see p. 49).

Heusler, *Nibelungensage*, 55, maintains that there are two distinct figures in **N**: the retainer of Kriemhilt and the warner. Panzer, op. cit. 393, accepts this, but considers that the second figure stems from local traditions connected with a 'Harlungeburch' near Pöchlarn (MHG Bechelâren), Rüedegêr's seat (see Harlunge, pp. 62–3). However, the warning motif appears in the earliest versions of the 'Destruction of the Burgundians', and in the ON Am and Völss the messenger Vingi warns the Niflungar before

ELSE (1)

they enter Atli's hall (see p. 138 and n. 1). It seems possible that the name of the traditional warner, Eckehart, may derive from that of Eckewart, of which it is a variant (see pp. 33 f. above, also W. Richter, 'Beiträge zur Deutung des Mittelteils des Nibelungenliedes', *ZfdA* LXXII (1935), 18).

ECKNAD, see ECKENÔT (1)

ECKWIT
Son of Mentiger (see genealogy of Ecke, p. 33 n. 2).

ref: **AHb** p. 4, 7

EGGERÎCH, see ECKERICH (2)

EGWALDUS, see EUGEL

EGWARD(US), see NIBELUNC (1)

EHRENBERTUS, see GUNTHER (1)

pn: 8th-cent. German (Förstemann I. 455).

EKIVRID, after ECKESAHS

ELBERÎCH, see ALBERÎCH

ELEGAST
A dwarf banished by the elf-queen Virginâl; he takes refuge with her enemy Orgeis.

ref: **V(w)** 12, 5

pn: 13th-cent. German (Socin, 566): see îljas. The name is used for the Black Knight who helps Karl in exile, in *Karel und Elegast* (14th cent.); it also belongs to a master thief in traditions about Charlemagne (Lunzer, *Elegast*, 149–95).

ELEUTHIR
Byname of Helmnod.

ref: **W** 1008

pn: possibly *Leutheri* (*Liuthere*) is intended and has been distorted under Latin influence; cf. LG *Heleutherius* recorded in 817 (cit. Kögel I. ii. 317).

ELÎANT
Îmîan's messenger to Dietleip.

ref: **V(h)** 545, 1

pn: 8th-cent. German (Förstemann I. 80); Eliân is one of Fôre's minions in *Salman und Morolf* (12th cent.). The pn *Elinant*, for which the name in **V(h)** may be an accommodation, is frequent in OFr epic (Langlois, 187 ff.; see also Flutre, 65 f.).

ELIAS, ELIGAS, see ÎLJAS

ELSÂN, see ILSÂN

ELSE m. (1) brother of Gelpfrât
He and his brother control the right bank of

---

[1] See Davidson, 40 ff., regarding the significance of the term OE *seax* (ON *sax*), which is frequently used for a sword or dagger, usually with one edge.

ELSE (1)

the Danube. Hagen kills their ferryman, and they attack the Burgundians at night; after his brother and a thousand of his men have been killed, Else withdraws. In **B** he is among Gunther's men at Worms, where he fights Biterolf, Wolfrât, and Wîchêr in the combats against Dietrich's men.

ref: **B** 903; **Kl** 3835 (B); **N** 1545, 4; **N(k)** 1578, 3 (*Ilsung*)

In Þs, Elsungr controls the Rhine crossing (II. 286, 18). He and his men attack Þiðrekr and Hildibrandr at night. He wishes to avenge the death of his father (see Else m. (2) below). He is defeated and killed.

pn: recorded for a Roman mercenary in the 4th cent. (Amm. Marc. XXVI. 8, 9); frequent in Goth. and Lb (Schönfeld, 14), and occurs in OE genealogies (Searle, 226; Binz, 206);[1] 9th-cent. German (Förstemann I. 78; Schlaug I. 78); see also under Ilsunc, p. 85.

There may be a local reference in the naming of this figure: a Bavarian document of *c.* 1140 shows the brothers *Elso* and *Gelfrat* of Cholbach as Wittelsbach vassals (Müllenhoff, *ZE*, 414).

ELSE m. (2) father of Else and Gelpfrât
ref: **B** 862

In Þs, Elsungr (1. 26, 8), the ruler of Bern (Verona), is killed by Samson, Þiðrekr's grandfather (see Else m. (1) above).

ELSE m. (3) Dietrich's man
He is with Dietrich's forces at Bâdouwe (Padua).
ref: **DF** 8313

ELSE f.
In **Wd** a monstrous woman seizes Wolfdietrich's sword while he is asleep and then seeks his love: in **Wd(A)** she is a water-spirit who sloughs her rough skin and is revealed as a beautiful maiden; Wolfdietrich promises her one of his brothers in marriage, and she gives him a strength-giving herb.[2]
In **Wd(B)** 'diu rûhe Else von alter Troyen' comes from the forest on all fours; she bewitches Wolfdietrich, so that he wanders mad in the forest; finally he agrees to marry her; she shares her kingdom, 'diu alte Troye' (Troy),[3] with him, and is baptized 'Sigeminne', being transformed into a beautiful woman; she then gives Wolfdietrich a protective shirt. Later she is abducted by Drasîan but is rescued by Wolfdietrich. **AHb** follows the account of **Wd(B)**.

ref: **AHb** p. 6, 27; **Wd(A)** m 470, 2; **Wd(B)** 309, 1; **Wd(D)** IX. 56, 3; **Wd(Gr)** 513, 1

---

[1] An Elsa is named in the OE poem *Widsith* 117) in the same line as the Langobard Eadwine.
[2] This recalls the description of Aeneas' visit to 'vrowe Sibilla' in Heinrich von Veldeke's *Eneide* (*c.* 1175), in which the hideous prophetess gives

ÊRE

pn: 9th-cent. German (Förstemann I. 78), but *Els*- is a frequent element in river-names (H. Krahe, 'Süddeutsche Flußnamen: 12. Elsawa und Elsbach', *PBB* LXX (Halle, 1948), 457 f.), *Elsbaum* being another name for *Erle*, 'alder', a tree important in folk-medicine (Kluge, *EWb*, 172; Kaufmann, 30).

In *Wigalois* by Wirnt von Grafenberg (*c.* 1202–5), a monstrous woman named Rûêl seizes the hero after he has crossed a stream, and a similar episode occurs in the late-14th-cent. *Abor mit dem Meerweib* (see O. Jänicke, *DHB* IV. xlii; Schneider, *Wolfdietrich* (1913), 30 f.).

ELVEWINE
herzoge van Rine: he has driven Amelgêr von Tengelingen from his realm; Berhter (1) von Mêrân kills him and restores Amelgêr.

ref: **R** 3419

pn: in **R** the form is Middle Franconian; the pn is common from the 8th cent. in German (Förstemann I. 73; Schlaug I. 44) and very frequent in OE (Searle, 27 f., 533; Feilitzen, 181). It is equivalent to that of Alboin, the Langobard conqueror of Italy (†572), whose name, Ælfwine, occurs in *Widsith*, 70, and whose fame was widespread among Germanic peoples (Paul. Diac. I. 27).

ENGELWÂN
burcgrâve: the son of Hiutegêr and brother of Helmnôt (3) von Tuscân; he is in the service of Ortnît.

ref: **O** 30, 1; **O(k)** 21, 6 (*Engekan*)

pn: mainly UG, 8th cent. (Förstemann I. 118). It occurs for a peasant in *Neidharts Lieder*, 54, 14, etc.

ERCKAMBALDUS
A church dignitary to whom Geraldus dedicates W.

ref: **W** (prologus) 6

pn: 8th-cent. German (Förstemann I. 458 f.). This person used to be identified with Erckambald, Bishop of Straßburg (965–93) (K. Langosch, 'Waltharius', *VfL* IV (1953), 777 ff.; V (1955), 1114 f.), but it has recently been suggested that the Dedication is by the author, Geraldus, to Erckambald, Bishop of Eichstätt (884–916) (K. Hauck, 'Das Walthariusepos des Bruders Gerald von Eichstätt', *GRM* XXXV (1954), 11: see also Geraldus, p. 49, and the Introduction, p. xvi).

ÊRE
A personification, cf. MHG *êre*, 'honour'.
ref: **DF** 564; **Kl** 3452; **V(w)** 362, 9

the hero a herb to protect him against the stench of hell (2848 ff.).
[3] This is to distinguish it from Troja in Italy (see Jänicke, *DHB* III. lxx n. 2). The connection with Troy may derive from Heinrich von Veldeke's *Eneide* (see n. 2 above).

EREWÎN (1) son of Berhter (1) von Mêrân
He and his brothers lead Rother's embassy to Greece for the hand of King Constantin's daughter; he is imprisoned, but Rother obtains his release, and finally rewards him for his loyalty with Spain in lien.

ref: **R** 154

pn: 8th-cent. German (Förstemann I. 457; Schlaug I. 82); in OE the name occurs for a monier under Æthelred II (Searle, 234).

EREWÎN (2) Dietwart's man
He leads Dietwart's embassy to Ladiner von Westenmer for the hand of his daughter, Minne.

ref: **DF** 371

EREWÎN (3) von Elsentroye[1]
Etzel's man: he aids Dietrich against Ermenrîch.

ref: **DF** 3156; **Rs** 56, 1

See Näntwîn (3), p. 96.

EREWÎN (4) Îrinc's brother
Etzel's man in **Rs** (= Erewîn (3)?).

ref: **RS** 543, 1

EREWÎN (5) von Westvâlenlant (Westphalia)
Ermenrîch's man: his device is an ostrich on a black and white ground.

ref: **Rs** 491, 5 (R *Ellewin*, W *Ennewein*, AP *Enenum*)

## ERMENRÎCH

Son of Amelunc (3) and uncle of Dietrich (1) von Berne:[2] in **DF** he rules Gâlaber, Wernhêres marke, and Püllen (Calabria, Ancona, and Apulia); he is known to have treacherously sent his son Friderîch to Wilzenlant and to have had his nephews, the Harlunge, killed (2458 ff.; 2543 ff.). On the advice of Sibeche[3] and Ribestein he now plots against the life of his nephew, Dietrich von Berne[4]— God later punishes him for his misdeeds with a miserable end (2558):[5] he invades Dietrich's realm, but is defeated at Rabene (Ravenna) and flees, leaving his son Friderîch a prisoner. His leaders, Witege and Heime, capture a large number of Dietrich's men at Bôle (Pola); Ermenrîch, impervious to the fate of his son, forces Dietrich to withdraw from Italy by threatening to hang the prisoners.[6] Dietrich takes refuge in Hiunenlant (Hungary), but he returns with an army supplied by Etzel and defeats Ermenrîch at Meilân (Milan); Ermenrîch is again defeated at Bôlonje (Bologna), where Eckehart beheads his evil counsellor, Ribestein.[7]

In **A**, Ermenrîch besieges Dietrich at Berne (Verona), but flees, leaving a vast treasure in Dietrich's hands. In **Rs**, Ermenrîch flees before Dietrich's army in a great battle at Rabene (Ravenna). In **B**, Ermenrîch's men fight alongside those of Dietrich in support of Dietleip against Gunther at Worms.

In **ED**, Dirik van dem Bërne (= Dietrich von Berne) and his men set out against the köninck van Armentriken (= Ermenrîch): they pass a gallows before entering his castle at Freysack (= Breisach?);[8] he threatens to hang them, but Dirik beheads him.

ref: **A** 3, 1 (MS. *ementrich*, etc.; 330, 3 on *ermentrich*); **AHb** p. 3, 24 (*Ermentrich*, p. 3, 26 *Ementrich*, etc.); **B** 4589 (MS. *Erenreiche*); **DF** 2411 (A *Erenr(e)ich*, *Erentrich*, etc., R *Ermrich*); **ED** 2, 3 (*De Koeninck van Armentriken*); **Rg(D)** 623, 2; **Rs** 2, 1 (A *Eren(n)r(e)ich*, etc., R *Ermrich*); **V(h)** 654, 7; **Wu(B)** m 100, 2

The earliest reference to popular traditions about Ermanaric occurs in Flodoard's *Historia Remensis Ecclesiae* (c. 950), where Hermenricus is thought to have had his progeny put to death because of evil counsel (*MGH ss* XIII. 564; W. Grimm, *DHS*, 34).[9] In the *Ann. Quedl.* (c. 1000) Ermanricus, a cunning yet generous contemporary of Attila, is said to have caused the death of his son Fridericus and to have hanged his nephews Embrica and Fritla (see Harlunge, pp. 62 f.); Odoacer is the name of the evil counsellor who urges him to drive out Theodoricus from Verona into exile with Attila; Ermanricus dies when Hernidus (= Hemidus), Serila, and Adaocarus[10] cut off his hands and feet to avenge the death of their father (*MGH ss* III. 31; W. Grimm, *DHS*, 35 f.).[11] Eckehard's *Chronicon Urspergense*, which reaches A.D. 1126 (*MGH ss* VI. 130; W. Grimm, *DHS*, 41 f.), tells how Hermenricus is attacked by the brothers Sarus and Ammius ('vulgariter Sarelo et Hamidiecus'), but finds it strange for Theodoric to be contemporary with Ermanaric. In the *Genealogia*

---

[1] This seat very probably derives from **Wd**, i.e. Troy, which in that epic is the realm of 'diu rûhe Else' (see Else f., p. 36).

[2] In **AHb** only is he Dietrich's brother (see the genealogy, p. 26 n. 1).

[3] According to **AHb** and Þs, Sibeche (Sifka) gives him evil counsel because he has seduced Sibeche's wife (see Sibeche, p. 117).

[4] Heinrich von München in the early 14th cent. tells how 'Erntrîch' sent his son Friderîch 'in ein wildez lant', hanged the Harlunge, and drove his nephew Dietrich into exile with Etzel (W. Grimm, *DHS*, 225 f.).

[5] In the ON Hm he is maimed, in Þs diseased (see below).

[6] A frequent motif in OFr epic (Zink, *Légendes*, 112 f.).

[7] In **AHb** Eckehart slays Ermenrîch for hanging the Harlunge; this is repeated by Agricola in the 16th cent. (W. Grimm, *DHS*, 326 f.).

[8] See p. 62 n. 5.

[9] In the 10th-cent. *Miracula s. Bavonis*, Hermanricus is thought to have built a castle at Ghent (W. Grimm, *DHS*, 33).

[10] Possibly a corrupt form of Odoacer (see Ôtacher, pp. 103 f.).

[11] The *Chronicon Wurzburgense* (early 11th cent.) follows this (*MGH ss* VI. 23).

*Viperti* (12th cent.) Emelricus heads the family tree (see Harlunge, p. 62).

In the 13th cent. references in German literature outside the heroic epics are few: Wolfram von Eschenbach knows 'Ermrîch' as the patron of the coward Sibeche (*Parzival*, 421, 23–8) and as a great warrior (*Willehalm*, 384, 21). Der Wilde Alexander (*KLD* II. 24, 11–12; W. Grimm, *DHS*, 190) refers to Eckehart's hostility to him, Der Tanhûser (W. Grimm, *DHS*, 174 f.) to his generosity, and Ottokar von Horneck (*c.* 1295) to his hostility to Dietrich (W. Grimm, *DHS*, 189); his vast treasure is mentioned in the 15th-cent. *Reinke de Vos* (W. Grimm, *DHS*, 318).

In the OE poem *Widsith* the narrator travels to Eormanrīc's realm with Ealhhild (5), Eormanrīc's wife. Eormanrīc (8, 18, 88, 111) gives him a valuable ring (88–92), and he then lists the retinue (OE *innweorud*) of Eormanrīc (111–24), which includes Hēhca, the Herelingas, Emerca, Fridla, Seafola, Sifeca, Rūmstān, Freoþerīc, Wudga, and Hāma (see Hâche, Harlunge, Imbrecke, Frītele, Sabene (1), Sibeche, Rimstein, Friderîch (1), Witege, and Heime). In *Beowulf* the last-named, Hāma, is known to have taken the necklace of the Brōsingas (see Heime, p. 65) and incurred the hostility of Eormanrīc (1198–1201).[1] In *Deor* a strophe about Þeodrīc's thirty winters at Mǣringa burg (see p. 28 n. 4) is followed by one describing Eormanrīc's harsh rule (21–6).

In ON Eddic tradition, Hamðir and Sörli, the sons of Guðrún by Jónakr (see Kriemhilt, p. 20), cut off the hands and feet of Jörmunrekr (Rdr 8, 1; Hm 3, 3; Sg 64, 3; Ghv 2, 5; Hdl 25, 6; Sk ch. 50; Völss ch. 40) to avenge the death of their sister (Foglhildr in Rdr, Svanhildr in Hm, Sk, and Völss), whom her husband, Jörmunrekr, has had trampled to death by horses; they reject the help of their half-brother Erpr, who might have beheaded Jörmunrekr before he calls for them to be stoned to death (see Erpfe, p. 40): in Hm it is Guðrún who urges her sons to avenge Svanhildr, whom Jörmunrekr has had trampled to death for adultery with her stepson Randvér—the evil counsellor Bikki has urged Randvér to make love to her, and then informed Jörmunrekr, who also hangs his own son;[2] Svanhildr's brothers see Randvér's body on the gallows outside Jörmunrekr's hall. They enter and cut off Jörmunrekr's hands and feet; Jörmunrekr calls for them to be stoned because they are proof against metal (in Sk ch. 50 Guðrún gives her sons byrnies and helmets proof against iron).[3]

Saxo VIII. ix. 4–xi. 14 gives a long and confused account of the youthful exploits of the Danish King Iarmericus, a mighty conqueror, who kills Slav prisoners by hanging[4] and by tying them to wild bulls; he also builds a heavily guarded treasure-house. Bicco, whose brothers Iarmericus has killed, urges Iarmericus to hang his rebellious nephews, and accuses Iarmericus's son Broderus of adultery with his stepmother Swanilda: Iarmericus has Swanilda trampled to death, but only pretends to hang his son, who later succeeds him. Bicco informs Swanilda's kin, the Hellespontines, who besiege Iarmericus; a sorceress named Guthruna (VIII. x. 14) blinds Iarmericus's men, but Óðinn restores their sight and urges them to stone the Hellespontines, who are all slain; Iarmericus loses his hands and feet in the conflict.

In Þs, Erminrikr (I. 22, 23), son of Samson, rules at Bern. Sifka, because Erminrikr has seduced his wife Odilia, swears to destroy the race of the Aumlungar to which Erminrikr belongs (see Amelunc (1), pp. 5 f.): he contrives the deaths of his three sons, Friðrekr, Reginballdr, and Samson: the first dies in Villcinaland, the second is drowned on the way to England, and the third Erminrikr rides down after Sifka has accused him of ravishing his daughter. Sifka then incites Erminrikr against his nephews Egarð and Áki, whom Erminrikr hangs (see Harlunge), and against his nephew Þiðrekr; but Þiðrekr, warned by Viðga (MHG Witege), takes refuge with Attila; Viðga and Heimir, angered by Erminrikr's treatment of Þiðrekr, leave his court and plunder his realm. Þiðrekr with an army supplied by Attila defeats Erminrikr at Gronsport, Erminrikr dies after a long illness, and Sifka usurps the throne. Þiðrekr finally defeats Sifka at Ran (MHG Rabene = Ravenna) and assumes the throne at Bern.

pn: first recorded for the Ostrogothic King Ermanaric (†*c.* 375) (Schönfeld, 76 f.; Förstemann I. 482): *Erminrichus* (Amm. Marc. 4th cent.); *Hermanaricus* (Jordanes 6th cent.); it occurs for an early king of Kent, *Irminricus* (†560) (Binz, 209; Björkman, 21); otherwise it is rare: it occurs in German records from the 9th to the 13th cent.

---

[1] 'searonīðas fleah / Eormenrīces' (1200 f.), cf. 'flôh her Ôtachres nîd' (äH 18), which refers to Hildebrant fleeing with Dietrich from the wrath of Ôtacher, whom Ermenrîch later replaces as the enemy of Dietrich (see pp. 31, 37, 39 f.).

[2] In Sk ch. 50 and Völss ch. 40, Randvér, before being hanged, sends his father his plucked falcon as a symbol of his father's loss of power through his death.

[3] Von See, *GHS*, points out that the Völss links their vulnerability to stones with the murder of their brother, whose blood has desecrated the stones': an obvious connection may be seen with Cain's murder of Abel (*Genesis* IV, 10 ff. A detailed study of the Eddic material and Ermanaric's story in general may be found in *The Poetic Edda*, edited with translation, Introduction, and Commentary by Ursula Dronke, vol. i: *Heroic Poems* (Oxford, 1969), 142–242.

[4] He has a wolf tied to each victim; cf. his wolfish nature in OE tradition: 'wylfenne gehôht' (*Deor*, 22).

(Mone, 77 f.; Förstemann I. 482, also 473 under *Ermaricus*; Socin, 567). The first component is based on Gmc. *\*ermena-*, 'universal', cf. OHG *irmingot*, 'supreme god', and OE *eormengrund*, 'the earth' (see Zeuß, 45; Much, *Germania*, 25).

The development of traditions about the historical Ermanaric can be followed in some detail:[1] Ammianus Marcellinus, a contemporary, tells of his suicide in A.D. 375, when the Huns, having subjugated the Alans, crossed the Don and overwhelmed his Ostrogothic kingdom (Amm. Marc. XXXI. 3, 1–2). Jordanes, nearly two centuries later (*c.* 550), records that Hermanaricus, 'nobilissimus Amalorum', succeeded Gebericus as King of the Goths, and subjugated the Heruli, the Venethi, and the Aesti;[2] when the Huns overran the neighbouring Alans, the Rosomoni defected to the Huns, and Hermanaricus ordered Sunilda, a woman of their tribe, to be torn apart by wild horses because of the treason of her husband; her brothers, Sarus and Ammius, plunged a sword into his side;[3] Hermanaricus, unable to endure this wound and the inroads of the Huns, died at the age of 110 (Jordanes chs. XXIII (116)–XXIV (130)).[4]

Jordanes's story is reflected in the ON versions (Hm, Sk ch. 50), but in them the woman trampled to death is the young wife of Jörmunrekr in love with her stepson; the two lovers are put to death for adultery, to which the evil counsellor Bikki has incited them. By the 9th cent. Jörmunrekr's wife is made Guðrún's daughter (Rdr), thus linking Jörmunrekr's story with that of Sigurðr. It is possible that this story of Sunilda, Ammius, and Sarus was originally known in Germany, but was later displaced by other material to do with the Harlunge and Dietrich's exile: a deed of gift by *Heimo* and his daughter, *Suanailta*, was witnessed by *Saraleoz* and *Eghiart* at St. Gall in 786 (Wartmann I. 104);[5] the pn *\*Suanahilt* in its various forms is fairly frequent in South-West Germany, and also occurs elsewhere until the 11th cent. (Socin, 572; Schlaug I. 154; II. 150 f.), but her brothers' names are rarely recorded (Socin, 572; Bruckner, 302; Kögel I. ii. 217 ff.; Schlaug I. 149). In England the *Swanhild* recorded in the 13th cent. may well be of Norse origin (Binz, 209), and evidence for the brothers' names is doubtful (Feilitzen, 357 f.).

In German and English (?) traditions Ermanaric (MHG Ermenrîch, OE Eormanrīc) is famous for his violent character and great wealth; he sends his son (MHG Friderîch, OE Freoþerīc) to his death, hangs his nephews (MHG Harlunge, OE Herelingas, named MHG Frîtele and Imbrecke, OE Fridla and Emerca), and seizes their treasure and land, later localized at Breisach. In German tradition as early as the 10th cent., as in ON, he is incited against his relations by an evil counsellor;[6] in German tradition also, and possibly in English—the *Deor* passage is debatable—Ermanaric drives Theodoric (MHG Dietrich, OE Þēodrīc), who in heroic tradition becomes his nephew, into exile. Hostility to Theodoric could have two causes: Ermanaric's reputed hostility to his own kin—they are both Amals (see Amelunc (1), pp. 5 f.)—and his historical hostility to the Huns, with whom Theodoric's father, Theodemer (see Dietmâr (1), pp. 25 f.), in historical fact, and Theodoric (MHG Dietrich) in heroic tradition, take service.[7]

ERMENTRÎCH, ERMRÎCH, see ERMENRÎCH above

ERNST
burcgrâve ze Grimiure, father of Triutlint: he entertains Wolfdietrich after the latter's encounter with the robbers.

ref: **Wd(D)** v. 28, 2; **Wd(Gr)** 866, 2

pn: 8th-cent. German (Förstemann I. 484 f.). The name here probably derives from that of the hero of the 'Spielmannsepos', *Herzog Ernst* (*c.* 1180).[8]

ERNTHELLE
In **AHb** 'künig Ernthelle von Trier' is thought to be the earliest hero: a brief

---

[1] Caroline Brady, *The Legends of Ermanaric* (Berkeley and Los Angeles, Calif., 1943), surveys the material exhaustively.
[2] The Ostrogothic realm extended from the Black Sea to the Baltic *c.* 350 (see Franz Altheim, *Goten und Finnen im dritten und vierten Jahrhundert* (Berlin, 1944), 17 ff.).
[3] The first component of Sunilda's name is based on Gmc. *\*swon-* (OHG *suona*, 'atonement, judgement'), and was possibly associated with *svanr*, 'swan', by popular etymology in ON, which is suggested by Foglhildr of Rdr and perhaps by Ealhhild of *Widsith* (see Chambers, *Widsith*, 21 ff., and Malone, *Widsith*, 136). Her brothers' names are also meaningful, being based on Gmc. *\*hama* and *\*sarwa*, both of which signify 'armour'.
[4] In Þs, Milias, the aged King of Húnaland, dies in despair when Attila invades his kingdom (I. 49; II. 85).
[5] See p. 56 n. 6.

[6] Bikki (ON) and Sibeche (MHG) both contrive the destruction of Ermanaric's sons. Such a figure was not required in the original Gothic story as told by Jordanes. Odoacer (see Ôtacher, p. 104) temporarily becomes Ermanaric's evil counsellor when the cycles of Theodoric and Ermanaric are linked, some time between 700 and 1000, and Ermanaric replaces Odoacer as the main enemy of Theodoric (see Dietrich(1), p. 31). It is conceivable that Odoacer's wife's name, Sunigilda, influenced the linking of the two cycles (Chambers, *Widsith*, 40).
[7] Witege and Heime (OE Wudga and Hāma) are early associated with Ermenrîch: their ambiguous position between him and Dietrich in *MHG* epic exemplifies the contradictions in Dietrich's hostile relationship with Ermenrîch, a fellow Amelunc, and in his dependence on Etzel, a Hun.
[8] hrsg. von Karl Bartsch (Wien, 1869).

account of his adventures is given (see below).

ref: **AHb** p. 1, 5

In the 'Spielmannsepos' *Orendel* (12th cent.?) the hero, Orendel, experiences adventures in the Orient, wins the warrior-maiden Brîde (see Brigida), and acquires the 'grauer rock', a relic thought to be Christ's seamless robe (see Wolfdietrich, p. 149 n. 4).

pn: 8th-cent. German (Förstemann I. 211; Mone, 74); possibly related to OE *ēarendel*, 'morning star, beam of light', a term used for Christ in Cynewulf's *Elene* (cf. IE *ausos*, 'dawn': Kluge, *EWb*, 525), and to ON Aurvandill (Sk ch. 25), the name of a hero, whose frozen toe is placed in the sky by Þórr and named 'Aurvandilstá' (Berger, *Orendel*, lxxvii ff.).

## ERPFE (SCHARPFE)
Son of Etzel and Helche: in **Rs** he (Scharpfe) and his brother Orte are killed by Witege at Rabene (Ravenna).

ref: **B** 3334 (MS. *Erpse*); **Rs** 158, 2 (Scharpfe)

In ON Eddic tradition Erpr is the name of (1) Atli's son by Guðrún (Akv 37, 3; Hm 8, 2; Dr prose, p. 223), killed together with his brother Eitill by her (see Kriemhilt, p. 20), and (2) the son of Jónakr and half-brother of Guðrún's sons, Hamðir and Sörli (Rdr 8, 4; Hm 14, 1; Sk ch. 50; Völss ch. 39):[1] in Hm they scornfully reject his offer of aid against Jörmunrekr and kill him, terming him a 'little brown fellow' and 'bastard' (ON 'jarps-kammr' 12, 3, 'hornungr' 14, 8),[2] for they misunderstand his enigmatic description of how he can help: 'sem fótr öðrom' (like one foot the other) (13, 4); they realize too late that his help could have saved them (28) (see Ermenrîch, p. 38.).

In Þs, Erpr (II. 105, 5) and his brother Ortvin, the sons of Attila and Erka, are killed by Viðga in Þiðrekr's battle against Erminrikr at Gronsport (Ravenna ?).

pn: 1st-cent. Chattic leader, *Arpus* (Schönfeld, 30);[3] 8th-cent. German (Förstemann I. 485 f.; Mone, 83; Schlaug I. 80; II. 194; Kaufmann, 109); it is used in the 13th cent. for a peasant in *Neidharts Lieder*, 94, 7.

The name is based on Gmc. *erp(p)a-* (OHG *erph*, ON *iarpr*, 'dark brown'), but in the context of the 'Heldensage' it may well represent an accommodation for a Hunnish pn such as *Arpad*, a name borne by a Hungarian prince (†907), whose son was named after a son of Attila, Ellac (Moravcsik II. 74 f., 125).

ERWÎN, see EREWÎN

ESPRIAEN, see ASPRÎÂN

ETENE, see HETEL(E)

ETZEL(E)[4]

In **äH**, Hiltibrant has received an arm-ring from 'der chuning . . . / Hûneo truhtîn' (34 f.) (= Etzel?).

In **W**, Attila, ruler of the Huns, by threatening war, obtains hostages from three kings: Gibicho, King of Francia, sends his vassal Hagano; Heriricus, King of Burgundia, his daughter Hiltgunt; Alphere, King of Aquitania, his son Waltharius. All three hostages escape (see Hagen (1), Hildegunt (1), and Walther).

In **N**, Etzel, son of Botelunc (1314, 2, etc.), ruler of Hiunenlant (see Hiunen), after the death of his first wife Helche, marries Kriemhilt, the widow of Sîfrit, who is at first reluctant because he is a heathen: Rüedegêr, Etzel's emissary, persuades her to accept him by suggesting that she might convert him (1262 f.).[5] Etzel's power is demonstrated by the exotic peoples welcoming her at Tulne (Tulln in Austria): Riuzen, Kriechen, Pœlân, Walâchen, men of Kiev, Petschenære (1338 ff.), but his leaders, apart from his brother Blœdel, bear Germanic names: Râmunc, Gibeche, Hornboge, Hâwart, Îrinc, Irnfrit. Kriemhilt, wishing to be avenged on Hagen for the death of Sîfrit, persuades the unwitting Etzel to invite her brothers Gunther, Gêrnôt, and Gîselhêr, the Burgundian kings, to Etzelnburc (see Wärbel, p. 137); she then incites Etzel's brother Blœdel to attack their men: her son by Etzel, Ortliep, is killed by Hagen at the start of the conflict, in which Blœdel, most of Etzel's men, and all the Burgundians are killed. Kriemhilt is executed by Hildebrant after she has slain Hagen, and Etzel is left with Dietrich lamenting the loss of his men. In the Kl he curses his gods, Machmet and Machazên, and regrets his apostasy; the author does not know his end (4703 ff.).

In **DF** and **Rs**, Etzel supplies Dietrich with men for his campaigns against Ermenrîch in Italy; in **Rs** his sons, Scharpfe and Orte (in **B** Erpfe and Orte), join Dietrich's army and are killed by Witege at Rabene; through the intercession of Rüedegêr, Etzel

---

[1] In Ghv prose, p. 263, Hamðir, Sörli, and Erpr are said to be the sons of Jónakr and Guðrún.
[2] See Hœrninck, p. 82.
[3] Cf. also the 6th-cent. Goth. *Erpamara* (Jordanes ch. v), which probably represents two names, *Erp* and *Amara*.
[4] See Helmuth de Boor, *Das Attilabild in Geschichte, Legende und heroischer Dichtung* (Bern, 1932), for a detailed discussion of this character.

[5] According to the **Kl** and **N(C)** he has been converted, but has later relapsed into heathendom (Kl 1086; N(C) 1261, 5–8). The renegation of Attila is referred to in Heinrich von Veldeke's *Servatius* (c. 1170), in which St. Servatius converts Etzel, who later reverts to heathendom (1987 ff.). See also p. 41 below.

ETZEL(E)                                                              ETZEL(E)

and Helche forgive Dietrich their loss (**Rs** 1114 ff.).

In **B** the magnificence of Etzel's court attracts Biterolf and his son Dietleip to serve him. He personally leads an army against the Prussians to rescue Biterolf and Rüedegêr from captivity, and later supplies Dietleip with an army to exact vengeance on Gunther.

In **Rg(D)** he sets out with Dietrich to the rose-garden at Worms, but takes no part in the combats against the men of Gibeche, who finally becomes his vassal (see p. 51).

In **Wu(B)** Frau Sælde takes refuge at his court from a cannibal monster which Dietrich kills (see Wunderer, pp. 153 f.).

ref: **AHb** p. 1, 22; **B** 285; **DF** 4999; **DuW** 69; **äH** m 34 f.; **Kl** m 75 n 83 (C), 92 (B); **N** 5, 4; 1143, 2; **Rg(C)** 677; **Rg(D)** 14, 1; **Rg(P)** 13; **Rs** 17, 1; **W** 11 (Attila: H *attala*, E *etcilo*); **WuH** I (Wien), 12, 2; **Wu(B)** 1, 3; **Wu(k)** m p. 1, 6 n p. 2, 9

Certain German chronicles attempt to reconcile the actions of the historical Attila with those of Etzel of the 'Heldensage': in the *Ann. Quedl.* (c. 1000) Attila is known to have devastated Gaul, but also to have restored Theodoric to his kingdom in Italy (*MGH ss* III. 31; W. Grimm, *DHS*, 35 f.);[1] Eckehard in his *Chronicon Urspergense* (up to 1126) notes the contradiction between Jordanes's history and the 'Heldensage', in that the latter makes Attila and Ermanaric contemporary (*MGH ss* VI. 130; W. Grimm, *DHS*, 41); in the mid-12th-cent. *Kaiserchronik* (13840 ff.) it is related how Etzel seizes Mêrân from 'der alte Dietrich', whose son Dietmâr retakes it and defeats Etzel's sons, Plôdel and Frîtele, after Etzel's death of a haemorrhage (see Dietrich, p. 28); in Heinrich von München's *Weltchronik* (early 14th cent.), Attila is the patron of Dietrich, marries Chreimhilt (= Kriemhilt) after the death of Helche, and (in a variant MS.) is said to have conquered France and Germany (W. Grimm, *DHS*, 226 f.); in a late-14th-cent. MS. from the Tyrol he is said to have acquired a chariot when he conquered Spain and Scotland (W. Grimm, *DHS*, 317); the Saxon Chronicle (15th cent.) tells how Attila was turned back from Italy by the Pope; his nose bled and he then plunged into the Danube and disappeared (W. Grimm, *DHS*, 320). Others localize his activities: in the *Swabian Chronicle* of Crusius (c. 1550) the peasants are said to connect Attila with ruins, and he is thought to have devastated Württemberg on his return from the battle of Châlons (W. Grimm, *DHS*, 356); in the *Thuringian Chronicle* (16th cent.) he is said to have visited Eisenach to marry Grymhilda, Gunther's daughter (W. Grimm, *DHS*, 344).

German literary references to Etzel outside the heroic epics are rare: Heinrich von Veldeke in *Servatius* (c. 1170) deals with Etzel's depredations into western Europe (1066 ff., 3261 ff.), and refers to him as 'Bodelinghes son' (3369) (see also p. 40 n. 5); Wolfram von Eschenbach in *Willehalm*, 384, 20, refers to him as a great warrior; Seifrid Helbling (late 13th cent.) knows of him from N (W. Grimm, *DHS*, 185); Frauenlob lists him among departed worthies (ibid. 196); in the MDu *Karlmeinet* (c. 1300), Karl finds a great treasure buried by a 'konynck Etzelin' (ibid. 191).

In Simon Kéza's *Chronica Hungarorum* (1282–90), material from German tradition is blended with historical matter (ibid. 181 ff.; see also Bleyer, 429 ff.): Ethele, a Hungarian leader, murders his brother Buda (see Blœdel, p. 13) for naming the town of Buda after himself (see also Dietrich (1), p. 28, Helche, p. 67, and Hiunen, p. 80 n. 1).

In OE the ruler of the Huns is mentioned in *Widsith*: 'Ætla wēold Hūnum' (18); and the Huns are termed 'Ætlan lēode' (122). In *Waldere* Waldere is 'Ætlan ordwyga' (l. 6) (see Walther, p. 136).

In ON Eddic tradition Atli (Akv 1, 1; Am 2, 3; Gðr 1 25, 3; Gðr II 26, 8; Gðr III 1, 1; Dr prose: p. 233; Od 2, 2; Ghv 11, 6; Br 5, 5; Sg 32, 4; Sk ch. 50; Völss ch. 25)[2] is the son of Buðli and brother of Brynhildr (see Botelunc, p. 14):[3] in Akv, Atli invites Gunnarr and his brother Högni to visit him;[4] he has them seized on arrival, but they refuse to divulge the hiding-place of the Niflungar treasure (see Nibelunge, p. 98);[5] after Atli has had Högni's heart cut out, Gunnarr knows that their secret is safe. Atli then has Gunnarr thrown into a snake-pit (see Gunther (1), p. 55, and Hagen (1), p. 59). Guðrún, the wife of Atli and sister of Gunnarr (see Kriemhilt, p. 20), kills her sons Erpr and Eitill,[6] and serves their hearts for Atli to eat;[7] she then kills Atli with a sword

---

[1] Etzel's connection with Dietrich is also attested by the letter of the schoolmaster Meinhard regarding Bishop Günther of Bamberg in 1061, deploring the latter's interest in Attila and Amalung (= Dietrich) (see p. 28).

[2] 'Artala kongur í Húnalandi' is referred to in the Faroese ballads *Brynhildur táttur* and *Høgna táttur* (*CCF* I. 8–22, 22–31); in the Danish ballads he is not mentioned by name, but Her Loumer in *Frændehævn* takes his role in a story similar to that of Akv (*DgF* I. 26–32: see also Kriemhilt, p. 20).

[3] In Dr, Guðrún is given to Atli as a wife in compensation for the loss of his sister Brynhildr (see Brünhilt).

[4] In Am 14 ff. and Völss ch. 34, before the visit of Gunnarr and Högni, Högni's wife dreams of Atli in the form of a fire, an eagle, and a bear.

[5] In Völss ch. 36, Atli demands the treasure from them as the property of Guðrún, Sigurðr's widow.

[6] The name Eitill (Akv 37, 3) for Atli's son occurs elsewhere: Dr prose, p. 223; Hm 8, 3. For Erpr see under Erpfe.

[7] In Völss ch. 33, after his marriage to Guðrún, Atli dreams that she thrusts him through with a sword and that he eats two saplings, two of his hawks, and two of his dogs.

and sets fire to the hall over the drunken Huns.[1]

In Þs, Attila (1. 56, 8), son of the Frisian King, Osið, conquers the kingdom of Húnaland from Milias, who dies of despair (see pp. 18, 39 n. 4),[2] and sets up his capital at Susat (Soest in Westphalia). He has Erka, the daughter of Osantrix of Villcinaland, abducted and makes her his queen (see Helche, p. 66): from then on he is at war with Osantrix and his successors; Þiðrekr, an exile at his court, conducts many of these campaigns against the Slavs (see Dietrich (1), p. 29, Ôserîch, p. 103, Riuzen, p. 108, and Wilzen, p. 144). Attila supports Þiðrekr in his efforts to win back Amlungaland from the usurper Erminrikr; his sons are killed in the campaign, but Roðingeirr reconciles him with Þiðrekr after their loss (see Rüedegêr, p. 111). After Erka's death he weds Grimilldr, who persuades him to invite her brother Gunnarr and his men to Susat, but he refuses to have them attacked, and Grimilldr bribes Irungr to start the conflict (see Kriemhilt, p. 20). Högni's son Aldrian later locks Attila in a cave where the Niflungar treasure and that of Sigurðr are stored, and he starves to death. Þiðrekr rules Húnaland subsequently.

pn: two forms: (1) showing *i*-mutation of *a* (Gmc. \**Attila*, cf. *Attila* of Jordanes):[3] OHG *Ezzilo*, first recorded in 782 (Förstemann I. 153 f.; Socin, 316; *Etzele* is used for a peasant in the mid 13th cent. in *Neidharts Lieder*, 35, 23; 80, 39); 8th-cent. OE *Etla* (Sweet, 160).

(2) syncopated (Gmc. \**Atlo*: see Fr. Kluge, 'Zeugnisse zur germanischen Sage in England', *Englische Studien* XXI (1895), 447): OE *Ætla* c. 650 (Searle, 62); ON *Atli*.

It is often argued that the name is equivalent to the diminutive of Goth. *atta*, 'father' (Feist, 62; Baesecke, *Vorgeschichte*, 253; Kralik, *Trilogie*, 470), and such semantic accommodation may well have taken place, as with ON *Atli* and *atall*, 'harsh, terrible' (Jóhannesson I. 85; S. Gutenbrunner, 'Über einige Namen in der Nibelungendichtung', *ZfdA* LXXXV (1954/5), 58), but the pn occurs in an early list of kings of the Bulgars, the probable descendants of Attila's Huns (Moravcsik II. 81; Zeuß, 710 f.; Altheim I. 15 ff.), and can be related to the Turkish pn *Ätli*, originally a river-name (ibid. 229).

This central figure of the 'Heldensage' represents the historical Attila (†453):[4] after the death of their uncle Ruas in 434, Attila and his brother Bleda, the sons of Mundzucus, became joint rulers of the Huns. In 445 Attila murdered his brother and became sole ruler (see Blœdel, p. 13): his dominion extended from the Alps to the Baltic and from just east of the Rhine to the Caspian. In the years 443 and 447 he ravaged the East Roman Empire and imposed a heavy tribute in gold. The discovery of the sword of the 'war-god', which was brought to him, imbued him with ambitions of world conquest (Priscus, 314; Jordanes ch. xxxv (183)).

Priscus, the historian, who accompanied the East Roman envoy, Maximinus, to the wooden encampment of Attila beyond the Danube, has left an account of his visit to Attila's wife Kreka (see Helche, p. 67) and of the banquet attended by the East Romans, at which two barbarians—their race is not stated—sang songs in praise of Attila's warlike deeds, and other entertainments took place: Attila remained indifferent to all of this and only showed a trace of tenderness when his youngest son Ernac entered the hall.

When his demand for the hand of Honoria, the sister of the Emperor Valentinian III, together with half the Roman Empire, was rejected, Attila invaded Gaul with a vast army, which included the Ostrogoths led by Valamer, Vidimer, and Theodemer (see Dietmâr, p. 25) in 451, but met his first reverse at Orleans. The West Roman leader Aetius, with a small force of Roman troops, supported by the Visigoths of Toulouse and other Germanic contingents, including Burgundians, Franks, and possibly some Saxons, opposed Attila at the Catalaunian Fields (Châlons-sur-Saône) in Southern Gaul; after tremendous slaughter, in which the Visigothic King Theodoric was slain, Attila retreated to his wagon-camp, but was allowed by Aetius to withdraw.[5] The next year he invaded Italy and destroyed Aquileia, but withdrew to Pannonia without attacking Rome.

In 453, at a time when he was preparing to attack the East Roman Empire, Attila added a beautiful girl named Ildico (Gmc. \**Hildiko*?) to the number of his wives:[6] on the wedding night, after drinking heavily, he

---

[1] In Am, which recounts the same story as Akv, but emphasizes Atli's cruelty and avarice, Guðrún accuses him of murdering her mother for her treasure, and starving her sister to death in a cave. Her own vengeance, too, is intensified: she gives him beer mixed with the blood of their children and served in their skulls; her son by Högni, Hniflungr, helps her to kill Atli (also in Völss ch. 38).

[2] It may be noted that in the mid-12th-cent. *Kaiserchronik*, Mîlîan is the name given to two heathen kings of Babylon (5183, 16632), both of whom are humiliatingly defeated, the first by the Roman Titus and the second by the crusader Godfrey of Bouillon.

[3] The forms *Attila* of **W** and *Attilo* of OE *Domesday* (Binz, 205) depend on the Latin form of Jordanes; an *Attila* is recorded for the Bishop of Laon (634–64) (Förstemann I. 153).

[4] This account is based on E. A. Thompson, *A History of Attila and the Huns* (Oxford, 1948), and the relevant chapters (xxxv–lii) in *Jordanis Romana et Getica*, ed. Th. Mommsen (Berlin, 1882: = *MGH auct. ant.* v. i). Priscus' report of the East Roman embassy to Attila is well translated in Gustav Freytag, *Bilder aus der deutschen Vergangenheit*, Bd. I (Leipzig, I), 143–72.

[5] See p. 17 n. 2.

[6] Jordanes gives Priscus as his source for the account (Thompson, 149 n. 2).

died of suffocation caused by bleeding of the nose.¹ Attila's sons quarrelled after his death, and the Gepid king, Ardaric, led a revolt of the Germanic subject peoples, in which the Huns were utterly defeated at Nedao in 454 (?), Attila's eldest son, Ellac, being killed in the battle; remnants of the Huns under his other sons fled to the Black Sea region, where they were again defeated. The Ostrogoths under Valamer, who took no part in the battle of Nedao, defeated the Huns in a separate battle, from which only a few Huns under Attila's youngest son, Ernac, escaped into the East Roman Empire. Dengizec, the last son of Attila of whom there is any record, was killed on a raid into the East Roman Empire in 469.

In Germanic heroic tradition Attila's last wife becomes the sister of the Burgundian kings, for whose death Attila is held responsible (see Burgonde, pp. 16 ff., Kriemhilt, p. 21, and Gunther, pp. 55 f.); in the most archaic versions of the 'Destruction of the Burgundians' in ON (Am and Akv)² she is thought to have murdered him in revenge for her brothers; in the later versions in MHG (**N** and **Kl**) she brings about the deaths of her brothers, and the manner of Attila's death is left uncertain (see Kriemhilt, p. 21).

In German tradition Attila has taken the place of the emperors Leo and Zeno, the historical patrons of Theodoric the Great, the Ostrogothic ruler of Italy (MHG Dietrich von Berne); this may have come about through a confusion of Theodoric with his father, Theodemer, who served Attila loyally. Although it may be assumed from **äH** (*c*. 700), the first certain record of Attila's patronage of Theodoric occurs in the *Ann. Quedl.* (*c*. 1000) (see Dietrich (1), p. 28).

The killing of the sons of Etzel and Helche by Witege is not recorded before the 13th cent.:³ their names: *Erpfe*, *Orte* (**B**); *Erpr*, *Ortv*in (Þs), resemble significantly those of the sons of Etzel/Atli by his second wife Kriemhilt/Guðrún: *Erpr*, Eitill (Akv); Ortliep (**N**).

## EUGEL
A dwarf, son of Nybling (see Nibelunc (1), p. 97): in **hS** he greets Seyfrid by name and tells him who his parents are. Seyfrid pulls his beard and smashes his crown, after which he agrees to help the hero against the dragon on the 'Trachenstain' (see Alberîch, p. 3). He aids Seyfrid against the giant Kuperan with the help of the cloak of invisibility (*nebelkappe*). When the dragon arrives, he and his dwarf relatives hide a treasure. Seyfrid kills the dragon and takes the treasure, thinking it belongs to the dragon. Eugel finally prophesies Seyfrid's marriage to Krimhilt, his murder by Hagen, and Krimhilt's revenge.

ref: **gS** p. 72, 29 (*Egwaldus*, later also *Egwald*); **hS** 42, 5 (*Eugleyne*, later also *Eugel*; **H** always *Ogel*); **hS(Sachs)** 411 (*Ewgelein*)

pn: possibly descriptive, cf. NHG *Äuglein* and the name in the Czech version of **hS**, *Vocáček*, 'little big-eyes' (Golther, *Hürnen Seyfrid*, x). In *Orendel* (12th cent.?) the hero's father is named *Ougel* (6).

In **hS** Eugel has replaced Alberîch of **N**, but he has also been made the third son of Nibelunc (1), although the first two sons are unnamed (see Schilbunc, p. 115. and Nibelunc (2), p. 97). A similarly helpful dwarf named Lorandin aids Seyfrid in the late-13th-cent. romance *Seifrid de Ardemont* (see p. 119 n. 8).

# F (V)

## FALENTRINS
Daughter of Helferîch (1) von Lûne and wife of Baldunc von Tirol.

ref: **V(h)** m 214, 9 n 240, 5 (Falentrins, 537, 3 Valiklius, 801, 9 Volentrins, 969, 7 Volentrîn)

## VALKE
A horse renowned for its speed: in **Rg(A)** Dietrich gives Schemminc to Witege in exchange for Valke. In **Rs** Wolfhart gives it to Dietrich von Berne for saving his life, but Dietrich on Valke is unable to overtake Witege, who is riding Schemminc, at Rabene (Ravenna).

In **E(L)** and **jSn** Dietrich owns it.

In **Wd(A)** Wolfdietrich inherits the horse from Hugdietrich; the major-domo, Berhtunc, hands it over to him when he is about to break out of the besieged fortress of Lilienporte; later it saves his life by fighting

---

¹ Jordanes (ch. XLIX) gives a detailed description of Attila's funeral, which has elements characteristic of the accounts of Germanic funerals, e.g. that of Bēowulf (*Beowulf* 3137 ff.). See G. N. Garmonsway and J. Simpson, *Beowulf and its Analogues* (London, 1968), 340 ff.

² A detailed study of the Eddic material and parallel literature to do with Attila and the 'Destruction of the Burgundians' may be found in *The Poetic Edda*, edited and translated by Ursula Dronke, vol. i: *Heroic Poems* (Oxford, 1969), 3–141.

³ Cf. p. 147 n. 2.

## VALKE

off a dragon while he sleeps (see Schemminc, p. 115).

ref: **E(L)** 152, 2; **Rg(A)** 232, 3; **Rg(C)** 1300; **Rs** 626, 1; **jSn** m 28, 6 n 59, 2; **Wd(A)** m 351, 2 n 423, 3

In Þs Þiðrekr receives Falka (I. 162, 16) from Heimir, son of the horse-dealer Studas; Falka is the brother of Skemmingr and Grani, the horses of Viðga and Sigurðr. Falka aids Þiðrekr against Ekka by breaking the giant Ekka's back (see Schemminc, p. 115), and Þiðrekr later lends the horse to Ulfrað, who breaks out of a besieged castle mounted on it (see Wolfhart, p. 152).

pn: related to MHG *valke*, 'falcon', and *val*, *valwe*, 'pale, dun' (Kahle, 171; *DWb* III. 1269 f.; Kluge, *EWb*, 179 ff.).

## VALWEN pl.

Members of this tribe in the service of Constantin are routed by Arnolt as they are about to lead Rother to the gallows.

In **B** they are archers in Etzel's army.

ref: **B** 9728 (MS. *Valben*); **R** 4089 (H *ualewin*, R *Valwin*)

This tribe is referred to in German literature in the mid 12th cent.: *Kaiserchronik*, 14023 (see Dietrich (1), p. 28), and in the 13th cent.: *Wigalois*, 9898, Johannes von Würzburg's *Wilhelm von Österreich*, 907, and *Neidharts Lieder*, 102, 28.

This is the German name for the Kumans or Polowci, a brutal Finnish people, who harried the Byzantine Empire in the 11th and 12th cents. (Zeuß, 743 ff.; Frings–Kuhnt, *Rother*, 193; Hempel, *Nibelungenstudien*, 15).

## VÂSOLT (FASOLT)

In **E** Dietrich von Berne encounters the long-haired giant Vâsolt pursuing a maiden through the forest with hounds and blowing his horn. Dietrich takes the maiden into his protection, and Vâsolt threatens to hang them both. Dietrich defeats him and he swears fealty, but breaks his oath and attacks Dietrich when he learns that Dietrich has killed his brother Ecke; he also leads Dietrich into conflict with his giant kin. We learn from **E(ds)** that Dietrich finally kills him. **hS(Sachs)** mentions his death at the hands of Dietrich.[1]

ref: **AHb** p. 3, 38 (*Vasat*); **E(d)** 2, 4 (*Fassolt*); **E(L)** 2, 4; **E(s)** 2, 4 (*Fasolt*); **hS(Sachs)** 830 (*Fasolt*)

In Þs, Fasold (1. 175, 9), brother of Ekka and Vildiver, accuses Þiðrekr of killing Ekka in his sleep. Þiðrekr defeats him, and he joins Þiðrekr's band of heroes. On the Bertangaland expedition he is defeated by the fifth son of Isungr. Later he marries the daughter of Drusian (see Drasîân). He dies at the hands of Hertnið, son of Osanctrix (see Hertnît (1), p. 70).

pn: no occurrence before 1100 in German records (Mone, 96 f.; Förstemann I. 500; Socin, 570; Müllenhoff, *ZE*, 357; Jänicke, *ZE*, 313; Holthausen, 500); the Lb pn *Faro(a)ld* is possibly cognate (Ploß, 59).

The name probably refers to the long, flowing locks of Vâsolt, being based on the same stem (IE *\*pēs*, 'to blow': Kluge, *EWb*, 185) as OHG *faso*, 'fringe, edge, thread' (see O. Plaßmann, 'Agis: eine Untersuchung an Wörtern, Sachen und Mythen', *PBB* LXXXII (Sonderband, Halle, 1961), 129 f.), and suggests the characteristics of a storm-demon.[2]

It is probable that Vâsolt was originally a weather-spirit connected with the weather-witches of Jochgrîm (see Sêburc (1), pp. 116 f.): W. Grimm refers to the Munich weather-spell, 'Ich peut dir Fasolt dass du das wetter verfirst mir und meinen nachpauren ân schaden' (W. Grimm, *DHS*, 371). In **E** Vâsolt appears in the cannibal variant of the folk-tale of 'Der Wilde Jäger' (Röhrich, *Erzählungen* II. 1–52, 393–407; see also Wunderer, pp. 135 f.).

## FELIX

In **E(s)** Dietrich is said to have ruled in his day.

ref: **E(s)** 284, 5

Felix III was elected Pope six weeks before the death of Theodoric the Great in 526.

## VELLE (HELLE)

A giant: in **O** he brings dragons' eggs into Ortnît's land (see abrahemisch (adj.), p. 3, and Machorel, p. 92). His wife is named Runze (Rütze). In **Wd(B)** Ortnît kills them both.

ref: **AHb** m 5, 28; **O** 494, 6 (Helle: ac *Velle*); **Wd(B)** 474, 1 (Helle: H *helt*, a *velle*, c *walle*, z *welle*); **Wd(Gr)** 789, 1 (Velle)

pn: possibly based on MHG *velle*, 'fall, crash', but *Heinrichus Velli* recorded at Müllhausen in the 13th cent. suggests a by-name based on MHG *vel*, 'hide', and, in a transposed sense, 'person'; cf. NHG Bälglein (Socin, 446). The name occurs in a list of giants in the late-13th-cent. *Reinfried von Braunschweig* (W. Grimm, *DHS*, 195).

## VELLENWALT

A giant in the service of Nîtgêr killed by Heime (see Wîcram).

ref: **V(h)** 510, 2; **V(w)** 656, 7

pn: an appellative based on an imperative phrase, i.e. 'fell the forest!'

---

[1] Hans Sachs mentions Fasolt and other heroes in his *Fechtspruch: Ankunft und Freiheit der Kunst* (1545) (cit. Drescher, 425).

[2] J. de Vries, 'Das germanische Sakralkönigtum', *GRM* XXXIV (1953), 185, considers that Vâsolt's long hair indicates dedication to Woden (ON Óðinn).

## VELSENSTÔZ
A giant in the service of Nîtgêr; killed by Wolfhart (see Wîcram).

ref: **V(h)** 732, 1; **V(w)** 663, 1

pn: an appellative based on a phrase, i.e. 'crash of rock' (cf. MHG *stôz*, 'crash').

## FELSENSTRAUCH, see BITTERBÛCH
pn: an appellative based on a phrase, i.e. 'fall of rock' (cf. MHG *strûch*, 'fall, crash').

## VENUS
Eckart stands as warner before 'frau Venus berg' (see Eckehart, pp. 33 f.).

ref: **AHb** p. 3, 27

## VERSÂBE, see BERSÂBE

## VIDELNSTÔZ (BALDEGRÎN)
A giant killed by Dietleip (see Wîcram).

ref: **V(h)** 867, 4; **V(w)** 714, 4 (*Baldegrein*)

pn: appellative, i.e 'fiddle-stroke', possibly obscene.

## VIGAN(T), see TERFÎANT

## VIGAS, see TRIUREIZ

## VIRGINÂL
An elf-queen (unnamed in **V(d)**), who rules at Jeraspunt (Zetugein in **V(d)**) in the Tyrol; her kingdom is ravaged by the heathen Orkîse (because she has exiled Elegast, according to **V(w)**), who demands a maiden as yearly tribute. Hildebrant and Dietrich defeat and kill Orkîse, and Virginâl prepares to welcome the victors. She sends her messenger, Bîbunc, to find them; after many adventures Dietrich arrives at Jeraspunt and marries Queen Virginâl, who then hands over her kingdom to him.

ref: **V(d)** m 3, 4; **V(h)** m 2, 3 n 87, 8; **V(w)** 9, 7

pn: of uncertain origin: it has been related to Goth. *faírguni*, 'mountain', OE *firgen*, 'mountain woodland' (Feist, 139), and ON *Fjörgyn* (Vsp 56, 10), an earth-goddess (Jiriczek, *DHS* (1898), 234 f.; von der Leyen, *Sagenbuch* I. 65 f.), cf. *Virgunnia*, at one time the name of a vast forest between Ellwangen and Ansbach (Zeuß, 10). It has also been surmised that it is a latinization of the Greek *Parthenopé* (Lunzer, *Elegast*, 151 f.),[1] and the obvious connection with Lat. *virgo* occurred to the author of **V(d)**, in which Hildebrant hides under the bridal bed to witness the consummation of Dietrich's marriage to the elf-queen (125 ff.).

## VLÂCHEN, see WALÂCHEN

## FLORIGUNDA, see KRIEMHILT

## FLORIS
King of Denmark: he and Hildebrant escort Virginâl to Berne (Verona) after her marriage to Dietrich.

ref: **V(w)** 846, 1

pn: of Romance origin (see Flutre, 79, under *Flori*).

## VOLKÊR von Alzeye[2]
In **N**, Volkêr, 'der starke spileman' (196, 2), bears Sîfrit's banner in the campaign against the Saxons and Danes. Later he becomes Hagen's close companion on the journey of the Burgundians to Hiunenlant. At Bechelâren he receives twelve gold rings from Rüedegêr for his minstrelsy. In the fighting with the Huns at Etzel's court his sword is frequently compared to a fiddle-bow and his blows to melodies (184, etc.);[3] he kills Irnfrit and Sigestap, and is killed by Hildebrant.

In **WuH** he escorts Walther and Hildegunt through the Vosges and warns them against the hostility of Ortwîn.

In **Rg(A)** he is among the men of Worms opposing the champions of Dietrich and Etzel; he is defeated by 'der junge Ortwîn'. In **Rg(CDP)** he is defeated by Ilsân; in **Rg(DP)** he is thought to be the son of Kriemhilt, and has a fiddle depicted on his shield (in **AHb** he is her nephew).

In **DF** and **Rs** he is Ermenrîch's man: he fights Wolfhart at Bôlonje (Bologna) and Baltram at Rabene (Ravenna).

ref: **AHb** p. 2, 37 (*Felscher*, p. 7, 22 *Felcker*, print of 1509 *Fölcker*); **DF** 9235; **Kl** 456; **N** 9, 4; **Rg(A)** 7, 2; **Rg(C)** 28; **Rg(D)** 45, 1; **Rg(P)** 75; **Rs** 705, 1; **WuH** (Wien) I. 2, 1

In Þs, Folker (II. 283, 9) is the close companion of Högni; in the fighting between the Niflungar and the Huns he fights bravely, but is finally beheaded by Þiðrekr.

In the Danish ballad, *Grimilds Hævn*, Falquor Spilmand is Hagenn's comrade, his fiddle-playing being frequently referred to (*DgF* I. 44 ff.); in *Kong Diderik og hans Kæmper* and *Kong Diderik i Birtingsland* he is one of Diderik's companions (ibid. 94 ff., 124 ff.).

pn: *Fulcaris*, 6th-cent. Herulean (Schönfeld, 96; Much, *Germania*, 107); 8th-cent. German (Förstemann I. 550 f.; Schlaug I. 84 f.; II. 93); rare in South-East Germany before 1140 (Kromp I. 26; III. 30), but frequent generally later in the 12th cent. (Socin, 38). The occurrence of this name in OE is probably of continental import (Searle, 242 f.; Feilitzen, 256); the OFr

---

[1] Cf. Portalaphê, p. 106.
[2] Alzei, 23 km. north-west of Worms. On the connection between Volkêr and the lords of Alzei, whose coat of arms was a fiddle, see W. Grimm, *DHS*, 371 f., 402 f.; Ploß, 56; Rosenfeld, *Namen*, 249.
[3] Fischart, in his *Peter von Stauffenberg* (1588), refers to Volkêr's fiddling (Jänicke, *ZE*, 330).

## VOLKÊR

equivalent, *Fouchier* or *Fouchard*, is frequent in the *ch.d.g.* (Langlois, 226 f.; Ploß, 56).[1]

A document from the monastery of Oudenburg in West Flanders, dealing with tax on land due to the Count of Flanders from 'Folkirus ioculator' and dated 27 May 1130 (or 1131), suggests that the name was already connected with minstrelsy in the early 12th cent. (H. Breßlau, 'Volker der Spielmann', *AfdA* XXXIV (1910), 120 f.; see also Rosenfeld, *Namen*, 248).

## VOLCNANT

Dietrich's man: in **DF** he is sent by Sabene von Rabene to warn Dietrich of the approach of Ermenrîch's forces. In **Rg(F)** he is Hâwart's brother.

ref: **DF** 2903; **Rg(F)** III. 14, 1

pn: 9th-cent. German (Förstemann I. 554; Schlaug II. 93), and is recorded in OE (Searle, 243).

## VOLCWÎN

In **B**, the brother of Näntwîn (2), he aids Gunther against Dietrich's men. In **A**, on the other hand, he is among Dietrich's men.

ref: **A** 73, 2; **B** 10277

In the *Kaiserchronik* (mid 12th cent.) Volcwîn is the name of one of Duke Adelgêr's men (7061) (see p. 3).

pn: 8th-cent. German (Förstemann I. 558; Schlaug II. 94), and occurs in OE (Searle, 243); *Fouquin*, the OFr equivalent, occurs in the *ch.d.g.* (Langlois, 230).

## VORDECK, see GÊRWART

## FRANKE (FRANKEN, FRANCIA, FRÄNKISCH adj.)

Ethnic name: also applied to a German region, Franken, 'Franconia'. *Frankrîche* (**B** 6639; **DF** 2351; **DH** F 44, 1, 2; **E(d)** 317, 11; **E(L)** 66, 12; **ED** 1, 1; **Kl** 2457; **gS** p. 68, 30 (*Franckreich*); **hS(Sachs)** 82; **Wd(D)** VIII. 333, 4) applies to France (see Kerlingen, p. 18).

In **W** Guntharius and Hagano are termed 'Franci nebulones' (555) (see Nibelunge, p. 97, and Sicamber, p. 118); in the **Kl** Gunther and his men are termed 'Rînvranken' (347); otherwise the term 'Franken' is used for the people of Franconian areas, apart from the Burgundians of the 'Heldensage' (see Burgonde, pp. 16 f.).

ref: the people: **B** 9310; **Ku** 366, 4; the Burgundians in particular: **B** 5963; 9734; **W** 483, etc. (Francus, Franci)

the region: **DF** 538; **V(h)** 581, 10; **V(w)** 841, 6; **W** 87 (Francia); **Wd(D)** VIII. 13, 1; **Wd(Gr)** 1549, 1

fränkisch adj.: **B** 3121 (f. wîn); **R** 5021 (f. lant)

It is probable that the Chauci, who inhabited the region between the Ems and the Elbe in the 1st cent. A.D., represent the original confederation later joined by the Salii and the Ripuarii to constitute the later tribes designated 'Franci', a name known from the 3rd cent. (Much, *Germania*, 311 ff.). Under Clovis (Chlodovech) the Franks conquered Gaul in 486, defeated the Alemanni in 496 and 506, and colonized the Main region. Under Theodoric, the son of Clovis, they destroyed the Thuringian realm in 532. Later the Saxons, Bavarians, and Frisians were subjugated. From the point of view of the 'Heldensage' the incorporation of the Burgundian kingdom in South-East France into the Frankish realm in the 6th cent. is all-important (see Burgonde, p. 17).

## FREISE (FREISSAN)

Hildebrant's sword (see also Brinnic, p. 15).

ref: **jSn** 148, 4 (Freissan: MS. readings: v *frygsam*, h[1] *friessen*, d *weihe*); **V(h)** 62, 8 (Vreisen: MS. *freisem*); **V(w)** 112, 7 (*Freise*, also *Fraise*)

In the late-13th-cent. *Ritterpreis*, Vreise (175) is mentioned together with other swords (Schieb-Frings, *Eneide* II. 188).

pn: based on MHG *vreise*, *vreissam*, 'terrible'.

## FRIDEBOLT ûz Kriechenlande (Greece)

Attends Wolfdietrich's wedding to Sîdrât.

ref: **Wd(D)** VIII. 334, 1; **Wd(Gr)** 1873, 3

pn: 6th-cent. WFr, 8th-cent. German (Förstemann I. 530; Schlaug I. 87; II. 94).

## FRID(E)GÊR

Companion of Dietwart.

ref: **DF** 565 (Fridgêr)[2]

pn: 8th-cent. German (Förstemann I. 532; Schlaug I. 88; II. 95). It is used for a peasant in *Neidharts Lieder*, 144, 8.

## FRID(E)LEIP ûz Swâben (Swabia)

Aids Gunther against the men of Dietrich and Etzel.

ref: **B** 5073 (MS. *Fridlieb*)

pn: 8th-cent. German (Förstemann I. 535), 9th-cent. OE (Searle, 248).

## FRIDERÎCH (1) son of Ermenrîch

In **DF** Ermenrîch is known to have sent him to Wilzenlant with treacherous intent (2458 ff.) (see p. 37 n. 4); in this epic he is taken prisoner by Dietrich's men, but Ermenrîch is not prepared to exchange him for prisoners taken from Dietrich's forces. When Dietrich returns to Italy, Friderîch is in command at Bâdouwe (Padua), but is put to flight by Wolfhart. In **AHb** Ermenrîch has two sons, whom he refuses to ransom from Dietrich.

ref: **AHb** m p. 9, 1; **DF** 2458

The hostility of Ermanaric (ON Jörmunrekr, MHG Ermenrîch) to his sons and his responsibility for the death of his son

---

[1] See also p. 60 n. 8.

[2] Omitted from the index to *DHB* II.

## FRIDERÎCH (1)

Fridericus are recorded in the 10th cent. (see Ermenrîch, p. 37).

In the OE poem *Widsith* the name Freoþerîc (124) occurs in the same line as Wudga and Hāma (see Witege and Heime), but no sure identification is possible (Malone, *Widsith*, 145: see also Friderîch (2) below).

In Þs, Friðrekr (II. 161, 7) is sent by his father, Erminrikr, to Osanctrix, the ruler of Villcinaland, to demand tribute; Friðrekr is killed through the machinations of Sifka, Erminrikr's counsellor, who has suggested the undertaking.

In ON Eddic tradition, Jörmunrekr's son is named Randvér; in Saxo's Danish history, Broderus (see Ermenrîch, p. 38).

pn: 5th-cent. continental Germanic; 7th-cent. German (Schönfeld, 94; Förstemann I. 536 f.; Schlaug I. 88 f.; II. 95); rare in OE (Searle, 249; Feilitzen, 254).

The historical Ermanaric is said to have had a son named Hunimundus, who, according to Cassiodorus (5th cent.), was exceedingly handsome (cit. Panzer, *Heldensage im Breisgau*, 46). The name may well derive from that of the 5th-cent. Rugian king (see Friderîch (2) below).

## FRIDERÎCH (2) von Rabene (Ravenna)

Dietrich's man: in Rs he warns Dietrich of the approach of Ermenrîch's army.

ref: **A** 76, 1; **DF** 2719; **Rs** 261, 4

This figure has been identified as Fridericus, son of the Rugian king, Felectheus, put to death by Odoacer. He fought with Theodoric in Italy against Odoacer, but later deserted to the enemy (see also Wielant, p. 143).[1]

## FRIDERÎCH (3) von Sêlande[2]

Ermenrîch's man: he fights Ruodwîn at Rabene (Ravenna).

ref: **Rs** 726, 4 (MS. A *Frideger*)

## FRIDERÎCH (4) Constantin's man

He quarrels with Asprîân, the leader of Rother's giants, about the precedence of their respective masters.

ref: **R** 1609

See Dietrich (3), p. 31, regarding the incognito 'Friðrik' in Þs.

## FRIDESCHOTTEN

Uote (4), the mother of Hagen (2) in **Ku**, comes from 'Frideschotten lande', apparently part of Norway (9, 3; 30, 1). Later we learn that Ludewîc rules it (611, 1).

ref: **Ku** 9, 3

Various explanations have been put forward for this ethnic name (Bach I, § 177 c; Martin, *Kudrun*, note to str. 9, 3; Rosenfeld, *Namen*, 245).

## FRIDUNC von Zæringen (Zähringen, near Freiburg, Breisgau?)

Ermenrîch's man.

ref: **DF** 8637

pn: 9th cent. in German place-names (Förstemann II. ii. 952); the simplex *Frido* is recorded in the 9th cent. (ibid. I. 528).

## FRIESEN pl.

Ethnic name, referring to the people and region of Frisia. In **R**, Rother grants this territory to certain men in his service. In **Ku** the region is part of Hetel's realm of Hegelingen.

ref: **Ku** 208, 1; **R** 4830

The main area of Frisian settlement is on the North Sea coast between the Ems and the Issel (Zeuß, 136 ff., 397 ff.). The Frisians are referred to in OE heroic poetry (cf. *Beowulf*, 1093, etc., and *Widsith*,[1] 27, etc.). They play no part in German heroic tradition as it has been recorded.

## FRÎTELE[3]

One of the Harlunge: brother of Imbrecke.

ref: **B** 4595 (MS. *Fritelen*, etc., but 4765 *Freyteln*, 5657 *Fridel*)

Ermanaric's nephew Fritla is mentioned in the *Ann. Quedl.* (c. 1000), and the *Genealogia Viperti* (12th cent.) names Vridelo as one of the Harlungi (W. Grimm, *DHS*, 35, 55); in the *Kaiserchronik* (mid 12th cent.), however, Frîtele is thought to be one of Etzel's sons (13862).

In the OE poem *Widsith* the name Fridla, together with that of Emerca, occurs immediately after the pl. Herelingas (112 f.).

In Þs, Fritila (II. 166, 1) is the name of the foster-father of the brothers Áki and Egarð, and Fritilaborg (I. 30, 17)[4] is the residence of their father, Áki Aurlungatrausti (see Harlunge, p. 63, and Hâche, p. 56).

pn: 4th-cent. Gothic (Förstemann I. 528), 8th-cent. German (ibid. 529; Socin, 16; Schlaug II. 196); OE place-name *Friþela byrig* in a document of 957 (Binz, 208).

Probably a hypocoristic form of a pn with first component *Friðu- (OHG *fridu*, 'peace, protection') and the diminutive suffix *-ilo* (Henzen, 141 f.).

## FRÔMUOT

Sigeminne's handmaiden.

ref: **Wd(B)** 426, 9; **Wd(Gr)** 674, 1

pn: 9th-cent. German (Förstemann I. 520; Schlaug II. 197). It occurs as a personification in *Neidharts Lieder*, 31, 38. That it is a

---

[1] For a discussion of this figure see Jiriczek, *DHS* (1898), 134, 144; G. Eis, 'Ein Rugier im Buch von Berne', *GRM* XXXIX (1958), 417 f.

[2] Possibly Zealand in Denmark, but the title may stem from **Ku**; cf. Herwîc von Sêlant, p. 71 n. 3.

[3] The spellings with -î- in Jänicke's edition of *Biterolf* in *DHB* I are uncertain (see Kaufmann, 124 ff.).

[4] Boer, *Sagen*, 68, identifies the place as Vercelli, whereas Paff, 77 f., takes it to be Feltria (!).

meaningful name is shown by the comment of Wolfdietrich, 'daz ist ein sæleger name ... heizent ir Frômuot, mit fröiden müezt ir sîn ...' **(Wd(B)** 426, 21 f.).

## VROUENZART
A nickname given to Dietrich by Nîtgêr's giants.

ref: **V(h)** 338, 2

pn: refers to the character of young Dietrich in this epic, 'tender towards the ladies'.

## FRUOTE (1) von Tenelant (Denmark)
In **Ku**, Fruote, old and wise ('altgrîs'), is chamberlain to Hetel, to whom he is related. On the expedition to win Hilde von Îrlant for Hetel, he lures Hilde on board ship with a display of rich wares, and she is then abducted. After the unsuccessful battle at Wülpensant, he advises against further pursuit of the Normans, who have abducted Kûdrûn, the daughter of Hetel and Hilde; later he restrains Wate from destroying the Norman castle after Kûdrûn's rescue.

In **B**, Biterolf assumes his name (according to the editor, but not according to the MS., which has *Diete*).[1]

In **Rs**, Fruote, 'der tugenthafte, milte, guote' (797, 1-3), supports Ermenrîch at Rabene (Ravenna). His device is a golden lion on a white ground. Dietrich captures him and hands him over to Hildebrant.

In **Rg(D)** he is a young king driven from his kingdom by Gunther, whom he defeats in the combats at Worms. His device is three martens (in **Rg(P)** a Moor's head).

In **Wd(A)** he is the nephew of Hugdietrich, who makes warlike preparations against him.

ref: **AHb** p. 3, 10; **B** 1910 (MS. *Diete*); **Ku** 219, 4; **Rg(D)** m 72, 4 n 161, 2; **Rg(P)** 117; Rs 478, 4; **Wd(A)** 6, 2

In German tradition Herger (*c.* 1150-80) refers to Fruote von Tenemarke as an example of good fortune and generosity (*MF* 25, 19-20); Seifrid Helbling (late 13th cent.) does likewise (Müllenhoff, *ZE*, 370).

In OE *Beowulf* the name Frōda is used for the King of the Heaðobeardan (2025);[2] in fact Bēowulf I, the Dane (18, 53), takes the place of Fróði Friðr ('the peaceful') of Danish genealogies, i.e. of Saxo's Frotho I and Frotho III (Saxo II. i. 1 ff.; v. i. 1 ff.), for he is the son of Scyld and father of Healfdene, while Fróði is the son of Skjöld and father of Hálfdan.

The Danish historian Saxo Grammaticus mentions six persons named Frotho; two are of interest here: the first (II. i. 1-iv. 3), son of Hadingus, kills a dragon by slitting its belly open (see Sîfrit (1));[3] the second (v. i. 1-xvi. 3), son of Fridlevus, rules peacefully for thirty years (but see p. 79 n. 3), but fails to reconcile Hithinus and Höginus (see Hetel, Hagen (2), and Hegelinge). After his death, one Hiarno, a minstrel (see Hôrant, p. 81), is elected king for verses composed in his honour; Frotho's son, Fridlevus, returns to claim the throne.

In ON Eddic tradition Fróði, son of Friðleifr, is remembered for his peaceful reign (Grt 1, 5; HHu I. 13, 5; Sk ch. 44; Hátt 43, 5), and his generosity is proverbial.[4] In Grt he has a magic mill from which two giantesses, Fenja and Menja, grind wealth and happiness. Finally they produce a hostile army and his golden age ends. A different Fróði is the father of Hlédís (Hdl 13, 5).

pn: rare before 1000 in German (Förstemann I. 541); it is recorded in OE (Binz, 174; Feilitzen, 256).

OHG *fruot* means 'wise, old' (cf. OE *frōd*, OS *frôd*); in MHG *vruot* can also mean 'handsome, noble, gay, healthy' (Lexer III. 554).

FRUOTE (2) Biterolf's incognito (see Froute (1) above) ref: **B** 1912 (MS. always *Diete*)

# G

## GABEIN
A former owner of Ecke's sword (see Eckesahs, p. 34).

ref: **E(d)** 88, 2

pn: probably a variant of the name of the Arthurian hero, Gâwein.

## GALERANT
A giant killed by Gêrnot (2) at Mûter (see Wîcram, p. 140, and Wolfrât (3), p. 152 n. 5).

ref: **V(w)** 677, 9

pn: probably of OFr origin: the name occurs in OFr romance (Flutre, 84; see also Kalbow, 44, 92).

---

[1] Jänicke's emendation is justified by the preceding lines, which refer to Biterolf's thoughts: 'er gedâhte im eines namen: / ... er was ein recke ûz Tenelant ...' (**B** 1905 ff.).

[2] See Klaeber, *Beowulf*, xxxiv, and Malone, *Widsith*, 155 ff.

[3] See Klaeber, *Beowulf*, xxii.

[4] The rune for F is interpreted in this light (*CPB* II. 370).

## GAMAZITUS (MAZITUS, MARTIKOS, MADIUS)
A maiden pursued by Orkîse.

ref: **V(d)** 12, 1 (Macitus); **V(h)** m 23, 10 n 260, 7 (343, 1 Martikos); **V(w)** m 60, 7 n 64, 1 (*Madius*)

pn: possibly a descriptive name based on Romansh *gamoscio*, 'chamois' (Lunzer, *Elegast*, 151).

## GANGOLF
Dietrich, when pursuing Witege at Rabene (Ravenna), calls on this saint (see also Zêne).

ref: **Rs** 937, 1

St. Gangolf is the patron saint of tanners and shoemakers (†*c*. 760).

pn: 7th-cent. German (Förstemann I. 597).

## GEISELBRANT, see GÎSELRANT

## GELASIUS
Pope during Dietrich's reign in Italy (see Anastasius and Felix).

ref: **E(s)** 284, 5

Gelasius was Pope between 492 and 496.

## GELPFRÂT
Brother of Else m. (1): he is killed by the Burgundians in **N**.

ref: **B** 845; **Kl** m 3840 (B); **N** 1531, 3

pn: 12th-cent. German (Socin, 17, 569; Müllenhoff, *ZE*, 414; see Else m. (1), pp. 31 f.).

## GENEFERIS
A heathen killed by Wolfdietrich in the Holy Land.

ref: **Wd(w)** 945, 1

## GERALDUS
He dedicates **W** to Erckambaldus.

ref: **W** (prologus) 11

Geraldus was formerly not considered to be the author of **W**, but recently his authorship has been proposed, and the Dedication has been assumed to be to Erckambald, Bishop of Eichstätt (884–916); in consequence a date for the composition of **W** *c*. 890 is now suggested (see Erckambaldus, p. 36, and the Introduction, p. xvi).

## GÊRBART (1) Dietrich's man (GÊRHART, GÊRWART)
Brother of Wîchart (**N**, **B**), killed by Gîselhêr (**Kl**).

In **V(h)** he is one of the Wülfinge and kills the giant Senderlîn at Mûter (see Wîcram).

ref: **A** 73, 3 (Gêrhart); **B** 5249 (MS. *Gerhart*, later also *Gebart*); **Kl** 1759 (A *Gerharten*, b *gebharten*, d *gewarten*); **N** 2281, 1 (Ih *Gerhart*, g *Gerbrat*, b *Gebhart*; 2323, 2 A *Gerhart*); **N(k)** 2335, 1 (*Gerwart*); **V(h)** 463, 12 (Gêrwart); **V(w)** 590, 12 (*Gerwart*)

pn: rare in German records (Förstemann I. 575; Bach I, § 87, 7).

## GÊRBART (2) Ermenrîch's man
Fights Marholt von Sibenbürgen at Rabene (Ravenna) in **Rs**. In **A** he is killed by Alphart.

ref: **A** 159, 1 (MS. *Derbart*); **Rs** 739, 5

## GÊRDRÛT
In **Ru** the custom of drinking 'Gerdrudis amore' when starting a journey is mentioned.

In **R** Rother is made the father of Pippin, whose children are Karl and St. Gerdrut; her house (a convent) is at Nivelles.

ref: **R** 3479; **Ru** IV. 162

This popular saint of North-West Germany has been related to Charlemagne (†814) in **R**; in fact she was a daughter of Pepin of Landen and died in 659.

## GÊRE (1) marcgrâve
Vassal of the Burgundian kings in **N**, he accompanies Kriemhilt part of the way to Hiunenlant. In **B** he is among Gunther's men at Worms and leads Stûtfuhs's forces against Rienolt in the combats against Dietrich's men. In **DF** he is among Dietrich's men opposing Ermenrîch at Bâdouwe (Padua).

ref: **B** 7779; **DF** 8312; **N** 9, 3

pn: 8th-cent. German (Förstemann I. 573; II. i. 1001 f.; Schlaug I. 94; II. 198) and is recorded in OE (Searle, 253).

This figure in **N** probably derives from the historical margrave Gero of North Thuringia (†965), a victorious leader against the Slavs under Otto I, referred to as 'dux et marchio' in a document of 946 (Panzer, *Nibelungenlied*, 396 f.; see also Eckewart, p. 35).

## GÊRE (2) father of Gotelint
ref: **B** 6089

## GÊRE (3) brother of Stûtfuhs
Ermenrîch's man: killed by Eckehart.

ref: **A** 358, 3

## GÊRE (4) von Îrlant (Ireland)
Father of Sigebant (1).

ref: **Ku** 1, 2

## GÊRE (5) = WERNHÊR (2)
A heathen pirate forcibly baptized 'Wernhêr' by Wolfdietrich.

ref: **Wd(D)** V. 94, 3; **Wd(Gr)** 932, 1

## GÊRHART, see GÊRBART (1) and GÊRWART
pn: 8th-cent. German (Förstemann I. 578 f.; II. i. 1006; Schlaug I. 92; II. 98).

## GÊRLINT
Wife of Ludewîc and mother of Hartmuot von Ormanîe (Normandy): she incites Ludewîc and Hartmuot to abduct Kûdrûn, whose father, Hagen (2), has rejected Hartmuot as a suitor. During Kûdrûn's captivity

## GÊRLINT

Gêrlint sets her menial tasks. When the rescuing Hegelinge army captures the Norman fortress, Wate beheads Gêrlint. She is referred to as 'tiuvelinne' (738, 1), 'vâlantinne' (629, 4), and 'wülpinne' (1015, 1).

ref: **Ku** 588, 1

pn: 8th-cent. WFr and German (Förstemann I. 582; Schlaug I. 93), frequent in the South-East (Kromp III. 32).

## GÊRNÔT (1) brother of Gunther (1)

In **N** he restrains Ortwîn from attacking Sîfrit, when the latter challenges Gunther on his arrival at Worms, but he takes an active part in the war against the Saxons and Danes, capturing the Saxon leader, Liudegêr. Hagen consults him about the plan to murder Sîfrit, but he takes no part in the fateful hunt. Later he and his younger brother, Gîselhêr, persuade their sister, Kriemhilt, to let them fetch her husband Sîfrit's treasure from Nibelungelant, and Hagen has it sunk in the Rhine. He and Gîselhêr accompany her part of the way to Hiunenlant when she sets out to wed Etzel. When the Burgundians halt at Bechelâren (Pöchlarn) during their journey to Etzel's court, Rüedegêr gives Gêrnôt a sword. Gêrnôt and Rüedegêr later kill each other in the fighting between the Burgundians and Etzel's men; the sword is found by Hildebrant in the **Kl**.

In **B** he organizes the combats between Gunther's men and the supporters of Dietleip at Worms: he fights Dietleip and Biterolf.

In **Rg(A)** he is defeated by Helmschrôt (by Rüedegêr in **Rg(CDP)**) in the combats against Dietrich's men in the rose-garden at Worms.

In **DF** and **Rs** he is among Ermenrîch's men and fights Eckewart at Rabene (Ravenna).

In **Vhw** he wishes never to listen to a traitor.

ref: **AHb** p. 7, 20; **B** 2741; **DF** 8654; **Kl** 233; **N** 4, 2; **N(T)** 1049, 1 (*Geernoet*); **Rg(A)** 6, 4; **Rg(C)** 26; **Rg(D)** 27, 3; **Rg(F)** v. 20, 3; **Rg(P)** 45; **Rs** 723, 1; **gS** 97, 12 (*Walbertus*); **hS** 176, 1 (*Gyrnot*); **hS(Sachs)** 1003; **Vhw** 11 (*Geernot*).

In ON Eddic tradition Gutþormr (Gotþormr) (Grp 50, 3; Br 4, 3; Sg 20, 1; Gðr II 7, 7; Hdl 27, 5; Sk ch. 48; Völss ch. 25), the son of Gjúki (stepson in Sk, half-brother of Gunnarr and Högni in Hdl), having sworn no oaths to Sigurðr, is urged by Gunnarr to kill him (Sg); the dying Sigurðr throws his sword Gramr at him and cuts him in half (see Sîfrit (1), p. 121). Gutþormr, therefore, takes no part in the journey of the Niflungar to Atli's court.

In Þs, Gernoz (I. 322, 3), son of Aldrian, is the brother of Gunnarr and Gisler; he is in the plot against Sigurðr, but takes no part in the fateful hunt. At Bakalar (MHG Bechelâren) Roðingeirr gives him a new shield. In the fight between the Niflungar and Atli's men at Susat (Soest), Gernoz kills Bloðlin, and is killed by Hildibrandr.

In the Danish ballads, *Grimilds Hævn* and *Diderik i Birtingsland* (*DgF* I. 44, 124 ff.), a certain Gierlo (Germer) accompanies Gynter, and in the Faroese ballad *Høgna táttur* (*CCF* I. 22–31), Jarmer is the companion of Gíslar: both probably represent MHG Gêrnôt.

pn: 8th-cent. German (Förstemann I. 584; II. i. 1009; Mone, 61), rare in the 10th and 11th cents., but popular on the Middle Rhine c. 1150–1250 (Socin, 18; E. Schröder, 'Codex Laureshamensis', *AfdA* LVI (1937), 56), remaining rare in the South-East (Kromp I. 25), and not occurring in OS before 1000 (Schlaug II. 99) or in Lb before the Frankish conquest (Ploß, 58).

The second component of this pn possibly derives from the same stem as OHG *hnôtôn*, 'swing a spear', being later confused with OHG *nôt*, 'need' (E. Schröder, *DNK*, 8 f.); it has also been equated with OS *nôt*, giving the meaning 'spear-companion', which has been further interpreted as 'brother-in-law' (Kralik, *Nibelungenlied*, xxxvii).

ON Gutþorm (Gotþormr), then, approximates to *Gundomaris* (*Godomaris*) of the *Lex Burgundionum* (see Burgonde, p. 17); the original Burgundian name—the later Burgundian kings, Gundioch I and Gundobad II, had sons named Godomaris (index to *MGH script. rer. Merov.* II); apparently it has been replaced in German tradition by the typically Frankish *Gêrnôt* (**N**),[1] possibly when Sîfrit's murder was attributed to Hagen (Baesecke, *Vorgeschichte*, 268).

## GÊRNÔT (2) Dietrich's man

A Wülfinc: he kills the giant Wolfrât at Mûter (Galerant in **V(w)**: see Wîcram).

ref: **V(h)** 747, 1; **V(w)** 677, 1

## GÊRNÔT (3) keeper of the bear Wisselau (GERNOUT)

A knight in the service of Karl.

ref: **BW** 106 (*Gernout*)

## GÊROLT von Sahsen (Saxony)

Ermenrîch's man: he fights Îsolt at Rabene (Ravenna).

ref: **Rs** 715, 5

pn: 7th-cent. WFr, 8th-cent. German (Förstemann I. 585 f.; II. i. 1009; Schlaug I. 93; II. 99; Ploß, 59).

## GÊRWART von Troyen[2] (GÊRHART, VORDECK, WILDUNC von Biterne (= Viterbo))

In **O** he rules Nutschîr and Bônavente

---

[1] See Wisniewski, *Thidrekssaga*, 185 ff., regarding the form of the name *Gernoz* in Þs.

[2] Troja in Italy. See p. 36 n. 3.

(Nocera and Benevento); he supplies Ortnît with 5,000 men for his bridal quest.
In **Wd** he pretends to have killed the dragons, which were in fact slain by Wolfdietrich. In **Wd(BC)** Wolfdietrich kills him for this imposture; in **Wd(D)** he pardons him.

ref: **AHb** p. 5, 17; **O** 39, 1; **O(k)** 26, 2 (*Gerepart*); **O(w)** 34, 1 (*Gerhart*); **Wd(B)** 753, 2 (Wildunc); **Wd(C)** VIII. 16, 1 (Gêrharten); **Wd(D)** III. 46, 1; **Wd(Gr)** 306, 1; **Wd(k)** 300, 4 (*Vordeck*)

pn: 8th-cent. German (Förstemann I. 586; II. i. 1011; Schlaug I. 94; II. 100). See also Gêrbart.

## GERWITUS
A count from Worms, one of Guntharius's men killed by Waltharius.

ref: **W** 914

pn: 8th-cent. WFr and German (Förstemann I. 586; Kögel I. ii. 313 f.).

## GHERÎNS
Merchant at Berne (Verona): he gives lodgings to the ladies, Wendelmuot and Sêburc, on their embassy from Kriemhilt to Dietrich.

ref: **Rg(F)** II. 6, 1

pn: origin uncertain: such forms as *Guarin-*, *Guerin-* occur in WFr and Lb for *Warn-*, but German *Gh-* spellings for *Gêr-* are also recorded (Förstemann I. 573 f., 1540). In OFr epic *Gerin* is a frequent pn (Langlois, 274 f.).

## GHISELEER, see GÎSELHÊR

## GIBALDUS, see GIBECHE (1)

## GIBECHE (1) father of Gunther (1)[1]
In **W**, Gibicho, the ruler of Francia, has his capital at Worms. He sends Hagano as a hostage to Attila. When his son Guntharius succeeds him, Hagano returns to Worms.
In **Rg(AD)**, Gibeche, the father of Kriemhilt, rules at Worms; he is defeated by Hildebrant in the combats at the rosegarden and becomes Dietrich's vassal. In **Rg(D)** he is the owner of the rose-garden (see Kriemhilt, p. 19).
In **hS**, **gS**, and **AHb** he is the father of the Burgundians and rules at Worms.

ref: **AHb** p. 1, 24; **B** 2620 (?); **N(k)** 7, 2; **Rg(A)** 1, 4; **Rg(C)** 12; **Rg(D)** 7, 2; **Rg(F)** V. 20, 3 (MS. *gebiche*); **Rg(P)** 2 (MS. *geybich*); **Rg(V)** 10; **gS** p. 66, 7 (*Gibaldus*); **hS** 11, 7; **hS(Sachs)** 20; **W** 14 (Gibicho)

In the 8th-cent. OE poem *Widsith* Gifica is the ruler of the Burgundians (19).

[1] In **N** the father of Gunther is named Dancrât, whereas the name Gibeche is borne by a subject king at Etzel's court (see Gibeche (2)). This confusion is maintained in **B**, in which Gunther and his brothers are referred to as 'Dancrâtes kint'

In ON Eddic tradition Gjúki is the father of Gunnarr, Högni, and Guðrún (Grp 13, 7; Fm 41, 1; Br 6, 2; Gðr I 4, 2; Sg 1, 2; Hlr 4, 5; Gðr II 1, 5; Gðr III 2, 2; Od prose, p. 234; Akv prose, p. 239; 1, 5; Am 1, 7; Ghv 9, 2; Hm 2, 8; Hdl 27, 2; Sk chs. 48, 50, and 80; Völss ch. 24); the name is also used for Högni's son (Dr prose, p. 223). Gjúkungar, as an alternative term for Niflungar, is often used for Gunnarr and his brothers (Sg 35, 3; Dr prose, p. 223; Sk chs. 48 and 50; Völss ch. 25); it is also used in the Faroese ballad *Høgna táttur* (*CCF* I. 22–31), and occurs once in a chapter heading of Þs (II. 302, 19), in which Aldrian is in fact the father of the Niflungar.

pn: 9th-cent. German (Förstemann I. 631 f.; II. i. 1048); rare in OE (Searle, 257; Binz, 202). The name *Gibica* appears at the head of the list of ancestors of the Burgundian King Gundobad in the *Lex Burgundionum* of 516 (see Burgonde, p. 17).

## GIBECHE (2) an exile
In **N** this exiled king is among Etzel's retinue greeting Kriemhilt at Tulln; she honours him with a kiss. Later he jousts with the Burgundians, his name being linked with that of Schrûtân.
In **B** he and Schrûtân, in Etzel's service, fight the Poles; later they oppose Gunther's men at Worms.

ref: **B** 1231; **N** 1343, 4

## GIBECHE (3) von Gâlaber (Calabria)
Ermenrîch's counsellor.

ref: **DF** 7114

## GILEGE
This saint is invoked to protect Rother and his men.

ref: **R** 2926 (3945 H *gilies*, 4068 H *ylien*, B *Ylien*)

This is St. Ägidius, popular in Western Germany and especially on the Lower Rhine. He is of Provençal origin (Frings–Kuhnt, *Rother*, 189; see also Flutre, 91), and is frequently invoked in the *Chanson de Roland* (Langlois, 278).

## GIPPITO, see JUPITER

## GÎSELHÊR
In **N**, Gîselhêr, the younger brother ('der junge', 'daz kint') of Gunther and Gêrnôt, takes no part in the murder of their brother-in-law, Sîfrit, and comforts their sister, Kriemhilt, after his death; nevertheless, he and Gêrnôt fetch Sîfrit's treasure from Nibelunge lant (see Gêrnôt (1), p. 50).

(**B** 2617), but Gibeche is known to have formerly kept a company of warriors at Worms (2616 ff.). The 15th-cent. modernization of **N**, **N(k)**, has Gibich, quite correctly, as Gunther's father (7, 2; 123, 1).

## GÎSELHÊR

When the Burgundians halt at Bechelâren (Pöchlarn) during their journey to Etzel's court, Gîselhêr is betrothed to Dietlint, Rüedegêr's daughter. On arrival in Etzelnburc he is the only one of her brothers whom Kriemhilt greets with a kiss. In the ensuing fight against Etzel's men the dead and wounded are thrown from the hall at Gîselhêr's suggestion. He and Wolfhart kill each other.

In the Kl he is also said to have killed Wolfwîn, Nîtgêr (2), and Gêrbart.

In B he aids his brother, Gunther, at Worms against the men of Etzel and Dietrich.

ref: **AHb** p. 7, 20; **B** 6208; **Kl** 232; **N** 4, 3; **N(T)** 1049, 1 (*Ghiseleer*)

In the 8th-cent. OE poem *Widsith*, Gīslhere (123) appears among Eormanrīc's '*innweorud*' (retinue), many lines from Gifica (19) and Gūðhere (66).

In Þs, Gisler (I. 322, 4) is the brother of Gunnarr and Gernoz. At Bakalar (MHG Bechelâren) Roðingeirr gives him his daughter in marriage, as well as Sigurðr's sword, Gramr; in the fight against Attila's men he kills Roðingeirr with it, and is himself wounded by Hildibrandr; he dies when his sister, Grimilldr, sticks a firebrand into his mouth.

Gíslar in the Faroese ballad *Høgna táttur* (*CCF* I. 22–31) probably derives from Þs, for the name is unknown in ON Eddic tradition.

pn: 9th-cent. German (Förstemann I. 653; II. i. 1060; Schlaug I. 95; II. 194); peasants bear this name in *Neidharts Lieder*, 144, 8; 59, 31c.

The name *Gislaharius* appears in the list of ancestors of the Burgundian King Gundobad in the *Lex Burgundionum* in 516 (see Burgonde, p. 17), and is found in place-names in South-East France and North Italy, areas of Burgundian, Gothic, and Langobardic settlement (Gamillscheg I. 60; II. 194); it occurs only in early OE records (Searle, 259; Binz, 204).

## GÎSELRANT (GEISELBRANT)

A giant killed by Ortwîn (5) (see Wîcram).

ref: **V(h)** 887, 4; **V(w)** 734, 4 (*Geiselbrant*)

## GLESTE

Eckehart's sword.

ref: **A** 380, 3

pn: based on MHG *gleste*, 'glow, glitter, gleam'.

## GLOCKENBÔZ

A giant killed by Îmîan (see Wîcram).

ref: **V(h)** 862, 7; **V(w)** 709, 1

pn: a phrase-name based on MHG *glocke*, 'bell', and *bôzen*, 'strike'.

## GÔDÎAN, see MACHOREL

pn: probably derives from such names as *Gaudisse, Gaudin*, etc., in OFr epic (Voretzsch, 330 f.; Heinzel, *Ostgotische Heldensage*, 88 f.); the name *Gaudon* appears in the prose *Oswald* (15th cent.) for a heathen king, whose daughter is won by the hero (ibid.).

## GOEDELE, see UOTE (2)

pn: a hypocoristic name based on the equivalent of Goth. *gōds*, OE *gōd*, OHG *guot*, 'excellent', cf. Gūden.

## GOLDELÎN von Walhen lande (Italy)

A retainer of Queen Virginâl: she writes a letter for Hildebrant to Dietrich, when the latter has been captured by Nîtgêr's giants at Mûter.

ref: **V(h)** 494, 11

pn: a byname for a woman (Socin, 142); the simplex *Golda* is recorded in Germany in the 11th cent. (Förstemann I. 664).

## GOLDEMÂR

A dwarf king: in **G** Dietrich sees a lady held captive by Goldemâr; in **AHb** we learn that she is Hertlîn, daughter of the King of Portugal, and that Dietrich wins her from Goldemâr and marries her.

ref: **AHb** p. 8, 5; **G** 6, 12

This dwarf king is referred to in *Reinfried von Braunschweig* (c. 1300), and a house-haunting spirit of this name is known (see W. Grimm, *DHS*, 195 f.).

## GOLDRÛN

Daughter of Liudegêr von Vrancrîche: attendant to Helche (see p. 66).

ref: **Kl** 2454 (C *Winelint*)

pn: 9th-cent. German (Förstemann I. 664; Müllenhoff, *ZE*, 315); 11th-cent. OE in *Domesday* (Feilitzen, 273).

## GOLTWART

Herbort claims to have killed him and his companion Sêwart.

ref: **B** 6491

## GOTELE (1) Etzel's man

'der marcman': in **DF** and **Rs** he aids Dietrich against Ermenrîch. In **B** he leads Etzel's army against the Poles and fights a champion from Nâvarre in the combats at Worms against Gunther's men. In **A**, too, he is among Dietrich's men.

ref: **A** 74, 2 (MS. *Bottel*); **B** 1223; **DF** 5149; **Rs** 44, 1

pn: 8th-cent. German (Förstemann I. 660).

## GOTELE (2) Wolfhart's incognito

Wolfhart assumes this name when captured at Worms by Stûtfuhs.

ref: **B** 8923

## GOTELINT

Wife of Rüedegêr: in **N** she gives Hagen the shield of Nuodunc when the Burgundians halt at Bechelâren (Pöchlarn). In the **Kl** she has dreams of ill omen before she hears the news of Rüedegêr's death: of his retinue covered with snow (death's pallor), and of her husband and herself entering a dark room (the grave). She is said to be Dietrich's niece (**N**, **B**), the daughter of Gêre (2) (**B**), the daughter of Gunther (**AHb**), and related to Dietlint, Biterolf's wife (**B**).

ref: **AHb** m p. 3, 12; **B** 980; **Kl** 2049;[1] **N** 1159, 3; **Rg(D)** 88, 1

In Þs the name Gudelinda is used for Roðingeirr's wife (II. 178, 6), and for the daughter of Drusian, who marries Þiðrekr (II. 60, 17).

pn: 8th-cent. German (Förstemann I. 662, 682 f.; Kromp I. 32). It occurs in the 13th cent. in *Neidharts Lieder*, 39, 20, and Wernher der Gartenære's *Meier Helmbrecht*, 117, for peasant-girls.

## GRAMABET
The heathen Beliân's gate-keeper.

ref: **Wd(D)** VI. 23, 1; **Wd(Gr)** 1082, 1

pn: the first component may show the WFr Romanized form of *\*Hraban-* (Kaufmann, 152), but an appellative might be intended based on MHG *gram*, 'hostile, angry', and *abbet, abet*, 'abbot'.

## GRANDENGRÛS (PISRANDENGRUSZ)
Son of the giant Wîcram: killed by Dietrich at Mûter.

ref: **V(h)** 385, 7; **V(w)** 571, 7 (*Pisrandengruß*)

pn: possibly derives from the name of a heathen giant *Grandin* in OFr epic (Langlois, 297), the last component representing MHG *grûs*, 'horror, terror'.

## GRÎME (GRÎNE)
In **E(L)**, Ebenrôt tells how Dietrich has killed the giant pair, Grîme and Hilte (see Hilde (3)), and taken a byrnie from them; he states that Dietrich has killed the giant while he slept, but Vâsolt denies this.[2]

In **E(d)**, Dietrich is known to have taken the helmet Hildegrîn from Grîme and Hilte.

In **äSn** and **jSn** the giant Sigenôt occupies the cave of Grîme and Hilte; he attacks Dietrich because he is wearing his uncle Grîme's helmet (see Hildegrîn, p. 78) and throws him into a snake-pit. Dietrich escapes by means of Grîme's ladder after Hildebrant has killed Sigenôt.

ref: **E(d)** 5, 3 (Greymen, Greimen, etc.); **E(L)** 7, 3 (MS. *grinen*); **E(s)** 3, 3 (*Greymen*); **äSn** 3, 5 (6, 11 MS. *grinen*); **jSn** 7, 5 (prints *greimen*, etc.).

---

[1] Edzardi in his edition reads 'Dietlint' here; Bartsch's reading, 'Gotelint', is preferable.

[2] In **äSn** Dietrich has killed Grîme, whereas Hildebrant has killed Hilde; in **jSn** Hilde has been killed by Dietrich, too.

In Þs, the dwarf Alfrikr (see Alberîch, p. 4) gives Þiðrekr the sword Naglringr, which he has stolen from Hildur and Grímur, and with which the giant pair can be defeated; he then leads Þiðrekr and Hildibrandr to their cave. Þiðrekr kills them, and he and Hildibrandr seize their treasure, which includes Hildigrímur, the helmet subsequently worn by Þiðrekr.

pn: 8th-cent. WFr, 11th-cent. German (Förstemann I. 670), 10th-cent. OE (Searle, 268); the pn is probably based on the equivalent of OE *grima*, 'mask, helmet', ON *gríma*, 'cowl, hood', cf. OHG *grînan*, 'grimace'.

## GRIMME
A giant: he leaps and throws a stone to divert the onlookers[3] when he accompanies Rother in Constantinople (see Asprîân, p. 7). Rother grants him Scotland in lien.

ref: **R** 1657

This giant is referred to in *Reinfried von Braunschweig* (c. 1300) (cit. W. Grimm, *DHS*, 195).

pn: probably an appellative based on MHG *grim(me)*, 'grim, fierce'.

## GRÎNE, see GRÎME

## GRIPPÎÂN, *kûnec ze den wilden Riuzen* (King of the savage Russians) Father of Beliân.

ref: **Wd(B)** 266, 31; **Wd(C)** II. 10, 4; **Wd(Gr)** 343, 3; **Wd(w)** 333, 3 (*Cyprian*)

pn: possibly based on the legendary griffon's name (Lat. *grȳphus*), which appears in names as Gmc *\*grip-*; short forms such as *Grippo* are found in WFr (see Kaufmann, 155).

## GÚDEN, see UOTE (2)
pn: see Goedele.

## GUDENGART, see BIRKHILT

## GUNTHER (1) King at Worms
In **W**, the son of Gibicho, the King of Francia. Greedy for the treasure carried by Waltharius and Hiltgunt on their flight from the land of Attila, he sets out with twelve men to attack them; however, his leading vassal Hagano refuses to fight against his former comrade Waltharius (see Hagen (1), pp. 57 f.). Guntharius rejects Waltharius's offer of a hundred gold arm-rings and demands the entire treasure;[4] he sends his men one by one against Waltharius, who kills eleven of them; he then takes flight, but the next day he and

---

[3] **DH** Witolt diverts the crowd by juggling with his iron rod (see p. 147).

[4] See OE *Waldere* below, p. 54.

# GUNTHER (1)

Hagano attack Waltharius from ambush; in this fight Guntharius loses a leg (see Walther, pp. 135, 136 and n. 8).

In **N**, Gunther, son of Dancrât and Uote, rules at Worms 'in Burgonden' with his brothers, Gêrnôt and Gîselhêr. Sîfrit, in order to win the hand of Gunther's sister, Kriemhilt, takes service at his court, in the course of which he defeats the Saxons and Danes, and then accompanies Gunther as his vassal[1] on his bridal quest for Brünhilt: in Iceland, Sîfrit, using the cloak of invisibility (MHG *tarnhût*), represents Gunther and defeats Brünhilt in athletic contests, so that she reluctantly agrees to become Gunther's queen. On her wedding night she refuses to submit to Gunther until she knows why Gunther's sister has married a subject, Sîfrit (620 ff.), and binds him in her girdle, with which she hangs him on the wall by a nail till morning; at Gunther's request Sîfrit, once more invisible, subdues her the next night, but he also takes a ring and girdle from her, which he gives to his wife Kriemhilt. Later the two queens quarrel, and Kriemhilt accuses Brünhilt of unchastity with Sîfrit, producing the ring and girdle as evidence (see Brünhilt, p. 15, and Kriemhilt, pp. 18 f.). Gunther takes no action against Sîfrit, but Hagen persuades him that Sîfrit must die for the humiliation of Brünhilt. Gunther connives at the plot against Sîfrit's life and takes no action against his murderer, Hagen. A reconciliation between Kriemhilt, Sîfrit's widow, and Gunther is brought about by her younger brothers, Gêrnôt and Gîselhêr, but Gunther connives at the seizure of Sîfrit's treasure and its sinking in the Rhine, which Hagen arranges.

Against the advice of Hagen, Gunther agrees to Kriemhilt's marriage to Etzel; in spite of the opposition of Hagen and Rûmolt,[2] and the warning dream of Uote, he accepts Etzel's invitation to Hiunenlant. Hagen assumes command of the Burgundian forces on the journey, during which they are entertained by Gunther's uncle, Bishop Pilgerîn, at Passau, and by Rüedegêr at Pöchlarn (MHG Bechelâren), where the latter gives Gunther a suit of armour. When the conflict with the Huns breaks out in Etzel's hall, Gunther fights valiantly; he and Hagen are the last Burgundians left alive, but they refuse to surrender. Dietrich binds them and hands them over to Kriemhilt, who has Gunther beheaded, and executes Hagen herself when, after seeing Gunther's severed head, he refuses to divulge the hiding-place of the treasure (see Kriemhilt, p. 19).

In the **Kl**, Gunther's headless body is found among the slain; in the fighting he is said to have killed Sigehêr, Wîchart, and Wîcnant.[3]

In **Rg(A)**, Gunther, son of Gibeche, is[4] defeated by Amelolt in the combats in the rose-garden at Worms (in **Rg(D)** by Fruote); in **Rg(F)** he fights a drawn combat with Nuodunc. His device is three peacocks on a brown field (**Rg(F)** IV. 20, 1 f.).

In **B**, Gunther urges Gêrnôt and Hagen to attack Dietleip for his splendid equipment, but all three are wounded by the young hero,[5] who later enlists the help of Etzel and Dietrich to exact vengeance: in the ensuing combats at Worms Gunther fights Dietleip twice; finally, he makes peace when Rüedegêr brings the enemy banner to the city gate. Gunther's device is a silver boar (9846).

In **DF** Gunther supports Ermenrîch against Dietrich, but his men are put to flight at Bôlonje (Bologna); he fights Îmîân at Rabene (Ravenna) in **Rs**.

ref: **AHb** p. 3, 11; **B** m 2704 n 2833; **DF** 8653; **Kl** 143; **N** 4, 2; **N(T)** 944, 1 (*Guntheer*); **Rg(A)** 6, 4; **Rg(C)** 26; **Rg(D)** 27, 3; **Rg(F)** IV. 18, 1; **Rg(P)** 63; **Rs** 488, 3; **gS** 97, 11 (*Ehrenbertus*); **hS** 173, 7; **hS(Sachs)** 1003; **Vhw** m 1 n 10 (*Gontier*); **W** 16 (Guntharius); **WuH** (Wien) 1. 16, 1

Wolfram von Eschenbach in the early 13th cent. refers to the advice of Rûmolt to Gunther (see Rûmolt, p. 112); other German literary references outside the heroic epics also depend on **N** and are rare (W. Grimm, *DHS*, 227, 318, 344).

In the OE poem *Widsith* the narrator states that Gūðhere had given him a ring when he visited the Burgendas (65 f.); in *Waldere* Gūðhere (1. 25) is boastful and has refused the sword, treasure, and rings offered him by Waldere, with whom he unjustly seeks conflict; he is termed 'wine Burgenda' (11. 14); in the *Finnsburg* fragment the pn Gūðere [*sic*] is borne by a Frisian warrior (18), who attempts in vain to restrain the youthful Gārulf from attacking Sigeferð, the defender of the entrance to a hall.[6]

In ON Eddic tradition Gunnarr, son of Gjúki (Grp 34, 1; Br 11, 5; Gðr I 21, 5; Gðr II 7, 1; Gðr III 8, 1; Sg 7, 4; Dr prose, p. 223; Od prose, p. 234; 12, 3; Akv 1, 2; Am 6, 6; Ghv 3, 2; Hm 7, 8; Hdl 22, 1; Skr 84; tion of the Burgundians' (ON Akv) he is fettered at once (see below, p. 55). In **AHb** Gunther is said to have killed Hildebrant in a conflict at Berne (**AHb** p. 11, 14 f.) subsequent to the fight against the Huns.

---

[1] At Brünhilt's castle of Îsenstein Sîfrit leads Gunther's horse ashore and holds the stirrup for him to mount (**N** 385 ff., 396 ff.). See Panzer, *Nibelungenlied*, 332, regarding a possible historical parallel.

[2] In **Vhw** Gontier's only wish, could he live for ever, is to enjoy hunting, women, eating, drinking, and dancing, which recalls Rûmolt's advice in **N** 1465 ff. (see p. 112).

[3] In **N** no names of opponents slain by him are given; in the archaic version of the 'Destruc-

[4] The traditional father of Gunther (see Gibeche (1), p. 51).

[5] These motifs stem from the 'Walthersage' (see **W** above).

[6] Similar episodes occur in **W** and **N** (see p. 151 and n. 8).

Sk ch. 28; Völss ch. 25), has two brothers, Högni[1] and Gutþormr,[2] and a sister, Guðrún. Gunnarr and his people are usually termed 'Gjúkungar' (see Gibeche (1), p. 51). Once Gunnarr is termed 'vin Borgunda' (Akv 18, 3) (see Burgonde, p. 17).

Gunnarr and Högni swear oaths of brotherhood with Sigurðr, the husband of their sister Guðrún. Sigurðr changes shapes with Gunnarr and passes through the wall of flame (ON *vafrlogi*) to win Brynhildr for him. Later she quarrels with Guðrún and learns of the deception (see Brünhilt, p. 15, and Kriemhilt, pp. 19 f.); Gunnarr, wrongly imagining Sigurðr has broken his oath and seduced Brynhildr, decides that he must die. Högni refuses to break his oaths to Sigurðr, so they arrange for Gutþormr to kill him (see Gêrnôt, p. 50); Högni and Gunnarr take Sigurðr's land and the gold he won from the dragon Fáfnir.[3]

Atli, who has married Sigurðr's widow, Guðrún, invites Gunnarr to Húnaland; despite warnings (see pp. 20, 41, 59 n. 3, 132 f.), Gunnarr decides that they must make the journey. Atli's men seize and bind them on arrival.[4] Gunnarr refuses to reveal the hiding-place of the Niflungar treasure; when he is shown the heart of Högni he knows the secret is safe for ever.[5] Atli then has him thrown into a snake-pit (ON *ormgarðr*),[6] where he plays the harp with his toes until a snake kills him.[7]

In later Eddic tradition Gunnarr is thought to have sought the love of Oddrún, Atli's sister (see Ortrûn, p. 102).

In Þs, Gunnarr (I. 322, 3), son of Aldrian and Oda, is King of Niflungaland; he has two brothers, Gernoz and Gisler, a half-brother Högni (see p. 59), and a sister, Grimilldr, who marries Sigurðr. Gunnarr takes part in Þiðrekr's expedition to Bertangaland, where he is defeated and bound by the eleventh son of Isungr (see Dietrich (1), p. 29).[8]

At Sigurðr's suggestion Gunnarr weds Brynilldr, but, after she has hung him from a nail by her girdle on the wedding night (see N above), he persuades Sigurðr to exchange clothing and represent him in the bridal chamber; Sigurðr deflowers her and exchanges rings with her. Later, when the two queens quarrel, Sigurðr's wife Grimilldr sees his ring on Brynilldr's finger and accuses her of unchastity with Sigurðr; Brynilldr demands vengeance on Sigurðr for dishonouring her and Gunnarr by his talk. Högni murders Sigurðr on a hunt, and the brothers rejoice at his death.

Grimilldr then weds Attila and urges him to invite her brothers to Húnaland; in spite of the warning dreams of his mother Oda (see Uote (1), pp. 132 f.), Gunnarr accepts the invitation: en route at Bakalar (MHG Bechelâren) Roðingeirr gives Gunnarr a golden helmet. In the fight with Attila's men at Susat, Gunnarr is captured by Osið and cast by Grimilldr to his death in a snake-pit,[9] but Högni survives the combat long enough to beget an avenger (see Hagen (1), p. 60).[10]

pn: recorded in Late Antiquity for the Burgundian King *Gundaharius* (†437) (Schönfeld, 118); 8th-cent. German (Förstemann I. 702, 709; II. ii. 1133 ff.; Socin, 19; Schlaug I. 98; II. 103; Kromp I. 22; III. 35 ff.); Lb after the Frankish conquest in 8th cent. (Bruckner, 23; Ploß, 58), but not OE (Binz, 203; Searle, 273, gives two, probably continental, moniers).

First component \**Gunð*- (OHG *gund-*, OE *gûð*, 'war, conflict'), frequent among the Burgundians and Vandals, occurs also in pn of Gothic and Frankish rulers (Förstemann I. 693 f.; Schönfeld, 118 f.).

The Burgundian King, Gundaharius, together with his entire family and 20,000 of his people, is reported to have perished in 437 in a battle against a force of Huns in the employ of Aetius, the Roman Governor of Gaul (see Hiunen, p. 80). However, Gundobad, King of the new Burgundian realm in southern Gaul, claimed Gundaharius as an ancestor in his *Lex Burgundionum*, issued in 516 (see Burgonde, p. 17).

In the 8th cent. Paulus Diaconus (ch. xiv. 5) makes Attila responsible for the destruction of the Burgundians, led by Gundicarius, who marched eastward to his death.[11]

---

[1] Cf. the Faroese ballads, *Brynhildur táttur* and *Høgna táttur* (*CCF* I. 8 ff., 22 ff.), in which Högni is Gunnarr's brother.

[2] Gutþormr is a stepbrother in Sk, a half-brother in Hdl.

[3] After Sigurðr's death Brynhildr commits suicide; in Am and Dr Gunnarr has another wife named Glaumvor.

[4] In Akv only Gunnarr and Högni go; in the later Am the number is increased.

[5] The positions are reversed in N 2366–73, where Hagen dies after seeing Gunther's severed head and declaring the treasure safe till doomsday.

[6] In the 12th cent. a Scandinavian bishop identified the snake-pit near Luna in Italy (W. Grimm, *DHS*, 46).

[7] The scene of Gunnarr in the snake-pit is depicted on the carved Oseberg cart (*c.* 850), on a Götland stone (8th cent.), on the Överhogdal tapestry (12th cent.); Gunnarr is shown playing the harp with his feet on the carved church door of Hylestad (12th cent.), which also shows scenes from Sigurðr's youth (see Hauck, *Bilder-Edda*, 52; *Bilderdenkmäler*, 367; von See, *GHS*, 127 f.; Sven B. F. Jansson, 'A Newly Discovered Runic Stone from Västerljung, Södermanland', *Nordica et Anglica: Studies in Honor of Stefán Einarsson* (The Hague and Paris, 1968), 115–20).

[8] In the Danish ballad *Diderik i Birtingsland* (*DgF* I. 124 ff.), Gynter is one of Diderik's companions.

[9] A 'Schlangenturm' existed in Soest till the 18th cent. (Raßmann, *DHS* I. 11 n. 1).

[10] In the Danish ballad *Grimilds Hævn* (*Dg* FI. 44–50), which depends on Þs to a large extent, Gynter accompanies Hagenn on the fatal visit to their sister.

[11] In the 6th cent. Jordanes (ch. xxxvi) maintains that the Burgundians fought alongside

GUNTHER (1)

The impressive figure of the historical Gundaharius (as reflected in the ON Akv)[1] may well have been gradually modified by traditions about the Frankish King, Gunthram (†592),[2] who was succeeded as ruler of Burgundy by Brunihildis, his brother Sigebert's widow, until her death in 613: the contrast of the weak royal figure of Gunther (ON lays on Sigurðr's death, and MHG **N**) with the resolute major-domo figure of Hagen/Högni and the ruthless female characters, Brünhilt/Brynhildr and Kriemhilt/Guðrún, suggests a later context of Merovingian family intrigue.

GUNTHER (2) son of Sîfrit and Kriemhilt (LÖWHARDUS)
In **N**, after Sîfrit's murder, Kriemhilt allows her father-in-law Sigemunt to take the boy to Xanten.
In **gS** the adventures of Siegfried's son, Löwhardus, are referred to: he fights the Sultan of Babylon and weds a Sicilian princess.[3]

ref: **N** 716, 2; **gS** p. 97, 20 (*Löwhardus*)

In ON Eddic tradition Sigurðr's son is named Sigmundr (Gðr II 28, 7; Sk ch. 48); after Sigurðr's murder Gunnarr and Högni kill him (Sk ch. 49; Völss ch. 26).

GUT, see UOTE (2)
pn: see Goedele.

# H

HÂCHE
Father of Eckehart (**B**, **Wd(D)**) and son of Berhtunc von Mêrân (**Wd(B)**, **AHb**); in **B** one of the Harlunge in Etzel's forces; in **A**, Dietrich's man; in **V(h)** he is one of the Wülfinge who aids Dietrich at Mûter.
In **Wd(D)** he defeats Bouge and Wahsmuot, Wolfdietrich's hostile brothers, and later he aids Wolfdietrich at Tischcâl.

ref: **A** 73, 1; **AHb** p. 6, 5; **B** 5229; **V(h)** 619, 1; **Wd(B)** 294, 3; **Wd(D)** VII. 23, 1; **Wd(Gr)** 506, 4

In the OE poem *Widsith* the pn Hēhca (MS. *heðcan*) appears in the same line as Herelingas (112) at the head of Eormanrīc's company (OE *innwearud*).[4]

In Þs, Áki, an equivalent name,[5] is used for (1) Áki, Aurlungatrausti (I. 30, 20), father of Egarð and Áki (see Harlunge, p. 63) and half-brother of Þiðrekr and Erminrikr: he kills the lover of his unfaithful wife, Bolfriana, who marries Viðga after his death; Fritila is the foster-father of Áki's sons (see Frítele, p. 47); (2) the son of Áki (II. 157, 3).

pn: 8th-cent. German, *Hacho*, *Haccho* (Förstemann I. 720),[6] OE *Domesday*, *Haca*, *Hacco* (Feilitzen, 281).
The name may be based on a stem \**Hāha*- (Gmc. \**hanhan*, OHG *hâhan*, 'hang'), appropriate, perhaps, to one connected with the Harlunge (see Kaufmann, 163).

HADAWARDUS
A warrior of Guntharius killed by Waltharius.

ref: **W** 782

pn: 9th-cent. German (Förstemann I. 797; Schlaug I. 101).

Wilhelm Grimm equates the pair Hadawardus and Ekivrid of **W** with Hâwart and Irnfrit of **N** (W. Grimm, *DHS*, 129 n.).

(HADEBRANT) (1) = OHG HADUBRANT, MHG ALEBRANT: son of Hildebrant (1)

Aetius against the Huns at the battle of Châlons in 451 (see Etzel, p. 42). Although the historical Gundaharius was killed in battle, most poetic tradition tells of his capture and torture by Attila to obtain the Burgundian treasure; episodes in Vandal history have sometimes been adduced to account for the details of the end of Gunther/Gunnar: King Gundaric was captured and crucified by the Romans in 427, and the last Vandal king, Gelimer, besieged on a mountain in North Africa by Byzantine troops in 534, asked his opponents for a harp with which to sing a lay about his own sad fate (Procopius, *Vand.* I. 3; II. 6–7).

[1] In the ON *Njálssaga* (ed. E. Ó. Sveinsson (Reykjavík, 1954)), composed c. 1280, Gunnarr is the name of an honourable man who faces death resolutely (ch. 77); his avenger is named Högni (ch. 78).

[2] See Brünhilt, p. 16, and Sîfrit, p. 122.
[3] A 'Volksbuch' entitled *Ritter Löwhardus*, describing his adventures, appeared shortly after 1657 (see H. Jantz, 'The Last Branch of the Nibelungen Tree', *MLN* LXXX (1965), 433–40).
[4] Malone, *Widsith*, 161, takes the name to represent that of the father of Ermanaric, *Achiulf* (<\**Hāhiwulf*), of which it would be a hypocoristic form.
[5] This pn is an accommodation, but is not cognate with MHG *Hâche*. The 12th-cent. LG pn *Aki* is possibly of ON origin (Schlaug II. 171).
[6] In the year 807 *Hecho* is a witness to a gift in Breisgau by a man whose daughter is named *Swanahilt* (Wartmann I. 186): this is, however, uncertain evidence for a knowledge of the 'Ermanarichsage'.

(HADEBRANT) (1)

In **äH** he and his father meet as champions between two armies, and, although his father realizes the relationship, they fight (see Hildebrant (1), p. 74).

In **jH** father and son fight when Hildebrant returns to Berne (Verona): the father defeats the son, but they are reconciled[1] and go together to Hildebrant's wife, Uote (2) (see p. 133).

ref: **äH** 3 (MS. *haðubrant*; *hadubrant* 17, *hadubraht* 14 and 36); **jH** 2, 3 (Alebrant)

The fragments of verse, the so-called 'Lost Lay of Hildebrand', in ch. 8 of the 14th-cent. ON *Ásmundar saga kappabana* (*FAS* I. 399 ff.), indicates that the father kills the son in the earliest version of the lay (see Hildebrant (1), p. 76).

In Þs, as in **jH**, Hildibrandr and his son, Alibrandr (II. 329, 22), are reconciled after their fight. Later Alibrandr kills the usurper, Sifka (see Sibeche, p. 117). On his deathbed Hildibrandr leaves his weapons to his son for the protection of Þiðrekr. The name Alibrandr is also used for the son of Otnið (I. 69, 26).

pn: 8th-cent. German (Förstemann I. 793; II. i. 1294; Schlaug II. 103) and OE (Searle, 287, 559). At Fulda, where the MS. of **äH** was written down *c*. 810–20, until 826 *-braht* spellings for this name preponderate in the records (Baesecke, *Hildebrandlied*, 45 f.). The components *Hadu-* and *-brant* are common in Lb personal names (ibid.). *Höðbrandr* in a genealogy of the 14th-cent. *Flateyjarbók* is the ON equivalent.[2]

See Alebrant (1) regarding the MHG nameform.

HADEBRANT (2) von Stîrmarke (Styria)
Aids Dietleip against Gunther's men at Worms.

ref: **B** 8783

HADEBURC
Hagen, seeking a crossing over the Danube, comes upon two sibyls (MHG *wîsiu wîp*) floating like birds on the water of a stream (**N** 1533 ff.) and seizes their garments. Hadeburc, addressing Hagen by name, prophesies that the Burgundians' journey to the Huns will be full of honour, but, after he has returned them their garments ('wunderlîch gewant', possibly feathered garments?),

HAGEN(E) (1)

her sister, Sigelint, adds that not one of those who make the journey will return home; she also states that only the king's chaplain will survive: this last prophecy is fulfilled later, when Hagen casts the chaplain overboard and he gains the home shore of the Danube without drowning (1574 ff.).

ref: **N** 1535, 1; **N(k)** 1561, 1 (*Heidburg*)

In Þs, II. 285 f., Högni cuts the two waternymphs—here mother and daughter—in half when he learns that the Niflungar will never return from Húnaland. The same episode is related in the Danish ballad *Grimilds Hævn* (*DgF* I. 44–50).

pn: 9th-cent. German (Förstemann I. 794; Schlaug I. 100; II. 1030); recorded in OE (Searle, 287).

Such prophetic water-nymphs are not uncommon in Germanic tradition (see Panzer, *Nibelungenlied*, 385 f.), and supernatural beings who marry mortals or prophesy in return for their garments are frequently found in fairytale (see *Der Trommler*, *KHM* no. 193; Bolte–Polívka III. 412 ff.; cf. Wielant, pp. 141 f.).

HADEMÂR von Diezen (Dießen)
Usurps Rother's throne, but his rebellion is put down (see Wolfrât (1), p. 152).

ref: **R** 2942

This episode may reflect a feud between members of the Bavarian nobility in the 12th cent. The counts of Andechs, whose possessions included Dießen, acquired the dukedom of Meran (Dalmatia) in 1178 in succession to the counts of Dachau (W. Grimm, *DHS*, 60; Panzer, *Italische Normannen*, 61 f.; de Boor, *GDL* I. 254).

pn: 1st-cent. leader of the Chatti, 8th-cent. German (Förstemann I. 795 f.; Schlaug I. 100); recorded in OE (Searle, 287).

HADUBRANT, see HADEBRANT (1)

HAGATHIO
The father of Hagano (see Aldrîan, p. 9).

ref: **W** 629[3]

pn: WFr, recorded in 755 and 860 (Förstemann I. 718).

HAGEN(E) (1) von Tronege[4]
In **W**, Hagano refuses to aid Guntharius,

---

[1] Der Marner (13th cent.) in the Kolmar MS. refers to 'des jungen Albrandes tôt', which Wilhelm Grimm emends to 'des jungen Alphartes tôt' (W. Grimm, *DHS*, 466).
[2] Here Hildir, son of Hálfdan, has a son named Höðbrandr, the father of Hildir and Herbrandr; the first Hildir possibly represents Hildibrandr (see *CPB* II. 519).
[3] See E. Schröder, *DNK*, 365 f., regarding the form of this pn in **W**.
[4] 'von Tronege Hagene' (**N** 9, 1, etc.): Hagen's seat has been localized most plausibly at Kirchheim in Alsace, formerly Nova Troja (see Hempel, *Nibelungenstudien*, 21 f.); other local-

izations suggested are Xanten (see Sîfrit, p. 118 n. 2), Tournay (Flemish Doornik), Troneck in the Hunsrück, and Tongres in Belgium (see Gerd Backenköhler, *Untersuchungen zur Gestalt Hagens von Tronje in den mittelalterlichen Nibelungendichtungen* (Bonn, 1961), 188). In **W**, Hagano is referred to as of Trojan origin, 'veniens de germine Troiae' (28), which tallies with the fictitious Trojan origin of the Franks; 'Högni af Troia' of Þs II. 322, 10 may well depend on **W**; in **AHb**, too, he is termed 'Hagen von Troy' (p. 2, 35), and in a 15th-cent. document of the bishop's court at Xanten 'Haegen van Troien' (W. Grimm, *DHS*, 322; Müllenhoff, *ZE*, 427).

King of Francia, against Waltharius, his former formidable fellow-hostage at Attila's court (see Etzel, p. 40)[1]; he reinforces his warning by recounting his dream, in which a bear bites off Guntharius's leg and bites out his own (Hagano's) eye.[2] After Waltharius has killed eleven of Guntharius's men, including Hagano's nephew Patavrid, Hagano agrees to join Guntharius in an attack on him from ambush: in this fight Hagano loses his right eye and six teeth, but he cuts off Waltharius's right arm (see Walther, p. 135).

In **N**, Hagen is the vassal and relative of the Burgundian kings, Gunther, Gêrnôt, and Gîselhêr;[3] he is knowledgeable (86 ff.) and of awesome appearance (413, 1734).[4] After Kriemhilt, Sîfrit's wife, has publicly humiliated her brother Gunther's wife, Brünhilt, Hagen plots Sîfrit's death: by pretending a desire to protect Sîfrit in a fictitious war, he learns from Kriemhilt the secret of Sîfrit's vulnerability between the shoulder-blades; he then hurls Sîfrit's own spear through this spot, while Sîfrit is drinking in a stream after hunting.[5] He has Sîfrit's corpse placed outside Kriemhilt's door, but she knows that Hagen has committed the murder, and not robbers as has been given out; later the dead man's wounds bleed when Hagen passes before the bier (1044), a further proof of his guilt (see p. 119). Hagen then has Sîfrit's treasure seized and sunk in the Rhine.

Hagen opposes Kriemhilt's marriage to Etzel, and is at first against acceptance of Etzel's invitation to the Burgundian kings; however, he takes command of the thousand men accompanying the royal brothers on their journey to Hiunenlant (see Nibelunge, p. 97). While seeking a crossing over the Danube he encounters two water-nymphs, who prophesy that, apart from Gunther's chaplain, none of the company will return (see Hadeburc, p. 57). Hagen kills a ferryman and ferries the Burgundians across the river in his boat—an oar breaks and he repairs it with his shield-strap.[6] Then he tests the water-nymphs' prophecy by throwing the chaplain overboard: since the priest reaches the home shore, Hagen destroys the boat and informs the Burgundians of their fate. That night he and his brother Dancwart beat off the attack of the ferryman's lords (see Else (1), pp. 35 f., and Gelpfrât, p. 49). At the frontier Eckewart gives a further warning. At Bechelâren (Pöchlarn) Gotelint, Rüedegêr's wife, gives Hagen the shield of her dead nephew Nuodunc.[7] At Etzelnburc he is once more warned against Kriemhilt's hostility by Dietrich. Kriemhilt demands the treasure, but Hagen tells her it is sunk in the Rhine; he openly flaunts Sîfrit's sword Balmunc before her and admits to the murder of Sîfrit. That night he and Volkêr protect the sleeping Burgundians against a Hunnish attack instigated by Kriemhilt. During a feast Dancwart brings the news of the slaughter of the Burgundian squires (see Blœdel, p. 13), at which Hagen immediately beheads Ortliep, the son of Kriemhilt and Etzel,[8] and the boy's tutor, and cuts off the hand of Etzel's messenger, Wärbel.[9] In the ensuing conflict Hagen fights valiantly:[10] he kills Îrinc and Hâwart and puts Hildebrant to flight, but he is finally bound by Dietrich and handed over to Kriemhilt. She demands the treasure once more, but Hagen refuses to reveal its hiding-place while his lord yet lives: she has Gunther's severed head brought before him, but he then declares the treasure to be safely hidden from her for ever;[11] she beheads him with Balmunc.[12]

In the **Kl**, Hagen is held responsible for the whole conflict ('der vâlant der ez allez riet' 1394) and Kriemhilt is exonerated, since she has acted from loyalty to Sîfrit and desired vengeance on Hagen alone (303 ff.).[13]

---

[1] In **W** he escapes from Hunnish captivity, but in **N** and **WuH** Etzel has apparently sent him home.
[2] Cf. the warning dreams of Högni's wife in ON Eddic tradition, Am and Völss (see p. 41 n. 4, and Uote (1), pp. 132 f.).
[3] In **AHb** and **hS** he is the brother of Gunther, which tallies with ON Eddic tradition (see below); in Þs he is a half-brother.
[4] In Þs, too, full descriptions of him are given: Högni is troll-like, ashen-pale, dark-haired, tall, strong, intelligent, and ruthless, with one piercing eye—the other he has lost in his encounter with Valtari (Þs I. 343 f.; II. 302).
[5] In two 15th-cent. MSS. of **N**, the scene is illustrated: correctly in the Vienna Piarist MS. k; in the Hundeshagen MS. b, Hagen is shown shooting an arrow (see p. 118 n. 4).
[6] In late ON Eddic tradition (Am and Völss) the Niflungar break the rowlocks when rowing across a fjord. In Þs, Högni kills the ferryman because the rowlocks break, whereas in the Danish ballad *Grimilds Hævn* (*DgF* I. 44–50), the Niflungar use a shield when the steering-oar breaks.
[7] In the conflict at Etzel's court it is hacked to pieces, and Hagen avoids fighting Rüedegêr by asking him to give him his shield (**N** 2194 ff.).
[8] In Þs and **AHb** Grimilldr/Kriemhilt incites her son to slap Högni/Hagen's face in order to provoke the conflict (see Ortliep, p. 100). Hagen's statement before beheading the child, 'nu trinken wir wîn und gelten's küneges wîn' (**N** 1960, 3), is recalled in Högni's words after beheading Attila's son Aldrian in Þs, 'i þessum apalldrs garðe dreckum gott vin. oc þat uerðum ver dyrt at kaupa' (Þs II. 309, 6 f.).
[9] In late ON Eddic tradition (Am and Völss), the Niflungar kill Vingi, Atli's messenger, on arrival.
[10] He urges the Burgundians to quench their thirst in blood (also in the Danish ballad, *Grimilds Hævn*), and to protect themselves with their shields against falling timber when Kriemhilt has the hall set on fire (in ON Guðrún burns the hall over Atli and the drunken Huns: see Kriemhilt, p. 20).
[11] The roles of Gunther and Hagen are reversed in **N**: cf. the archaic version of the ON Akv below.
[12] In **gS** (17th cent.) Siegfried's father brings about the death of Hagenwald (= Hagen) (see Sigemunt (1), p. 125).
[13] **N(C)** also emphasizes Hagen's guilt.

In **Rg(A)**, Hagen is among Kriemhilt's champions at the rose-garden; he is defeated by Eckehart; in **Rg(CDP)** by Wolfhart (an undecided combat in **Rg(F)**): his device is a pair of gold bison-horns (**Rg(D)** 290, 3).

In the wish-poem **Vhw**, Hagen desires the horse Scimminc (= Schemminc) and the sword Nimminc, and he also wants to take part in a tournament with a thousand men before a thousand ladies.

ref: **AHb** p. 2, 35; **B** 771; **DF** 2052; **Kl** 144 (B), 274; **N** 9, 1; **N(T)** 1040, 4; **Rg(A)** 7, 1; **Rg(C)** 27; **Rg(D)** 44, 3; **Rg(F)** 1. 3, 1; **Rg(P)** 65; **gS** m p. 66, 17 n p. 97, 11 (*Hagenwald*); **hS** 175, 1; **hS(Sachs)** 1003; **Vhw** m 1 n 9; **W** 27 (Hagano); **WuH** (Graz) VII. 2, (Wien) II. 19, 3

The occasional references to Hagen, occurring in German literary and historical works outside the heroic poems from the 14th cent. on, depend on **N** (W. Grimm, *DHS*, 226, 273, 307, 313, 316, 318, 320).

In the second fragment of OE *Waldere*, Hagena (II. 15) is with Gūðhere during the encounter with Waldere (see Walther, p. 136), but, although he possesses an excellent sword that is superior to Mimming (see Mimminc, p. 94), he keeps it in its scabbard.[1]

In ON Eddic tradition Högni (Grp 37, 3; Br 7, 1; Sg 14, 7; Dr prose, p. 223; Gðr II 7, 2; Gðr III 8, 2; Od 8, 4; Hm 6, 4; Ghv 3, 4; Akv 6, 2; Am 6, 2; Hdl 27, 1; Skr 84; Sk ch. 48; Völss ch. 25) is the son of Gjúki and the brother of Gunnarr: he and Gunnarr swear brotherhood with Sigurðr, the husband of their sister Guðrún. When Sigurðr's murder is planned, Högni refuses to kill him because of his oaths, and Gutþormr does the deed (see Gêrnôt, p. 50, and Gunther, p. 55).[2]

In Akv, Atli, Guðrún's second husband, invites Gunnarr and Högni to Húnaland. Högni interprets the wolf's hair Guðrún has twisted into a ring as a warning.[3] However, he accompanies Gunnarr to Atli's hall;[4] Atli's men attack them, and Atli demands the Niflungar treasure (see Nibelunge, p. 98 ):[5] Gunnarr is bound at once, but Högni kills seven and casts one into the fire before being overpowered.[6] Gunnarr demands to be shown Högni's heart before he will reveal the treasure's hiding-place, but he is not deceived by the trembling heart of Hjalli, the cook, when it is brought before him (in the Am Hjalli is spared); on seeing Högni's heart he declares that the Niflungar treasure is now safe in the Rhine for ever.[7]

In late Eddic tradition (Völss ch. 38; Sk ch. 50), Högni's son (by Guðrún in Am; named (H)niflungr in Am and Völss) helps Guðrún kill Atli (see Kriemhilt, p. 20 n. 6, and Nibelunge, p. 98).[8]

In Þs, Högni (I. 321, 2) is the son of Oda, wife of Aldrian, by a demon who has ravished her when she was asleep in a garden;[9] he is, therefore, the half-brother of Gunnarr, Gisler, Gernoz, and Grimilldr, but, like Gunnarr, he has an eagle depicted on his shield (see Gunther, p. 55).[10] He accompanies Þiðrekr to Bertangaland, where he is defeated by the eighth son of Isungr.[11] Later he serves Attila. Attila sends Högni with eleven men in pursuit of the fugitives, Valtari and Hilldigundr; Valtari kills eleven men and Högni flees, but he later makes a surprise attack on them at night; Valtari knocks out Högni's eye with a bone from the boar they are eating.[12] Later Högni rules at Verniza (Worms), and after Sigurðr's wife, Grimilldr, has accused Gunnarr's wife, Brynilldr, of unchastity with Sigurðr, he plots Sigurðr's death (see p. 55); for this purpose he arranges a hunt, in the course of which he kills a large boar; after quartering it the company drink at a stream, and Högni plunges a spear between Sigurðr's shoulder-blades while he is drinking. Sigurðr's corpse is brought to Grimilldr's

---

[1] It is possible to interpret the first speech of this fragment as belonging to Waldere and referring to his second sword (see Norman, *Waldere*, 15 ff., and Walther, p. 136). See Hagen (2), p. 62, regarding the sword, Dáinsleif, possessed by Högni in ON tradition.

[2] Only in Hm and Ghv, where Högni and his brothers are said to have wakened Sigurðr, is Högni apparently directly implicated in his murder; in Br and Gðr II he openly tells Guðrún of Sigurðr's death.

[3] In Am and Völss it is Högni's wife, Kostbera, who interprets the warning runes and wolf's hair sent by Guðrún; she also has ominous dreams (see pp. 41 n. 4, 132 f.). Högni rejects these warnings, as does Gunnarr those of his wife, Glaumvor.

[4] In Am and Völss Högni's sons, Snævarr and Sólarr, and his brother-in-law, Orkingr, go with them.

[5] In Völss, Atli intends to avenge Sigurðr's murder, a secondary motif, since his wife Guðrún sides with her first husband's murderers in what follows.

[6] In Am they kill 19 out of 30 Huns.

[7] The cutting out of Högni's heart is depicted in a late-12th-cent. carving from the church at Austad, Setesdal, in Norway.

[8] In Þs he is named Aldrian (Aldrias in the Faroese ballad *Høgna táttur* (*CCF* I. 22 ff.); in the Danish ballad *Grimilds Hævn* (*DgF* I. 44 ff.) and the *Hven. Chron.*, it is Hagenn's son Rancke, who kills Grimild (W. Grimm, *DHS*, 345).

[9] For this incubus motif see Alberîch, p. 3, Dietrich (1), p. 27 and n. 10, and Machmet, p. 91. Note Högni's troll-like appearance in Þs (see p. 58 n. 4): Þiðrekr calls him 'alfs son' (II. 324, 18).

[10] Cf. Kriemhilt's dream that two eagles kill her falcon in **N** (see p. 18).

[11] He is among Diderik's heroes in the Danish ballads to do with this expedition, *Kong Diderik og hans Kæmper* and *Kong Diderik i Birtingsland* (*DgF* I. 94 ff., 124 ff.).

[12] This recalls that after the fight in **W** Waltharius advises Hagano to avoid roast pork, since he has lost six teeth (**W** 1436) (see Walther, p. 135).

bed: she knows that Högni himself is the 'boar' which he alleges has killed Sigurðr.[1]

Högni approves of Grimilldr's marriage to Attlila, but prophesies disaster if Gunnarr accepts Attila's invitation to Húnaland: however, he takes a leading part on the journey. As in N, Högni receives warnings from two water-nymphs, whom he kills, and from Ekkivorðr (see Eckewart): the ferry-boat sinks at the Rhine crossing and the Niflungar are drenched when they reach the shore. Högni then tells Gunnarr that none of them will return. At Bakalar, Roðingeirr's wife, Gudelinda, gives Naudungr's shield to Högni (see Nuodunc, pp. 99 f.). Once more the Niflungar are soaked by a rain-storm.

On arrival at Susat, Grimilldr sees the armour underneath their clothing when the Niflungar are drying themselves at the fire and she realizes that they are prepared for fighting. She demands from Högni the treasure of Sigurðr: he replies that he has only brought his weapons. Grimilldr arranges for Irungr and his men to attack the squires of the Niflungar, but at a feast in an orchard she incites her son Aldrian to slap Högni's face, at which Högni beheads the boy and hurls the head at her breast (see N above); he also beheads the boy's tutor. When the general conflict starts, Grimilldr has fresh oxhides spread at the entrance to the orchard, so that many Niflungar fall and are killed.[2] After Gunnarr has been cast into a snake-pit, Högni sets fire to the town, so that the fight can be continued in the lighted streets; he finally surrenders rather than be roasted like a fish by Þiðrekr's fiery breath.[3] Before he dies of wounds he begets a son, Aldrian, to whom he bequeaths the keys of the treasure-house containing the treasure of Sigurðr (see pp. 98, 121); the boy locks Attila in the treasure-house to starve to death, and later he rules Niflungaland (see p. 42).[4]

In the Danish ballad *Sivard og Brynild* (*DgF* I. 16–23), Hagenn (Nielus in version C) weds Brynild, whom Sivard has won from a glass mountain: when she sees her own rings on the fingers of Sivard's wife, Seineld (see Kriemhilt, p. 20), she incites Hagenn to kill Sivard; he beheads Sivard with Sivard's own sword, Adelryng, and brings her the severed head, then cuts her to pieces and kills himself by falling on the sword (see Brünhilt, p. 16, and Sífrit (1), p. 121).[5] *Grimilds Hævn* (*DgF* I. 44–50) follows Þs, but Hagenn and Falquor (MHG Volkêr) are the leading heroes in the fight against their sister Kremold's men. After his father's death, Hagenn's son, Rancke, locks Kremold in a treasure-cave to starve. In the *Hven. Chron.* the story is localized on an island between Zealand and Scania, where Hogne, who has killed Sigfrid for seducing his wife, Gluna, lives: Gluna[6] warns him not to attend his sister Chremild's second wedding. Here, too, his death is avenged, as in *Grimilds Hævn*, by his son Rancke, but his son by Gluna rules Hven after his death.

In the Faroese ballad *Brynhildur táttur* (*CCF* I. 8–22), Högni and Grímur (ON Gunnarr, MHG Gunther) are known to have murdered Sigurðr; in *Høgna táttur* (ibid. 22–31) Högni takes a leading part in the journey to Artala (ON Atli, MHG Etzel); finally he kills Tíðrikur (MHG Dietrich), but he is himself killed by Tíðrikur's dragon-like venomous breath (see Þs above). His son Aldrias kills Artala.

pn: Many of the records for this pn must derive from short forms of compound names with the first component *Hagan-.[7] The one-stemmed name is recorded as follows: 7th-cent. WFr, 8th-cent. German (Förstemann I. 718 f.; Socin, 567, 572 f.; Schlaug II. 201; Müllenhoff, *ZE*, 295 ff.; Kromp I. 12 f.), 9th-cent. Lb (Ploß, 58); 7th-cent., but not beyond 8th-cent., OE (Binz, 192 f.; Sweet, 429 ff.; Searle, 277 f.; Feilitzen, 282, gives an 11th-cent. reference in *Domesday*, probably Norman). The OFr *Haguenon* occurs in the *ch.d.g.* for the associate of traitors (Langlois, 322 f.; Kalbow, 22; C. Voretzsch, 'Zur Geschichte der Nibelungensage in Frankreich', *ZfdA* LI (1909), 41).[8]

This one-stemmed name is most probably based on the Gmc. root *hag- with -n-extension to the stem (*DWb* IV. ii. 137; Kluge, *EWb*, 280), cf. OHG *hac*, OE *haga*, 'thorn-bush, hedge, enclosure, fence', and OHG *hagan*, OE *hagona*, 'thorn-hedge' (Kaufmann, 161 f.);[9] the name is semantically

---

[1] See p. 61 n. 1.
[2] This ruse is described in the Danish ballad *Grimilds Hævn* (C version) and in the *Hven. Chron.*
[3] The western town-gate of Susat (Soest in Westphalia), where Högni fell, is said to be named after him (Þs II. 328, 3), and the 'Höggenstraße' of Soest may indicate a localization of the Nibelungen story there (K. Bohnenberger, 'Nibelungenstätten', *PBB* XLII (1917), 535).
[4] In the Danish ballad *Grimilds Hævn*, as in *Hven. Chron.*, Rancke, Hagenn's son, treats Kremold thus; in the Faroese ballad *Høgna táttur*, Högni's son kills Artala, but in one version he locks Guðrún (MHG Kriemhilt) in a cave, which contains treasure (see H. de Boor, *Die färöischen Lieder des Nibelungenzyklus* (Heidelberg, 1918), 209 ff., regarding the role of Hagen's son in Þs and the Scandinavian ballads).
[5] Here the roles of Gunther and Hagen are combined.
[6] Here, too, the roles of Gunther and Hagen are combined; the name of Hogne's wife recalls that of Gunnarr's wife, Glaumvor, in Am.
[7] e.g. *Agenaricus* in the 4th cent. (Amm. Marc. XVI. xii. 5); names in *Chagn-, Chain-*, occur for Burgundian royalty c. 600 (Ploß, 54).
[8] The names *Haguenon* and *Fouchard* (= Volkêr?) are associated in the *ch.d.g. Gaydon* (Ploß, 56).
[9] In W *Waltharius* refers to Hagano as 'paliurus' (1351) and 'spinosus' (1421); in B a battlement (MHG *burgzinne*) is depicted on his banner (9819).

### HAGEN(E) (1)

suitable for the protector of a maiden: a 'Hagen' protects a 'Hild' in both N and Ku.[1]

Hagen/Högni is always involved in the plot against the life of Sîfrit/Sigurðr, but whether or not his original role was that of the daemonic slayer of a fertility god (see n. 1 below), it is only in the German account of 'Siegfried's Death' (and Þs) c. 1200 that he is the actual murderer; in the ON Eddic versions he refuses to kill Sigurðr because of his oaths, a scrupulosity he also shows towards Waltharius in W.

In ON Eddic tradition Högni is made the brother of Gunnarr (Þs makes him a daemonic half-brother), but in W and N Hagen is a close relative and powerful vassal.[2] This relationship to the Burgundian kings is probably secondary, for Hagen's name does not alliterate with theirs on G-. His ultimate origin may be sought in the 'Hildesage', in which the leading role-names alliterate on H-: Hagene (1) von Tronege and Hagene (2) von Îrlant are both guardians of a 'Hild' (see F. R. Schröder, 'Die Sage von Hetel und Hilde', DVjs XXXII (1958), 52 ff.).

In the ON Akv, the most archaic version of the 'Destruction of the Burgundians', Högni's role is subsidiary to that of Gunnarr, whereas in the Eddic lays concerning Sigurðr's death, Gunnarr's position, contrasted with Sigurðr's eminence, appears in an adverse light. Hagen rises above his discredited lord, Gunther, in W and N; in the latter epic, where the story of Sîfrit's murder (Part I) is joined to that of the destruction of the Burgundians (Part II), and Attila's greed for the gold of the Burgundians is replaced by Kriemhilt's desire to avenge the death of her husband, Sîfrit, the character of Gunther is discredited throughout: he must, therefore, play a subsidiary role in Part II as well as in Part I, whereas Hagen becomes the actual murderer and daemonic adversary of Sîfrit, assuming more importance than his lord: hence the reversal of roles in the final scene, i.e. Hagen is the last Burgundian to die in N, whereas in the Eddic poems it is Gunnarr (MHG Gunther).

### HAGEN(E) (2) father of Hilde (1)

In **Ku** the son of Sigebant von Îrlant and Uote (4): in childhood he is seized by a griffon and carried to an island, where he kills the griffons and rescues three princesses; he also kills a 'gabilûn' (chameleon?) and tames a lion. A pilgrim ship takes him and the princess to Ireland,[3] and he weds one of the princesses, Hilde (2) von Indîân. He becomes a harsh ruler ('Vâlant aller künige' 168, 2, etc.; 'der wilde Hagene' 124, 1, etc.), and keeps his daughter, Hilde, in strict seclusion (see pp. 72 f.). Hetel von Tenelant sends an expedition, led by Wate and Hôrant, to abduct her. Hagen pursues and overtakes them on the shore of Wâleis; he wounds Hetel but is stunned by Wate; Hilde brings about a reconciliation, and Hagen agrees to her marriage to Hetel.

In DH, 'der wilde Hagene' (F 45, 2, 1, etc.) is the father of Hilde von Krichenlant, whom he refuses to give in marriage. Etene (= Hetel) sends an expedition under Horant to win her.

ref: DH F 45, 2, 1; Ku 22, 4

The earliest reference to Hagen (2) in German literature occurs in Lamprecht's *Alexander* (mid 12th cent.), and indicates that Wate originally kills Hagen:

man saget von dem sturm der ûf
  Wolfenwerde gescah,[4]
dâ Hilten vater tôt gelach
zewisken Hagenen unde Waten:
sô ne mohter herzô nieth katen.
iedoch ne mohte nechain sîn,
noch Herewîch noch Wolfwîn,[5]
der ie gevaht volcwîch
dem chunige Alexander gelîch.

(1321–8 Vorau MS.)

In the OE poem *Widsith*, Hagena is mentioned in close proximity to Heoden and Wada (see Hetel and Wate):

Hagena (wēold) Holmrycgum,[6] Heoden
  Glommum.
Witta wēold Swǣfum, Wada Hælsingum.
(21 f.)

In ON Högni (Rdr 5, 1; Skr 88; Sk chs. 61 ff.; Hátt str. 49, 3) fights Heðinn, who has abducted his daughter, Hildr; each night Hildr raises the dead, so that their battle is

---

[1] Various interpretations of the name have been suggested: the equivalent of OHG *hagustalt*, 'unmarried man', with extended meaning of 'vassal' (E. Mueller, 'Deutung einiger Namen im Nibelungenlied', *Monatsheft* XXXI (1931), 281; Marion Sonnenfeld, 'An Etymological Explanation of the Hagen Figure', *Neophil.* XLI (1959), 301 ff.); a demon, cf. *hagupart*, 'mummer's mask' (Kögel I. ii. 208); an accommodation of the name of Aetius, the 5th-cent. Governor of Roman Gaul (Heinzel, *Nibelungensage*, 4 ff.), or of the title of the leader of the Alans, the 'Chagan', allied to Aetius (Schütte, *Gotthiod* II. 152 f.). In his interpretation of Hagen representing a 'boar' in his role as the slayer of the fertility god (Siegfried?), F. R. Schröder ('Sigfrids Tod', *GRM* XLI (1960), 121) relates the name to *Häckel*, a Swabian dialect word for 'boar' (see also Heinrich Beck, *Das Ebersignum im Germanischen* (Berlin, 1965), 172 ff., regarding Hagen as the boar in the murder of Sîfrit in the Nibelungen versions of N and Þs).

[2] It is probably fortuitous that he is made Gunther's brother in hS.

[3] The capital, Baljân (**Ku** 161, 2), possibly represents the Irish place-name Ballyghan.

[4] The Straßburg MS. has *wlpinwerde*. This is the Wülpensant of **Ku** 809, 4, etc., where a battle takes place in the abduction story of Kûdrûn (see Stackmann, *Kudrun*, liii, and Hegelinge, p. 64).

[5] Straßburg MS. *herwich vnde wolfram*.

[6] For the identification of this Baltic Rugian tribe, see Much, *Germania*, 388 f., and Malone, *Widsith*, 168.

## HAGEN(E) (2)

eternal (see Hegelinge, p. 64).[1] In Sk Högni draws his sword Dáinsleif,[2] which cannot be sheathed till it has tasted blood.

In Saxo's Danish history (Saxo v. vii. 8–ix. 1), Höginus fights Hithinus, after accusing him of seducing his daughter, Hilda; finally they kill each other.

In HHu II and Völss ch. 9, Högni is the name of the father of Sigrún, whom Helgi abducts.

The earliest reference to Hagen (OE Hagena, ON Högni) makes him a ruler on the Baltic (*Widsith*); ON tradition places him in Denmark (Saxo; *Sörla þáttr*) or South Norway (Sk). The Irish localization in **Ku** may be influenced by the somewhat similar tale of Isolde.

Hagen's role as the sinister guardian of a 'Hilde' suggests the possibility that he is ultimately identical with Hagen (1) von Tronege (see p. 61).

## HAGEN(E) (3) brother of Hildebrant (1)

ref: **Rg(F)** III. 18, 3

## HAGENWALD, see HAGEN(E) (1)

## HAIDANGERNOSZ
Eckenôt's horse.

ref: **E(d)** 308, 2 (MS. *Haid anger noß*)

## HARDENACKE, see ECKEHART

## HARLUNG
Son of Dietmâr and brother of Dietrich and Ermenrîch: father of the Harlunge.

ref: **AHb** p. 6, 35

The father of the Harlunge is given various names: Herlibo (12th-cent. *Genealogia Viperti*, W. Grimm, *DHS*, 55); Harelus (16th-cent. Beatus Rhenanus, Jänicke, *ZE*, 312); Diethêr (13th-cent. **DF**, and Heinrich von München, W. Grimm, *DHS*, 225); Áki (Ps: see Hâche). All agree that the father of the Harlunge is the brother of Ermanaric, apart from Saxo, who has Iarmericus killing his sister's sons (see Ermenrîch, p. 38).

pn: see Harlunge pl. below.

## HARLUNGE pl.
Nephews of Ermenrîch (sons of Diethêr in **DF**,[3] of Harlung in **AHb**): in **DF**, Ermenrîch has them killed and seizes their land and gold; Eckehart avenges them by killing Ermenrîch's evil counsellor, Ribestein. In **Rs**, Eckehart captures Sibeche with the intention of hanging him for his part in the death of the Harlunge. In **Rg(CDF)**, Eckehart is their guardian. In **B**, the Harlunge, who aid Dietleip against Gunther, are named Frîtele and Imbrecke; Wahsmuot carries their clover-green banner; Hâche, Eckehart, Regentage, Herdegen, and Rimstein are among their men.

In **AHb**, Eckart is said to have killed Ermentrich for hanging the Harlinge, whose father is Harlung, the son of Dietmar (p. 3, 22 ff.),[4] but later we learn that Sibich, whose wife Ermentrich has seduced, urges Ermentrich to seize the land and castle of Harlinge at Breisach while their guardian, Eckart, is absent. Ermentrich hangs them, and he and Sibich escape the wrath of Eckart in spite of the support given to Eckart by Dietrich (p. 8, 11 ff.).[5]

ref: **AHb** p. 3, 23 (*herlinge*, p. 8, 33 *harlingen*); **B** 4594; **DF** 2548; **Rg(C)** 666; **Rg(D)** 63, 2; **Rg(F)** III. 13, 2; **Rs** m 864, 5

The earliest German reference to the Harlunge, that of the *Ann. Quedl.* (c. 1000), states that Ermanricus hanged his nephews, Embrica and Fritla (*MGH ss* III. 31; W. Grimm, *DHS*, 35);[6] Eckehard von Aura in his *Ursperg Chronicle* (c. 1126) states that the people of Breisach are called 'Harelungi' (*MGH ss* VI. 185; W. Grimm, *DHS*, 42);[7] in the 12th-cent. *Genealogia Viperti*, a certain Herlibo von Brandenburg, an alleged ancestor of Wiprecht von Groitsch, is the brother of Emelricus (= Ermanaric?), whose sons, the Harlungi, are named Emelricus, Vridelo, and Herlibo (*MGH ss* XVI. 232; W. Grimm, *DHS*, 54 f.); a 'Harlungberg' is recorded in 1166 near Brandenburg an der Havel (W. Grimm, *DHS*, 457; see also Eckewart, p. 35).[8] Fischart in the 16th cent. associates Eckart with the 'Harlunger' (ibid. 352).

In the OE poem *Widsith* the names Herelingas (112), Emerca, and Fridla (113) appear among the '*innweorud*' of Eormanrîc.

According to Ordericus Vitalis (*Historia Ecclesiastica* VIII. 17, cit. Malone, *Studies*, against the 'köninck van Armentriken' (= Ermenrîch), who resides at 'Freysack' (= Breisach?), in **ED** is possibly undertaken to avenge the Harlunge, since 'Hardenacke' (= Eckehart?) accompanies it.

[6] The *Würzburg Chronicle* (early 11th cent.) follows this (*MGH ss* VI. 23). E. Schröder, 'Die Heldennamen in den Jahrbüchern von Quedlinburg', *ZfdA* XLI (1897), 24 ff., points out that the suffixes of these pn are Anglo-Frisian.

[7] Similarly the Harlunge are associated with Breisach and the Breisgau in the 16th cent. (W. Grimm, *DHS*, 355; Jänicke, *ZE*, 312 f.). See n. 5 above.

[8] See also Martin Zeiller's *Itinerarium Germaniae* (1652) (W. Grimm, *DHS*, 490).

---

[1] The story is also told in the *Sörla þáttr eða Heðins saga ok Högna* (*FAS* I. 365–82), and the battle lasts 143 years, until King Óláfr Tryggvason visits Háey (Hoy in the Orkneys), where the battle takes place, and one of his men, Ívarr Ljómi, puts an end to it (ch. 9).

[2] The work of the dwarf Dáinn, who is mentioned in the Vsp (quoted *SnE*: Gylf ch. 14) and in Hdl 7, 10; in Háv 143, 2 there is an elf named Dáinn.

[3] In **DF** there are three, also in Heinrich von München's 14th-cent. *Weltchronik* (W. Grimm, *DHS*, 225).

[4] Joh. Agricola (16th cent.) follows this account (W. Grimm, *DHS*, 326 f.).

[5] The expedition of Dirik (= Dietrich)

193), the English priest Gualchelm saw the 'familia Herlechini', a company of damned souls preceded by a warning giant wielding a club (cf. Eckehart, pp. 33 f.), in January 1092 in Normandy. Walter Map about a century later refers to the curia of Henry II of England as 'familia Herlethingi', and tells of Herla, an ancient British king, who is doomed to ride until the dog given him in the dwarf-world is taken from his back.[1]

In Saxo VIII. x. 9, Iarmericus hangs his sister's two sons, who have been brought up in Germany, and demolishes their castles (see Ermenrîch, p. 38).

In Þs, Sifka persuades Odilia, his wife, whom Erminrikr has dishonoured, to defame Egarð and Áki of Aurlungaland (II. 157, 2–3), the sons of Áki Aurlungatrausti of Fritilaborg (see Hâche, p. 56): in a passage (II. 164 f.) that gives the impression that the coming of the two young men is a spring phenomenon,[2] she tells Erminrikr's queen to be on her guard, as they would not spare even her virtue; Erminrikr overhears the conversation, attacks the castle of Egarð and Áki at Trelinnborg, and has them hanged, in spite of the warning given to them by their fosterfather, Fritila. Their stepfather, Viðga (MHG Witege), accepts the town of Ran (Ravenna) in compensation.

pn: 9th-cent. German (Förstemann I. 764; see Kaufmann, 175); frequent in placenames, especially in association with mountains (Förstemann II. i. 1255 f.); it also occurs in OE place-names (Binz, 209).

The basis for this pn is the hypocoristic *Haralo or *Harilo, cf. OHG Herilo (Kaufmann, 175), comprising OHG hari + the suffix -ilo; the additional suffix -ung/-ing indicates that the Harlunge 'belong to the race or kin of Harilo', or that they are simply 'men of the host or army';[3] *Haralo/*Harilo could well represent a byname of Woden (Flasdieck, 325); cf. the terms 'Herföðr' (Vsp 29, 1) and 'einherjar' for Óðinn and his followers in ON (Much, Germania, 385).[4]

Their name, the passage of Þs referred to above, and the behaviour of their guardian, Eckehart, in **Rs** (see p. 33) suggest a connection between the Harlunge and the folk belief in 'wuotes heer' (Woden's host) or the 'Wilde Jagd' widespread in western Europe in the Middle Ages (Harvey, 249).[5] Apparently the Harlunge have replaced the brothers Ammius and Sarus of Jordanes's account (ON Hamðir and Sörli) as the victims of Ermanaric in German and English tradition (see p. 39). It is, indeed, significant that Ermenrîch has the Harlunge hanged in German tradition, just as Jörmunrekr has his own son hanged in ON tradition.

HARTMAN von Tuscân (Tuscany) Brother of Herman (3).[6]

ref: **Wd(B)** m 755, 2; **Wd(D)** VIII. 169,3; **Wd(Gr)** 1705, 4; **Wd(w)** 1660, 3 (*Hartmut*; 1840, 4, etc., *Hartman*)

pn: 8th-cent. German (Förstemann I. 755; Schlaug II. 105)

HARTMUOT von Ormanîe[7] (Normandy) In **Ku**, Hartmuot is rejected as a suitor for the hand of Kûdrûn, although she shows tender feelings towards him when he visits her secretly. During the absence of Kûdrûn's father and her bridegroom, Herewîc, Hartmuot and his father, Ludewîc, abduct Kûdrûn and sixty-two of her handmaidens; they defeat the pursuing Hegelinge led by Hetel, Kûdrûn's father, and Ludewîc kills Hetel at a battle at Wülpensant (see p. 64). Kûdrûn refuses to marry Hartmuot and she is ill-treated by his mother, Gêrlint, during her captivity in Normandy. When the avenging Hegelinge surround the Norman fortress, Hartmuot prevents Gêrlint having Kûdrûn put to death. He is taken prisoner, but Kûdrûn arranges his marriage to her handmaiden, Hildeburc, and he is allowed to return to Ormanîe.

In **B**, Herbort tells how he has abducted Hartmuot's sister, Hildeburc, and defeated their father Ludewîc.

ref: **B** 6468; **Ku** 587, 4 (1650, 4 *Hartman*)

pn: 9th-cent. German (Förstemann I. 756; Socin, 20; Schlaug I. 99; II. 105; Kromp I. 35).

HARTNÎT, see HERTNÎT (1)

---

[1] Walter Map, *De Nugis Curialium*, ed. M. R. James (Oxford, 1914), I. 11; IV. 13; see also Flasdieck, 250 ff.

[2] Panzer, *Heldensage im Breisgau*, 61, relates their individual names (MHG Frîtele and Imbrecke, OE Emerca and Fridla) to ON *friðr*, 'beautiful', and *ömurligr*, 'terrible', to suggest the dual nature of seasonal dioscors. See also A. H. Krappe, 'Der Tod der Etzelsöhne im Dietrichepos', *ZfdA* LXIX (1932) 143, and Baesecke, *Vorgeschichte*, 51, regarding the Harlunge as dioscors.

[3] Attempts have been made to relate the name to that of the Heruli, who were in fact defeated by Ermanaric in the 4th cent., but the Herulian tribal name is based on Gmc. *erilaz/erlaz* (OS *erl*, OE *eorl*, 'nobleman'), the initial unorganic *H*- deriving from Latin scribes (Kaufmann, 108). If a case for a connection with any one Germanic tribe can be made, it is surely with the Harii of Tacitus, *Germania*, ch. 43, a Vandalic tribe, who painted their bodies and shields black to terrify their enemies (Much, *Germania*, 382, 385 f., considers that they thus represent the 'Totenheer').

[4] Those dedicated to Óðinn (Woden) were hanged according to Scandinavian cult rites.

[5] This ghostly rout was imitated in Germany at certain seasons as late as the 16th cent. (Neckel, *Deutsche Sagen* I. 9 f.).

[6] Cf. Herman and Hartvin in Þs (Herman (1), p. 69).

[7] See Symons, *Kudrun*, notes to strs. 587, 1 and 588, 3, regarding the various spellings of this place-name in the manuscript of **Ku**.

## HARTUNC (1) son of Immunc
A dwarf captured by Ruodlieb.

ref: **Ru** XVIII. 8 (MS. *hartunch*)

pn: 8th-cent. German (Förstemann I. 752; Socin, 20; Schlaug I. 99; II. 105), rare in OE (Searle, 286; Binz, 201; Feilitzen, 287).

See also Hertnît (1).

## HARTUNC (2) Dietrich's man
ref: **A** 74, 1

## HÂWART von Tenemarken (Denmark)
An exile at Etzel's court, he is Îrinc's liege lord. In **N** he and Irnfrit attack the Burgundians to avenge the death of Îrinc; he is killed by Hagen. In the **Kl**, Dancwart is said to have killed him. In **B** he is among Etzel's men fighting the Poles; he also takes part in the combats against Gunther's men at Worms, where he fights Berhtolt (see Hadawardus, p. 56).

ref: **B** 1241; **Kl** 423; **N** 1345, 1

pn: 9th-cent. German (Förstemann I. 721; Mone, 73; Socin, 567, 572; Schlaug I. 112; II. 115).

## HEGELINGE pl.
Ethnic name: Hetel's men (**Ku** 429, 4), his realm, 'ze Hegelingen' (207, 1), 'von Hegelingen' (232, 4), and 'Hegelinge lant' (314, 1).

ref: **Ku** 207, 1

In the OE poem *Deor*, Heorrenda becomes the '*scop*' of the Heodeningas (36) in place of Dēor (see Hôrant, p. 81).

In the ON Sk ch. 62, the terms 'Hjaðninga veðr' (Hjaðning weather, i.e. 'battle'), 'Hjaðninga eldr' or 'Hjaðninga vendir' (fire or staves of the Hjaðnings, i.e. 'weapons'), are explained by the story of Hildr and the eternal battle between her abductor, Heðinn, and her father, Högni, which is called the 'Hjaðningavíg'; this battle is referred to in other ON monuments (see Hagen (2), pp. 61 f., and Hilde (1), pp. 72 ff.).

In **Ku** the battle between Hagen and Hetel is not eternal.[1] A tragic outcome to their fight in earlier German tradition is indicated by the reference to the battle at Wolfenwerde in Lamprecht's *Alexander* (see Hagen (2), p. 61).

The site of the battle in ON tradition is an island, Höð (Hod off Norway) or the island of Háey (Hoy in the Orkneys) (see p. 73); in German tradition Wolfenwerde (Lamprecht) or Wülpensant (**Ku**)[2] on the Scheldt estuary, in an area where the Franks and Scandinavians were in contact from the 9th cent. on. The original setting may well have been on the Baltic island of Hiddensee to the west of Rügen ('Hithinsö' of Saxo), in an area from which the story of the conflict between Hagen and Hetan (= Hetel) for the sake of Hilde probably stemmed.[3]

pn: *Heðanings (OE *Heodeningas*, ON *Hjaðningar*), the original name of Hetel's people,[4] corresponds to the OHG pn *Hetan* (see Hetel, p. 72); the form *Hegelinge* of **Ku** is of uncertain origin: the Bavarian place-name *Högling* near Tegernsee (c. 1144 *Hegelingen*) possibly influenced it (Müllenhoff, *ZE*, 314), but a purely phonetic change from -*dl*- to -*gl*- is also possible (Boesch, *Kudrun*, xix n. 2).

## HEIME
Son of Madelgêr (**B**, of Adelgêr in **A** and **AHb**) and the companion of Witege; he has four elbows (**AHb**, **Rg**, Swedish Þs); his sword is named Nagelrinc (**A**, **B**, **Rg**): in **Rg** and **V** he is Dietrich's man: in **Rg(AD)** he kills the giant Schrûtân in the combats against the men of Worms in the rosegarden; in **V(hw)** he kills the giants Vellenwalt and Klingelbolt at Mûter (see Wîcram).

In **A**, **B**, **DF**, and **Rs** he is the leader of Ermenrîch's men: in **A**, although owing allegiance to Dietrich (8 ff.), he and Witege kill one of Dietrich's men, the youthful Alphart; Heime is bound to aid Witege in this fight, because he had saved his life and that of Dietrich at Mûtâren on an occasion in the past (253). In **DF** Heime fights Dietleip at Bôlonje (Bologna); in **Rs** he fights Walther but flees from Rüedegêr.

ref: **A** 2, 2; **AHb** p. 3, 28; **B** 5194; **DF** 3395; **Rg(A)** 97, 4; **Rg(C)** 374; **Rg(D)** 64, 1; **Rg(F)** III. 7, 1; **Rg(P)** 121; **Rs** 712, 5; **V(h)** 610, 3; **V(w)** 619, 3

---

[1] Kemp Malone, 'An Anglo-Latin Version of the Hjaðningavíg', *Speculum* XXXIX (1964), 35–44, discusses the Norse versions, but does not consider the eternal battle to be part of the original story. K. W. von Sydow, 'Märchenforschung und Philologie', *Universitas* III (1948), 1056 f., thinks this motif was brought into the West Norse version from Ireland during the Viking period. See also Panzer, *Hilde-Gudrun*, 329 f.

[2] In **Ku** the name is used for the site of Hetel's unsuccessful battle with the Norman abductors of his daughter, Kûdrûn, whereas Hagen's fight against Hetel, the abductor of his daughter, Hilde, is sited on the shore of Wâleis (see Hagen (2), p. 61).

[3] Helgi's ships muster at Heðinsey in HHu II 22, 8, and Völss ch. 9, before his battle with Högni. Wulpen (*wulpa insula*, cf. Du *de groote wulp*, 'curlew') at the Scheldt mouth is first recorded in 1096. In 1198 the arm of the Scheldt separating the islands of Wulpen and Coesant is named *Hiddeneze* (in 1250 *Hedinzee*); it is possible that the name of this channel influenced the localization, when the story came to the Low Countries from the North (Boesch, *Kudrun*, xxxv). See Th. Frings, 'Zur Geographie der Kudrun', *ZfdA* LXI (1924), 192 ff.; 'Hilde', *PBB* LIV (1930), 394 ff.; Stackmann, *Kudrun*, lii.

[4] F. R. Schröder, 'Die Sage von Hetel und Hilde', *DVjs* XXXII (1958), 46 f., suggests that *Heðanings, 'people of the skins', was the starting-point and that the pn *Heðan was abstracted from it.

Heime's sword Nagelrinc is mentioned by Heinrich von Veldeke in the 12th cent. (see Eckesahs, p. 34), but the earliest German literary references to Heime himself, outside the epics, are first recorded in the 13th cent. (W. Grimm, *DHS*, 179, 186, 196; Müllenhoff, *ZE*, 364); he is still remembered in the 15th cent. (W. Grimm, *DHS*, 316, 318). Local traditions about him grow up at the monastery of Wilten at Innsbruck, which he is said to have founded: Albert von Stade (mid 13th cent.) mentions his grave as being 13 feet in length (ibid. 178 f.); in later reports he is said to have killed a hostile giant named Thürss as well as a dragon (ibid. 179, 490; Mone, 288 f.); baroque statues of Haymo and Thürss flank the door of the monastery church; within the church is a large wooden effigy of the hero (c. 1500).

In the OE poem *Widsith*, Wudga and Hāma are named among Eormanrīc's followers (OE *innweorud*) (124); apparently they are exiles or adventurers (OE *wræccan*) in control of people and wealth (125–30). In *Beowulf* Hāma (1198) is thought to have fled from the wrath of Eormanrīc, after carrying off the necklace of the Brōsingas (1197–1201)[1] to the 'bright stronghold';[2] then he died.[3]

'Hame' is mentioned in the same passage as 'Widie' and other heroes known to OE tradition in a late version of the *Brut* in the MS. Cotton Vesp. D. IV (fol. 139b) (see Chambers, *Beowulf*, 252 n. 2; Klaeber, *Beowulf*, xxxiv n. 7).

In late ON Eddic tradition (13th cent.), Heimir, the husband of Brynhildr's sister, Bekkhildr (Völss ch. 24), is visited by Sigurðr after his first meeting with Brynhildr (see also Grp 19, 2); later he visits Brynhildr at the house of Heimir (Völss ch. 29). Heimir brings up Áslaug, the daughter of Sigurðr and Brynhildr (Sk ch. 5; Völss ch. 29).

Saxo in his Danish history tells of a Saxon champion named Hama (VI. v. 17) whom the Danish champion Starkad cuts in half.

In Þs a full account of the life of Heimir (I. 40, 3) is given: he is the son of Studas (I. 38, 18), the manager of Brynilldr's stud.[4] Þiðrekr defeats him in single combat, but not before he has broken his sword Blodgang on Þiðrekr's helmet. He joins Þiðrekr's company and brings him the horse Falka (see Valke, p. 44), but his own steed Rispa (I. 40, 7)[5] is peerless. Þiðrekr gives him the sword Naglringr, which angers Viðga, who reveals that Heimir has left him to fight twelve robbers single-handed at Briktan (see Witege, p. 146); for this Þiðrekr banishes Heimir from Bern (Verona).[6] He lives for a short time as a robber before being reconciled with Þiðrekr. On Þiðrekr's Bertangaland expedition he is defeated by Isungr's youngest son. Heimir and Viðga remonstrate with Erminrikr for forcing his nephew, Þiðrekr, into exile from Bern, and Heimir knocks out the teeth of Erminrikr's evil counsellor, Sifka (see Sibeche, p. 117); he then lives as an outlaw, pillaging Erminrikr's realm for thirty years. On Erminrikr's death Heimir enters the monastery of Wadincusan in Lombardy under the name of 'Lodvígur' (II. 376, 3). The monastery is threatened by the giant Asplian. 'Lodvígur' forces the abbot to return his weapons and his horse, Rispa, who is at first too weak from starvation to carry him;[7] Heimir eventually kills the giant. Þiðrekr visits the monastery and recognizes the broad-shouldered monk with the long grey beard; he rejoins Þiðrekr in Romaborg (Rome), then returns to destroy the monastery by fire and to kill all the monks.[8] Heimir is finally killed by an aged giant, who is subsequently slain by Þiðrekr.

pn: based on Gmc. *haima-, 'home' (cf. OHG *heimo*, OE *hāma*, 'house-cricket', and OHG *heim*, OE *hām*, 'home'); 8th-cent. German (Förstemann I. 731; Socin, 20; Schlaug I. 104 f.), it occurs occasionally together with Witege (Müllenhoff, *ZE*, 308; E. Schröder, *DNK*, 97), and in a St. Gall document of 786 together with Suanailta (Wartmann I. 104: see p. 39). It is rare in OE (Searle, 279; Binz, 212), but is more frequent in the 11th cent. in the continental form *Haimo* (Searle, 278).

A number of persons bear the name (H)*aymon* in OFr epic (Langlois, 13 f., 323),

---

[1] The manuscript is corrupt at three points in this passage, and *Brōsinga* (1199) may well be an error for *Brīsinga*; thus the necklace would be the famous '*Brīsinga men*' of ON mythology (Þrk 13, 6), the necklace of Freyja won back from Loki by Heimdallr, with whom Hāma has possibly been confused (see S. Bugge, 'Studien über das Beowulfepos', *PBB* XII (1887), 73 ff.).

[2] 'tō þære byrhtan byrig' (1199) is obscure: the rainbow, the abode of Heimdallr in ON myth (see n. 1 above), and Verona (MHG Berne) have both been suggested (Boer, *Sagen*, 195 f.), but it could be a Christian reference to the kingdom of heaven.

[3] The final phrase 'gecēas ēcne rǣd' (1201) means 'he gained eternal benefit', i.e. 'he died' (cf. *Beowulf*, 2469, 'Godes lēoht gecēas'); a reference to Heime's 'moniage' is unlikely.

[4] Heimir's own name was originally Studas too (I. 39, 6); cf. OHG *stuot*, OS *stôd*, 'stud'; his device in Þs is a white stallion. He is said to be named Heimir after a terrible dragon (I. 39, 26).

[5] Cf. MHG *rispe*, 'branches, bushes', *rispeln*, 'curl'.

[6] Þiðrekr uses the name 'Heimir' (I. 176, 17) when trying to avoid fighting Ekka (Witege reproaches Heime for cowardice in A 261 f.).

[7] The most famous 'moniage' is that of Guillaume in OFr epic, but a similar encounter between Ogier and his aged horse occurs in the *Chevalerie Ogier* (see also Ilsân, pp. 84 f., Walther, p. 136, and Wolfdietrich, p. 150). H. P. Pütz, 'Heimes Klosterepisode. Ein Beitrag zur Quellenfrage der Thidrekssaga', *ZfdA* C (1971), 178–95, discusses the 'moniage' of Heimir, its relationship to other such 'moniages', and its bearing on the provenance and authorship of the source material of Þs.

[8] The monastery of Wedinghausen near Arnsberg, Westphalia, was destroyed by fire in 1210.

the best-known being the brother of Maugis (see Madelgêr, p. 92) and father of Renaut, to whom he gives the famous horse, Baiart (see Benary, 38 ff.).

Heime's comradeship with Witege and his service with Ermenrîch, whose hostility he incurs, are attested in the earliest monuments (OE *Widsith*, *Beowulf*);[1] his service with Dietrich appears to be secondary and probably results from the later coalescence of traditions about Dietrich and Ermenrîch (see pp. 31, 39). His 'moniage' shows the influence of OFr epic.

HEINRICH (1) der Vogelære
The name taken by the narrator of **DF**, who comments on the meanness of princes (7949–8015).

ref: DF 8000

The name possibly refers to Henry the Fowler (†936), who was thought to have been a just ruler by 13th-cent. authors. The redactor of **DF** and **Rs** was an Austrian of the late 13th cent., and he indicates his support of the nobility whose revolt was suppressed by Albrecht von Habsburg in 1296 (Martin, *DHB* II. li ff.).

pn: 8th-cent. German (Förstemann I. 733 f.).

HEINRICH (2) von Ofterdingen
The fictitious author of **L(D)**.

ref: L(D) 2822

The champion of the Duke of Austria in the *Wartburgkrieg* (13th cent.), a poem about the contest of 'Minnesänger' at the Wartburg in Thuringia (see G. Rosenhagen, 'Heinrich von Ofterdingen', *VfL* II (1936), 324).

HEINRICH (3) der schœne
He exposes the deception of Wildunc (see Gêrwart, pp. 50 f.).

ref: Wd(B) 765, 1

HELCHE (HERCHE) wife of Etzel (OSPIRIN)
In **W**, Ospirin treats Hiltgunt with great kindness while she is a hostage at Attila's court, and puts her in charge of the treasury. She regrets the loss of her 'foster-child' when Hiltgunt escapes with Waltharius (see Hildegunt (1), p. 78).

In **B**, a company of heathen (presumably Etzel's men) are known to have escorted Helche from her father, Ôserîch (376 ff.). She and Etzel reside at Treisenmûre (also in **N(C)**, in **N** Zeizenmûre).[2]

In **N**, the virtues of Helche, Etzel's first wife, are recalled (in **N(k)** she is thought to have converted him to Christianity, 1271, 2). After her death, Etzel seeks the hand of Kriemhilt, who, on her marriage to Etzel, receives Helche's former retinue; their names are given in the **Kl**: Herrât, Sigelint, Goldrûn, Hildeburc, Herlint, and Adellint.

In **DF** she is known to have persuaded Etzel to aid Dietrich against Ermenrîch, and she arranges Dietrich's marriage to her niece, Herrât.

In **Rs** she dreams that a dragon has carried off her sons, Scharpfe and Orte: they are killed subsequently by Witege at Rabene (Ravenna) when in Dietrich's care (see pp. 26 f., 145), Rüedegêr persuades her to forgive Dietrich for their loss.

ref: **AHb** p. 4, 1 (*herriche*; p. 7, 33 *Herche*); **B** 341; **DF** 4662; **E(L)** 199, 1; **E(s)** 174, 1 (*Helde*); **Kl** 100; **N** 1143, 1; **Rg(C)** 680 (*Herche*); **Rg(D)** 130, 3 (Herche); **Rg(P)** 83 (*Herche*; 120 *Helchen*); **Rs** 11, 6; **W** 123 (Ospirin); **WuH** (Wien) I. 12, 2; **Wu(B)** m 6, 3; **Wu(k)** 2, 30 (*heillig*)

The death of Helche's sons is referred to in the 13th cent. in Wernher der Gartenære's *Meier Helmbrecht* (76–81) and in *Der Wolf und der Geiß* (W. Grimm, *DHS*, 185), and in the 14th cent. in Heinrich von München's *Weltchronik* (ibid. 226).

In the late ON Eddic poem Gðr III, Herkja (2, 4), Atli's concubine, accuses his wife, Guðrún, of adultery with Þjóðrekr, and is executed for the slander (see p. 20).

In Þs, Attila first sends his nephew Osið (together with 'hertugi Roðolfr' in Version 2), then Roðolfr af Bakalar ('margræivi Roðingeirr af Bakalar' in Version 2), for the hand of Erka (I. 57, 29; II. 83, 21), the daughter of King Osanctrix of Villcinaland (land of the Wilzi), but without success. Roðolfr (Version 2 'hertugi Roðolfr') returns once more to Osanctrix's court, disguised as an old man and calling himself 'Sigurðr', and becomes well trusted by the King; he and Osið then abduct Erka and her sister Berta. Attila marries Erka, and Roðolfr Berta.[3] Later, in a confused episode reminiscent of **E**, Erka urges Þiðrekr to recapture her relative, Þiðrekr son of Valldemarr; Þiðrekr beheads him and casts the head at her feet (see pp. 31, 33). Erka persuades Attila to aid Þiðrekr against Erminrikr; her sons Erpr and Ortvin are killed by Viðga in the campaign, but she urges Attila to forgive Þiðrekr for their loss. On her deathbed she gives her niece, Herrað, to Þiðrekr in marriage. She is buried in the town-wall of Susat (Soest).

pn: *Herche*, *Heriche*: 9th-cent. German (Förstemann I. 764; II. ii. 1255; Socin, 56; Schlaug II. 202), such names being based on the equivalent of OHG *heri*, 'army'; *Helche*: 13th-cent. German (Socin, 56).

Treisenmûre, i.e. Traismauer, at the confluence of the Traisen and the Danube.
[3] The name Roðolfr (Gmc. \**Hrōð-wulfs*) recalls that of the hero of **R**, Rother (Gmc. \**Hrōð-hari*), whose daughter-in-law is named Berte.

---

[1] Schütte, *Gotthiod* I. 164, equates Heime with the Gothic hero, Hanale, mentioned together with Vidigoia by Jordanes in the 6th cent. (ch. v) (see p. 147).
[2] See Fr. Panzer, 'Der Weg der Nibelungen', *Helm Festgabe* (Tübingen, 1951), 97 ff., regarding

## HELCHE (HERCHE)

The historical basis for this person and the origin of her name could well be the 'Kreka' (Greek woman), Attila's wife, whom Priscus visited in the 5th cent. (Priscus, 310, 318: see Etzel, p. 42). In Kéza's late-13-cent. Hungarian chronicle (W. Grimm, *DHS*, 183), one wife of Ethele (Attila) is said to be the daughter of the Greek Emperor Honorius (see Kriemhilt, p. 21 n. 2, and Dietrich, p. 28).[1]

## HELENA
Mother of Constantin (2).

ref: **R** 4395

Julia Flavia Helena, mother of Constantine the Great, was the alleged discoverer of the True Cross and held to be the foundress of many Rhineland churches (Frings–Kuhnt, *Rother*, 190).

## HELFERÎCH (1) Dietrich's man

In **N** he brings the news of Rüedegêr's death to Dietrich, and kills Dancwart in the fighting against the Burgundians that then ensues. In the **Kl** he is found among the dead in Etzel's hall.

ref: **A** 73, 4; **B** 5248; **Kl** 1543 (C *Gelpfrat*); **N** 2241, 1

The name occurs in ON Eddic tradition for Hjálprekr, the King of Denmark, who is the foster-father of Sigurðr (Sf prose, p. 163; Rm prose, p. 173;[2] Sk ch. 47; Völss ch. 12).

pn: 4th-cent. WFr, 5th-cent. Burgundian (Schönfeld, 138); 8th-cent. German (Förstemann I. 841; Socin, 22; Schlaug I. 104).

The appearance of this typically Frankish name in the Nibelungen-complex may not be entirely fortuitous: Chilperic I of Tournai (†584) was the brother of Sigebert of Metz (see pp. 16, 122); Hjálprekr's helpful role in ON tradition, however, indicates an appellative interpretation of the name.[3]

## HELFERÎCH (2) von Lunders (London)[4]

Etzel's man: in **DF** and **Rs** he aids Dietrich against Ermenrîch; in **DF** he fights Ladiner at Bôlonje (Bologna); in **Rs** he fights Baldunc at Rabene (Ravenna) and later brings the news of the death of Helche's sons to Dietrich.

ref: **DF** 5157; **Rs** 51, 2

In Þs, Hjalprikr (II. 228, 2) has charge of Erka's sons, Ortvin and Erpr (see Ilsân). Viðga kills Hjalprikr and the youths at Gronsport (see Witege, p. 146).

## HELFERÎCH (3) twelfth son of Berhter (1) von Mêrân

He has died fighting the heathen beyond the Elbe (see Wilzen).

ref: **R** 469

## HELFERÎCH (4) von Lütringen (Lorraine)

In **E** Ecke finds him by the roadside suffering from wounds inflicted by Dietrich, who has also killed his companions, Ortwîn, Liudegast, and Hûc. In **AHb** Dietrich is said to have killed him. In **DF** he appears among Etzel's men.

ref: **AHb** p. 3, 35 (*Helfferich von bunn*); **DF** 5156; **E(B)** 1;[5] **E(d)** 64, 7 (Helffreich von Lone); **E(L)** 59, 7 (MS. *Helfrich von lun*); **E(s)** 56, 7

## HELFERÎCH (5) von Lûne (Luna in Italy)

In **V**, Helferîch and Portalaphê are the parents of Rentwîn. After Dietrich and Hildebrant have rescued Rentwîn from the jaws of a dragon, Helferîch entertains them at his castle of Ârône (Arona), and takes part in their subsequent adventures with giants and dragons.

ref: **V(d)** 51, 12; **V(h)** 155, 9; **V(w)** 279, 9

HELFFART, see HELMSCHART (2)

HELLE, see VELLE

## HELMNÔT (1) Guntharius's man (HELMNOD)

Killed by Waltharius. His byname is Eleuthir.

ref: **W** 982 (Helmnod)

pn: apparently a late creation like Gêrnôt (Holz, *Sagenkreis*, 95 n. 1).

## HELMNÔT (2) Dietrich's man

ref: **A** 74, 1 (MS. *helmschrot*); **B** 10653; **N** 2261, 1

## HELMNÔT (3) von Tuscân (Tuscany)

In **O** he aids Ortnît in his bridal quest for the daughter of Machorel. After Ortnît's death he protects his widow; Helmnôt is mentioned in **Wd**.

In **A** he is among Dietrich's men opposing Ermenrîch.

ref: **A** 77, 2; **O** 10, 1; **O(k)** 9, 2 (*Helmschrot*; 18, 7 *Helmbolt*, etc.); **Wd(C)** VIII. 21, 3; **Wd(D)** VIII. 331, 1; **Wd(Gr)** 1841, 2

---

[1] A confusion: in fact the Visigoth Athavulf married Placidia, the daughter of Honorius, whereas Attila claimed the hand of Honoria, sister of the Western Emperor Valentinian (*CMH* I. 415).
[2] Cf. the Faroese ballad *Regin smiður* based on Rm (*CCF* I. 1–8).
[3] Cf. the translation 'adjutor fortis' by Venantius Fortunatus (cit. A. Scherer, 'Zum Sinngehalt der germanischen Personennamen', *BzNf* IV (1953), 3).
[4] Probably via OFr Lundres (Flutre, 262).
[5] The opening line of the fragment **E(B)**, 'Vns seit von Lutringen Helfrich . . .', suggests that this may be a poet's name, about which the incident of the wounded knight was later woven; cf. Wolfram von Eschenbach's *Parzival* 504, 7 ff. (Jiriczek, *DHS* (1898), 193; Schneider, *GHS* I 259).

**HELMSCHART (1)** Dietrich's man
Killed by Reinhêr at Bôlonje (Bologna) in
**DF**; Dietrich laments his death in **Rs**.

ref: **DF** 2999; **Rs** 10, 6

pn: a late creation, with second component based on MHG *scharten, scherten*, 'cut off, injure, wound' (see Helmschrôt below).

**HELMSCHART (2)** a robber
Killed by Wolfdietrich (see Rûmelher).

ref: **Wd(D)** v. 11, 1; **Wd(Gr)** 849, 1; **Wd(w)** 791, 1 (*Helffart*)

**HELMSCHRÔT**
Dietrich's man (possibly identical with Helmschart (1) above): he defeats Gêrnôt in the combats at Worms in **Rg(A)**.

ref: **A** 73, 4; **Rg(A)** 101, 4

pn: a late creation, with second component based on MHG *schrôt*, 'wound, cut, chip'. It is used for one of the soldiers of Herod and Pontius Pilate in miracle plays of the 15th and 16th cents. (W. Grimm, *DHS*, 478, 480); Fischart refers to it in his *Gargantua* (ed. 1594) (ibid. 352; Bach 1, § 313).

**HELPFERÎCH**, see HELFERÎCH

**HERBORT** von Tenelant (Denmark)
In **B** the uncle of Boppe: he is among Gunther's men and fights Dietrich in the battle for the gates of Worms. He gives an account of his past adventures (6452 ff.): he has abducted Hildeburc von Ormanîe, and defeated her father Ludewîc and her brother Hartmuot; he has killed a giant (named Hugebolt in **E(L)**) and two persons named Goltwart and Sêwart; later he has taken Hildeburc to the Rhine, overcoming the opposition of Dietrich and Hildebrant. His device is a stag with golden antlers.

In **Rg(D)** he is among Gibeche's men opposing those of Dietrich at Worms: he is killed by Dietrich von Kriechen; in **Rg(F)** 'Herbort von dem Rîn' fights Eckehart.

In **E(L)** his father, Ruotliep (see Heriburg, p. 69), has given him the sword that Ecke is carrying.

ref: **AHb** p. 3, 3 (*Herbot*); **B** 6227 (MS. *Herwart*, otherwise *Herbort*); **E(L)** 83, 1; **Rg(D)** 47, 2; **Rg(F)** 1. 5, 2; **Rg(P)** 70 (*Hazwart*; 325 *Herwart*, etc.)

In Þs, Herburt (II. 43, 13) joins his uncle Þiðrekr after the death of his brother Herðegn (see Herdegen (1) below). Þiðrekr sends him to Bertangaland to win for him the hand of Hilldr, the daughter of King Artus. Herburt attracts the attention of the princess while she is in church by means of mice ornamented with gold and silver; by painting a hideous picture of Þiðrekr on the wall he persuades Hilldr to accept him as a suitor instead of Þiðrekr. He abducts her, kills twenty-four men sent in pursuit by Artus, and takes service with another king.

pn: 11th-cent. German (Förstemann 1. 767; Socin, 23; Schlaug II. 110; Jänicke, *ZE*, 311).

It is possible to assume the existence of a 'Herbortlied' on the basis of the accounts in **B** and **Þs** (Schneider, *DHS* (1930), 84 f.; Norman, *Dukus Horant*, 100 ff.).

**HER(E)BRANT (1)** Hildebrant's father (OHG HERIBRANT)
In **äH** he is the father of Hiltibrant and grandfather of Hadubrant.

In **DF** and **V(h)** he appears among Dietrich's men.

In **Wd(B)** he is the eldest of the sons of Berhtunc imprisoned by Wolfdietrich's brothers; Wolfdietrich frees him and his brothers.

In **Wd(D)** he brings up Wolfdietrich's son, Hugdietrich, and receives Garten (Garda) in lien. He marries Âmîe, daughter of Wernhêr: their children are Hildebrant, Nêre, Elsân, and Mergart (see the genealogical tree, p. 75 n. 3). He leads Hugdietrich's men aiding Wolfdietrich at Tischcâl.

ref: **AHb** p. 6, 1; **DF** 5867; **äH** 7 (MS. *heribrantes*, also 44; 45 *heribtes*); **V(h)** 653, 9; **Wd(B)** 876, 1; **Wd(D)** IV. 115, 2; **Wd(Gr)** 505, 2

In Þs, Herbrandr (I. 252, 12), the 'far-travelled', is the son of Reginballdr—his relationship to Hildibrandr is not stated.[1] He summons Þiðrekr's eleven companions for the expedition to Bertangaland and is defeated there by Isungr's second son. In the Danish ballad *Kong Diderik i Birtingsland* (*DgF* I. 124 ff.), Brand Vefferlin (4, 1 = Herbrant?) tells Diderik about King Isac (= Isungr?).

pn: 8th-cent. German (Förstemann 1. 767 f.; II. i. 1257 f.; Schlaug II. 110).[2] At Fulda *-braht* spellings preponderate for this pn till *c.* 840 (see Hadebrant (1), p. 57). In the 13th cent. the name occurs for a peasant in *Neidharts Lieder*, 77, 17.

In OE the name with *-brand* is isolated (Searle, 292), but with *-beorht* it is recorded from the 7th cent. (ibid.). It occurs in the late-12th-cent. Anglo-Norman *Romance of Horn* (see Hildebrant (1), p. 76).

**HER(E)BRANT (2)** von Biterne (Viterbo)
Hildebrant's brother.

ref: **Rg(F)** III. 18, 4

**HERCHE**, see HELCHE

**HERDEGEN (1)** a retainer of the Harlunge
ref: **B** 5229

---

[1] See p. 57 and n. 2 regarding the name Herbrandr in a 14th-cent. ON genealogy.

[2] The common noun *herebrant* occurs in the *Annolied* (11th cent.) with the meaning 'flame of battle' (see Fr. Kluge, 'Die Heimat des Hildebrandsliedes', *PBB* XLIII (1918), 502).

## HERDEGEN (1)

In Þs, Herðegn (II. 43, 6) of Iverne (Ireland) is married to Isollde, Þiðrekr's sister; their son, Herðegn (II. 43, 9), is killed in swordplay by his brother, Tristram; the elder brother, Herburt, is held responsible and leaves home (see Herbort above).

pn: 9th-cent. German (Förstemann I. 779; Schlaug II. 110).

## HERDEGEN (2) Walgunt's man

He is sent to meet 'Hiltgunt' (= Hugdietrich) at Salnecke (Salonika).

ref: **Wd(B)** 40, 1; **Wd(Gr)** 48, 1

## HEREGART

The most high-born of Kûdrûn's attendants; she avoids the discomfort of her mistress's captivity in Normandy by marrying the cupbearer at the Norman court. For her treachery Wate beheads her when the Hegelinge rescue Kûdrûn.

ref: **Ku** 1007, 4

pn: 9th-cent. German (Förstemann I. 770).

HERIBRANT, see HER(E)BRANT (1)

## HERIBURG

Daughter of Hartunch: Ruodlieb marries her.[1]

ref: **Ru** XVIII. 11

In the ON Eddic Gðr I, Herborg (6, 1), a German princess ('Húnalands dróttning'), comforts Guðrún by recounting her own story: she has lost her father, mother, four brothers, her husband, and seven sons, and she has been captured and ill-treated by her captor's wife (see p. 22).

In Þs the name is used for the wife of King Salomon (II. 111, 6), and for his daughter, whom Apollonius abducts (see p. 82 n. 1).

pn: 8th-cent. German (Förstemann I. 768; Schlaug I. 105; II. 110) and OE (Searle, 292; Sweet, 146).

## HERIRICUS

The ruler of Burgundia, he sends his daughter Hiltgunt as a hostage to Attila (see Hildegunt (1)). His capital is at Cabillonae (Châlons-sur-Saône).

ref: **W** 35

pn: 4th-cent. Goth.; 6th-cent. WFr; 7th-cent. German (Förstemann I. 777; II. i. 1261; Schlaug I. 107; II. 111) and OE (Searle, 294, 560). The name also occurs in the OE poem *Beowulf*: Hererīc (2206), the uncle of Heardrēd.

## HERLEIP von Westvâle (Westphalia)

Gunther's man.

ref: **B** 5076 (MS. *Herliep*).

pn: 8th-cent. German (Förstemann I. 773; Schlaug I. 106); it occurs among the names

---

[1] She is the mother of Herbort, who is the son of Ruotliep in **E(L)**.
[2] They are rewarded with Westerîche (**Wd(D)**

## HERMAN (4)

of the Harlungi in the 12th-cent. *Genealogia Viperti* (see Harlunge, p. 62).

## HERLINT (1) confidante of the daughter of Constantin (1)

An old woman, who acts as go-between for 'Dietrich' (= Rother) and Constantin's daughter.

ref: **R** 280

pn: 8th-cent. German (Förstemann I. 773 f.; II. i. 1261; Socin, 588; Kromp III. 32; Bach I, § 284). The name occurs in Wolfram von Eschenbach's *Parzival* (c. 1210) for the lady wooed by Fridebant von Schotten (25, 5).

## HERLINT (2) von Kriechen (Greece)

Attendant to Helche.

ref: **Kl** 2461

## HERMAN (1) Rother's man

'marcgrâve': he suggests to Rother that Luppolt should lead an embassy to Constantinople for the hand of Constantin's daughter (see Rother, p. 109).

ref: **R** 86

In Þs there are three persons named Herman: (1) a knight sent in pursuit of Herburt and Hilldr by Artus (II. 57, 20) (see Herbort, p. 68); (2) a messenger of King Osanctrix imprisoned by King Milias (II. 81, 22) (cf. Herman (1) and (2) below); and (3) a Swabian count ('greifar i Svava') who, together with Hartvin, is involved in the plot against Queen Sisibe and is ordered by her husband, King Sigmundr, to murder her; he saves the queen by killing Hartvin (I. 288, (10)) (see p. 124, and Herman (2) and (5) below).

pn: 7th-cent. German (Förstemann I. 744; II. i. 1261 f.; Schlaug I. 106; II. 110); in OE of late continental origin (Searle, 293; Feilitzen, 290).

## HERMAN (2) Ortnît's man

'grâve': sent to demand tribute from Hugdietrich in **Wd(D)**; in **Wd(A²)** he woos Ortnît's widow.

ref: **Wd(A²)** 538, 1; **Wd(D)** III. 54, 1; **Wd(Gr)** 314, 1; **Wd(k)** 207, 6

## HERMAN (3) von Tuscân (Tuscany)

He is defeated by Wolfdietrich in a tournament at Tervîs (Treviso) for the hand of Âmîe. He and his brother, Hartman, aid Wolfdietrich against the impostor Gêrwart and help him rescue his eleven vassals.[2]

ref: **Wd(D)** VII. 139, 4; **Wd(Gr)** 1447, 4

## HERMAN (4) von Pôlân (Poland)

In **B** he is defeated by Etzel and becomes his vassal; in **Kl** and **N(k)** he is at Etzel's court.

ref: **B** m 3422 n 3583; **Kl** 389; **N(k)** 2127, 2

IX. 209, 2), the name of this lien probably deriving from the designation of Rother's seat 'bi dem westeren mere' (see Ladiner (1), p. 88).

## HERMAN (4)

This figure possibly represents Ladislaus Hermann of Poland († 1102) (Panzer, *Nibelungenlied*, 80).

## HERMAN (5) von Swâben (Swabia)
Gunther's man.

ref: **B** 6249

See under Herman (1).

## HERMAN (6) von Normandîe (Normandy)
Ermenrîch's man: he leads the men of Messîe (Messina).[1]

ref: **Rs** 482, 2

## HERMAN (7) von Ôstervranken (East Franconia)
In **DF** he is among Dietrich's men at Bôlonje (Bologna); in **Rs** he is one of Etzel's men aiding Dietrich.

ref: **DF** 5732; **Rs** 63, 2

## HERMAN (8) Dietwart's companion
Uncle of Berhtunc (3).

ref: **DF** 397

## HERRÂT
Wife of Dietrich (1) von Berne (in **AHb** his second wife): in **B** and **DF** she is the niece of Helche, in **N** the daughter of Näntwîn, and in **AHb** the daughter of Etzel's sister. In **DF**, Dietrich marries her after his victory over Ermenrîch at Meilân (Milan), in **Rs** after his victory at Bôlonje (Bologna). In **N** she controls Etzel's household after the death of Helche, and instructs her new queen, Kriemhilt, in her duties. In the **Kl** she accompanies Dietrich and Hildebrant back to Berne (Verona).

ref: **AHb** p. 8, 8 (*Herrot*); **B** 4351; **DF** 7556; **E(a)** 281, 1; **E(s)** m 281, 1; **Kl** 2447; **N** 1381, 1; **äSn** m 32, 12; **Rs** 36, 1

In Þs, Erka (see Helche, p. 66) on her deathbed gives her niece, Herrað (II. 255, 22), in marriage to Þiðrekr. She finally returns to Bern (Verona) with Þiðrekr and Hildibrandr. Her name is also used for a relative of Þiðrekr (II. 326, 11).

pn: m. and f. 8th-cent. German (Förstemann I. 777; II. i. 1263; Schlaug I. 106; II. 111).

Theodoric the Great had two known wives, one in Moesia before he entered Italy, the other, named Audefleda, sister of Clovis, the Frankish King. In German traditions he has several (see p. 30 n. 7). It may be significant that his mother's name was Erelieva (\**Hereliufu*) (Wrede, 60), which shows the same first component as Herrât.

## HERRICHE, see HELCHE

## HERROT, see HERRÂT

## HERTINC, see HERTNÎT (1) von Riuzen (Russia)

## HERTLÎN
Daughter of the King of Portugal (**AHb**): in **G** she is held captive by the dwarf Goldemâr. In **AHb** Dietrich rescues her from Goldemâr, and she becomes his first wife; on her death he marries Herrât.

ref: **AHb** p. 8, 3; **G** m 2, 9

pn: possibly a contracted form of Herrât (see above) with a diminutive suffix.

## HERTNÎT (1) von Riuzen (Russia)[2]
Etzel's man: in **DF** he aids Dietrich against Ermenrîch. In **Rg(D)** he is among Dietrich's champions at Worms; his device is a wheel; he fights a drawn combat with Walther. In **Rg(C)** he kills the giant Stüefinc.

ref: **AHb** p. 3, 13 (*Hartung*); **DF** 5908 (A *Hortrit*); **Rg(C)** 382; **Rg(D)** 74, 1 (Hartnît: sh *hartung*, fT *Hertnit*); **Rg(P)** 119 (MS. *Herting*)

In Þs four persons are named Hertnið: (1) the King of Hólmgarðr[3] (I. 44, 2) and father of Osanctrix, Valldemarr, and Ilias; his brother is named Hirðir; (2) the son of Ilias (I. 51, 1): he and his brother Osið (Hirðir in Version 2) are sent by their uncle Osanctrix, King of Villcinaland, to Milias, King of Húnaland, to ask for the hand of his daughter Oda (see Ôserîch, p. 103); (3) the son of Osanctrix (II. 269, 18) who is married to the enchantress Ostacia: in the form of a flying dragon, she helps her husband against Isungr, Þetleifr, and Fasold, who are invading Villcinaland;[4] she destroys the enemy but is killed by Þetleifr.[5] Hertnið survives, and there is said to be a long story about him;[6] (4) Hertnið af Bergara (II. 359, 13) (see Ortnît (1), p. 101).

pn: 9th-cent. German (Förstemann I. 756; II. i. 1245; Socin, 20; Schlaug II. 105).

## HERTNÎT (2) father-in-law of Wielant
Wielant marries his daughter: their sons are named Wittich and Wittich owe.

ref: **AHb** p. 3, 20 (*hertwich*; Straßburg MS. *hertnicht*)

In the OE poem *Deor*, Nîðhād (5) fetters (or hamstrings) Wēlund's legs; later Nîðhād's daughter, Beadohild, becomes pregnant. In *Waldere*, Nîðhād (II. 8) is related to Widia, the son of Wēland (see Wielant, pp. 141 f.).

In the ON Eddic poem Vkv, Níðuðr (6, 1), King of the Niárar (a king in Sweden according to the prose introduction), has Völundr hamstringed and forces the smith

---

[1] This suggests that he is a Norman from South Italy.
[2] See Eckehart, p. 33 n. 5
[3] 'Novgorod' (MLG Nôgarden): see Ortnît (1), p. 101.
[4] 'land of the Wilzi' (see Wilzen(lant), p. 144).
[5] W. von Unwerth, 'Ostacia and Kára', *PBB* XL (1915), 160, discusses similar episodes in Eddic poems where the valkyrie, Kára, intervenes to help Helgi.
[6] Possibly a confusion with Hertnið (4).

## HERTNÎT (2)

to work for him. Völundr escapes by rising into the air, after killing Níðuðr's two sons and ravishing his daughter, Böðvildr (see Wielant, pp. 141 f.).[1]

In Þs, Niðungr (I. 2, 9; I. 83, 5, etc.) rules in Jutland. Velent kills his court smith with the sword Mimungr, and the King has him lamed for trying to poison him. Velent then kills the King's two youngest sons, ravishes his daughter (named Heren in MS. A: I. 120, 9), and flies off on self-made wings (see Wielant, p. 142). After Niðungr's death, Velent becomes reconciled with his heir, Otvin (MSS. AB Nidungur: I. 131, 12), and marries Heren; their son is named Viðga (MHG Witege). The name Niðungr is also used for the father of Sisibe (I. 282, 17: see Sigelint (I), p. 124).

pn: the name of Wielant's father-in-law always contains the element Gmc. *niþ- (OHG nîð, OS nîth, OE nið, 'hate, anger', ON nið, 'scorn, dishonour'); in **AHb** it is the second component (see Hertnît (1)). OE hād means 'state, condition, kind, nature'; thus OE Niðhād (Níðuðr of Vkv is an approximation) could well be equated with OE niðing, ON niðingr, 'treacherous villain', as in Þs, Niðungr (cf. Nîtgêr (1), p. 99). Gmc *niþ-, however, also indicates 'valour, battle-fury' (Kluge, EWb, 506) and was a reputable name-component: Nidada, 6th-cent. Goth. (Schönfeld, 173); Nidhad, St. Gall in 799 and Trier in 960 (Förstemann I. 1159; Socin, 572); Nithung, Nydung, 9th-cent. LG (Förstemann I. 1158; Socin, 155; Schlaug I. 135).

## HERTRÎCH

A smith in Wasconje lant (Aquitaine: see p. 137), the only equal of Mîme; together they have made twelve swords (see Mîme, p. 94).[2]

ref: **B** 149

pn: 5th-cent. for the Gepid leader, Ardaric; 6th-cent. WFr, 8th-cent. German (Förstemann I. 757 f.).

## HERTWICH, see HERTNÎT (2)

## HERWÎC von Sêlant (Sêwen)[3]

A suitor for the hand of Kûdrûn, whose suit is only accepted after he has attacked the realm of her father, Hetel. He takes part in the unsuccessful battle at Wülpensant against the Normans, Hartmuot and Ludewîc, who have abducted Kûdrûn, while he and Hetel are away fighting another suitor, Sîfrit von Môrlant. Herwîc is associated with Kûdrûn's brother, Ortwîn, in the final rescue of Kûdrûn from the Normans (see Kûdrûn, p. 22). His heraldic device is the foliage of the water-lily (MHG sêbleter) on a blue ground (1373).[4]

ref: **Ku** 586, 4

In Lamprecht's Alexander (mid 12th cent.), Herwîc and Wolfwîn (= Ortwîn (3)?) take part in the battle of Wolfenwerde (1325) (see p. 61).

A Shetland ballad taken down on the island of Foula in 1774 (Symons, Kudrun, 14 ff.) contains a story in which a rival suitor carries off the bride, Hildina, and is eventually killed by the bridegroom, Hiluge, but it is unlikely that this represents an original 'Herwigsage' (Schneider, GHS I. 375). In the Olimpia episode of Ariosto's Orlando Furioso (ed. 1532), which may derive from **Ku**, Bireno di Selandia plays the same role as Herwîc (see Kûdrûn, p. 22).

pn: 7th-cent. Goth. and WFr, 8th-cent. German (Förstemann I. 781 f.; Socin, 20; Schlaug II. 111 f.; Kromp I. 35; III. 46 ff.).

## HESSEN pl.

The people and region of Hesse:[5] see Marchunc and Sturmgêr (4).

ref: people, **B** 10772; region, **DF** 8643; **N** 176, 1; **Rs** 494, 1

## HETEL(E)

In **Ku** his realm, 'ze Hegelingen', with its capital of Matelâne,[6] comprises Friesen, Dietmers, Stürmen, Holzsæzen, Nîflant, Nortlant,[7] and Wâleis.[8] He sends an expedition led by Wate, Fruote, Hôrant, and Môrunc to Ireland to win the hand of Hilde, the daughter of Hagen (2): Hôrant wins her for Hetel by his singing, telling her that his master sings even better, but she is finally abducted when inspecting merchandise on the Hegelinge ship. Hagen and his men overtake the abductors as Hetel is greeting them on the shore of Wâleis: in the ensuing fight Hagen wounds Hetel and is himself wounded by Wate; Hilde intervenes, and Hagen agrees to her marriage with Hetel. Hilde bears Hetel two children, a son Ortwîn and a daughter Kûdrûn, whom Hetel keeps in strict seclusion. He accepts Herwîc von Sêlant as a suitor for her hand after Herwîc

---

[1] The term 'grjót-Níðuðr' is known in ON as early as the 9th cent. (de Vries, Altn. Litg. I. 54).
[2] It is possible that Eckerîch (1) is intended (see p. 34).
[3] Possibly the Danish island of Zealand, but more probably the North Sea islands generally, i.e. 'Sea Land'.
[4] Probably word-play on Sêlant: but see Müllenhoff, ZE, 314, and H. Rosenfeld, 'Die Kudrun: Nordseedichtung oder Donaudichtung', ZfdPh LXXX (1962), 304.
[5] See Zeuß, 347 ff.; Much, Germania, 286.
[6] Possibly this place-name recalls that of Matlinge in South Holland (Symons, Heldensage, 111 f.).
[7] For the variant MS. spellings, Ortlant, Hortlant, etc., see Boesch, Kudrun, 35.
[8] Hegelinge comprises then: Frisia, Dithmarschen, Stormarn, Holstein; Nîflant and Nortlant possibly represent Livland and Denmark respectively. Hetel is said to have grown up in Denmark. Wâleis—Wales or Valois are impossible here—is unidentified.

has attacked his realm; but Kûdrûn is abducted by the Normans, Hartmuot and Ludewîc, while Hetel is aiding Herwîc against a rival, Sîfrit von Môrlant. Hetel and the Hegelinge overtake the Normans at Wülpensant:[1] in the ensuing battle Ludewîc kills Hetel, and the Hegelinge break off the fight; the Normans sail away with their captive (see Kûdrûn, pp. 21 f.).

In **DH**, Etene rules in 'tuschen richen' (Germany): his realm comprises Lamparten, Pulen, Zizilion, Tuskan, Denemarkten, Spangenlant, Ungarn, and Vrankrich.[2] He sends Horant to win Hilde von Krichenlant (Greece), the daughter of 'der wilde Hagene': Horant is accompanied by Morunck and the giants, Wate, Witolt, and Asprion; Horant wins Hilde for his master by his singing, as in **Ku** (see Hôrant, pp. 80 f.).

ref: **DH** F 41, 1, 2 (Etene); **Ku** m 200, 1 n 206, 3 (MS. *Hettelein*; also *Hettlein, Hettelin, Hettel*, etc.)

In the OE poem *Widsith*, Heoden (MS. *Henden*),[3] the ruler of the Glomman (21),[4] is mentioned together with Hagena (see Hagen (2), p. 61).

In ON, Heðinn (Rdr 5, 3; Skr 88; Sk ch. 62; *Sörla þáttr* (*FAS* I. 365 ff.)) abducts Hildr, the daughter of Högni: the ensuing battle between Heðinn and Högni continues till doomsday, since Hildr raises the dead by spells each night (see Hilde (1), p. 73). In Rdr 6, 3, *Sörla þáttr* ch. 5 (*FAS* I. 373), and *Göngu Hrólfs saga* ch. 17 (*FAS* II. 207), Heðinn is the son of Hjarrandi (see Hôrant, p. 81) and rules Serkland (Africa?); Heðinn is the name of the brother of Helgi in HHv 31, 1 (see p. 79).

In Saxo v. vii. 8–ix, Hithinus is betrothed to Hilda, the daughter of Höginus, with whom, together with Onef and Glomerus,[5] he goes on an expedition to the Orkneys. Höginus accuses Hithinus of seducing Hilda, and ultimately they kill each other in a fight on the island of Hithinsö (Hiddensee, west of Rügen on the Baltic), although it is said that Hilda raises the dead each night.

pn: *Hetan (Hetin), the original name for this person, is found in West and North Germanic: 6th-cent. WFr (Greg. Tur. x. 3);[6] early 8th-cent. German (Förstemann I. 806), also compounds such as *Mardhetin* (ibid. I. 1099), *Wolfhetin* (ibid. I. 1653), and in place-names (ibid. II. i. 1353 f.; *Bach* II. §59); rare in OE, but it occurs in place-names (Binz, 195); in ON the names *Heðinn, Biarnheðinn, Úlfheðinn* are recorded (Schramm, 77). The name is thought to be based on the equivalent of OE *heden*, ON *heðinn*, 'cape or hood of skin or fur', possibly an animal mask or skin worn in disguise (ibid.; Schwarz, *Deutsche Namenforschung* I. 25);[7] the common noun is not recorded in German.

*Hetel(e)*, as printed by the editors of **Ku**, represents a South German variant form not recorded before the 12th cent. (Mone, 84; Fr. Wilhelm, 'Ein wichtiges Regensburger Zeugnis für die Heldensage im 12. Jahrhundert', *PBB* XXXIII (1908), 570); forms like *Hettilo* recorded as early as the 8th cent. at Freising (Kromp III. 45) are probably based on OHG *hadu*, 'conflict', with the suffix -*ilo* (E. Schröder, 'Hetele von Hegelingen', *ZfdA* LXV (1928), 256); apparently Hans Ried, the 16th-cent. scribe of **Ku**, has replaced *Hetan* by the more familiar *Hettile* (Rosenfeld, *Namen*, 255 f.).

The omission of *H*- in *Etene*, the form of **DH**, is a riddle (see Norman, *Dukus Horant*, 107), but may well result from a Jewish accommodation of an unfamiliar name to a well-known one, *Ethan*, the poet of the 18th Psalm (Rosenfeld, *Namen*, 256).

HIBERI pl.
The Iberians (Spaniards).

ref: **W** 1132

HILDE (1) daughter of Hagene (2)
In **Ku** Hilde, daughter of Hagene (2) von

---

[1] See Hegelinge, p. 64 n. 2.
[2] His dominion covers most of western Europe, like that of Rother (see p. 109): Lombardy, Apulia, Sicily, Tuscany, Denmark, Spain, Hungary, and France.
[3] Malone, *Widsith*, 15 f., 68, argues for the retention of the MS. reading on the basis of *hendinos*, a Burgundian word for 'king' (Amm. Marc. XXVIII. 5, 14), yet accepts the identification with Hetel of **Ku** and Heðinn of ON tradition.
[4] Probably a Baltic tribe; their name has been related to ON *glammi*, 'barkers', a *heiti* for 'wolf' (Rdr 14), and equated with that of the *Lemovii* of Tacitus, *Germania*, ch. 43, giving a Gmc. stem *lemi*, 'bark' (see Much, *Germania*, 389 f.). It is, perhaps, significant that Hetel/Heðin's people, the *Heðaningas*, may be interpreted as 'the people of the skins' (see Hegelinge, p. 64 n. 4). Hauck, *Bilderdenkmäler*, 308, makes out a wolf depicted above the Hjaðningar on the 8th-cent. Swedish Lärbro Stone.
[5] Cf. Glomman of *Widsith* above.
[6] Kaufmann, 181, suggests that a Romanized form of the word for 'heathen' may be the basis for such WFr names as *Chedenus*, etc. (OS *hēthin, hēdin*; OHG *heithin, heidan, heidin*).
[7] Cf. ON *úlfheðnar*, 'warriors in wolf-shape', and the appellative use of the name Heðinn in *Njálssaga* (ed. E. Ó. Sveinsson (Reykjavík, 1954)): for a person in disguise (Kaupa-Heðinn, ch. 22) and for a sorcerer (Galdra-Heðinn, ch. 101). It may be noted that the Hegelinge/Hjaðningar fight at Wolfenwerde in Lamprecht's *Alexander* (Wülpensant in **Ku**), and that Helgi plays a similar role to Hetel/Heðinn at Frecasteinn ('wolf-rock') in the ON HHu I. Panzer, *Hilde-Gudrun*, 307, refers the name to the disguises used by suitors in the 'Goldener' type of folk-tale, whereas F. R. Schröder, 'Die Sage von Hetel und Hilde', *DVjs* XXXII (1958), 42 f., 65, relates it to initiation ceremonies of warriors dedicated to Óðinn, i.e. *úlfheðnar*', and suggests that the personal name derives from the appellative group-name *Heðaningas* (see note 4 above).

Îrlant and Hilde von Indîân, is brought up in well-guarded seclusion ('. . . ez beschein diu sunne selten noch daz ez der wint / vil lützel an geruorte . . .' 198, 2f.); her father hangs all messengers from suitors. Hetel von Hegelingen sends Wate, Hôrant, and Fruote with a large expedition to win her hand. Hôrant wins her favour by his singing, and she gives him her girdle as a pledge for Hetel; she is then abducted while inspecting 'merchandise' on board Hôrant's ship.[1] During the subsequent battle between Hagen's men and those of Hetel, Hilde intervenes to save her father's life from Hetel's grim leader, Wate; she then persuades Wate to heal the wounded ('er machtes vor dem tôde wol gesunde' 542, 4).[2] Hagen now agrees to her marriage with Hetel: their children are Ortwîn (3) and Kûdrûn. Her daughter, Kûdrûn, is abducted by a rejected suitor, Hartmuot von Ormanîe; in the pursuit of the Normans, Hilde's husband, Hetel, is killed by Ludewîc, Hartmuot's father, at the battle of Wülpensant (see p. 72). Finally Hilde sends an army led by Hôrant and Wate to Normandy, and Kûdrûn is brought home (see p. 22).

In **DH**, Hagene, father of Hilde von Krichenlant (Greece), refuses to give his daughter in marriage to any suitor. Etene (see Hetel, p. 72), who rules in Germany, sends Horant of Denmark with a splendid retinue to win the maiden. Hilde, on her way to church, protected from the sun's rays by a baldachin in the shape of peacocks' wings (F 64, 3–4),[3] is impressed by Horant; later he wins her love by his singing, and she gives him a powerful protective stone. At first she wishes to marry him, but finally she agrees to become Etene's queen.

ref: **DH** F 44, 6, 4; **Ku** 197, 4

Hilde is mentioned in Lamprecht's *Alexander* (mid 12th cent.), but her part in the conflict between Hagen and Wate is not made clear (see Hagene (2), p. 61). In the late-13th-cent. *Wartburgkrieg* (W. Grimm, *DHS*, 379), she and Hôrant are mentioned together.

The only English reference to Hilde occurs in the 13th-cent. ME poem *Annot and Johon*, 48, where her name appears among famous persons of Welsh and Scandinavian tradition.[4]

Already in the 9th-cent. Rdr, Hildr is the instigator of the conflict between her abductor Heðinn and her father Högni in ON tradition—in this poem she is termed 'sorceress' (ON *fordǽða*); the fight takes place on an island, possibly Hod, off Normarr in Norway (ON Höð);[5] in HHu II the pn 'Hildr' is used appellatively for a woman who incites conflict (Stackmann, *Kudrun*, lxiv). In Saxo v. vii. 8–ix, the scene of battle is Hiddensee, near Rügen on the Baltic, and Hilda is thought to raise the dead each night by magic songs. The whole story of Hildr's abduction by Heðinn and the fight between him and her father, Högni, on the island of Hoy in the Orkneys (ON Háey) is told in Sk ch. 62:[6] Hildr eggs them on to conflict, and each night she raises the slain by singing magic spells; thus the battle called 'Hjaðningavíg' continues till doomsday (see Hegelinge, p. 64).

pn: frequent from the 8th cent. in German records (Förstemann I. 821; Socin, 57; Schlaug I. 110; II. 204; Kromp III. 35); 10th-cent. Lb (Bruckner, 265); 7th-cent. OE (Binz, 194; H. Ström, *Old English Personal Names in Bede's History* (Lund, 1939), 170). Many of these names probably represent compounds with first or second component based on Gmc. \**hildjō* (OHG *hiltia*, 'strife conflict'), though this name-component, in both the simplex and compound pn, may well have originated as a feminine equivalent of Gmc. \**heldaz*, 'warrior' (see Schramm, 162 f.; Kaufmann, 185); it is used appellatively, in the sense of Gmc. \**hildjō*, to name valkyries in ON: Hildr (Vsp 30, 7; Grm 36, 4; Hlr 7, 3 (= Brynhildr); Gylf ch. 36; Sk chs. 10 (= Brynhildr), 60, 61; Hátt str. 54, 3, etc.).

The story of Hilde is obviously based on human experience: the story of the flight of a man and woman pursued by the woman's guardian, with whom the abductor must fight, is frequently met in fairytale and myth (Panzer, *Hilde-Gudrun*, 251 ff.; Betz, *Aufriß* III (1957), 1529); such a story, in which the woman stands between her father and her lover,[7] was probably known to the Germanic peoples of the North Sea–Baltic region, i.e. the Danes and Angles, as early as the 5th cent.,[8] but, since the Rugians (OE

---

[1] In **R** a 'merchant' abducts Rother's wife by luring her on board ship to see strange merchandise. In **Ku** Hilde has already been won by Hôrant's singing (see Hôrant, p. 81 n. 1).

[2] The task of Hildr in the ON versions; see also Hildegunt (1), p. 78.

[3] See under Hildeburc (1) the Þs account of a similar device protecting Hildr (p. 77).

[4] No. 76 in *English Lyrics of the XIIIth Century*, ed. Carleton Brown (Oxford, 1932).

[5] Where Vigfusson, *CPB* II. 7, reads 'Höð Glamma' and 'Höð í holmi' in the relevant passages, Ernst A. Kock, *Den Norsk-Isländska Skaldadiktningen*, vol. i (Lund, 1946), 1, reads 'höðglamma' and 'hond í holmi', giving an entirely different meaning (ON *höð*, 'strife'), and thus no name for the island.

[6] She is mentioned together with Heðinn and Högni in the 15th-cent. Skr. 88.

[7] Apparently the original Germanic story was of the abduction of a man's daughter by his blood-brother, whereas the later MHG epics deal with a Mediterranean type of 'bridal quest' (Stackmann, *Kudrun*, lx f.).

[8] Engraved stones in Götland, Sweden, dating from c. 800 or possibly even earlier, are said to show pictorial representations of Hilde's story (Hauck, *Bilderdenkmäler*, 360 f.; Stackmann, *Kudrun*, lxviii f.; von See, *GHS*, 118 f.).

Holmrycgas), over whom Hagena rules in *Widsith*, left their Baltic seat in the 4th cent. at the latest, the *Widsith* references to persons of the Hilde story may well go back to the 4th or even the 3rd cent. (Stackmann, *Kudrun*, lxix; see also Hetel, p. 72, and Wate, p. 138).[1] The raising of the dead and the eternal battle are probably of Celtic origin (see p. 64 n. 1), and are likely to have been added by Scandinavians in contact with the British Isles during the 9th and 10th cents., for in West Norse versions the setting of the battle is in the Orkneys as well as off Norway.

The story of Hilde, as it appears in **Ku**, probably comes from the North via the Low Countries, which were settled by Scandinavians in the 9th cent. In **DH**, details from a variant, in which the messenger woos Hilde for himself instead of for his master, have been added, i.e. from a 'Herbortlied' (see the Þs account of Hildr, under Hildeburc (1), pp. 77 f.).[2]

HILDE (2) von Indîân (India)
Wife of Hagen (2) and mother of Hilde (1).

ref: **Ku** m 73, 3 n 170, 1

HILDE (3) a giantess
Wife of the giant Grîme (**E** and **äSn**):[3] in **E(L)** Dietrich is known to have killed them both.[4]

ref: **E(d)** 5, 3; **E(L)** 7, 3; **E(s)** 3, 3; **äSn** m 7, 7; **jSn** m 3, 8

In Þs, Hilldur (1. 35, 1) is the wife of Grímur: Þiðrekr kills them both (see pp. 53, 96).

HILDE (4) = HILDEGUNT (1)

ref: **WuH** (Wien) 1. 18, 4 (MS. *vrouwen Hilden*)

HILDEBRANT (1) son of Herebrant (1)
In **äH** (MS. *c.* 810–20), Hiltibrant, returning to Italy with the army supplied to Deotrîch by the lord of the Huns (= Etzel), faces his son Hadubrant, a champion of the opposing army, presumably that of Ôtacher, whose hostility has caused Deotrîch's exile (see Dietrich (1), p. 26, and Ôtacher, p. 103). Hadubrant refuses to believe that Hiltibrant is his father, and scornfully rejects the gift of a gold arm-ring; Hiltibrant realizes that he must now fight his own son, whom he left with his wife when he accompanied Deotrîch into exile for thirty years. The poem breaks off as father and son engage in combat.

In **jH** (15th-cent. prints),[5] Hildebrant returns to Berne (Verona) after an exile of thirty-two years (thirty years in the version of the *Dresdner Heldenbuch* of 1472),[6] and, although warned by Abelon (see Amelunc (2), p. 6), he seeks out his son Alebrant, and a fight ensues: Hildebrant overpowers the youth and forces him to reveal his identity,[7] after he has received from him a blow that makes him leap back, exclaiming: 'nun sag, du vil junger, den streich lert dich ein wip' (10, 4);[8] reconciliation takes place, and father and son return together to Hildebrant's wife Ute (see Uote (2), p. 133).[9]

This grizzled warrior is the constant companion and loyal mentor of Dietrich von Berne in the later epics (13th cent. on): his device is three wolves (**Rg(D)**, **Wd(D)**, **V(w)**: see Wülfinc (1)),[10] and his helmet is adorned with a golden serpent (**A**, **Rg(D)**, **jSn**); in **V(h)** a wheel is depicted on his banner; his sword is named variously: Brinnic (**A**), Freise (**V**), and Freissan (**jSn**).[11]

In **N**, Hildebrant is sent by Dietrich to investigate the lamentation caused by Rüedegêr's death, but becomes involved in fighting with the Burgundians by his hotheaded nephew Wolfhart: he kills Volkêr, but is forced to retreat by Hagen. Nevertheless, he strikes Kriemhilt dead with his sword, after seeing her behead the defenceless Hagen, whom Dietrich has bound. In the **Kl** he returns to Berne with Dietrich and Herrât.

In **Rg**, Hildebrant organizes the combats between Dietrich's champions and those of Kriemhilt and Gibeche in the rose-garden at

---

[1] The name of the guardian of the abducted woman, it may be noted, remains remarkably constant: Hagen (MHG)—Hagena (OE)—Högni (ON) appears in most stories about a 'Hilde' (cf. also *Hildegunt*, *Brünhilt*, and *Kriemhilt*).

[2] See Norman, *Dukus Horant*, 129.

[3] In some texts there is uncertainty about the relationship of Hilde to Grîme: the *Dresdner Heldenbuch* version of **jSn** in str. 108, 7 makes her his sister, MSS. s¹ hv Sigenôt's sister; in all texts of **jSn** at str. 7, 6 she is Grîme's sister (see Schoener, *Sigenot*, 203).

[4] In **äSn** Dietrich kills Grîme, whereas Hildebrant kills Hilde.

[5] Although **jH** is recorded at least 600 years later than **äH**, the two lays are treated together here, since their content is similar.

[6] Some prints of **jH** make it thirty-three years.

[7] In **äH**, Hiltibrant does not hesitate to reveal his identity but the son in **jH**, in accordance with the usage of chivalry, only reveals his parentage after being defeated (see p. 153).

[8] This suggests a foul blow: cf. the Þs, where Alibrandr pretends to surrender his sword and treacherously tries to cut off Hildibrandr's hand, whereat Hildibrandr exclaims 'þetta slagh mun þier hafa þin kona enn æigi þinn fader' (11. 350, 23 f.). Originally it may have been a secret blow, known only to Hildebrand (see F. Norman, 'Das Lied vom alten Hildebrand', *Studi Germanici* I (Roma, 1963), 29 f.): cf. Þs I. 348, where Hildibrandr is said to win his fights with a single sword-stroke.

[9] In some versions Hildebrant places a gold ring in Ute's cup of wine as a sign of recognition. In the version of the *Dresdner Heldenbuch* father and son fight a mock combat in front of Frau Ute before Hildebrant is finally reunited with her.

[10] In Þs, a white castle with golden towers representing Bern is depicted on his shield.

[11] In Þs II. 322, 23, his sword is named Lagulfr ('fire-wolf'?).

## HILDEBRANT (1)

Worms (see Kriemhilt); he himself defeats Gibeche, but has difficulty in persuading Dietrich to face Sîfrit. In **B**, too, Hildebrant marshals Dietrich's men in the combats at Worms and again has difficulty urging Dietrich to fight Sîfrit.

In **DF** and **Rs**, Hildebrant leads Dietrich's men: before the battle at Rabene (Ravenna) in **Rs**, he surveys the opposing army of Ermenrîch and distinguishes the enemy leaders by their banners (474 ff.).[1] In **A** he is unable to dissuade his nephew Alphart from taking up outpost duty against Ermenrîch's forces attacking Berne. In the defence of Berne he kills Berhtram (2).

In **L(AD)**, Hildebrant accompanies Dietrich to the rose-garden of the dwarf Laurîn, and advises him to stun the dwarf and seize his strength-giving belt in order to overpower him.[2] Hildebrant takes part in the battle against Laurîn's men in his underground kingdom, and finally instructs the defeated dwarf in Christianity before his enforced baptism. In **L(K)II** Hildebrant and Laurîn separate Dietrich and Walberân when they engage in single combat before Berne.

In **äSn**, Hildebrant kills the giant Sigenôt and rescues Dietrich from the snake-pit into which the giant has thrown him. In **jSn** and **E** we learn of the fight of Dietrich and Hildebrant against the giant pair, Hilde and Grîme (see Hilde (3), p. 74).

In **V(h)**, Hildebrant urges the youthful Dietrich to fight dragons rather than dally with ladies at court: in the course of their adventures, Hildebrant rescues a maiden from the heathen Orkîse, kills a dragon, frees his relative Rentwîn from its jaws (see p. 27), and summons the Wülfinge to the rescue of Dietrich, who has been captured by Nîtgêr's giants at Mûter; finally, he returns with Dietrich to the court of the elf-queen Virginâl at Jeraspunt. In **V(dw)** he kills the giant Janapas at Ortneck.

In **Wd(D)**, Hildebrant, the grandson of Berhtunc von Mêrân and son of Herebrant and Âmîe, has a sister Mergart married to Amelolt von Garten.[3]

In **AHb** Hildebrant and Dietrich are the sole survivors of the battle at Etzel's court, but Hildebrant has received two wounds in the head which never heal.[4] He is said to have been killed by Gunther at Berne (AHb p. 11, 15; earlier by Gunther's son (!), p. 3, 29).

ref: in many manuscripts from the 14th cent. on, the *t* of the first component of this name is omitted and such spellings as *Hillebrant* abound: **A** 65, 4; **AHb** p. 3, 4; **B** 5247; **DF** 2539; **DuW** 37; **E(d)** 2, 12; **E(L)** 2, 13; **E(s)** 2, 13; **ED** 1, 4; **äH** 3 (MS. *hiltibraht*, also at 7, 30, 45; but *hiltibrant-* at 14, 17, 36, 44, 49, 58); **jH** 1, 1; **Kl** 368; **L(A)** 29; **L(D)** 107; **L(DrHb)** 5, 3; **L(K)II** 306; **N** 1718, 2; **Rg(A)** 56, 1; **Rg(C)** 217; **Rg(D)** 19, 3; **Rg(F)** II. 14, 2; **Rg(P)** 19; **Rg(V)** 20; **Rs** 114, 1; **gS** p. 89, 7; **hS** 15, 8; **hS(Sachs)** 39; **äSn** 8, 4; **jSn** 3, 1; **V(d)** 4, 1; **V(h)** 2, 6; **V(w)** 25, 8; **Wd(D)** IX. 211, 3; **Wd(Gr)** 2099, 3; **Wu(B)** 121, 1

Hildebrant is first referred to in medieval German literature outside the heroic poems in the 13th cent.:[5] Wolfram von Eschenbach in *Willehalm* (c. 1215) refers to Uote awaiting Hildebrant's return (439, 16); references to him continue in the 14th and 15th cents. (W. Grimm, *DHS*, 188, 196, 226, 313 f.; 316, 324, 478). In Wittenwiler's *Ring* (c. 1410), Hilprand is among the heroes involved in the final village battle (8067). In the 16th cent. he is known to the 'Meistersänger' and to Hans Sachs and Fischart (W. Grimm, 349, 352 ff.; Jänicke, *ZE*, 329, 331). The loss of the old songs about him and Dietrich is lamented by Konrad Gesner in his *Mithridates* (1555) (Müllenhoff, *ZE*, 378), but the Protestant Reformers disparage such tales (Jänicke, *ZE*, 325 f.); Hildebrant, however, survives to the 17th cent. (Müllenhoff, *ZE*, 431), even becoming a figure in puppet-plays (W. Grimm, *DHS*, 363, 491).

---

[1] In *Þs*, Hildibrandr meets his former comrade Reinaldr, now a leader in Erminrikr's army (see Rienolt, pp. 107 f.); together they review the leaders of the opposing forces (II. 232 ff.).

[2] The inscriptions to the frescoes at Lichtenberg in the Vinstgau (15th cent.) depicting this episode refer to Hildebrant's instructions (Müllenhoff, *ZE*, 425).

[3] Hildebrant's genealogical tree, according to **Wd(D)** and **AHb**, is as follows (see Wülfinge, p. 153):

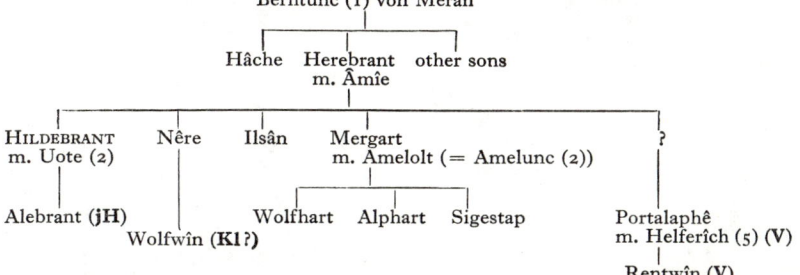

[4] Dietrich, according to Hungarian tradition, has such a wound in the head (see p. 28).

[5] He is referred to as Dietrich's companion in Eilhart von Oberg's *Tristrant* (5976), but the MSS. for this passage of this 12th-cent. work are not earlier than the 15th cent. (W. Grimm, *DHS*, 67; de Boor, *GDL* II. 34).

Apart from a confused reference in an early-13th-cent. Latin sermon on humility, in which Wade (MHG Wate) is alleged to say that Hildebrand alone is among elves, adders, and nickers ('water-spirits'),[1] the only reference to Hildebrand from the British Isles occurs in the 12th-cent. Anglo-Norman *Romance of Horn*, in which the brothers Herebrand, Hildebrand, and Goldbrand appear as heathen (Saracen) invaders of Horn's realm.[2]

Ch. 8 of the 14th-cent. ON *Ásmundar saga kappabana* (*FAS* I. 399 ff.) contains fragments of a poem about Hildibrandr's death, the so-called 'Lost Lay of Hildebrand' (Hild., *Edda*, 313 f.; *CPB* I. 190 ff.):[3] Hildibrandr encounters his younger half-brother, Ásmundr, by the Rhine; mortally wounded, Hildibrandr ('Húna kappi')[4] reveals to Ásmundr that they are both the sons of Drótt, but by different fathers.[5] Hildibrandr's broken shield lies at his head; on it are depicted the fourscore men he has slain, the last being his own son ('inn svási sonr'),[6] whom he has killed unwittingly.

In Þs, Hildibrandr (I. 32, 24), son of Reginballdr,[7] educates the young Þiðrekr at the court of Þetmarr in Bern (Verona): he aids Þiðrekr in his encounter with the giant pair, Hilldur and Grímur (see Gríme, p. 53), and is involved in the episode to do with Viðga's sword Mimungr, when the hero joins Þiðrekr's band of warriors (see Mimminc, pp. 94 f.). In Þiðrekr's Bertangaland expedition he is defeated by the tenth son of King Isungr.[8] Hildibrandr also takes a leading part in Þiðrekr's campaign against Erminrikr. In the fight against the Niflungar at Susat he kills Gernoz and severely wounds Gisler (MHG Gêrnôt and Gîselhêr).

After the death of Erminrikr he returns with Þiðrekr and Herrað to Amlungaland and aids Þiðrekr in defeating Elsungr's men, who oppose them (see Else m. (1)), killing Ingram and eight others (see p. 29); Amlungr, Elsungr's nephew, surrenders (see Amelunc (2), p. 6).[9]

In spite of the warning of Konrádur, Hildibrandr encounters his son Alibrandr; they both refuse to give their names and a fight ensues: Hildibrandr overpowers the youth after the latter has attempted a foul blow (see p. 74 n. 8), and forces him to reveal his name; they return to Bern, where Oda, Hildibrandr's wife, binds their wounds. Hildibrandr dies aged 150 (some say 200), leaving his weapons to Alibrandr for the protection of Þiðrekr.[10]

pn: 6th-cent. WFr (Förstemann I. 825; E. Schröder, *DNK*, 29 f.); it occurs for a member of the Arnulfingian dynasty in 791: *Hildebrandus comes et filius suus Nevelongus* (Jänicke, *ZE*, 310; see L. Levillain, 'Les Nibelungen historiques et leurs alliances de famille', *Annales du Midi* XLIX (1937), 337-408); 7th-cent. Lb (Förstemann I. 825; Bruckner, 268; E. Schröder, *DNK*, 29 f.; see W. Krogmann, *Das Hildebrandslied* (Berlin, 1959), 53 f.); in Germany the pn is fairly common, being first recorded at Fulda in 786 (Förstemann I. 825; II. i. 1361); it is among the three names in -*brant*, which is typically Langobardic, recorded there before 826 (Baesecke, *Hildebrandlied*, 45 f.; Bach I, § 384; see also Elfriede Ulbricht, 'Hildebrandslied und genealogische Forschung', *PBB* LXXXIV (Halle, 1962), 376-84).[11] The pn is recorded over the whole German area by the 11th cent. (Socin, 24; Schlaug II. 112;

---

[1] 'Ita quod dicere possunt cum Wade: "summe sende ylves and summe sende nadderes, summe sende nikeres, the biden pater [emended to *bi ðen watere*] wunien; nister man nenne bute Ildebrand onne"' (Fr. Kluge, *Angelsächsisches Lesebuch* (Halle, 1902³), no. xxxii; see also Chambers, *Widsith*, 98).
[2] Ed. M. K. Pope (Oxford, 1955), vv. 2912 ff., 3274 ff.
[3] See de Vries, *Altn. Litg.* II. 445 ff., and de Boor, *Kl. Schr.* II 73 ff., regarding the Faroese version in the *Snjólvskvæði*.
[4] Cf. the term 'altêr Hûn' used by Hadubrant in reference to his father, Hiltibrant (**äH** 39).
[5] A similar story about Hildigerus and Haldanus, the sons of Drota, is recorded in Saxo VII. ix. 3-16. See also de Boor, *Kl. Schr.* II. 88 ff., regarding a comparable conflict between two half-brothers, Angantýr and Hlöðr in Hlöð. A genealogy in the *Flateyjarbók* (14th cent) also contains the names of Hildibrandr's father and son (see p. 57 n. 2).
[6] Cf. 'suâsat chind' (**äH** 53).
[7] In Þs, Hildibrandr's genealogy is as follows (I. 32 f.) (see Jiriczek, *DHS* (1898), 289 ff.):

```
         Jarl af Fenedi ('jarl of Venice')
         |
    ┌────┴────┐
 Boltram   Reginballdr
    |         |
 Reginballdr  HILDIBRANDR
    |
 Sintram
```

[8] In the Danish ballads *Kong Diderik og hans Kæmper* and *Kong Diderik i Birtingsland*, Hillebrandt takes part in Diderik's expedition to *Birtingsland* (*DgF* I. 94-122, 124-9).
[9] This whole episode recalls **W**: during the journey the party avoids towns; a cloud of dust heralds the attack by Elsungr and his men; besides the riding-horses there is a pack-horse loaded with gold and silver (see Walther, p. 135, and Hildegunt, p. 78).
[10] See pp. 9 n. 2, 15, 74 n. 11 regarding the names of Hildebrant's sword in MHG epic and the Þs.
[11] The pn *Hildiberht* (cf. the forms in -*braht* of **äH** above) is frequent, being recorded for the Merovingian Frankish dynasty in the 6th cent. for the son of Clovis, and also for the son of Sigebert and Brunihildis (Förstemann I. 823 f.).

Kromp I. 30 f.; III. 51 ff.); in documents from the 13th cent. on it is met in association with that of Dietrich (Müllenhoff, *ZE*, 416; Jänicke, *ZE*, 312). In late OE the pn probably represents a continental import (Binz, 214).

The story of the combat between father and son is widespread among peoples speaking Indo-European languages (H. Rosenfeld, 'Das Hildebrandslied, die indogermanischen Vater-Sohn-Kampf-Dichtungen und das Problem ihrer Verwandtschaft', *DVjs* (1952), 413–32; see also Baesecke, *Hildebrandlied*, 55 ff., where direct derivation from Persian traditions of Sohrab and Rustem is mooted): apart from the Greek versions (Telegonos and Oedipus), the story ends with the father killing the son, as may also be assumed for the German version (**äH**) from the ON evidence (see above); in OFr epic, which most probably influenced the later German version (**jH**), reconciliation takes place (see B. Buße, 'Sagengeschichtliches zum Hildebrandsliede', *PBB* XXVI (1901), 1–92).[1] The placing of this conflict between father and son in the setting of Dietrich's exile (**äH** 15–27) may well have occurred in Langobardic Italy, as the names in -*brant* suggest,[2] for the return from exile links the two themes (Boer, *Sagen*, 179) and also supplies the context.[3]

This lay (**äH**), with its tragic outcome, probably composed among the Langobards in Italy at the beginning of the 8th cent.,[4] was copied by two scribes at Fulda c. 810 from a manuscript, in which an attempt had been made to transpose it into LG, of which the scribe was partially ignorant;[5] it reached Scandinavia, where the context was altered, since Theodoric, as an epic hero, was not known there till the 13th cent. (see Dietrich (1), p. 29). Its popularity in Germany is attested by the many and widespread records of the later ballad (**jH**), which derive from an early 13th-cent. version with a happy end (H. Rosenfeld, 'Hildebrandslied', *VfL* v (1955), 413–16), and by Hildebrant's constant presence at the side of Dietrich von Berne in the MHG epics.

Any one of the following historical persons, who have been put forward at various times, could have contributed to the ideal figure of Hildebrand, which embodies the qualities of experience, courage, and loyalty required in the entourage of princes: Gensimund, the loyal servant of the Gothic royal dynasty of the Amals (Cassiodorus, VIII. 9:[6] see Müllenhoff, *ZE*, 254); Hibba,[7] Theodoric's general, who saved the Visigoths from defeat by the Franks in 511 (Jordanes, ch. lviii), and is termed by Cassiodorus 'Ibba vir sublimus dux' (IV. 17); Ansprant, the guardian of the youthful Langobard King, Liutpert, who himself ruled the Langobards for three months before his death, and was succeeded by his son, Liutprant, whose nephew, Hildeprant, fought against the Byzantines at Ravenna in 732 and became co-regent in 735 (Paul. Diac. IV. 17–57).

HILDEBRANT (2) son of Berhtunc (1)
ref: **AHb** p. 6, 5

HILDEBURC (1) von Ormanîe (Normandy)
In **Ku**, originally a princess from Portigâl (Portugal), she is rescued from the griffon island by Hagen (2). She accompanies his daughter Hilde (1) when she becomes the wife of Hetel, then shares the captivity of their daughter Kûdrûn, when the latter is abducted by the Normans, Hartmuot and Ludewîc. Finally she marries Hartmuot and becomes Queen of Ormanîe.

In the **Kl** she is named among Helche's attendants.

In **B**, Herbort relates how he abducted Hildeburc, the daughter of Ludewîc and sister of Hartmuot;[8] he has defeated Dietrich and Hildebrant on his return with her to the Rhine.

ref: **B** m 6463 n 6503; **Kl** 2461; **Ku** m 73, 3 n 485, 1

It seems probable from **B** above that Hildeburc is ultimately to be identified with the Hilldr, daughter of King Artus af Bertangaland, in Þs II. 47, 8: Þiðrekr sends his nephew Herburt with a splendid retinue to win her for him. Herburt sees her going to church under a canopy shaped like two peacocks to protect her from the rays of the sun (see the account of **DH**, p. 73); in the church he attracts her attention by letting gold- and silver-ornamented mice run to the wall near which she is sitting. Finally Hilldr persuades her father to let Herburt be her personal servant; Herburt tells her that he has been sent by his uncle Þiðrekr to win her

---

[1] The Marner's reference to 'des jungen Albrandes tôt' (see p. 57 n. 1) suggests that a tragic version may still have been in circulation in the 13th cent.

[2] Traditions about two champions meeting between opposing armies are known from records of early Germanic warfare, especially among the Langobards, who may well have been influenced by Roman models (F. Norman, 'Das Lied vom alten Hildebrand', *Studi Germanici* I (Roma, 1963), 31 f.).

[3] F. R. Schröder, 'Mythos und Heldensage', *GRM* XXXVI (1955), 4, would make the context more precise: Theodoric's crossing of the Isonzo in August 489.

[4] Baesecke, *Hildebrandlied*, 49, considers that it was composed at the court of King Liutprant (†744). See below.

[5] Baesecke, op. cit. 14 ff., 41 ff., suggests that this original manuscript derived from a Bavarian version of the lay.

[6] De Boor, *Kl. Schr.* II. 100 ff., links Gensimund with Gizurr, the ancient Hunnish warrior of the ON Hlöð ('Battle of the Goths and Huns').

[7] For the personal name see Schönfeld, 145; Förstemann I. 814, 942; Kaufmann, 184: it is possible that it represents the short form of a compound name with first component \*Hildi-.

[8] In **Ku** Ortrûn is the name of Hartmuot's sister.

for him, but draws so hideous a picture of Þiðrekr on the wall that she refuses to marry such a 'devil' and persuades Herburt to elope with her.

pn: 8th-cent. German (Förstemann I. 826; II. i. 1362; Socin, 57; Schlaug I. 108; II. 112; Kromp III. 54 f.); in the 13th cent. it is used for a village maiden in *Neidharts Lieder*, 42, 10. It is recorded from the 9th cent. in OE (Searle, 297; Sweet, 154; Binz, 179).[1]

HILDEBURC (2) mother of Wolfdietrich (cf. DIETLINT (3))

In **Wd(A)**, Hugdietrich's wife, the sister of Botelunc, although a Hunnish princess, converts her husband to Christianity ('Si was ein heideninne und geloubte doch an got' 19, 3).[2] After failing to seduce her, Sabene, Hugdietrich's evil counsellor, plots against the life of her son, but the child, 'Wolf hêr Dietrich' (113, 4), after he has played unharmed with wolves, is saved by the loyal Berhtunc (see Wolfdietrich, p. 148).

In **Wd(B)**, Hildeburc's father, Walgunt, the heathen King of Salnecke (Salonika), keeps her locked in a tower;[3] Hugdietrich, disguised as a woman and calling himself 'Hildegunt', seduces her (see p. 82), and she bears him a son, later named 'Wolfdietrich', after he has been found in a wolf's den (see Wolfdietrich, p. 148).

ref: **AHb** p. 6, 21; **Wd(A)** m 3, 1; **Wd(B)** 16, 1; **Wd(D)** v. 34, 3; **Wd(Gr)** 22, 1

HILDEGRÎN

Dietrich's helmet: in **E** it illuminates the forest at night, so that the young giant Ecke is able to see Dietrich; its brightness increases with age (**E(L)** 71, 12 f.);[4] a jewel is the source of light (**E(d)** 201, 12).[5] In jSn, Sigenôt recognizes the helmet Dietrich is wearing as that belonging to his uncle Grîme, whom Dietrich has slain.

ref: **A** 42, 4; **B** 9237; **E(d)** 79, 7; **E(L)** 70, 7; **E(s)** 57, 13; **L(D)** 1091; **jSn** 26, 2; **Wu(H)** 168, 8[6]

In the Þs the full story is told of how Þiðrekr kills the giant pair, Hilldur and Grímur, and wins the helmet Hildigrímur from them (I. 38, 2) (see p. 53).

[1] In *Beowulf*, Hildeburh (1070), a Danish princess, daughter of Hōc and sister of Hnæf, is carried off to Denmark after fighting between Hnæf's men and those of her husband Finn, King of the Jutes and Frisians, has taken place (see Hûc, p. 82).
[2] In the 12th-cent. 'Spielmannsepos' *Oswald*, Pamige is described in the same terms (239 f.).
[3] Cf. the seclusion of Hilde (1) in **Ku** and Hildr in Þs (see pp. 73, 77).
[4] The helmet of Detricus in Kéza's *Chronica Hungarorum* (late 13th cent.) has the same quality (W. Grimm, *DHS*, 182).
[5] In **V(h)** 36, 4 the term 'hiltegrîn' is used for a light-giving jewel in the helmet of Orkîse. This light-giving quality is also found in the jewel on the helmet of the chevalier in the OFr analogue to

pn: based on \*hildi- (OHG hiltia, 'battle') and \*grima (OE grima, 'mask, helmet', ON gríma, 'hood; spectre'; cf. OHG grînan, 'grimace'); the pn *Hiltigrim* (-grin) is recorded in the 9th cent. in Germany (Förstemann I. 830); *Heldegrin* is the name of an innkeeper in OFr epic (Langlois, 329).

The name of Dietrich's helmet appears to be old, but the tale of Hilde and Grîme in MHG and Þs is late aetiological fiction to account for it; the power of illumination by means of a jewel seems also to be secondary (perhaps first in the 13th cent. in E), though Hauck (*Bilder-Edda*, 58 f.) makes out a bejeweled helmet belonging to Dietrich in the Swedish textile frieze of Överhogdal (*c.* 1100) (!).

HILDEGUNT (1) Walther's wife

In **W**, Hiltgunt, daughter of Heriricus, the King of Burgundia, is sent to Attila as a hostage. She escapes from the land of the Huns with Waltharius (see Walther), and brings armour, treasure, and food for their flight from the storehouse of her mistress, Attila's queen Ospirin (see Helche, p. 66); on the journey westward she leads the packhorse and carries a fishing-rod. When the fugitives reach the Vosges mountains, Hiltgunt keeps watch while Waltharius sleeps with his head in her lap. During the night watch after the first encounter with Guntharius's men, Hiltgunt keeps herself awake by singing. After Waltharius has fought Hagano and Guntharius, she tends the wounds of the three warriors[7] and serves them wine. Finally she marries Waltharius.

In **B**, Hildegunt recalls how she made the Huns drunk before her flight with Walther (12633 ff.).[8]

ref: **B** 767; **N** 1756, 4; **Rg(F)** IV. 3, 4; **W** 26 (Hiltgunt);[9] **WuH** (Graz) V. 2; (Wien) I. 8, 4

Outside the epics, references to Hildegunt first occur in Germany in the early 13th cent.; Walther von der Vogelweide, playing on his own name, declares:

mînes herzen tiefiu wunde
   diu muoz iemer offen stên, sie enwerde heil
von Hiltegunde.        (*Gedichte*, 74, 18 f.)

Walther and Hildegunt are mentioned by the husband in *von einem übelen wîp* (W. Grimm, *DHS*, 173). Otherwise there is only a confused

**E**, *Le Chevalier du Papagau* (O. Freiburg, 'Die Quelle des Eckenliedes', *PBB* XXIX (1904), 17; see p. 33).
[6] Here the term refers to the helmets of both Dietrich and the 'Wunderer'.
[7] In the ON *Njálssaga* (ed. E. Ó. Sveinsson, Reykjavík, 1954), composed *c.* 1280, a woman named Hildigunnr læknir (H. the Healer, ch. 57) tends the wounded Starkaðr and Þorgeirr (ch. 63).
[8] In **W** it is Waltharius who makes the Huns drunk (304 ff.).
[9] The form of the name without the linking vowel is conditioned by the demands of the hexameter (Hans Kuhn, 'Zur Geschichte der Walthersage', *Festgabe für Ulrich Pretzel* (Berlin, 1963), 338).

## HILDEGUNT (1)

reference in the *Annales Bojorum* (1554) of Aventinus, where 'Hyldegunda filia Herrici reguli Francorum' is taken to be Attila's last wife (Müllenhoff, *ZE*, 432), an obvious confusion.

In the OE *Waldere* the name does not occur, but it is assumed by most critics that \*Hildegȳþ speaks words of encouragement to Waldere (I. 1–25).

In the 10th-cent. ON Hdl, the name Hildigunnr occurs for the daughter of Sváva and a sea-king, apparently Heðinn, Helgi's brother (*CPB* II. 517 n. 3).[1]

In the Þs, Hilldigundr, daughter of Ilias af Greca (II. 106, 2), elopes from Húnaland with Valtari, and they are pursued by Attila's men led by Högni (see Walther, p. 136).

In the version of the Walther story found in the late 14th-cent. *Polish Chronicle* of Boguphalus (W. Grimm, *DHS*, 174; Heinzel, *Walthersage*, 28 ff.), a Polish hero named Walczerz wins Helgunda, daughter of the Frankish king, by his singing (cf. Hôrant), and kills a German rival while returning with her across the Rhine. Helgunda elopes with another lover named Wislaw (see Wisselau, p. 144 and n. 6); Walczerz kills them both, and Helgunda is buried at the castle of Tyniec.

pn: 6th-cent. WFr; 9th-cent. German (Förstemann I. 830; Socin, 571; Schlaug II. 112; Holthausen, 498; Bach I, § 301). In OE the name *Hildegȳþ* is recorded *c*. 700 on a runic inscription at Hartlepool, Co. Durham, and in the 9th-cent. *Liber Vitae* (Sweet, 128, 155).

## HILDEGUNT (2) incognito of Hugdietrich (1)

Hugdietrich, disguised as a woman, pretends to be his own sister 'Hildegunt', who has been exiled for refusing to marry a heathen; by this ruse he obtains entry to the tower where Walgunt keeps his daughter, Hildeburc, in seclusion (see Hugdietrich (1), p. 82).

ref: **Wd(B)** 56, 4; **Wd(Gr)** 62, 4

HIL(L)-, HYL-, etc., see under HILD-

HILT-, see under HILD-

## HIUNE(N) (HIUNENLANT, HIUNENRÎCHE; HIUNISCH adj.)

The people and kingdom ruled by Etzel, whose capital is at Etzelnburc (Gran or Ofen in Hungary): see also Ungern.

ref: Hiune sg.: **äH** 39 ('altêr Hûn' = Hiltibrant); **N** 1889, 3

Hiunen pl.: **DuW** 409; **äH** 35 ('Hûneo truhtîn = Etzel?); **N** 1239, 1; **Rg(D)** 17, 2; **Rg(P)** 246; **Rs** 492, 6; **W** 5 (Hunos acc. pl.); **WuH** (Wien) I. 12, 4; region (von den H., ze den H., etc.): **DF** 4534; **Kl** 108; **N** 1170, 4; **Rg(C)** 675; **Rg(D)** 4, 3; **Rs** 398, 4; **Wd(A)** 3, 1; (der) Hiunen lant: **AHb** p. 1, 21 (= Vnger); **B** 284; **DF** 7767; **N** 1166, 3; **Rg(D)** 193, 1; **WuH** (Graz) VII. 1; Hiunen rîche: **B** 309; **Kl** 77 (C) 121

hiunisch adj.: **AHb** p. 10, 19 (die h. held = Wölffinge); **B** 4843 (the language); **Wd(k)** 1, 7 (*Haunisch* = region); hiunisch (-ez, -iu) lant: **DF** 4861; **N** 1180, 4; **Rs** 6, 5; hiunisch (-ez, -iu) rîche: **DF** 4538; **DuW** 147; **Kl** 77 (B); 3610 (C); hiunisches gemerke: **Wd(A)** 2, 2; hiunisch marke: **DF** 5885

In the catalogue of epic figures in OE *Widsith*, it is recorded that 'Ætla wēold Hūnum'(18); the fictitious 'scop' of the poem, Wīdsīð himself, visits the Huns (57) as well as a number of Germanic peoples.[2] In ON the Húnar are the subjects of Atli (MHG Etzel), but the term also applies to the peoples of the South in general, i.e. Germany: Húnar pl. Gðr II 15, 6; Akv 2, 4; Ghv 12, 1; Hlöð 15, 5; Völss ch. 37 (Hýnir); Húnaland: Gðr I 6, 2; Od 4, 4; Hlöð 1, 2; Völss ch. 1; Húnmörk: Akv 13, 2.

In the Þs, Attila's realm of Húnaland (1. 49, 21), which he has seized from Milias (see p. 42), also termed 'Saxland', lies in North Germany, its capital being at Susat (Soest in Westphalia).[3]

pn: probably related to Kumanic \**kun*, 'power, strength' (Altheim I. 7); the people were termed *Huni* (Latin), Χοῦνοι (Greek), by Classical authors; in Gmc. a long vowel appears: OHG *Hûni*, MHG *Hiune* (MHG *hiune*, Early NHG *heune*, mean 'giant'). The modern forms with a short vowel, NHG *Hunne*, Engl. *Hun*, stem from MLat. *Hunni*.

The Huns, a Turco-Tatar race of nomadic horsemen, appeared in eastern Europe in the 2nd cent. A.D. (Altheim I. 3; *CMH* I. 323–66). Their impact on European history was first felt with their crossing of the Don and sudden defeat of the Alans and Ostrogoths in 375 (see Ermenrîch, p. 39); they next advanced to the Danube and subjugated not only the Ostrogoths but also other Germanic tribes of central Europe. Their first appearance struck terror in the minds of contemporaries (Amm. Marc. xxx. iv. 1–4); in Ostrogothic tradition they were thought to

---

[1] Cf. Hilde (1), pp. 73 f.

[2] In Bede's *History*, ch. v, 9, names of Germanic peoples are listed, and the Huns are included among the Frisians, Rugini, Danes, and Boructuari, which, taken together with the *Widsith* evidence, suggests that in northern Germanic tradition the dominion of Attila and the Huns extended far to the north and reached the Baltic.

[3] His realm approximates to the Duchy of Saxony between 900 and 1180 (Paff, 91). This may, however, reflect the tradition of the northern extent of Hunnish rule (see previous note); Saxo, v. vii. 12–13, relates how Frotho (see Fruote, p. 48) defeats the Huns, and then rules from Russia to the Rhine; he permits Hun, the brother of the King of the Huns, to rule Saxony as his vassal.

have been sired by evil spirits on witches in the wilderness (Jordanes, ch. xxiv); in fact, their hardy horses and effective short horn bows, their mobile existence and simple needs, enabled them to produce superb cavalry forces. From their base in the Pannonian Plain they were able to threaten and harass both the East and the West Roman Empires, and in 434, under their leader Ruas, they even undertook the siege of Constantinople. Nevertheless, in the late 4th and early 5th cent. the Romans employed the as yet disunited Huns as allies and mercenaries; thus in 437 Aetius, Governor of Gaul, used a force of Huns to destroy the Burgundian power (see Burgonde, p. 17). Under Attila, who ruled the Huns from 445 till his death in 453, they were united for a few years, but on his death the Germanic tribes rebelled, his sons were defeated at the battle of Nedao in 454, and the Hunnish confederation dispersed; it is probable that the Bulgarians are descended from the remnants of the Huns (Zeuß, 710 f.; see also Blœdel, p. 13, and Etzel, pp. 42 f.).

The Huns were succeeded in Pannonia by other Asiatic horsemen: the best-known of these were the Avars in the 6th to 8th cent. and the Magyars or Hungarians in the 9th, both of whom are frequently confused with them (see Avares, p. 8, and Ungern, p. 132).[1] In German medieval epics 'Hiunenlant' and 'Ungern' are identical, i.e. both terms refer to the Kingdom of Hungary, for by the 12th cent. the Germans, especially the Bavarians and Austrians, regarded the Hungarians as Christian neighbours worthy of respect,[2] and in 1187 King Bela of Hungary entertained the German Emperor, Frederick I, at Gran, when he was on his way to the Holy Land.[3]

## HIUTEGÊR
Ortnît's steward: father of Engelwân and Helmnôt (3).

ref: **AHb** m p. 515; **O** 33, 1

pn: possibly derived from Wolfram von Eschenbach's *Parzival*, where Hiutegêr von Schotlant (25, 9) is in the service of Fridebrant; it may be an accommodation of OFr *Audigier* (Martin, *Parzival* II. 36), though

*Hút(t)inger* is recorded in Germany as a second name in the 13th cent. (Socin, 356).

## HIUZOLT (1) Ermenrîch's man
He fights Walther at Bôlonje (Bologna) in **DF** and Îrinc at Rabene (Ravenna) in **Rs**.

ref: **DF** 8635 (von Norwæge H.);[4] **Rs** 709, 5 (H. von Grüenlande)[5]

pn: *Hiuz-* is apparently a late hypocoristic form (Socin, 179); it is possibly related to MHG *hiuzen*, 'defy'.

## HIUZOLT (2) von Priuzen (Prussia)
Etzel's man: he aids Dietrich at Meilân (Milan).

ref: **DF** 5907

## HÔHERMUOT
A giant killed by Biterolf (see Wîcram).

ref: **V(h)** 890, 9

pn: descriptive, cf. MHG *hôher muot*, 'sense of well-being; pride'.

## HOLZSÆZEN pl.
Holsteiners, led by Îrolt and Fruote (**Ku** 1374, 1415). Holzânelant (Holstein) is part of Hetel's realm (**Ku** 1089, 1).

ref: **Ku** 1374, 3

The NHG regional designation *Holstein* derives from LG *Holtseten*, *Holsten*, 'forest-dwellers' (Zeuß, 396), and refers to the region of the Cimbric peninsula south of Denmark.

## HÔRANT von Tenemarke (Denmark)
In **Ku** and **DH** Hôrant is sent by his lord (Hetele in **Ku**, Etene in **DH**) to win the hand of Hilde (von Îrlant in **Ku**, von Krichenlande in **DH**), whose father, 'der wilde Hagene', keeps her in strict seclusion and hangs all messengers for her hand. Hôrant sails with a splendid retinue (including Môrunc, Îrolt, Wate,[6] and Fruote in **Ku**; Morunk, and the three giants, Wate, Asprion, and Witolt,[7] in **DH**); on arrival in Hagen's realm, Hôrant and his men give themselves out to be 'merchants' exiled by Hetele/Etene, and impress the population with their generosity.[8] Hôrant wins Hilde's

---

[1] Cf. the 12th-cent. Regensburg gloss of 'Huni' by 'Vnger' (Müllenhoff, ZE, 415). In the mid-12th-cent. *Kaiserchronik*, the terms 'Unger' and 'Hûne' are used for the Magyars (15544 ff.), but the Huns are always referred to as 'Hûne' (7046 ff.). In Hungarian tradition, too, the Hungarians are identified with the Huns, e.g. the *Gesta Hungarorum* (1172–90), in which the entry of the Hungarians into Pannonia is regarded as the second invasion by the same people (see Bleyer, 441 ff.). The original name of the Hungarians, *Ugri*, developed an -*n*- in Old Slavonic, giving *Ungarii* in Latin records, which received an initial *H*- in MLat.; hence *Hungarii*, which added to the confusion with the *Huni* of old (F. P. Magoun, 'Geographical and Ethnic Names in the Nibelungenlied', *Mediaeval Studies*, VII (1945), 128 f.).

[2] Soon after their defeat by Otto the Great at the Lechfeld in 955, Christianity reached the Hungarians under King Geisa (†997).

[3] Panzer, *Nibelungenlied*, 397, relates this to the visit of Gunther and his men to Bechelâren in **N** (see p. 110 n. 10).

[4] Norway.     [5] Greenland.

[6] In **Ku**, Wate is in practical command of the warlike expedition.

[7] In **DH**, Horant has difficulty in preventing Witolt from killing Greeks (F62, 4 ff.); Rother's giants cause similar alarm in Constantinople (**R** 825 ff., 1039 ff.).

[8] In **Ku** they sell valuable wares cheaply; in *DH* they have golden horseshoes nailed to their horses' hooves by a single nail, so that they are cast off as largesse to the populace (see Harvey, 175, regarding this motif).

favour by his Orpheus-like singing,[1] and she gives him a token of her affection (in **Ku** her girdle for Hetel, in **DH** a protective ring for Hôrant himself); initially she is attracted to Hôrant, and only agrees to become the wife of Hetele/Etene when Hôrant agrees to continue singing for her, and also assures her that his master sings even better than he.

In **Ku**, Hilde then allows herself to be abducted while inspecting the wares of the 'merchants' on board their ship. Kûdrûn, the daughter of Hetele and Hilde, is abducted by Hartmuot von Ormanîe, and Hôrant takes a leading part in the battles against the Normans and the rescue of Kûdrûn (see p. 22).

**DH** breaks off after Hôrant has won Hagen's esteem by his prowess in jousting and by his generosity.

ref: **DH** F 42, 3, 1; **Ku** 206, 2 (MS. *Horrannt*)

In German literature Hôrant is first mentioned in the late-12th-cent. 'Spielmannsepos', *Salman und Morolf*,[2] and references to his minstrelsy occur in the late 13th and early 15th cents. (W. Grimm, *DHS*, 379 f.; Müllenhoff, *ZE*, 423 f.).

In the OE poem *Deor* (c. 900), the narrator complains that Heorrenda (39), a man skilled in song ('lēoðcræftig monn' 40), has supplanted him as the court poet of the Heodeningas ('Heodeninga scop' 36).

In Saxo's Danish history, Hiarno (VI. i. 1)[3] achieves the crown of Denmark by composing a poem for inscription on the tomb of Frotho III (see Fruote, p. 48), but he is deposed and slain by the rightful heir, Fridlevus. In ch. 12 of the 14th-cent. *Bósa saga* (*FAS* III. 312), Hjarrandi is connected with a certain dance-song, the 'Hjarrandahljóð'. Otherwise, in West Norse tradition, where pursuit and combat are more important than the methods of abduction in the story of Hildr,[4] Hjarrandi, also a byname of Óðinn (Hátt str. 53, 6), is the name of the father of Heðinn (Rdr 6, 3; Sk ch. 62; *Sǫrla þáttr* ch. 5 (*FAS* I. 373); *Göngu Hrolfs saga* (*FAS* II. 207)).

pn: two forms in German records (Heusler, *Heldennamen*, 100 f., and Norman, *Dukus Horant*, 112 ff.):

(1) *Herrant*, 9th-cent. German (Förstemann I. 777, under *Herirant*;[5] Socin, 572 f.; Schlaug II. 138; Müllenhoff, *ZE* 312 f.; Kaufmann, 176), corresponds to ON *Hjarrandi*[6] and OE *Heorrenda*, being a participial form based possibly on the same root as MHG *\*herren*, deduced from *hurren*, 'move quickly', cf. OHG *hirlîh*, 'sudden, vigorous'; OE *heorr* and ON *hjarri*, 'door-hinge', possibly also 'plectrum', i.e. 'that which plays' (see Müllenhoff, *ZE*, 312; Jóhannesson, 830), probably derive from the same root. Such an appellative name would be suitable for a minstrel (cf. Wärbel, p. 138).

(2) *Hôrant*, first recorded c. 1100 in UG at Tegernsee, then in the mid 12th cent. in Franconian (Förstemann I. 866; Müllenhoff, *ZE*, 313; E. Schröder, *DNK*, 96); it is the only form in German epics, and is possibly influenced by the verb 'to hear' (OHG *hôren*) because of Hôrant's minstrelsy.[7]

HORNBÎLE
One of Biterolf's three swords.

ref: **B** 12262 (MS. *hornpeyl*)

pn: The name may suggest a weapon for cutting the horn of giants and dragons (Wackernagel, 137), but it is far more likely to refer to a sword with a horn grip (Davidson, 58, 62, 181); cf. MHG *bîl*, MLG *bîle*, 'axe, cutting-iron' (Kluge, *EWb*, 62), and such OE sword terms as *hildebill*, *guðbill*, etc. (Keller, 155).

HORNBOGE (1) Etzel's man
Associated with Râmunc as the leader of the Walâchen (Vlâchen).

ref: **B** 3452; **N** 1344, 1; **N(k)** 1358, 1 (*Hornebung*; 1914, 2 *Hornebrande*)

In Þs, Hornbogi af Vendland (I. 139, 12) is among Þiðrekr's men: he aids Viðga against the robbers at Briktan, but he is defeated by Isungr's seventh son in the Bertangaland expedition. He is an excellent bowman and has two flying birds depicted on his shield.[8]

pn: descriptive, referring to horn bows of

---

[1] In **Ku** Hôrant first wins the favour of Hilde's mother, Hilde (2) von Indîan, for whom he sings three melodies ('dœne', 384, 1), cf. Rother's three songs (see p. 109 n. 6); for Princess Hilde, when he later visits her apartment with Môrunc, he sings a song from Amilê (Arabia? **Ku** 397), which a Christian might only hear at sea (see W. Grimm, *DHS*, 375, regarding songs learnt from nixes). When Hôrant sings for Hilde, the birds and beasts attend (**Ku** 372, 389, etc.), and in **DH**, even the wild boars cease rooting (F 66, 3 f.); in **DH**, mermaids approach the ship to listen when he sings on embarkation 'in gotes namen varn wir' (F 51, 6 ff.; cf. Gottfried von Straßburg's *Tristan*, 11531 ff.).
[2] Salmân's messenger states that, even if he sang as well as Hôrant, he could not win back Salme, Salmân's wife (155, 3 ff.); in fact, Môrolf later sings a song he learnt in Endîan (251–6). See also Môrunc (1), p. 95.

[3] See F. Detter and R. Heinzel, 'Hœnir und der Vanenkrieg', *PBB* XVIII (1894), 547, for discussion of this myth.
[4] Schneider, *GHS* I. 381.
[5] Rosenfeld, *Namen*, 252 f., also derives *Herrant* from an original *\*Hari-rand* (OHG *heri*, 'army', and *rand*, 'shield').
[6] The name *Hiarrende* also occurs in Saxo v. xiii. 4 for one of the sons of Arngrimus.
[7] Rosenfeld, *Namen*, 253, considers the first component to be *Hô-* (OHG *hôch*, 'high'); see Kaufmann, 179, 193.
[8] In **N**, the Petschenære, mentioned in the same passage as Hornboge, Râmunc, and the Walâchen, are said to be able to shoot birds on the wing (1340); Râmunc and his horsemen are said to ride like flying birds (1343).

HORNBOGE (1)

steppe horsemen (see Hiunen, pp. 79 f., and Walâchen, p. 134), cf. MHG *hornboge*, 'bowman' (*Rolandslied*, v. 2625).
See Hœrninck below.

HORNBOGE (2) von Pôlân (Poland)
A hostage at Etzel's court in **B**, he aids Dietrich against Ermenrîch in **DF** and **Rs**.

HŒRNINCK
In **ED**, 'eyn Hœrninck mit synen hœrnen Bagen' is a companion of Dirik (= Dietrich von Berne) on his expedition against the 'kœninck van Armentriken' (= Ermenrîch).

ref: **ED** 16, 3
Hornboge (1) above is probably intended.

pn: the distortion of the name may not be entirely fortuitous: Hamðir and Sörli refer to their half-brother, Erpr, as 'hornungr' (bastard) (Hm 14, 8) when they set out to kill Jörmunrekr (see Erpfe, p. 40). *Hornung* occurs as a pn in German records from the 8th cent. (Förstemann I. 867; Socin, 219).

HORTLIEB
Counsellor to Sigmund.

ref: h**S**(Sachs) 79

pn: a corruption of Ortliep (?).

HÛC von Tenemarke (Denmark)
In **A** he aids Dietrich against Ermenrîch, yet in **E** he is one of the companions of Helferîch killed by Dietrich. In **AHb** his seat is Mencz (Mainz).

ref: **A** 307, 3; **AHb** p. 1, 19; **E(d)** 64, 10; **E(L)** 59, 10; **E(s)** 56, 10

In OE *Widsith*, the patronymic Hōcingas (9) applies to the Danes, whose ruler is Hnæf; in *Beowulf*, Hōc (1076) is the father of Hildeburh and Hnæf, chief of the Healfdene. This genealogical complex is reflected in an ON name-list, where Hnefi and Hökingr appear as sea-kings (Malone, *Widsith*, 167); it is not clear how it became involved in the Alemannic ducal genealogy of Charlemagne's queen, Hildegard, in the 8th cent.: 'Godefridus dux genuit Huochingum, Huochingus genuit Nebi, Nebi genuit Immam, Imma vero genuit Hiltigardam . . .' (Thegan's *Vita Hludovici*, ch. 11: cit. Müllenhoff, *ZE*, 285).

pn: 8th cent. (Förstemann I. 922; Schlaug I. 116); OE place-names (Binz, 181). See also Hugdietrich below.

Epic connections, now lost, are suggested by the following: in OE Hōc, a Dane, is the father of Hildeburh (*Beowulf*); in MHG, Dietrich kills Hûc von Tenemarke (**E**) and

[1] The seduction of a secluded princess by a suitor in female disguise is a widespread European ballad and folk-tale motif (see O. Jänicke, *DHB* IV. xli f.; I.-M. Greverus, *Skandinavische Balladen des Mittelalters* (Hamburg, 1963), 108 f.): in ON it is represented by the stories of Hagbard and Signe (Saxo VII; I. 258 ff.), Óðinn and Rinda

HUGDIETRICH (1)

fights Herbort von Tenemarke, Hildeburc's abductor (**B**); Herbort himself kills *Huge*bolt (**E(L)**), and *Hug*dietrich woos a Hildeburc (**Wd(B)**).

HUGDIETRICH (1) father of Wolfdietrich
In **Wd(A)**, Hugdietrich rules at Constantinople: his realm includes Greece, Bulgaria, and the Hunnish March. His queen is a heathen princess; their youngest son, Wolfdietrich, is born during Hugdietrich's absence on a campaign against Fruote von Tenemarke. A plot by the evil counsellor Sabene against the life of Wolfdietrich is foiled by the loyal major-domo Berhtunc (1), to whose care Hugdietrich, on his deathbed, commends his wife, sons, and realm.

In **Wd(B)**, Hugdietrich, son of Antzîus of Greece, decides to win the hand of Hildeburc, whose father Walgunt, the heathen King of Salnecke (Salonika), keeps her confined in a tower. Disguised as a woman and giving himself out as his own sister 'Hildegunt', Hugdietrich wins the favour of Walgunt and is permitted to teach Hildeburc embroidery in her tower; he seduces her, and she bears him a son, Wolfdietrich.[1] The pair are forgiven, Hildeburc becomes Hugdietrich's queen, and she bears him two more sons, Bouge and Wahsmuot. Before he dies, Hugdietrich divides his kingdom, leaving Constantinople to Wolfdietrich and the rest to Bouge and Wahsmuot;[2] he commends Wolfdietrich and the Queen to the protection of Berhtunc.

In **Wd(D)**, Olfân von Babilônje invades Hugdietrich's realm, and Wolfdietrich defeats him in a battle at Constantinople. Later Hugdietrich agrees to pay tribute to Ortnît, but Wolfdietrich disputes this.

ref: **AHb** p. 5, 40; **O** 521, 8 (ae only);[3] **O(w)** 443, 1 (*Haüge Diterich*); **Wd(A)** 2, 4 (7, 2 MS. *huge Diettreich*, etc.); **Wd(B)** 1, 2 (B always *hoch*-, other MSS. *haug*-, *hug*-, *hüg*-); **Wd(D)** III. 7, 2; **Wd(Gr)** 7, 2; **Wd(k)** 1, 4 (*Hogo dietereich*; 1, 8 *Hugo*, etc.)

pn: prefixal \**Hūg*- appears to be a byname of the Salian Franks, which may be related to the name of the Chauci of Tacitus, *Germania*, chs. 35 and 41 (< Gmc. \**hauhōz*, 'the high ones'; see Kluge, *EWb*, 311; Much, *Germania*, 312 f.).[4] As a pn it is well attested in Germany and France: *Hugi*, etc., 8th-cent. German (see under Hûc above); *Hu(g)on* for a large number of persons in OFr epic (Langlois, 348 ff.), including 'Hugon le fort, emperere de Grece et de Constantinoble' (ibid. 350; Voretzsch, 314); *Hugo* in OE *Domesday* is a continental import (Feilitzen, 294).

(Saxo III), and Apollonius and Herborg (Þs II. 109 ff.).
[2] 'bi der Ipper' (Hungary?) to Wahsmuot and 'Blibort' (Lilienporte, i.e. Durazzo?) to Bouge.
[3] See *DHB* IV. 260.
[4] The editors of the MHG texts keep to short *u* for *Hugdietrich*.

## HUGDIETRICH (1)

Widukind in the 10th cent. refers to Clovis (Chlodovech) as 'Huga' (Widukind I. 9: see Baesecke, *Vorgeschichte*, 137); in OE *Beowulf*, the Hūgas (2502, 2914) are the Salian Franks who defeated Hygelāc the Geat (Chochilaicus in Greg. Tur. III. 3) between 516 and 521,[1] and they were the subjects of the son of Clovis (†511), Theodoric of Metz (†534), the Merovingian ruler of Gaul, to whom the *Ann. Quedl.* (c. 1000) refer: 'Hugo Theodoricus iste dicitur, id est Francus, quia olim omnes Franci Hugones vocabantur a suo quodam duce Hugone' (*MGH ss* III. 31; J. Grimm, *GDS*, 468 f.).

Thus *Hugdietrich* could indicate the 'Frankish Dietrich' or 'Dietrich, son of Clovis' (see also Wolfdietrich, pp. 150 f.). On the other hand, there are parallels to the Hugdietrich of MHG epic in anecdotes of a folk-tale nature recorded about Clovis himself (Fredegar II. 17–20):[2] his messenger for the hand of the Burgundian princess, Chrotehild, was disguised as a beggar and was said to have abducted her by force of arms, and Clovis, originally a heathen, was thought to have been converted to Christianity by divine intervention. According to the *Poeta Saxo* (*MGH ss* I. 268 f.), there were songs about Clovis and his son Theodoric in the 9th cent.; 'Þēodrīc wēold Froncum' of OE *Widsith* 24 undoubtedly refers to the son.

Hence the name of this figure apparently derives from that of the son of Clovis, whereas the prefix *Hug-* and the role suggest Clovis himself. The transfer of this ostensibly Frankish figure to Constantinople has been explained by the fact that Clovis was the first Christian ruler of importance in the West after the collapse of the Roman Empire, an equivalent to Constantine in the East, since stories closely resembling those of Wolfdietrich are met in OFr epics about Floovant (< \**Chlodovinc*, 'son of Clovis' ?), whose father is sometimes named Constantine (Schneider, *DHS* (1930), 130). Another explanation might well be that much of the Wolfdietrich complex is a derivative from OFr epic, in which some names are borrowed and some accommodated to German taste. It is, therefore, open to doubt whether Hugdietrich derives from heroic tradition about any one historical person: as a figure in German epic he is first recorded *c*. 1215.

## HUGDIETRICH (2) son of Wolfdietrich

In **Wd(D)** he is brought up by Herebrant (1), and brings aid to his father when the monastery of Tischcâl is attacked by Tarîas.

In **DF** he marries Sigeminne (2) von Francrîche; their son is Amelunc (3) (see the genealogy, p. 26 n. 1).

ref: **DF** 2316; **Wd(B)** 863, 2; **Wd(D)** IX. 219, 4; **Wd(Gr)** 2107, 4

## HUGDIETRICH (3) son of a knight

In **Wd(A²)** Wolfdietrich gives aid to a woman in labour, whose husband, a knight, has been killed by a dragon; he tells her to baptize the infant 'Hugdietrich'. In **Wd(BD)** the mother and the unnamed child die (**Wd(B)** 842 ff.; **Wd(D)** VIII. 51 ff.).[3]

ref: **Wd(A²)** 575, 4 (Huge Dietrich); **Wd(k)** 219, 6 (*Hugo dietereich*)

## HUGEBOLT
A giant killed by Herbort.

ref: **B** m 6480; **E(L)** 83, 4

pn: 8th-cent. German (Förstemann I. 923 f.; Schlaug I. 116; II. 115).

## HÜLLE
A giant killed by Dietrich at Mûter (see Wîcram).

ref: **V(h)** m 510, 5 n 517, 11

pn: possibly an appellative based on MHG *hülle*, 'cloak, headgear' (?), or *hülwe, hül*, 'quagmire' (?).

## HÛNBREHT
Dietrich's man.

ref: **A** 74, 1 (MS. *hünbrecht*)

pn: 7th-cent. German (Förstemann I. 931 f.; Schlaug I. 117; II. 115).

## HÛNOLT (1) Gunther's man

In **N**, chamberlain (MHG *kameræere*) at the Burgundian court at Worms (in **B**, cupbearer (MHG *schenke*)): he is usually associated with Sindolt.

In **B**, Heime refers to his blows as 'Hûnolts wîn' (1270 ff.); at Worms Hûnolt fights together with Sindolt and Rûmolt against Dietrich's men.

ref: **B** 7747; **N** 10, 2

pn: 8th-cent. German and Lb (Förstemann I. 935; Schlaug I. 117; Ploß, 56), 7th-cent. OE (Searle, 308); the OFr equivalent *Hunaut* occurs for several persons in the *ch.d.g.* (Langlois, 347 f.).

## HÛNOLT (2) Dietrich's man

In **DF** he takes a leading part against Ermenrîch at Rabene (Ravenna) and Bôlonje (Bologna); in **Rs** he is among Etzel's men aiding Dietrich.

ref: **A** 74, 2; **DF** 3007; **Rs** 114, 3

## HÛNOLT (3) Dietwart's man

Companion to Dietwart: he rules from Swabia to beyond the Rhine.

ref: **DF** 526

---

[1] See Chambers, *Beowulf*, 385 ff.
[2] See p. 16 n. 3.
[3] See Wolfdietrich, p. 149 n. 2.

# I

**IBELÎN (LORINA)**
Sister of Nîtgêr: she succours Dietrich when he is the prisoner of her brother's giants at Mûter, and summons Hildebrant to his aid, yet she warns Nîtgêr, when his castle is about to be attacked by Dietrich's rescuers.

ref: **V(h)** m 369, 2 n 395, 2; **V(w)** m 555, 2 n 581, 2 (*Lorina*)

pn: origin uncertain; possibly based on MHG *îbe, îwe*, 'yew'.

**ILION von Troien**
= Helen of Troy: Hilde is said to be more beautiful than she.

ref: **DH** F 44, 7, 2

pn: confusion with Ilium, the other name of Troy (?).

**ÎLJAS von den Riuzen (Russia)**
Uncle of Ortnît: in **O** he leads Ortnît's expedition to Muntabûr (Mons Tabor) to win the daughter of the heathen Machorel. In the fighting Ortnît has to restrain Îljas from killing prisoners and women, and from trampling on the wounded.[1] He also enters the heathen temples, destroys their idols, and breaks their tombs. When the heathen princess has been abducted, he and Alberîch assist at her baptism.

ref: **AHb** p. 4, 37 (*Eligas*; p. 5, 14 *elegast*); **O** 11, 1 (Ŷljas); **O(C)** 234, 4 (*Elyas*); **O(k)** 10, 2 (*Illias*); **O(w)** 10, 1 (*Helias*, etc.; 273, 1 *Elias*)

In Þs, Ilias (I. 47, 29; II. 68, 22), son of Hertnið, the King of Holmgarðr (Russia), is the half-brother of Valldemarr and Osanctrix: he rules Greece. His children are named Hertnið and Hilldigundr, and he also has a nephew named Hertnið (see Hertnît (1), p. 70).

pn: *Ilias*, late 12th-cent. Bavarian (Müllenhoff, *ZE*, 354; Jänicke, *ZE*, 311).

This figure apparently derives from Russian traditions about Ilya Murometsch, the violent follower of Vladimir of Kiev;[2] Þs, possibly using LG tales brought from Russia, relates him to Vladimir.

**ILSAM**, see ILSÂN

[1] See Witolt, p. 147.
[2] See Bowra, *Heroic Poetry* (London, 1952), 61; R. Trautmann, 'Die Dietleibsage und die Bylinendichtung', *PBB* LXVI 1942, 146–52, discusses various adventures attributed to Ilya in the 15th cent. or later; some of these resemble those of Þetleifr in Þs (see Dietleip, pp. 24 f.). Ilya is also said to have killed his own son (see Hildebrant, p. 77).
[3] In Þs, Hjalprikr is the guardian of the young princes (see Helferîch (2), p. 67).

**ILSÂN (ELSÂN, ILSAM, ILSUNC)**
Hildebrant's brother: in **DF**, Elsân and Starchêr are left in command at Berne (Verona) when Dietrich leaves the city to raise Ermenrîch's siege of Meilân (Milan). In **Rs** he is the guardian of Scharpfe and Orte, the sons of Etzel and Helche, and of Diethêr, Dietrich's younger brother. The three youths are killed by Witege at Rabene (Ravenna); Dietrich beheads Elsân when he hears of their deaths from Helferîch.[3]

In **L(A)**, Ilsunc instructs Laurîn in the Christian religion before his baptism.[4] In **Rg(A)**, a monk at Îsenburc (Münchgezell in **Rg(C)**), Ilsân joins Dietrich's champions in the combats at Worms and defeats Stûtfuhs (Volkêr in **Rg(D)**; he kills Aldrîân in **Rg(F)**), then insists on fighting fifty-two additional champions, demanding the prize of fifty-two kisses and rose-wreaths from Kriemhilt, whose face bleeds from his rough beard; on his return to the monastery he crams the wreaths on to the heads of his terrified fellow monks. In **Rg(D)**, during the journey to Worms, he overpowers the troublesome Rhine ferryman (see Norpreht).[5] In **A** he brings eleven hundred monks to aid Dietrich against Ermenrîch.

ref: **A** 319, 1 (MS. *Ilsam*); **AHb** p. 6, 4 (*ylsam*, p. 7, 35 *Ylsan*); **DF** 3014 (Elsân); **L(A)** 1779 (Ilsunc); **L(K)II** 389 (Ilsunc); **Rg(A)** 104, 4; **Rg(C)** 398; **Rg(D)** 76, 3; **Rg(F)** III. 20, 3; **Rg(P)** 131 (*Ilsam*); **Rg(V)** 110 (*ilsam*); **Rs** 114, 2 (Elsân: 282, 6 R *Elsam*); **Wd(D)** IX. 221, 2 (Elsân: e *eilsan*, f *ylsan*); **Wd(Gr)** 2109, 2 (Elsân); **Wd(w)** 2022, 2 (*Lÿfant*)

Ilsân is mentioned among Dietrich's men by Heinrich von Meissen (†1318) (W. Grimm, *DHS*, 196), but the earliest reference in German literature outside the epics to the rough-bearded warrior-monk occurs in Brant's *Narrenschiff* (1498) (ibid. 323); numerous references appear in the 16th and early 17th cents. (ibid. 352 ff., 357, 361, 488; Jänicke, *ZE*, 330).

'Munck Alsing' ('Monich Broder Helsing') appears among Diderik's champions in the Danish ballads *Kong Diderik og hans Kæmper, Kong Diderik i Birtingsland*, and

[4] Aventinus in his *Bavarian Chronicle* (1580) makes 'Ylsing' the son and successor of 'Lareyn' as ruler of Germany (W. Grimm, *DHS*, 340 f.).
[5] This episode possibly derives from a name association with Else (1), the liege lord of the difficult Danube ferryman in **N**. In Þs, Elsungr controls the Rhine crossing (see Else m. (1), p. 36).

# ILSÂN

*Den skallede Munk* ('the bald-headed monk') (*DgF* I. 108 ff., 124 ff., 219 ff.).

pn: *Ilsunc*: 8th-cent. German (Mone, 20; Förstemann I. 948 f.; Socin, 571 ff.). The name occurs for a peasant in *Neidharts Lieder*, 31, 37; 92, 6. It is possibly based on Gmc. *\*ali-* (OHG *eli-*, 'strange, other', showing *e/i* variation, cf. MHG *iltis, eltes*) + *-s-* component (Henzen, 122), as for *Else* m., and the suffix *-unc*. The last two components are varied with *-sam* (Henzen, 205 f.) or *-sân* cf. OHG *seltsâni*: Kluge, *EWb*, 702).

In Fischart's works the name is printed as follows: *Ilsän* (1570), *Ilsung* (1574), *Illsung* (1582), *Illzam* (1594) (W. Grimm, *DHS*, 352 ff.).

It seems probable that Ilsân's primary role was that of guardian to the young princes, and that he was originally forgiven, but later emerged from the monastery to which he had fled from Dietrich's wrath (Jiriczek, *DHS* (1898), 316 f.). It is uncertain whether his 'moniage' is based on that of Heime (Schneider, *GHS* I. 324); this turbulent monk is likely to be a creation of the 13th cent., when a coarsening among members of the spiritual orders is thought to have set in (W. Grimm, *DHS*, 403, 420).

## ILSUNC

Dietrich's man.

ref: **DF** 8315

pn: see under Ilsân above.

## IMBRECKE

One of the Harlunge: brother of Frîtele.

ref: **B** 4595 (MS. *Imbrechen*)

The names Emerca[1] in OE *Widsith*, 113, and Embrica in the *Ann. Quedl.* probably represent the same person (see Harlunge, p. 62).

pn: *Ambricus, Ambricho*, etc., 5th cent.; various forms with or without extraneous *-b-, Imbrico, Emricho, Embricus, Empricho*, 8th-cent. German (Förstemann I. 98; Schlaug I. 78; II. 117, 193). A hypocoristic form, *\*Amrika*, may well be the basis, possibly related to the name of one of the Vandalic dioscors, *Ambri* and Assi, and with the *Ambrones* of Jutland (Baesecke, *Vorgeschichte*, 50 f.; Zeuß, 147 ff.).

## YMELOT von Babilonie (Cairo)

Father of Basilistium: he twice attacks Constantin's realm at Constantinople and is twice defeated by Rother's forces.

ref: **R** 2561

## ÎMÎÂN

In **DF** and **Rs**, Îmîân von Antîoch (Antioch) is one of Etzel's men aiding Dietrich against Ermenrîch.

In **V** Îmîân von Ungern (Hungary) aids Dietrich at Mûter and kills the giants Adelrant and Glockenbôz (see Wîcram).

ref: **DF** 5150 (A *Yman*); **Rs** 545, 1 (A *yman*); **V(h)** 302, 11 (MS. *ynnan*); **V(w)** 651, 2 (*Morilean*)

pn: possibly from Arthurian epic, cf. Ênîte's uncle in Hartmann von Aue's *Erec* (1180–5),[2] Îmâin von Tulmein (175 f.); however, the manuscript spellings suggest Arabic *imam*, 'leader, priest', as a possible basis.

## IMMUNC

Father of the dwarf Hartunc (see Ruotliep, p. 113).

ref: **Ru** XVIII. 8 (MS. *Immunch*)

pn: *Immo*: 7th-cent. German (Förstemann I. 949; II. i. 1561; Schlaug I. 119 f.); the *-ung* suffix characterizes this as a dwarf-name.

(IRAM) see p. 118 n. 6.

## ÎRINC von Tenemarke (Denmark)

An exile at Etzel's court, usually associated with his liege lord, Hâwart von Tenemarke, and with Irnfrit von Düringen: in **N** his sword is named Waske; Hagen kills him with his spear in his second onslaught against the Burgundians.

In **DF** and **Rs** he aids Dietrich against Ermenrîch and fights Hiuzolt at Rabene (Ravenna); his brother is named Erwîn. In **B** 1589 and **Kl** 448 (B) he is said to be 'von Lütringen'.[3]

ref: **B** 1241; **DF** 5144; **Kl** 423; **N** 1345, 2; **N(k)** 1359, 2 (*Arnald*); **Rs** 54, 1

In his Saxon history (c. 970), Widukind of Corvey records the story of Iring, the majordomo of Irminfrid, King of the Thuringians (Widukind I. 9–13): Irminfrid's queen, Amalaberga, incites Iring to advise his master to reject an embassy from Theodoric the Frank; in the ensuing hostilities Irminfrid is defeated by Theodoric and his allies, the Saxons. Theodoric, by means of promises and bribes, persuades Iring to kill his master while the latter is doing homage. Iring does so, but kills Theodoric as well; he then places Irminfrid's corpse above that of his victor and cuts his way from the hall.[4] Because of this exploit, the Milky Way is said to be named after him.

In Þs Grimilldr incites Irungr (II. 307, 10) to kill the young knights of the Niflungar (see Blœdel, p. 13); in the subsequent fighting Högni kills Irungr with a spear. The place

---

[1] Malone, *Widsith*, 139, takes this to be the name of a Gothic hero, equating it with the name *Amara*, which occurs in the compound *Erpamara* (Jordanes, ch. v (43)), based on the equivalent of OHG *amara*, the name of a finch (Kluge, *EWb*, 190). See p. 40 n. 3.

[2] hrsg. von A. Leitzmann (Tübingen, 1963³), 5.
[3] No doubt a confusion in manuscript transmission between 'Düringen' and 'Lütringen', as in the manuscripts of **R** (see Lütringen).
[4] Saxo tells a similar tale about the murder of King Ole of Denmark by Starkad (ch. viii).

# ÎRINC

where he fell in Susat is called 'Irungs vegr to this day' (II. 320, 14).

pn: 8th-cent. German (Mone, 74 f.; Förstemann I. 967; Schlaug II. 116); unknown in England, apart from glosses referring to the Milky Way as *Iringes weg* (Binz, 202).

This figure is not mentioned by contemporary historians when reporting the destruction of the Thuringian realm (see Irnfrit below): Jacob Grimm suggests that the name derives from an eponym for the Thuringians, *Epurduring (J. Grimm, GDS, 314, 415) (see also Düringen, p. 32).

## IRNFRIT von Düringen (Thuringia)

An exile at Etzel's court:[1] in **N** he and Hâwart (see Hadawardus, p. 56) support Îrinc in his attack on the Burgundians; Volkêr kills him; in the **Kl** his body is found with those of Îrinc and Hâwart.

In **B** he takes part in Etzel's Polish campaign; in the combats at Worms he fights a 'lantgrâve von Düringen' responsible for his exile.

ref: **B** 1238; **Kl** 422; **N** 1345, 3

pn: *Hermenefridus* for the 6th-cent. Thuringian king (Schönfeld, 134); *Irminfrid, Erminfrid, Irinfrid, Irmfrid*, etc., 8th-cent. German (Förstemann I. 476 f., 969; Kaufmann, 108 f., 217; Mone, 73; Schlaug I. 120; II. 117); an *Eormenfrith* appears in OE *Domesday* (Searle, 231). The first component of this pn is probably based on Gmc. *ermena*, 'universal' (see Ermenrîch, p. 39).

In 531, according to the contemporary historian Procopius (*Goth.* v. xii ff.), the Franks led by Theodoric and Chlotachar conquered the Thuringians and slew their king, Hermenfrid; his queen, Amalberga, the niece of Theodoric the Ostrogoth, fled with her children to the protection of her brother, Theodahad, in Italy. Amalafrid, Hermenfrid's son, later became an East Roman general under Justinian. Gregory of Tours records (Greg. Tur. III. 4 ff.) that Irminfrid was treacherously thrown to his death from the walls of Zülpich. There is no contemporary account of Iring, Irminfrid's majordomo (see Îrinc above).

The 13th-cent. *De Suevorum Origine* (W. Grimm, *DHS*, 130 f.) reports that Irminfrid took refuge with Attila. It is doubtful whether memories of Attila's one-time sway over the Thuringians are reflected in these later traditions. Perhaps the fortunes of Amalafrid in exile have been transferred to his father.

## ÎROLT von Nortlande (= Denmark?)

Plays a subsidiary role as mediating court official in **Ku**, and is usually mentioned together with Môrunc. He takes part in the expedition led by Hôrant to win Hilde for Hetel, and fights in the various campaigns of the Hegelinge. He leads the Frisians and Holsteiners in the final battle against the Normans, when Kûdrûn is rescued.

ref: **Ku** 231, 4

pn: apparently a fusion of name-components from **N**, cf. *Îrinc* and the court officials *Rûmolt, Sindolt*, and *Hûnolt*. An accommodation for *Heriold*, the name of a Dane given dominion over Frisia by the Franks in 826, is suggested by Jungandreas, *Gudrunsage*, 105 f.; but forms equivalent to OHG *Heriwald* with omission of *H-* occur mainly in WFr and Lb, indicating Romance influence (Förstemann I. 779 f.).

## ISAAK

Accompanies Dirik against the 'köninck van Armentriken'.

ref: **ED** 18, 2

The name appears to be a corrupt form of Isungr, the name of the ruler of Bertangaland in Þs (I. 255, 14), against whose sons Þiðrekr pits his twelve champions (de Boor, *Kl. Schr.* II. 45); the same corrupt form, Isac, occurs in the Danish ballad *Kong Diderik i Birtingsland* (DgF I. 124–9).

## ÎSENHART (ÎSENHER)

A robber killed by Wolfdietrich (see Rûmelher).

ref: **Wd(D)** v. 9, 1; **Wd(Gr)** 847, 1 (Îsenher); **Wd(w)** 789, 1 (*Isenher*)

pn: descriptive, yet recorded from 8th cent. in German documents (Förstemann I. 976 f.). In Wolfram von Eschenbach's *Parzival*, 25, 24, the opponent of Fridebrant bears this name, and it occurs in *Neidharts Lieder*, 139, 7, for a peasant.

## ÎSOLDE (1) von Îrlant (Ireland)

The heroine of Arthurian epic: Hilde is said to be more beautiful than she.

ref:: **DH** F 44, 7, 1

In Þs the name Isollde is used for Þiðrekr's sister (II. 43, 7), Iron's wife (II. 112, 5) and daughter (II. 135, 21), and for Hertnið's widow (II. 359, 14).

pn: This name would be well known from Eilhart von Oberg's *Tristrant* (c. 1170) and from Gottfried von Straßburg's *Tristan* (c. 1210). See under Îsolt, below, regarding the masculine form of the name which occurs in non-literary records.

## ÎSOLDE (2) von Wiene (Vienna)

Attendant on Kriemhilt.

ref: **Kl** 3041 (Isalde)

---

[1] In the **Kl**, Îrinc, Hâwart, and Irnfrit have been twenty years in exile under the imperial ban (**Kl** 418–55). Presumably, if this reference has any historical basis, the 'keiser' concerned would be Theodoric, son of Clovis, and the Burgundians would represent Irnfrit's historical enemies, the Franks.

ÎSOLT
Etzel's man: in **DF** and **Rs** he aids Dietrich against Ermenrîch; he fights Gêrolt von Sahsen at Rabene (Ravenna).

ref: **DF** 5147; **Rs** 49, 3

pn: 8th-cent. German (Förstemann I. 972). It occurs for Fôre's nephew in the 12th-cent. *Salman und Morolf*, 554, 1.

ISRAHELISCH adj.
Reference is made in **R** to the crossing of the Red Sea by the 'israhelischiu diet' (People of Israel).

ref: **R** 3935

ÎWÂN von Tuscân (Tuscany)
He and Reinhêr act as regents when Dietwart sets out on his bridal quest for Minne.

ref: **DF** 404 (P *Twan*, A *Tiban*; 1516 A *Yban*)

pn: possibly a derivative of the name of the hero of Hartmann von Aue's *Iwein*.[1] However, names in Îw- (OHG *îwa*, 'yew') are recorded: cf. *Iwo*, 8th-cent. German Förstemann I. 978).

# J

JÂCOB
Ortnît rules 'sant Jâcobes lant' (= Lombardy?).

ref: **Wd(D)** III. 47, 4; **Wd(Gr)** 307, 4

JANAPAS
The son of the Saracen, Orkîse. At his castle of Ortneck he sets four lions on Dietrich and Hildebrant. The heroes kill his lions, his warriors, and Janapas himself.

ref: **V(d)** 90, 7 (*Janibus*); **V(w)** 418, 12

pn: probably from OFr epic, where *Jambus* (*Jambuz*) is used to name Saracens (Langlois, 367).

JÊSUS
His name is used in pious invocations and exclamations, usually in conjunction with 'Krist'.

ref: **DF** 4370; **E(d)** 140, 11; **L(A)** 1776; **O(k)** 194, 6; **O(w)** 33, 5; **Rs** 97, 1; **hS** 29, 2; **V(h)** 49, 13; **V(w)** 146, 13; **W** 1456; **Wd(B)** 571, 2; **Wd(D)** X. 111, 3; **Wu(B)** 126, 5

JOCHFRÎT von Spangen (Spain)
Attends Wolfdietrich's wedding to Sîdrât.

ref: **Wd(D)** VIII. 333, 1 (g *gerfried*, ac *hartnit*); **Wd(Gr)** 1872, 3; **Wd(w)** 1790, 1 (*Jofreÿt*)

pn: possibly from OFr *Jofroi* (Langlois, 377 ff.; Flutre, 88), cf. *Jofrit* in *Willehalm von Orlens*, by Rudolf von Ems 263, and *Jokfrit* in *Friedrich von Schwaben*, 7445.

JÔHAN (1) the Apostle
'Sant Jôhans segen' is given on setting out on a journey (**Rs** 287, 1; **V(w)** 43, 12); in **Rg(V)**, Ilsân offers it to his opponent Stûtfuhs. In **Wd(D)** Wolfdietrich visits 'sant Jôhans alter' at Constantinople to speak with the spirit of Berhtunc.

ref: **Rg(V)** 290; **Rs** 287, 1; **V(w)** 43, 12; **Wd(D)** IX. 150, 4; **Wd(Gr)** 2038, 4

JÔHAN (2) the Baptist
Arnolt invokes this saint when he leads his men to rescue Rother from the gallows.

ref: **R** 4069

The Langobard King, Rothari, was said to have revered this saint (Paul, Diac. IV. 48: cit. Frings–Kuhnt, *Rother*, 190).

JÔNAS
Wolfdietrich in distress recalls God's help to Jonas (see Danîêl and Nôê).

ref: **Wd(D)** VIII. 124, 1; **Wd(Gr)** 1660, 1

JORCUS
A cowardly bailiff of King Gibaldus.

ref: **gS** p 92, 11

JÖRGE
His saint's day is mentioned in **DF** and **Rs**. Wolfdietrich, in the later versions of his story, stands in a special relationship to this saint: his godfather is 'sant Jörge' (**Wd(D)** VI. 182, 1; 'ritter Jörge' in **Wd(B)** 173, 3); he wins the protective shirt called 'sant Jörgen hemt' (**Wd(D)** IV. 58, 1) from the giant Belmunt; finally the hero joins the 'sant Jörgen orden' (**Wd(D)** X. 11, 3) at the monastery of Tischcâl. His loyal vassal Berhtunc is buried in 'sant Jörgen münster' at Constantinople (**Wd(B)** 900, 3); 'sant Jörgen arm' (= the Bosphorus) is mentioned in **Wd(D)** VII. 1, 4.[2]

ref: **DF** 355; **Rs** 148, 4; **Wd(B)** 173, 3; **Wd(D)** IV. 58, 1; **Wd(Gr)** 447, 3

St. George and Wolfdietrich have three characteristics in common (Schneider *Wolfdietrich* (1913), 305 f.): they are Christian fighters of the Saracens, dragon-slayers, and

---

[1] hrsg. von G. F. Benecke und Karl Lachmann (Berlin, 1926⁵).

[2] See O. Jänicke, *DHB* IV. 287.

have close links with Constantinople, of which St. George is the patron saint. Salonika and Athens, both given as the birth-place of Wolfdietrich, were centres of the cult of St. George. The *Legenda Aurea*, which recounts the saint's life, dates from *c*. 1270, but was not generally known in Germany till the early 14th cent.

JUBART von Latrân (Papal States?)
Dietrich's man: killed by Reinhêr von Pârise at Bôlonje (Bologna).

ref: **DF** 3013 (A *Iwart*)

pn: probably from OFr, cf. *Jobert* (*Joibert*) in the *ch.d.g.* (Langlois, 374 f.).

JUDAS
ref: **R** 3339
pn: biblical.

JUPITER
A Saracen god.

ref: **V(d)** 27, 7 (Gippito; 100, 2 Jupiter); **V(h)** 63, 5; **V(w)** 93, 12; **Wd(D)** v. 4, 3 (Juppiter); **Wd(Gr)** 842, 3

pn: frequent in OFr *ch.d.g.* (Langlois, 387).

# K

(See under C)

# L

LADINER (1) von Westenmer (Adriatic?)
Father of Rother and Minne.

ref: **DF** 892 (A *Ladimer*)

The title of this person probably derives from the location of Rother's capital, Bari, 'bi dem westeren mere' (1). 'Ladinor von Westerlant', father of Minne, is mentioned by Heinrich von München in his 14th-cent. *Weltchronik* (W. Grimm, *DHS*, 224).

LADINER (2) von den Bergen
Ermenrîch's man: fights Helferîch (2) at Bôlonje (Bologna).

ref: **DF** 8645 (W *ladimer*; 9243 R *ladimer*)

LADISLAU
Follower of Witzlân: aids Gunther in the combats at Worms.

ref: **B** 11720 (MS. *Ladislaw*)

LAMPARTE(N) (LAMPARTÆRE; LAMPARTENLANT)
Lombard, Lombardy: both Dietrich (1) and Ortnît (1) rule Lamparten(lant), which is the scene of Dietrich's campaigns against Ermenrîch in **DF**, **Rs**, and **A**. Often the meaning is extended to include all Italy.

ref: Lamparte sg. (= Ortnît): **O** 20, 1; Lampartære: **O(C)** 178, 1; Lampartner: **O(k)** 28, 2
    Lamparten pl. (people): **O** 23, 3; **Rs** 204, 6; **Wd(A)** 504, 4

[1] The silken thread encircling Kriemhilt's rose-garden in **Rg(A)** has no function; this gives

Lamparten (region): **A** 53, 1; **B** 8538; **DF** 2234; **DH** F 41, 2, 2; **E(L)** 21, 7; **E(s)** 16, 7; **L(DrHb)** 4, 1; **L(K)II** 12; **O** 2, 3; **O(C)** 317, 2; **jSn** 1, 2; **V(w)** 564, 5 **Wd(A)** 417, 2; **Wd(B)** 656, 2; **Wd(C)** VIII. 21, 1; **Wd(D)** VII. 113, 3; **Wd(Gr)** 1420, 3; **Wd(k)** 154, 1
    Lampartenlant (der Lamparten lant): **AHb** p. 4, 11; **B** 8209; **Rg(A)** 33, 2; **Rg(C)** 112; **Rg(F)** I. 1, 4; **V(h)** 378, 5; **Wd(D)** v. 50, 4; **Wd(Gr)** 888, 4

The name of this region of North Italy derives from that of the Langobards, a Germanic people who entered Italy under Alboin in 568; their rule lasted till 773, when Charlemagne sent their last king, Desiderius, to a monastery and assumed the Langobard crown. In OHG *Lancpartolant* is usually synonymous with *Italia* (Zeuß, 476 n.).

LAURÎN
A dwarf-king, the owner of a rose-garden in the Tyrol, which is encircled by a silken thread;[1] he rides a horse the size of a roebuck and is magnificently accoutred; he wears a golden crown with singing birds upon it. Dietrich and Witege visit the rose-garden; Witege breaks the thread and tramples on the roses. Laurîn, alerted by the broken thread, challenges the intruders. He overpowers Witege, and is about to cut off his right hand and left foot as a penalty, when Dietrich, who has been joined by Hildebrant, Wolfhart, and Dietleip, intervenes: Dietrich subdues

priority to Laurîn's rose-garden (see J. Lunzer 'Rosengartenmotive', *PBB* L (1927), 164).

the dwarf with considerable difficulty by wrestling—Laurîn possesses sword-proof armour, a cloak of invisibility (MHG *tarnkeppelîn*), and a strength-giving girdle.¹ Dietleip, in spite of the fact that Laurîn has abducted his sister (**L(A)** Künhilt, **L(D)** Sîmilte), prevents Dietrich from killing him. Laurîn and the four heroes swear oaths of loyalty; the dwarf entertains them with marvels in his underground kingdom, then drugs and imprisons them. Künhilt frees the heroes, who defeat Laurîn and his dwarfs and giants.² On the intercession of Künhilt, Dietrich once more spares Laurîn's life; his kingdom is placed under the regency of the dwarf Sintram, and is only restored to him after he has accepted baptism and sworn allegiance to Dietrich (in **L(D)** he is kept as court fool (MHG *goukelære*) at Berne).³ In **L(K)II** Laurîn's uncle, Walberân, sails to the West and lands at Venice with a vast host to rescue him. Walberân worsts Dietrich in a combat before the walls of Berne (Verona); Laurîn and Hildebrant separate them, and peace is restored.

In **AHb**, when all the heroes are dead, a little dwarf (Laurîn?) leads 'der Berner' (= Dietrich von Berne) to another world (**AHb** p. 11, 17–24).⁴

ref: **AHb** m 11 19; **L(A)** 61; **L(D)** 78; **L(DrHb)** 16, 8; **L(K)II** 57

The earliest German references to Laurîn outside the epics occur in the 13th-cent. *Wartburgkrieg* (W. Grimm, *DHS*, 192 f.), Spiegel's *Abenteuer* in the 14th cent. (ibid. 314), and Wittenwiler's *Ring c.* 1410; in this last poem, Laurîn (8146) and his dwarfs aid Dietrich against the giants. Further references occur in the 16th and 17th cents. (ibid. 340, 349, 352, 357, 362; Jänicke, *ZE*, 328; Müllenhoff, *ZE*, 431).

pn: rare in German records:⁵ *Laurinus de Insbruck* 13th cent. (Wolff, 169), Br. Joh. *Lawrin* 14th cent. in Breisgau (Socin, 538). The name is used for one of Herod's soldiers in a 15th-cent. religious play (W. Grimm, *DHS*, 478).

The form of the name in the manuscripts and prints is sometimes thought to show 13th-cent. Bavarian *au* from MHG *û*, if it is indeed related to the stem *\*lûr-*, cf. MHG *lûren*, 'lie in wait', *lûre*, 'deceiver' (Holz, *Laurin*, xxxxi f.). A connection with the non-IE root *\*lawa-* or *\*lauwa-*, 'stone', has also been suggested (J. Lunzer, 'Rosengarten-motive', *PBB* L (1927), 216), but, although this root is met in place-names of the Alpine region and elsewhere, *Laurein* in the South Tyrol and *Laureberg* and *Lurley* (*Lorelei*) on the Middle Rhine (ibid. 211 f.), no dwarf or rose-garden has been associated with it.⁶

The poem about Laurîn was probably composed in the Tyrol *c.* 1250 (de Boor, *GDL* III. i. 166); its widespread popularity is attested by Low German, Czech, and Danish translations; a Faroese ballad, *Lavrin Dvörgakongur*, is based on the Danish version.⁷

LENGESÆRE = Walther
Walther is connected with Lengers (Langres).

ref: **Rs** 47, 1

LEO
Walthariu's horse.

ref: **W** 327

pn: derives from Lat. *leo*, 'lion' (see Lewe).

In **Rg(D)** Walther has a lion depicted in blue on his shield.

LEWE
Hildebrant's horse.

ref: **V(h)** 108, 7

pn: derives from MHG *lewe*, 'lion' (see Leo above).

LIBERTÎN von Palerne (Palermo)
Libertîn, having already defeated Sigestap, challenges Dietrich at Ârône (Arona): Dietrich defeats him, and the two heroes swear oaths of loyalty.⁸ Libertîn aids Dietrich against Janapas at Ortneck.

---

¹ Sîfrit and Ortnît engage in such wrestling-bouts with the dwarf Alberich in **N** and **O**. The fight between Dietrich and Laurîn is depicted in the 15th-cent. frescoes at the castle of Lichtenberg in Vinstgau (see Zingerle, 79; Müllenhoff, *ZE*, 425 ff.).
² In **L(DrHb)** Laurîn has six giants: Signit, Zanck, Spross, Slachvore, Streitpas, and Stauer. Wolfdietrich is also added to Dietrich's companions in this version.
³ This motif also occurs in a folk-tale of the Ladine Valley (see P. B. Wessels, 'König Laurin, Quelle und Struktur', *PBB* LXXXIV (Tübingen, 1962), 247 ff.).
⁴ In a 14th-cent. addition to the *Wartburgkrieg*, Laurîn leads Dietrich to Palackers (Baghdad?), the kingdom of his brother Sinnels (= Sintram?) near India, where he is destined to live a thousand years, although people will believe he has vanished into a volcano (O. Jänicke, *DHB* I. lvi ff.; see also p. 27).

⁵ *Luaran* in a Salzburg document dated 1041–50 (Müllenhoff, *ZE*, 310) probably represents a different name (Holz, *Laurin*, xxxix; Symons, *Heldensage*, 94).
⁶ Wolff, *Laurin*, 119 ff., finds no connection between the name Laurîn and the rose-garden story in oral tradition, but he nevertheless localizes the 'Laurinsage' in Meran (Merano) in the South Tyrol. He relates Laurîn's rose-garden to the myth of the 'lost paradise', associated in the Ladine with the sunset glow on the mountain peaks. See also Bach II, § 449, regarding the possible connection of the rose-garden with the Roman Rosalia festival for the dead.
⁷ Torsten Dahlberg, *Zum dänischen Lavrin und dem niederdeutschen Lorin* (Lund, 1950), 13.
⁸ Such combats occur between Þiðrekr and his subsequent followers in Þs (see Heime, Witege, and Vâsolt).

ref: **V(d)** 78, 11; **V(w)** 376, 2

pn: probably of Romance origin.

LIEBGART (1) wife of Ortnît and Wolfdietrich (SÎDRÂT (1))
In **O**, Ortnît abducts the daughter of the heathen king, Machorel, and has her baptized 'Sîdrât' before marrying her. In **Wd**, Ortnît's widow marries Wolfdietrich after he has slain the dragon which killed Ortnît; she is named 'Liebgart' in **Wd(AB)**.

ref: **AHb** p. 5, 26 (*Sydrat*); **DF** m 2077 n 2139 (Liebgart); **O** m 11, 3 n 481, 6 (a *Siderat*, c *siderott*);[1] **O(w)** 403, 2 (*Libgart*); **Wd(A)** m 33, 4; **Wd(A²)** m 525, 4 n 548, 1 (Liebgart); **Wd(B)** 354, 2 (Liebgart: abcdefg *siderat*); **Wd(D)** III. 44, 2 (Sîdrât); **Wd(Gr)** 304, 2 (Sîdrât); **Wd(k)** m 26, 8 n 329, 2 (*Liebgarta*); **Wd(w)** 295, 2 (*Libgart*)

pn: 8th-cent. German (Förstemann I. 1024).

LIEBGART (2) wife of Walgunt

ref: **AHb** p. 6, 21; **Wd (B)** 15, 3; **Wd(Gr)** 21, 3

LIMHÊR (?)
Brother of Barûc: a giant follower of Belmunt killed by Wolfdietrich.

ref: **Wd(D)** IV. 83, 2 (ab *lumer*, cd *lumen*, z *römer*; x. 40, 3 e *lymmer*, f *luner*, a *lumer*, c *lamar*); **Wd(Gr)** 472, 2; **Wd(w)** 2064, 2 (*Lymmus*; 2065, 3, etc., *Lifinus*; 2106, 1 *Limers*)

pn: transmission corrupt; the component *\*Lim-* is doubtful (see Kaufmann, 236).

LIMME
Witege's helmet: made by Wielant (**B**).

ref: **A** 449, 3 (MS. *lonen*); **B** 161 (MS. *Lymme*)

pn: origin uncertain; possibly from MHG *limmen*, 'growl' or 'grind the teeth' (Wackernagel, 140), or Gmc. root *\*leuhma-*, 'shine, flash' (OS *liomo*, OE *lēoma*, ON *liómi* (Kluge, *EWb*, 438; Raßmann, *DHS* II. 378).

LINDUNC (?)
A dwarf: leader of Walberân's army.

ref: **L(K)II** 137 (MS. *lingun*; 148 *lingbundes*; 164 *lingbunk*)[2]

LIUDEGAST (1) von Tenemarke (Denmark)
Brother of Liudegêr von Sahsen, with whom he is usually mentioned (see Liudegêr (1) below).

ref: **B** 5049; **DF** 5900; **N** 140, 3; **Rs** 734, 2 (L. von Sahsen)

pn: recorded once, in 6th cent. (Förstemann I. 1041); probably introduced to chime with Liudegêr.

---

[1] See A. Amelung, *DHB* IV. 255.
[2] See Holz, *Laurin*, 199, note to v. 137, etc., in

LIUDEGAST (2) companion (brother?) of Helferîch (4)
In **E**, the wounded Helferîch tells Ecke that Dietrich has killed his companion, Liudegast (brother in **E(s)**).

ref: **AHb** p. 1, 19 (*lugegast*; p. 3, 32 *ludegast*); **E(d)** m 64, 8; **E(L)** 59, 9; **E(s)** 56, 8

LIUDEGÊR (1) von Sahsen (Saxony)
Brother of Liudegast von Tenemarke: in **N**, the brothers declare war on Gunther, but Sîfrit, leading the Burgundian forces, defeats and captures them; Gunther releases them, on Sîfrit's advice, without demanding tribute. In **B**, Liudegêr is King of Denmark (5043 ff.) and ruler of Saxony (6561 ff.); he and his brother support Gunther in the combats at Worms, where they oppose the Harlunge.
In **DF**, the brothers first appear among Etzel's men supporting Dietrich against Ermenrîch (5899 ff.), then with Ermenrîch's men (8629 ff.); in **Rs**, Liudegêr von Mîssen and his brother, Liudegast von Sahsen, are among Ermenrîch's men: Liudegêr fights Biterolf at Rabene (Ravenna).

ref: **B** 5043; **DF** 5899; **N** 140, 1; **Rs** 735, 1 (L. von Mîssen)

pn: 7th-cent. WFr and Lb; 8th-cent. German; frequent in LG (Förstemann I. 1039; Schlaug I. 125; II. 122). The LG form of the first component *Liud-* (Gmc. *\*leud-*, as in OS *liudi*, but OHG *liuti*, 'people, war band') is fixed by the name of St. Liudger (†809) (J. Lunzer, 'Kleine Nibelungenstudien', *ZfdA* LXIX (1932), 231).
It is possible that Liudegêr and Liudegast reflect notions of a Danish–Saxon alliance against the Empire (Heusler, *Nibelungensage*, 80; Panzer, *Nibelungenlied*, 320): Duke Liudeger of Saxony opposed the Emperor Henry V in 1115 (Lunzer, op. cit. 229), and in 1171 a treaty and betrothal between the Danish and Saxon ruling families took place; Waldemar I of Denmark and Henry the Lion, Duke of Saxony, were also allied in campaigns against the Slavs (ibid. 236 f.).

LIUDEGÊR (2) von Vrankrîche (France)
Father of Goldrûn.

ref: **Kl** 2456

Possibly an inexact recollection of Ludewîc von Ormanîe, abductor of Kûdrûn in **Ku** (see below, also p. 52).

LIUTWAR
Ermenrîch's man.

ref: **B** 5677

pn: fem. only: 6th-cent. WFr; 8th-cent. German (Förstemann I. 1048).

LODOBER, see DOLOBER

which he rejects Müllenhoff's conjecture 'Nibelunc'.

## LOFHART

**LOFHART**, see WOLFRÂT

**LORINA**, see IBELÎN

**LŎWHARDUS**, see GUNTHER (2)

### LÛCIFER
ref: **Wd(A)** 463, 2

pn: biblical (Isaiah 14: 12).

### LUDEWÎC von Ormanîe (Normandy)
In **Ku** he aids his son Hartmuot in the abduction of Kûdrûn and kills her father Hetel at the battle of Wülpensant (see Kûdrûn, pp. 21 f.). He is beheaded by Herewîc, Kûdrûn's bridegroom, when the Hegelinge army storms the Norman fortress of Kassiâne[1] to rescue Kûdrûn.

In **B** Herbort boasts that he has defeated Ludewîc and his son Hartmuot and abducted Ludewîc's daughter, Hildeburc.

ref: **B** 6163; **Ku** 588, 3

pn: borne by the 5th-cent. Frankish conqueror of Gaul, Clovis (*Chlodovechus*), the name was apparently reserved for royal persons, *\*Hludowig* being rare in early German records (Förstemann I. 855 ff.; Schlaug II. 124). *Ludewîc* occurs for a Christian warrior in Pfaffe Konrad's *Rolandslied* (4826) in the 12th cent.

In ON, *Hlöðvér*, the name of the father of Völundr's swan-maiden wife (Vkv 10, 6) and the ruler of a kingdom promised to Guðrún (Gðr I 25, 6), refers to the Frankish king. In Þs, *Loðwígr* (I. 201, 9) is the name of the margrave of Aldinflis, '*Loðvígur*' (II. 376, 3) the incognito used by Heimir on entering a monastery, and *Hlodver* (II. 343, 8) the name of the father of Konrádur (see Kuonrât, p. 22).

## MACHOREL

**LUMMERT**, see AMELUNC (2)

### LUPPOLT
Son of Berhter (1) von Mêrân: leads the embassy to Constantinople to ask the hand of King Constantin's daughter for his master Rother. Constantin imprisons him with his eleven companions. Rother rescues them when he visits Constantinople to win the princess. Luppolt takes part in the subsequent campaign in Greece to rescue Rother's queen. Rother makes him 'koninc zo Karlungin' (= France).

ref: **R** 50 (*lupolt*; other spellings: *liupolt*, *lipolt*)

pn: *\*Hludobald*: 8th-cent. WFr; 9th-cent. German (Förstemann I. 850; Schlaug I. 124; II. 122).

### LÜTRINGEN
Duchy of Lorraine: Helferîch (4) in **E** and **DF**, and Îrinc in **Kl** and **B**, are from Lütringen, yet in **B** the latter fights the 'herzoc von Lütringen' in the combats at Worms (7720).

ref: **B** 1589; **DF** 5156; **E(B)** 1; **E(s)** 56, 7; **Kl** 448; **R** 4829 (H *Dorringin*, RB *Lotringin*)

This term originally applied to the subjects of Lothar I (†855), but by *c*. 1000 was restricted to those living north of the South Vosges. In the 10th cent. it refers to that region.

**LŸFANT**, see ILSÂN

# M

### MACHAZÊN
Heathen god: cursed by Etzel.

ref: **Kl** 1065

pn: in OFr epic *Maca-* is frequently a component of Saracen names (Langlois, 411 f.); Mohamet is also termed *Macon* (ibid. 418).

### MACHMET
Heathen god: cursed by Etzel in the **Kl** (see Machazên above), worshipped by Machorel in **O** and by Orkîse in **V**. In **Wd(B)**, when he defeats the heathen Beliân in knife-throwing, Wolfdietrich suggests that Machmet has dozed off (625, 3–4).[2]

In **AHb** Machmet is the name of a demon, who visits Dietrich's mother before his birth and prophesies great strength and fire-breathing power for her son; he also builds the city of Berne (Verona) in three nights.

ref: **AHb** p. 6, 38; **Kl** 1065; **O** 271, 2; **V(d)** 27, 4; **V(h)** 63, 1; **V(w)** 93, 11; **Wd(B)** 545, 4; **Wd(D)** v. 4, 2; **Wd(Gr)** 842, 2; **Wd(k)** 260, 5

As in OFr epic, the prophet Mohamet is thought to be a heathen god (Langlois, 413).

### MACHOREL von Muntabûre (GÔDÎÂN)
He rules at Jerusalem, yet his capital is Suders in Sürie (Tyre in Syria). Seventy-two heads of messengers for his daughter's hand

---

[1] Symons, *Heldensage*, 111, relates the name to Cadzund in Holland.

[2] In the OFr epic *Gaufrey* the heathen Naisier, in a similar knife-throwing duel, complains that Mohamet is asleep (cit. Hermann Schneider, 'Die Quellen des Nibelungenliedes', *Euphorion* XLV (1950), 495).

adorn the battlements of his fortress of Muntabûre (Mons Tabor). Ortnît, with the aid of Îljas and the dwarf Alberîch, abducts the princess; Alberîch plays tricks on the heathen and, protected by his cloak of invisibility, casts down his idols. Machorel, pretending to be reconciled to the marriage of his daughter to Ortnît, sends dragons' eggs to Ortnît's land: one of the dragons that hatch out kills Ortnît.

ref: **AHb** p. 5, 23 (*küniges . . . zû rachaol*); **DF** 2137 (Gôdîan); **O** 13, 1 (W *Marchorel*, A *Nachorel*, K *Zacherel*, e *achahel*, c *nachael*, a *nachaol*); **O(w)** 13, 1 (*Machabell*); **Wd(A)** m 417, 4; **Wd(D)** m III. 43, 4

pn: based on that of the Sultan Malek-el-Adel, whose Syrian fortress of Mons Tabor, built in 1212, was besieged during the crusade of 1217 (Amelung, *DHB* III. xxviii; Schneider, *GHS* I. 351).

MACITUS see GAMAZITUS

## MADELGÊR (ADELGÊR)
Father of Heime: mentioned among Ermenrîch's men, together with Madelolt, in **DF**.

ref: **A** 32, 3 (*Adelgêres*); **AHb** p. 3, 28 (*adelgers*); **B** 6371; **DF** 8663

In Þs the father of Heimir is named Studas (see Heime, p. 65).

pn: frequent in WFr; 8th-cent. German (Förstemann I. 1113; II. ii. 246; Socin, 152; Schlaug I. 131).

There is a possible connection between Madelgêr and Maugis (Amaugis), brother of Haymon in OFr epic (Langlois, 444; Kalbow, 45; Benary, 44 ff.); he is a skilful thief and steals the swords of Charlemagne and his peers. In Konrad's *Rolandslied* (12th cent.), Madelgêr (1600) is the name of a smith known to have made twelve swords at Regensburg, but he is not mentioned in the OFr source, the *Chanson de Roland*. In *Salman und Morolf* (12th cent.), a dwarf, who introduces Môrolf to a mermaid, is also named Madelgêr (730, 3).

## MADELOLT
Ermenrîch's man: mentioned together with Madelgêr.

ref: **DF** 8663

pn: 8th-cent. German (Förstemann I. 1115; II. ii. 246).

MADIUS, see GAMAZITUS

## MÂL
A sword: Arnolt's in **R**; Wolfhart's in **Rg(F)**.

ref: **R** 4153; **Rg(F)** v. 22, 3

pn: probably related to MHG *mâl*, 'decoration, ornament', especially on weapons and equipment (Lexer I. 2014), cf. OE *brodenmæl*, 'sword ornamented with a serpentine pattern' (Keller, 179 f.; Davidson, 122 ff.).

MALGERAS, see RŪMEROC

pn: cf. OFr Saracen name *Malgariz* (Langlois, 432).

## MAMBOLT (MAMEROLT)
A giant who threatens Dietrich at Mûter.

ref: **V(h)** 388, 1; **V(w)** 574, 1 (*Mamerolt*)[1]

pn: possibly a short form of *Maginbold*, recorded in Germany from the 8th cent. (Förstemann I. 1072).

## MARCELLÎÂN
This saint appears to Liebgart (1) in the shape of a white-robed old man.

ref: **Wd(B)** 734, 2

St. Marcellian (†202) was Bishop of Auxerre.

## MARCHUNC von Hessen
Ermenrîch's man.

ref: **DF** 8643

pn: the one-stemmed *Marcho* is recorded in Germany from the 8th cent. (Förstemann I. 1095). The basis can be either OHG *marah*, 'horse', or *mark*, 'march' (see Kaufmann, 248 f.).

## MARHOLT (1) von Sibenbürgen (Transylvania)
Etzel's man: aids Dietrich and fights Gêrbart at Rabene (Ravenna).

ref: **Rs** 739, 1

pn: 8th-cent. German (Förstemann I. 1097; Schlaug II. 126).

## MARHOLT (2) von Gurnewâle (Cornwall)
Ermenrîch's man.

ref: **DF** 8656 (W *Marolt*; 9050 R *Morholt*)

Perhaps a confusion of Marke von Gurnewâle and Môrolt von Îrlant from Gottfried von Straßburg's *Tristan* (*c*. 1210).

## MARÎA
The name of the Virgin Mary is frequently invoked, especially in the later epics.

ref: **DF** 9916; **E(d)** 142, 1; **E(s)** 99, 5; **hS** 30, 1; **jSn** 101, 11; **V(d)** 12, 6; **V(w)** 64, 11; **Wd(B)** 573, 2; **Wd(D)** VII. 18, 1; **Wd(Gr)** 686, 3; **Wu(B)** 120, 5

## MARKE
Ermenrîch's man: he fights Dietleip at Rabene (Ravenna).

ref: **Rs** 704, 2 (RA *Marche*)

pn: see Marchunc.

---

[1] In *Salman und Morolf* (12th cent.), the father of Fôre is named Memerolt (22, 3).

**MARKÎS**, lantgrâve ze Düringen (Thuringia)
Ermenrîch's man: he fights Ortwîn at Rabene (Ravenna).

ref: **Rs** 731, 1

pn: based on MHG *markîs* from OFr *marquis*, the equivalent of MHG *lantgrâve*.

## MARPALY
Daughter of the heathen Belîan: when Wolfdietrich arrives at Belîan's castle at Falkenîs, the heathen challenges him to a knife-throwing contest, but allows the hero to spend the night with his daughter. Marpaly knows by her prophetic powers that Wolfdietrich will kill her father, and throws away the drugged drink Belîan has sent him; however, she fails to seduce Wolfdietrich, who refuses to make love to her unless she becomes a Christian. The next day Wolfdietrich kills Belîan in the knife-throwing contest, and Marpaly vainly exercises her magic arts to prevent his departure: she conjures up mountains, lakes, mists, a burning forest, and fearsome demons (in **Wd(D)** they carry her off to hell); she even takes the shape of a bird (a magpie in **Wd(B)**, a crow in **Wd(D)**).[1]

ref: **Wd(B)** m 535, 3; **Wd(D)** VI. 9, 2; **Wd(Gr)** 1068, 2; **Wd(k)** m 256, 1

pn: probably a corrupt form of an OFr name for a Saracen princess, cf. *Malatrie, Margalie, Marsabile* (Langlois, 422, 432, 438); in the OFr epic *Floovant* the hero is captured by an emir, whose daughter, *Maugalie*, helps him escape (Heinzel, *Ostgotische Heldensage*, 73 f.; see also Wolfdietrich, p. 149 n. 2).

The Falkenîs episode resembles in some details the experiences of Lanzelet with Galagrandeiz and his daughter in Ulrich von Zazikhoven's *Lanzelet* (c. 1200) (O. Jänicke, *DHB* IV. xliii; Schneider, *Wolfdietrich* (1913), 261 ff.), and those of Þetleifr with Sigurðr the Greek and his daughter at the castle of Marsteinn in Þs (see p. 25).

## MARSILJÂN von Ceciljenlant (Sicily)
Wolfdietrich rids his country of the giant Baldemar.

ref: **Wd(D)** VII. 53, 1; **Wd(Gr)** 1354, 1

pn: probably from *Marsille* (*Marsillion*), the name of the Saracen King of Spain and opponent of Charlemagne in the OFr *Chanson de Roland* (Langlois, 438 f.; *Marsilie* in Konrad's *Rolandslied*, 381); the name *Mersilîan* (*Marsilîan*) also occurs for heathens in the 12th-cent. 'Spielmannsepen' *Orendel*, 2931, and *Salman und Morolf*, 302, 3.

**MARTIKOS**, see GAMAZITUS

[1] In the late-15th-cent. version of **Wd** in the *Dresdner Heldenbuch*, **Wd(k)**, she sends him dreams of a folk-tale nature: an enchantress locks him and his horse in a box for refusing to marry her; he sees rolls walking and wine pouring itself,

**MARYNA**, see MERGART

## MEDELBOLT
Heathen god.

ref: **V(h)** 91, 12;[2] **Wd(D)** v. 4, 3; **Wd(Gr)** 842, 3

pn: WFr 8th-cent. *Madelbald*, based on Gmc. *\*mapla-*, 'meeting-place' (Förstemann I. 1112; Kaufmann, 254); it is possible that a derogatory accommodation to MHG *madel, medel,* 'maggot, worm', has taken place.

## MEIZLÎN
A dwarf who entertains Wolfhart in his mountain kingdom (see Merzelîn below).

ref: **V(h)** 642, 2

pn: perhaps based on MHG *meizen*, 'hew, cut', with reference to mining activities of dwarfs.

## MENELOUS
Husband of Ilion (= Helen of Troy).

ref: **DH** F 45, 1, 3

**MENTIGER**, see NETTINGER

## MERCURIUS
Saracen god.

ref: **V(w)** 440, 12

## MERGART
Daughter of Herebrant and sister of Hildebrant: she is married to Amelolt von Garten (see Amelunc (2)); their sons are Wolfhart, Alphart, and Sigestap (see Hildebrant's genealogy, p. 75 n. 3).

ref: **AHb** m p. 6, 4; **Wd(D)** IX. 221, 3; **Wd(Gr)** 2109, 3; **Wd(w)** 2022, 3 (*Maryna*)

pn: 11th-cent. German (Förstemann I. 1104; Schlaug II. 129; Bach, §§ 284, 287).

## MERZELÎN
A dwarf: Wolfhart jousts with him at Virginâl's court.

ref: **V(h)** 984, 9

Probably identical with Meizlîn above.

pn: possibly based on MHG *merz*, 'treasure, rarity, ornament' (Lexer I. 2119).

## MERZÎAN (1) uncle of Delfîan and brother of Schudân
At Jerusalem Wolfdietrich is captured by forces led by Schudân. Merzîan is about to have him hanged, but a friendly Saracen frees him; Wolfdietrich's forces take the city, and Merzîan flees.

ref: **Wd(D)** v. 165, 1; **Wd(Gr)** 1001, 1

pn: In the 12th cent. a *Martian*, not known

and a rose-wreath that turns into a snake, etc. (290 ff.).

[2] J. Zupitza would amend to Apolle (*DHB* v. 277).

## MERZÎAN (1)

in the OFr original, appears in Pfaffe Konrad's *Rolandslied*, 4831, and in *Orendel*, the hero encounters two heathen brothers, *Merzîan* and *Sûdân* (910 f.).

## MERZÎAN (2) von Babilône (Cairo)

Etzel is said to be more magnificent than he.

ref: **B** 307

## MICHAEL

In L, Laurîn's appearance causes Witege to take him for St. Michael. Elsewhere this saint is referred to as the protector of the souls of the dead (**Kl, R, jSn**).

ref: **Kl** 2609; **L(A)** 239; **L(D)** 497; **L(DrHb)** 53, 4; **R** 4437; **jSn** 153, 2

## MÎME

A master smith living at Azzarîâ near Tôlêt (Toledo): he has made three swords, one of which, Schrit, is owned by Biterolf. He and Hertrîch have made twelve swords, and Wielant has made Mimminc, the thirteenth.

ref: **B** 139 (Mime)

In ON Eddic tradition Mímir is connected with wisdom: the head of Mímir first spoke and told the runes clearly (Sd 14, 4), for Mímir drinks mead each morning from Mímisbrunni, 'the pledge of Óðinn', where Óðinn hid his eye (Vsp 28, 10 f.),[1] and Óðinn is his friend (Sk ch. 9). The waves are termed 'Míms synir' (Vsp 46, 1).

Saxo, III. ii. 5 ff., tells how Hotherus (ON Höðr) captures a dwarf Mimingus, who ransoms his life by handing over a sword, with which Hotherus can kill Balderus (ON Baldr),[2] and a magic arm-ring, which increases its owner's wealth.[3]

In Þs, Mimir is a smith, who brings up Sigurðr (I. 303, 10 ff.); Sigurðr kills him and his brother, the dragon Reginn (see Eckerîch (1), p. 34, and Sîfrit, p. 119).[4]

In the Danish ballads *Ravengaard og Memering* and *Memering* (DgF I. 204 ff., 214 ff.), Miemerinng (Mimering) is a dwarf knight.

pn: *Mimo* (*Memmo*) 9th-cent. German (Förstemann I. 1124); *Mimmung* 15th-cent. German (Müllenhoff, ZE, 360 f.); the name, with or without the suffix *-ing/-ung*, is thought to occur in place-names (Mone, 90; Förstemann II. ii. 296 f.; but see Kaufmann, 259). Its basis is possibly Gmc. \**mîm-*, 'measure, think', cf. OE *mâmrian*, LG *mimeren* (F. Detter and R. Heinzel, 'Hœnir und der Vanenkrieg', *PBB* XVIII (1894), 549).

---

[1] A. Mentz, 'Schrift und Sprache der Burgunder', *ZfdA* LXXXV (1954/5), 7 ff., interprets the inscription on a 5th-cent. Burgundian buckle as a reference to Mimo (Mima), the 'beast of the dead', which conveys the spirit to the other world. Depicted on the buckle is a horse or stag drinking from a vessel, which Mentz takes to be Mímisbrunni.

[2] Cf. Alfrikr, p. 4, and Ruotliep, p. 113.

[3] Such a ring is the basis of Andvari's treasure in ON Eddic tradition (see p. 97 n. 6).

Apparently Mîme (ON Mímir), originally a supernatural being, has become a smith in German tradition—this includes the Danish and Þs references.

## MIMMINC (MIMMUNC)

The sword of Witege, made by his father Wielant.

ref: **A** 450, 4 (MS. *Mynfurges*); **B** 178 (Mimminc: MS. 8557 *mynningen*; 12273 *Miningen*); **L(A)** 1543 (m *mūnick*, r *minich*, K *munigtlich*); **Rg(A)** 239, 4 (a *menung*, b *merungen*); **Rg(C)** 1337 (Mîmingen: MS. *mymeng*); **Rg(D)** 278, 4 (Mîmingen: b *schemningē*); **Rg(P)** 316 (Mêmingen: MS. *mẽȳgen*; 444 Mîmunge); **Rs** 402, 5 (Mimmingen: A *myningen*; 901, 6 R *miminiges*, A *mynniges*); **V(h)** 730, 12 (MS. *mimig*; 873, 12 *mimmg*); **V(w)** 720, 12 (MS. *memmenunge*); **Vhw** 143 (*Nimminc*)

In German literature outside the 'Heldensage', Heinrich von Veldeke in his *Eneide* (c. 1175) first mentions this sword (5729 MS. G *Mynning*)[5] (see Eckesahs, p. 34, and Nagelrinc, p. 96); in the 14th cent., '*Mimminc*' is referred to in another LFr poem, *Heinric en Margriete van Limborch* (Müllenhoff, *ZE*, 365 f.). A corrupt form of the name is used appellatively for a sword in *Neidharts Lieder*, 91, 37; 92, 7 (R *mæchenich*, C *mesching*, c *menink*, *meñingk*, d *mǣchting*). In an LG Easter play of 1464, one of Pilate's soldiers bears a sword named '*Mummink*' (ibid. 366). Seyfrid is made the owner of '*Menig*' by Spangenberg in the 16th cent. (Golther, *Hürnen Seyfrid*, xxiii) and of '*Meynunc*' by Joh. Staricius in the 17th (W. Grimm, *DHS*, 364).

In the OE *Waldere* fragments, Mimming, 'Wēlandes worc', is borne by Waldere (I. 2 f.): formerly Þēodrīc has considered giving this excellent sword (Mimming?) to Widia (MHG Witege) for his help against giants (II. 4 ff.).[6] In the 14th-cent. ME romance of *Horn*,[7] it is known that Weland made Bittefer, the equal of Miming (397 ff.).

In Þs, Mimungr (I. 101, 8: A *Minnungur*) is made by Velent, who kills a rival smith at Niðungr's court with it (see Wielant, p. 142). He gives it to his son Viðga (MHG Witege); Hildibrandr exchanges his own sword for it when Viðga arrives at Bern; Viðga challenges Þiðrekr, but when Þiðrekr is about to kill the defenceless Viðga, whose sword has broken, Hildibrandr returns Mimungr to him; he defeats Þiðrekr and then joins Þiðrekr's band of warriors. Later

---

[4] In Rg(A) Eckerîch brings up Sîfrit in the smithy. ON Eddic tradition makes Reginn Sigurðr's smith foster-father; in Þs the name Reginn has been transferred to the dragon (see Sîfrit (1), pp. 119 ff.).

[5] Other manuscript readings are: H *Minnenc*, h *Mynnemyng*, M *Minnichleich*, B *Mimminch*.

[6] The author thus refers to Mimming's traditional owner.

[7] *King Horn*, ed. J. Hall (Oxford, 1901).

Heimir picks up Mimungr during the fighting against Osanctrix, but Þiðrekr forces him to return it to Viðga (I. 272 ff.).[1] In the Bertangaland combats Þiðrekr borrows Mimungr from Viðga and defeats Sigurðr with it, his own sword, Ekkisax, being inadequate for cutting Sigurðr's horn skin.

In the Swedish version of Þs, after killing Viðga (Sv *Wideke*), Þiðrekr (Sv *Didrik*) casts Mimungr (Sv *Mimingh*) into a lake (see Witege, p. 146 n. 10).

In the Danish ballad *Kong Diderik og hans Kæmper* (Version B), Viderick (MHG Witege) bears the sword Menning (*DgF* I. 99 ff.); in *Ulv van Jærn* (Version G) it is named Mimmering (ibid. 154 ff.). In the Faroese ballads, Virgar (MHG Witege) owns the sword Mimring (W. Grimm, *DHS*, 368).

pn: The short vowel of this sword-name makes any association with the smith Mîme unlikely, especially as its fashioning is always attributed to Wieland. The numerous German *-n-* spellings, also reflected in the MSS. of the Þs and in the Danish ballads, suggest the Gmc. root \**min-*, 'remember', as a basis; cf. MHG *minnen*, 'think of with love' (see Kluge, *EWb*, 479; Kaufmann, 259).

MÎMUNC von Isterrîch (Istria)
He and his brother, Tûriân, are the companions of Dietwart.

ref: **DF** 449 (A *Minnunckh*)

MINNE (1) daughter of Ladiner (1) von Westenmer
Wife of Dietwart.

ref: **DF** 899

pn: 9th-cent. German (Förstemann I. 1125; Socin, 61): the name is based on the abstract, OHG *minna*, MHG *minne*, 'love, remembrance'.

MINNE (2) personification

ref: **V(h)** 349, 11; **V(w)** 812, 7

MÎSSENÆRE pl.
The men of Mîssen (Meißen), who aid Gunther at Worms.

ref: **B** 10775

MŒRE pl. (MÔRLANT, MÔRRÎCHE)
The subjects of Sîfrit (3) von Môrlant in **Ku**: his country is also termed Môrrîche. In **Rs**, Biterunc von Môrlande supports Ermenrîch. Fraw Seld in **Wu(B)** was born 'zu Moren'.

ref: Mœre pl.: **Ku** 670, 3; **Wu(B)** 20, 3
Môrlant: **Ku** 580, 1; **Rs** 714, 1; Môrrîche **Ku** 729, 3

MHG *môre* is taken to be synonymous with 'Saracen' or 'heathen'; hence Sîfrit (3), a heathen viking figure in **Ku**, is thought of as a ruler of the Moors. The basis for the name is MLat. *Maurus*, 'Moor'.

MOREAN, see BŒMRÎÂN
pn: see MŒRE above.

MOREIN, see SENDERLÎN (2)
pn: see MŒRE above.

MORGÂN
A robber killed by Wolfdietrich (see Rûmelher).

ref: **Wd(D)** v. 16, 4 (z *Marckan*, ef *mortgram*); **Wd(Gr)** 853, 4

pn: possibly a corrupt form of OFr *Morgant*, a Saracen name (Langlois, 471).

MORILEAN, see ÎMÎÂN

MÔROLT (1) von Îrlant (Ireland)
Ermenrîch's man: he is killed by Dietrich at Rabene (Ravenna).

ref: **Rs** 806, 5 (Môrholt: A *Morolt*)

pn: probably derives from that of Môrolt von Îrlant, the giant killed by Tristan in Gottfried von Straßburg's *Tristan*, 6742; in Wolfram von Eschenbach's *Parzival* he is an ally of Fridebrant.

The name is recorded in the 7th cent. in Lb and the 8th cent. in German (Förstemann I. 1118); *Morault* is frequent in OFr epic (Langlois, 469). The basis is MLat. *Maurus*, 'Moor'.

MÔROLT (2) von Arle (Arles in Provence)
Brother of Karle; Ermenrîch's man.

ref: **DF** 8649

MÔRUNC (1) Hetel's man
The close companion of Hôrant on the quest for Hetel's bride, Hilde (1): in **Ku** his realm is thought variously to be Wâleis (641, 4), Nîflant (211, 1), and Frieslant (481, 1);[2] he is frequently mentioned together with Îrolt.

In **DH** he is the brother of Horant.

ref: **DH** F 47, 3, 3; **Ku** 211, 1

pn: 8th-cent. German (Förstemann I. 1117; Schlaug I. 134); place-names like *Moringen*, etc. (Förstemann II. ii. 250), are probably of different origin.

It is possible that the name in **Ku** and **DH** is a variant of that of Môrolf, King Salmân's minstrel, who does in fact compare himself to Hôrant (see p. 81 n. 2).

MÔRUNC (2) von Dietmarse (Dithmarschen)[3]

---

[1] In **B** a similar sword story is told about Heime's sword, Nagelrinc (see p. 96).
[2] See p. 71 regarding these regions which in **Ku** are included in the dominions of Hetel.
[3] This name and seat very probably derive from **Ku**: cf. Hetel, part of whose realm is Dietmers.

MÔRUNC (2)

Ermenrîch's man: killed by Dietrich at Rabene (Ravenna) in **Rs**.

ref: **DF** 8657 (A *Maysunck*); **Rs** 738, 1

MÔRUNC (3) von Engellant (England)
Ermenrîch's man: a silver-white panther on a black ground is depicted on his shield.

ref: **Rs** 496, 1

MÔRUNC (4) von Tuscân (Tuscany)
Ermenrîch's man.

ref: **Rs** 1008, 1

MOYSES
Rother recalls God's help to Moses in time of need.

ref: **R** 3933

# N

NAGELRINC
Heime's sword (**A**, **B**, **Rg**); in **L(A)**, Wolfhart uses it; in **B** during the fighting at Worms (10926 ff.) it is knocked from Heime's hand by Sîfrit; Hildebrant picks it up and gives it to his nephew Wolfhart; after Heime and Hildebrant have come to blows about it, Dietrich orders Hildebrant to return it to Heime.[1]

ref: **A** 272, 3; **B** 10551; **L(A)** 1543 (m *natinck*, r *nagel*); **Rg(A)** 221, 1; **Rg(C)** 1249; **Rg(D)** 342, 3 (b *Nach gerling*)

The first reference to this sword in German literature outside the 'Heldensage' occurs *c.* 1175 in Heinrich von Veldeke's *Eneide*: Nagelring (5730) (see Eckesahs, p. 34, and Mimminc, p. 94). It is mentioned among other swords in the late 13th-cent. *Ritterpreis* (Schieb-Frings, *Eneide*, 188).

In Þs, Naglringr (I. 35, 5) was made by the dwarf Alfrikr (see Alberîch, p. 4), who, when captured by Þiðrekr, ransoms his life by stealing it from its owner, the giant Grímur, and giving it to Þiðrekr, who is thus able to kill the giant pair, Grímur and Hilldur, with it (see Grîme, p. 53).[2] Later he gives it to Heimir, whose first sword was Blodgang (I. 40, 10).

In the Danish ballads, a sword with the corrupt name 'Adelryng' is used by Miemeringg in *Ravengaard og Memering* (*DgF* I. 204 ff.); Sivard (MHG Sîfrit) is the owner in *Sivard og Brynild* (Version A) (ibid. 16 ff.); in *Kong Diderik og Löven* (Version A) (ibid. 132 f.), Dhyryk (MHG Dietrich) finds the dead Syfred's sword Adelryng in the dragon's lair and kills the dragon with it (see Wolfdietrich, p. 149, and Rôse, p. 109).[3]

pn: based on the equivalent of OHG *nagal*, OE *nægl*, ON *nagl*, 'nail'; this component is met in other sword names, e.g. OE *Nægling* (*Beowulf*, 2680),[4] ON *naglfari* (Sk ch. 51). The name may indicate a sword with a ring attached by decorative nails; cf. MHG *genagelt*, for *gemâlet*, 'brightly decorated' (**N(C)** 1294, 1).[5]

NÄNTWÎN (1) father of Herrât
His wife is the sister of Helche.

ref: **N** 1381, 4

pn: 6th-cent. Goth. (Schönfeld, 170); 8th-cent. German (Förstemann I. 1152); 9th-cent. Lb (Ploß, 57).

NÄNTWÎN (2) von Regensburc (Regensburg)
Brother of Volcwîn and nephew of Witege: he aids Gunther in the combats at Worms; he is killed by Hildebrant.

ref: **B** 5069

NÄNTWÎN (3) Dietrich's man
In **DF** Dietrich sends him to Ermenrîch to demand ransom for prisoners captured at Meilân (Milan). In **Rs** he fights Wolfgêr at Rabene (Ravenna).

ref: **DF** 7071; **Rs** 724, 1 (N. von Elsentroye)[6]

NEBULONES, see NIBELUNGE pl.

NÊRE
Dietrich's man, brother of Hildebrant and father of Wolfwîn; in **DF** he is killed by Reinhêr von Parîse at Bôlonje (Bologna).

ref: **A** 44, 2; **DF** 3009; **Kl** 1743; **V(w)** 843, 8; **Wd(D)** IX. 221, 2; **Wd(Gr)** 2109, 2

pn: in the 12th-cent. *Rolandslied* of Pfaffe Lamprecht, a Saracen of this name is killed by Ludewîc (4827); the name is absent from the OFr original, the *Chanson de Roland*.

---

[1] In Þs, a similar story is told about Viðga's sword Mimungr: see Mimminc, pp. 94 f.

[2] In the frescoes at Runkelstein (14th cent.) 'Fraw Riel', a giantess, is depicted holding Nagelrinc, possibly a confusion of Rûêl from *Wigalois* with Hilde (3), wife of Grîme (W. Grimm, *DHS*, 493).

[3] See under Balmunc (1), p. 9, regarding swords found in dragons' dens.

[4] Beowulf uses it against the dragon, but it shatters, and he finishes the fight with another sword (see Balmunc (1), p. 9 n. 4).

[5] See Davidson, 66, 125, regarding this ancient type of sword with a ring on the hilt.

[6] Erwin (3) von Elsentroye may be intended (see p. 37 n. 1).

NETTINGER (MENTIGER)
Brother of the giantess Runze, husband of Gudengart, and father of Ecke, Vâsolt, Ebenrôt, Eckwit, and Eckenôt (1) (see the genealogy of Ecke, p. 33 n. 2).

ref: **AHb** p. 3, 38 (*mentigers*); **E(s)** 187, 4

pn: a family name in the 14th cent. (Mone, 96). It is possibly a corrupt form of *Nîtgêr* (see p. 99).

NEVELUNGEN, see NIBELUNGE pl.

NIBELÔT von Pârîse (Paris)
Etzel is more magnificent than he.

ref: **B** 295

pn: possibly a variant of *Nibelunc*, cf. *Amelôt* and *Amelunc* (p. 6).

NIBELUNC (1) father of Nibelunc (2) and Schilbunc
The original owner of a treasure and the sword Balmunc (see Nibelunge pl.).

ref: **B** 7227; **N** 88, 3; **gS** p. 82, 39 (*Egward*);[1] **hS** 13, 8

pn: see Nibelunge pl.

NIBELUNC (2) son of Nibelunc (1)
See Nibelunge pl.

ref: **B** 7819; **N** 87, 3; **hS** m 14, 3 (?)

NIBELUNGE pl.[2]
In **W**, Waltharius terms Guntharius and Hagano 'Franci nebulones' (555).[3]
In **N**, Schilbunc and Nibelunc ('die küenen Nibelunge' 87, 2) give Sîfrit the sword Balmunc as an advance payment for dividing between them the treasure left them by their father, Nibelunc, which is brought from a mountain; when Sîfrit is unable to perform this task, a fight ensues, and he kills the brothers, their twelve giants, and seven hundred of their men with Balmunc;[4] he then rules 'Nibelunge lant'[5] and wins the cloak of invisibility (MHG *tarnkappe* 97, 3) and the treasure from the dwarf Alberîch, whom he appoints as his treasurer.[6] A thousand Nibelunge warriors (501, 3) become his subjects (also termed 'Schilbunges recken' 721, 3); after Sîfrit's death they return to 'Nibelunge lant' (1082), and the 'Nibelunges golt' is seized and lowered into the Rhine at Lôche (= Lochheim, near Worms) on the orders of Hagen. With Âventiure xxv ('Wie die Nibelunge zen Hiunen fuoren') the thousand 'Nibelunge helde' (1523, 1) join Gunther's men,[7] who also number a thousand (1478); from then on the term 'Nibelunge' refers to the Burgundians and to Hagen, their leader on the journey to Etzel's kingdom ('er was den Nibelungen ein helflîcher trôst' 1526, 2).[8] Kriemhilt, on the arrival of the Burgundians at Etzel's court, demands the return of the 'hort der Nibelunge' (1741, 2) from Hagen,[9] who uses Balmunc, 'Nibelunges swert' (2348, 4), in the subsequent fighting against the Huns. The account of this conflict is summed up in the last half-line of the poem: 'daz ist der Nibelunge nôt' (2379, 4).[10] In the **Kl**, the term 'Nibelunge' occurs once for the Burgundians (see Franke), otherwise only for Nibelunc and his sons; in **B** for the original owners of the treasure; and in **Rg(A)** for Gibeche's men, the Burgundians.

In **hS**, the treasure of the Nibelunge is confused with that won by Seyfrid from a dragon: 'der Nyblinger hort' (13, 2) is removed from its hiding-place by 'Nyblings sone' (134, 1)[11] during Seyfrid's fight with the man-dragon holding Krimhilt prisoner. They place it in a cave under the 'Trachenstain', and Seyfrid, after killing the dragon, loads it on to his horse in the belief that it belonged to the dragon (166, 7), but then sinks it in the Rhine, when the dwarf Eugel prophesies that his life will be short (167). It has been earlier stated that dwarfs give Seyfrid a treasure when he kills his first dragon, from whose melted horn he obtains his horn skin (38).

ref: (1) The original owners of a treasure and their men, who become subjects of Sîfrit and Sigemunt:[12] **AHb** p. 7, 25; **B** 7848; **Kl** 1403 (C); **N** 87, 2; **hS** 13, 2; der Nibelunge lant: **N** 92, 3

---

[1] This name (MHG *Eckewart*) may derive from **N**.
[2] For a full account of the journey of the Nibelunge (ON *Niflungar*) to the land of the Huns, and their final destruction there, see Hagen (1), pp. 58 ff.
[3] Possibly a latinization of OHG *nibulunc*, understood as 'son of the misty, dark underworld, son of mist' (Strecker, *Waltharius*, 55), cf. *scrato*, 'goblin', as a gloss for Lat. *nebulo* (Kögel I. ii. 301); an ironic pun, Lat. *nebulones*, 'windbags', for Lat. *nobiles*, 'noble', is likely in the context (E. Schröder, 'Franci Nebulones', *ZfdA* LXXIV (1937), 80).
[4] This episode is paralleled in fairytale; see Panzer, *Sigfrid*, 63 ff., regarding the so-called 'Erbteilungsformel'.
[5] In **N**, this realm, Niderlant, and Norwæge, which are all subject to Sîfrit, are thought of as contiguous.
[6] A small golden wand with marvellous power

(1124, 1) is part of the treasure; cf. the wealth-giving ring of the dwarf Andvari in ON Eddic tradition (see pp. 120 n. 5), and the similar ring given by the dwarf Mimingus to Hotherus in Saxo (see p. 94).
[7] The matter is ambiguous, since the original Nibelunge have already returned to Xanten with Sigemunt and there are never more than a thousand warriors accompanying Gunther to Etzel's kingdom.
[8] In **N(k)**, the term 'Nibelunge' is restricted to the men of Nibelunc and Schilbunc.
[9] In the **Kl**, the loss of the treasure, which is inexhaustible according to the C-version (1407 ff.), is given as one reason for Kriemhilt's relentless hostility to Hagen (1403 ff., 3736 ff.).
[10] In the C-version 'daz ist der Nibelunge liet'.
[11] Eugel is the only son of Nybling named.
[12] In an LG fragment of **Rg**, Sîfrit is 'der van Nevelungen' (Holz, *Rosengarten*, lxx).

(2) Gunther's and Gibeche's men, i.e. the Burgundians (see Burgonde, pp. 16 f.): **Kl** 1754; **N** 1523, 1 (?), 1526, 2; **Rg(A)** 177, 3; **W** 555 (Franci nebulones: **N** *Nivilones*) (?)

Apart from Wolfram von Eschenbach's reference to 'den küenen Nibelungen' (*Parzival*, 421, 7), from the late 12th to the 16th cent. references outside the heroic epics are to the Nibelungen treasure in the Rhine (W. Grimm, *DHS*, 173, 179, 191, 309, 314, 320, 352; Müllenhoff, *ZE*, 424,);[1] in the *Minneburg* (14th cent.), for example, although the 'niblung...schatz' is mentioned, Gunther's men are termed 'frenkisch ingesinde' (W. Grimm, *DHS*, 315). The proverbial phrase, 'Da das Gold im Rhein ligt', of Sebastian Franke (16th cent.) must refer to the Nibelungen treasure (ibid. 348).

In ON Eddic tradition the name 'Niflungar' refers to Gunnarr's people (Br 16, 10; Dr title, p. 223; Akv 11, 2; Am 47, 5; Sk chs. 48, 50; Hniflungar: HHu I. 48, 10; Ghv 12, 6), also termed 'Gjúkungar' (see Gibeche (1)); Högni's son is named Niflungr (Völss ch. 38; Hniflungr: Am 88, 5).[2] The name is connected with the treasure demanded from Gunnarr by Atli and which has been sunk in the Rhine: 'Niflunga skattr' (Sk ch. 50; Hátt II str. 41); 'hodd Niflunga' (Akv 26, 7); the *kenningar* for gold of the *Bjarkamál* (10th cent.) quoted in Sk ch. 58, str. 128, are: 'Rínar rauðmalmi' (the Rhine's ruddy ore); 'rógr Niflunga' (strife of the Nibelungen), cf. 'rógmalmr' (ore of strife) of Akv 27, 6. The name is not applied to the treasure Sigurðr wins from the dragon, about which a story is preserved (Rm; Fm; Sk chs. 46–7; Völss ch. 14),[3] the supernatural beings involved bearing names different from those of the beings who possess the treasure won by Sîfrit in **N** (see pp. 118, 120).

In Þs, Gunnarr's people are termed 'Niflungar' (I. 1, 9; II. 258, 3, etc.), and his realm south of the Rhine 'Niflungaland' (I. 282, 5); the treasure possessed by Gunnarr and Högni, later identified with that of Sigurðr (see pp. 42, 60), is the 'Niflungaskattr' (II. 279, 26); Högni's son Aldrian locks Attila in the treasure-house to starve to death beside it (II. 369–74: see Hagen (1), p. 60). The sagaman states that the garden where Gunnarr and his men fought the men of Attila in Susat (Soest) is still called 'Niflunga garðr' (II. 327, 22).

In the Danish ballad *Grimilds Hævn* (C-version: *DgF* I. 48–50), Hagenn's son Rancke locks Grimild in a treasure-cave with 'Nidings Skat' (Niding's treasure). Likewise in the *Hven. Chron.*, Chremild is locked in a cave by Hogne's son, where she dies among the treasure of 'Nögling', here the father of Hogne (W. Grimm, *DHS*, 345).

pn: first recorded in 752 among the Salian Franks for *Nibelungus* (*Nivelongus*), a nephew of Charles Martel, and several times in the same Arnulfingian family in the 8th and 9th cents. (Müllenhoff, *ZE*, 290 f.; Jänicke, *ZE*, 310 f.; Förstemann I. 1161; Kaufmann, 268); in Germany *Nibelungus* is first recorded in 774 in a Lorsch document referring to land near Worms (Müllenhoff, *ZE*, 292), being rarely recorded in the 9th and 10th cents.: *Nipulunc* in 802 at Freising,[4] *Nebulunc* in 815 in a document regarding land near Worms, *Nevelungus* in 993 in Alsace (ibid. 292 f.); *Neuelunchus* occurs in a Worms document of 1106 and becomes more frequent from then on (ibid. 294 f.).

In WFr records the name *Nevelongus* (*Nivelongus*) occurs more frequently in the 11th and 12th cents. (ibid. 292 ff.); the pn *Nevelon*[5] is frequent in OFr *ch.d.g.* (Langlois, 484; see also Flutre, 145, and C. Voretzsch, 'Zur Geschichte der Nibelungensage in Frankreich und Deutschland', *ZfdA* LI (1909), 41). The name does not occur in OE (Binz, 204).

The Arnulfingian family, among whom the name *Nibelungus*, etc., was common, were descended from Pepin of Landen (*CMH* II. 123 ff.), whose daughter St. Gertrude (†659) founded the monastery of Nivelles in South Brabant (Gmc. \**Niuwi-alha*, 'new sanctuary': Kaufmann, 268 f.).[6] Pepin of Heristal, Pepin of Landen's grandson, exercised, as majordomo, dominion over Merovingian Gaul from 697 to 714; his later descendants were Charles Martel and Charlemagne. It seems possible that this name derives from the association of this distinguished family with Nivelles (see L. Levillain, 'Les Nibelungen historiques et leurs alliances de famille', *Annales du Midi* XLIX (1937), 408, for a family tree).

Whatever the origin of the name, accommodation to the Gmc. root \**neðula-* (OHG *nebul*, *nibulnisse*, MHG *nebel*, *nibel*, *nibelunge*, 'mist, darkness', OS *neðal*, OFris. *nevil*, MDu *nevel*, 'mist', ON *njól*, 'night') or \**niðila-* (OE *nifol*, *neowol*, 'low, deep, dark', ON *nifl-*, cf. *Niflheimr*, 'underworld')

---

[1] The Nibelungen treasure, constituting and symbolizing royal power, may well derive from the gold-bearing property of the Rhine sands, from which, according to Otfrid I. 1, 72 (9th cent.), the Franks obtained gold: 'joh lesent thar in lante gold in iro sante' (Otfrids Evangelienbuch, hrsg. von O. Erdmann (Tübingen, 1965⁵), 13).

[2] See Hagen (1), p. 59.

[3] Some confusion certainly exists: in Dr and Sk ch. 49, Gunnarr and Högni seize the gold Sigurðr won from Fáfnir, and in Völss ch. 36, Atli demands the treasure from Gunnarr and Högni as the inheritance of Gúðrun, Sigurðr's widow.

[4] A *Nebolugno genere Bavario*, a personage connected with the Frankish royal house, is recorded in a document from Pistoja for the year 812 (W. Grimm, *DHS*, 30, 455); there is no further record for the South-East till 1250 (Kromp I. 11).

[5] Gmc. ð becomes OFr *v* (Kalbow, 38).

[6] H. Grégoire, 'La patrie des Nibelungen', *Byzantion* IX (1934), 34 ff., suggests a Celtic origin for the name, \**Nivialah*, 'new temple'.

appears to have taken place (Kluge, *EWb*, 504 f.; see also Kaufmann, 268 f.). In **N**, at any rate, the name has been applied to supernatural beings, and the treasure Sîfrit wins from them has been equated with Gunther's royal treasure; the name *Nibelunc* may well have been interpreted as 'mist man' in this context (see also Schilbunc, p. 115); cf. the translation of 'Nybling' by *Mhaček* (Czech *mha*, 'mist') in the Czech version of **hS** (Golther, *Hürnen Seyfrid*, x).

Whether the name originally belonged to historical persons and was then applied to supernatural beings, i.e. 'Nebelwesen' (Heusler, *Nibelungensage*, 28), or vice versa (S. Gutenbrunner, 'Über einige Namen der Nibelungendichtung', *ZfdA* LXXXV (1954/5), 44 ff.), the pn appears first with certain authenticity on the Lower Rhine among members of a great Frankish dynasty. In all probability it became attached to the heroes of the story about the destruction of the Burgundians, Gunther and his men, when this story was absorbed into Frankish traditions before transmission to Scandinavia (see Burgonde, pp. 16 f.).[1]

NIMMINC, see MIMMINC

NÎTGÊR (1) ruler at Mûter
The leader of Nîtgêr's giants, Wîcram, captures Dietrich von Berne, who is then kept prisoner at Mûter.[2] When Dietrich's men defeat the giants,[3] Nîtgêr becomes Dietrich's vassal. Nîtgêr's sister Ibelîn and his wife Simelîn succour Dietrich during his captivity.

ref: **V(h)** 317, 7 (MS. usually *Nitinger*); **V(w)** 505, 7

pn: 8th-cent. German (Förstemann I. 1158; Schlaug I. 135; II. 130); see Nettinger, p. 97.

NÎTGÊR (2) Dietrich's man
Father of Sigelint (3) in **B**: he is killed by Gîselhêr in the **Kl**.

ref: **A** 306, 3; **B** 13192; **Kl** 1755

NÔÊ
Wolfdietrich in adversity recalls God's help to Noah (see Danîêl and Jônas).

ref: **Wd(D)** VIII. 122, 3; **Wd(Gr)** 1658, 3

(NORDÎÂN), see p. 118 n. 6.

In the Þs Nordian, huntsman of Iron, is the father of the giants Asplian, Ædgæir, Avæntroð, and Viðolfr.

NORPREHT (1) Rhine ferryman (RUOPREHT)

In **Rg(D)** he demands a fee of a hand and a foot for his services. Ilsân overcomes him and ferries Dietrich's company across the Rhine at Worms. Hildebrant pays him thirty gold marks on the return journey (in **Rg(C)** he waives the fee).

ref: **AHb** p. 7, 28 (*Rûpreht*); **Rg(C)** 818; **Rg(D)** m 166, 4 n 192, 4 (610, 4 s *Ruprehht*)

pn: 8th-cent. German (Förstemann I. 1168; Schlaug I. 135; II. 131); it is recorded in OE (Searle, 358).

A document of Worms dated 1290 refers to the quarrel between the monastery of Schönau and the ferrymen, Burkard, *Norpertus*, and Gnanno, who refuse to pay dues to the monastery (Holz, *Rosengarten*, xciii ff.). Nevertheless, the incident probably has literary antecedents: cf. Gunther's ferryman in **W**, Else's ferryman in **N**, and Laurîn's penalty in **L** (see pp. 35 f., 88, 135).

NORPREHT (2) von Bruoveninge (Prüfennig, nr. Regensburg)
Etzel's man: he aids Dietrich and fights Môrunc at Rabene (Ravenna).

ref: **DF** 5155; **Rs** 55, 1

NUODUNC
Rüedegêr's son (**B** 3335 ff.; **Rg(D)** 320, 2; **Rg(F)** III. 17, 3). In **N**, Rüedegêr refers to 'mîniu kint' (2164, 3) when Nuodunc is already dead, yet only one other child, his daughter (see Dietlint (2)), is otherwise mentioned. Rüedegêr's wife, Gotelint, laments the death of Nuodunc at the hands of Witege (also known to **Rg(CD)**) when she gives his shield to Hagen (1698 ff.); later Kriemhilt promises his widow and lands to Blœdel (1903 ff.), the latter being variously identified: Bruoveninge (Prüfennig) (**Rs**), Stîrelant (Styria) (**B**), Swanvelden and 'ze Nüerenberc der sant' (**A**).

In **A**, **B**, **DF**, and **Rs**, Nuodunc supports Dietrich—he is his nephew in **Rg(F)** IV. 18, 1: in **Rs** he fights Fruote at Rabene; in **Rg(F)** he is matched against Gunther in the combats at Worms. In **B** he accompanies Etzel's sons, Orte and Erpfe, in the service of Queen Helche.

ref: **A** 78, 3 (MS. *nydong* always); **B** 3335; **DF** 5154; **N** 1699, 3 (b *Nidunges*, etc.); **N(k)** 1729, 5 (*Neidung*); **Rg(C)** 1325; **Rg(D)** 320, 2; **Rg(F)** III. 17, 3 (MS. *nvdinge*; IV. 18, 1 *nodungk*, etc.); **Rs** 41, 2

In Þs, Nauðungr (II. 227, 23), Duke of Valkaborg (Wallachia?), is the brother of Gudelinda, Roðingeirr's wife. He is killed by Viðga at the battle against Erminrikr at

---

[1] W. Richter, 'Beiträge zur Deutung des Mittelteils des Nibelungenliedes', *ZfdA* LXXII (1935), 10, and Gamillscheg III. 86, 141, argue for Burgundian origin of the family name, \**Nibilingōs*, in the 5th cent.; against this it may be noted that in OE, Gūðhere is known to be a Burgundian,

but the Nibelungen name is unknown (see Gunther, p. 54).
[2] Cf. the role of Hertnît (2) in the story of Wielant( see pp. 70 f).
[3] See under Wîcram the names of the giants defeated by Dietrich and his men (p. 140).

Gronsport, where he bears Þether's standard.[1] Gudelinda later gives his shield to Högni.

pn: *Noding* (*Noting*), 9th-cent. German (Förstemann I. 1164 f.; Socin, 570; Schlaug I. 135; II. 131;[2] W. Grimm, *DHS*, 111) and Lb (Ploß, 57).

Although the vowel of the first component presents considerable problems,[3] it is probable that the first component of the name is based on Gmc. *nauði- (OS *nôd*, OHG *nôt*, ON *nauðr*, 'distress, need').

# O

OLFÂN (1) von Babilônje (Cairo in Egypt) Brother of Belmunt: he attacks Hugdietrich's kingdom and is defeated by Wolfdietrich.

ref: **Wd(D)** III. 10, 4; **Wd(Gr)** 271, 4
pn: possibly based on OFr *olifant*, 'warhorn'.

OLFÂN (2) Belmunt's gate-keeper
A giant killed by Wolfdietrich.

ref: **Wd(D)** IV. 71, 1; **Wd(Gr)** 460, 1

ORENDEL, see ERNTHELLE

ORKÎSE (ARABAN)
A heathen who exacts the yearly tribute of a maiden from the elf-queen Virginâl: he tracks his quarry with hounds and blows a huntinghorn. Hildebrant kills him. In **V(d)** his father and son are named Terevas and Janibus; in **V(w)** Teriufas and Janapas. In **V(w)** the exiling of the dwarf Elegast is given as the cause of his hostility to Virginâl.

ref: **V(d)** m 3, 9 n 16, 1 (Araban; 100, 12 Origreis; 104, 3 Origens); **V(h)** m 1, 2 n 82, 12; **V(w)** m 1, 11 n 255, 8 (Orgeis: MS. *argeisen*)

pn: probably of Romance origin, cf. *Orgaie* (*Orgais*), a name used for heathens in the *ch.d.g.* (Langlois, 502); nevertheless, the name has been associated with *Orco*, an Alpine forest demon (Jiriczek, *DHS* (1898), 237; Schneider, *GHS* I. 271).
Cf. *Vâsolt*, p. 44, and Wunderer, pp. 153 f.

ORT(E)
Son of Etzel and Helche: he and his brother Scharpfe are killed by Witege at Rabene (Ravenna) in **Rs**; in **B**, his brother is named Erpfe.

ref: **B** 3334; **Rs** m 124, 5 n 172, 2
In Þs the sons of Attila and Erka killed by Viðga are named Ortvin (II. 105, 5) and Erpr.

pn: 8th-cent. German (Förstemann I. 1180 f.).

ORTFELS
A dwarf who helps Wolfdietrich rescue Sigeminne from Drasîan.

ref: **Wd(B)** 454, 108; **Wd(Gr)** 747, 4

ORTLIEP
Son of Etzel and Kriemhilt: in **N**, Kriemhilt has him brought to the feast with the intention of provoking a conflict between the Huns and the Burgundians (1912);[4] Hagen, on hearing that the Burgundian squires have been slain, cuts the boy's head off, and it falls in Kriemhilt's lap; then the conflict begins.
In **AHb**, Crimhilt urges her son to strike Hagen on the cheek; Hagen beheads him the second time he does it, and the conflict starts.

ref: **AHb** m p. 10, 23; **N** 1388, 3
In Þs, Grimilldr urges her son Aldrian (II. 281, 10) to strike Högni on the cheek at the feast; Högni beheads him and hurls the severed head at Grimilldr's breast; the conflict starts.

pn: 9th-cent. German (Förstemann I. 1181; Socin, 29, 156); frequently confused with *Ortleip*, Förstemann I. 1180). 'Ortliep der hün' is the name of a peasant in the 14th-cent. *Metzen hochzît*, v. 97.[5]
The killing of a child as the starting-point of a conflict occurs in the 10th-cent. Spanish *Infantes de Lara* (Wais, *Frühe Epik*, 147) and the 11th-cent. Welsh tale *Branwen*;[6] see Hempel, *Nibelungenstudien*, 203, and Hermann Schneider, 'Die Quellen des Nibelungenliedes', *Euphorion* XLV (1950), 493.

ORTNÎT (1) von Lamparten (Lombardy)
In **O**, the ruler of Lamparten (Lombardy),

---

[1] In **A** he bears Dietrich's standard at the defence of Berne against Ermenrîch's forces (**A** 418, 436).
[2] Kaufmann, 269, bases OS *Nôthung*, however, on Gmc. *nanþ-, 'daring' (cf. *Näntwîn*).
[3] See Heusler, *Heldennamen*, 104; G. Baesecke, 'Gudrun-Kriemhilt, Grimhild-Uote, Guthorm-Gernot', *PBB* LX (1936), 377; Th. Frings, 'Nuodunc, Naudung', *PBB* LXXX (Halle, 1961), 278 f.
[4] In ON Eddic tradition, Guðrún kills her sons Erpr and Eitill (see pp. 20, 40).
[5] In *Der Bauernhochzeitsschwank*, hrsg. von E. Wießner (Tübingen, 1956).
[6] *The Mabinogion*, trans. Gwyn Jones and Thomas Jones (London, 1950), 36 f.

with his capital at Garte (Garda):[1] his true father is the dwarf Alberîch (see p. 3), who gives him splendid equipment, including golden armour and the sword Rôse. He decides to seek the hand of the daughter of the heathen Machorel, the battlements of whose castle at Muntabûre (Mons Tabor) are adorned with the heads of the messengers of her suitors. Ortnît's uncle, Îljas von Riuzen (Russia), takes command of the expedition which sets sail from Messîn (Messina); with the help of Alberîch, who outwits Machorel and overturns his idols, and after fierce fighting, in which the ruthless Îljas excels, Ortnît abducts the princess; she is baptized, and Ortnît celebrates his marriage to her at Garte. Machorel, pretending to be reconciled, sends a messenger with dragon's eggs to Lamparten, and Ortnît is carried off by one of the dragons and devoured by its brood;[2] before setting out on this fatal adventure, Ortnît makes his wife promise not to marry any man unless he has killed the dragon. Ortnît's avenger is to be the ancestor of Dietrich von Berne (597, 3).[3]

In **Wd**, Wolfdietrich kills the dragon with Ortnît's sword Rôse, which he finds in its lair,[4] and returns to Garte in Ortnît's armour to wed Ortnît's widow, Sîdrât.[5]

In **E**, it is known that Wolfdietrich gave Ortnît's armour to the monastery of Tischcâl, from which the queens of Jochgrîm acquired it; Sêburc, one of the latter, gives it to the giant Ecke. Dietrich kills Ecke and puts on the armour, first cutting off a piece to make it fit. The excellence of Ortnît's armour is also attested in **L(DrHb)** and **hS**.

ref: **AHb** p. 4, 9 (*Otnit*); **DF** 2035 (A *Ottenit*); **E(d)** m 21, 5 n 196, 4 (Ottene(y)t); **E(L)** 21, 7 (MS. *otenit*); **E(s)** 16, 7 (*Otnit*); **L(DrHb)** 65, 4 (*Ortney*); **L(K)II** 18 (Ortneit); **O** title (A *Ottnides*, W *Ornitt*, e *Otnit*, c *otnid*), 5, 2 (W *Ortneit*, K *Ortney*, later *Ortneit*, A *Ottnit*, later *Otnit*, a–g *Otnit*); **hS** 70, 7 (NH *Ornit*, F *Otnits*, Ba *Otnis*); **Wd(A)** 417, 2 (A *Otnit*, K *Ortney*); **Wd(B)** 343, 4 (B *Ortneit*, KH *ortnayden*); **Wd(C)** VIII. 12, 1 (*otnides*); **Wd(D)** III. 42, 2 (title e *Otnit*); **Wd(Gr)** 302, 2 (Otnit); **Wd(w)** 293, 2 (*Ortnit*)

In German literature outside the epics, Ortnît is referred to in the 14th-cent. *Weltchronik* of Heinrich von München and in *der zunge strît* (W. Grimm, *DHS*, 224 f., 308 f.), and by Fischart and Goldast in the 16th cent. (ibid. 352, 362); 'Kinig Orthneit' is depicted as a giant on the late-14th-cent. frescoes at the castle of Runkelstein (ibid. 493).

In the Þs, the story of Hertnið af Bergara[6] has many parallels with that of Ortnît (II. 359 ff.): a dragon lays waste his kingdom and carries him off to its brood. Þiðrekr kills the dragon with Hertnið's sword, which he finds in its lair, dons Hertnið's armour,[7] and weds Hertnið's widow, Isollde (see also Dietrich (1), p. 29, and Wolfdietrich, p. 150).

pn: *Ortnit*, first recorded in Germany 1160 (Mone, 75; Förstemann I. 1181). In the literary manuscripts and prints, *Ot-* spellings (OHG *ôt-*, OS *ôd*, 'wealth, property') outnumber *Ort-* spellings (OHG *ort*, 'point of weapon, spearhead of army'), but the form *Ōtnit* has not been recorded outside these literary monuments.[8]

Ortnît's story, as we have it in **O** and **Wd**, consists of a bridal-quest scheme very similar to that in the early-13th-cent. OFr *Huon de Bordeaux* (Voretzsch, 344 ff.; Hempel, *Nibelungenstudien*, 151 ff., 166 ff.; Schneider, *GHS* I. 353), in which the hero's real father, the fairy Auberon, helps him win the hand of a heathen princess (see Alberîch, p. 3).

It is generally accepted (Amelung, *DHB* III. xix f.; Jiriczek, *DHS* (1911), 168; Schneider, *Wolfdietrich* (1913), 385 f.; *GHS* I. 354; Baesecke, *Vorgeschichte*, 402 f.; de Boor, *GDL* II. 207) that a conflation of South German Ortnît von Garten (Garda in Italy) with North German *Hardnið fan Nôgarden (= Hertnið (1) von Riuzen: see p. 70 and n. 3) has taken place, bringing the Russian hero Ilya Murometsch (see Îljas von Riuzen, p. 84) into the story as formidable helper and counsellor. This North German *Hardnið (Þs Hertnið) has sometimes been associated with the alleged dioscoric myth of the Hartunge (ON Haddingjar) (Symons, *Heldensage*, 73; G. Dumézil, *La Saga de Hadingus* (Paris, 1953), 123 ff.),[9] but otherwise the joining of the stories of Ortnît and Wolfdietrich does not appear to be primary

---

[1] His dominions include Brescia, Verona, Rome and the Lateran, Trient, Troja, Luceria, and Benevento, and his suzerainty extends to Sicily and Apulia, whose heathen ruler, Zacharîs, equips his expedition to Syria. It has been argued that this realm reflects the unified Italy sought by Frederick II in the third decade of the 13th cent. (Amelung, *DHB* III. xxv ff.).

[2] In **Wd(B)**, Ortnît kills Machorel's giant messenger Helle (see Velle) and his wife Runze (487 ff.).

[3] In **DF**, Wolfdietrich is brought into the genealogy of Dietrich (2109–2294), whereas Ortnît is made the son of Sigehêr and Amelgart, and is the brother of Sigelint; thus he is the uncle of Sîfrit (see p. 26 n. 1).

[4] See p. 9 n. 4.

[5] In **Wd(B)**, as a youth, Wolfdietrich fights Ortnît because of his demand for tribute, but they are later reconciled (49 f., 343 ff.).

[6] This is usually taken to represent Bergamo in N. Italy (Symons, *Heldensage*, 75), but Bulgaria seems more likely, cf. OFr Borgarie (Flutre, 209); in **Wd(A)**, Hugdietrich rules 'der Bulgerîe walt' (2, 2) and Baltram has his seat there (190, 1).

[7] In Þs, Mimir gives Sigurðr the helmet, shield, and armour he has made for King Hertnið af Holmgarðr (I. 314, 4–6), possibly a confusion with Hertnið af Bergara (see Hertnît (1), p. 70).

[8] In Þs, Otnið (also *Ortnið*, *Ortnit*) is the name of Attila's brother (I. 56, 27; II. 84, 5).

[9] Wolfdietrich is said to kill the dragon to avenge his dioscoric twin, Ortnît.

## ORTNÎT (1)

(Jiriczek, *DHS* (1911), 165): Ortnît's tragic dragon fight, like Bēowulf's, could well be the fitting end to his career.[1] It is unlikely that the two epics were joined before 1150, for the author of **R** knew the 'loyal vassals' story of **Wd** independently of **O** (Symons, *Heldensage*, 75; Schneider, *Wolfdietrich* (1913), 400 f.).

The reference in the *Kaiserchronik* (mid 12th cent.) to Ôtacher as the usurper in Lancpartenlant defeated by Dietrich (13840 ff.) suggests a possible link (see Ôtacher, p. 104, and Wolfdietrich, p. 151), and the preponderant *Ot-* spellings of the hero's name support a correlation with Odoacer, whom Theodoric (Dietrich von Berne in MHG epic) defeated and succeeded in Italy (Mone, 75; Schütte, *Gotthiod* II. 66 ff.; J. de Vries, 'Die Sage von Wolfdietrich', *GRM* XXXIX (1958), 15 f.).[2]

## ORTNÎT (2) brother-in-law of Îljas

Ruler of Lamparten (Lombardy): his heir, Ortnît (1), is in fact the son of the dwarf Alberîch.

ref: **AHb** m p. 4, 10 n p. 4, 30 (*Otnit*); **O** m 169, 1; **Wd(D)** VII. 181, 3 (Otnîdes);[3] **Wd(Gr)** 1490, 3 (Otnit)

See Sigehêr (4) von Rœmischlant, the father of Ortnît (1) in **DF**.

## ORTRÛN

Sister of Hartmuot von Ormanîe: she treats Kûdrûn kindly during her captivity; finally she marries Ortwîn, Kûdrûn's brother.

ref: **Ku** 977, 4

In late ON Eddic tradition the sister of Atli and lover of Gunnarr is named Oddrún (Sg 58, 1; Dr prose, p. 223; Od 2, 1; Völss ch. 31).

pn: 11th-cent. German (Socin, 60; Schlaug II. 134; Kromp I. 35).

## ORTWÎN (1) von Metzen (Metz)

Steward at Gunther's court in **N**: hostile to Sîfrit; he takes no part in the journey of the Burgundians to Hungary.

In **B** he fights Wolfhart and Berhtunc in the combats at Worms.

In **DF** and **Rs** he appears among Dietrich's men and fights Markîs von Düringen at Rabene (Ravenna).

ref: **B** 6007; **DF** 3016; **N** 9, 2; **Rs** 577, 1; **WuH** (Wien) I. 4, 3

pn: 6th-cent. Goth.; 8th-cent. German (Förstemann I. 1181; Kromp I. 35 f.; III. 58 ff.; Schlaug II. 135); post-Conquest OE (Searle, 369).

See Orte, p. 100, regarding Attila's son, Ortvin, in Ps.

## ORTWÎN (2) uncle of Ortwîn (1)

ref: **B** 2482

## ORTWÎN (3) von (N)ortlant[4] (Denmark?)

Son of Hetel and Hilde (1): he takes part in the unsuccessful battle of Wülpensant against the Normans Ludewîc and Hartmuot, the abductors of his sister Kûdrûn.[5] He and Kûdrûn's bridegroom, Herwîc, lead the Hegelinge expedition which rescues Kûdrûn (see Kûdrûn, p. 22). He marries Hartmuot's sister, Ortrûn. Zigzag bars (MHG *örter*) are depicted on his banner (1371, 2; 1460, 2).[6]

ref: **Ku** 574, 1

## ORTWÎN (4) a giant

Brother of Pûsolt and nephew of Schrûtan: he is one of Kriemhilt's champions at the rose-garden; in **Rg(AC)**, Sigestap kills him (Dietrich in **Rg(F)**).

ref: **Rg(A)** 7, 4; **Rg(C)** 30; **Rg(F)** IV. 16, 3

## ORTWÎN (5) Dietrich's man

He defeats Volkêr at the rose-garden in **Rg(A)**. In **V** he kills the giant Gîselrant (see Wîcram).

ref: **Rg(A)** 99, 4; **V(h)** 887, 1; **V(w)** 734, 1

See also Râtwîn, p. 107 n. 2.

## ORTWÎN (6) companion of Helferîch (4)

Killed by Dietrich.

ref: **AHb** p. 1, 20; **E(a)** 56, 9; **E(d)** m 64, 9; **E(L)** 59, 9; **E(s)** 56, 9

Possibly the same person as Ortwîn (4) above.

## ORTWÎN (7) a watchman

At Constantinople, Wolfdietrich learns from him that 'Punting' (= Berhtunc (1)) is dead.

ref: **Wd(k)** 312, 2

---

[1] Like Bēowulf, he kills a giant and giantess before succumbing to the dragon in **Wd(B)** (see Velle and Runze).

[2] In **Wd(B)** Ortnît fights Wolfdietrich, who later succeeds him (see p. 101 n. 5). In the mid-13th-cent. *Österreichische Genealogie*, Wolfdietrich is made the son and successor of another usurper, 'Ôtacher von Bêheimlant', and his wife, Margret (W. Grimm, *DHS*, 177); this is the historical Ottokar II of Bohemia (†1278), who married Margaret of Babenberg and thus laid claim to Austria, which he seized in 1251.

[3] Âmîe lends the hauberk of 'der alte Otnît' to Wolfdietrich. It is not clear which Ortnît is intended.

[4] See Symons, *Kudrun*, 72, for the manuscript spellings.

[5] In Lamprecht's *Alexander* (mid 12th cent.), Herwîch and Wolfwîn (= Ortwîn?) are mentioned together in a reference to the battle at Wolfenwerde (see Boesch, *Kudrun*, xxxi ff.). See Wolfwîn, p. 153 and n. 1.

[6] Rosenfeld, *Namen*, 245, refers this device to the Wittelsbach coat of arms of the counts of Ortenburg.

## ORTWÎN (8) a robber
Killed by Wolfdietrich (see Rûmelher).

ref: **Wd(D)** v. 10, 1; **Wd(Gr)** 848, 1

## ÖSENWALT, see RÛMENWALT

## ÔSERÎCH
The father of Etzel's first wife, Helche.

ref: **B** m 377 n 1962

In Þs, Osantrix (I. 47, 27; II. 68, 20), the son of Hertnið af Holmgarðr, rules Villcinaland (see Wilzenlant, p. 144).[1] Asplian and his giant brothers, Ædgæir,[2] Avæntroð, and Viðolfr, are in his service (see Asprîân, Ebenrôt, and Witolt). He wishes to win the hand of Oda (I. 49, 23; II. 71, 7), daughter of Milias, King of Húnaland; Milias imprisons his messengers, so Osanctrix sets out for Húnaland with his giants and a large army: at Milias's court he assumes the name 'Þiðrekr' (II. 78, 6; 'Friðrik' in Version 1 (I. 53, 24)) and pretends to have been exiled by himself. He offers his services to Milias; when Milias rejects them, Osanctrix's men attack, Milias flees, and the messengers are freed. Oda is brought before Osanctrix, who puts her feet in his lap and fits her with one gold and one silver shoe, and then reveals his true identity (the shoe episode is only found in Version 2).[3] He returns with her to Villcinaland and makes her his queen. Their daughter is named Erka. Attila has Erka abducted (see Helche, p. 66) and makes her his queen. Hostility continues between him and Osanctrix, who is killed leading his men against the forces of Attila and Þiðrekr at Brandinaborg (Brandenburg).[4] Osanctrix's son, Hertnið, succeeds him as King of Villcinaland.

pn: 8th-cent. German (Förstemann I. 130; Schlaug I. 140); 7th-cent. OE (Searle, 377 f.). The form of the name in Þs probably derives from LG (Heusler, *Heldennamen*, 101). In **W**, the name of Attila's wife Ospirin has the same first component, Ôs- (Goth. *ans*, ON *áss*, 'god').[5] See Antzîus, pp. 6 f.

## OSPIRIN, see HELCHE
The name of Attila's queen in **W**.

pn: 8th-cent. German (Förstemann I. 122, 1182). Cf. Ôserîch, the name of Helche's father in **B**.

## ÔSTERVRANKEN
East Franconia (see Franke, p. 46).

ref: **B** 3114; **DF** 5732; **N** 1524, 2; **Rs** 63, 1

## ÔTACHER
In äH, Hiltibrant has fled with Deotrîch from the hostility of Ôtacher. He faces his son, Hadubrant, who is with Ôtacher's army opposing Deotrîch's forces (see Hildebrant, p. 74).

In **E(s)**, 'Octaher von Lampart' is known to have driven out Augustulus and taken possession of Rome.

ref: **E(s)** 283, 2; äH 18

Odoacer,[6] son of Edeco, one of Attila's generals, seized power in Italy in 476 at the head of an army of Germanic mercenaries, and deposed the Emperor Romulus Augustulus. The East Roman Emperor, Zeno, concurred by granting him the title of patrician.[7] In 487 Odoacer destroyed the realm of the Rugians in Lower Austria; their King, Felectheus, was killed, and his son, Fridericus, took refuge with Theodoric (see Friderîch (2), p. 47). In 489 Zeno commissioned Theodoric (see Dietrich (1), p. 30) to win back Italy for the Empire (*CMH* I. 437 ff.): after varying fortunes he besieged Odoacer at Ravenna from 490 to 493. Bishop John of Ravenna arranged a treaty, according to which Theodoric and Odoacer would rule Italy jointly. According to John of Antioch, Theodoric stabbed Odoacer at a banquet, and, as he did so, declared: 'This is what you did to my friends' (cit. Hodgkin, 212); Odoacer's family and followers were massacred and his, wife Sunigilda was starved to death.[8]

Ennodius in his *Panegyricus* (A.D. 507) suggests that Odoacer had previously murdered Theodoric's kin, and by the *Anonymus Valesianus* in the year 526, a year after Theodoric's death, Odoacer is said to have attempted to assassinate Theodoric (*MGH auct. ant.* VII. 203 ff.; IX. 320: cit. Betz, *Aufriß* III (1962), 1906).

In Germanic heroic tradition Theodoric's patron, the Emperor Zeno, is replaced by Attila (MHG Etzel), and the conquest of Italy becomes a reconquest by the exiled Theodoric (MHG Dietrich von Berne); this is the stage reached in äH.[9] Later, Ermanaric

---

[1] There are two versions of his bridal quest, which have close parallels with that of Rother (Þs I. 44–56; II. 61–84); a gap in Version 1 can be filled by the Swedish version of Þs (Sv). The parallel versions are given in de Vries, *Rother*, 90–100.

[2] Probably derives from OFr Ogier (see pp. 7 n. 6, 138 n. 6).

[3] See de Vries, ibid. lxxxi, regarding this passage.

[4] In Version 1 of the 'Vilkinasaga', Vildiver kills Osanctrix (Þs I. 269) (see Wisselau, p. 144 n. 5).

[5] Kaufmann, 36, points out that in OHG the first components of such names can be based on *\*Aus-* (Gmc. *\*ausan-*, 'ear').

[6] See *Enc. Brit.* XVI (1964), 707 f.

[7] A contemporary portrait of Odoacer exists on a silver half-siliqua issued during his rule in Italy (Hodgkin, 649, plate).

[8] Cf. Svanhildr, the wife of Jörmunrekr in ON Eddic tradition (see p. 39 n. 6).

[9] In the OE poem, *Wulf ond Eadwacer*, a woman, apparently the wife of the tyrannical Eadwacer, longs for her lover, Wulf, who is in exile and by whom she is expecting a child. The poem is extremely obscure, but it is possible that the traditional enmity between Odoacer and Theodoric is reflected here, since 'Wulf' may signify 'outlaw' or 'exile'; on the other hand, the woman's lament, 'uncerne earme hwelp / bireð wulf tō wuda' (16 f.), recalls how Wolfdietrich was

ÔTACHER          PETER

replaces Odoacer as Dietrich's adversary (see Ermenrîch, pp. 37 ff.). In the *Ann. Quedl.* (*c.* 1000), Odoacer has become the evil counsellor of Ermanaric and urges him to exile Theodoric (see p. 37). In MHG epic Ermenrîch's evil counsellor is named Sibeche (see pp. 117 f.). The *Kaiserchronik* (mid 12th cent.), combining history and heroic tradition, records that Ôtacher, having entered Lancparten (Lombardy) and Mêrân (Maronia), was defeated by Dietrich, who returned from exile at the court of Zeno (13840 ff.) (see Dietrich, p. 28, and Ortnît, p. 102).

pn: For the 5th-cent. ruler of Italy (Schönfeld, 174 f.); 8th-cent. Lb and WFr, 9th-cent. German (Förstemann I. 201 ff.; II. i. 265; Schlaug I. 137); it also occurs in OE (Searle, 189).[1]

ÔTNÎT, see ORTNÎT

OTTE (1) brother of a vassal of Hagene (2)
ref: **Ku** 611, 2

pn: 7th-cent. Lb, WFr, and OE; 8th-cent. German (Förstemann I. 186 f.; II. i. 253 ff.; Schlaug I. 138; II. 216; Searle, 175).

The reference in **Ku** has been taken to apply to Otto IV, who received York in fief from Richard I (Stackmann, *Kudrun*, 124).

OTTE (2) Etzel's man
ref: **B** 1239

# P (see also under B)

PALDNER
= Libertîn von Palerne (Palermo).

ref: **V(d)** 83, 2

PALLUS
Father of Amelgart (1) von der Normandîe.

ref: **DF** 1945

pn: *Pallo* recorded in WFr and at Straßburg in the 8th cent. (Förstemann I. 243); *Pallu*(s) is also found in OFr romance (Flutre, 151). In **DF** the name possibly derives from that of Pallas, son of Evander in the *Aeneid* (cf. Heinrich von Veldeke's *Eneide* (*c.* 1175), 6081 ff.).

PALMUNC, see BALMUNC

PALTHER, see BALTHER

PALTRAM, see BALTRAM

PANDARUS
Ancestor of Werinhardus, who is also termed 'Pandarides' (739).

ref: **W** 728

pn: the name is that of the famous Trojan archer of the *Iliad*.

PANGRÂZIEN
A holy relic of this saint is attached to the shirt of St. George (see Jörge), which Sigeminne gives to Wolfdietrich in **Wd(B)**; in **Wd(D)** it protects him in his knife-fight against Belîân. A similar relic is fixed in the pommel of Ortnît's sword Rôse (**Wd(B)** 729, 2).

born out of wedlock and carried off and reared by wolves in **Wd(BC)** (see *The Anglo-Saxon Poetic Records*, vol. iii, ed. G. P. Krapp and E. V. K. Dobbie (Columbia University Press, 1936), liv ff.).

ref: **Wd(B)** 349, 3; **Wd(D)** VI. 160, 4; **Wd(Gr)** 570, 3

The cult of St. Pancratius (†304) was especially widespread in France: Karl in the 13th-cent. MLG *Karlmeinet* is under his protection (Schneider, *Wolfdietrich* (1913), 284), and a relic of his is in the pommel of Brîde's sword in the 12th-cent. 'Spielmannsepos', *Orendel* (v. 1639).

PARIS
In **DH** he is known to have killed Menelous.

ref: **DH** F 45, 1, 4

PARZIVÂL
In **DF**, reference is made to his search for the grail, in **V(h)** to his fighting ability.

ref: **DF** 490; **V(h)** 1045, 12

This is the Arthurian figure, the hero of Wolfram von Eschenbach's *Parzival* (*c.* 1200–10).

PATAVRID
Nephew of Hagano: he is the sixth warrior of Guntharius to be killed by Waltharius. Hagano fails to restrain him from attacking (see p. 151 and n 8).

ref: **W** 846

pn: rare; 7th-cent. WFr; recorded in 709 at Salzburg (Förstemann I. 228).

PETER
The saint is invoked by Constantin's minstrel when he asks Rother's queen to heal the sick with a 'magic' stone (see p. 109).

ref: **R** 3178

[1] The OE common noun *ēadwacer* means 'watchman of property' (Bosworth-Toller, 216).

## PETSCHENÆRE pl.
Subject to Etzel: 'die wilden Petschenære' can shoot birds on the wing (see Hornboge (1), p. 81).

ref: **N** 1340, 2

In the *Kaiserchronik* (mid 12th cent.) they are among the peoples led by Dietrich against Ôtacher (see p. 28).

The Patzinaks, a Turkish people, attacked Constantinople in the mid 11th cent., but were later employed as mercenaries by the Byzantine emperors; they were famed for their archery and for their ferocity in war (Moravcsik I. 46; Altheim I. 120).

## PILGERÎN (1) bischof von Pazzouwe (Passau)
Brother of Uote, and thus uncle of Gunther and his brothers: in **N** he greets his niece, Kriemhilt, at Passau, when she is on her way from Worms to Hungary to wed Etzel; he accompanies her as far as Melk (MHG Medelicke). Later he entertains Gunther and his men at Passau.

In the **Kl** he decides to question all the survivors of the battle at Etzel's court in order to have the story of the disaster recorded (377 ff.; 4675 ff.); he also collects information from Etzel's messenger Swämmel and has it set down by his scribe Kuonrât; the story was later told in German (4694 ff.) (see Kuonrât, p. 22).

ref: **Kl** 3597 (C); 3604 (B); **N** 1296, 4

Pilgrim was Bishop of Passau from 971 to 991, the period when the Hungarians, during the reign of King Geisa, were being converted.[1] In 1181 a fire destroyed the cathedral at Passau, and miracles occurred when Pilgrim's tomb was moved during rebuilding. Reference to him in **N** may be in deference to Wolfger, Bishop of Passau from 1191 to 1204; he succeeded a Bishop Peregrinus at Aquileia in 1204 (Tonnelat, 313 ff.).

## PILGERÎN (2) von Troyen[2]
Wolfdietrich's incognito at Falkenîs (see Marpaly, p. 93).

ref: **Wd(B)** 551, 4

## PIP(P)IN
The son of Rother by Constantin's daughter: he marries Berte, who bears him Karl and Gêrdrût. On Pippin's initiation into knighthood at Aachen, Rother hands over his realm to him (see p. 109).

ref: **R** 3476

Pepin III became King of the Franks in 751; he was the father of Charlemagne (see Karl); Rother's connection with this dynasty is fictitious.

## PISRANDENGRUSZ, see GRANDENGRÛS

## PITEROLF, see BITEROLF

## POCZPOSTEL (POSOBEL, POSEL)
A heathen, one of Janapas's men killed by Hildebrant.

ref: **V(d)** 97, 11 (99, 1 Posobel); **V(w)** 436, 4 (*Posel*)

pn: Lunzer, *Elegast*, 152, considers it possible that the variant name is based on Hebrew *pasul*, *posel*, 'useless, perfidious'.

## PÔLÂN (BÔLÂN)
The people and country of Poland: in **N** and **B** subject to Etzel; in **B**, Rüedegêr leads Etzel's army against the Russians and the rebellious Duke of Poland, Herman (**B**, **Kl**);[3] Hornboge (**B**, **DF**, **Rs**) and Wenezlân (**DuW**) both stem from Poland.

ref: sg.: **B** 3650; **DuW** 114; pl. **B** 3448; **N** 1339, 2

region: **B** 1232; **DF** 5904; **DuW** 67; **Kl** 390; **Ku** 288, 3 (MS. *Polay*);[4] **R** 4865; **V(w)** 841 (*Polant*)

## POLIAS
One of Walberân's subject kings.

ref: **L(K)II** 181

## POMERÂN
The people and region of Pomerania: in **B**, Dietleip, in the service of Etzel, conquers them (see p. 24).

ref: **B** 4022

In the mid-12th-cent. *Kaiserchronik* they are among the peoples led by Dietrich against Ôtacher (see p. 28).

The Pomorani, later Germanized, were a Slavonic tribe inhabiting the Baltic region east of the Oder (Zeuß, 663 f.).

## PORCILLIA (PORTECILIA)
Cousin of the elf-queen Virginâl: together with Potrune and Rossilia, she is rescued by Dietrich and Hildebrant from captivity in the castle of Janapas at Ortneck.

ref: **V(d)** m 102, 12 n 104, 10; **V(w)** m 451, 1 n 455, 5 (*Portecilia*)

## PORTALAPHÊ von Tuscân (Tuscany)
Hildebrant's niece, and wife of Helferîch (5) von Lûne: Rentwîn is her son.

ref: **V(d)** 52, 1 (*Partolape*); **V(h)** 156, 1; **V(w)** 280, 1 (*Portelaf*)

---

[1] In **N(C)**, Pilgerîn urges Kriemhilt to convert Etzel (1330).
[2] This title probably derives from the name of the realm of Wolfdietrich's wife, Else (see p. 36).
[3] In the mid-12th-cent. *Kaiserchronik*, the Poles are among the peoples led against Ôtacher by Dietrich (see p. 28).
[4] The strophe apparently refers to the harsh rule of Hagen (2) in Poland, but interpretation is uncertain.

## PORTALAPHÊ

pn: possibly a corrupt form of *Parthenopé*, the Greek name for Naples (W. Grimm, *DHS*, 283, 296).[1]

## PORTECILIA, see PORCILLIA

## POSEL, see POCZPOSTEL

## POTRUNE (POTBRÜNNE)
See Porcillia.

ref: **V(d)** m 102, 12 n 104, 9; **V(w)** m 451, 1 n 455, 6 (*Potbrünne*)

## POYTÂN von Wuscherât (Wissehrad, near Prague)
Brother of Witzlân: he supports Gunther in the combats at Worms.

ref: **B** 5061

## PREISELUNG
A relative of Dietrich. He attends Dietrich's wedding to Virginâl.

ref: **V(w)** 843, 7

## PRIUZEN
The people and land of Prussia: in **B**, Rüedegêr, Biterolf, and Schrûtân lead Etzel's forces against the Prussians; Bodislau, the Prussian King, is captured and forced to take part in Etzel's campaign against the Poles. Hiuzolt stems from Prussia in **DF**; Schrûtân rules the Prussians in **AHb** and **Rg(D)**. The master of the Teutonic Order in Prussia is mentioned in **Wd(w)**.

ref: people: **AHb** p. 3, 1; **B** 1518; **Rg(D)** 46, 4; **Rg(P)** 74
region: **DF** 5907; **V(h)** 623, 7; **Wd(w)** 887, 1; der Priuzen lant: **B** 1391; der Priuzen wâc (frontier between the Huns and Prussians): **B** 3551

The Prussians, a heathen Baltic people, were first mentioned in German sources at the end of the 10th cent. They were exterminated or subjected by the Teutonic Order, whose territory acquired their name (Zeuß, 671, 674 ff.).[2]

## PÜLLÆRE (PÜLLESCHÆRE, PÜLLOYSÆRE)

Apulian: as rulers of Apulia (MHG Pülle), Zacharîs in **O** and Stuotfuhs in **B** are so termed; in **B**, Stuotfuhs's followers aid Gunther at Worms.

ref: sg.: **B** 8839 (Pülloysære); **O** 66, 1 (Pülleschære)
pl.: **B** 9205 (Püllære)

## PUNTUNG, see BERHTUNC (1)

## PÛSOLT
Brother of Ortwîn (4) and nephew of Schrûtân, a heathen giant: he is one of Kriemhilt's champions killed by Wolfhart in **Rg(A)** (by Eckewart in **Rg(C)**).[3]

ref: **Rg(A)** 7, 3; **Rg(C)** 29; **Rg(V)** 194
pn: see Buozolt.

# R

## RABENÆRE pl.
The people of Ravenna (MHG Rabene).

ref: **B** 5188; **DF** 6978

## RABESTEIN, see RIMSTEIN

## RABINA, see SIMELÎN (2)

## RACHAOL, see MACHOREL

## RACHIN, see RUNZE
pn: The name *Rachin* occurs for a Saracen woman in OFr epic (Langlois, 543). The inscription for one of the giantesses depicted in the frescoes at Runkelstein (14th cent.) reads 'Fraw rachyn rauck' (W. Grimm, *DHS*, 493).

## RÂMUNC (1) ûzer Walâchen lant (Rumania)
Etzel's man: usually associated with Hornboge (1); in **B** he fights Stuotfuhs in the combats at Worms.

ref: **B** 1218; **N** 1343, 1

pn: 8th-cent. German; 9th-cent. Lb (Förstemann I. 1244).[4] It is possibly used meaningfully here for the leader of bowmen; cf. MHG *râmen*, 'aim' (cf. Hornboge (1), pp. 81 f.).

## RÂMUNC (2) von Îslande (Iceland)
Ermenrîch's man.

ref: **DF** 8647

## RANDOLF
The eighth warrior of Guntharius to be killed by Waltharius.

ref: **W** 962

pn: 8th-cent. German (Förstemann I. 1247 f.).

---

[1] Cf. Virginâl, p. 45.
[2] In the mid-12th-cent. *Kaiserchronik* they are among the peoples led by Dietrich against Ôtacher (see p. 28).
[3] In Rs, Wolfhart fights Buozolt von Norwæge (see p. 16).
[4] Ploß, 57, suggests a folk-etymology from *Romanicus* (Rumanian).

## RANDOLT von Ankône (Ancona)
Brother of Rienolt: in **DF**, Randolt, Ermenrîch's messenger, warns Dietrich of Ermenrîch's hostile intentions.¹ He joins Dietrich's forces, when the latter returns to Italy from exile. In **B**, the brothers, Randolt and Rienolt von Meilân, are among Ermenrîch's men opposing Gunther at Worms.

ref: **A** 199, 4; **B** m 4601 n 5205; **DF** 2661

pn: 8th-cent. German (Förstemann I. 1247). It is the name of the stag in the late-12th-cent. beast-epic *Reinhart Fuchs*, 1105 (ed. G. Baesecke, Halle, 1952²), and occurs for a peasant in *Neidharts Lieder*, 31, 35, in the 13th.

## RATEBOR
Witzlân's man: he fights Gunther at Worms.

ref: **B** 11720

## RÂTWÎN
Dietrich's man.

ref: **A** 73, 1 (MS. *rotwin*)²

pn: 8th-cent. German (Förstemann I. 1219; Schlaug I. 143; II. 138); recorded in OE (Searle, 393 f.).

## REGENTAGE (-TAC)
Uncle of Eckehart and Wahsmuot: among the Harlunge forces which accompany Ermenrîch's men against Gunther at Worms.

ref: **B** 4770 (10239 Regentac)

pn: 9th-cent. German (Förstemann I. 1227; II. ii. 527; Schlaug I. 145).

## REINHÊR (1) von Meilân (Milan)
Dietrich's man.

ref: **Rs** 205, 1

pn: 6th-cent. WFr; 8th-cent. German (Förstemann I. 1231 f.; Schlaug I. 145; II. 140); recorded in OE (Searle, 397). The OFr form *Renier* occurs in the *ch.d.g.* (Langlois, 553; Schneider, *Kl. Schr.* 74).

## REINHÊR (2) von Pârîse (Paris)
Ermenrîch's man: he kills Alphart, Nêre, Berhtram, Amelot, Eckenôt, Helmschrôt, Eckewart, and Starchêr at Bôlonje (Bologna), and is killed by Wolfhart.

ref: **DF** 9561

## REINHÊR (3) von Cêciljenlant (Sicily)
Companion of Dietwart (see Îwân, p. 87).

ref: **DF** 511

¹ See Rienolt, below, regarding a similar role played by Reinaldr in Þs
² It is possible that Ortwîn (5) is intended (W. Grimm, *DHS*, 263).
³ See p. 75 n. 3, regarding his relationship to Hildebrant. A 12th-cent. bas-relief on a capital in Basel Cathedral depicts a knight with a lion on his shield, possibly Dietrich, freeing another knight from the jaws of a dragon (Müllenhoff, *ZE*, 329; Jiriczek, *DHS* (1898), 246 f.; Schneider, *GHS* I. 273). See also Baltram (1), p. 9, and Sintram (1), pp. 127 f.

## REIN(H)OLT, see RIENOLT

## RENTWÎN
Son of Helferîch (5) and Portalaphê: Hildebrant kills a dragon which has half swallowed him.³ He aids Dietrich and Hildebrant in subsequent adventures after his father has entertained them at Ârône (Arona).⁴

ref: **V(d)** m 50, 9 n 52, 4; **V(h)** m 147, 9 n 157, 1; **V(w)** m 271, 9 n 281, 1 (*Rotwein*)

pn: 8th-cent. WFr and German (Förstemann I. 1247; Schlaug I. 144).

## RIBESTEIN⁵
Eckehart beheads him for his evil counsel to Ermenrîch (see Eckehart, p. 33, Sibeche, p. 117, and Harlunge, p. 62).

ref: **DF** 2567

In OFr epic, *Ripeu de Ribemont* (Langlois, 562)⁶ plays a similar role: he offers to hang the sons of Haymon for Charlemagne; Renaut, their guardian, hangs him.

pn: in a late-13th-cent. Basel record, *H. Ribstein* occurs (Socin, 434).

## RÎCHART (RITSCHART)
Dietrich's man: in **B** he is the brother of Wolfwîn and Wolfbrant.

ref: **A** 73, 3; **B** 5250 (Ritschart); **N** 2281, 1 (Ritschart: b *Reichart*)

pn: 6th-cent. WFr; 8th-cent. German (Förstemann I. 1263; Schlaug I. 148; II. 142); in OE *Domesday*, *Ricard* is probably of continental origin (Feilitzen, 349). The spelling *Ritschart* in MHG probably reflects the French pronunciation; it occurs in Wolfram von Eschenbach's *Parzival*, 665, 7, for Ritschart von Nâvers.

## RICHE, see ALBERÎCH

## RÎCHOLT von Ormanîe
Etzel's man: he aids Dietrich against Ermenrîch.

ref: **Rs** 69, 1

pn: 7th-cent. WFr; 8th-cent. German (Förstemann I. 1270; II. ii. 586; Schlaug I. 148).

## RIENOLT (REIN(H)OLT) von Meilân (Milan)
Ermenrîch's man: in **DF** he is killed by Wolfhart, in **Rs** by Dietrich.
In **B**, he and his brother Randolt fight

⁴ The coat of arms of the Milanese dynasty of Visconti, who at one time owned the castle of Arona, is a naked child half swallowed by a dragon (J. O. Plaßmann, 'Agis: eine Untersuchung an Wörtern, Sachen und Mythen', *PBB* LXXXII (Sonderband, Halle, 1961), 114 f.).
⁵ See Rimstein.
⁶ Possibly a name-equivalent of Ribestein (Benary, 69).

## RIENOLT

Stuotfuhs and Gêre. In **A** he commands Ermenrîch's army attacking Berne (Verona).

In **Rg(D)** he is one of Gibeche's champions at the rose-garden at Worms: he is defeated by Sigestap.

In **V(hw)**, as one of the Wülfinge aiding Dietrich, he kills the giants Ulsenbrant and Schelledenwalt at Mûter (see Wîcram).

In **ED**, 'De gude Reinholt van Meilan' is the porter at the castle of the 'köninck van Armentriken' (= Ermenrîch). Dirik and his men, after killing everyone in the castle, spare Reinholt because of his loyalty to his lord.

ref: **A** 199, 3; **B** m 4601 n 5205; **DF** 3331 (R Rinolt, A reinolt, etc.); **ED** m 10, 2 n 11, 4 (reinholt); **Rg(C)** 1125 (Reinolt); **Rg(D)** 47, 1 (s reinbolt); **Rg(P)** 67 (Reinolt); **Rs** 222, 1; **V(h)** 749, 3 (Reinolt); **V(w)** 679, 3 (Reinolt)

In Þs, Erminrikr's leader, Reinaldr (II. 170, 17), warns Þiðrekr of Erminrikr's plot against him (see Randolt, p. 107). He and Þiðrekr's leader, Hildibrandr, survey together the opposing forces before the battle of Gronsport (Ravenna?); in the battle Reinaldr kills his kinsman, Ulfrað (see Wolfhart, p. 152), and is killed by Roðingeirr. Another Reinaldr (I. 161, 6) is named among Þiðrekr's men.

pn: 6th-cent. WFr; 8th-cent. German (Förstemann I. 1237 f.; II. ii. 529; Schlaug I. 146; II. 140). 10th-cent. OE (Searle, 397 f.). In OFr *ch.d.g.* the equivalent name *Renaut* occurs very frequently (Langlois, 550 ff.). The first component *Rein-* derives from OHG *ragan-*, *regin-*, an emphatic prefix (see Henzen, 63, 65), which is frequently replaced by *Rien-* in the manuscripts of the MHG epics. The replacement of the second component -olt (OHG *waltan*, 'rule') by -holt may be influenced by MHG *holt*, 'friendly, loyal'.

## RIMSTEIN

Among the men of the Harlunge with Ermenrîch's forces opposing Gunther at Worms.

ref: **B** 4771 (10677 MS. *Rabestain*)[1]

In Þs, Rimsteinn (I. 274, 1) refuses tribute to Erminrikr, whose forces besiege his castle at Gerimsheimr; Viðga (= Witege) kills Rimsteinn, and the castle is taken and placed in the charge of Valtari (= Walther).

pn: 8th-cent. German (Förstemann I. 1276). Any connection with OE Rûmstän of *Widsith*, 123, must remain speculative (Malone, *Widsith*, 182 f.).

## RÎNFRANKEN pl.

Gunther's people (see Burgonde and Franke).

ref: **B** 9730; **Kl** 347

## RÎNHERREN

The men of Worms (see above).

ref: **Rg(C)** 1935

## RISENKINT

The leader of Laurîn's giants.

ref: **L(D)** 2007

pn: allusive, 'giant's child', or 'giant youth'.

## RITSCHART, see RÎCHART

## RITZSCH

A giantess: she is among the company which entertains Dietrich and Vâsolt when they visit the giant pair, Zere and Rachin (see Runze, p. 112).

ref: **E(d)** 274, 3

pn: see Runze (Rütze).

## RIUZE(N)

The people and land of Russia: in **N** subject to Etzel; in **B** allied with the Poles in rebellion against him (see Pôlân, p. 105). Îljas (**AHb**, **O**), Hertnît (1) (**AHb**, **DF**, **Rg**), Grippîan (**Wd**), and Belîan (**Wd**) stem from Russia.

ref: sg.: **B** 8053; **O** 56, 1; **O(C)** 310, 1
pl. (people): **AHb** p. 3, 13 (*rüssen lant*); **B** 3770; **DuW** 478; **O** 11, 1; **Wd(B)** 266, 31; **Wd(C)** II. 10, 4; **Wd(D)** VI. 1, 3
(region): **AHb** p. 4, 13; **DF** 5908; **N** 1339, 1; **O** 17, 1; **O(C)** 234, 4; **Rg(C)** 282; **Rg(D)** 74, 1; **Rg(P)** 119

In the *Kaiserchronik* (mid 12th cent.) they are among the peoples led by Dietrich against Ôtacher (see p. 28). The Marner (fl. c. 1230–67) refers in his repertoire to 'der Riuzen sturm' (W. Grimm, *DHS*, 179), possibly the same material as in **B** (above) and Þs (below).

In Þs, the Russians (Ruzi, Ruzciiland, etc.: I. 1, 13; 144, 1, etc.; II. 62, 12, etc.) play an important part: Hertnið leaves Russia (which includes Greece and Hungary) and Poland to his son, Valldemarr; Valldemarr invades Attila's realm of Húnaland (equivalent to Saxony) to avenge his brother, Osanctrix of Villcinaland (see Ôserîch, p. 103); in the subsequent campaigns against the Russians and Wilzi, Attila is aided by Þiðrekr (see p. 31 regarding Dietrich's campaigns against the Slavs). Finally Valldemarr is killed at Smolensk and the Russians pay tribute to Attila.

## RŒMÆRE pl.

Romans.

ref: **DF** 2325; **R** 4003

## RÔME

A giantess: she helps Wolfdietrich by carrying him and his horse across the mountains to Lombardy.

ref: **Wd(D)** m VII. 116, 1 n VII. 128, 1 (f *ranne*, c *romina*, z *rüny*, *rümy*)

pn: *Roma* f. occurs in Lb records (Förste-

---

[1] Wilhelm Grimm takes this to be Ribestein (W. Grimm, *DHS*, 158).

mann I. 883), but the transmission in **Wd** is too corrupt for firm identification.

In Wirnt von Grafenberg's *Wigalois* (c. 1205), the giantess Rûêl seizes the hero and his horse; a ballad, *De Jager uyt Grieken* (printed in Amsterdam in 1818), is based on a similar episode (Meier, *Balladen* I. 48 f.).

RÖSCHLÎN, see RUSCHE

RÔSE
The sword given by Alberîch to Ortnît. It remains in the lair of the dragon which kills Ortnît in **O**. In **Wd**, Wolfdietrich finds it there and kills the dragon with it.[1]

In **Rg**, Rôse is borne by different heroes: Dietrich (**Rg(CD)**); Ilsân (**Rg(P)**).

ref: **O** 116, 3; **O(k)** 62, 1 (*Rosa*); **Rg(C)** 1837; **Rg(D)** m 491, 3 n 513, 2; **Rg(P)** 590; **Wd(B)** 482, 6; **Wd(C)** VIII. 16, 3; **Wd(D)** m VIII. 126, 1; **Wd(Gr)** 794, 3; **Wd(k)** 244, 3 (*Rosse*)

This sword is mentioned in the fragmentary *Ritterpreis* (late 13th cent.) together with other swords (Schieb–Frings, *Eneide* II. 188), and in the MDu *Seghelihn van Jherusalem*, which has certain affinities to **Wd**, the hero bears a similarly named sword, Rosebrant (see Schneider, *Wolfdietrich* (1913), 368).

pn: based on MHG *rôse*, 'rose', i.e. the most excellent sword.

ROSSILIN (ROSILIA)
A maiden rescued from Janapas by Dietrich and Hildebrant (see Porcillia).

ref: **V(d)** 104, 8 (*Rossilin*); **V(w)** 455, 4 (*Rosilia*)

ROTHER
In **R**, King Rother, to whom most of western Europe is subject,[2] has been crowned in Rome and resides at Bari 'bi deme westeren mere'.[3] He sends an embassy of twelve to Constantinople for the hand of King Constantin's daughter; among the twelve are the seven sons of Rother's major-domo, Berhter von Mêrân (see p. 10). Constantin imprisons the messengers, so Rother sails to Constantinople, where he takes service with Constantin under the name of 'Dietrich'; his great generosity, and escort of twelve giants led by Asprîân,[4] impress the populace. 'Dietrich' sends Constantin's daughter a silver and a gold shoe, and then reveals his true identity while fitting her feet with the correct pair.[5] She persuades Constantin to free Rother's messengers, who recognize their master by his singing to the harp.[6] Ymelot von Babilônie (Cairo) invades Greece: 'Dietrich' and his giants defeat and capture him; Rother, however, brings the false news of a defeat to Constantinople and urges the Queen and princess to take refuge on his ship; he then sails to Bari with the princess, who becomes his queen.

Disguised as a merchant, Constantin's minstrel lures Rother's wife on board ship at Bari to inspect an alleged 'healing stone', and then sails back with her to Greece. Rother sets out for Constantinople, and lands his army near the city, where it is concealed in a forest; then, disguised as pilgrims, he, Berhter, and Luppolt enter the city; here Constantin is held prisoner by Ymelot, and the wedding of Rother's wife to Ymelot's son, Basilistium, is being celebrated. Rother is captured by the heathen and led out to be hanged; he is rescued through the intervention of Count Arnold and his own hidden army, which emerges from the forest at the sound of Luppolt's horn.

Rother returns with his queen to Bari; he finally retires to a monastery; his son, Pippin, and grandson, Karl, succeed him as rulers of his empire.

ref: **DF** 1315 (Ruother: P *Rùcker*); **R** 2 (H *rŏther*, R *Rothere*: other manuscript spellings are *Rŏther*, *Rvther*, *Rocther*, *Rochtere*, *Rocher*, etc.: see Frings–Kuhnt, *Rother*, 192 f.)

The Marner (*fl. c.* 1230–67) refers to 'künig Ruther' in his repertoire, and Hugo von Trimberg (*c.* 1300) mentions 'künic Rücker' in *Der Renner* (W. Grimm, *DHS*, 179, 191); in *Reinfried von Braunschweig* (*c.* 1300), 'Ruther' and his giants are mentioned (ibid. 195); references in the 16th cent. probably derive from Hugo von Trimberg (ibid. 356, 482).

Although Rother is not named there, the bridal quest and abduction themes of **R** may be found in Þs (see Helche, p. 66, and Ôserîch, p. 103).[7]

pn: Gmc. *Hrōðhari*, widespread and frequent (de Vries, *Rother*, xci): 7th-cent. WFr and Lb (Förstemann I. 904); 8th-cent. German (Förstemann I. 904 f.; II. i. 1457 f.; Socin, 34; Schlaug I. 114).

The historical model for the figure of Rother has been much disputed (see W. J. Schröder, *Spielmannsepik* (Stuttgart, 1962), 26 ff.): probability rests with the Norman, King Roger II of Sicily (†1154), whose name

---

[1] Cf. Balmunc, p. 9 and n. 4.
[2] At the end of the epic he distributes the following liens (4820 ff.): Scotland, Reims, Lorraine, Frisia, Holland, Spain, Saxony, Thuringia, the Sorbic March, Austria, Bohemia, Poland, France, Apulia, and Sicily. Maronia (MHG Mêrân) is the fief of his major-domo, Berhter (see p. 10).
[3] See Ladiner von Westenmer, p. 88.
[4] Besides Asprîân, two others, Witolt and Grimme, are named. Three giants go with Hôrant in **DH** on the bridal quest for Hilde (see p. 80).
[5] See Ôserîch, p. 103.
[6] Before their departure, these three songs ('leike' 172) have been sung to them by Rother as a sign of recognition in time of need.
[7] The pn is possibly reflected in that of Attila's messenger, Roðolfr, in the Þs (see p. 66).

corresponds to Gmc. *Hrōðgār*,[1] and who is referred to in the mid-12th-cent. *Kaiserchronik*, 17087, as 'Ruocher' (later MS. readings are *RûtgeR*, *Ruther*), and in the *Saxon Chronicle* (c. 1230) under the year 1137 as 'Rother von Pülle' (cit. Panzer, *Italische Normannen*, 44):[2] Bari, the main harbour of his South Italian realm, was an important embarkation-point for Palestine (Th. Frings, 'Rothari-Roger-Rothere', *PBB* LXVII (1944), 368 ff.);[3] in 1143 his suit for the hand of the Byzantine Emperor's daughter was rejected; he was involved later in wars with Byzantium and Egypt, the capital of which was Cairo, i.e. 'New Babylon' (Panzer, op. cit. 40 ff.).

Rother's name may well derive from that of the famous Langobard conqueror and lawgiver, King Rothari (636–52);[4] his bridal quest, on the other hand, and that of the Langobard, King Authari (584–90), for Theudolinda (see Dietlint (1), p. 25) have only general similarities.

The character of Rother in **R**, however, is that of an ideal Emperor of the West, the model being Charlemagne, to whose realm that of Rother corresponds (de Boor, *GDL* I. 256), and with whom Rother is connected genealogically in **R**.[5]

ROTOLF
A robber killed by Wolfdietrich (see Rûmelher).

ref: **Wd(D)** v. 13, 1; **Wd(Gr)** 850, 5; **Wd(w)** 793, 1 (*Rotolt*)

pn: recorded for the Herulian King in the 5th cent., and for the 6th-cent. Bishop of Constance; frequent in German from the 8th cent. (Förstemann I. 918 f.; Schlaug I. 115; II. 146), and occurs in OE (Searle, 303).

In Þs, the name Roðolfr (I. 58, 10; II. 87, 9) is used for Attila's messenger to Osanctrix for the hand of Erka (see p. 66).

ROTWEIN, see RENTWÎN
pn: see under Ruodwîn.

RÛAN von Bârût (Beirut?)
Companion of Dietwart.

ref: DF 411

RÜEDEGÊR von Bechelâren[6]
In **N** he is an exile serving Etzel as a marcher lord (marcgrâve): he is famed for his generosity (1692, etc.).[7] Etzel sends him to Worms to ask for the hand of Gunther's sister, Kriemhilt; Rüedegêr emphasizes Etzel's power and wealth (1235 ff.), and swears to uphold Kriemhilt's cause against those who may wrong her (1255 f.); after he has pointed out the possibility that she can convert Etzel from heathendom (1262, 3), she finally agrees to become Etzel's queen. Rüedegêr escorts her to Hungary. The Burgundians, on their way to Etzel's court, are directed by Eckewart, Rüedegêr's border guard, to Bechelâren,[8] where they are lavishly entertained: Rüedegêr gives his daughter Dietlint[9] in marriage to Gîselhêr, Gunther's younger brother;[10] to Gunther he gives a suit of armour and to Gêrnôt a sword; Rüedegêr's wife, Gotelint, gives Hagen a shield once owned by Nuodunc,[11] whose death at the hands of Witege she still mourns; to Volkêr she gives twelve gold arm-rings for his singing. Rüedegêr escorts his guests to Hungary. When the fighting breaks out between the Burgundians and Huns at Etzel's court, Rüedegêr first withdraws with Dietrich; he is torn between loyalty to his guests, the Burgundians, and loyalty to his liege lord, Etzel; Kriemhilt reminds him of his oath to her. After Etzel and Kriemhilt have begged him on bended knee to intervene, he enters the fray, but first he gives a shield to Hagen—his last act of generosity: he and Gêrnôt kill each other.[12] The recovery of Rüedegêr's body from the hall involves Dietrich and his men in the conflict (see Hildebrant, p. 74, and Wolfhart, p. 151).

In the **Kl**, the arrival at Bechelâren of Rüedegêr's horse Boymunt with an empty saddle confirms the dreams of ill omen of Gotelint and Dietlint.

In **DF**, Rüedegêr, an exile at Etzel's court, accompanies Dietrich on his campaigns against Ermenrîch and successfully leads his men in battles at Meilân (Milan) and Bôlonje (Bologna). After the battle of Rabene (Ravenna) in **Rs**, Rüedegêr persuades Helche and Etzel to forgive Dietrich for the loss of their sons.[13]

[1] See Rüedegêr, p. 111.
[2] He appears in Þs as Roðgeirr, the mighty ruler at Salerno (I. 8, 4), great-grandfather of Þiðrekr, and takes a place in Þiðrekr's genealogical tree equivalent to Rother's in that of Dietrich, in **DF** (see pp. 26 n. 1, 29 n. 1).
[3] See following note.
[4] Bari was in Langobard hands for over two centuries (670–875) (Panzer, *Italische Normannen*, 44).
[5] The Carolingian aspirations of the Hohenstaufen dynasty, especially of Frederick I (1152–90), may be reflected here. The date of **R**, which was probably written by a Rhinelander for a Bavarian patron, would be prior to the defection of Henry the Lion, Duke of Saxony, from Frederick I at the battle of Legnano in 1176, but after the restoration to him of the duchy of Bavaria in 1156; Roger II of Sicily had earlier supported Henry the Lion against the Emperor.
[6] See the thorough monograph by J. Splett, *Rüdiger von Bechelaren* (Heidelberg, 1968).
[7] In the MDu **Vhw**, Rudigeer wishes to be like a god dispensing gold coins to all the world.
[8] Pöchlarn, at the confluence of the Erlaf and Danube in Lower Austria.
[9] Her name only occurs in the **Kl**.
[10] Panzer, *Nibelungenlied*, 397, relates this idyll to Frederick I's sojourn in Hungary in 1187 before his tragic death leading a crusade; his younger son was betrothed to the Hungarian King's daughter.
[11] Rüedegêr's son in **B** and **Rg(DF)**.
[12] In **Rg(D)**, Rüedegêr defeats Gêrnôt in the combats against the champions of Kriemhilt in the rose-garden.
[13] In the **Kl**, Dietrich recalls how Rüedegêr won back Etzel's favour for him (2215 ff.).

In **B**, Rüedegêr and Biterolf lead Etzel's forces against the Prussians and Poles; they are captured by the Prussians at Gamalî but escape. Rüedegêr later takes a prominent part in the combats at Worms and leads Etzel's forces in support of Dietleip against Gunther; in the fighting he and Walther wound each other.

In **AHb**, Dietrich comes to Bechelâren after being forced to leave Berne (Verona) by Ermentrich; there Riediger kneels before him, but Dietrich tells him to stand up, as he, Dietrich, is but a poor man; then Riediger gives him food and drink and escorts him to Etzel (p. 9, 12 ff.).

In **Wu(B)**, Rüdinger declines the honour of championing Fraw Seld against the Wunderer, and Dietrich kills the monster.

ref: **AHb** p. 3, 11 (*Riediger von bethelar*); **B** 749 (MS. *Rudeger*); **DF** 4668; **DuW** 189; **Kl** 493; **N** 1147, 3; **N(k)** 1157, 3 (*Rudingere*, etc., also 1159, 4 *Rudigere*, etc.); **Rg(A)** m 113, 4; **Rg(C)** 386; **Rg(D)** 73, 2; **Rg(F)** III. 17, 3 (MS. *rudinger*); **Rg(P)** 118; **Rs** 15, 2; **Vhw** m 1 n 12; **Wu(B)** 48, 8 (*rüdinger*, etc.); **Wu(H)** 49, 8 (*Rudiger*, also *Rudinger*)

The earliest record of Rüedegêr in connection with the 'Heldensage' occurs in the *Quirinalia* of Metellus von Tegernsee (c. 1160), who refers to songs about 'Rogerius comes' and 'Tetricus vetus' (= Dietrich von Berne) in the Erlaf region (W. Grimm, *DHS*, 49; Splett, 25 f.). Herger (*fl. c.* 1150–80) knows of Rüedegêr's generosity (*MSF* 26, 1–5). Subsequent references to Rüedegêr from the 13th to the 15th cent. link his name with those of Etzel and Dietrich (W. Grimm, *DHS*, 196, 313, 316; Müllenhoff, *ZE*, 419).

In Þs (Version 2 only) Attila sends 'margreifi Roðingeirr af Bakalar' (II. 88, 14) to ask King Osanctrix for the hand of his daughter Erka, but without success (see Ôserîch and Helche).[1] When Þiðrekr is forced by Erminrikr to withdraw from Bern (Verona), he is entertained by Roðingeirr (II. 178, 2) and Gudelinda at Bakalar (MHG Bechelâren, = Pöchlarn) on the Rhine (!); Roðingeirr accompanies him to Húnaland, and both take part in the campaigns of Attila against the Russians and Wilzi (see Wilzen, p. 144). Roðingeirr finally returns with Þiðrekr to Bern. After the battle against Erminrikr at Gronsport (Ravenna?), he persuades Attila and Erka to forgive Þiðrekr for the loss of their sons (see Helche, p. 66).

At the wedding of Grimilldr to Attila in Worms, Gunnarr gives Roðingeirr Sigurðr's sword Gramr. Gunnarr and his men are entertained on their way to Húnaland at Bakalar: Roðingeirr gives his daughter in marriage and the sword Gramr to Gisler, a helmet to Gunnarr, a shield to Gernoz, and to Högni the shield of Gudelinda's brother, Nauðungr.[2] In the conflict between the Niflungar and the Huns, Roðingeirr is killed by Gisler.[3]

In the Danish ballad *Grimilds Hævn* (Version A: *DgF* 1. 44–6), a hero named Obbe Iern (42, 1) makes a gesture similar to that of Rüedegêr in **N**: during the fight incited by Grimild, he offers Falquor (MHG Volkêr) a sword, much prized by his own brother.[4]

pn: 8th-cent. German (Förstemann I. 898; II. i. 1456; Socin, 160; Schlaug I. 114; II. 144), becoming common in the 12th cent. in Bavaria (Kromp I. 31 f.); in the 9th cent., syncopated forms, *Rodker*, *Rvotger*, etc., are the rule, but trisyllabic forms emerge in the 11th cent., especially in the South-East; mutated forms also arise first in the South-East (E. Schwarz, 'Alte und neue Fragen der deutschen Personennamenforschung', *GRM* XLVIII (1967), 17 ff.). Forms with *-ing-* are recorded from *c.* 1200 (Kromp III. 77), which suggests that the Þs draws on material not earlier.

In OE, the equivalent *Hrōðgār* is recorded for a monier under Æthelstan (925–41) (Searle, 303), and in epic poetry it is known for the Danish King Hrōðgār (*Beowulf*, 61, *Widsith*, 45).[5] In OFr epic, the pn *Rogier* is frequent (Langlois, 568 f.).

This figure probably represents a late addition to the 'Heldensage', though the existence of a historical margrave of the Eastern March (Austria) of this name cannot be disproved.[6] The fame of the Spanish hero Rodrigo Diaz de Vivar, 'El Cid' (†1099), in all probability influenced the development of the figure of Rüedegêr: in **B**, Rüedegêr is an exile from Arâbî (Arab Spain) and his comrade Biterolf comes from Toledo; 'El Cid' was in fact twice banished by Alfonso of Castile and served the Moorish King of Saragossa; in popular tradition he was a

---

[1] The name of the successful emissary is 'hertugi Roðolfr' (in Version 1 'margreifi Roðolfr af Bakalar': see Rotolf, p. 110).

[2] The gift of a sword to Gêrnôt in **N** has probably been altered in Þs, which also duplicates the gift of a shield.

[3] Probably altered by Þs from **N**, where Gêrnôt kills Rüedegêr (see above). Þs also omits Rüedegêr's divided loyalties in **N**.

[4] Splett, 37, rejects the identification with Rüedegêr. In another Danish ballad, *Kong Diderik og hans Kæmper* (Version A), Raadengaard (= MHG Rüedegêr?) is among Diderik's men; he also is the hero of his own ballad, *Raadengaard og Örnen* (*DgF* 1. 94–9, 174–6).

[5] Hrōðgār's reign (*c.* 500) was peaceful and glorious (Klaeber, *Beowulf*, xxxi f.); the name of his nephew and co-regent Hrōðulf (*Beowulf*, 1017, *Widsith*, 45) equates with that of *Rolpho* (Saxo II), a Danish king renowned for his generosity.

[6] Records of a 10th-cent. 'Ru(d)gerus de Preclara', an alleged predecessor of Duke Leopold I of Austria, occur in 13th-cent. documents (Müllenhoff, *ZE*, 418 f.); the reference to 'Rudegerus marchio' in the necrologue of St. Andrae an der Traisen, compiled *c.* 1260–70, possibly stems from a 12th-cent. original (Splett, 35).

guiltless exile (B. Q. Morgan, 'Rüedegêr', *PBB* XXXVII (1912), 330 ff.): the exile motif would draw him into the company of Dietrich in Etzel's entourage.

## RÛMELHER (RUMELHER?)
On his pilgrimage to the Holy Sepulchre, Wolfdietrich encounters twelve heathen robbers led by Rûmelher: the remaining eleven are named Widergrîn, Betewîn, Biterolf, Îsenhart, Ortwîn, Helmschart, Rotolf, Betlî, Wolfram, Billunc, and Morgân. The robbers disagree about the apportioning of Wolfdietrich's equipment: Wolfdietrich kills them all, and remarks that they now all have an equal share.[1]

ref: **Wd(D)** v. 5, 1 (c *rumeler*, a *rümelher*); **Wd(w)** 785, 1 (*Amelhere*)

pn: recorded at Basel in 1295 (Socin, 160): possibly a byname based on Late MHG *rumelen*, *rummeln*, 'make a loud noise, rumble' (Lexer II. 535).

## RÛME(DE)NWALT (ÖSENWALT)
A giant killed by Blœdelîn (see Wîcram).

ref: **V(h)** 874, 7; **V(w)** 721, 7 (*Ösenwalt*)

pn: a phrase-name: 'clear the forest' or 'lay bare the forest', based on MHG *rûmen*, 'clear', or *œsen*, 'destroy, lay bare'.

## RÛMEROC (MALGERAS)
A giant killed by Witege (see Wîcram).

ref: **V(h)** 872, 5; **V(w)** 719, 5 (*Malgeras*)

pn: a phrase-name: 'clear the bark' (MHG *roc*, 'bark of a tree'). The name in **V(w)** resembles the typical Saracen names found in OFr *ch.d.g.*; cf. *Malacras*, *Margoras* (Langlois, 421, 433).

## RÛMOLT
In **N**, Rûmolt, Gunther's 'kuchenmeister',[2] is mentioned together with other court officials, Sindolt and Hûnolt, and takes an active part in the campaign against the Saxons and Danes. When Etzel's invitation to Hiunenlant (Hungary) is being discussed, Rûmolt advises Gunther to remain at Worms and enjoy the comforts of his court rather than risk his life on such a childish enterprise (1465 ff.). Although the Burgundians take the opposite course, Rûmolt is left as regent at Worms during Gunther's absence (1517 ff.). In the **Kl**, after the destruction of Gunther and the Burgundians in Hiunenlant, he arranges for the coronation of Gunther's son (see Sîfrit (2), p. 123).
In **B**, Rûmolt is among Gunther's men at Worms and fights Wolfhart, Heime, and Witege in the combats; humorous reference is made to his office: the 'brâten' (roasts) he distributes are wounds (10562 ff.), and his shield is soot-coloured (10610 ff.).

ref: **B** 7696; **DF** 8633; **Kl** 4373; **N** 10, 1; **N(k)** 23, 1 (*Rimult*); **Rs** 224, 1

In Wolfram von Eschenbach's *Parzival*, Liddamus, when charged with cowardice, states that, rather than be a 'Wolfhart', he prefers to act like Rûmolt:

Ich tæte ê alse Rûmolt,
der künec Gunthere riet,
do er von Wormz gein Hiunen schiet:
er bat in lange sniten bæn
und inme kezzel umbe dræn.
(420, 26 ff.)[3]

pn: 7th-cent. Lb (Bruckner, 301; Ploß, 54 f.); 8th-cent. German (Förstemann I. 884; II. i. 1472); rare and late OE (O. Ritter, 'Anglistische Notizen zur deutschen Namenkunde', *PBB* LXV (1942), 122. Although it may have come to be associated later, in the context of Rûmolt's role in **N**, with MHG *rûme* pl., 'remnants of food', the first component of this pn probably derives from OHG *Rûma*, 'Rome' (E. Schröder, *DNK*, 109), although Gmc. *\*hrōma-*, 'fame', as a basis cannot be ruled out (Kaufmann, 201).

## RUNZE (RÜTZE, RACHIN)
In **O** and **Wd(B)** a giantess, the wife of Velle (Helle): in **Wd(B)**, Ortnît kills them both. In **E(d)** and **AHb** she is the mother of Zere (Zorre) and the aunt of Ecke (see the genealogy on p. 33 n. 2). In **hS(Sachs)**, Dietrich is said to have killed her.[4]

ref: **AHb** p. 4, 3 (*Rûncze*); **E(d)** 273, 5 (Rachin); **E(s)** 185, 9 (*Rützze*); **O** 494, 6 (ac *Rütze*); **Wd(B)** 474, 2 (K *rantz* or *röntz*, a *rütze*, Hc *rucz*, e *rüsse*); **Wd(Gr)** 776, 2; **Wd(w)** 745, 2 (*Runtsch*)

pn: the form *Rütze* is probably related to MHG *rütschen*, *rützen*, 'slide' (cf. Ritzsch), while *Runze* can be related to MHG *runse*, 'river, flowing water' (Kluge, *EWb*, 615), and may be identified with *Runsa*, a Tyrolean mountain spirit thought to cause avalanches (Jiriczek, *DHS* (1898), 197); however, an appellative for a hideous woman, based on MHG *runze*, 'wrinkle' (Kluge, loc. cit.), seems more likely; cf. *Ruczela* (*Runzela*), the name of the peasant's wife in the late-12th-cent. *Reinhart Fuchs*, 20, 28, 36 (ed. G. Baesecke, Halle, 1952²).

**RUODLIEB**, see RUOTLIEP

## RUODWÎN von Treisenmûre (Traismauer)
Etzel's man: he aids Dietrich against about the Burgundians (Akv 22, 2; Am 61, 3; Völss ch. 37).

---

[1] In Þs, Viðga also defeats twelve robbers who share out his equipment before the fight (I. 145–59: see p. 146 and n. 3).

[2] The office of 'kuchenmeister' was first instituted in Germany in 1202 (Heusler, *Nibelungensage*, 83), but Gunther's cook plays a role in **W** (438), and a cowardly cook, Hjalli, in the service of Atli is known in ON Eddic traditions

[3] Wolfram apparently knew the C-version of N, in which Rûmolt offers 'sniten in öl gebrowen' (1468, 7) to the Burgundians.

[4] Also in a 16th-cent. 'Meisterlied' (Jänicke, *ZE*, 329).

RUODWÎN

Ermenrîch and fights Friderîch (1) at Rabene (Ravenna).

ref: **Rs** 725, 1

pn: 8th-cent. German (Förstemann I. 917 f.).

RUOLANT
A messenger: he brings Dietrich the news that Berne (Verona) is besieged.

ref: **V(h)** 1056, 5 (MS. *roltant, rolrant, rollant*, etc.)

pn: 10th-cent. German (Förstemann I. 909); it becomes well known through the hero of the OFr *Chanson de Roland* (see Langlois, 570 f.), Rûlant (109) in the German version, Pfaffe Konrad's *Rolandslied*.

RUOPREHT, see NORPREHT

RUOTHER, see ROTHER

RUOTLIEP
In an episode of Section XVIII of **Ru**, the hero Ruodlieb catches a dwarf, who ransoms his life by showing Ruodlieb the treasure of King Immunch and his son Hartunch (see also Alfrikr, p. 96, and Mimingus, p. 94). The dwarf declares that Ruodlieb will defeat them and marry the heiress to the treasure, the King's daughter, Heriburg; this prophecy confirms the dream of Ruodlieb's mother (Section XVII), in which Ruodlieb kills two boars (= Hartunch and Immunch) and a great herd of sows which attack him;[1] she also dreams that a white dove (= Heriburg) brings a crown to her son.

In **E(L)**, Ruotliep is the original owner of Ecke's sword; he gives it to his son Herbort (see Eckesahs, p. 34).

ref: **E(L)** 82, 6; **Ru** v. 223 (MS. *Rŏdlieb, Ruodlieb*, etc.)

In the Þs, Ekka recounts how Alfrikr originally made the sword Ekkisax and, having stolen it from where a subsequent owner had hidden it, gave it to Rozeleif (I. 180, 15), who passed it on to his like-named son (I. 181, 1).

pn: forms of the name with final component based on the equivalent of OHG *leiba*, 'what is left', occur in German from the 8th cent. (Förstemann I. 908 f.; Schlaug I. 114; see Kögel II. ii. 402).[2] *Hrodliup* occurs at Freising in the 9th cent. (Förstemann I. 910), but forms such as *Rûtliebus* (cf. OHG *liob*, 'dear') are more common in the 13th cent. (Socin, 161).

RUSCHE (RÖSCHLÎN)
Eckehart's horse.

ref: **A** 445, 1 (Röschlîn); **B** 10228 (Ruschen dat.)

pn: in **A**, the name-form is probably based on MHG *rosch, rösch(e)*, 'quick, fresh, brave' (see Bach I, § 255 a; Wackernagel, 142).[3] The nickname *Rosche* occurs in the 13th cent. (Socin, 435). The form of the name in **B** is possibly an alternative; however, MHG *rusch(e)*, 'brush', could well be the basis. In Þs, a fast hunting-dog is named *Ruska* (II. 127, 4).

RÜTZE, see RUNZE


# S

SABENE (1) son of Sibeche
Ermenrîch's man: in **DF**, Wolfhart captures and hangs him at the battle of Bâdouwe (Padua) (8352 ff.); in **B** it is known that some of the Amelunge are subject to him (6375 ff.); he often appears with Berhtunc (4) von Rabene.

ref: **B** 5197; **DF** m 8352 n 8365

In the OE *Widsith*, the equivalent name Seafola (115) occurs in the same line as Þeodrīc, but the relationship is uncertain;[4] the ON equivalent Sevill is used in the early-13th-cent. *Skjöldungasaga* for an evil character (cit. Malone, *Widsith*, 185).

[1] Cf. the dream of Kriemhilt in **N**, in which two boars kill Sîfrit (see pp. 19, 118).
[2] Kaufmann, 224, considers Gmc. *\*laiƀaz* m. or *\*laiƀō* f., 'offspring, heir, descendant', to be the basis for the second component.
[3] French influence has also been suggested: Fr.

pn: probably based on Gmc. *\*saƀa-* (cf. OE *sefa*, 'understanding', OS *\*afsebbian*, OHG *\*intseffen*, 'perceive, understand', MHG *entseben*, 'feel, perceive') with *-n-* extension to the stem: the stem occurs in the 4th-cent. Visigothic pn *Saphrax* (Werle, 51); *Savinus* occurs in Lb in 881 (Bruckner, 301). Forms with *-l-* extension occur from the 7th cent. in German (Förstemann I. 1286, 1301), and from the 8th cent. in Lb (Bruckner, 301).

The name is possibly a Germanic accommodation for that of Sabinianus, the East Roman general, who captured 5,000 men and 2,000 wagons sent by Theodoric the Great *rouge*, 'red' (Schneider, *Kl. Schr.* 74).

[4] Malone, *Widsith*, 184 f., takes Seafola to be Sabene (3), Hugdietrich's treacherous counsellor, whereas Chambers, *Widsith*, 41 ff., identifies him with Sabene (2) von Rabene.

SABENE (1)

to the relief of Durazzo in 479 (see Diethêr, p. 24, and Dietrich (1), p. 30); his son, also named Sabinianus, was defeated by Theodoric's general Pitzia in 505 (see Jiriczek, *DHS* (1898), 123; *CMH* I. 475 ff., 483).

SABENE (2) von Rabene (Ravenna)
Dietrich's man: he warns Dietrich of the approach of Ermenrîch's army.

ref: **DF** 2708

SABENE (3) Hugdietrich's counsellor
herzoc Sabene ('der ungetriuwe', 'der valsche'), formerly in the service of Botelunc, attempts to seduce Hugdietrich's queen during Hugdietrich's absence campaigning; he then alleges that her new-born babe has been begotten by the Devil, and urges Hugdietrich to have the child killed; the infant, later named Wolfdietrich, is saved by the loyal Berhtunc. On Hugdietrich's death, Sabene incites Wolfdietrich's two brothers against him. In **Wd(k)**, Wolfdietrich defeats his brothers and executes Sabene.

ref: **Wd(A)** 7, 4; **Wd(k)** 3, 7

Sabene's name may well derive from that of Ermenrîch's evil counsellor (see Sabene (1) above), but his role in **Wd(A)** is that of a typical traitor in OFr epic (Schneider, *GHS* I. 348 f.): cf. the story of Sigurðr's birth in the Þs (see Sigelint (1), p. 124).

SABÎN von Brâbant
He takes Kriemhilt's challenge to Dietrich, for which he is rewarded with the hand of Bersâbe and a dukedom.

ref: **Rg(A)** m 15, 1 n 34, 2; **Rg(C)** 116; **Rg(V)** m 60; **hS(Sachs)** 850

SÆLDE
'vrô Sælde' (Fortuna) is referred to in **DF**, **V**, and **E(d)**; in **E(L)**, the maiden Bâbehilt prophesies that 'vrô Sælde' will protect Dietrich (160).

In **Wu**, 'fraw Seld' assumes the role of a maiden pursued by a cannibal monster, 'der Wunderer'; the monster is killed by Dietrich, whose future fame she then prophesies.

ref: **DF** 566; **E(d)** 245, 7; **E(L)** 10, 7; **V(h)** 39, 6; **V(w)** 121, 6; **Wu(B)** m 11, 1 n 208, 1; **Wu(k)** m p. 2, 35 n p. 4, 20

The role of a maiden pursued by a monster is usually taken by an unnamed 'Waldfräulein' (see Vâsolt and Orkîse, pp. 44, 100, 153 f. [Wunderer]);[1] the name, based on MHG *sælde*, 'good fortune, blessing', may well derive from the prophecy of Bâbehilt in **E(L)** (see Zink, *Wunderer*, 76).

SAHS, see ECKESAHS

SAHSE(N)
The people and region of Saxony in North Germany; their proverbial ferocity is referred

[1] Connection with the 'sälige Lütt' or 'selige Fräulein' of popular tradition is uncertain (cf.

SARRAZÎN

to (**G** 9, 10; **Ku** 1503, 4; **V(h)** 623, 6). Ekivrid (**W**), Gêrolt (**Rs**), Liudegêr (**B**, **N**), Liudegast (**Rs**), and Ortwîn (1) (**B**) are from Saxony. Berhtwîn receives Saxony from Wolfdietrich (**Wd(D)**), and a count in the company of Luppolt receives it from Rother (**R**).

ref: sg. (people): **Ku** 366, 4; pl. **B** 2709; **G** 9, 10; **N** 140, 2; **W** 768 (Saxonibus dat. pl.)
(region): **B** 2749; **N** 170, 1; **R** 4841; **Rs** 715, 5; **V(h)** 623, 6; **V(w)** 614, 6; **Wd(D)** IX. 214, 2; **Wd(Gr)** 2102, 2
adj.: **W** 756 (Saxonicis dat. pl.)

In Þs, Saxland (I. 2, 17; 206, 6, etc.) is a general term for North Germany; in fact Attila's realm of Húnaland, with its capital Susat (Soest in Westphalia), corresponds approximately to the duchy of Saxony c. 900–1180 (Paff, 91 ff.).

The Saxons, first mentioned by Ptolemy in the 2nd cent. A.D. as inhabiting the neck of the Cimbric peninsula, extended their territory southward during the next two centuries (Zeuß, 150); their confederation was finally subdued and Christianized by Charlemagne (772–804).

SALOMÔN
Biblical king: in **B**, his magnificence is referred to, in **V** his skill in magic.

ref: **B** 287; **Rg(P)** 832; **V(h)** 312, 11; **V(w)** 499, 11

In the 12th-cent. 'Spielmannsepos' *Salman und Morolf*, Salme, Salmân's wife, is abducted by Fôre and won back by Môrolf.

In the Þs, Herborg, the heroine of an abduction story, is made the daughter of Salomon (II. 111, 4), King of Frakland (France) (see Heriburg, p. 69).

In medieval traditions, which derive from Jewish legend, Solomon is a powerful, wise, and Christian king, opposed by a demon.

SAMPSON (SIMSON)
Biblical figure: in **V(w)** and **gS** his strength is referred to.

ref: **gS** p. 70, 27 (*Simson*); **V(w)** 108, 3 (*Sampson*)

In Þs, the name Samson is used for the grandfather of Þiðrekr (I. 8, 10) and for the third son of Erminrikr (II. 163, 20).

SARRAZÎN
Saracen: a general term for heathen in the later epics, also used for individuals: Zacharîs (**O**); Janapas (**V**); Orkîse (**V**); Kober (**V**); Belmunt (**Wd(D)**); Belîân (**Wd(D)**).

ref: sg.: **O(k)** 180, 6; **V(d)** 90, 1; **V(h)** 35, 12; **V(w)** 32, 12; **Wd(D)** IV. 54, 4; **Wd(k)** 252, 8
pl.: **O** 326, 4; **O(w)** 282, 4; **V(h)** 244, 8; **V(w)** 138, 8; **Wd(D)** III. 18, 1

Baesecke, *Vorgeschichte*, 13, 36; Röhrich, *Erzählungen* II, 401).

## SARRAZÎN

The Saracens, the Mahometan opponents of the crusaders in the Middle East, were well known to western Europe after the First Crusade of 1096–9; the term *Sarrasin* occurs frequently in the *ch.d.g.* as a synonym for heathen (Langlois, 604 ff.).

## SCARAMUNDUS
Byname of Kimo.

ref: **W** 688

pn: recorded as a family name at Reichenau *c.* 1189 (Socin, 161).[1]

## SCHADESAM
The dragon which carries off Ortnît and is later killed by Wolfdietrich.

ref: **Wd(B)** 529, 1 (ac only *schadesam*); **Wd(D)** VIII. 62, 4 (63, 2, f *freysam*); **Wd(Gr)** 1598, 4

pn: based on MHG adj. *schadesam*, 'harmful'.

## SCHARPFE, see ERPFE

pn: recorded in the form *Scherfin* at St. Gall in 809 (Förstemann I. 1305); a *Sarpo* occurs in OE *Domesday* (Feilitzen, 351).

## SCHELLE(DE)NWALT
A giant killed by Reinolt (see Wîcram).

ref: **V(h)** 877, 7; **V(w)** 724, 7

pn: a phrase-name, 'make the wood resound', based on MHG *schellen*, 'make resound'.

## SCHEM(M)INC
Witege's horse: in **Rg(A)**, Dietrich gives it to Witege in exchange for the horse Valke, in order to persuade Witege to fight the giant Asprîân (232 ff.).[2] In **DF**, Dietrich gives it to Witege when he reaffirms his oath of allegiance (7194 f.); after the battle of Rabene (Ravenna) in **Rs**, Dietrich on Valke is unable to overtake the treacherous Witege on Schemminc (958 ff.).[3]

In **V**, Dietrich rides Schemminc.

ref: **A** m 207, 4 n 234, 2 (MS. *schymig*); **DF** 7195 (A *Scheminungen*); **Rg(A)** 232, 3 (f *schēmȳg*, b *schȳnnig*, m *schimling*); **Rg(C)** 1300 (*Scheming*); **Rg(D)** 112, 2; **Rg(P)** 442 (Schimmunc); **Rs** 394, 5 (A *scheminingen*, etc.); **V(h)** 185, 5 (Scheminc); **V(w)** 210, 13 (Schamung); **Vhw** 143 (*Scimminc*)

In **Þs**, Velent gives his son Viðga the horse Skemmingr (I. 108, 5), which is from the stud of Studas (see Heime, p. 65), being the brother of Heimir's Rispa, Þiðrekr's Falka, and Sigurðr's Grani. At the battle of Gronsport, Þiðrekr's brother, Þether, kills Skemmingr: Viðga then kills Þether and flees from Þiðrekr on Þether's horse.

In the Danish ballad *Kong Diderick og hans Kæmper* (Version A: *DgF* I. 94–9), Viderick's horse, Skeminng, helps him defeat Lanngebeen Redsker (a giant) by breaking the giant's back (see Valke, p. 44).[4]

pn: based on the same root as OHG *scimo*, 'shine, glitter', cf. late MHG *schimel*, 'white or grey horse', ON *skemmingr*, 'grey seal', it probably refers to a white horse (Kluge, *EWb*, 643, 649 f.; Kahle, 221; Wackernagel, 142). An *Albertus Scymminch* is recorded at Hannover in 1311 (Müllenhoff, *ZE*, 416).

## SCHILBUNC
Son of Nibelunc (1).

ref: **B** 7820; **N** 87, 3 (A *Silbunch*, D *Schylbunt*, b *Schiltung*; 721, 3 A *schilbundes*)

pn: rare; 9th-cent. German (Förstemann I. 1307; Kromp I. 11; E. Schröder, 'Bunte Lese', *ZfdA* LXI (1924), 36 f.). The cognate Swedish dynastic name occurs in OE and ON: Scylfingas (*Beowulf*, 2381), Skilfingar (Hdl 11, 6; Sk ch. 80); in ON *skilfingr*, it is a *heiti* for 'prince' and the byname of Óðinn, whose throne is Hliðskjálf, 'High Seat' (Grm prose, p. 56).

The name is possibly based on the equivalent of OE *scilfe*, 'shelf, ledge' (cf. OE *scylf*, *scylp*, 'peak, tower'), from which it has been suggested that it means 'rock- or cave-man' (Kralik, *Trilogie*, 218 ff.); a connection with OE *scelfan*, ON *skjalfa*, 'shake, tremble', has also been suggested, giving the meaning 'frost-man' (Kögel I. ii. 209; F. Detter, 'Zur Ynglingasaga', *PBB* XVIII (1894), 80).

## SCHILTBRANT (1) Dietrich's man

ref: **A** 80, 2

pn: Gmc. \**skeld*-, 'shield', is an extremely rare name component (Bach I, § 197; Förstemann I. 1307); names containing it are usually late formations (but see Schiltunc, p. 116).

## SCHILTBRANT (2) son of Berhtunc (1)
Wolfdietrich's man, killed at Tischcâl.

ref: **Wd(D)** IX. 56, 1 (c *hiltebrant*, a *helbrant*, yz *herbrant*); **Wd(Gr)** 1941, 1

---

[1] Förstemann, I. 1305, gives *Bertoldus Scarmundus* and cites Graff II. 814, where no date is given; Kögel, I. ii. 306, finds no early evidence, but takes it to be an old name, i.e. 'protector of the troop of warriors'.

[2] In **Rg(D)**, Dietrich promises to return Schemminc to Witege, who has forfeited it when he fought Amelolt at Garte; Witege originally obtained it from inside a mountain as a gift from his father Wielant (316 f.).

[3] Witege whispers into Schemminc's ear:

'linse unde lindez heu / daz wil ich dir geben' (959, 1 f.). This motif, also found in Wolfram von Eschenbach's *Willehalm*, 591 ff., derives from the OFr *Chanson d'Aliscans* (Martin, *Parzival*, lxxxvii f.).

[4] In the Faroese ballads Virgar (MHG Witege) rides Skjemming (W. Grimm, *DHS*, 368). In the Danish ballad *Sivard Snarensvend* (Version A: *DgF* I. 9–10), Sivard's horse is named Skimling Gram (3, 4; later Skamling, Skemling).

## SCHILTRANT
Dietrich's man (= Schiltrant (1)?).
ref: **DF** 5858 (A *Siltrant*)
pn: see Schiltbrant (1).

## SCHILTUNC
A dwarf: he brings Walberân's challenge to Dietrich, and defeats Wolfhart in the subsequent combats at Berne (Verona).
ref: **L(K)II** 199
pn: recorded in the Saxon region in 802 (Förstemann I. 1307); Wolfram von Eschenbach uses the name for Fridebrant's father-in-law (*Parzival*, 48, 18).
  The cognate name occurs in OE and ON for a Danish dynasty (see Schiltbrant (1), p.115): Scyldingas (*Beowulf*, 30); Skjöldungar (Hdl 11, 5); the founder is named Scyld in OE (*Beowulf*, 4), and Skjöld, the son of Óðinn, in ON (Sk ch. 52).

## SCHILTWÎN (1) son of Berhtunc (1)
Wolfdietrich's man, killed at Tischcâl.
ref: **Wd(D)** x. 100, 2 (g only); **Wd(Gr)** 2212, 2
In *Orendel* (12th cent.), Schiltwîn is the name of Brîde's messenger to Orendel (1125).
pn: cf. Schiltbrant (1).

## SCHILTWÎN (2) Dietrich's man
He kills the giant Bitterbûch (Felsenstrauch) at Mûter (see Wîcram).
ref: **V(h)** 463, 9; **V(w)** 590, 9

## SCHIRN
Witzlân's man: he aids Dietrich against Gunther at Worms.
ref: **B** 11721

## SCHRIT
A sword made by Mîme and owned by Biterolf (see also Hornbîle and Welsunc).
ref: **B** m 115 n 123
pn: possibly based on OHG *scrîtan*, 'go, stride' (cf. OE *scrîðan*, 'go, wander, glide', ON *skríða*, 'crawl, glide'), indicating 'that which glides like a serpent' (Wackernagel, 137); MHG *schrit*, 'pace', i.e. describing its length, however, seems a possible derivation.

## SCHROTENHELM
A giant killed by Dietrich (see Wîcram).
ref: **V(w)** 737, 12
pn: a phrase-name, 'hew the helmet', based on MHG *schrôten*, 'hew with the sword'.

## SCHRÛTÂN (1) Etzel's man
In **N** and **B** he appears with Gibeche (2); in **B** he is 'herzoc von Mêrân'.

[1] The name depends on a conjecture (see Holz, *Rosengarten*, 257, 274).
[2] The name, against the MSS., is conjectured from that of the brother of Merziân in *Orendel*

ref: **B** 1235; **N** 1880, 1; **N(k)** 1914, 1 (*Schrethan*)
pn: surname at Regensburg in 1276; by-name for a retainer at Winkelried in 1300 (Müllenhoff, ZE, 361; Socin, 570; W. Grimm, *DHS*, 272 n. 2). The name may be based on the same Gmc. root, *skraud-*, as the simplex *Scrot*, *Scroto* (OHG *scrôtan*, 'cut, hew'), met from the 9th cent. in German records (Förstemann I. 1309; Kaufmann, 308).

## SCHRÛTÂN (2) a giant
In **Rg** he is one of Kriemhilt's champions at the rose-garden: he rules the Prussians (**Rg(D)**, **AHb**), and is the uncle of Ortwîn (4) and Pûsolt (**Rg(A)**); Heime kills him.
ref: **AHb** p. 3, 1 (*Schruthan*); **Rg(A)** 7, 3 (afm *Schruthan*); **Rg(C)** 29 (*Strûthan*); **Rg(D)** 46, 3; **Rg(F)** IV. 6, 4;[1] **Rg(P)** 73 (*Strûtân*)
In the 16th cent., Fischart refers to this giant (W. Grimm, *DHS*, 353; Jänicke, ZE, 330).

## SCHUDÂN (SCHUDIG)
Brother of Merziân (1): a heathen killed by Wolfdietrich.
ref: **Wd(D)** v. 192, 3 (MSS. *schüdig*, *schuldig*, *schündig*, etc.);[2] **Wd(Gr)** 1028, 3 (*Schudig*)

## SCIMMINC, see SCHEM(M)INC

## SCOTTIGENI
The Irish.
ref: **W** 1132

## SEBEL (ABILA)
A heathen queen, the former owner of Orkîse's spear (**V(h)**); she incites him to kill Christians (**V(w)**).
ref: **V(h)** 33, 5; **V(w)** m 2, 2 n 97, 7 (*Abila*)
pn: possibly from OFr *Sebile*, from Lat. *Sybilla* (Langlois, 611; cf. Sibille, p. 118).[3]

## SÊBURC (1) one of the three queens at Jochgrîm
She equips the young giant Ecke for his fight with Dietrich, giving him Ortnît's golden armour, which Wolfdietrich has left at the monastery of Tischcâl. Dietrich finally casts Ecke's severed head at the feet of the queens at Jochgrîm (**E(ds)**).
ref: **E(d)** 19, 2; **E(L)** 19, 2; **E(s)** m 1, 7 n 14, 2; **Wd(k)** m 333, 1
pn: 9th-cent. German (Förstemann I. 1313; Schlaug I. 150; II. 148; Socin, 61); 11th-cent. OE (Searle, 406).
According to popular tradition, three ancient (12th cent.), which is Sûdân (911) (see O. Jänicke, *DHB* IV. 329).

[3] Lunzer, *Elegast*, 152, relates it to Hebrew *zeðel*, 'mist'.

SÊBURC (1)

witches dwell on the Jochgrimm, a mountain in the South Tyrol (W. Grimm, *DHS*, 470).¹

SÊBURC (2) herzoginne von Beiern (Bavaria)
She takes Kriemhilt's challenge to Dietrich, from which the combats between the men of Worms and Dietrich's champions ensue (see p. 19).

ref: **Rg(F)** I. 1, 3

SEIFRID, see SÎFRIT (1)

SELD, see SÆLDE

SENDERLÎN (1) Virginâl's minstrel
ref: **V(h)** 1006, 7

pn: a diminutive of MHG *senedære*, 'lover' (?).

SENDERLÎN (2) a giant (MOREIN)
Killed by Gêrwart at Mûter (see Wîcram).

ref: **V(h)** 744, 7; **V(w)** 675, 4 (*Morein*)

SENEREIS, see TRIUREIZ

SÊWART (1) companion of Goltwart
Herbort claims to have killed them both.

ref: **B** 6491

pn: 9th-cent. German (Förstemann I. 1313; Schlaug I. 150); the name of the hero's father (1568) in *Oswald* (12th cent.)

SÊWART (2) Ermenrîch's man
Killed by Wolfhart.

ref: **A** 200, 1 (MS. *Sewalt*)

SEYFRID, see SÎFRIT (1)

SIBECHE
Ermenrîch's evil counsellor and father of Sabene (1): in **DF**, he and Ribestein incite Ermenrîch against his nephew Dietrich; Sibeche flees in the subsequent battle against Dietrich's forces at Bâdouwe (Padua). In **A** he is responsible for the defection of Heime and Witege from Dietrich to Ermenrîch; here too he flees from Eckehart in the battle for Berne (Verona). In **Rs**, Sibeche flees at the battle of Rabene (Ravenna), but Eckehart captures him and binds him naked across his saddle, with the intention of hanging him for inciting Ermenrîch against his nephews, the Harlunge; according to the **AHb**, Sibeche has done this because of Ermentrich's seduction of his wife (see Þs below).²

¹ Cf. Vâsolt, p. 44.
² This motif, also found in the biblical story of David and Uriah, occurs in the Danish ballad *Marsk Stig* (*DgF* III. 358 ff.); in **AHb**, Sibeche is also a 'marschalk' (p. 8, 11).
³ In some records the Bishop's name has been replaced by the innocuous name *Sigebodo* (Mllüenhoff, *ZE*, 309).
⁴ It is difficult to identify this person, since the context suggests a female, i.e. Sifka, an evil

ref: **A** 41, 4; **AHb** p. 8, 12; **B** 10995; **DF** 2567; **Rs** 863, 3

Treachery was already linked with the name of Sibeche in the 11th cent., for in the life of Bardo, who became Archbishop of Mainz in 1031, the term 'perfidus Sibicho' is applied to a certain Bishop Sibicho of Speyer, whose name is recorded between 1039 and 1054 (Müllenhoff, *ZE*, 308 ff.).³ In the 13th cent. further references to Sibeche's treachery and evil counsel occur in literary sources (W. Grimm, *DHS*, 171, 187, 189; Müllenhoff, *ZE*, 313, 354 f.); Wolfram von Eschenbach presents Sibeche as a coward (*Parzival*, 421, 23 ff.).

In ON Eddic tradition, Bikki is the name of Jörmunrekr's evil counsellor (Rdr 11, 1; Sg 64, 2; Akv 14, 3; Ghv prose, p. 263; Sk ch. 50; Völss ch. 31): he urges Randvér, Jörmunrekr's son (see Friderîch (1), p. 47), to seduce his stepmother Svanhildr, and then informs Jörmunrekr, who has Randvér hanged and Svanhildr trampled to death by horses.

In Saxo XVIII. x. 8–13, Bicco sets Iarmericus against his German nephews (see Harlunge, p. 63) and his son Broderus (see Friderîch (1), p. 47), whom he accuses of seducing the Queen; Iarmericus has the Queen trampled to death; her kin, the Hellespontines, being informed by Bicco, kill Iarmericus.

In Þs, Sifka (I. 244, 20) becomes disloyal to Erminrikr and swears to destroy the Aumlungar (MGH Amelunge), after the King has seduced his wife Odilia (see **AHb** above). He contrives the deaths of Erminrikr's three sons (see Friderîch (1)) and of his nephews, Egarð and Áki (see Harlunge), and urges Erminrikr to attack his nephew Þiðrekr. He usurps the throne on Erminrikr's death, but is killed by Alibrandr at the battle of Ran (Ravenna).

pn: possibly based on Gmc. \*saða-, 'understanding' (Malone, *Widsith*, 188; cf. Sabene, p. 113), or \*seƀ-, 'kinship' (cf. OHG *sippa*: Kluge, *EWb*, 710); 8th-cent. German (Förstemann I. 1314; Schlaug II. 223; Müllenhoff, *ZE*, 310). A *Sifeca* appears in the OE poem *Widsith*, 116,⁴ and a placename, *Seofecan wyrð*, recorded in 957 in Berkshire possibly comprises the same name (Binz, 208). ON *Bikki* (Saxon *Bicco*) appears to be a hypocoristic form of LG \**Sibiko* (Kögel, I. ii, 211), possibly accommodating to the masculine counterpart of ON *bikkja*, OE *bicce*, 'bitch' (Naumann, 33).⁵

heroine of the ON *Hervarar saga*, whereas the form here (Sifecan, acc. sg.) is masculine (see Malone, *Widsith*, 187 ff.).
⁵ The pn *Bicco* is recorded from the 7th cent. in WFr, and from the 8th cent. in German (Förstemann I. 300 f.; II. i. 450 f.; Schlaug II. 178; Socin, 30), also in OE *Domesday* (Feilitzen, 202) and OE place-names (Chambers, *Widsith*, 33; Searle, 106).

## SIBECHE

The origin of this figure is uncertain; his name is connected with treason in the early 11th cent.;[1] in the MHG epics of the 13th cent. he appears as Ermenrîch's evil counsellor, replacing Odoacer in this role (see Ôtacher, p. 104, and Ermenrîch, pp. 38 f.); he resembles the traitor figures of OFr epic in some respects (cf. Ribestein, p. 107).

## SIBILLE

Marpaly possesses the book of 'der alten Sibillen', from which she knows Wolfdietrich's age and destiny.

ref: **Wd(D)** VI. 92, 2; **Wd(Gr)** 1151, 2 (Sibilla)

The name *Sebile* (*Sibile*) was used for Saracen queens in OFr romance and epic (Flutre, 171; Langlois, 611): see Sebel, p. 116; it stems from that of the prophetic women, who in Roman tradition sold the prophetic Sibylline Books to King Tarquin (see Smith, 485). Heinrich von Veldeke in his *Eneide* (c. 1175) describes Aeneas' visit to the hideous prophetess 'vrowe Sibilla' (2687 ff.).

## SICAMBER

Waltharius calls Hagano 'lusce Sicamber' ('one-eyed Sigambrian') after he has put out his eye.

ref: **W** 1435

The Sigambri belonged to the Istvaeonic tribal group, and later appeared in the federation of the Franks, among whom their name remained as a dynastic one (Zeuß, 83).

## SÎDERAM, see SIGRAM

## SÎDRÂT (1), see LIEBGART (1)

## SÎDRÂT (2) Wolfdietrich's daughter

ref: **AHb** p. 6, 33; **Wd(D)** IX. 219, 2; **Wd(Gr)** 2107, 2

## SIEGFRIED, see SÎFRIT (1)

## SIEGHARDUS, see SIGEMUNT (1)

## SÎFRIT (1) son of Sigemunt (SEYFRID, SIEGFRIED)

At the opening of **N**, Kriemhilt dreams that two eagles kill her tame falcon; her mother Uote interprets this dream as presaging the death of her future husband (see p. 18). Sîfrit, son of Sigemunt and Sigelint, is brought up at 'Santen in Niderlanden' (20, 1).[2] He sets out for Worms to win the hand of Kriemhilt, sister of the Burgundian King, Gunther, whose powerful vassal, Hagen, gives his lord an account of Sîfrit's youthful exploits: the winning of a vast treasure and the sword Balmunc[3] from the Nibelungen, and a cloak of invisibility (MHG *tarnhût, tarnkappe*) from their dwarf treasurer, Alberîch (see Nibelunge, pp. 97 ff.); the slaying of a dragon in whose blood he has bathed to make his skin horny and proof against weapons. Sîfrit defeats Saxon and Danish invaders of Burgundy (see Liudegast and Liudegêr (1), p. 90), and, acting as Gunther's vassal, he wins for him the hand of Brünhilt, whom he defeats in athletic contests, invisible in the '*tarnkappe*' while Gunther makes the appropriate movements. For these services Gunther gives Sîfrit the hand of his sister, Kriemhilt, but at Gunther's request Sîfrit, invisible in the '*tarnkappe*', subdues Brünhilt in the bridal chamber for him. The two queens quarrel about the merits of their husbands while watching jousting, and Kriemhilt, displaying the girdle and ring Sîfrit has taken from Brünhilt in the bridal chamber, accuses her of being Sîfrit's mistress (MHG *kebse*). For this dishonour to Brünhilt, Hagen, with the connivance of Gunther, plots Sîfrit's death: under the pretext of wishing to protect him in a fictitious war, Hagen learns from Kriemhilt that a linden-leaf has fallen on the spot between Sîfrit's shoulder-blades as he bathed in the dragon's blood (she indicates the spot by sewing a cross on his tunic there);[4] a hunt is arranged, before which Kriemhilt dreams that two boars attack Sîfrit and that two mountains crush him;[5] Sîfrit, after excelling at the hunt[6] in the

---

[1] In the ON Rdr (early 9th cent.), the context suggests that he is among Jörmunrekr's entourage, but gives no hint about evil counsel.

[2] The cult of St. Victor is associated with Xanten (MHG *Santen* < Lat. *ad sanctos*), and, although originally a martyr, he and St. Gereon are depicted spearing a lion and a dragon on a relief above the entrance to the cathedral there (c. 1000); although Siegfried's name corresponds semantically to that of the saint, he is only localized at Xanten in **N**, and nowhere else (see Th. Frings, 'Siegfried, Xanten, Niederland', *PBB* LXI (1937), 364–8; Baesecke, *Vorgeschichte*, 244 ff.; Bach I, § 313 a; Höfler, *Siegfried*, 92; K. C. King, 'On the Naming of Places in Heroic Literature', *OGS* II (1967), 13–24).

[3] Sîfrit is depicted holding Balmunc on the late-14th-cent. frescoes at Runkelstein (W. Grimm, *DHS*, 372; Müllenhoff, *ZE*, 386).

[4] In Norse myth (Gylf ch. 49), Baldr's vulnerability is revealed to his enemy Loki by the goddess Frigg; this motif of betrayal of a mythic hero's secret strength by a woman is widespread: it occurs also in the Middle Eastern stories of Gilgamesh and Samson.

[5] For parallels to these dreams in OFr epic, see Hempel, *Nibelungenstudien*, 199 f.; Panzer, *Nibelungenlied*, 358 f. E. Ploß, 'Byzantinische Traumsymbolik und Kriemhilds Falkentraum', *GRM* XXXIX (1958), 226, shows that the boar occurs in dreams in Oriental and late Classical literature; such a boar dream also occurs in **Ru** (see Ruotliep, p. 113).

[6] Sîfrit kills a variety of game (934 ff.), including a bison (MHG *wisent*); in the Þs a bison-hunt by Iron and Nordian is also set in the Vosges (ON Valslönguskogr: II. 111, 3); cf. the likewise disastrous bison-hunting of Iram and Nordiân mentioned c. 1230 in *Der Weinschwelg*, 98 ff. (*Der Stricker*, Bd. II, hrsg. H. Fischer (Tübingen, 1967), 46 f.

Vosges (MHG Waskenwalt),[1] is killed by Hagen, who plunges a spear between his shoulder-blades while he is drinking from a spring.[2] Before succumbing, Sîfrit fells Hagen with his shield, then commends his wife and son to the care of Gunther (see p. 121 n. 3). Hagen has Sîfrit's corpse cast before Kriemhilt's door, and she realizes from his undamaged shield that Sîfrit has been murdered:[3] the murderer is subsequently revealed when Sîfrit's wounds bleed in the presence of Hagen.[4] Sîfrit is buried at Worms,[5] and his treasure is seized and sunk in the Rhine (see Nibelunge, p. 97); Kriemhilt's vengeance on Hagen and her brothers for the murder of Sîfrit and their seizure of his treasure comprises the second part of the epic (see Kriemhilt, p. 19, Gunther (1), p. 54, and Hagen (1), p. 58).

In **Rg**, Kriemhilt wishes to match Sîfrit against Dietrich, and in the final combat in her rose-garden between Dietrich's champions and those of Worms, Dietrich defeats Sîfrit by melting his horny skin with fiery breath. In **B**, likewise, Dietrich defeats Sîfrit at Worms; in **Rs**, Dietrich takes him prisoner at Rabene (Ravenna). In **AHb** it is thought that Crimhilt provoked the fight at Etzel's court, to take revenge on Dietrich for killing Seifrit in the rose-garden (**AHb** pp. 7, 25 f.; 10, 6 f.).

In **hS**, Seyfrit is too unruly to remain at the court of his father Sigmunt—he hangs lions on trees (33)—and he takes service in a smithy, where he fights the smiths and cleaves the anvil asunder; the master smith sends him into the forest for charcoal, hoping a dragon will kill him, but Seyfrid kills it, crushes others with uprooted trees, burns them all, and anoints his body with the molten horn, rendering his skin horny and invulnerable, apart from a spot between the shoulder-blades he cannot reach. At the 'Trachenstain', with the help of the dwarf Eugel, he wins a sword from the giant Kuperan, frees Krimhilt from captivity, and slays the flying dragon that has abducted her; he loads treasure, which belongs to dwarfs, on to his horse, under the assumption that it was the dragon's hoard, but sinks it in the Rhine when he learns from Eugel that he has but eight years to live (see Nibelunge, p. 97).[6] He weds Krimhilt, whose brother Hagen murders him by a spring in the Odenwald. gS follows hS,[7] but adds the following: after Siegfried's death, Florigunda (= Kriemhilt) and Siegfried's son Löwhardus (see Gunther (2)) take refuge with Sieghardus (= Sigemunt), who brings about the death of Hagenwald (= Hagen (1)).

ref: **AHb** p. 7, 19 (*Seifrit*); **B** 5099; **DF** 2049 (A *Seyfrid*); **E(L)** 209, 13; **Kl** 55(C) (a *Seyfrid*), 74; **N** 21, 1 (a *Seyfrid*); **N(k)** 21, 3 (*Seifrid*, *Seifert*, etc.); **N(m)** Av. 1 (*siferit*); **N(T)** 945, 1 (*Zegevrijt*); **Rg(A)** 3, 2; **Rg(C)** 18; **Rg(D)** 47, 3; **Rg(F)** v. 19, 4 (gen. Sigevrides; v. 26, 3 Sigevrit); **Rg(P)** 77; **Rg(V)** 36 (*Seyfrid*); **Rs** 495, 1 (A *Seyfrid*); gS p. 64, 1 (*Siegfried*); **hS** 1, 6 (NHF Ba *Seyfrid*; BOO¹X *Sewfrid*); **hS(Sachs)** 9 (*Sewfrit*)

Sîfrit apparently enters German literature with **N** c. 1200:[8] Wolfram von Eschenbach (c. 1210) knows of the revenge taken on the Nibelunge for his death (*Parzival*, 421, 10); the Marner (c. 1250) refers to 'Sigfrides . . . tôt', 'der Ymlunge hort', and 'wen Kriemhilt verriet' separately (W. Grimm, *DHS*, 179 f.); likewise, Hugo von Trimberg, in *Der Renner* (c. 1300), mentions 'Sîfrides wurm', 'Kriemhilde mort', and 'der Nebelunge hort' as separate themes (ibid. 191). Sîfrit's steadfastness in love is mentioned c. 1350 in *Die Minneburg* (ibid. 315); c. 1442 Joh. Roth states that 'Sifrid, Hagin und Kunehilt' are still the subject of song (W. Grimm, *DHS*, 319 f.).

Sîfrit's combat with Dietrich in the rose-garden is mentioned by Ottokar von Horneck c. 1295 (ibid. 190). A knowledge of Sîfrit's (**Rg(A)** 3, 329 ff.). The 15th-cent. MS. m of **N**, consisting of âventiure-headings only, indicates an attempt to reconcile the contents of **N** with material similar to that of **hS**: in Av. 1 Sîfrit acquires a horn skin and treasure; Av. 6-9 recount Kriemhilt's abduction by the flying dragon after Sîfrit's arrival at Worms.

[1] The murder takes place with better geographical probability near Ôtenhein (now Edigheim) in the Odenwald, on the left bank of the Rhine, in **N(C)** 1001, 7; for localizations of the spring, see W. Grimm, *DHS*, 169.
[2] The scene is illustrated in the 15th-cent. MSS. b and k, incorrectly in the former, where Hagen is using a bow and arrow.
[3] Kriemhilt reacts as if he has died in battle, an inconsistency carried over into the Ps, where no fictitious war is mentioned.
[4] This 'Bahrprobe' helps date the **N** c. 1200 (see Panzer, *Nibelungenlied*, 360 f.).
[5] In **N(C)**, Kriemhilt has Sîfrit's remains transferred to the abbey of Lorsch (MHG Lôrse), which is said to have been founded by her mother, Uote (1142, 29 ff.). See K. C. King, op. cit. 21 f., regarding the traditions about Siegfried associated with the abbey, and p. 132 n. 4.
[6] That a story containing similar episodes existed in the 13th cent. is suggested by references in Rg(A): to Sîfrit's hanging lions by their tails; to his upbringing by the smith Eckerich; and to his slaying the dragon 'ûf eime steine'
[7] Through a misunderstanding of 'gehörnt' in the title, the woodcuts of **gS** show the hero with horns.
[8] In one later literary monument it is hardly possible to identify the hero with Sîfrit of the 'Heldensage', in spite of the identity of names: in *Seifrid de Ardemont*, by Albrecht von Scharfenberg (c. 1280), only preserved in Ulrich Füetrer's *Buch der Abenteuer* (1490), the hero, who bears the name 'Seyfrid', takes part in a medley of adventures in the service of the ladies Condiflor and Mundirosa, some of which derive from Arthurian romance, others recalling those of Seyfrid in **hS** (see p. 123 n. 1). A similar poem is probably represented by the late-14th-cent. fragment, *Her Syfrid* (W. Grimm, *DHS*, 317).

## SÎFRIT (1)

youthful adventures is indicated in a poem about the battle of Göllheim (1298), in which a smith bears the name 'Syverit' (Müllenhoff, ZE, 364); Jacob Ayrer (†1605) refers to Seyfrid's encounter with the giant Kuperan (ibid. 379).

Traditions about Seyfrid became localized at Worms: his tomb was first reported there at the convent of St. Cecilia in the 16th cent. (W. Grimm, DHS, 178, 339, 360 f., 489 f.; Müllenhoff, ZE, 435), when he was also portrayed on the new tower of the town hall (W. Grimm, DHS, 352, 359); up to the mid 17th cent. the city authorities avidly cultivated his memory (ibid. 363 f.).

The bulk of references to Siegfried from the 13th to the 18th cent. are to do with his horny skin (ibid. 194, 196, 309, 314 ff., 351 f., 356, 362 f., 367, 474, 489 f.; Jänicke, ZE, 325, 328 ff.).[1]

In ON Eddic tradition, Sigurðr (Sf prose, p. 163; Grp prose, p. 164; Rm prose, p. 173; 17, 1; Fm prose, p. 180; 4, 4; Sd prose, p. 180; 1, 8; Br (1, 1); 2, 1; Sg 1, 1; Gðr I 1, 4; Gðr II 1, 8; Dr prose, p. 223; Hlr prose, p. 219; 13, 3; Od 19, 8; Ghv prose, p. 263; 4, 5; Am 98, 4; Hm 6, 5; Hdl 25, 7; Skr 85; Sk ch. 47; Völss ch. 13), frequently termed 'Fáfnis bani' (slayer of Fáfnir) or 'sveinn' (youth), the son of Sigmundr[2] and Hjördís (see Sigelint (1)), is born at the court of King Hjálprekr in Denmark. His foster-father, the smith Reginn,[3] reforges the sword Gramr from the fragments left by Sigmundr for Sigurðr, who cleaves the anvil in two when testing it; Reginn urges the youth to kill the dragon Fáfnir,[4] Reginn's brother, who guards treasure[5] on the Gnitaheiðr:[6] Sigurðr digs a trench, from which he plunges his sword into the underside of the dragon as it comes to drink.[7] Reginn instructs Sigurðr to cook the dragon's heart: Sigurðr burns his finger in the fat, licks it, and immediately understands two birds discussing Reginn's intention to kill him for the sake of the treasure.[8] Sigurðr beheads Reginn and loads his horse Grani[9] with the treasure (see Nibelunge, p. 97).[10]

Sigurðr comes to Hindarfjall in Frakland (land of the Franks), where he awakens a valkyrie sleeping on a mountain-top surrounded by a blaze of light—her name is Sigrdrífa (Fm, Sd) or Brynhildr (Sk ch. 48); they plight their troth[11] and exchange rings.[12] Later he weds Gjúki's daughter, Guðrún (MHG Kriemhilt),[13] and swears oaths of loyalty with her brothers, Gunnarr and Högni. Sigurðr exchanges shapes with Gunnarr, passes once more through the wall of flame (ON *vafrlogi*) to win Brynhildr for Gunnarr, and again exchanges rings with her. Brynhildr weds Gunnarr under the illusion that he has won her, but she still longs for Sigurðr. She and Guðrún quarrel while they

---

[1] A Franconian tradition recorded in the mid 19th cent. tells of a swineherd named Säufritz who became invulnerable by bathing in the water haunted by a dragon (Müllenhoff, ZE, 385).

[2] Grp and Völss ch. 17 recount Sigurðr's vengeance on the sons of Hundingr for Sigmundr's death.

[3] The pn, recorded in OS c. 900 (Schlaug I. 147), could have significance (cf. Goth. *ragin*, 'counsel'; OE *regn*-; OHG, OS *regin*-, 'strong').

[4] This name is probably appellative: *Fáfnir* < \**Faðmir*, 'the embracer', in which is the IE root \**pet*-, 'spread out the arms' (Jóhannesson, 539).

[5] This treasure is of supernatural origin (Rm, Fm, Sk ch. 46 f., Völss ch. 14): the gods Hönir, Óðinn, and Loki kill Otr, son of Hreiðmarr; to obtain the compensation demanded, Loki forces the dwarf Andvari to surrender his gold, which includes the ring Andvaranautr, by means of which the treasure may be increased (cf. the golden wand of the Nibelungen treasure (N 1124)); the dwarf lays a curse upon the treasure (see Nibelunge, p. 98). Hreiðmarr's son, Fáfnir, kills his father, seizes the treasure, and guards it in the shape of a dragon: the treasure includes the sword Hrotti (see p. 9), a golden byrnie, and the helmet Ægishjálmr. (The dragon which kills the hero in OE *Beowulf* (2756 ff.) likewise possesses an ill-omened treasure that includes helmets and, like the treasure in N, is removed by the cart-load.)

[6] Höfler, *Siegfried*, 110 f., equates the Gnitaheiðr with the Knetterheide near Minden in the vicinity of the Teutoburger Wald (see p. 123 n. 7).

[7] In Saxo II. i. 1–iv. 3, Frotho kills a dragon thus (see Fruote (1)).

[8] In the German account (hS 10), Seyfrid first dips his finger into the molten horn before anointing himself with it, and his finger becomes horny. Sigurðr's invulnerability is mentioned in Sk ch. 51, where it is stated that Sinfjötli and Sigurðr have such hard skins that poison cannot harm them externally; in Þs, Sigurðr's skin is said to be as hard as boar-hide or horn, and invulnerable to weapons (I. 345, 3 f.) (see Sigemunt, p. 125 n 9).

[9] Sigurðr's horse Grani (Vkv 14, 2; HHu I 42, 1; Grp 5, 8; Rm prose, p. 73; Fm prose, p. 188; Sd 17, 6; Gðr I 22, 4; Sg 39, 4; Hlr 11, 1; Gðr II 4, 1; Od 21, 7; Sk ch. 47; Hátt I 41, 4; Völss chs. 9, 13; Þs I. 314, 8) is famous in Scandinavia, but Sîfrit's possession of a renowned horse is only touched on once in the German epics (Rg(A) 349).

[10] An engraved runic stone at Ramsundberget in Södermanland, Sweden (c. 1020), shows Sigurðr killing the dragon, roasting its heart, the birds talking, Reginn beheaded, and Grani loaded with the treasure; similar scenes are carved on the late-12th-cent. church doors from Hylestad, Setesdal, near Christiansand in South Norway (see Gunther, p. 55 n. 7). Regarding Scandinavian pictorial representation of Sigurðr's deeds, some allegedly as early as the 6th cent., see Hauck, *Bilderdenkmäler*, 375.

[11] Völss, chs. 23 f., tells of another meeting at the house of Heimir (see Brünhilt, p. 15 n. 2, and Heime, p. 65); their daughter Áslaug is the ancestress of Norwegian kings (Völss ch. 51).

[12] In Sk no exchange is mentioned, hence Sigurðr gives Andvaranautr, the ring belonging to the treasure, to Brynhildr when he wins her later for Gunnarr (see pp. 15, 19 f., 97 n. 6); but in Völss ch. 21 he has already given it to her at this first meeting, so, at the second meeting, he takes it back and later gives it to his wife Guðrún.

[13] In Völss ch. 25, Guðrún has dreams of ill omen about her marriage to Sigurðr; cf. Kriemhilt's dream in N (see pp. 18, 19 n. 6).

are bathing in the river (in Sk ch. 49 while washing their hair in the river) about the merits of their husbands (see Brünhilt and Kriemhilt, pp. 15 f., 19 f.); when Guðrún recognizes Andvaranaut on Brynhildr's finger, Brynhildr realizes that she has been deceived.[1] Brynhildr now urges Gunnarr to have Sigurðr murdered; Gunnarr and Högni incite Gutþormr to kill Sigurðr in his bed (see Gêrnôt (1));[2] the dying Sigurðr hurls his sword at Gutþormr, cutting him in half.[3]

In the Þs, Sigurðr (I. I, 8), son of Sigmundr and Sisibe (see Sigelint (1), p. 124, regarding Sigurðr's marvellous birth in Þs), is reared by a hind, then adopted by the smith Mimir; but Sigurðr[4] proves so unruly (see Eckerîch (1), p. 34) that Mimir sends him to burn charcoal in the forest haunted by his brother, the dragon Reginn; Sigurðr kills the dragon with a burning tree-trunk and boils it in a pot; he tastes the stew with his finger and is able to understand two birds talking of Mimir's intention to kill him; he also anoints himself with the dragon's blood, which renders his skin horny, except for the place between his shoulder-blades.[5] He returns with the dragon's head to Mimir, who then attempts to placate him with the gifts of a helmet, armour, and a shield, as well as the sword Gramr, with which Sigurðr immediately kills him. Sigurðr now goes to Brynilldr's castle and kicks open the iron gates to it;[6] he demands the horse Grani from her stud, tames it, and rides off to Bertangaland to become the standard-bearer of King Isungr. In the thirteenth combat between Isungr's champions and those of Þiðrekr, Sigurðr is defeated by Þiðrekr, who uses Vidga's sword Mimungr to cut through his horn skin (see Mimminc, p. 95).[7]

Sigurðr marries Grimilldr, Gunnarr's sister, and arranges Gunnarr's marriage to Brynilldr; at Gunnarr's request they exchange clothing, and Sigurðr subdues Brynilldr in the bridal chamber for him; he also deflowers her and purloins her ring, which he gives to Grimilldr. On Brynilldr's entry into the hall, Grimilldr omits to rise:[8] in the course of the ensuing quarrel she shows Brynilldr the ring Sigurðr took from her. Högni, to avenge Brynilldr's humiliation, arranges a hunt, in the course of which Sigurðr is to be murdered: after a large boar has been killed and quartered, Gunnarr, Högni, and Sigurðr quench their thirst at a stream; Högni then plunges his spear between Sigurðr's shoulder-blades while he is drinking. Gunnarr has the corpse thrown on to the bed of the sleeping Grimilldr; she wakes and, seeing Sigurðr's undamaged shield and helmet, realizes that he has been murdered,[9] and accuses Högni of being the 'boar' (ON *villigaultr*) he alleges has killed Sigurðr.[10]

Grimilldr mentions to her second husband Attila that her brothers now possess Sigurðr's great treasure (II. 279, 16 ff.);[11] this induces Attila to invite them to Húnaland, where they are all slaughtered (see Gunther, p. 55, Hagen, p. 60, and Etzel, p. 42). After the death of Grimilldr and her brothers, Aldrian, Högni's son, lures Attila into Sigurðr's treasure-vault ('Sigisfroð kialara' II. 326, 21) and locks him in to die (see pp. 42, 60).

In the Danish ballad *Sivard og Brynild* (*DgF* I. 16–23), Sivard rescues Bryneld from a glass mountain and gives her to Hagenn (see Hagen (1), p. 60). While washing clothes at the river, she sees the rings on the fingers of Seinild, Sivard's wife (presumably those she originally gave to Sivard), and urges Hagenn to kill Sivard: Hagenn beheads Sivard with Sivard's own sword, Adelryng, and brings Bryneld the head; he then cuts her in two, and kills himself by falling on the sword. Sivard is also mentioned in *Sivard Snarensvend*, *Grimilds Hævn*, *Kong Diderik og hans Kæmper*, *Kong Diderik i Birtingsland* (ibid. 9–12, 44–55, 94–129); in *Kong Diderik og Löven* he is thought to have been killed by a dragon (ibid. 132–41). In the *Hven. Chron.* (16th cent.), Hogne kills Sigfrid for seducing his wife Gluna (see Hagen (1), p. 60).

The Faroese ballad *Regin smiður* (*CCF* I. 1–8) follows Eddic tradition (Rm; Fm; Völss chs. 11–19) in recounting Sigurðr's youthful exploits, and *Brynhildar táttur* (ibid. 8–22) completes the Eddic account up to his death. The account of Guðrún's vengeance on her brothers in *Hogna táttur*

---

[1] In Völss ch. 28, Guðrún shows Brynhildr Andvaranaut (see p. 120 n. 12).
[2] In Br. prose, p. 201 (*Frá dauða Sigurðar*), it is stated that some say Sigurðr was killed out of doors, while others say he was killed in bed, but that in Germany he is said to have been killed in the forest. In Gðr II Grani returns empty-saddled from the assembly.
[3] In later Eddic tradition, Sigurðr tells Guðrún that her brothers will protect her, although he is anxious about his infant son (Sg. 25, 5–8; Völss ch. 30: cf. N 996; see also p. 119).
[4] The spelling *Sigfræð* occurs throughout this episode (Þs I. 305, 12; 306, 6, etc.); see H. de Boor, 'Die Handschriftenfrage der Þiðrekssaga', *ZfdA* LX (1923), 104 f.
[5] German and Scandinavian motifs are combined here.
[6] In Od and the Faroese ballad *Brynhildar táttur* (*CCF* I. 8–22), he also breaks into her castle (see below).
[7] See Amelunc (2), p. 6, regarding Sigurðr's previous encounter with Þiðrekr's messenger, Amlungr.
[8] See p. 122 n. 5.
[9] Cf. N, where a fictitious war has been cancelled and the hunt is arranged in its stead (see p. 119 n. 3).
[10] See p. 61 n. 1.
[11] This is the first mention of Sigurðr's treasure in Þs; according to Attila it has three sources: the dragon's lair, booty, and the wealth left by Sigmundr. Later Grimilldr refers to Sigurðr's former possession of the 'Niflungaskattr' (II. 298, 18), i.e. the Nibelungen treasure.

## SÎFRIT (1)

(ibid. 22–34), on the other hand, recalls Þs.[1] Sigurðr also features in ballads about adventures with dwarfs and giants (Raßmann, *DHS* I. 48).

pn: \*Sigifrið: 7th-cent. WFr; 8th-cent. German, very frequent and widespread by 12th cent. (Förstemann I. 1324; II. ii. 721; Socin, 572; Schlaug I. 151; II. 149; Kromp I. 26 ff.; III. 101 ff.; see also O. Behaghel, 'Sîfrit, der Sohn des Sigemunt und der Sigelint', *PBB* XLIII (1918), 157),[2] occurring with the appellative 'Hürnein' in 14th cent. (Müllenhoff, *ZE*, 362; Socin, 163; see also A. Wallner, 'Zeugnisse zur Heldensage', *ZfdA* LXV (1928), 224). The contracted forms appear early in WFr records (Kaufmann, 312), and the contraction *i* <*-igi-* occurs as early as the 9th cent. in documents from the Lower Rhine (Förstemann I. 1325); *Sîfrit* is the usual MHG form—*Sigevrit* of **Rg(F)** and MDu *Zegevrijt* of **N(T)** are exceptional (see Behaghel, op. cit. 156 f., and P. B. Salmon, 'The Nibelungenlied in Mediaeval Dutch', *Mediaeval German Studies* (London, 1965), 134); diphthongization occurs in the 14th cent.: *Seifrid* (Bavarian *Seufrid*) (see Golther, *Hürnen Seyfrid*, xxii n. 1).

The name is recorded as early as the 7th cent. in OE, and becomes especially frequent in 9th-cent. Kentish documents (Sweet, 160, 166, 179, 439 f., 445 f., 452 f.; Searle, 418 f.; II. 241; Binz, 184 f.; Chambers, *Widsith*, 199; Schütte, *Gotthiod* I. 184 f.).[3] The first component of this name, \**Sigi-* (OHG *sigu*, 'victory'), occurs in the names of the kin of Arminius, the Cheruscan leader (†A.D. 17), is frequent in the names of Frankish leaders in the 5th and 6th cents. (Schönfeld, 205 f.), and occurs among those of Burgundian rulers in the 6th cent. (see H. de Boor, 'Hat Siegfried gelebt?', *PBB* LXIII (1939), 252; Karsten, 150; cf. Sigemunt, p. 126), and of Saxon and Anglian kings in Britain in the 7th and 8th cents. (Schütte, op. cit. 184 f.). The second component, \**-frið* (OHG *fridu*, 'protection'), is rather rare, and in ON the pn *Sigurðr* (< \**Sigvörðr*) represents a WGmc. \**Sigiward*, with component \**-ward* (OHG *wart*, 'protection') (Heusler, *Heldennamen*, 102).

Parallels to the story of Siegfried have been seen in the life of the historical ruler of Austrasia, the Frankish King Sigebert of Metz, the son of Chlotar I: in 565 he defeated the Danes and Saxons; in 572 he aided his brother Gunthram, the ruler of Burgundy, against the Saxons (see Gunther, p. 56); in 566 he married the Visigothic princess Brunihildis, who brought a vast treasure from Spain as dowry (see Brünhilt, p. 16). Sigebert's brother, Chilperic (see Helferîch (1), p. 67), married Brunihildis's sister, but had her strangled at the instigation of his mistress, Fredegunda (see Kriemhilt, p. 21); Sigebert, urged on by Brunihildis, attacked and defeated Chilperic; Sigebert's murder at a meeting in 575[4] was then contrived by Fredegunda.[5]

Certain motifs in the various accounts of 'Siegfried's Youth' are the common stock of folklore: unusual birth and upbringing by an animal foster-parent (a hind in Þs; in **hS** and elsewhere he does not know his parentage); immense strength and unruly behaviour as a child (see *KHM* no. 90, and Bolte–Polívka II. 287, 295 f.); special powers (horny skin in German traditions and understanding of bird language in Scandinavian); winning of magic objects from supernatural beings (sword, cloak of invisibility, and golden wand in **N**; sword, byrnie, helmet, and ring in ON Eddic tradition);[6] slaying of a treasure-guarding dragon;[7] awakening of a maiden,[8] to whom he is

---

[1] See H. de Boor, *Die färöischen Lieder des Nibelungenzyklus* (Heidelberg, 1918), regarding the relationship between the Faroese ballads and Norse and German traditions as represented in the Eddic material and Þs.

[2] See also Sigemunt (1), p. 126.

[3] Sigeferð of the Secgan, a tribe of the north coast of Germany, appears in the OE *Finnsburg*, 15, 24, probably the same person as Sæferð of the Sycgan in *Widsith*, 31 (see Chambers, *Widsith*, 199).

[4] The setting of the murder in German tradition (**N** and Þs) resembles more closely that of an earlier Sigebert, the last King of the Ripuarian Franks, who was murdered out hunting in the forest of Buchonia, which included the present Odenwald, in 510; a variant version of 'Siegfried's Death', in which the hero is murdered in bed, was current in Scandinavia. In **N** and Þs, a combination of the two traditions is attempted (see Hempel, *Nibelungenstudien*, 141).

[5] The quarrel of these two queens probably supplies the *motive* for the murder of Siegfried in the German and ON versions of the story; it has also been suggested that the quarrel of two women resulting in the murder of the Goth, Urajas, in 540 contributed the motifs of omission of greeting (Þs) and the quarrel while bathing (ON Eddic poems) (see p. 16 n. 5).

[6] This is paralleled by the so-called folk-tale 'Erbteilungsformel', whereby a mortal weds and loses a supernatural wife ('gestörte Mährtenehe'), but regains her with the aid of magic objects which he wins from supernatural beings while they are quarrelling about their possession (Panzer, *Sigfrid*, 63 ff.).

[7] The Eddic version (Rm, Fm) is a variant in which this 'Erbteilungsformel' is combined with the winning of the treasure from the dragon by turning one brother into the treasure-guarding dragon and the other into the hero's smith foster-father. There are two, possibly fortuitous, parallels in **hS**: the wer-dragon slain by Seyfrid when rescuing Krimhilt, and the confusion of the treasure belonging to dwarfs with that guarded by the dragon (see Nibelunge, p. 97 ). The rescue of a maiden from a flying dragon (**hS**), probably not earlier than the 13th cent., may well be influenced by the legend of St. George (H. W. J. Kroes, 'Die Erweckung der Jungfrau hinter dem Flammenwall', *Neophil.* XXXVI (1952), 156).

[8] See Hempel, *Nibelungenstudien*, 135, and J. de Vries, *Betrachtungen zum Märchen* (Helsinki, 1954), 104 ff., regarding the relationship between the awakening story and the folklore type of 'Dornröschen' (*KHM* no. 50); it has also been

betrothed but whom he later forgets;¹ bridal quest as 'strong helper' to win a bride for his 'master'.² Furthermore, Siegfried has acquired the characteristics of an archetypal semi-divine hero, and his death has sometimes been related to seasonal fertility cults, in which the god or his representative is killed by an evil demon:³ his death and that of Baldr in ON myth may well have an ultimately common origin (F. R. Schröder, 'Balder und der zweite Merseburger Spruch', *GRM* XXXIV (1953), 171).⁴

It is probable, then, that Sigebert's marriage to Brunihildis, and his murder at the instigation of a woman, provide names for the roles in the story of Siegfried's murder, as well as the setting into which older traditions about the death of a mythic hero have been drawn (F. R. Schröder, 'Mythos und Heldensage', *GRM* XXXVI (1955), 8 ff.; Rosenfeld, *Namen*, 235 f.);⁵ but the precise equation of 'Siegfried' and his slaying of the dragon with Arminius, the Cheruscan leader,⁶ and his destruction of the Roman legions in the Teutoburger Wald in A.D. 9 remains in the realm of speculation.⁷

## SÎFRIT (2) son of Gunther and Brünhilt

In the **Kl**, Brünhilt has him crowned after Gunther's death. In **AHb** he kills Hildebrant in a final battle at Berne (Verona).

ref: **AHb** m p. 3, 29; **Kl** m 3765; **N** 718, 4

suggested that the wall of flame representing the original thorn hedge in the ON versions is possibly of Celtic origin (J. de Vries, 'Über keltisch-germanische Beziehungen auf dem Gebiet der Heldensage', *PBB* LXXV (Tübingen, 1953), 241).
¹ This motif is frequent in Arthurian romance, and occurs in *Seifrid de Ardemont* (see p. 119 n. 8), where the resemblance of the encounters between the hero and Mundirosa to those between Sigurðr and Brynhildr in ON Eddic tradition need not necessarily show dependence of one story on the other, though a remote common origin is possible (see Kroes, op. cit. 154, and 'Der sagengeschichtliche Gehalt des Liedes vom Hürnen Sewfrid', *GRM* XXXIX (1958), 198).
² See p. 16.
³ F. R. Schröder, 'Die Sage von Hetel und Hilde', *DVjs* XXXII (1958), 56 ff., sees in Hagen, the murderer of Siegfried and guardian of a 'Hild', an ancient demon of death. H. Grégoire, on the other hand ('La patrie des Nibelungen', *Byzantion* IX (1934), 16–22), discusses the 'martyrdom' of a non-existent St. Evermar (OHG *ebur-mâri*, 'famous boar'): it was a May Day folk festival at Russon, near Tongres in Belgium, said to date from the 10th cent., in which the mob is led by 'Hacco'; this Grégoire takes to be a reflex of Hagen's murder of Siegfried in the 'Heldensage', and not vice versa.
⁴ Cf. p. 118 n. 4.
⁵ By the time of the death of Brunihildis in 613, the Anglo-Saxons were firmly established in Britain, and it appears that their heroic repertoire did not include these names and roles stemming from 6th-cent. Merovingian family feuds: a dragon-fight is attributed to Sigemund in *Beowulf*, and his exploits with his son Fitela are referred to (see Sigemunt (1), p. 125), but there

## SÎFRIT (3) von Môrlant⁸

His suit for the hand of Kûdrûn, daughter of Hetel, having been rejected, he attacks the successful suitor, Herewîc von Sêlant; Herewîc and Hetel besiege Sîfrit's forces in a river fortress. A truce is arranged when Kûdrûn is abducted by the Normans, and Sîfrit takes part in subsequent campaigns to rescue her and finally marries Herewîc's sister. Sîfrit himself, who is apparently swarthy when Kûdrûn first sees him (**Ku** 583, 3), is later of a 'Christian' appearance, although his men are dark, since his parents are of different races (1663 f.); his realm of Môrlant comprises Alzabê, Abakîe, Ikarjâ, and Karadê;⁹ his device is a golden head on a brown field.¹⁰

ref: **Ku** 580, 1 (MS. *Seyfrid*, etc.)

Sîfrit's role in **Ku** stems perhaps from recollections of the encirclement of the Viking forces of 'Gotfrid' and 'Sigifrid' in their fortified camp at Elsloo, near Maastricht, by Charles the Fat in 882, and the designation of heathen vikings as 'Mœre' suggests the influence of OFr epic, in which Norsemen are frequently called 'Sarrasin' (Stackmann, *Kudrun*, lxxviii f.).

## SIGANT

A Saracen god.

ref: **V(w)** 202, 2

is no reference to any other son of his, although the pn Sigeferð is not uncommon in OE records (see p. 122).
⁶ Höfler, *Siegfried*, 27 ff., arguing from the name of the tribe, the Cherusci (cf. Gmc. *\*herut*, 'stag'), to which Arminius was supposed to belong, considers that Siegfried's death can be traced back to the killing of a 'stag-man' in a cult-rite; the various references to stags in connection with Sigurðr in Eddic tradition and in Þs (ibid. 49 ff.), and the name of Sigurðr's mother, Hjördís (cf. ON *hjörtr*, 'stag'), and of the mountains, Hindarfjall ('hind fell'), that he has to traverse to find Brynhildr in Eddic tradition, appear to bear this out; in addition, Höfler relates Siegfried's death to a cult-rite in which the hero is killed by a boar (see p. 61 n. 1). However, the Cheruscan name may well derive from Gmc. *\*heru*, 'sword' (see von See, *GHS*, 39 ff.).
⁷ The dragon-standards were not used by the Roman army until a century after this battle, and were employed in the West another century after that; and the only known early localization of Siegfried's dragon-slaying lies considerably to the south of the Teutoburger Wald: the Icelander, Abbot Nikulús of Þverá, was shown the 'Gnitaheiðr' just south of Paderborn in the mid 12th cent. (W. Grimm, *DHS*, 46).
⁸ See Mœre, p. 95.
⁹ These names have a Mediterranean or Middle Eastern ring consistent with the conception of Sîfrit as a 'Saracen'.
¹⁰ F. Rosenfeld, 'Die Kudrun: Nordseedichtung oder Donaudichtung', *ZfdPh* LXXXI (1962), 301 ff., connects this with the Pappenheim coat of arms, Caesar's head, and equates Mœre and Karadê with the Pappenheim seats of Moeren and Kalden in Bavaria.

**SIGEBANT (1) von Îrlant (Ireland)**
In **Ku** the son of Gêre and Uote: he marries a princess Uote von Norwæge (Norway); their son is Hagen (2).
In **Rs** he is among Ermenrîch's men; he fights Helferîch at Bâdouwe (Padua).

ref: **Ku** 1, 2; **Rs** 248, 6

pn: rare: 12th-cent. German (Mone, 83; Müllenhoff, *ZE*, 317, 416; Schlaug II. 73, 148); it occurs in Konrad's *Rolandslied* (c. 1170) for a Christian warrior (v. 4952),[1] and in *Neidharts Lieder*, 31, 35, for a peasant in the early 13th cent.

**SIGEBANT (2) von Mêrân (Maronia)**
Sigehêr (4) sends him with Sindolt to Normandy to ask for the hand of Amelgart.

ref: **DF** 1965

**SIGEBANT (3) Dietrich's man**
He fights Tirolt von Brûnswîc at Rabene (Ravenna).

ref: **A** 76, 2; **DF** 3007; **Rs** 729, 4

**SIGEHÊR (1) von Walâchen**[2]
Etzel's man: in the **Kl**, Gunther has killed him; in **B**, 'Sigehêr von Turkîe', who leads the Vlâchen, is with Etzel's forces in Poland and takes part in the fighting against Gunther's men at Worms.

ref: **B** 3453; **Kl** 391; **N(k)** 2127, 3 (?)

pn: 6th-cent. German. WFr, 8th-cent. German (Förstemann I. 1326; II. ii. 722 f.; Schlaug I. 152; II. 149); 7th-cent. OE (Searle, 420 f.; Binz, 169).[3]

**SIGEHÊR (2) Dietrich's man**
In **A** the father of Alphart.

ref: **A** 80, 2; **B** 5250; **DF** 5859; **Rg(F)** III. 19, 1 (MS. *Yseher*)

**SIGEHÊR (3) von Zæringen)**[4]
Ermenrîch's man: he fights Berhtram von Salnicke at Rabene (Ravenna).

ref: **Rs** 716, 4

**SIGEHÊR (4) von Rœmischlant (Italy)**
Son of Dietwart: marries Amelgart von der Normandîe; their children are Ortnît (1) and Sigelint (1) in **DF** (see Sigemunt (1), p. 125 n. 4).

ref: **DF** 1884

Heinrich von München in his *Weltchronik*

---

[1] The name is absent from the OFr original, *La Chanson de Roland*.
[2] Rumanians (?); see Walâchen (Vlâchen), p. 134.
[3] Sigehere, ruler of the Sædene, is named in OE *Widsith*, 28. Cf. ON Siggeirr (p. 125 and n. 4).
[4] Zähringen, near Freiburg, Breisgau (?).
[5] In Þs, her brother's name is Ortvangis (l. 282, 17).
[6] This pn may derive from the passage in **hS**: 'Deyn mûter hieβ Siglinge / Vnd was von Adel geporn' (48, 5 f.).
[7] -*ng*- for -*nd*- (-*nt*-) is characteristic of MG

(14th cent.) gives Sigehêr as ruler of Lamparten (here Italy) (W. Grimm, *DHS*, 224).
See Ortnît (2), the father of Ortnît (1) in **O** and **Wd**.

**SIGEHÊR (5) von Westvâle (Westphalia)**
Companion of Dietwart.

ref: **DF** 542

**SIGELINT (1) wife of Sigemunt (1)**
Mother of Sifrit (**B, DF, Kl, N, gS, hS**); daughter of Sigehêr (4) and sister of Ortnît (1) in **DF**.[5]

ref: **B** 6403; **DF** 2042; **Kl** 73 (C); (B) 163;[1] **N** 20, 2; **gS** m p. 64, 4 n p. 73, 24 (*Adelgunda*);[6] **hS** m 1, 5 n 48, 5 (*Siglinge*);[7] **hS(Sachs)** 420 (*Siglinga*)

In ON Eddic tradition, Hjördís (Grp 3, 7; Hdl 26, 3; Sk ch. 47; Völss ch. 11)[8] bears Sigurðr after the death of her first husband, Sigmundr, when she is married to Álfr, son of King Hjálprekr of Denmark; she is named in the Faroese ballad *Regin smiður* (*CCF*) 1. 1–8).

In Þs, Sisibe (l. 282, 18),[9] daughter of King Niðungr of Spain,[10] is left by her husband, Sigmundr, in the care of Hartvin and Herman while he is campaigning in Poland; Hartvin fails to seduce Sisibe, and on Sigmundr's return, he and Herman accuse her of adultery with a servant (see Herman (1), p. 69); Sigmundr orders them to kill her in the Black Forest (Þs Svavaskogr); she gives birth to Sigurðr while the two conspirators are quarrelling, places the babe in a glass container, and then dies. The container falls into a stream and floats out to sea; it is found by a hind, which rears Sigurðr together with its fawns (see Sîfrit (1), p. 121).

pn: 8th-cent. German and Lb (Förstemann I. 1328; Ploß, 58). It is used for a village maiden in *Neidharts Lieder*, 165, 23.
The name is based on the equivalents of OHG *sigu*, 'victory', and *lindi*, 'supple, soft'; whether the last component may be equated with OHG *lind*, ON *linnr*, 'dragon, serpent',[11] which go back ultimately to the same Gmc. root \**linþ*-, is uncertain (Kluge, *EWb*, 441; Kaufmann, 237).

**SIGELINT (2) a water-nymph**
See Hadeburc, p. 57.

---

(Karl Weinhold, *Mittelhochdeutsche Grammatik* (Paderborn, 1883²), § 219).
[8] Cf. ON *hjörtr*, 'stag': in Þs, young Sigurðr is reared by a hind (see p. 123 n. 6).
[9] Höfler, *Siegfried*, 152 n. 190, argues from earlier Gmc. name material that Sisibe could be the original name for Siegfried's mother (see Kaufmann, 317, regarding the component *Sis*-).
[10] Cf. Sigelint (3) below, the daughter of Nîtgêr (2) in the **Kl**.
[11] The cognate ON pn *Sigrlinn* is used for a woman wooed by Atli in HHv 1, 1.

## SIGELINT (2)

ref: **N** m 1533, 3 n 1539, 1 (a *winelint*); **N(k)** 1565, 1 (*Wilint*)

## SIGELINT (3) daughter of Nîtgêr (2)
Attendant to Helche.

ref: **Kl** 2452

See Sigelint (1) above.

## SIGEMÂR (1) von Brâbant (Brabant)
Ermenrîch's man.

ref: **DF** 8640 (A *Sigemair*)

pn: recorded for the father and brother of Arminius the Cheruscan in the 1st cent., and in German records from the 8th (Förstemann I. 1329; II. ii. 724; Schlaug I. 152; II. 149). It occurs in *Neidharts Lieder*, 49, 37.

## SIGEMÂR (2) von Engellant (England)
Ermenrîch's man (possibly identical with Sigemâr (1) above); he is killed by Stûtfuhs at Rabene (Ravenna).

ref: **Rs** 727, 6 (A *Sigmair*)

## SIGEMINNE (1) = 'diu rûhe Else'

ref: **AHb** p. 6, 27; **Wd(B)** 337, 2; **Wd(Gr)** 608, 4; **Wd(w)** 526, 2 (*Sigmunda*)

See Else f.

pn: see Sigeminne (3) below.

## SIGEMINNE (2) von Francrîche (France)
Wife of Hugdietrich (2).

ref: **DF** 2353

## SIGEMINNE (3) personification
She holds sway at the wedding of Dietrich to Virginâl.

ref: **V(h)** 1026, 12

pn: the name suggests the victory of courtly love ('Die Siegerin Minne'), since Dietrich is thought of as being in the service of 'minne', love for the elf-queen Virginâl (see also Minne (2), p. 95).

## SIGEMUNT (1) von Niderlant[1]
Husband of Sigelint (1) and father of Sîfrit (1): in **N**, his capital is Santen (Xanten); he abdicates in favour of his son when the latter returns with his bride, Kriemhilt. He accompanies them to Worms, and returns to Santen with their son, Gunther (2), after Sîfrit's murder.

In **hS**, his counsellors advise him to let the unruly boy Seyfrid leave his court. In **gS** he leads an army against his son's murderers, and Hagenwald (= Hagen (1)) dies in the campaign.

ref: **AHb** p. 7, 24; **B** 7857; **DF** 2044; **Kl** 70 (C) 160; **N** 20, 2; **Rg(D)** 466, 1; **gS** p. 64, 1 (*Sieghardus*); **hS** 1, 4 (H *Sigismund*); **hS(Sachs)** 8

In the OE poem *Beowulf* (867–902), as a parallel to Bēowulf's slaying of Grendel, a minstrel recites the deeds of Sigemund (875), the son of Wæls (see Welsunc, p. 139): he tells of his campaigns abroad and of his terrible deeds in the company of his nephew, Fitela (879),[2] with whom he killed many giants; his most famous deed was to kill a dragon, whose treasure he loaded into his ship.

The name of Sigmundr, father of Sigurðr, is mentioned frequently in ON Eddic tradition (Em 16; Grp 3, 6; HHu I 6, 2; HHu II prose, p. 150; str. 12, 6; Sf prose, p. 162; Sd 1, 5; Rm 13, 2; Fm 4, 5; Sg 39, 6; Hdl 2, 7; Sk ch. 47), and a full account of his ancestry and deeds is given in Völss chs. 1–12: Sigmundr and his twin sister, Signý, are the children of Völsungr by Hljóð, daughter of the giant Hrímnir. Óðinn, Völsungr's great-grandfather,[3] appears at the wedding of Signý to King Siggeirr[4] of Gautland (Götland), and plunges the sword Gramr into the oak-trunk (ON *barnstokkr*) in the middle of Völsungr's hall; only Sigmundr can withdraw it.[5] Siggeirr invites Völsungr and his sons to a feast: although Signý warns of treachery,[6] Siggeirr has Völsungr killed and his ten sons set in stocks in the forest; Siggeirr's mother in wolf-shape devours nine, but Sigmundr escapes with Signý's help. Sigmundr, with Signý's connivance, kills her two sons by Siggeirr,[7] and she then bears her brother a son named Sinfjötli[8] who is proof against external poison.[9] After a period in the forest clad in wolfskins (ON *úlfhamir*), when they kill many men, Sigmundr and Sinfjötli set fire to Siggeirr's hall, and Signý perishes voluntarily with her husband in the flames. Sigmundr marries Borghildr, by whom he has two sons, Helgi

---

[1] 'Lowlands', i.e. the region round about Xanten, on the German side of the Dutch border (see K. C. King, 'On the Naming of Places in Heroic Literature', *OGS* II (1967), 18 f.).

[2] Cf. ON Sinfjötli.

[3] See Welsunc, p. 139, for the ancestry of Völsungr.

[4] Equivalent to MHG Sigehêr: in **DF**, Sigehêr (4) is the father of Sigelint (1), Sîfrit s mother.

[5] The Celtic hero, Arthur, likewise pulls his sword from a stone.

[6] Cf. the destruction of the Niflungar in Akv and the Nibelunge in **N** (see Etzel, p. 41, and Gunther, pp. 54 f.).

[7] Cf. Guðrún's murder of her sons by Atli (see Kriemhilt, p. 20).

[8] Other references to Sinfjötli are: Em 16; HHu I 8, 8; HHu II 23, 1; Sf prose, p. 162; Sk ch. 51. Apart from Fitela of *Beowulf*, no equivalent pn is recorded in OE, but *Sintarvizzilo* occurs quite frequently in Bavarian documents of the 9th and 10th cents. (Förstemann I. 508, 1338; Müllenhoff, *ZE*, 306 f.). It may be a byname, a *kenningr* for a 'wolf', based on the equivalents of OHG *sintar*, 'cinder', and *fezzil*, 'fetlock', i.e. 'bright foot (Baesecke, *Vorgeschichte*, 285).

[9] Sigmundr himself is proof against internal poison (cf. Sk ch. 51, where Sigmundr's ability to drink poison, and the hard skins of his sons, Sigurðr and Sinfjötli, are mentioned).

and Hámundr, but she poisons Sinfjötli for killing her brother.¹ Sigmundr then drives her out and weds Hjördís. He is mortally wounded in battle against the former suitor of Hjördís, Lyngvi, the son of Hundingr, after Óðinn has appeared on the battlefield and broken his sword; Sigmundr gives the fragments of Gramr to Hjördís² for the son she will bear after his death; Sigurðr is born when Hjördís has become the wife of Álfr, son of King Hjálprekr of Denmark (see Sigelint (1), p. 124). Sigurðr's vengeance on the sons of Hundingr for Sigmundr's death is described in Grp and Völss ch. 17.

In Þs, Sigmundr (I. 182, 11), son of Sifian, is the King of Tarlungaland (MS. B Jarlungaland);³ his queen is Sisibe, daughter of King Niðungr of Spain. When he returns from campaigning with his brother-in-law, Drasolfr, who is married to Signy (only named in MS. A), his counsellors, Hartvin and Herman, accuse the Queen of adultery,⁴ and Sigmundr orders them to take her to the Black Forest and kill her; she dies giving birth to Sigurðr, while the two villains are quarrelling (see Sigelint (1), p. 124).

pn: 1st-cent. Cheruscan leader, *Segimundus*, son of Segestes (Schönfeld, 205); 5th-cent. Burgundian king, *Sigismundus* (Förstemann I. 1317); 8th-cent. German (op. cit. I. 1317, 1330; Socin, 36, 164; Schlaug I. 152); contracted form as early as 909 for *Simundus*, Bishop of Halberstadt, and *Seymund* in Lorraine in 962 (Förstemann I. 1330); a rare pn in Bavaria, and unknown in the extreme south-east (Kromp I. 28; III. 101); 9th-cent. Lb (Bruckner, 303) and OE (Searle, 421; Binz, 191; Feilitzen, 363; see also F. W. Moorman, 'English Place-names and Teutonic Sagas', *Essays and Studies* v (1914), 93). The second component, Gmc. *mundō (OHG munt, 'protection'), gives the same significance as that of the name of Sigemunt's son, *Sîfrit* (see p. 122).⁵

The historical King Sigismund of Burgundy (†523) is possibly reflected in the figure of Sigemunt (ON Sigmundr): according to Gregory of Tours (Greg. Tur. III. 5), at the instigation of his second wife, he had his son Sigiric strangled.⁶ In 523 he was defeated by the Franks (*CMH* II. 117); Sigismund, his wife, and two children were thrown down a well.⁷ His son, Godomar, later defeated the Franks, but Burgundy was finally incorporated into the Frankish realm in 534 (see Burgonde, pp. 16 f.). The early contracted form of the pn in the Rhine Frankish area also suggests a strong Frankish element in the origin of this epic figure.

It appears that traditions about Sigemund's dragon-slaying and outlaw life with his nephew or son were known to the Anglo-Saxons in Britain by at least the 7th cent. During the same century, traditions about him must have reached Scandinavia, linked with those about Siegfried (ON Sigurðr); the various explanations of Siegfried's birth and his ignorance of his parentage (see Sîfrit (1), p. 122) suggest that the genealogical connection of the two heroes is fictitious. The two names occur in father–son relationship as early as the 8th cent. on the Middle Rhine; cf. *Sigfridus filius Sigimundi* at Weißenburg in 744 (Socin, 572).

SIGEMUNT (2) Îmîân's man
ref: **V(h)** 701, 1

SIGENANT
He jousts with Blœdelîn at the wedding of Dietrich and Virginâl.
ref: **V(h)** 999, 4
pn: 8th-cent. German (Förstemann I. 1330; Schlaug I. 152; Socin, 36). It occurs in Rudolf von Ems's *Willehalm von Orlens*.

SIGENÔT
In **Sn**, Dietrich kicks awake this giant, who is sleeping under a tree (**äSn** 2; **jSn** 62);⁸ Sigenôt attacks the hero who is wearing the helmet of Grîme, Sigenôt's uncle; he carries off Dietrich and shuts him in a cave (a dragon-pit in **jSn**). Hildebrant is also carried off by the giant; he finds Dietrich's sword in the cave and kills Sigenôt with it.

In **hS(Sachs)**, Dietrich is thought to have killed Sigenôt. In **L(DrHb)** this giant appears among Laurîn's minions; Wolfdietrich kills him.
ref: **L(DrHb)** 257, 2 (Signit); **hS(Sachs)** 831; **äSn** m 2, 2 n 6, 4; **jSn** m 2, 12 n 7, 7
References to this giant occur from the 13th cent. to the end of the 16th in German literature (W. Grimm, *DHS*, 196, 316, 343, 482; Müllenhoff, *ZE*, 379, 431; Jänicke, *ZE*, 326 f., 329); the name is also used for one of Herod's soldiers in a 15th-cent. miracle play (K. Bartsch, 'Über ein geistliches Schauspiel des XV. Jahrhunderts', *Germania* III (1858), 282). In Wittenwiler's *Ring* (c. 1410), the giant 'Sigen' aids the Nissinger in the village battle.

---

¹ Óðinn bears away the body in a little boat (cf. Arthur's last voyage).
² The Faroese ballad *Regin smiður* (*CCF* I. 1–8) mentions the visit of Hjördís to the dying Sigmundr to obtain the fragments of Gramr.
³ = MHG Kärlingen, 'France' (?).
⁴ Cf. Sabene (3) in **Wd(A)**, p. 114.
⁵ Anton Scherer, 'Zum Sinngehalt der germanischen Personennamen', *BzNf* IV (1953), 7 f., derives it from *mundaz, 'mindful of' (OHG gimunt, 'remembrance').

⁶ Possibly represented by Sinfjötli in ON tradition (Baesecke, *Vorgeschichte*, 286).
⁷ The legend of St. Sigismund (7th cent.) records that Sigismund fled to the mountains after his defeat, but was betrayed (*MGH script. rer. Merov.* II. 329 ff.: cit. Baesecke, op. cit. 285).
⁸ In Þs, Viðga kicks the giant Ædgæir awake and later kills him (I. 361) (see Witege, p. 146 n. 5).

**SIGENÔT**

pn: apart from the 9th-cent. *Sigenoð* in OE (Searle, 421), there is no record of this pn.

**SIG(E)STAP**
Dietrich's man;[1] son of Amelunc (2) and brother of Wolfhart, thus Hildebrant's nephew: in **N**, Volkêr kills him; he fights Näntwîn (2) at Worms in **B**; in **Rg(A)** he kills the giant Ortwîn (4) in the combats against Kriemhilt's men in the rose-garden at Worms; in **Rg(D)** he defeats Rienolt; in **V(h)** he kills the giant Bitterkrût at Mûter (see Wîcram); in **V(dw)** he is defeated by Libertîn.

ref: **A** 76, 3 (MS. *Segenstap*, also *segestap*); **AHb** p. 3, 8; **B** 5252; **Kl** 1697; **N** 2258, 1; **Rg(A)** 96, 4; **Rg(C)** 422; **Rg(D)** 71, 1; **Rg(P)** 116 (Segestap); **jSn** 93, 9; **V(d)** 81, 5; **V(h)** 463, 11; **V(w)** 384, 7

In Þs, Sigstaf (*Segistop* in the Swedish version) is the name of one of the robbers defeated by Viðga at Briktan (I. 153, 14).[2]

pn: isolated *Sigistab* at Fulda in 866, then *Siegestappus* at Cologne in 1191, and *Sistappus* at Trier c. 1200, etc. (Förstemann I. 1331; Müllenhoff, *ZE*, 358 f.); a *Sigestef* is recorded in the 9th cent. in OE (Binz, 215).

The last component is probably based on Gmc. \*staða-, 'staff' (Heusler, *Heldennamen*, 102; Kaufmann, 325).

**SIGEVRIT**, see SÎFRIT (1)

**SIGEWÎN**
Ermenrîch's man: Alphart kills him.

ref: **A** 154, 1

pn: 8th-cent. German (Förstemann I. 1333; Schlaug I. 152).

**SIGLINGA, SIGLINGE**, see SIGELINT (1)

**SIGMUND**, see SIGEMUNT (1)

**SIGMUNDA**, see SIGEMINNE (1)

**SIGNIT**, see SIGENÔT

**SIGRAM (SÎDERAM)**
A dwarf: in **V(h)** he jousts with Wolfhart at Virginâl's court; in **V(w)** he entertains him in his mountain kingdom.

ref: **V(h)** 484, 2 (Sideram, 935, 5 Sigram); **V(w)** 629, 1

pn: 7th-cent. WFr; 8th-cent. German (Förstemann I. 1327).

**SIMELÎN (1)** wife of Ymelot von Babilonîe
ref: **R** 2569

pn: masc. for Alsatian peasant in 1298 (Socin, 164, 633). This is perhaps a descriptive name based on MHG *semele, simele*, 'fine white roll'.

**SIMELÎN (2)** wife of Nîtgêr (1)
She aids Dietrich when he is imprisoned by Nîtgêr's giants.

ref: **V(h)** 317, 5 (MS. 467, 5 *sinelin*, 1094, 12 *sybelin*); **V(w)** 505, 5 (*Rabina*)

**SÎMILTE**, see KÜNHILT

**SIMSON**, see SAMPSON

**SINDOLT (1)** Gunther's cup-bearer
Usually mentioned together with Rûmolt and Hûnolt.

ref: **B** 7741; **Kl** 4079; **N** 10, 2; **N(k)** 9, 3 (*Gundram*; 10, 2 *Gerbrant*; 158, 2 *Gundolt*)

pn: 9th-cent. German (Förstemann I. 1344).

**SINDOLT (2)** Dietrich's man
In **DF** he is captured by Ermenrîch's men at Bôle (Pola), but released on Dietrich's withdrawal from Italy. In **Rs** he fights Witegouwe at Rabene (Ravenna).

ref: **DF** 3008; **Rs** 578, 1

**SINDOLT (3)** Sigehêr's man
See Sigebant (2).

ref: **DF** 1967

**(SINNELS)**
Laurîn's brother (see Laurîn, p. 89 n. 4, and Sintram (2), p. 128).

pn: *Sinnol* is recorded at Basel in 1297 (Socin, 440); possibly based on MHG *sinewel*, 'round'.

**SINTRAM (1)** Etzel's man
In **DF** and **Rs** he is named together with Baltram (1) among Etzel's men aiding Dietrich against Ermenrîch. In the **Kl** he is the father of Adellint, and resides at Püten (Pitten, Austria); in **B**, although termed 'von Kriechenlant', his seat is apparently Ôsterlant (Austria).

ref: **B** 1107; **DF** 5152; **Kl** 2470; **Rs** 58, 1

In Þs, Sintram (Sistram) af Fenedi (Venice) (I. 33, 3), son of Reginballdr and grandson of Boltram, is rescued from the jaws of a dragon by Þiðrekr and Fasold (see Baltram (1), p. 9 and Rentwîn, p. 107). He joins Þiðrekr's company and is defeated by the fourth son of Isungr in the Bertangaland combats. His equipment is grass-green, and a dragon is depicted on his shield. Heimir, when he first meets Viðga, assumes the name 'Sintram' (I. 200, 8).

According to a Swiss tradition, two brothers, Baltram and Sintram, Dukes of Lenzburg, founded Burgdorf in Emmental, Canton Bern: a dragon devoured Baltram, in the battle against Ermenrîch's forces at Berne (451 f.).

---

[1] In the **Kl** he is erroneously stated to be Dietrich's cousin.
[2] In **A**, Sigestap seeks out Witege and Heime

## SINTRAM (1)

and Sintram killed it; he found Baltram still alive inside it; to commemorate the event he founded the chapel of St. Margaret (Krappe, *Mythologie*, 159; Schneider, *GHS* I. 273).

pn: 8th-cent. German (Förstemann I. 1343; Socin, 36, 164; Schlaug II. 148); 9th-cent. Lb (Bruckner, 304).

## SINTRAM (2) a dwarf

In **L(A)**, after Laurîn's capture, Dietrich places Laurîn's kingdom in his charge; in **L(K)II** he sends the news of Laurîn's capture to Alberîch, who summons the help of Walberân.

ref: **L(A)** 1643 (MS. *smoran*); **L(K)II** 3 (MS. *sindron*)[1]

It is possible that this is Laurîn's brother, Sinnels (see also Laurîn, p. 89 n. 4).

## SÎVRIT, see SÎFRIT (1)

## SLACHVORE

One of Laurîn's giants: Dietrich kills him.

ref: **L(DrHb)** 257, 5

pn: phrase-name based on MHG *slagen*, 'strike', and *vor(e)*, 'forward', meaning 'lay on!' (?).

## SPROSS

One of Laurîn's giants: Hildebrant kills him.

ref: **L(DrHb)** 257, 4

pn: based on MHG *sproz*, 'sapling' (?).

## STARCHÊR (1) Dietrich's man

Killed by Reinhêr (2) at Bôlonje (Bologna).

ref: **DF** 3014

pn: 8th-cent. German (Förstemann I. 1361); twice in OE *Domesday* (Feilitzen, 373).

## STARCHÊR (2) Dietwart's man

He is sent by Dietwart as a messenger for the hand of Minne (see Erewîn (2)).

ref: **DF** 955

## STARCHÊR (3) Ermenrîch's man

Killed by Dietrich at Rabene (Ravenna).

ref: **Rs** 628, 3

## STARKÂN

He joins Dietrich's forces at Meilân (Milan).

ref: **DF** 5731

pn: *Starco*, *Starchand*, recorded from 8th cent. in Germany (Förstemann I. 1361); the suffix *-ân* is usually reserved for giants or foreign persons.

## STAUER

One of Laurîn's giants: Wolfhart kills him.

ref: **L(DrHb)** 257, 7

pn: possibly based on MHG *stöuwen*, *stouwen*, 'lament, scold'.

## STIEFFUNG, see STÛTFUHS

## STÎRÆRE, STÎRÊRE (STÎREHELT)

Biterolf and Dietleip are designated thus: in **B**, Biterolf receives Styria (MHG Stîre) in lien for twelve years; his son Dietleip is usually associated with this region of Austria.

ref: (= Biterolf): **B** 13349; **DF** 5151; **Rs** 42, 1

(= Dietleip): **L(D)** 93; **Rg(F)** III. 19, 2; **Rs** 278, 1; **V(h)** 848, 12 (Stîrehelt); 1047, 5 (Stîrer)

## STOYNE

Witzlân's man: he aids Gunther in the combats at Worms.

ref: **B** 11724

## STRANDOLF, see WOLVESMAGE

## STREITPAS

One of Laurîn's giants: Witege kills him.

ref: **L(DrHb)** 257, 6

pn: a phrase-name based on MHG *strîten*, 'fight', and *baz*, 'better'.

## STRÎTGÊR von Grüenlant (Greenland)

Ermenrîch's man.

ref: **Rs** 498, 4

pn: no record found; compounds based on Gmc. *\*strīda-*, 'strife', are rare: such compound names are apparently new creations (see Förstemann I. 1366; Kaufmann, 329).

## STRÎTHÊR (1) Dietrich's man

ref: **DF** 5851

pn: no record: see Strîtgêr above.

## STRÎTHÊR (2) von Tuscân (Tuscany)

Ermenrîch's man.

ref: **DF** 6485

## STRÛTHAN, see SCHRÛTÂN (2)

## STÛDENFUHS, STÛDENFUSZ, STUOTFUHS, STÜEFINC, see STÛTFUHS

## STURMGÊR (1) Etzel's man

Aids Dietrich.

ref: **DF** 5160 (A *Sturinger*)

pn: no record found: compound names based on Gmc. *\*sturm* appear to be late creations (Förstemann I. 1367).

## STURMGÊR (2) von Engellant (England)

Ermenrîch's man.

ref: **DF** 8639

It is possible that Sturmgêr (3) and (4) represent the same person.

## STURMGÊR (3) von Îslant (Iceland)

Ermenrîch's man.

ref: **DF** 9300 (W *Sturmger*, R *Stumbger*)

---

[1] O. Jänicke prints *Sindrân*: see *DHB* I. 238.

STURMGÊR (4) von Hessen
Ermenrîch's man.

ref: **Rs** 494, 1 (R *Stvrmbger*, A *Stringer*; 832, 1 RA *Stvringer*)

STURMHOLT von Swangöu (Schwangau) Ermenrîch's man: he fights Blœdelîn at Rabene (Ravenna).

ref: **Rs** 710, 6

pn: no record found; see Sturmgêr (1) above.

STÛTFUHS (STÛDENFUHS, STÜEFINC)
This giant warrior is associated with various regions: 'von dem Rîne' (**A**, **Rg(A)**, **DF**, **Rs**); 'von Palerne' (Palermo) and 'künec von Pülle' (Apulia) (**B**); 'von Îrlant' (**Rg(CD)**); 'von Ypperlant ... in Vngerlant' (**AHb**).[1] In **A**, he and his brother Gêre (3) are among Ermenrîch's men opposing Dietrich; in **Rg** he is one of Kriemhilt's champions opposing those of Dietrich: he is defeated by Ilsân in **Rg(A)**, killed by Dietleip in **Rg(D)** and by Hertnît in **Rg(C)**. In **B** he supports Gunther's men against Dietrich and captures Wolfhart, but he is finally killed by Dietrich.

In **DF** and **Rs** he is among Dietrich's men opposing Ermenrîch, and kills Sigemâr (2) at Rabene (Ravenna). In **V(h)** he is again one of Dietrich's men, and kills the giant Wolvesmage at Mûter (see Wîcram).

ref: **A** 326, 4 (MS. *Stüdenfusz* always); **AHb** p. 2, 39 (*Stieffung*); **B** 5038 (MS. *Stûtfuchs*, also *Stautfuchs*); **DF** 3015 (Stûtfuhs: A *Stûtfisch*; 5853 R *Stovdfvhs*); **Rg(A)** 9, 1 (Stûdenvuhs); **Rg(C)** 34 (*Stuffing*); **Rg(D)** 45, 3 (Stüefinc: h *stüeffing*, s *schiffing*); **Rg(P)** 68 (Stûtfûz); **Rg(V)** 271 (*staudnfues*); **Rs** 727, 1 (Stûtfuhs: R *Stovtfvhs*, A *Stautfuhs*); **V(h)** 882, 2 (Stûtvuhs: MS. *stutfus*); **V(w)** 729, 1 (*Straußfus*)

In the 1582 edition of Fischart's *Gargantua*, 'Strausfüssige(r) Staudenfuß' is mentioned among other giants (W. Grimm, *DHS*, 353); Michael Sachse mentions 'Staudenfuß' in his *Neue Kaiserchronik* of 1606 (ibid. 488).

In the Þs, 1. 45, (3), etc., the name Studfus is used for one of the robbers defeated by Viðga at Briktan (A *Stodfuss*, B *Stofn(er)*).

pn: the form *Stûtfuhs*, *Stûdenfuhs*, etc., is of uncertain composition: possibly LG, cf. MLG *stût*, 'thick part of the thigh' (Kluge, *EWb*, 762),[2] and OS *fûs*, 'ready, eager' (Müllenhoff, *ZE*, 420 f.); variety of form indicates early folk-etymology for this unfamiliar name; cf. NHG *Staude*, *Strauß*, *Fuß*, and *Fuchs*. The family name of *Diemudis Staudfuchsinn* is recorded at Vienna in 1314 (ibid. 419). In the 15th cent., a Jew in an Eger miracle play is named *Staudenfues* (W. Grimm, *DHS*, 478).

The form *Stüefinc*, etc., apparently a re-

[1] See W. Grimm, *DHS*, 278.
[2] Müllenhoff, *ZE*, 419, equates the first com-

placement for the earlier unfamiliar name, is based on MHG *stüefe*, 'strong, brave'.

SURBEN pl.
In **R**, Rother gives 'Plisnin und Svurven' (Pleißen and the Sorbic March, i.e. East Thuringia) to ten counts in Luppolt's company. In **B**, the 'Dürenge und die Surben' from 'Ôsterlande' aid Gunther at Worms (5056).

ref: **B** 5056; **R** 4842

The Sorbs, a Slavonic tribe, the Sorabi of Latin chroniclers, inhabited the region to the north of Bohemia on both sides of the Elbe from the 8th cent. on (see Zeuß, 642 f.; Frings–Kuhnt, *Rother*, 191).

SURGEN pl.
The Syrians ruled by Machorel.

ref: **AHb** p. 5, 23 (*surgen land*); **O** 218, 2 (Sürie: W *svrie*; *sorgen*)

SWÂBE(N)
'der Swâbe(n) lant' (Swabia) is traversed on journeys between the Rhine region and Hungary or Italy in **N**, **Kl**, **B**, **Rg(A)**, and **Wd(D)**. The following heroes are connected with it: Berhtolt, Frideleip, and Herman (5) in **B**; Hûnolt (3) in **DF**; Ortnît rules it in **Wd(D)**.

ref: (people): sg. **B** 10771 (= Berhtolt); pl. **B** 6249
(region): Swâben: **B** 5073; **DF** 525; **E(L)** 66, 11; **Kl** 3824; **Ku** 744, 2; **N** 1493, 3; **V(h)** 581, 10; **Wd(D)** III. 47, 2; **Wd(Gr)** 307, 2 der Swâben(n) lant: **B** 8787; **Rg(A)** 22, 4

In the first half of the 13th cent., the dukedom of Swabia comprised a large area of South-West Germany and included part of present-day Switzerland (Paff, 175 ff.).

Svava, the name of Norðungr's kingdom in Þs (1. 28, 17), refers to South Germany in general, and the Black Forest is termed 'Svavaskogr' (1. 297, 2). In the Eddic poem HHj, Svávaland is a land to the south.

The ethnic name corresponds to that of the *Suebi*, a tribe known to Caesar on the Rhine; a large number of the North German tribes are referred to under this name in chs. 38–45 of the *Germania* of Tacitus, A.D. c. 100 (see Much, *Deutsche Stammeskunde*, 102 ff.; *Germania*, 29, 330 f.).

SWÄMMEL(ÎN) (SWEMMEL(ÎN))
Etzel's minstrel: in **N**, Etzel sends him and his fellow minstrel Wärbel to Worms with the invitation to Gunther and his brothers to visit Hungary (see Wärbel, p. 137).

In the **Kl**, Swämmel brings the news of the death of Gunther and his brothers to Worms; he also visits Bishop Pilgerîn at Passau, who has Swämmel's account of the destruction of Gunther and his men set down by the scribe Kuonrât (see Pilgerîn,

ponent with OHG *stuot*, 'stud'.

p. 105); subsequently he visits Bechelâren to bring the news of Rüedegêr's death to Gotelint.

ref: **Kl** 2858; **N** 1374, 1; **N(k)** 1462, 1 (*Schwebelein*)

See Wärbel, pp. 137 f., regarding Atli's messengers in Eddic tradition, and those of Attila in Þs.

pn: possibly a descriptive name for a minstrel based on MHG *swemmelîn*, the diminutive of *swam*, 'sponge'.[1]

## SYTOMER
Witzlân's man: he aids Gunther at Worms.

ref: **B** 11721

# T (see also under D)

## TANASTUS
The eleventh warrior of Guntharius killed by Waltharius: he comes from Speyer.

ref: **W** 1010

pn: origin uncertain (see Kögel I. ii. 318; Baesecke, *Vorgeschichte*, 430; also Kaufmann, 91, regarding the first component, Gmc. \**Dana-*).

## TARÎAS (KARINAS)
Heathen king who threatens the monastery of Tischcâl, to which Wolfdietrich has retired; he is defeated by Wolfdietrich and his son Hugdietrich (2).

ref: **Wd(D)** x. 22, 2; **Wd(Gr)** 2134, 2; **Wd(w)** 2047, 2 (*Karinas*)

pn: possibly a corrupt form of *Darius*, the name of the Persian King of Antiquity (cf. *Daria*, a Saracen king in OFr epic (Langlois, 172)).

## TARNUNC
A dwarf: his kingdom has been usurped by Billunc (1); Wolfdietrich kills Billunc and restores the kingdom to Tarnunc's son.

ref: **Wd(B)** 839, 1

pn: based on MHG *tarnen*, 'conceal', giving obvious association with *tarnhût*, *tarnkappe*, 'cloak of invisibility', often possessed by dwarfs. The pn *Tarnink* is recorded at Salzburg in the 9th cent. (Socin, 185).

## TENE(N), TENEMARKE, etc.
In **N**, the Danes and Saxons, led by Liudegast and Liudegêr, are defeated by the Burgundians under Sîfrit. Elsewhere the following persons are associated with Denmark: Boppe (**B**), Diezolt (**DF**), Floris (**V(w)**), Fruote (**AHb, B, Ku, Rg(D), Rg(P), Rs, Wd(A)**), Hâwart (**B, Kl, N**), Herbort (**B**), Hetel (**DH, Ku**), Hôrant (**DH, Ku**), Hûc (**A, E**), Îrinc (**Kl, N**), Liudegast (**N**),

Liudegêr (**B**). In **Wd(k)** it is part of Wolfdietrich's realm.

ref: Tene: sg.: **Kl** 1230 (= Îrinc); **Ku** 401, 4 (= Hôrant); pl.: **Ku** 33, 4; **N** 2074, 1
Tenen, the region: **Ku** 317, 1
Tenemarke: sg.: **Ku** 1544, 3 (= Fruote); **N(C)** 2045, 4 (= Îrinc); pl.: **Ku** 938, 2
Tenemarke, Denemarcke, the region: **A** 307, 3; **AHb** p. 3, 10; **B** 4958; **DF** 8634; **DH** F 41, 3, 1; **E(d)** 64, 10; **E(s)** 56, 10; **Kl** 446; **Ku** 200, 1; **N** 140, 3; **Rg(D)** 72, 4; **Rg(P)** 117; **Rs** 686, 1; **V(w)** 846, 1; **Wd(A)** 6, 2; **Wd(k)** 1, 5
Tenelant: **B** 1909; **Kl** 447 (C); **Ku** 204, 1; **N** 2058, 1; **Rs** 478, 4
Tenelender sg.: **N** 2045, 4 (= Îrinc)
Tenerîche: **Ku** 354, 3

## TENGELÊRE
= Wolfrât (1), son of Amelgêr (1) von Tengelingen (see p. 5).

ref: **R** 4207 (H *tengelere*, RB *Tengelingere*)

## TEREVAS
A heathen, the father of Orkîse.

ref: **V(d)** 1, 2; **V(w)** 1, 2 (*Teriufas*)

pn: origin obscure; possibly from Turkish *derwiš*, 'mendicant priest', but *Derwisch*, 'dervish', does not occur in German till the 16th cent. (Kluge, *EWb*, 128);[2] cf. Treferîs.

## TERFÎANT (TREVÎANT, AFFIGANT, VIGAN(T))
A heathen god.

ref: **V(d)** 17, 10 (Affigant, also 27, 7 Vigant, 100, 2 Vigan); **V(h)** 62, 12 (Trevîant); **V(w)** 93, 11 (*Terfîant*); **Wd(D)** v. 4, 2 (Tervîân, vii. 49, 1 Tervîant); **Wd(Gr)** 842, 2

pn: probably from OFr epic, in which *Tervagan(t)* is frequently the name of a Saracen god (Langlois, 633 ff.; Flutre, 179); cf. Wolfram von Eschenbach's *Willehalm*, 17, 20 f.

---

[1] See F. Detter and R. Heinzel, 'Hoenir und der Vanenkrieg', *PBB* xviii (1894), 553, for another derivation which relates it to MHG *sweimen*, 'soar, hover': the form of the 15th-cent. **N(k)**, *Schwebelein*, seems to support this; cf. NHG *schweben*, 'hover'. See also Henzen, 144 f., regarding the suffix -(*i*)*līn*.

[2] Lunzer, *Elegast*, 152, suggests a derivation from Hebrew *tərefā*, 'unclean, devilish'.

**TERLEPEIN**
A heathen, Orkîse's man.
ref: **V(w)** 190, 7

**TÎBALT** (1) von Püllenlant (Apulia)
Dietwart's companion: he is killed by a dragon on Dietwart's bridal quest for Minne.
ref: **DF** 482
pn: Gmc. *Þeudobald (see Diepolt (1), p. 23); this form probably derives from OFr epic, *Tiebaut* (*Thiebaut*) (Langlois, 635 ff.); cf. the name of the first husband of Gyburc, *Tybalt*, in Wolfram von Eschenbach's *Willehalm*, 8, 2.

**TÎBALT** (2) von Sibenbürgen (Transylvania)
Brother of Herrât, Dietrich's wife: he is one of Etzel's men aiding Dietrich against Ermenrîch.
ref: **Rs** 67, 1

**TÎBÂN** von Gurdenwâle (Cornwall)
Ermenrîch's man: he fights Hildebrant at Rabene (Ravenna).
ref: **Rs** 720, 5

**TÎDAS** von Meilân (Milan)
Dietrich's man.
ref: **DF** 5720

**TÎROLT** von Brûnswîc (Brunswick)
Ermenrîch's man: he fights Sigebant (3) at Rabene (Ravenna).
ref: **Rs** 729, 1 (R *Tyerolt*, A *Turolt*)
pn: the manuscript readings suggest that this may represent the common Norman name *Turold* (< ON *Þórvaldr*).

**TIUTSCH** adj.
This adjective refers to
   the German language: *tiutsch* **Wd(D)** VIII. 236, 2; *in tiuscher zungen* **Kl** 4697; *diz diutsche buoch* **A** 45, 2;
   the people of Germanic race: *manic man, / bêde tiutsch unde walch* **B** 7993; *von den tiuschen gesten* **N** 1354, 4;
   the country: *tiuschiu rîche* **DH** F 41, 1, 1; **E(d)** 10, 10;
   the house of the Teutonic Order at Acre: *daz tiutsche hûs* **Wd(D)** v. 106, 4; its officials: *die tiuschen bruoder* **Wd(D)** v. 134, 4; *Teütsche gsellen* **E(s)** 17, 5;
   German units of measurement: *ein tiutsche raste* **DF** 9726; *Teütsche meilen* **E(s)** 239, 2.
   The base is Gmc. *þeudō-, which gives OHG *diot*, MHG *diet*, 'people', and the adj. OHG *diutisc*, MHG *tiu(t)sch* (see Kluge, *EWb*, 129).

**TÎWALT** von Westvâle (Westphalia)
Ermenrîch's man.
ref: **DF** 8655
pn: probably a variant of Tîbalt (see above).

**TÔT** (1) personification
ref: **E(L)** 145, 4; **Ku** 1419, 4; **V(h)** 79, 5; **V(w)** 127, 11
pn: cf. MHG *tôt*, 'death'.

**TÔT** (2) heathen god
Wolfdietrich breaks Belîân's idol of this god before killing him.
ref: **Wd(D)** VI. 114, 3

**TRAWTENMUNT**
Wolfdietrich leaves Ortnît's widow in his care.
ref: **Wd(k)** 321, 1
pn: 8th-cent. German (Förstemann I. 426).

**TREFERÎS**
A heathen: one of Merzîân's men killed by Wernhêr (2). His sword is named Beierlant.
ref: **Wd(D)** v. 168, 1 (b *terferis*, c *derffis*, etc.); **Wd(Gr)** 1004, 1
pn: cf. Terevas.

**TREVÎANT**, see TERFÎANT

**TRIPPEL** von Athênis (Athens)
Husband of Dietlint (3): their son is Wolfdietrich.
ref: **Wd(C)** II. 4, 3

**TRIUREIZ (VIGAS, SENEREIS)**
A heathen: one of Orkîse's men killed by Dietrich and Hildebrant.
ref: **V(d)** 38, 1 (*Vigas*); **V(h)** m 99, 1 n 107, 1 (*Triureiz*: B *trivereis*); **V(w)** 228, 1 (*Senereis*)

**TRIUTLINT** (1) daughter of Ernst
ref: **Wd(D)** v. 31, 2; **Wd(Gr)** 869, 2
pn: 8th-cent. German (Förstemann I. 426).

**TRIUTLINT** (2) wife of Ernst
ref: **Wd(D)** m v. 31, 2; **Wd(Gr)** m 869, 2

**TROGUS**
The tenth warrior of Guntharius killed by Waltharius; he comes from Straßburg (Lat. Argentina).
ref: **W** 1009
pn: 7th-cent. WFr *Drogo* and German *Truogo*, etc. (Förstemann I. 420; Schlaug I. 73; II. 189), based on the Gmc. root *draug- (Goth. *driugan*, 'do war service') (see Kaufmann, 97 f.).

**TRONEGÆRE**
= Hagen (1), whose seat is Tronege (see p. 57 n. 4).
ref: **B** 6020; **Kl** 1218; **N** 234, 1

**TRUSÎÂN**, see DRASÎÂN

## TÛRÎAN (1)

**TÛRÎAN** (1) Isterrîch (Istria)
Brother of Mîmunc and companion of Dietwart.

ref: **DF** 433

In *Orendel* (12th cent.), the heathen Dûrîan (2384) beheads the abductor of Brîde, Wolfhart. In Wolfram von Eschenbach's *Parzival*, a certain Taurîan is the brother of Dodines (271, 12).

**TÛRÎAN** (2) von Spôlît (Spoleto)
Ermenrîch's man.

ref: **DF** 6524

**TÛSUNC** von Normandîe (Normandy)
Ermenrîch's man.

ref: **DF** 8641

pn: Förstemann, 1. 436, gives simplex names, such as *Duso*, *Doso*, from the German records, which possibly show the same base (see Kaufmann, 101 f.).

The pn may, however, be based on the variant MHG form *tûsinc* for *tûsent*, 'thousand'.

# U

**ULSENBRANT**
A giant killed by Reinolt at Mûter (see Wîcram).

ref: **V(h)** 751, 1; **V(w)** 681, 1 (*Waldeprant*)

pn: first component possibly based on MHG *ülse*, 'fool'. The name is used for a giant in *Reinfried von Braunschweig* (W. Grimm, *DHS*, 195).

**UNGER(N)** (UNGERLANT, UNGERMARKE, UNGERISCH adj.)
Hungary (see Hiune(n), pp. 79 f.).

ref: Unger(n): **AHb** p. 1, 21; **DH** F 41, 3, 3; **N** 1162, 1; **R** 489; **Rs** 49, 3 (A *Hungern*); **V(h)** 302, 12; **Wd(w)** 830, 1
   Ungerlant: **AHb** p. 9, 38; **B** 1119 (MS. *Hungerlant*); **N** 1373, 1; **Rg(C)** 1128; **V(h)** 532, 5; **V(w)** 792, 2; **Wu(B)** 1, 1
   Ungermarke: **Kl** 2473 (d *Hunger-*, D *ungerischer* . . .)
   ungerischiu rîche: **Wd(D)** v. 50, 1

pn: see Hiune(n), p. 80 n. 1.

**UODELGART**
A giantess: she attacks Dietrich, who has killed her brother Ecke and her mother Birkhilt (see Ecke's genealogy, p. 33 n. 2).

ref: **E(L)** 239, 7

pn: 8th-cent. German (Förstemann 1. 1187)

**UOLRÎCH** von Tegelingen[1]
Ermenrîch's man: he fights Alebrant (2) at Rabene (Ravenna).

ref: **Rs** 735, 5

## UOTE (1)

ref: **DF** 6524

pn: 8th-cent. German (Förstemann 1. 1190 ff.; Schlaug 1. 141). The full form *Uodelrîch* is used for a peasant in *Neidharts Lieder*, 64, 29.

**UOTE** (1) mother of the Burgundian kings
Mother of Gunther, Gêrnôt, Gîselhêr, and Kriemhilt: in **N** she is the wife of Dancrât[2] and sister of Bishop Pilgerîn von Pazzouwe (Passau). When her daughter Kriemhilt dreams that two eagles kill her tame falcon, Uote interprets this as presaging the death of Kriemhilt's future husband, i.e. Sîfrit (see p. 18). Later she warns Gunther not to accept Etzel's invitation to Hungary, and recounts her dream in which all the birds in the land die.[3] Hagen persuades Gunther to reject the warning. In **N(C)**, after the death of Dancrât, she founds an abbey at Lôrse (Lorsch),[4] to which Sîfrit's remains are later transferred. In the **Kl** it is known that she is buried at Lôrse, having died of grief at the death of her sons in Hungary.

ref: **Kl** 37; **N** 7, 1

In ON Eddic tradition, the wife of Gjúki (see Gibeche (1), p. 51), and mother of the Niflungar, i.e. of Gunnarr, Högni, and Guðrún, is named Grímhildr[5] (Grp 33, 3; Gðr 17, 1; Od 15, 8; Am 72, 5; Sk ch. 48; Völss ch. 25; also in the Faroese ballad *Brynhildur táttur* (*CCF* 1. 8–22)): by means of a magic potion, she causes Sigurðr to forget Brynhildr and marry her own daughter, Guðrún.

In the Þs, Oda (1. 282, 6) is the mother of Gunnarr, Gernoz, Gisler, and Grimilldr by her husband Aldrian (Mb2 Irungr), but wives of Högni and Gunnarr recount dreams of ill omen to warn against acceptance of Atli's invitation (see pp. 20, 41 n. 4, 59 n. 3).

---

[1] See Amelgêr (1), p. 5, regarding this title, which probably derives from **R**.
[2] Outside **N** and **Kl**, the mother of the Burgundians, Gibeche s wife, is unnamed: **Rg(A)** m 2, 1; **Rg(F)** m 24, 1; **gS** m p. 66, 26; **hS** m 16, 5; **W** m 30.
[3] In ON Eddic tradition, Guðrún warns her brothers by sending a wolf s hair twisted into a gold ring (Akv); in Am and Völss chs. 34 f., the
[4] J. R. Dieterich, *Der Dichter des Nibelungenliedes* (Frankfurt am Main, 1923), 41 f., notes that an Uta von Calw founded a convent at Lorsch in 1130.
[5] See Kriemhilt, pp. 20 f., regarding this pn.

Högni is her son by a demon, who has ravished her when she was sleeping in a garden (cf. Alberîch, p. 3, Laurîn, p. 89, and Machmet, p. 91). Högni rejects her warning against accepting Attila's invitation to Húnaland, when she recounts her dream that many of the birds in Niflungaland are dead (also in the Faroese ballad *Högna táttur* (*CCF* I. 22–33)). The name Oda is also used for the wife of Osanctrix (see Ôserîch, p. 103) and for the wife of Biturulfr (see Dietlint (1), p. 25).

pn: LG *Ōda*, UG *Uote*: 8th–cent. WFr, Lb, and German (Förstemann I. 187 f.; Schlaug I. 138; II. 216; G. Baesecke, 'Gudrun-Kriemhilt, etc.', *PBB* LX (1936), 376 f.; E. H. Mueller, 'Deutung einiger Namen im Nibelungenlied', *Monatshefte* XXXI (1939), 279 f.; Bruckner, 220); rare in South-East German (Kromp I. 21; III. 122).

It is possible that the figure of Uote stems from the historical Oda, ancestress of the Liudolfingian Saxon dynasty of German emperors; she died in 913, aged 106 (E. Schröder, *DNK*, 99 ff.).

UOTE (2) Hildebrant's wife
In **äH**, according to Hiltibrant's son, Hadubrant, Hiltibrant has left his wife and infant son defenceless and unprovided for (20 ff.).
In **jH**, although she has not seen her husband for thirty-two years (see p. 74), Ute welcomes him on his return home with their son Alebrant.

In **DF**, **Rg(D)**, and **AHb**, Hildebrant leaves Uote with his brother-in-law, Amelolt, when he sets out with Dietrich. In **A** she brings up her nephew, Alphart; in **Rg(D)** she cares for the Harlunge.

ref: **A** 103, 4; **AHb** p. 7, 37; **DF** 4305; **ED** m 4, 1; **äH** m 21; **jH** 1, 4 (3, 4 q *Gûden*, N *Goedele*); **L(D)** 125; **Rg(A)** m 320, 4; **Rg(C)** 661; **Rg(D)** 41, 4; **Rg(F)** III. 5, 4; **jSn** 20, 1; **V(d)** 7, 4 (Gut); **V(h)** 587, 8; **V(w)** 42, 8

In Wolfram von Eschenbach's *Willehalm* (c. 1210–20), Uote's devotion to Hildebrant is recalled (439, 16).

In Þs, Oda (I. 159, (5)) is the name of Hildibrandr's wife. After the destruction of the Niflungar, Hildibrandr returns with Þiðrekr to Bern; he thinks that Oda (II. 329, 26) was pregnant when he left her and that their son, Alibrandr, would now be ruling at Bern. After defeating his son in combat, he returns home with him to Oda, who tends their wounds and feeds them.

UOTE (3) wife of Gêre (4) von Îrlant (Ireland)
Mother of Sigebant (1).

ref: **Ku** 1, 3

UOTE (4) von Norwæge
Wife of Sigebant (1) von Îrlant and mother of Hagen (2).

ref: **Ku** m 8, 3 n 42, 4

# V

(see under F)

# W

WÂCHILT
A mermaid: she gives refuge to Witege, when he rides into the sea at Rabene (Ravenna) to escape the wrath of Dietrich.[1]

ref: **Rs** m 964, 5 n 969, 3 (R *Wæchilt*, A *Nothilt*)

In Þs, King Villcinus of Villcinaland begets Vaði by a mermaid (ON *sækona*: I. 73, 19; II. 63 ff.);[2] Vaði is the father of Velent, whose son is Viðga. In the Swedish version, Wideke plunges into the sea to escape Didrik and the mermaid brings him to Sioland (Zealand) in Denmark (Þs II. 395 ff.) (see Wate, pp. 138 f., Wielant, p. 142, and Witege, pp. 145 f.).

pn: the first component is probably based on MHG *wâc*, 'wave, moving waters'.

WAHSMUOT (1) leader of the Harlunge forces
He supports Dietleip against Gunther's men in the combats at Worms: he is unhorsed by Herbort. Regentage and Hâche are his relatives.

ref: **B** 4769

[1] In the 12th-cent. *Salman und Morolf*, 726, 4, a similar 'merminne' entertains her nephew, Môrolf, under the sea.

[2] It may be noted that in **Ku** 529, 3, Wate is thought to have learnt the art of healing 'von einem wilden wîbe' (see p. 138).

## WAHSMUOT (1)

pn: rare: 8th-cent. at Lorsch (Förstemann I. 1497), possibly confused with the commoner pn *Hwasmuot* (*Wasmuot*), recorded from the 8th cent. (Förstemann I. 937, 1548; Schlaug II. 155; see also Kaufmann, 377). The Marner (*c*. 1231) refers to a 'Minnesänger' named 'Wahsmuot' (XIV. 18, 276).

## WAHSMUOT (2) Wolfdietrich's brother
(cf. Dietrich (4), (5), and (6), p. 31)
See Bouge (1), p. 14.

ref: **AHb** p. 6, 9 (*waßmût*; p. 6, 25 *wasmût*); **Wd(B)** 258, 3 (B *waschmût*); **Wd(D)** III. 6, 1 (III. 57, 3 a *waszmüt*); **Wd(Gr)** 261, 3; **Wd(w)** 308, 3 (*Wachsmut*)

**WALACH**, see WALBER

## WALÂCHEN pl. (VLÂCHEN)
Among Etzel's subject peoples greeting Kriemhilt at Tulne in **N**: led by Râmunc, they ride 'sam vliegende vogele' (like flying birds, 1342); they are followed by Gibeche and Hornboge with their men (1344).

In **B**, Râmunc and Hornboge lead the Vlâchen, who are redoubtable bowmen (10187 ff.), against Gunther's men at Worms. Otherwise Blœdel (**B**) and Sigehêr (1) (**Kl**) are associated with this people.

ref: **B** 1218 (MS. *Walhen*; 1358 *Walachen*); **Kl** 391 (d *Flachen*, Ca *Vlachen*); **N** 1339, 2 (BD *Walachen*, d *Walechen*, Igh *Valwen*, b *polachen*)

pn: this name refers to a nomadic people of South-East Europe, probably the Rumanians (Zeuß, 264); cf. OSlav. *Vlachŭ* (Kluge, *EWb*, 836).

## WALBER ûz Türkîe (Turkey)
Aids Etzel and Kriemhilt against Gunther and his men.

ref: **Kl** 400; **N(k)** 2127, 4 (*Walach*)[1]

pn: possibly represents a name like *Waldbern*, *Walpero*, recorded from the 9th cent. in German records (Förstemann I. 1501).

## WALBERÂN
The ruler of all dwarfs; his kingdom comprises Armeniâ, Sinâî, Tabôr, Judêâ, Kaukasas, and Kanachas (Canaan). He lands with an invisible host at Venice in order to rescue his nephew, Laurîn, who has been captured by Dietrich. Laurîn acts as mediator, and single combats are arranged before the walls of Berne (Verona). In the first combat he forces Dietrich to retreat; then peace is made.

ref: **L(K)II** 59

pn: possibly a corruption of OFr *Auberon* (see Alberîch, p. 4).

## WALBERTUS, see GÊRNÔT (1)
Son of Gibaldus (see Gibeche (1)) in gS.
pn: *Waldobert*: 7th-cent. WFr and Lb; 8th-cent. German (Förstemann I. 1501 f.; Schlaug I. 168).

## WALBURC
A book containing the story of Wolfdietrich is said to have been found at the monastery of St. Walburc at Eistet (Eichstätt).

ref: **Wd(D)** I. 4, 3; **Wd(Gr)** 4, 3 (Waltburg)

St. Walpurgis (†*c*. 780) was abbess of Eichstätt from 754 till her death; her real name was Wealdburh (OE) (E. Schröder, *DNK*, 60 ff.; Searle, 479).

pn: \*Waldeburg 8th-cent. German (Förstemann I. 1502; Schlaug I. 168); *Walburc* 13th-cent. German (Socin, 62).

**WALDEMAR**, see BALDEMAR

pn: 7th-cent. WFr, 8th-cent. German (Förstemann I. 1509; Schlaug I. 168).

**WALDEPRANT**, see ULSENBRANT

pn: 8th-cent. Lb, 9th-cent. German (Förstemann I. 1502).

## WALDERÎCH
Dietrich's man.

ref: **A** 76, 2

pn: 8th-cent. German (Förstemann I. 1511; II. ii. 1213; Schlaug I. 169; II. 154).

## WALGUNT von Salnecke (Salonika)
Father of Hildeburc (2), whom he keeps secluded in a tower; Hugdietrich, disguised as a woman, seduces her. Their child, later christened Wolfdietrich, is smuggled from the tower, but is carried off by a she-wolf, with whose litter Walgunt finds him when he is out hunting. His wife Liebgart persuades him to forgive the lovers, and Hildeburc becomes Hugdietrich's queen.

ref: **AHb** p. 6, 20; **Wd(B)** 15, 2; **Wd(Gr)** 21, 2

pn: fem., isolated 8th-cent. WFr (Förstemann I. 1506 (*Waldegundis?*) 1517 (*Walegundis*)); \*-*gunþaz*, the corresponding m. form of the final component, f. \**gunþi*, one of the most common Gmc. components for fem. pn, must be assumed (see Kaufmann, 159).

## WALHE(N) (WALHENLANT, WALHISCH adj., WELSCHLANT)
The people and country of Italy

ref: Walhe sg.: **Wd(k)** 216, 5 (=Ortnît);
pl.: **O** 357, 1 (= Italians)
Walhen (=Italy): **E(d)** 72, 10; **E(L)** 66, 10; **O** 3, 3: **O(k)** 177,5; **Wd(k)** 215, 7;
Walhenlant: **O** 393, 4; **V(h)** 494, 12
walhisch (welsch) adj.: **O** 353, 2; **Wd(A)** 75, 2; **Wd(D)** VIII. 236, 2; **Wd(Gr)** 1776, 2;
Welschlant: **O(k)** 2, 5; hS(Sachs) 827

This ethnic name derives from that of the

---

[1] A confusion with the ethnic name, Walâchen (see above).

## WALHE(N)

*Volcae*, a Celtic tribe known to Caesar in the 1st cent. B.C., and was used originally by the Gmc. peoples for those of Celtic race, in OHG *walah, walh*, 'Celt' (Gmc. *\*Walhōs*), later being applied to the Romanized Celts of Gaul and Italy (see Kluge, *EWb*, 853).

## WALKÊR von Messîe (Messina)

Ermenrîch's man.

ref: **Rs** 487, 1 (A *Walckner*)

pn: based on the equivalent of OHG *walah, walh*, 'Roman' or 'Celt' (see above), and *heri*, 'army' or *gêr* (*kêr*): 6th-cent. Burgundian, 8th-cent. German (Förstemann I. 1517), 9th-cent. OE (Searle, 480); with second component OHG *gêr* (*kêr*): 9th-cent. German (Förstemann I. 1517).

## WALRÎCH (WELDERICH)

Brother of the giant Zere and son of the giantess Runze (see the genealogy of Ecke, p. 33 n. 2).

ref: **AHb** p. 4, 5 (*welderich*); **E(d)** 282, 11 (Welderich); **E(L)** 226, 1

pn: 6th-cent. WFr, 9th-cent. German (Förstemann I. 1520).

## WALTHER (WALTHARIUS)

In **W**, Walthariusis sent by his father, King Alphere of Aquitania, as a hostage to the court of Attila the Hun (see Etzel, p. 40), where he achieves high military command. After a successful campaign, he invites Attila and his nobles to a banquet; leaving Attila and his men in a drunken stupor, he escapes with Hiltgunt, a Burgundian princess (see Hildegunt (1), p. 78)). They travel by night and live by catching birds and fishing. At the Rhine crossing by Worms, Walther gives the ferryman an alien fish, which causes his presence to become known to the Frankish King, Guntharius. Guntharius, against the advice of Hagano, Waltharius's former comrade at Attila's court, sets out with eleven men in pursuit of the fugitives, who have reached a defile in the Vosges; he demands the treasure and refuses Waltharius's offer of a hundred gold rings, in spite of Hagano's warning, reinforced by a dream in which a bear bites off Guntharius's leg, and knocks out Hagano's eye and six teeth.[1] Waltharius kills Guntharius's eleven warriors: Kamalo, Kimo, Werinhardus, Ekivrid, Hadawardus, Patavrid, Gerwit, Randolf, Trogus, Tanastus, and Helmnod; Guntharius flees. The next day, Waltharius and Hiltgunt leave the defile. Guntharius and Hagano, who has now agreed to take part in the fight after the death of his nephew, Patavrid, attack from ambush: Waltharius cuts off Guntharius's leg; Hagano intervenes, Waltharius's sword shatters, and Hagano cuts off his right hand; Waltharius draws his second sword with his left hand and cuts out Hagano's right eye and six teeth. Hiltgunt tends their wounds and dispenses wine. Hagano and Waltharius joke about their injuries and renew their oaths of friendship. Guntharius and Hagano return to Worms. Waltharius returns to Aquitania, weds Hiltgunt, and reigns for thirty years.[2]

In the fragmentary **WuH**, Volkêr escorts Walther and Hildegunt from the Rhine through the Waskenwalt (Vosges)[3] to Lengers (Langres),[4] and preparations are made for their wedding.

In **N**, Etzel recalls Hagen and Walther as hostages at his court (1756 f.), and references are made during the fighting to Walther's exploits with Hagen in Etzel's service (1796 f.) and to his reluctance to fight Walther at the Waskenstein (2344).

In **B**,[5] Biterolf fights with his nephew, Walther von Spanjenlant (Spain)—Walther also rules Kärlingen (France), Arragûn, and Nâvarren—whom he encounters returning from the land of the Huns; they are reconciled when Biterolf discovers their relationship. Later in the epic, Walther appears among Gunther's men at Worms, where he fights Wolfhart; in the combats he is chosen to fight Rüedegêr, who states that he will let him escape as he has done in the past (7656 ff.);[6] the fight is undecided, as is also Walther's subsequent combat with Dietrich.

In **Rg(A)**, Walther von dem Wasgenstein is among the Burgundian champions at Worms and fights a drawn combat with Dietleip (with Hertnît von Riuzen in **Rg(D)**; in **Rg(F)** he defeats Witege). In **Rg(D)** the device on his shield is a blue lion (see Leo, p. 89).

In **A**, Walther von Kerlingen aids Dietrich against Ermenrîch. In **DF** and **Rs**, Walther von Lengers is among Etzel's men aiding Dietrich: he fights Hiuzolt at Bôlonje (Bologna) in **DF** and Heime at Rabene (Ravenna) in **Rs**.[7]

---

[1] Cf. the warning dream about a bear in the ON Am 16 (see p. 41 n. 4).

[2] Hans Kuhn, 'Zur Geschichte der Walthersage', *Festgabe für Ulrich Pretzel* (Berlin, 1963), 341 ff., suggests that the original story ended with the death of the hero, and supports this by a reference to similarities of detail in the description of Kjartan's death in ch. 49 of the early-13th-cent. ON *Laxdæla saga* (ed. E. Ó. Sveinsson (Reykjavík, 1934), 151 ff.).

[3] In **N**, Sifrits murder takes place in the Waskenwalt (Vosges); it is placed more correctly at Ôtenhein in the C-version (see p. 119 n. 1).

[4] Walther is associated with Langres in **DF** and **Rs**. Baesecke, *Vorgeschichte*, 442, points out that a Bishop Walter (†1179) was also Count of Langres.

[5] The first five âventiure of **B** (see Dietleip, p. 24) are thought to be modelled on the lost Walther-epic (see Schneider, *GHS* I. 334, and Baesecke, op. cit. 443 ff.).

[6] This suggests that in the lost Walther-epic, Rüedegêr led a half-hearted Hunnish pursuit of the eloping pair.

[7] In **DF**, a Walther von Kerlingen is named among Ermenrîch's men, by an oversight (8638); no separate entry has been made in the Catalogue.

ref: **A** 77, 2; **AHb** p. 2, 36; **B** 575; **DF** 5902; **N** 1756, 3; **Rg(A)** 8, 3; **Rg(C)** 32; **Rg(D)** 44, 4; **Rg(F)** IV. 2, 1; **Rg(P)** 66; **Rg(V)** 328; **Rs** 47, 1; **W** 79 (Waltharius); **WuH** (Graz) III. 1; (Wien) 1. 9, 4

In German literature, apart from the epics, Walther and Hildegunt are mentioned in the 13th-cent. *von einem übelen wîbe* (W. Grimm, *DHS*, 173), and Walther von der Vogelweide makes play with his own name through reference to the story of Walther and Hildegunde (see Hildegunt (1), p. 78).

In the first fragment of the OE *Waldere*, a fight has already taken place by a rock face (I. 15), and Waldere (II. 11), the son of Ælfhere and leading warrior of Ætla ('Ætlan ordwyga': I. 6), whose sword is Mimming, the work of Wēland (I. 5),[1] is being urged (by Hildegȳð?) to oppose Gūðhere, who has unjustly sought battle and refused Waldere's offer of a sword, treasure, and arm-rings.[2] In the second fragment, Hagena speaks of his excellent sword resting in its scabbard;[3] Waldere then challenges Gūðhere, who has been depending till now on Hagena, to win his (Waldere's) armour from him, although he (Waldere) is battle-weary.[4]

The early 11th-cent. *Chronicon Novaliciense* (W. Grimm, *DHS*, 40; Heinzel, *Walthersage*, 288), in recounting the story of a Waltharius connected with the Piedmontese monastery of Novalese, follows **W** word for word for the most part, but includes also the hero's retirement to the monastery, which he defends against robbers (cf. the 'moniages' of Heime and Wolfdietrich, pp. 65, 150).

In the Þs, Valtari af Vaskasteini (I. 245, 19) is the nephew of Erminrikr, who ransoms Valtari's life after his defeat in stone-putting and shaft-throwing by Þetleifr (see Dietleip, p. 25) and later puts him in charge of the castle of the rebel Rimsteinn at Gerimsheimr (see Rimstein, p. 108). In an exchange of hostages with Attila, Erminrikr sends Valtari to Attila's court at Susat. During a feast, Valtari and Hilldigundr, the daughter of the Greek King Ilias, escape together; Attila sends twelve men led by Högni in pursuit.[5] Valtari kills Högni's eleven companions and Högni flees.[6] That night, Högni attacks from the darkness of the forest as the pair are eating a leg of roast boar-meat: Valtari hurls the leg-bone at him and puts out his eye.[7] The pair return to Erminrikr's court. In the battle between Erminrikr's forces and those of Þiðrekr at Gronsport, Valtari is Erminrikr's standard-bearer: he and Vildiver kill each other, Vildiver cutting off Valtari's leg in the encounter.[8]

A Polish version of the Walther story is contained in the late-14th-cent. *Polish Chronicle* of Boguphalus (W. Grimm, *DHS*, 174; Heinzel, *Walthersage*, 28 ff.): Walczerz wdały (Walther the Strong) elopes with Helgunda, a Frankish princess, whose love he wins by his singing (cf. Hôrant, pp. 80 f.). Walcherz's German rival has all the Rhine crossings guarded. A ferryman refuses his offer of a gold coin, so Walczerz, with Helgunda behind him on the horse, rides across the river. His rival overtakes them, and Walczerz kills him. The pair return to Walczerz's castle at Tyniec near Cracow. Later Helgunda proves unfaithful, and Walczerz kills her and her lover, Prince Wislaw of Wislica.[9]

pn: based on the equivalents of OHG *waltan*, 'rule', and *hari*, people, army',[10] it does not belong to the earliest type of Gmc. name-formation (Anton Scherer, 'Zum Sinngehalt der germanischen Personennamen', *BzNf* IV (1953), 10); earliest record for Langobard King *Valdarus* (†546) (Schönfeld, 252); frequent from 8th cent. in Lb, WFr, and German (Förstemann I. 1506 f.; Schlaug I. 168; II. 153; Socin, 40; Bach I, §§ 301, 529; Kögel I. ii. 285); German family name *c.* 1200 (Socin, 172); rare in OE: late-7th-cent. and early-8th-cent. spellings *uualdhere*, etc. (Sweet, 427), the expected

---

[1] In **W**, Waltharius s armour is the work of Wieland (965), in *Waldere* it is the heirloom of Ælfhere (II. 18) (see Wielant, p. 141).

[2] See **W** above.

[3] This speech could also be attributed to Waldere, who would thus refer to his second sword (see Hagen (1), p. 59 n. 1).

[4] 'Feta, gyf ðū dyrre, / æt ðus heaðuwērigan hāre byrnan!' (II. 16 f.), a topos of heroic diction, cf. 'Doh maht dū nū aodlīhho, ibu dir dīn ellen taoc, / in sus hēremo man hrusti giwinnan . . .' (äH 55 f.); in the *Laxdæla saga*, Kjartan in a like situation is termed 'vígmóðr' (battle-weary) (ed. E. Ó. Sveinsson (Reykjavík, 1934), 154).

[5] Either the Þs has simplified here or is drawing on a version, possibly the lost MHG Walther-epic, in which the Huns were the only pursuers (see H. W. J. Kroes, 'Die Walthersage', *PBB* LXXVII (Halle, 1955), 77 ff.).

[6] In the Þs, the attack by Elsungr and his men on Þiðrekr, Hildibrandr, and Herrað during their return to Amlungaland from Attila's court also appears to be modelled on similar events in **W** (see Hildebrant, p. 76).

[7] This reflects the grim suggestion by Waltharius, after the second fight in **W**, that Hagano should avoid eating roast boar-meat and stick to porridge (see Hagen (1), pp. 58 f.).

[8] A reflection of Guntharius s injury in **W** (see Gunther (1), p. 54).

[9] Hermann Schneider, 'Das Epos von Walther und Hildegunde', *GRM* XIII (1925), 385 ff., connects the latter part of this Polish version with the postulated campaign of Walther against the Poles in the lost Walther-epic, which can be deduced from Biterolf's exploits against the Poles and the capture of their king and queen in **B**; the fights between Valtari and Vildiver-Vizleo in the Þs, and between Walczerz and Wislaw in the Polish version, support this (see Wisselau, pp. 144 f.).

[10] The author of **W** falsely relates the name to OHG *wald*, 'forest' for Waltharius's Saxon opponent, Ekivrid, compares him with a wood-spirit: 'Saltibus assuetus faunus mihi quippe videris' (763).

OE form *Wealdhere* occurring in 6th- and 7th-cent. topographical names (Binz, 218 f.); rare in ON: *Valdarr*, ruler of the Danes, mentioned in Hlöð (*CPB* I. 349)[1] and a late Skjöldungar genealogy (*CPB* II. 522), also appears as the suitor of Guðrún in Gðr II 19, 1.

The pn *Gautier* (*Gualter*) is frequent in OFr *ch.d.g.* (Langlois, 266 ff.); in the *Chanson de Roland*, 'Gualter del Hum' (v. 803, etc.), nephew of Ogier le Danois, is one of Roland's men.[2]

It is probable that traditions about Walther existed in South-West German in the 8th or 9th cent. (Baesecke, *Vorgeschichte*, 434; see also Fr. von der Leyen, *Das Heldenliederbuch Karls des Großen* (München, 1954), 120, regarding motifs of the Walther story in certain ON sagas): the original story may well have been about the pursuit of an eloping pair, and a combat between abductor and guardian, similar to the story of Hilde (see Hilde (1), pp. 73 f.), and Hagen could most probably have been Walther's opponent. A historical setting has been supplied later by making the eloping pair fugitives from Hunnish captivity, the attack on them by Gunther, motivated by greed for the treasure altering Hagen's role to one in which he suffers a conflict of loyalties.

Apparently the name of the scene of the fight (by a rock face in *Waldere*, at the Waskenstein in **N**), and thence Walther's byname ('von dem Wasgenstein' **Rg(A)**, 'af Vaskasteini' Þs) and possibly his sword's name (Waske in **B**) derive,[3] became associated not only with the Vosges (*Vosagus* in **W**: OHG *Wascgo silva* 802, *Wesge, Wasge* 992, *Wascgo* 992 (Bach II, § 431)), but also with Aquitaine as the land of the Basques (*Equitania* is glossed '*uuasconolant*' in the early 8th cent.: Steinmeyer-Sievers Gl. III. 610, 5),[4] although the route from the land of the Huns to this region would not normally pass through the Vosges (MHG *Waskenwalt*, cf. **WuH** above); hence Walther's realm in medieval German tradition fluctuates between France and Spain: Aquitania (**W**), Spanje (**N**, **WuH**, B), Kerlingen (**A**, **B**, **Rg(D)**, **DF**, **AHb**); Lengers (**DF**, **Rs**), Arragûn (**B**), and Nâvarren (**B**).[5]

The author of **W** elaborated on the traditional fight, using classical models, especially the *Thebais* of Statius (Panzer, *Wasichenstein*, 13 ff.), and his version was incorporated into the *vita* of another Waltharius connected with the monastery of Novalese (see above). The lost MHG Walther-epic, based on traditional material as well as on **W**, can only be surmised from fragments (**WuH**) and from its influence on other epics (**N**, **B**); together with **W**, it is the source for Þs and for the Polish version, the latter adding motifs from elsewhere. It is not possible to decide whether the OE *Waldere* fragments represent an archaizing reflection of **W** or whether *Waldere* is indeed a short epic deriving from an original early lay similar to the source of **W**.

WANDELBAR von Francrîche (France) Attends Wolfdietrich's wedding with Sîdrât (1).

ref: **Wd(D)** VIII. 333, 4 (e *wandels bar*, a *wendelnar, wendewar*, bc *wedelfar, z adelgar*); **Wd(Gr)** 1873, 2

pn: possibly a corruption of *Wandelmar* (6th-cent. WFr, 8th-cent. German: Förstemann I. 1529). *Wandelber* is recorded in the 13th cent. near Zürich (Socin, 448), and possibly represents a byname based on MHG *wandelbære*, 'changeable, fickle' (ibid. 617).

WÄRBEL(ÎN) (WERBEL(ÎN))
Etzel's minstrel: he and his fellow minstrel Swämmel are sent to Worms with the invitation to Gunther and his brothers to visit Hungary; Kriemhilt, Etzel's queen, instructs the minstrels to make sure that Hagen comes too. When the fighting breaks out between the Huns and Burgundians in Etzel's hall, Hagen cuts off Wärbel's right hand for bringing the treacherous invitation.

ref: **N** 1374, 1

In ON Eddic tradition, the name of the messenger bearing the treacherous invitation from Atli to Gunnarr varies: Knéfröðr (Akv 1, 4; Dr prose, p. 223); Vingi (Dr prose, p. 223; Am 4, 2; Völss ch. 35).[6] In Am and Völss Vingi confuses the warning runes sent by Guðrún to her brothers (see Kriemhilt, p. 20); when Gunnarr and his men arrive in Húnaland, Vingi belatedly warns them

---

[1] Omitted as a late accretion in the Neckel-Kuhn edition (1962) of the *Edda*.

[2] Wilhelm Tavernier, 'Waltharius, Carmen de prodicione Guenonis und Rolandsepos', *ZffrSL* XLII (1914), 56, considers that Gualter derives from **W**. He appears in the MHG *Rolandslied* of Pfaffe Konrad (c. 1170) as 'Walthere der wigant' (v. 1189).

[3] The Wasichenstein, possibly a sharp rock (cf. OHG (*h*)*was*, 'sharp'), localized as a specific rock formation near Obersteinbach, between the Palatinate and Alsace. In the 14th cent. the Wasichenstein family, which can be traced back to 1227, had six silver hands on its coat of arms (Panzer, *Wasichenstein*, 11 f., 54).

[4] Cf. Hertrîch, a smith in Wasconje lant in **B** (p. 71).

[5] The 16th-cent. Spanish ballad *Asento está Gaiferos* contains features suggesting an association with the story of Walther (R. Menéndez Pidal, *Romancero Hispánica* (Madrid, 1953, vol. I), 286 ff.); it is impossible to say whether these associations derive from **W** or from an earlier Germanic lay known to the Visigoths.

[6] A messenger's name; cf. OHG pn *Wingiboto*, recorded in the 9th cent. (Raßmann, *DHS* I. 242), possibly based on Gmc. \**wîha*- with -*n*-infix, 'sacred' (see Kaufmann, 404, and Kluge, *EWb*, 849, under *weihen*).

against entering Atli's hall,[1] but they cut him down.

In Þs, Attila's messengers are unnamed (II. 280, 10–281, 19): Grimilldr gives them secret instructions before they leave.

pn: possibly a descriptive name based on MHG *werben*, 'strive, beg', with perhaps an association with MHG *wirbel*, 'plectrum' (Müllenhoff, *ZE*, 312).

## WASKE
A sword: used by Îrinc in **N** and by Walther in **B**.

ref: **B** 12286 (MS. *Waschen*); **N** m 2033, 2 n 2051, 4 (B *Waschen*, C *wasechen*; Ih *wasgen*, a *wachsen*, d *wahen*, D *valken*)

pn: probably based on OHG (*h*)*was*, 'sharp', + suffix -*k*- (Henzen, 196), cf. the ON sword-names *Hvati*, *Langhvass* (Davidson, 177): it may be given to Walther in **B** because of his fight at the *Wasken*stein (see p. 137).

## WAẞMUOT, see WAHSMUOT (1)

## WATE (1) von Stürmen (Sturmlant)[2]
In **Ku**, this grizzled and ferocious warrior,[3] with his wide knowledge of the sea-ways, leads the expedition to win Hilde, daughter of Hagen von Îrlant, for his master Hetel von Hegelingen. In Ireland, Wate and his men give themselves out as 'merchants' exiled by Hetel. After Hôrant, by his singing, has won Hilde's love for Hetel, Wate organizes her abduction (see pp. 72 f.). Hagen overtakes Wate and the Hegelingen as they are disembarking in Wâleis; a fight ensues, and Hilde intervenes to prevent Wate's killing her father Hagen. Wate then heals the wounded (an art he has learnt 'von einem wilden wîbe' (529, 3), see Wâchilt, p. 133), and Hagen agrees to Hilde's marriage to Hetel. Wate takes part in the unsuccessful battle at Wülpensant against the Norman abductors of their daughter Kûdrûn. He is in command at the final battle against the Normans, and his war-horn that can be heard thirty miles away signals the Hegelingen army; the Normans are routed, and he beheads Gêrlint, the Norman queen, who has ill-treated Kûdrûn, and Hergart, Kûdrûn's faithless handmaiden;[4] he is restrained from destroying the Norman fortress by Fruote. He finally acts as steward at Kûdrûn's wedding to Herwîc.

In **DH**, the giants Wate von den Krichen,[5] Witolt, and Aspriôn accompany Hôrant on his expedition to Greece to win the hand of Hilde for Etene (= Hetel). On arrival in Greece, the giants terrify the townsfolk (see Hôrant, p. 80 and n. 7). Wate is described as wearing golden armour and a golden helmet, on which is a golden linden-tree (F 62, 1 f.), more like an angel than a man, 'er schein ein engel unde nicht ein man' (F 73, 2, 4).

ref: **DH** F 42, 1, 1; **Ku** 205, 1 (252, 4 *Watte*)

German literary references to Wate are limited to the 12th cent.: in Lamprecht's *Alexander* (mid 12th cent.), Wate is said to have killed Hilde's father, Hagen (see p. 61), at the battle of Wolfenwerde; in Pfaffe Konrad's *Rolandslied* (c. 1170), the Emperor Karl addresses Oigir von Denemarke as 'des Waten chunnes' (7801).[6]

In the name-list of the OE *Widsith* it is stated in line 22: 'Witta wēold Swǣfum, Wada Hælsingum'.[7] The preceding line contains the names of Hagena and Heoden (see Hagen (2) and Hetel, pp. 61, 72).[8]

Later Wade is well known in England (see Binz, 196 ff.): Walter Map (c. 1180) relates that Gado, the son of the Vandal King, is well able to handle his ship, which has brought him with ease through tempests from India to Essex, and that he defeats the Romans for King Offa. His appearance is like that of an angel, with his grey hair and splendid armour[9] (see the account of **DH** above).

Chaucer (†1400) lets Januarie remark of old women in *The Marchantes Tale*, 'They conne so michel craft on Wades boot' (1424),[10] and in his *Troilus and Criseyde*, Pandarus tells a 'tale of Wade' (III. 614).[11] Local traditions about Wade are attested in England by 'Wade's Causeway', a Roman road near Pickering, and 'Wade's Grave', a megalithic monument near Whitby (Chambers, *Widsith*, 97 f.).

In the Þs, the giant Vaði (I. 73, 18) is the son of King Villcinus (see Wilzen, p. 144) by a mermaid (II. 65, 4) (see Wâchilt, p. 133);

---

[1] It has been suggested that Eckewart has assumed this warning role in **N** (see W. Richter, 'Beiträge zur Deutung des Mittelteils des Nibelungenliedes', *ZfdA* LXXII (1935), 18).

[2] Stormarn in Schleswig-Holstein.

[3] The young Hilde hesitates to kiss him in greeting (340 f.); in battle he grinds his teeth with fury (1508).

[4] Cf. Hildebrant's execution of Kriemhilt (N 2375 f.).

[5] His connection with Greece is obscure (see Norman, *Dukus Horant*, 119 n. 81).

[6] Cf. **Ku** 1416, 3, where Hôrant is referred to as 'daz Waten künne' (Stackmann, *Kudrun*, lii f.). It should be noted that Ogier of *La Chanson de Roland* has probably also given his name to the giant Ædgæir in the Þs (see p. 7 n. 6).

[7] The Hælsingas are probably a Baltic tribe (see Malone, *Widsith* (1962), 158).

[8] See Norman, *Dukus Horant*, 115, regarding the relationship between Wada, Hagena, and Heoden here.

[9] Walter Map, *De Nugis Curialium*, ed. M. R. James (Oxford, 1914), II. xvii, 85–90.

[10] Chaucer, *Works*, 117. The name Gringalet given to Wade's boat by Speght in his edition of Chaucer's works in 1598 is that of Gawain's horse: this horse-name occurs in OFr in the 12th cent., and is probably of Celtic origin; cf. Cymric *gwyngalet*, 'white-hard' (Flutre, 97).

[11] Chaucer, *Works*, 427.

## WATE (1)

Vaði's son is Velent (MHG Wielant). Vaði wades across the Grönasund, which is nine ells deep, with Velent on his shoulders, when he is taking the child to be apprenticed to two dwarf smiths in Ballofa (I. 75, 9–76, 2); Velent is later the possessor of a marvellous boat (see Wielant, p. 142).

pn: the name is probably based on Gmc. *wað- (OHG waten, OE wadan, ON vaða, 'stride, wade') (Norman, *Dukus Horant*, 114; Kluge, *EWb*, 842).¹ It is recorded from the 7th cent. in WFr and the 8th cent. in German (Förstemann I. 1491; Müllenhoff, *ZE*, 317); 9th-cent. OE (Sweet, 154, 156, 162; Searle, 472 f.; Feilitzen, 407; Max Förster, 'Proben eines englischen Eigennamen-Wörterbuches', *GRM* XI (1923), 108).

## WATE (2) Ermenrîch's man

In the fighting against Dietrich's men at Meilân, he is killed by Dietleip.

ref: **DF** 3919

## WEIGANT von Yban

He formerly owned Ecke's sword (see Eckesahs, p. 34).

ref: **E(d)** 87, 6

pn: based on MHG *wîgant*, 'warrior': 8th-cent. German (Förstemann I. 1578).

## WELDERICH, see WALRÎCH

pn: see Walderîch, p. 134.

## WELFFEN

'der junge Welffen' = Wolfdietrich.

ref: **Wd(k)** 287, 2

pn: 9th-cent. German (Förstemann I. 937; Schlaug I. 118); recorded at Goslar in 1152 for the father of Henry the Lion; it is common later in the Bavarian ducal family (Schlaug II. 227; Bach I, § 329).

This byname is based on the equivalent of OHG *hwelf*, OS *hwelp*, 'young wolf' (Bach I, § 336. 1); it refers here to the first part of Wolfdietrich's name.

## WELSCH, WELSCHLANT, see WALHE

## WELSUNC

A sword: used by Biterolf (**B**)² and Dietleip (**B, L(D), Rg(P)**).³

ref: **B** 561 (636 H *Welfunge*, 12265 H *Welffunge*); **L(D)** 2272 (s *erklungen*, d *walsung*); **Rg(P)** 509 (Weisenuge)

In German literature outside the epics, the only reference is in the late 13th-cent. manuscript fragment of the *Ritterpreis*, where 'Wilssunk' (247) is mentioned as Dietleip's sword (W. Grimm, *DHS*, 312; Schieb–Frings, *Eneide* II. 188).

In the OE epic *Beowulf*, Sigemund, the son of Wæls (897), is termed 'Wælsing' (877).

In Eddic tradition, Völsungr (HHu II prose, p. 150; Sf prose, p. 162; Hdl 26, 2; Sk chs. 47 and 80; Skr 76; Völss ch. 2) is the name of Sigmundr's father, and the term 'Völsungar' refers to Sigmundr's kin (HHu I 52, 7; HHu II prose, p. 150; Form ch. 4; Sk chs. 51 and 80; Völss ch. 2; Þs I. 2, 8); thus Sigurðr, Sigmundr's son, is also a 'Völsungr' (Rm 18, 3; Sg 1, 3). In Völss chs. 1–2, details about the ancestry and birth of Völsungr, the father of Sigmundr, are given: he is the grandson of Sigi, the son of Óðinn (see Form ch. 4); Óðinn helps Sigi win the kingdom of Húnaland (Frakland is his realm in Form ch. 4); Rerir, Sigi's son, is childless until Óðinn sends his wife an apple: after a six years' pregnancy, the child Völsungr is cut from her body, and she dies.⁴ Völsungr weds Hljóð, the daughter of the giant Hrímniir, and she bears him the twins Sigmundr and Signý. Völsungr is killed by Signý's husband Siggeirr (see Sigemunt (1), p. 125).

pn: from *c*. 800 German (Förstemann I. 1555; Socin, 572; Müllenhoff, *ZE*, 288); possibly present in such English place-names as *Walsingham*, recorded in 1035 (Ekwall, 494). It is probably based on Gmc. *wala-, cf. Goth. *valisa*, 'select, beloved' (Holthausen, *GEWb*, 120).

Evidently the author of **B** connected this pn with a sword story.⁵

## WENDELMUOT f.

The messenger of Sêburc (2).

ref: **Rg(F)** II. 5, 1

pn: m. and f. 9th-cent. German (Förstemann I. 1529; Schlaug I. 172). It occurs for a village maiden in *Neidharts Lieder*, 29, 5.

## WENEZLÂN von Bôlân (Poland)

He fights a drawn combat with Dietrich von Bern.

---

¹ F. R. Schröder, 'Die Sage von Hetel und Hilde', *DVjs* XXXII (1958), 63 f., relates it to Gmc. *wōð- (OHG *wuoten*, 'to rage'), and thence to the god Woden, (OHG *Wuotan*, ON *Óðinn*); in this connection it may be noted that in the OE *Widsith* name-list, Wada is preceded by Witta, whose grandfather, according to Bede's *History* I, 15, II, 5, was Woden (see K. Sisam, 'Anglo-Saxon Royal Genealogies', *Proc. Brit. Acad.* XXXIX (1953), 324).

² In **B**, Biterolf uses it against Walther (561 ff.), but, by an oversight of the author, Dietleip, his son, takes his father's old sword (2157) when he sets out to look for Biterolf and uses Welsunc against him (3658); Dietleip keeps possession of it (12265).

³ Dietleip is shown bearing the sword *'Belsung'* on the frescoes at Runkelstein (late 14th cent.) (Müllenhoff, *ZE*, 386).

⁴ Cf. *Van den Machandelboom* (*KHM* no. 47), in which this motif occurs and the mother of the murderered boy also dies in childbirth.

⁵ See Sigemunt (1), p. 125, regarding the sword that Óðinn plunges into the oak-trunk at the centre of Völsungr's hall in Völss, ch. 3.

## WENEZLÂN

ref: **DuW** m 13 n 139
pn: see Witzlân
This figure possibly represents Wenzel II of Bohemia (1278–1305), who became King of Poland in 1300 (de Boor, *GDL* III. ii. 177).

WERBEL(ÎN), see **WÄRBEL(ÎN)**

## WERINHARDUS
Descended from Pandarus: the third of Guntharius's men killed by Waltharius.

ref: **W** 725 (P *uuirinhardus*, etc.)

pn: 8th-cent. German (Förstemann I. 1543; Schlaug I. 173; see also Kögel I. ii. 307).

## WERNHÊR (1) von Wernhêres marke
In **Wd(D)** a wealthy burgher of Tervîs (Treviso) and ruler of Wernhêres marke,[1] father of Âmîe (see Wolfdietrich, p. 149 n. 11).
He is among Ermenrîch's men opposing Dietrich in **DF**, and is killed at Rabene (Ravenna) in **Rs**.

ref: **AHb** p. 6, 2; **DF** 2432; **Rs** 848, 1; **Wd(D)** VII. 138, 1; **Wd(Gr)** 1445, 1

pn: 7th-cent. WFr; 9th-cent. German (Förstemann I. 1544 f.; II. ii. 1246; Socin, 40; Schlaug I. 173).

The March of Ancona was ruled by a 'Wernhêr' as early as 1094; many of his successors bore the same name; the region was known, therefore, as *marcia Guarnerii* in the 13th cent. (Jänicke, *DHB* IV. xv).

## WERNHÊR (2) = GÊRE (5)
Gêre, a heathen pirate, takes this name when he is forcibly baptized by Wolfdietrich. He fights with Wolfdietrich in the Holy Land against the heathen, where he kills Treferîs.

ref: **Wd(D)** V. 98, 1; **Wd(Gr)** 935, 1

WIBURG, see **BÎBUNC (1)**

## WICHART (WITSCHACH)[2]
Dietrich's man: he is killed by the Burgundians in **N**, by Gunther in the **Kl**. He is mentioned together with Ritschart (Rîchart), Gêrbart (Gêrhart), and Helferîch (1) in **A**, **B**, and **N**; in **B** he is the brother of Gêrbart.[3]

ref: **A** 73, 3 (MS. *wytzschach*); **B** 5249; **Kl** 1775; **N** 2281, 1

pn: 8th-cent. German (Förstemann I. 1583; II. ii. 1321; Schlaug I. 176; II. 161; see Ploß, 57, regarding this pn among the retainers of the Babenberg dukes of Austria); 7th-cent. OE (Searle, 489). W. Grimm, *DHS*, 263, takes 'Wytzschach' to be a Slavonic name.

## WÎCHÊR (WÎCKÊR) (1) Dietrich's man
In **A** and **B** he is among Dietrich's men opposing Ermenrîch; in **Rs**, 'Wîckêr von Kunstenôbel'[4] appears among Etzel's men aiding Dietrich against Ermenrîch.

ref: **A** 76, 1 (MS. *wiker*); **B** 7795 (MS. *Wickher*; 9261 MS. *Wicker*); **Rs** 72, 1 (R *Wichker*, A *Weicher*)

pn: two names, based on OHG *gêr*, *kêr*, 'spear', and *heri*, 'army', respectively become confused in the records: 8th-cent. German (Förstemann I. 1582, 1584; II. ii. 1321; Schlaug I. 176; II. 161) and OE (Searle, 490).

## WÎCHÊR (WÎCKÊR) (2) Ermenrîch's man
He fights Gotel at Rabene.

ref: **Rs** 708, 5 (A *Weicker*)

## WÎCMAN
Dietrichs' man

ref: **DF** 5623

pn: 8th-cent. German (Förstemann I. 1586; II. ii. 1322; Socin, 42; Schlaug I. 176).

## WÎCNANT
Dietrich's man: killed by Gunther in the **Kl**;[5] in **B** he is the brother of Wolfbrant and Ritschart and bears Dietrich's standard against Gunther's men at Worms.

ref: **A** 76, 1; **B** 6355; **Kl** 1767

pn: 9th-cent. German (Förstemann I. 1587; II. ii. 1323; Schlaug II. 162).

## WÎCRAM
The leader of twelve giants in the service of Nîtgêr at Mûter: he seizes Dietrich and imprisons him at Mûter; he takes Dietrich's food, and excuses his hostility to Dietrich with the allegation that Dietrich's men, Hildebrant, Witege, Wolfhart, and Dietleip, have killed two hundred of his friends in Britanje (**V(h)** 377).[6] Dietrich kills Wîcram's son, Grandengrûs, and then Wîcram himself, when his men led by Hildebrant arrive at Mûter and kill the other giants.[7]

ref: **V(h)** 316, 1; **V(w)** 504, 1

pn: 8th-cent. German (Förstemann I. 1585; II. ii. 1322; Socin, 173).

also experiences difficulties with giants in OE *Waldere*. Regarding the conflict with giants in Brittany (or Britain?), see pp. 28 f.
[7] The other giants named are: Adelrant, Asprîân, Boemrîân, Vellenwalt, Velsenstôz, Galerant, Senderlîn, Ulsenbrant, Wolfrât, and Hülle. Dietrich and his men subsequently kill further giants on the way from Mûter to Jeraspunt; they are named: Bitterkrût, Bitterbûch, Klingelbolt, Videlnstôz, Gîselrant, Glockenbôz, Hôhermuot, Rûmedenwalt, Rûmeroc, Schellenwalt, Wolvesmage, and Schrôtenhelm.

---

[1] = Spoleto, Camerino, and Ancona in northern Italy.
[2] Cf. Rîchart (Ritschart).
[3] In Wolfram von Eschenbach's *Willehalm*, a Witschart appears together with a Gêrhart (13, 16; 25, 10).
[4] His title is thought to derive from **Wd**, in which Wolfdietrich is associated with Constantinople (see Jänicke, *DHB* III. lxix).
[5] Possible evidence for the existence of a Dietrich-epic *c.* 1200 (Schneider, *Kl. Schr.* 22).
[6] Viðga (MHG Witege) kills a giant during Þiðrekr's Bertangaland expedition in Þs; Þeodrīc

## WIDERGRÎN (BALDEGRÎN)
A robber killed by Wolfdietrich (see Rûmelher).

ref: **Wd(D)** v. 6, 1; **Wd(Gr)** 844, 1 (Baldegrîn); **Wd(w)** 786, 1 (*Baldegrin*)

## WIDOLT, see WITOLT

## WIELANT
The smith, father of Witege (**A, B, L, Rg, V**), whose armour, helmet Limme, and sword Mimminc he has made (**B** 157 ff.: see Mîme, p. 94), and to whom he has given the horse Schemminc (**Rg(D)** 316 f.); Waltharius's armour (**W** 965),[1] Ecke's helmet (**E(d)** 89, 2 f.), and the sword given by Helferîch (5) to Dietrich (**V(w)** 402, 3) are attributed to Wielant's workmanship.

According to **AHb**, he first serves King Elberich at Gloggensachsen (see p. 3 n. 4), and then King Hertwich, by whose daughter he has two sons, Wittich and Wittichowe (see Hertnît (2), pp. 70 f., Witege, pp. 145 ff., and Witegouwe, p. 147).

ref: **A** 262, 1; **AHb** p. 3, 16; **B** 157, 3; **L(A)** 21; **L(D)** 259; **L(K)II** 688; **Rg(A)** 239, 2; **Rg(C)** 1333; **Rg(D)** m 317, 1; **V(h)** 652, 13; **V(w)** 402, 3; **W** m 264 n 965 (BPE *Vuielandia fabrica,* T *walandia* f.)

Outside the epics, German references to Wielant are sparse.[2] In the 14th-cent. *Friedrich von Schwaben*, the hero uses the name 'Wielant' when he is searching for his beloved, Amelburg, who has been changed into a dove; he finds her bathing with two other maidens in a spring and steals their clothing, which he returns to them on being allowed to wed Amelburg; she dies nine years later.[3]

The OE poem *Deor* tells of the sinew-bonds[4] laid on Wēlund by Nīðhād (1–5), of the pregnancy of Beadohild, and of the death of her brothers (8–12); in *Waldere* it is known that Wēland's son, Widia, is related to Nīðhād (II. 8 f.) (see Witege,

p. 145). These oblique references to a knowledge of the 'Wielandsage' in England are supplemented pictorially by the carving on the left front panel of the *Franks Casket*, a whalebone casket first recorded in the 19th cent. in the possession of a family at Auzon, Haute-Loire, France, the runic inscriptions of which suggest a Northumbrian provenance *c*. 700 (see A. S. Napier, 'The *Franks Casket*', *Furnival Miscellany* (Oxford, 1901), 362–81; Baesecke, *Vorgeschichte,* 297 f.; Elliott, *Runes,* 98 f.; Düwel, *Runenkunde,* 46 f.): the smith stands with bent legs holding a head over an anvil by a pair of tongs in his left hand; a headless body lies on the floor below; with his right hand he receives an object (a broken ring?) from a standing woman (Beadohild?), who is accompanied by another woman (her maid?) holding a bag; what appear to be wings are hanging on the wall;[5] on the far right a man (Ægil?) is catching birds.[6]

Bēowulf's armour and the sword Mimming carried by Waldere are the workmanship of Wēland (*Beowulf,* 455; *Waldere* I. 2); in the ME romances of *Horn* (14th cent.) and *Torrent of Portugal* (15th cent.), he is famed as a sword-smith (W. Grimm, *DHS,* 306, 476), and his skill as a goldsmith is so well known that King Alfred (†899), in his translation of Boethius's *De Consolatione Philosophiae* (v. 1), replaces 'fidelis ossa Fabricii' with 'ðæs wīsan Wēlandes bān, ðæs goldsmiðes ðe wæs gēo mǣrost' (cit. W. Grimm, *DHS,* 31), and in a Latin poem by Geoffrey of Monmouth (12th cent.), King Rhydderich of Cumberland is said to have given a goblet fashioned by him to Merlin, 'pocula quae sculpsit Guielandus in urbe Sigenis'[7] (cit. W. Grimm, *DHS,* 45).

In the ON Vkv of the Edda, three brothers, Völundr (prose, p. 116, and str. 2, 10), Slagfiðr, and Egill, find three valkyries, Hlaðguðr, Hervor, and Ölrún, spinning linen by a lake, with their swan-garments (ON *álptarhamir*) lying near by:[8] the brothers take

---

[1] The smith's mark is on it (**W** 264); see Davidson, 45 f., regarding the marks made by sword-makers.

[2] A last echo of the 'Wielandsage' is thought to be the account of a Sachsenwald forester published in 1876, according to which a king retains an excellent smith named Mêland or Ammêland in his service by having his eyes put out (W. Grimm, *DHS,* 492 f.).

[3] The seizure of clothing from a supernatural being, whom the hero marries, but who departs or dies later, is a common folk-tale theme (cf. *Der Trommler, KHM* no. 193; Bolte–Polívka III. 407 ff.). Cf. also Hagen s encounter with the 'merwîp' Hadeburc (p. 57).

[4] 'seonobende' (6) could refer either to the hamstringing or to the fettering of Wēland (Malone, *Deor,* 6).

[5] On the Leeds Cross (10th cent.), the alleged figure of Wēland appears to have wings strapped to the back (see *The History of York,* ed. W. Page (London, 1912), 119 f.).

[6] This is probably the smith's brother, whose name is Egill in ON, for the name 'Ægili' is carved in runes on the lid of the casket, where Ægil's own story may well be depicted (see de Boor, *Kl. Schr.* II. 132 ff.; Baesecke, *Vorgeschichte,* 297 f., regarding Egill's role in the 'Wielandsage'). The pn *Baduhilt* occurs for the wife of the Frankish King, Chlodvic II (7th cent.), and in German documents from the 8th cent. (Förstemann I. 229); the names *Beadohild* and *Nīðhād* have not been found in OE documents (see Hertnît (2), pp. 70 f.), whereas *Wēland* and *Ægil* are frequent in OE place-names (Binz, 189; see also p. 143).

[7] Siegen, *c*. 30 miles east of Cologne.

[8] The prose prologue makes the brothers the sons of the Finnish King and their wives the daughters of the French King (Kjárr af Vallandi . . . Hlöðvér (= Clovis?)). These names are appellative: Slagfiðr, 'beat-wing', Egill, 'quick', Hlaðguðr, 'valkyrie with the headband ornament', Hervor, 'protection of the army', Ölrún, 'powerful spell', the first two women having bynames: svanhvít, 'swan-white', alvitr, 'very wise' (see Kögel I. i, 100; Jiriczek, *DHS* (1898), 21; de Vries, *Altn. Litg.* I. 56).

them to wife, but the women depart after nine years; while his brothers search for their wives, Völundr, the descendant of elves (*álfa ljóði* 10, 3), stays in his hut, setting gems in gold and making arm-rings. The men of Níðuðr take one of the rings and then fetter Völundr while he is asleep; he awakes to see his sword at Níðuðr's belt and his wife's arm-ring on the arm of Böðvildr, the King's daughter; at the instigation of Níðuðr's queen, Völundr is hamstrung and forced to serve Níðuðr as a smith on the island of Sævarstaðr. Völundr beheads the two sons of the King while they are inspecting his treasure-chest,[1] and throws their bodies under the bellows-pit; he makes goblets, set with gold and silver, from their skulls for the King,[2] gems from their eyeballs for the Queen, and brooches from their teeth for Böðvildr. Böðvildr breaks the arm-ring and goes to Völundr's smithy to have it mended, but he gives her beer and then rejoices at having taken revenge (he has evidently drugged the beer and ravished her). He rises into the air,[3] and alights on the wall of the King's hall; having obtained oaths from Níðuðr to ensure the safety of his wife and future child, he tells the King that he has killed his sons and that Böðvildr is pregnant. Níðuðr sends Þakkráðr to fetch the princess for questioning.[4]

In Þs, Velent (I. 2, 8), son of Vaði (see Wate, pp. 138 f.), is first apprenticed to Mimir (see Mîme, p. 94) in Húnaland (= Saxony), then to two dwarf smiths in the mountains at Ballofa (a cave near Balve, Westphalia): he kills the smiths with his father's sword and takes their treasure, then floats down the Weser and out to sea to Jutland, in a hollowed-out tree-trunk equipped with glass portholes, and takes service with King Niðungr. The royal smith Amelias becomes jealous, so a contest is arranged, in which Velent is to make a sword sharp enough to pierce armour made by Amelias: Velent forges the sword Mimungr,[5] cleaves Amelias to the girdle, and replaces him as court smith. During a military campaign Niðungr is without his 'victory stone';[6] Velent fetches it from the King's palace, five days' journey away, by riding the distance in twelve hours on his horse Skemmingr, but is refused the promised reward, the hand of Niðungr's daughter (named Heren in MS. A, I. 120, (9)). In revenge Velent tries to poison the King, for which he is hamstrung and kept in bondage to make gold and silver ornaments. Velent now kills Niðungr's two young sons and throws their bodies under the bellows; he sets their skulls in silver and gold as goblets for the King. The King's daughter breaks a ring and visits Velent's workshop with her maid to have it mended: Velent first deflowers her and then repairs the ring. Velent's brother Egill, an excellent archer,[7] shoots birds so that Velent can make a flying-garment (*flygil* I. 125, 18)[8] from their feathers. Velent puts on the flying-garment and flies to the topmost tower of Niðungr's castle, whence he tells Niðungr of his vengeance. Niðungr orders Egill to shoot Velent, and the archer punctures the bladder filled with the blood of the murdered princes concealed under Velent's left arm. Niðungr, seeing the blood, is deceived, but Velent flies back to Sioland (Zealand in Denmark). Niðungr's successor permits Velent to marry the princess, by whom he has a son named Viðga, whom he equips with armour, the sword Mimungr, a helmet, and the horse Skemmingr (see Witege, pp. 145 f.).

In the Danish ballads *Kong Diderik og hans Kæmper*, *Kong Diderik i Birtingsland*, and *Ulv van Jærn* (*DgF* I. 94 ff., 124 ff., 145 ff.), Viderick (MHG Witege) is the son of Verland (MHG Wielant), and in the B-version of the first-mentioned ballad (op. cit. I. 100), his mother's name is Buodell (15, 3; *Bodild* in Vedel's version, op. cit. I. 119).[9] In the Faroese ballad *Risin í Holmgörðum* (W. Grimm, *DHS*, 368), Virgar (MHG Witege) obtains the sword Mimring from his father's grave-mound.

In OFr epic, Galant (Galans) is famous as an armourer and sword-smith (Langlois, 247; W. Grimm, *DHS*, 46 f.; Benary, 53 ff.).

---

[1] The method of murdering children by shutting the lid of a chest on them is recorded of Merovingian royalty by Gregory of Tours (cit. Baesecke, *Vorgeschichte*, 56); the motif occurs in the folk-tale *Van den Machandelboom* (*KHM*, no. 47; Bolte–Polívka II. 422), which shows several other similarities to the story of Wieland.

[2] See p. 20 and n. 5.

[3] The Ardre Stone VIII (*c*. 800) of Götland, Sweden, shows the smith in the shape of a bird, his smith's tools, and two headless bodies of the boys (see Hauck, *Bilderdenkmäler*, 359); the smith in bird-shape is also depicted on the Klinte Hunnige Stone I (see von See, *GHS*, 120, plate).

[4] See Dancrât, p. 23.

[5] He forges this famous sword by filing it down and feeding the filings to birds, and then reforging them from the droppings (see Altheim I. 197 ff., Davidson, 159 ff., regarding this process).

[6] ON *sigrsteinn* from MHG *sigelstein*, *sigestein*, 'amulet' (J. de Vries, 'Bemerkungen zur Wielandsage', *Genzmer Festschrift* (1952), 175).

[7] Niðungr tests Egill by making him shoot an apple from his son's head; Egill succeeds, but keeps two arrows for use against Niðungr in case of failure (Þs I. 123 f.; see de Boor, *Kl. Schr*. II. 132 ff., regarding Egill and the 'Tellsage').

[8] The heading of this section of the Þs reads 'Velent gerir fiaðrham' (I. 125, 15), which suggests that '*flygil*' (MHG *vlügel*, 'wing') is taken to be a feathered garment (OS *feðerhamo*). Velent has his brother Egill test the *flygil*, but tells him to land with the wind, so that he shall crash, lest he fly off with it when he discovers its excellence (see de Boor, op. cit. 135, regarding this Ikaros-motif).

[9] Cf. OE Beadohild and ON Böðvildr above.

pn: 8th-cent. German (Förstemann I. 1553 f.; Socin, 571, 638; Schlaug II. 160)¹—for smiths in the 12th cent. (Müllenhoff, ZE, 361) and place-names from the 9th cent. (Förstemann II. ii. 1338; Raßmann, DHS II. 267 ff.); 9th-cent. Lb (Bruckner, 320). It occurs in English place-names, the most famous being that of *Wayland's Smithy*, a megalithic tomb near Lambourne in Berkshire, first recorded in a charter of 955 (*Welandes Smidthe*).² Traditions about Wieland's smithy are also attested by Danish place-names (W. Grimm, *DHS*, 369; Müllenhoff, *ZE*, 264).

Two forms of the name occur:

(1) with Gmc. *ē* in the root syllable: MHG *Wielant*, OE *Wēland*; possibly related to the same root as ON *vél*, 'cunning, deceit', and *véla*, 'create, construct with art', cf. ON *smidvéla*, 'art of metal-work' (Bach, § 72).

(2) with Gmc. *a* in the root syllable: ON *Völundr*; cf. also *walandia* of the Trier MS. of **W**. Distortion has probably taken place in transmission to the North; OFr *Galant* derives, via Norman *Galander*, ultimately from the ON form (see Heusler, *Heldennamen*, 97 f.; E. Schröder, *DNK*, 86 f.).

This participial name is, indeed, used appellatively, having the meaning 'cunning craftsman', like that of the Greek divine smith Daedalos; cf. 'ofnar völondom', 'woven by subtle craftsmen' (Hm 7, 3).³

Traditions about divine smiths are worldwide (Betz, *Aufriß* III (1962), 1919), but there are very striking parallels in the 'Wielandsage' to the Greek myths of Hephaestos (Vulcan), whom Zeus casts from Olympos, so that he breaks both his legs, and who attempts to ravish Athene when she enters his workshop; and of Daedalos, whom Minos of Crete confines in the labyrinth,⁴ which Daedalos himself has constructed, and who escapes by fashioning wings from birds' feathers.⁵ Such classical influences would be consistent with an origin for the story among the Rugians, who were settled on the Middle Danube and in contact with the Roman world in the late 5th and early 6th cent.⁶ (see H. Rosenfeld, 'Wielandlied, Lied von Frau Helchen Söhnen und Rabenschlachtlied',

*PBB* LXXVII (Tübingen, 1955), 204 ff.); evidence for the existence of the 'Wielandsage' among them at this time is suggested by an episode supposed to have taken place *c.* 480 and recorded in the *Vita S. Severini*, by Eugippius (*c.* 511): Gisa, the wife of Felectheus, the Rugian King, has kept barbarian smiths in confinement to make royal ornaments; the smiths seize the King's son, Fridericus (see Friderîch (2), p. 47), but, on the intervention of St. Severinus, free the boy in exchange for their liberty (cit. Baesecke, *Vorgeschichte*, 300).

The 'Sage' appears to have developed fully in North Germany and to have spread thence to the British Isles and Scandinavia. Certain motifs and names suggest that the Franks had a part in its transmission to the North (Rosenfeld, op. cit. 209); the swanmaiden prologue, possibly brought in through the flying motif, was probably introduced in North Germany after the story reached England. The role played by the smith's brother, depicted on the *Franks Casket* and recounted in detail in the Þs may well have been suppressed by the poet of Vkv (see von See, *GHS*, 114).

WÎGÂLEIS

Aids Hetel against Sîfrit (3) von Môrlant.

ref: **Ku** 582, 1 (MS. *wygolaises* gen.)

pn: probably derives from that of the Arthurian hero (see below).

WIGOLEIß

Arthurian hero; thought to have lived at the same time as Siegfried.

ref: **gS** p. 64, 3 (*Wigoleiß*)

pn: that of the hero of *Wigalois* by Wirnt von Grafenberg (1202–5).

WÎGOLT (1) von Zæringen (Zähringen, near Freiburg, Breisgau?)

Dietwart's man.

ref: **DF** 558

pn: 11th-cent. German (Förstemann I. 1588). It occurs for a peasant in *Neidharts Lieder*, 102, 6.

---

¹ *Wielant* (*Welant*) occurs in association with *Witigo* (*Witigovvo*) in two St. Gall documents of 864, but this may well be fortuitous (see Müllenhoff, *ZE*, 307; E. Schröder, *DNK*, 93 ff.).

² W. Grimm, *DHS*, 370, quotes a letter by Francis Wise of 1738 referring to a 'popular tradition', that a wayfarer whose horse had cast a shoe could tether it to the tomb, leave a groat on the cap-stone, and return later to find his horse shod and the groat gone. Professor R. J. C. Atkinson assures me in a letter that no coin earlier than 1850 was found during excavation of the site in 1962–3, a total of only five coins being found (see R. J. C. Atkinson, 'Wayland's Smithy', *Antiquity* XXXIX (1965), 126–33, for the report of the excavation).

³ The original significance of the name is apparently known to the compiler of Þs, who

states: 'Viðga var svn Velenz þess Væringer kall Volund firir hagleics sakar' (I. 360, 4), i.e. 'Viðga was the son of Velent, whom the Scandinavians call Völund because of his handicraft.'

⁴ The connection is known in ON, where *völundarhús* is the term for a labyrinth (cit. Raßmann, *DHS* II. 258).

⁵ On the *Franks Casket*, and in the Þs, the smith, like Daedalos, constructs wings: shapechanging by the use of a feather-garment (ON *fiaðrhamr*) is probably a later development, as in Vkv and on the Ardre Stone VIII (see p. 142 n. 3), possibly influenced by the swan-maiden prologue.

⁶ A Burgundian (Baesecke, *Vorgeschichte*, 303; Betz, *Aufriß* III (1962), 1919) and a Gothic origin (de Vries, *Altn. Litg.* I. 56 ff.; Genzmer *Festschrift*, 187) have also been put forward.

## WÎGOLT (2) Etzel's man
Aids Dietrich against Ermenrîch.

ref: **DF** 5159

## WILDUNC von Biterne (Viterbo), see GÊRWART

pn: 9th-cent. German (Förstemann I. 1591; Schlaug I. 178; Socin, 42, 173). It occurs for a peasant in *Neidharts Lieder*, 102, 6.

## WILHER
A giant in the service of Belmunt: Wolfdietrich kills him.

ref: **Wd(D)** IV. 19, 1; **Wd(Gr)** 407, 1

pn: 6th-cent. WFr and Lb, 8th-cent. German (Förstemann I. 1600 f.; Schlaug I. 179); 8th-cent. OE (Searle, 497).

## WILLUNG, see BÎBUNC (1)

## WILZEN(LANT)
Ermenrîch has sent his son Friderîch 'ze Wilzen lant'.

ref: **DF** 2460 (A *Vilze*)

The Marner's reference (13th cent.), 'war komen sî der Wilzen diet' (W. Grimm, *DHS*, 179 f.), suggests that the Wilzi featured in epic tradition.

In Þs, Villcinus (I. 44, 4; II. 61, 10) conquers Villcinaland (I. 44, 6; II. 61, 12) as well as Holmgarðr (= Russia). After Villcinus's death, Hertnið conquers Villcinaland, and his son Osanctrix succeeds him (see Ôserîch, p. 103). On the advice of Sifka, Erminrikr sends his son Friðrekr to demand tribute from Osanctrix; Friðrekr is killed by a noble in Villcinaland in league with Sifka (see Ermenrîch, p. 38).

pn: the *Wilzi* (OS *Wilti*, Lat. *Veletabi*) were a Slav people living between the Elbe and Oder; the name was extended to all Slavs in the area (Zeuß, 655 ff.; Paff, 220), with whom the Germans, especially the Saxons, were at war from the 8th to the 12th cent. (Müllenhoff, *ZE*, 340 f.).[1]

## WINDISCH adj.
'daz aller schœnste windisch wîp' = the Wendish wife of King Bodislau von Priuzen (**B** 1479, 1676 f.).

ref: **B** 1479

pn: the Wends (OHG *Winida*, Lat. *Venedi*) bear a name, originally applied to all Slavs by the Germanic peoples, but later restricted to the Slavonic tribes living between Holstein and the Vistula (Zeuß, 67 ff., 265 ff., 592 ff.).[2]

## WINELINT, see GOLDRÛN and SIGELINT (2)

pn: 8th-cent. German (Förstemann I. 1615).

## WISSELAU
A bear: he kills a giant on the sea-shore, and the giant's leader Espriaen (see Asprîân, p. 7) demands compensation from the bear's master, Gernout (see Gêrnôt (3), p. 50), who states that there are four similar bears on their ship. Gernout then clothes Wisselau in a four-quartered coat, and they accompany King Karl to Espriaen's castle, where the bear, on Gernout's instructions 'in gargoenischer tale', i.e. Gascon, a secret language (516), throws the master cook Brugigal into a caldron of broth and devours him. This intimidates the hostile giants.

ref: **BW** 1

In Þs, Vildiver (I. 250, 10),[3] whose companion Viðga (see Witege, p. 146) has been captured by Viðolfr, a giant in the service of King Osanctrix of Villcinaland, has himself sewn into a bear's skin in full armour;[4] he is then led on a chain to Osanctrix's court. The King wishes to bait 'Vizleo', the dancing 'bear' (I. 256, 11); Vildiver then kills twelve dogs and the two giants, Avæntroð and Viðolfr (see Ebenrôt, p. 32, and Witolt, p. 148).[5] Viðga breaks loose and the heroes ultimately return to Þiðrekr at Bern. In Þiðrekr's final battle against Erminrikr, Vildiver and Valtari (see Walther, p. 136) kill each other.[6] A boar and a bear are depicted on Vildiver's shield.[7]

pn: possibly based on Slavonic *Václav*, of which *Wenzel* is the Germanized form, perhaps a popular bear-name (Martin, *Wisselauwe*, 68).

The folk-tale about a helpful bear driving a demon from a haunted house is well known in northern Europe:[8] the 13th-cent. German version in verse, *Von einem schretel und von*

---

[1] Helferîch (3) dies doing God's work against the heathen beyond the Elbe (**R** 469 ff.).
[2] In the *Kaiserchronik*, the Wends (MHG Winde) are among the peoples led by Dietrich against Ôtacher (see p. 28).
[3] The saga-man explains Vildiver's name as the German for 'villdigolltr (ON *villigöltr*, 'wild boar') (Þs I. 339 f.). See Martin, *Wisselauwe*, 67 f., regarding the possible confusion of OHG *wildipero*, 'wild bear', with OS *wildeður*, 'wild boar'.
[4] W. Grimm, *DHS*, 33 f., suggests that Vildiver's gold arm-ring enables him to turn into a bear originally (cf. ON *berserkr*), and Höfler, *Sakralkönigtum*, 192 n. 411, characteristically assumes the ring to be that of a warrior dedicated to Óðinn.
[5] In Version 1 he also kills Osanctrix (see Ôserîch, p. 103).
[6] In the Polish version of Walther's story, Walczerz (= Walther) kills *Wislaw*, the lover of Helgunda (= Hildegunt): see p. 136.
[7] The saga-man interprets the boar as the symbol of a roving warrior, and the bear as commemorating Vildiver's bear disguise (Þs I. 339 f.).
[8] The main area of incidence is east central German, although Norway is a likely region of origin (see Röhrich, *Erzählungen* I. 1–26, 235–43). Bēowulf and Grettir, men of bear-like natures, also defeat house-haunting demons (see Chambers, *Beowulf*, 48 ff., 365 ff.; Klaeber, *Beowulf*, xiii ff., regarding the ON analogues to Bēowulf's fights with Grendel and his mother).

*einem wazzerbern* (Röhrich, *Erzählungen* I. 1–5), relates how a bear-keeper spends the night in a haunted house, where his bear mauls the demon haunting it (MHG *schrat, schretel*). The demon departs for ever when the owner of the house tells it that the large 'cat' has had five kittens. This tale has apparently been brought into the 'Karlssage' (**BW**) and also into the 'Dietrichsage' (Þs); in both cases the 'tame' bear (in **BW** a bear dressed like a man, in Þs a man disguised as a bear) kills giants subordinate to Asprîân, and has a similar name (**BW** Wisselau; Þs Vizleo).

## WITEGE

Son of Wielant and companion of Heime: his father has made him the sword Mimminc (**A, B, L, Rg(AD), V**) and the helmet Limme (**A, B**), and has given him the horse Schemminc (**Rg(D)**);[1] a golden hammer and tongs and a silver serpent are depicted on his banner (**V(h)** 652); a serpent is also depicted on his shield (**B** 11161).[2]

In **Rg(A)** he accompanies Dietrich to Worms and kills the giant Asprîân in the combats in the rose-garden (in **Rg(F)** he is defeated by Walther). In **L(AD)** he is also with Dietrich in Laurîn's rose-garden, the encircling silken thread of which he breaks in order to trample on the roses; Dietrich saves him from the dwarf's vengeance, and he later aids Dietrich against Laurîn's dwarfs and giants (in **L(DrHb)** he kills the giant Streitpas). In **V(h)**, he and Heime accompany Hildebrant to the rescue of Dietrich from Nîtgêr's giants at Mûter:[3] Witege kills two, Wolfrât and Rumeroc.[4]

In **B, DF,** and **Rs**, Witege and Heime are among Ermenrîch's leaders: in **B**, Witege fights Näntwîn, Hagen, and Rûmolt in the combats against Gunther's men at Worms. In **DF**, he and Heime capture a number of men sent by Dietrich to fetch gold from Bôle (Pola); Ermenrîch, by threatening to kill the prisoners, forces Dietrich to abandon Berne, but, after Ermenrîch's defeat at Meilân (Milan), Witege renews his oaths of allegiance to Dietrich, who then puts him in command at Rabene (Ravenna); Witege hands over the town to Ermenrîch after Dietrich's departure (7712 ff.); he flees once more after Ermenrîch's defeat at Bôlonje (Bologna). In **Rs**, Witege kills Scharpfe and Orte, the young sons of Etzel and Helche, and Diethêr, Dietrich's younger brother, before the battle of Rabene (Ravenna).[5] After Ermenrîch's defeat in the battle, Dietrich, belching flame, pursues Witege, but is unable to overtake him; Witege rides into the sea on Schemminc, and the mermaid Wâchilt receives him into her undersea realm.[6]

ref: **A** 14, 1; **AHb** p. 3, 14; **B** 159; **DF** 3678; **E(L)** 198, 7; **E(s)** 173, 7; **L(A)** 21; **L(D)** 259; **L(DrHb)** 8, 5; **L(K)II** 522; **N** 1699, 4; **Rg(A)** 98, 4; **Rg(C)** 255; **Rg(D)** 60, 1; **Rg(F)** III. 4, 1; **Rg(P)** 122; **Rg(V)** 109; **Rs** 364, 6; **V(h)** 378, 4; **V(w)** 564, 4

In German literature outside the 'Heldensage', Witege is not referred to before the early 13th cent., although his sword is already well known (see Mimminc, p. 94): Wolfram von Eschenbach, in his *Willehalm* (c. 1215), refers ironically to Witege cutting through eighteen hundred 'als ein swamp' (384, 23–385, 12); in Wernher der Gartenære's *Meier Helmbrecht* (c. 1260–80), his killing of the young princess at Ravenna is depicted on Helmbrecht's hat (72 ff.). References to his comradeship with Heime continue into the 15th cent. (W. Grimm, *DHS*, 173, 179, 186, 194, 316, 318, 466; Müllenhoff, *ZE*, 367 f.).

In the OE poem *Widsith*, Wudga and Hāma, vigorous fighters in the service of Eormenrīc, are described as 'wræccan', i.e. exiles or outlaws, who control people and wealth (124–30).[7] In the second fragment of *Waldere* it is said that Þeodrīc has considered sending an excellent sword (Mimming?) and treasure to Widia (ll. 4), the relative of Nīðhād and son of Wēland (ll. 8 f.), for saving him from the duress of giants (see Mimminc, p. 94).

In Þs, the twelve-year-old Viðga (I. 132, 1: MSS. AB *Virga*), son of Velent and

---

[1] In **Rg(A)**, Dietrich persuades Witege to face the giant Asprîân by offering to exchange Schemminc for Witege's horse, Valke; but in **Rg(D)** it is known that Witege originally received the horse from his father Wielant, and that he led it out of a mountain; apparently he lost it at Garten (Garda) when he fought against Amelolt (possibly a confused recollection of the latter's exploit against Sîfrit, preserved in the Þs (see Amelunc (2), p. 6); Dietrich now promises to return it if Witege will face the giant (see Schemminc, p. 115).

[2] In *Der jüngere Titurel* (c. 1270), 'Witege mit der slangen' is mentioned; in Þs, his helmet and saddle are adorned with a serpent, and the hammer and tongs are depicted on his shield (I. 136, 3–138, 10; elsewhere, Þs II. 2, 10, an anvil is painted on his shield (see W. Grimm, *DHS*, 194; Müllenhoff, *ZE*, 361).

[3] Wîcram, the leader of Nîtgêr's giants (see

p. 140), recalls Witege among Dietrich's men, who killed two hundred of his friends in Britanje (Brittany or Britain?) (**V(h)** 377).

[4] In **A**, Witege apparently recalls this episode when he urges Heime to help him against the redoubtable Alphart, by reminding him how he has saved the lives of Heime and Dietrich at Mûtâren (**A** 253 f.). See Heime, p. 64.

[5] Witege acquires a reputation for killing youths: he is known to have killed Nuodunc (**N** 1699; **Rg(D)** 319 f.); he and Heime kill Alphart (**A** 267 ff.).

[6] In the 13th-cent. *Chronicon imperatorum et pontificum Bavaricum*, Theodoric is supposed, according to popular tradition, to have been the son of a sea-monster (*belua marina*) and to have returned to the sea together with Witigo (W. Grimm, *DHS*, 464 f.).

[7] See Heime, p. 65.

Niðungr's daughter (see Wielant, p. 142), is equipped by his father with armour, helmet, shield, the sword Mimungr,[1] and the horse Skemmingr, when he sets out for Bern from Denmark. He meets Hildibrandr, Heimir, and Hornbogi at the river Eider and swears oaths of comradeship with them; at the crossing over the river Lippe at Briktan[2] he kills twelve robbers, although Heimir abandons him in the fight (see Heime, p. 65).[3] On arrival in Bern he challenges Þiðrekr and wounds him so severely that Hildibrandr intervenes;[4] they swear oaths of friendship, and Viðga joins Þiðrekr's band of heroes (see p. 94 f.).

In Þiðrekr's campaign against Osanctrix, Viðga is captured by the giant Viðolfr, but Vildiver rescues him (see Witolt, p. 148, and Wisselau, p. 144). On Þiðrekr's Bertangaland expedition, Viðga kills King Isungr's frontier guard, the giant Ædgæir,[5] in Bertangaskogr (the forest of Brittany), smears himself with the giant's blood, and rides back to his companions, pretending to be mortally wounded,[6] but then shares the giant's treasure with them.[7] In the combats against King Isungr's champions he defeats the eleventh son of the King.

Viðga becomes the vassal of Erminrikr when Þiðrekr arranges his marriage to Bolfriana, the widow of Áki Aurlungatrausti (see Hâche, p. 56): he and Heimir warn Þiðrekr when Erminrikr advances on Bern, and Viðga refuses to fight either Þiðrekr or his brother Þether, although he is prepared to fight the Huns. In the battle of Gronsport (= Ravenna?), Viðga kills Nauðungr, Attila's sons Ortvin and Erpr, and Hjalprikr (see Nuodunc, Orte, Erpfe, and Helferîch (2)), but only kills Þether after the youth has killed Skemmingr (see Diethêr, p. 24). Mounted on Þether's horse, he escapes Þiðrekr's wrath[8] by riding down the Moselle[9] and out to sea (see Dietrich (1), p. 29).[10]

pn: based on Gmc. *wiðu (OE widu, OHG witu), 'forest',[11] and *gawja (OE -gē, OHG gewi), 'district' (Schönfeld, 263), hence 'forest-dweller';[12] such forms as OHG Witigo, MHG Witege, Witiche, OE Wudga, Widia, Þs Viðga (Sv Wideke), etc., are usually held to be hypocoristic (Heusler, Heldennamen, 105; Malone, Widsith, 198 f.; but see Kaufmann, 397 f.):[13] the full form, Goth. *Widugōja or Widigōja (MHG Witegouwe), is represented by the 4th-cent. Vithigabius (Amm. Marc. XXVII. x. 3) and the 6th-cent. Vidigoia (Jordanes chs. v, xxxiv); the pn is frequently recorded from the 8th cent. in German documents (Förstemann I. 1568 f.; Socin, 174, 571, 573; Schlaug I. 175; II. 229; Müllenhoff, ZE 256 ff., 307 f., 360), e.g. Widugauuo in 774 in Alsace (Socin, 573), Witugauuo in 787 at St. Gall (Müllenhoff, ZE, 256), and the late-13th-cent. family name Witiche (Socin, 174). In 864 Witigo (Witigovvo) and Wielant (Welant) are named as witnesses in two St. Gall documents (Müllenhoff, ZE, 307 f.), but the reference to a Witigo frater Haimonis barbati in the mid 12th cent. at Salzburg is more positive evidence for the influence of the 'Heldensage' on name-giving (E. Schröder, DNK, 97 f.).

In OE the name is rare: Uydiga (?) 9th cent. (Sweet, 158); Widia and Wudia, 11th-cent. moniers, and Wdia in 1148 (Redin, 159 f.; Feilitzen, 417); the place-name Widian dun is also recorded (Searle, 486, no date).

---

[1] In the Faroese ballad, Risin! Holmgörðum, Virgar (= Witege) fetches his sword Mimring from his father's grave-mound so that he and Sigurðr can kill the giant Vilkus (Raßmann, DHS I. 48 f.).
[2] See Paff, 46 f., regarding the strange geography of this episode.
[3] The names of two of the robbers, Studfus and Sigstaf, recall those of statists in German epic (see Stûtfuhs and Sigestap); the robbers discuss the division of Viðga's equipment before the fight, as in Wolfdietrich's similar encounter with robbers (see Rûmelher, p. 112).
[4] This fight is mentioned in the MHG poem von einem übelen wîbe (c. 1250) (W. Grimm, DHS, 173; Müllenhoff, ZE, 367).
[5] Viðga kicks the giant awake. Dietrich wakes Sigenôt thus in **Sn** (see p. 126). In the Danish ballad Kong Diderik og hans Kæmper (Version B), Viderick wakes the giant with a spear-thrust (cf. Ortnît's waking of Wolfdietrich, **Wd(B)** 361 f.), and his horse helps him against the giant by breaking his ribs (DgF I. 99 ff.): cf. p. 149 n. 3.
[6] In the Danish ballads Kong Diderik i Birtingsland, Ulf van Jærn, Memring, and Greve Genselin, Viderick Verlanndz-sönn is among Diderick's champions (DgF I. 124 ff., 145 ff., 214 ff., 223 ff.); in Kong Diderik og hans Kæmper he kills a giant named Langben risi and plays the same trick on his companions as in Þs (op. cit. 94 ff.). In Danish local tradition, the grave and cave of Langben risi are to be found near Birkeby on Zealand, where a hill is also named after Viderick; the latter's grave is located near Grosby (W. Grimm, DHS, 369 f.).
[7] King Rother uses this ruse of a false defeat to confuse Constantin's forces when he abducts Constantin's daughter (see p. 109).
[8] In the church at Floda in Södermanland, Sweden, a fresco (15th cent.) shows Didrik belching flame in pursuit of Wideke (cit. W. Grimm, DHS, 477).
[9] This river is thought to flow into the sea (!).
[10] In the mid-15th-cent Swedish version of Þs, Viðga (Sv Wideke) rides into the sea and is brought by his great-grandmother, a mermaid (see Wâchilt, p. 133), to Sålandh (Zealand, Denmark), and later lives on the island of Fimber (Fehmarn?). Þiðrekr (Sv Didrik) discovers him and kills him after a long fight, but dies of wounds in Swabia on his way back to Italy; before he dies, he hurls Mimungr (Sv Mimingh) into a lake (Þs II. 395–8).
[11] See Hans Krahe, Sprache und Vorzeit (Heidelberg, 1954), 68, for the sacral significance of the IE root *u̯idhu.
[12] Schramm, 83, relates the second component to ON geyja 'to bark', hence 'forest-barker', i.e. 'wolf'.
[13] The Faroese Virgar and the Þs variant Virga are corrupt, while the Danish Viderick shows replacement of the second component.

In the 6th cent., Jordanes mentions Hanale and Vidigoia (see p. 66 n. 1) among the famous forbears, about whom the Goths still sing (ch. v); later he states that Priscus, the 5th-cent. East Roman historian, on his journey with a Roman embassy to Attila's court in Pannonia, came to the place where Vidigoia, the bravest of the Goths, perished through the guile of the Sarmatians (ch. xxxiv).[1] This early Gothic hero may well be the basis from which the figure of Witege developed (Heinzel, *Ostgotische Heldensage*, 58; Zink, *Légendes*, 209), but it seems very probable that the career of Vitigis (Procopius, *Goth.* V. xi–VII. xxxix; Jordanes ch. lx; Paul. Diac. xv f.) contributed to the sinister character of Witege at a later date (G. Matthaei, 'Die bairische Hunnensage', *ZfdA* XLVI (1902), 51; von der Leyen, *Sagenbuch* II. 226), although his name has a different base (see Witegîsen below): in 536 Vitigis was elected King of the Ostrogoths and had the last Amal king, Theodahad, Theodoric's nephew, put to death (cf. Witege's killing of Diethêr, Dietrich's brother, in **Rs**);[2] he led the Goths against the East Roman armies in Italy, but finally surrendered Ravenna to Belisarius in 540 (cf. Witege's treacherous betrayal of Rabene to Ermenrîch in **DF**)[3] and was taken as a prisoner to Constantinople, where he died in 542.[4]

Vidigoia, the hero of early Gothic tradition, appears to have been drawn first into the cycle of Ermanaric and then into that of Theodoric, for Witege (OE Wudga) is very early associated with Heime (OE Hāma) as one of Ermanaric's foremost warriors (*Widsith*), and is later involved with Dietrich (OE Þēodrīc) in fighting giants (*Waldere*, MHG epics, Þs, etc.). His association with Heime, who early becomes hostile to Ermanaric (*Beowulf*), and the influence of historical events connected with Theodoric and the end of Gothic rule in Italy, produce an ambiguity which results in the traitor figure and killer of young princes depicted in MHG epic. His relationship to Wielant is known at least by the 10th cent. (*Waldere*) and possibly suggests the further kinship to supernatural persons with alliterating names: Wate, Wâchilt, Villcinus (Þs).[5]

[1] Priscus, in the relevant passage of his report, makes no mention of Vidigoia, who may have met his death during Constantine's campaigns against the Goths c. 330 (see Müllenhoff, *ZE*, 255 f.).
[2] In **Rs**, Witege only admits killing Diethêr to the mermaid Wâchilt (970, 6), and in Þs, Þiðrekr pursues him specifically to avenge the death of his brother Þether (Þs II. 248). The death of the sons of Etzel and Helche in MHG epic may thus be a later elaboration (see p. 43).
[3] The double treachery of Witege in **DF** may also derive from events during Theodoric's campaign in Italy in 489: Tufa, Odoacer's general, defected to Theodoric, but then rejoined Odoacer and handed over a large Ostrogothic force to him at Faventia; because of this, Theodoric had to raise the siege of Ravenna and

## WITEGÎSEN

Ermenrîch's man: in **DF** he is named together with Witege, closely preceded by Heime and Witegouwe; in **Rs** he is named with Witegouwe.

ref: **DF** 8661; **Rs** 732, 5

pn: possibly a learned reintroduction of the name of the historical Vitigis (Goth. *Witigis), which should give MHG *Wîzigîs: the first component of this name is apparently equivalent to Goth. *witi, OE wite, OHG wizi, 'punishment' (Schönfeld, 269 f.; Holthausen, *GEWb*, 124; Kaufmann, 398 f.); in its MHG form, the second component may well represent an accommodation of the unfamiliar *gis (< gisil), 'arrow-shaft', 'stripling', to MHG îsen, 'iron' (A. Leitzmann, 'Kleinigkeiten zum deutschen Heldenbuch', *PBB* L (1927), 406).

## WITEGOUWE

Ermenrîch's man: in **DF** he is named with Heime, in **Rs** with Witegîsen. In **AHb** he is Wielant's son and Witege's brother.

ref: **AHb** p. 3, 15 (*Wittich owe*); **DF** 8659; **Rs** 732, 2

pn: see Witege above, of whose name it is the full form.

## WITOLT (WIDOLT, WITOLF)

A giant: in **R** he is one of the twelve giants led by Aspriân who accompany Rother on his bridal quest to Greece; he breaks loose from his chains at a banquet in Constantinople and, growling like a bear, attacks the Greeks with his iron rod (1649 ff.). He and his fellow giants help rescue Rother from the gallows, when Witolt tramples the wounded heathen into the ground and is barely restrained from destroying Constantinople.[6]

In **DH**, 'Witolt mit der stangen' (F 43, 2, 2; F 47, 4, 2, etc.) accompanies his brother Asprîon on Horant's embassy to Greece to win Hilde, the daughter of Hagen (2) for Etene (= Hetel); in Greece he hurls a duke in the air and entertains the crowd by juggling with his iron rod;[7] at a banquet he kills the tame lion of Hagen, Hilde's father.[8]

ref: **DH** F41, 4, 3; **R** m 752 n 767 (H *witolt*,

was himself besieged in Pavia, the situation being subsequently restored by the intervention of a Visigothic army (see Baesecke, *Vorgeschichte*, 207).
[4] H. Rosenfeld, 'Wielandlied, Lied von Frau Helchensöhnen und Hunnenschlachtlied', *PBB* LXXVII (Tübingen, 1955), 213 n. 2, daringly relates this to Witege's disappearance into the sea.
[5] See G. T. Gillespie, 'The Significance of Personal Names in German Heroic Poetry', *Mediaeval German Studies presented to Frederick Norman* (London, 1965), 17 f.
[6] See Îljas, p. 84.
[7] In **R**, the giant Grimme likewise diverts the crowd (see p. 53).
[8] In **R**, Aspriân kills Constantin's tame lion (see p. 7).

subsequently *widolt*, etc., E always *Witolf*, etc.)

In Þs, 'Viðolfr mitumstangi' (I. 48, 18, etc.; II. 69, 19, etc.),[1] son of Nordian, accompanies his brothers Asplian, Ædgæir, and Avæntroð on Osanctrix's bridal quest for Oda; Asplian keeps him chained to Ædgæir and Avæntroð (see Ebenrôt, p. 32). Milias, the father of Oda, refuses to accept Osanctrix as his vassal, and Viðolfr in fury stamps himself into the ground and breaks loose; in the ensuing conflict Osanctrix abducts Oda. Viðolfr later captures Þiðrekr's man Viðga (MHG Witege), but is killed by Vildiver (see Wisselau, p. 144).

pn: two forms: with component *-olf* (OHG *wolf*, 'wolf') 5th-cent. WFr, 10th-cent. German (Förstemann I. 1574); with *-olt* (OHG *waltan*, 'rule') 8th-cent. German, Lb, and OE (Förstemann I. 1573 f.; II. ii. 1311; Schlaug II. 1590; Bruckner, 321; Searle, 486).

It is possible that this figure 'Witolt mit der stangen' is based on that of the giant 'Rainoart au tinel' of OFr epic (Panzer, *Italische Normannen*, 76 f.).

WITSCHACH, see WÎCHART

WITTICH, see WITEGE

WITTICH OWE, see WITEGOUWE

WITZLÂN (1) von Bêheim (Bohemia) Witzlân and his brother Poytân, with their men Ladislau, Ratebor, Schirn, Sytomer, and Stoyne, support Gunther against Dietrich's men at Worms (see Bêheim, pp. 9 f.).

ref: **B** 5059 (6237 MS. *Wineslan*)

pn: 12th-cent. German (Socin, 571).

This figure possibly represents Wenzel I of Bohemia (†1253) (Jiriczek, *DHS* (1898), 174 ff.).

WITZLÂN (2) von Kriechenlant (Greece) Dietwart's man: father of Berhtunc (3).

ref: **DF** 473 (Wizlân)

WIWURGK, see BÎBUNC (1)

WOLF
Wolfdietrich's byname at baptism. He later refers to himself as 'der Wolf' (**Wd(B)** 369, 4).

ref: **Wd(B)** 175, 3; **Wd(D)** VIII. 119, 2

WOLFBRANT
Dietrich's man: killed in the fight against the Burgundians; in the **Kl**, Dancwart is said to have killed him. In **B** he is the brother of Wolfwîn and Ritschart, and fights Gelpfrât in the combats against Gunther's men at Worms.

ref: **B** 5251; **Kl** 1673; **N** 2261, 1 (Wolfprant); **V(w)** 843, 8

pn: 9th-cent. German (Förstemann I. (1648).

WOLFDIETRICH
The story of Wolfdietrich (**Wd**), which comprises the sequel to that of Ortnît (**O**), is preserved in divergent versions originating in the 13th cent. (see pp. xviii f., xxvi).

There are two different accounts of his birth and upbringing, in explanation of his byname (**Wd(A)** 1–155; **Wd(B)** 1–259): (1) In **Wd(A)** he is the third son of Hugdietrich of Constantinople; his mother, the sister of Botelunc, although she is a heathen, has him baptized 'Dietrich' like his two elder brothers (see Dietrich (4), p. 31). An evil counsellor, Sabene, having failed to seduce the Queen, alleges that the strong and unruly child[2] has been begotten by the Devil, and urges Hugdietrich to have him killed. Berhtunc is given the task and leaves the child by a lake to drown; when he finds him unharmed playing with wolves, he spares his life, and names him 'Wolf hêr Dietrich' (113). Wolfdietrich is restored to his parents. (2) In **Wd(B)**, Hugdietrich seduces Hildeburc, daughter of King Walgunt von Salnecke (Salonika), and their son is concealed outside the tower where Hildeburc's father has confined her; he is carried off by a wolf and is later found with its litter by Walgunt;[3] the child is christened 'Wolfdietrich' (175): 'ez heizet Wolfdietrich durch daz manz bî den wolven vant' (225, 4); Wolfdietrich's godfathers are Wülfwîn and Jörge.[4] Walgunt allows the pair to wed, and Hildeburc bears him two more sons, Bouge and Wahsmuot.

Berhtunc brings up the hero (**Wd(A)** 327 ff.; **Wd(B)** 262 ff.; **Wd(D)** III. 1 ff.). After Hugdietrich's death, Wolfdietrich's brothers dispute his inheritance of Constantinople (Sabene incites them against him in **Wd(A)** 255 ff.; they accuse him of bastardy in **Wd(B)** 267 ff.); Berhtunc loses six of his sixteen sons in the ensuing conflict (**Wd(A)** 310 ff., **Wd(B)** 283 ff.).[5] Wolfdietrich takes refuge at Lilienporte (Durazzo?) with Berhtunc, who equips him with his father's

---

[1] 'Viðolfr Mittumstangi' appears together with his brothers in the 15th-cent. ON Skr 76. In Hdl 33, 2, Viðólfr is the name of the ancestor of the sybils (ON *völur*) (quoted in Gylf ch. 5. Jónsson in his edition of the *Edda* places the relevant strophe in the Vspk str. 5).
[2] He hurls dogs against the wall (38, 4), cf. Seyfrid, who hangs lions on trees (**hS** 33; see Sîfrit (1), p. 119).
[3] The fragmentary **Wd(C)**, in which Wolf-dietrich is the son of Trippel von Athênis and Dietlint, indicates that Wolfdietrich has been reared by wolves (II. 1; II. 15 ff.).
[4] See Jörge (pp. 87 f.) regarding Wolfdietrich's affinities to St. George.
[5] In **Wd(D)** they are lost in battle at Constantinople against the heathen Olfân von Babilônje, and the dispute with his brothers is not recorded (III. 12 f.; IV. 109).

sword, armour, helmet, and the horse Valke (**Wd(A)** 423 ff.; Wolfdietrich and his vassals take refuge in a forest in **Wd(B)** 302); he sets out for Lamparten (Lombardy) to seek help from Ortnît for his vassals, Berhtunc and his ten remaining sons, whom his brothers subsequently imprison (**Wd(A)** 413 ff.).[1]

On reaching Garte (Garda), he learns from Ortnît's widow (Liebgart in **Wd(B)**, Sîdrât in **Wd(D)**) that Ortnît has been killed by a dragon, so he sets out to slay it (**Wd(A²)** 524 ff.; **Wd(B)** 656 ff.; **Wd(D)** VIII. 1 ff.).[2] In **Wd(A²)**, his horse, Valke, defends the sleeping hero against the dragon (**Wd(A²)** 586);[3] he then comes upon a lion fighting the dragon and aids it, because a lion is depicted on his shield; he is carried off together with the lion to the dragon's cave, where the young dragons eat the lion, but Wolfdietrich's life is preserved by his miraculous shirt;[4] in the cave he finds the dead Ortnît: he dons Ortnît's armour and kills the dragons with Ortnît's sword Rôse,[5] cuts their tongues out, removes Ortnît's ring,[6] and returns to Garte (Garda) (**Wd(B)** 667 ff.; **Wd(D)** VIII. 81 ff.; **Wd(A²)** breaks off where he is about to aid the lion (606)). An impostor (Wildunc in **Wd(B)**, Gêrhart in **Wd(C)**, Gêrwart in **Wd(D)**) claims to have killed the dragons, for which he demands the hand of Ortnît's widow; Wolfdietrich discredits him by producing the dragons' tongues,[7] and defeats him in battle (**Wd(B)** 753 ff.; **Wd(D)** VIII. 155 ff.; in **Wd(C)** VIII. 16, 1 Wolfdietrich executes him). Wolfdietrich then marries Ortnît's widow (**Wd(B)** 854 ff.; **Wd(D)** VIII. 330 ff.);[8] in **Wd(D)** she (Sîdrât) bears him two children: Hugdietrich and Sîdrât (IX. 218 f.).[9]

Wolfdietrich lands near Constantinople with an army supplied by Ortnît's widow, which he conceals in a forest; he enters the city disguised as a pilgrim (**Wd(B)** 858 ff.; **Wd(D)** IX. 35 ff.); there he finds his vassals, Berhtunc's sons, imprisoned, and speaks with the spirit of the dead Berhtunc; he summons his hidden army by a horn-blast, defeats his brothers, and rescues his loyal vassals; then he returns to Garte (Garda), having given Greece back to his brothers (**Wd(B)** 874 ff.; **Wd(D)** IX. 52 ff.); finally he grants fiefs to his followers (**Wd(B)** 930 f.; **Wd(D)** IX. 208 ff.),[10] and charges Herebrant, Berhtunc's eldest son, with the upbringing of his own son, Hugdietrich.[11]

**Wd(D)** provides a prologue and an epilogue linking Wolfdietrich's story with the Church: in the prologue it is stated that his

---

[1] The imprisonment of his vassals by his brothers is referred to in **Wd(D)** VII. 14. Before reaching Garte (Garda), he has various adventures: he is tempted by the blandishments of a 'wazzerwîp' (**Wd(A)** 470 ff.; **Wd(D)** IX. 56; in **Wd(B)** 308 ff. he marries her and rescues her from Drasîân: see Else f., p. 36), and defeats a band of robbers who unwisely share out his equipment before the fight (**Wd(A²)** 508 ff.; **Wd(D)** V. 3: see Rûmelher, p. 112).

[2] Wolfdietrich experiences a variety of adventures in **Wd(B)** and **Wd(D)**, which are variously placed before or after his visit to Garte (Garda): at Falkenîs he kills a heathen in a knife-fight and resists the allurements of the heathen's daughter (**Wd(B)** 534 ff.; **Wd(D)** VI. 242 ff.: see Beliân and Marpaly, pp. 10, 93); defeats the heathens Delfîân and Merziân (**Wd(D)** V. 141 ff., 165 ff.) and the giant Baldemar (**Wd(D)** VII. 27 ff.); is helped on his way to Lombardy by the giantess Rôme (**Wd(D)** VII. 116 ff.) and wins a tournament for the hand of Âmîe, the daughter of Wernhêr von Wernêres marke, at Treviso (**Wd(D)** VII. 137 ff.). Later he gives her in marriage to Berhtunc's son, Herebrant (**Wd(D)** IX. 202: see the genealogy, p. 75 n. 3). Before encountering the dragon, he comes upon a knight it has killed, and the knight's wife in labour (**Wd(A²)** 562 ff.; **Wd(D)** VIII. 51 ff.: see Hugdietrich (3), p. 83; the episode, which derives from *Revelation* 12: 2 ff., occurs after the dragon-fight in **Wd(B)** 842 ff.).

[3] In the Þs, Falka aids Þiðrekr by breaking the back of the young giant, Ekka; similarly in the Danish ballad *Kong Diderik og hans Kæmper*, Viderick's horse aids him against Langben risi (see pp. 33, 44, 146 n. 5).

[4] In **Wd(A)**, a hermit gives it to his mother for him at baptism (28 f.); the garment always fits and adds one man's strength to the wearer each year; cf. the legend of Christ's seamless robe (see Ernthelle, p. 40). In **Wd(B)**, Sigeminne (= Else f.) gives the hero the protective 'sant Jörgen hemt' (349), which in **Wd(D)** he wins from Belmunt (IV. 58; VI. 36, etc.).

[5] Cf. Balmunc, p. 9 n. 4, and Nagelrinc, p. 96.

[6] Wolfdietrich later makes himself known to Ortnît's widow by placing the ring in a winecup which he sends her (**Wd(B)** 771 ff.): this means of recognition occurs in **R** and other 12th-cent. 'Spielmannsepen' (see Jänicke, *DHB* IV. xliv f.).

[7] In Gottfried von Straßburg's *Tristan* (c. 1210), the hero exposes the imposture of the 'truchsæze' in the same way (see Bolte–Polívka IV. 170, regarding this motif).

[8] In **Wd(B)** she is abducted before the wedding by the dwarf, Billunc, but is rescued from Billunc's giants and dwarfs by Wolfdietrich with the help of the dwarf, Tarnunc (**Wd(B)** 795 ff.; Alberîch helps him in **Wd(k)**). Such a conflict with supernatural beings is reflected in **L(DrHb)**, in which Wolfdietrich aids Dietrich against Laurîn's minions and kills the giant Signit, and in Wittenwiler's *Ring*, in which Wolfdietrich is among Dietrîch's heroes opposing the giants (8069) (see Laurîn, p. 89 n. 2).

[9] See the genealogy of Dietrich (1) von Berne, p. 26 n. 1: in **DF**, Wolfdietrich is made the grandfather of Dietrich (2262 ff.). **AHb** follows **Wd(D)**, but makes his two children Sîdrât and Dietmâr, the latter being Dietrich s father (**AHb** p. 6, 4). In the mid-12th-cent. *Kaiserchronik*, 'der alte Dietrich' (= Wolfdietrich?) is Dietrich von Berne's grandfather (see Dietrich (1), p. 28).

[10] Westerîche (the Adriatic (?), see p. 69 n. 2) he grants to Herman and Hartman; to Hâche, land by the Rhine and Brîsach (Breisach); to Berhtêr, Mêrân (Maronia or Merano (?)); to Berhtunc the younger, Kernden (Carinthia); to Berhtwîn, Sahsen (Saxony); to Albrant, Brâbant (Brabant); and to the others, fiefs in Greece.

[11] He marries Âmîe, daughter of Wernhêr, to Herebrant (IX. 202), and grants their son, Hildebrant, a coat of arms with three golden wolves on it, in remembrance of his own name (**Wd(D)** X. 117 ff.: see Wülfinc (1), p. 153).

story derives from a book found at the monastery of Tagemunt (Admont in Styria?);[1] the chaplain of the Bishop of Eistet (Eichstätt)[2] brought the book to the convent of 'sant Walburc';[3] there the abbess had two experts broadcast the story (**Wd(D)** I. 1 ff.). In the epilogue, the aged hero retires to a monastery on the 'sant Jörgen orden' (Order of St. George) at Tischcâl (**Wd(D)** X. 3–11),[4] which, with the aid of his son Hugdietrich and Berhtunc's sons, he defends against the heathen giant Tarîas (X. 11–114),[5] and does penance for his sins by remaining throughout one night on a bier in the minster, where he is visited by the spirits of those he has slain (X. 121 ff.);[6] he dies sixteen years later.

In **Wd(k)**, Ortnît, Wolfdietrich, and Liebgart are said to be buried in the monastery, to which Wolfdietrich has presented Ortnît's golden armour; the queens of Jochgrîm later acquire this armour (**Wd(k)** 331 ff.: see Ortnît and Sêburc, pp. 101, 116).[7]

ref: **AHb** p. 5, 33; **DF** 2262 (Wolf her Dietrich, etc.; 2279 Wolfdietrich, etc.); **E(d)** 22, 2; **E(L)** 22, 2; **E(s)** 17, 2; **ED** 18, 1 (*Wulf främ dirick*; 18, 4 *wulffram diderick*?);[8] **L(DrHb)** 8, 3; **O** m 396, 3; **O(k)** 296, 2; **O(w)** 443, 6; **Rg(P)** 717; **Wd(A)** m 3, 4 n 113, 4 (Wolf hêr Dietrîch, etc.; 120, 4 Wolf Dietrîch, etc.); **Wd(B)** m 138, 4 n 175, 4 (Wolfdietrîch, etc.; 369, 2 Wolf hêrre Dietrîch); **Wd(C)** m II. 15, 3 n VIII. 6, 1 (Wolf hêr Dieterîch); **Wd(D)** III. 1, 1 (Wolf hêr Dietrîch, etc.; III. 5, 3 Wolfdietrîch, etc.); **Wd(Gr)** m 138 n 222, 3 (Wolfdietrîch, etc.; 262, 1 Wolfhêrdietrîch, etc.); **Wd(k)** m 5, 8 n 43, 8

German literary references to Wolfdietrich are all later than the probable date of composition of the earliest epic about him, **Wd(A)**, c. 1210–20 (Schneider, *Wolfdietrich* (1931), v); attempts are made to fit him into the historical record: in the mid-13th-cent. *Österreichische Genealogie*, 'Wolf Dietrich' is said to be the son of 'Ôtacher von Peheimlant' (W. Grimm, *DHS*, 177: see Ortnît, p. 102 n. 2); in Heinrich von München's early-14th-cent. *Weltchronik*, Wolfdietrich is said to have died aged 62 at Bari (W. Grimm, *DHS*, 225). In the 16th cent. he is known as a dragon-slayer (W. Grimm, *DHS*, 351 ff.).

The Þs identifies Wolfdietrich with Dietrich von Berne (II. 359–68): Þiðrekr, together with a lion he has aided, is carried off by a dragon; the young dragons devour the lion, but Þiðrekr kills the dragons with Hertnið's sword, which he finds in the dragon's cave;[9] he dons Hertnið's armour and helmet, defeats robbers attacking Hertnið's castle, and weds Hertnið's widow, Isollde. Motifs from Wolfdietrich's story occur in Þs in the adventures of other heroes: Þetleifr's adventures at Marsteinn are modelled on those of Wolfdietrich at Falkenîs (see Dietleip, p. 25, and Marpaly, p. 93); twelve robbers, who share out their opponent's equipment before the fight, are defeated by Viðga at Briktan (cf. Rûmelher, p. 112); Heimir retires to a monastery, which he defends against a giant (see Heime, p. 65).

pn: the byname 'Wolf'[10] in the sense of 'outlaw' or 'exile' would be appropriate both to Wolfdietrich and to Dietrich von Berne (Symons, *Heldensage*, 69; Schneider, *GHS* I. 358; Baesecke, *Vorgeschichte*, 407);[11] the meaning 'bastard' is also applicable to Wolfdietrich of the epic and to the historical Theodoric, allegedly son of a concubine (see Dietrich (1), p. 30).[12]

Important motifs in the story of Wolfdietrich are paralleled in early Merovingian history, and it has been thought that Wolfdietrich represents a conflation of two persons, the son and grandson of Clovis (see Hugdietrich, pp. 82 f.): Theodoric of Metz (†534) and Theodobert (†548) (Symons, *Heldensage*, 67 f.); both were born of concubines; the former faced the hostility of his brothers and the latter that of his uncles, whose opposition was overcome by the loyalty of the Frankish nobility.

Striking parallels to **Wd** in OFr epic have also been observed, and these are thought to reflect such Merovingian dynastic struggles (Schneider, *Wolfdietrich* (1913), 276 ff.): in *Parise la Duchesse*, the loyal major-domo, Clarembaut, and his fourteen sons support the Duchess, Parise, against her estranged

---

[1] See Jänicke, *DHB* IV. 323.
[2] Ibid.
[3] See p. 134.
[4] Possibly Dijon in Burgundy is intended (Jänicke, *DHB* IV, xxxiv).
[5] Cf. the 'moniages' of Heime and Walther, pp. 65, 136.
[6] Lothar I is said to have had such an experience (ibid. xlv f.).
[7] In **E**, Sêburc, the first queen at Jochgrîm, gives the armour to Ecke. Some uncertainty is shown in **Rg** as to the later ownership of Ortnît's sword (see Rôse and Eckesahs, pp. 109, 34).
[8] See Wolfhart, p. 152 n. 1.
[9] This episode is recounted in the Danish ballad *Kong Diderik og Löven* (*DgF* I. 132–40), except that the hero finds Syfred's sword Adelryng in the dragon's cave (see Nagelrinc, p. 96).
[10] *Wolf* (OHG *wolf*, 'wolf'), being the *kenningr* for 'warrior', represents one of the oldest Germanic name-components (Schramm, 78; Kaufmann, 416).
[11] The byname could possibly refer to Theodoric the Great's 'wolf years' before his entry into Italy (see S. Bugge, 'Die Heimat der altnordischen Lieder von den Welsungen', *PBB* XXXIX (1909), 269).
[12] Cf. Berhtunc's reply to Bouge's taunt that Wolfdietrich is a bastard (MHG *kebeskint*): 'waz saget ir mir von wolven die loufent dâ ze holz' (**Wd(B)** 279, 1); this is reflected in **jH** when Hildebrant overpowers his son, Alebrant, and offers to spare him should he be a 'Wölfinger', and the youth replies, 'Du sagst mir vil von wolfen die loufen in dem holz' (14, 1) (see Wülfinc (1), p. 153).

husband, Duke Raimond (see Berhtunc (1), p. 11); her youngest son, born in a forest, is kidnapped by robbers, adopted by King Hugo of Hungary, and named Huguet after him; with the help of Clarembaut and his sons, Huguet defeats his father's evil counsellors, and his mother is restored to the Duke's favour (see Heinzel, *Ostgotische Heldensage*, 68 f.). In *Floovant*[1] the hero, Floovant (< *Chlodovinc, 'son of Clovis'?), flees from his father and fights the heathen abroad; his hostile brothers aid the heathen; he is captured by a Saracen, whose daughter Maugalie helps him escape (cf. Marpaly, p. 93).

The OE poem *Widsith* confirms that there were traditions about Theodoric of Metz in the 7th cent.: 'Þēodrīc wēold Froncum' (24),[2] and in the late 9th cent. the *Poeta Saxo* mentions 'vulgaria carmina' celebrating Theodoric and other Frankish kings (*MGH* ss I. 268 f.). It remains uncertain, however, whether the common motifs in **Wd** and the OFr vassal epics can be accounted for by parallel native traditions in France and Germany; direct borrowing from French sources seems more likely,[3] since this obviates a complicated explanation for Wolfdietrich's connection with Greece (see Hugdietrich, p. 83).[4]

Wolfdietrich, whose name is not recorded in Germany before the 13th-cent. epics about him, has much in common with Dietrich von Berne, and the popularity of the Wolfdietrich-epics would account for the reciprocal influence in many details on the figure of Dietrich in the later Dietrich-epics.[5] It seems probable, however, that Wolfdietrich as the independent hero of the 13th-cent. epics was evolved with the figure of Dietrich von Berne in mind, the exile theme providing the common factor,[6] and, by learned inference, Ôtacher being correlated with Ortnît, whose name is recorded as early as 1160.[7]

[1] There are Italian, Dutch, and Norwegian versions of this epic.
[2] The identity of the 'Þēodrīc' mentioned in *Widsith*, 115, is still disputed (see Dietrich (1), p. 28 n. 3).
[3] The original Wolfdietrich lay and epic postulated by Schneider, *Wolfdietrich* (1913), 180 f., 377, in fact closely resemble a typical OFr vassal epic.
[4] Constantinople, Athens, and Salonika would in any case have been well known in the West after the Latin conquest of Byzantium in 1204.
[5] Both heroes have a lion depicted on their shields, fight dragons, possess the horse Valke and a protective shirt, and suffer exile; both lament excessively at their losses, for which they are reproved by their respective major-domos, Berhtunc and Hildebrant (**Wd(A)** 359 ff.; **DF** 4559 ff.). Wolfdietrich's loyal vassal, Berhtunc, is made the ancestor of Dietrich's loyal major-domo, Hildebrant, and of the Wülfinge; on the other hand, the name of Hugdietrich's evil counsellor in **Wd(A)**, Sabene, probably derives from that of Ermenrîch's henchman in **DF** (see Sabene (1), pp. 113 f.).
[6] Apparently the author of **R** (c. 1160) knew an exile story in which the hero rescues his loyal

WOLFERA(N)T, see WOLFRÂT (3)

WÖLFFING, see WÜLFINC (1) and (2)

WOLFGÊR von Gran
Etzel's man in **Rs**: he first aids Dietrich, but appears at Rabene among Ermenrîch's men (724, 4) and fights Näntwîn (3).

ref: **Rs** 66, 1

pn: 8th-cent. German (Förstemann I. 1649; II. ii. 1435; Schlaug I. 181); 9th-cent. OE (Searle, 507 f., 584).

WOLFHART
Dietrich's man, the son of Amelunc (2) von Garte and Mergart, the sister of Hildebrant; his brothers are Alphart and Sigestap.

In **N**, when the fighting breaks out between the Burgundians and Huns in Etzel's hall, Wolfhart urges Dietrich to fight his way out, but Dietrich bids him be silent (1993); later Dietrich sends Hildebrant to investigate the report of Rüedegêr's death, and the hotspur, Wolfhart, involves Dietrich's men in conflict with the Burgundians by attacking Volkêr, disregarding Hildebrant's efforts to restrain him (2265 ff.):[8] all but Hildebrant are slain; Wolfhart and Gîselhêr kill each other.

In the later epics, Wolfhart is depicted as an irascible hotspur,[9] frequently urging a reluctant Dietrich into combat, especially against Sîfrit in **Rg** and **B**. He is involved in most of Dietrich's fights and adventures: in **Rg(A)** he kills the giant Pûsolt (in **Rg(D)** he defeats Hagen); in **B** he is captured by the giant Stuotfuhs and wounded by Rûmolt; in **Rs** he fights Buozolt and Wernhêr; in **A** he kills Sêwart and a count from Tuscany; in **L** he fights dwarfs and giants (in **L(DrHb)** he kills the giant Stauer); in **L(K)II** he is defeated by the dwarf Schiltunc; in **V(h)** he kills the giant Velsenstôz at Mûter (see Wîcram).

major-domo, Berhter, and his sons from captivity in Constantinople; it is, indeed, significant that the hero, Rother, assumes the name 'Dietrich' when undertaking the rescue of his vassals during his pretended exile.
[7] Ôtacher von Lamparten, i.e. Odoacer, as the predecessor of Dietrich von Berne, i.e. Theodoric, possibly gives the clue to the structure of **Wd** and **O**, in which Ortnît von Lamparten is the predecessor of Wolf-Dietrich von Kriechen (see pp. 103 f.). Wolfdietrich is an exiled ruler who comes to North Italy from Greece, just as the historical Ostrogothic Theodoric did—Dietrich von Berne only comes from Hiunenlant once Attila (MHG Etzel) has replaced the East Roman Emperor Zeno as his patron in heroic tradition (see Etzel and Dietrich (1), pp. 28, 30 f., 43).
[8] Similar situations occur in the OE fragment *Finnsburg* with Gūðere and Gārulf, and in **W** with Hagano and Patavrid (see Panzer, *Nibelungenlied*, 426).
[9] In the **Kl** he has a red beard (1886), symbolic of fiery temper; he grasps his sword so firmly that it has to be prized from his dead hand with tongs (1681 ff.), and his teeth are clenched in death (1704).

WOLFHART

ref: **A** 74, 4; **AHb** p. 3, 4; **B** 5236; **DF** 3000; **DuW** 24; **E(d)** 288, 7; **ED** m 16, 1 f. (?) n 18, 3 (*De rasende Wulf främ diderick?*);[1] **Kl** 1864; **L(A)** 419; **L(D)** 754; **L(DrHb)** 8, 2; **L(K)II** 397; **N** 1719, 1; **Rg(A)** 32, 1; **Rg(C)** 107; **Rg(D)** 38, 1; **Rg(F)** II. 14, 4; **Rg(P)** 93; **Rg(V)** 52; **Rs** 64, 6; **jSn** 22, 2; **V(h)** 378, 5; **V(w)** 564, 5; **Wd(D)** IX. 221, 4; **Wd(Gr)** 2109, 4

In the 'Spielmannsepos' *Orendel* (12th cent.), the name Wolfhart (3218) for one of the abductors of Brîde may possibly derive from traditions about Dietrich's heroes, but the earliest certain reference to Wolfhart outside the 'Heldensage' is that of Wolfram von Eschenbach in *Parzival* (*c.* 1210-20), where Liddamus, who prefers the example of Rûmolt (see p. 112), declares:

Ich wil durch niemen mînen lîp
verleiten in ze scharpfen pîn.
waz Wolfhartes solt ich sîn?
(420, 20 ff.)

Sparse references occur in German literature from the 13th to the 15th cent. (W. Grimm, *DHS*, 196, 307, 316); Fischart in his *Gargantua* (ed. 1590) commends 'Wolffharte' as a good German name (Jänicke, *ZE*, 331).

In þs, Ulfrað (II. 176, 10: A *Wlfard*, B *Ulfar*) accompanies Þiðrekr to Attila's court and distinguishes himself in battle against King Osanctrix of Villcinaland. Later Þiðrekr's forces are surrounded by those of King Valldemar of Russia, and Þiðrekr lends Ulfrað his horse Falka, his helmet Hildigrímur, and his sword Ekkisax to fight his way out and bring relief from Attila. In the final battle against Erminrikr's men at Gronsport, Ulfrað is killed by his relative Reinaldr.

Ulff van Iern (= Wolfhart von Garten?)[2] is one of Diderik's companions in the Danish ballads, *Kong Diderik og hans Kæmper* and *Ulv van Jærn* (*DgF* I. 94 ff., 145 ff.).

pn: 7th-cent. OE (Searle, 509 f., 584; Binz, 215); 8th-cent. German (Förstemann I. 1651 f.; Schlaug I. 181; II. 166); 10th-cent. Lb (Bruckner, 324). The name is frequently confused with *Wolfrât* in the MHG epics.[3]

Wolfhart may well have belonged to Dietrich's entourage before Dietrich's entry into the Nibelungen complex. The hotspur role he plays in **N**, contrasting with Dietrich's noble calm, has been distorted in later epics, where Wolfhart becomes a comic braggart and Dietrich a coward.

WOLFHELM
Dietrich's man.

ref: **A** 76, 4

---

[1] Wolfhart and Wolfdietrich have become confused in this corrupt print (see de Boor, *Kl. Schr.* II. 56).
[2] See de Vries, *Rother*, lxi.
[3] Cf. Wolfrât (1) von Tengelingen below, with whom de Vries would identify Wolfhart (loc. cit.).

WOLFWÎN

pn: 9th-cent. German (Förstemann I. 1653; Schlaug I. 181), and OE (Sweet, 175; Feilitzen, 421; Searle, 510 f.).

WÖLFINGER, see WÜLFINC (1)

WOLFKÊR, see WOLFGÊR

WOLFPRANT, see WOLFBRANT

WOLFRAM (1) von Eschenbach
The fictitious author of **Wd(D)**.

ref: **Wd(D)** v. 133, 3; **Wd(Gr)** 969, 3

Wolfram's poetic works were completed between the years 1200 and 1220, and persons from the 'Heldensage' are referred to in them: Ermenrîch, Etzel, Gunther, Hildebrant, Rûmolt, Sibeche, Sîfrit, Uote (2), Wolfhart, and Witege.

pn: 7th-cent. WFr and German (Förstemann I. 1654 f.; Schlaug I. 182; II. 167).

WOLFRAM (2) a robber
Wolfdietrich kills him (see Rûmelher).

ref: **Wd(D)** v. 15, 1; **Wd(Gr)** 852, 1; **Wd(w)** 795, 1 (*albram*)

WOLFRÂT (1) von Tengelingen[4]
Son of Amelgêr (1): he suppresses the rebellion of Hademâr during Rother's absence. He takes part in Rother's second expedition to Greece and is rewarded with Austria, Bohemia, and Poland.

ref: **R** 2950 (H *lofhart*, subsequently *Wolfrat*, M *Wolfhart*, RB *Wolfrat*)

pn: 7th-cent. OE (Searle, 514); 8th-cent. German (Förstemann I. 1657; Socin, 42; Schlaug I. 182; II. 167); see also Wolfhart above.

WOLFRÂT (2) von Ôsterlant (Austria)
Brother of Astolt; they rule at Mûtâren (Mautern): in the combats at Worms they support Dietleip against Gunther, and Wolfrât fights Else.

ref: **B** 1051

WOLFRÂT (3) brother of Wîcram
A giant killed by Witege at Mûter.[5]

ref: **V(h)** 387, 1; **V(w)** m 573, 1 n 646, 1 (*Wolferat*; 659, 11 *Wolferant*)

WOLFWÎN
Dietrich's man: in **N** he is killed in the fight against Gunther's men: he is killed by Gîselhêr in the Kl. His relationship to Hildebrant is uncertain, since the various

---

[4] See Amelgêr (1), p. 5, regarding Te(n)gelingen.
[5] In **V(h)**, through an oversight of the author, he is also killed by Gêrnôt (2). In **V(w)**, the name of the giant killed by Gêrnôt (2) is Galerant.

WOLFWÎN

references conflict (see the genealogy of Hildebrant, p. 75 n. 3): in the **Kl** he is the son of Nêre, but **B** gives his brothers as Wolfbrant and Ritschart, whereas **Wd(w)** makes him the brother of Wolfhart.

ref: **A** 80, 2; **B** 5251; **Kl** 1733; **N** 2259, 1; **Wd(w)** 2022, 4

pn: 8th-cent. German, Lb, and OE (Förstemann I. 1661; Ploß, 57; Feilitzen, 427). It occurs in Lamprecht's *Alexander* (see Ortwîn (3), p. 102 n. 5).[1]

WOLVESMAGE (STRANDOLF)
A giant killed by Stûtfuhs (see Wîcram).

ref: **V(h)** 882, 7; **V(w)** 729, 7 (*Strandolf*)

pn: a descriptive name, 'wolf's gut', cf. such phrase-names for the robbers in Wernher der Gartenære's *Meier Helmbrecht*: Wolvesguome, Wolvesdrüzzel (v. 1195, 1203).

WULFFGRAMBÅHR, see KUPERAN

WÜLFÎN
Wolfdietrich's godfather.

ref: **Wd(B)** 173, 1; **Wd(Gr)** 220, 1; **Wd(w)** 209, 1 (*Wulfing*)

pn: 6th-cent. WFr, 8th-cent. German (Förstemann I. 1644).

WÜLFINC (1) (WÜLFINGE pl.) a family name
This name is used for Dietrich's men (**A**, **B**, **Rg**, **jSn**, **jH**, **Wd(D)**, **AHb**), especially for the relatives of Hildebrant (see Amelunc (1), p. 5, and the genealogy of Hildebrant, p. 75 n. 3);[2] in **A**, Ermenrîch's man, Wülfinc (3), is of this race.
In **Wd(D)**, the Wülfinge are descended from Mergart (IX. 221), Hildebrant's sister, and derive their name from Hildebrant's device, three golden wolves on a green ground within a blue ring, which Wolfdietrich has granted him in remembrance of his own name, hence the name Wülfinge (X. 117 ff.).
In **jH**, Hildebrant's son, Alebrant, replies: 'Du sagst mir vil von wolfen die loufen in dem holz' (14, 1), when his father offers to spare his life if he is a 'Wölfinger' (see p. 150 n. 12).

ref: sg.: **B** 10625 (= Wolfhart); **jH** 12, 4 (Wölfinger = Alebrant (1))

---

[1] H. W. J. Kroes, 'Die Hildestelle in Lamprechts Alexanderlied und die Kudrunsage', *Neophil.* XXXIX (1955), 259, considers it possible that this is, indeed, a reference to Dietrich's man, Wolfwîn.
[2] See Zink, *Légendes*, 134 f., regarding the name-lists of Dietrich's men in the 13th-cent. epics, and W. Grimm, *DHS*, 119, regarding Hildebrant's kin. In **V(h)**, Hildebrant is termed 'der Wülfinge trôst' (136).
[3] Hadubrant, the name of Hiltibrant's son in äH, has the same first component (Gmc. *haþu-, 'conflict').
[4] See Chambers, *Widsith*, 198, regarding the

WUNDERER

pl.: **A** 39, 4 (MS. *wolfingen*); **AHb** p. 10, 8 (*wölffing*); **B** 6359; **N(k)** 2039, 4; **Rg(A)** 12, 2; **Rg(C)** 44; **Rg(D)** 458, 3; **Rg(P)** 108 (Wolfingen); **jSn** 93, 6 (prints *wölffingen*); **V(h)** 136, 1; **V(w)** 257, 1; **Wd(D)** IX. 221, 4; **Wd(Gr)** 2109, 4

A reference in *Reinfried von Braunschweig* (c. 1300) suggests that the Wülfinge aided Dietrich against the dwarf Goldemâr (W. Grimm, *DHS*, 195), and in the early 16th cent. their prowess is recalled in a 'Meisterlied' entitled 'Ein Lied von dem Tod' (ibid. 355).
The Wylfingas of OE *Beowulf* (461, 471), the race to which Heaðolāf[3] belongs, are possibly identical with the Wulfingas ruled by Helm in *Widsith* (29),[4] and the Ylfingar, to which race Helgi belongs in ON Eddic tradition (HHu I 5, 2; HHu II prose, p. 150; 4, 14; Hdl 11, 8; Sk ch. 80).[5]
In Þs the name Ylfingar (II. 344, 21), like Wülfinge in MHG epic, is used for Þiðrekr's men, especially those associated with Hildibrandr, who is termed 'Ylfinga meistari' and 'Ylfinga ætt' (II. 344, 21; 350, 4, etc.).[6]

pn: 8th-cent. German (Förstemann I. 1645; Socin, 571, 573; Schlaug I. 182; II. 167); 10th-cent. OE place-names (Searle, 512; Binz, 214).

It is just possible that a Geatish tribal name from the Baltic region was used in the Amal royal family, to which Theodoric belonged (cf. Amelunc (1), pp. 5 f.); but the name itself, like *Wolf-* in Wolfdietrich, could well be appellative, suggesting wolf-like qualities required of a warrior, or even recalling Dietrich's fate as an exile;[7] in German literature, at any rate, the name does not occur before the 13th cent.

WÜLFINC (2) Dietrich's man

ref: **A** 74, 3

WÜLFINC (3) Ermenrîch's man
Alphart kills him and routs the eighty men he is leading (see Wülfinc (1) above).

ref: **A** 53, 4 (MS. *wolffing*)

WUNDERER
A cannibal monster, who pursues a maiden, Fraw Seld, with hounds. She takes refuge at Etzel's court, and 'der Wunderer' breaks

---

Helm- component in the names of Dietrich's men. Such names, however, are late in German epic (13th cent.): see Helmnôt, Helmschart, and Helmschrôt.
[5] See Wrenn, *Supplement*, 512 ff., regarding the possible connection with the East Anglian dynasty of the Wuffingas and the late-7th-cent. Sutton Hoo ship burial.
[6] See n. 2 above.
[7] The idea that the name suggests a warrior-cult connected with Oðinn seems far-fetched (see J. de Vries, 'Die Sage von Wolfdietrich', *GRM* XXXIX (1958), 15).

down the iron gate and enters. Dietrich first kills the hounds, then beheads the monster and brings the huge severed head to Fraw Seld (cf. Ecke, p. 33).

ref: **Wu(B)** m 21, 8 n 32, 6; **Wu(k)** p. 6, 9

This episode resembles those of **V** and **E** in which Orkîse and Vâsolt play roles similar to that of the 'Wunderer'; it is probably based on Arthurian models, but, as in the case of Vâsolt, 'der Wunderer' may well derive certain characteristics from native traditions; e.g. Etzel wishes to offer the monster food in propitiation, just as peasants put out food for 'der Wilde Jäger' and his rout.[1]

pn: MHG *wunderære* normally means 'worker of miracles'; here it is used in the sense of *wunder*, 'monster', as in *merwunder*, 'sea-monster'.

# Y

(see under I)

# Z

ZACHARÎS von Cecilje (Sicily)
Zacharîs, also termed 'der heide von Pülle' ('the heathen of Apulia'), equips Ortnît's expedition to win the daughter of Machorel, and it sails from his port of Messîn (Messina).

ref: **AHb** p. 5, 18 (*zacharias*); **O** 41, 1; **O(k)** 30, 6 (*Zachaeis*)

pn: possibly based on that of Zekeria of Tunis, an ally of Emperor Frederick II; the latter ruled Muslim subjects in Sicily and Apulia; an accommodation to the name of the Greek Pope Zacharias has apparently taken place (see Hempel, *Nibelungenstudien*, 148).

ZACHEREL, see MACHOREL

ZANCK
One of Laurîn's giants: Dietleip kills him.

ref: **L(DrHb)** 257, 3

pn: probably appellative, based on MHG *zank*, 'quarrel'; cf. 14th-cent. UG *zanken*, MG *zenken*, 'quarrel', originally to 'tear apart', as in the dog-name *Zänklein* used by Hans Sachs in the 16th cent. (cit. Kluge, *EWb*, 876).

ZARRASSEIN, see SARRAZÎN

ZEGEVRIJT, see SÎFRIT (1)

ZÊNE
Dietrich invokes the name of this saint and that of St. Gangolf when he is pursuing Witege.

ref: **Rs** 937, 1

St. Zeno is the patron saint of Verona (MHG Berne), of which he was Bishop c. 360. The names of St. Zeno and St. Gangolf are well known in North Italy and the Tyrol (G. Zink, *Le Cycle de Dietrich* (Paris, 1953), 120).

ZENO
Emperor at Constantinople in the time of Octaher.

ref: **E(s)** 283, 3

The Emperor Zeno (474–91) first accepted Odoacer as ruler of Italy in 476, but later he supported Theodoric's campaign against him in 489 (see Dietrich (1) and Ôtacher, pp. 30, 103).

ZERE (ZORRE)
A giant, the son of the giantess Runze (Rachin).

ref: **AHb** p. 4, 4 (*zorre*); **E(d)** 271, 8 (*Zer(e)*)

pn: appellative, based on MHG *zern*, 'tear to pieces' (Lexer II. 1065).

ZIVELLES
A cowardly soldier who kills Hagenwald in his sleep (see Hagen (1)).

ref: **gS** p. 92, 12

ZORRE, see ZERE

---

[1] Zink, *Wunderer*, 57 f.; see also Röhrich, *Erzählungen* II. 1–52, 393–407, regarding 'die Frauenjagd', a folk-tale variant of 'der Wilde Jäger'. Jiriczek, *DHS* (1898), 248, records a 17th-cent. saying: 'Der wunder möcht ein fressen.'

# INDEX

## LITERARY AND HISTORICAL NAMES NOT LISTED IN THE CATALOGUE

The names of the Catalogue are referred to in capital letters. Þ and ð are treated as Th and d respectively.

Abel, 38 n. 3
Achiulf (*Hāhiwulf), 56 n. 4
Adelryng, a sword, 9, 60, 96, 150 n. 9, see NAGELRINC
Ædgæir, 7, 32, 99, 103, 126 n. 8, 138 n. 6, 146, 148, see Ogier
Ægil, 141 and n. 6
Ægishjálmr, a helmet, 9, 120 n. 5
Ækkiharð, 34
Ælfhere, 5, 136 and n. 1, see ALPHERE
Ælfwine, 36
Aeneas, 34, 36 n. 2, 118
Aesti, 39
Aetius, 17, 42, 55 and n. 11, 61 n. 1, 80
Ætla, 41, 42, 79, 136, see ETZEL
Áki Aurlungatrausti, 25, 29 n. 1, 34, 47, 56, 62, 63, 146, see HÂCHE
— son of the above, 29 n. 1, 34, 38, 47, 56, 63, 117, see HARLUNGE
Aladarius, 28
Alans, 39, 61 n. 1, 79
Alaric, 5
Alban, 4 n. 1
Alboin, 20 n. 5, 36, 88
Albrecht von Habsburg, 66
Aldrian, father of the Niflungar, 4, 20, 23, 50, 51, 55, 59, 132, see ALDRÎAN
— son of Grimilldr, 4, 20, 58 n. 8, 60, 100
— son of Högni, 4, 42, 59 n. 8, 60, 98, 121
Aldrias, 4 n. 5, 59 n. 8, 60, see Aldrian, son of Högni
Alemanni, 6, 17, 46, 82
Alexius Comnenus, 7 n. 5, 18
Alfonso of Castile, 111
Álfr, 124
Alfrikr (Alpris), 4, 34, 53, 94 n. 2, 96, 113, see ALBERÎCH
Alibrandr, son of Hildibrandr, 9 n. 2, 13, 57, 74 n. 8, 76, 117, 133, see ALEBRANT (1)
— son of Osið, 57
Alsing (Helsing), 84, see ILSÂN
Amalaberga, 85, 86
Amalafrid, 86
Amals (Amalae, Amali), 6, 39, 77, 147, 153, see AMELUNC (1)
Amara, 40 n. 3, 85 n. 1
Amaugis, see Maugis
Ambri, 85

Ambrones, 85
Amelias, 142
Amelburg, 141
Amlungar, see Aumlungar
Amlungr, 6, 76, 121 n. 7, see AMELUNC (2)
Ammêland, see Mêland
Ammius, 37, 39 and n. 3, 63
Amulingas, 6, see AMELUNC (1)
Andvaranaulr, a ring, 120 nn. 5 and 12, 121 n. 1
Andvari, 3 n. 2, 94 n. 3, 97 n. 6, 120 n. 5
Angantýr, 76 n. 5
Angles, 73
Anglo-Saxons, 122, 123 n. 5, 126
Anseis, 7, see ANTZÎUS
Ansprant, 77
Apollonius, 7, 69, 82 n. 1
Apulians, 106, see PÜLLÆRE
Ardaric, 21 n. 2, 43, 71
Arminius, 122, 123 and n. 6, 125
Arnoldin, 7
Arnulfingians, 76, 98
Arpad, 40
Artala, 41 n. 2, 60 and n. 4, see ETZEL
Arthur, 125 n. 5, 126 n. 1
Artus, 7, 68, 69, 77, see ARTÛS
Aschenputtel, 22
Áslaug, 22, 65, 120 n. 11
Ásmundr, 14, 76
Asplian, 7 and n. 7, 32, 65, 99, 103, 148, see ASPRÎAN
Assi, 85
Athanagild, 16
Athavulf, 67 n. 1
Athene, 143
Atli, 13, 14, 19 n. 6, 29, 35, 41 and nn. 4–7, 42 n. 1, 43, 55, 58 nn. 9–10, 59 and n. 5, 66, 98 and n. 3, 102, 112 n. 2, 124 n. 11, 125 n. 7, 130, 132 n. 3, 137–8, see ETZEL
Attila, King of the Huns (†453), 13, 14, 17, 21, 25, 28, 31, 37, 40, 41 and n. 4, 43 and nn. 1–2, 55 and n. 11, 67, 79 n. 2, 80, 86, 103, 147, see ETZEL
— King of Húnaland (Þs), 4, 7, 20, 29, 38, 39 n. 4, 40, 42, 52, 58 n. 8, 59–60, 66, 79, 98, 100, 101 n. 8, 102, 103, 108, 109 n. 7, 110, 111, 114, 121 and n. 11, 130, 133, 136 and n. 6, 138, 146, 152, see ETZEL

# INDEX

Auberon (Auberi), 4, 101, 134, see ALBERÎCH
Audefleda, 30, 70
Aumlungar (Amlungar), 6, 38, 117, see AMELUNC (1)
Aurlungar, 63, see HARLUNGE
Aurvandill, 40, see ERNTHELLE
Austrechild, 16 n. 4
Authari, 25 and n. 3, 110
Avæntroð, 7, 32, 99, 103, 144, 148, see EBENRÔT
Avars, 8, 80
Aymon, see Haymon

Baduhilt, 141 n. 6, see Beadohild
Baiart, a horse, 66
Baldr (Balderus), 94, 118 n. 4, 123
Balthae, 14
Basques, 137
Bavarians, 3, 5, 6, 10 and n. 2, 15, 21 n. 2, 25, 46, 57, 80, see BEIER
Beadhkild, 70, 141 and n. 6, 142 n. 9
Bekkhildr, 65
Bela, 80
Belisarius, 30, 147
Bēowulf, the Dane, 48
— the Geat, 9 nn. 3–4, 43 n. 1, 96 n. 4, 102 and n. 1, 120 n. 5, 125, 141, 144 n. 8
Berta, 12, 66, see BERTE
Bicco, 38, 117 and n. 5, see SIBECHE
Bikki, 38, 39 and n. 6, 117, see SIBECHE
Billing, 12
Billung, Saxon dynastic name, see Hermann Billung
Billungr, 12, see BILLUNC
Bireno di Selandia, 71, see HERWÎC
Bittefer, a sword, 94
Biturulfr, 13, 25, 133, see BITEROLF (1)
Blanka, a horse, 13, see BLANKE
Bleda (Blæda, Bletla, Blêdla), 13, 42, see BLŒDEL
Blodgang, a sword, 65, 96
Bloðlin (Blodlenn), 13, 50, see BLŒDEL
Bodelingh, 14, 41, see BOTELUNC
Bodild, see Buodell
Böðvildr, 71, 142 and n. 9, see Beadohild
Boethius, 30, 31 and n. 1
Bohemians, 9–10, see BÊHEIM
Bohfrmund, 15
Bolfriana, 56, 146
Boltram, 9, 76 n. 7, 127, see BALTRAM (1)
— Hildibrandr's incognito, 9
Borghildr, 125
Borgundar, 17, 55, see BURGONDE
Boructuari, 79 n. 2
Brand Vefferlin, 68, see HEREBRANT (1)
Branwen, 100
Brísingar, 65 n. 1
Broderus, 38, 47, 117
Brîde, 4 n. 1, 15, 40, 104, 116, 132, 152, see BRIGIDA

Brōsingas, 38, 65 and n. 1
Brunehaut, 16 and n. 2, see BRÜNHILT
Brunihildis, 14, 16 and n. 2, 21, 56, 76 n. 11, 122, 123 and n. 5, see BRÜNHILT
Bryneld, 16, 20, 60, 121, see BRÜNHILT
Brynhildr, 14, 15 and nn. 1–3, 16, 19 and n. 6, 20 and n. 1, 41 and n. 3, 55, 56, 65, 73, 120 and n. 12, 121 and n. 1, 123 nn. 1 and 6, see BRÜNHILT
Brynilldr, 20, 55, 59, 65, 121 and n. 1, see BRÜNHILT
Buda, 13 n. 6, 41, see Bleda
Buðlanautar, two swords, 14
Buðli, 14, 41, see BLŒDEL
Buðlungar, 14
Bulgars, Bulgarians, 42, 80
Buodell (Bodild), 142, see Beadohild
Burgendas, 17, 54, see BURGONDE
Burgundians, 16–17 (Burgundiones, Burgiones, Burgundii, Burgundêre, Burguntare), 21 and n. 2, 42, 43, 46, 50, 51, 52, 55 and n. 11, 80, 99 and n. 1, 122, see BURGONDE
Buthlus, 14
Byzantines, 7 n. 5, 9, 18 n. 1, 55 n. 11, 77, 105, 110, 118 n. 5, see also East Romans

Cain, 38 n. 3
Celts, 74, 122 n. 8, 135
Chaba (Kewe), 21 n. 2, 28
Carolingians, 7, 110 n. 5
Charlemagne (Karl), 7 and nn. 1 and 6, 12, 17, 18, 28 n. 4, 35, 41, 49, 82, 88, 92, 93, 98, 105, 107, 110, 114, see KARL (1)
Charles the Fat, 123
— Martel, 98
Chatti, 40
Chauci, 46, 82
Cherusci, 122, 123 and n. 6, 125, 126
Chilperic I of Tournai, 16, 67, 122, see HELFERÎCH (1)
Chlodovech, see Clovis
Chlodio, 25 n. 4
*Chlodovinc, 83, 151
Chlodvic II, 141 n. 6
Chlotachar, 86
Chlotar I, Frankish King, 16, 122
Chochilaicus, see Hygelāc
Chremild, 60, 98, see KRIEMHILT
Chrotehild, 83
Clarembaut, 11 and n. 3, 150–1, see BERHTUNC (1)
Clovis (Chlodovech), 30, 46, 70, 76 n. 11, 83, 86 n. 1, 91, 141 n. 8, 150, 151
Cnut Lavard, 21 n. 4
Condiflor, 119 n. 8
Constantine, 18, 83, 147 n. 1
Crescentîâ, 31 n. 2
Crimild (Crumhelt), 21 n. 2, 28, see KRIEMHILT
Cypriân, 23

# INDEX

Daedalos, 143 and n. 5
Dáinn, 62 n. 2
Dáinsleif, a sword, 59 n. 1, 62
Danes, 21 n. 4, 73, 79 n. 2, 82, 86, 90, 116, 122, 130, see TENEN
David, 117 n. 2
Dengizec, 43
Dēor, 64, 81
Desiderius, 88
Detricus, 21 n. 2, 28, 78 n. 4, see DIETRICH (1)
Dettloff Danske, 25, see DIETLEIP
Dhyryk, 96, see DIETRICH (1)
Diderik, 29 n. 4, 45, 55 n. 8, 59 n. 11, 68, 76 n. 8, 111 n. 4, 146 n. 6, see DIETRICH (1)
Didrik, 30, 95, 133, 146 nn. 8 and 10, see DIETRICH (1)
Dieterîch, der scône, 31 n. 2, see DIETRICH (2)
— der ungetâne, 31 n. 2
Dornröschen, 16 and n. 8, 122 n. 8
Drasolfr, 126
Drota, 76 n. 5
Drótt, 76
Drusian, 25, 32, 33, 44, 53, see DRASÎAN
Drusus, 32
Durendart, a sword, 34

Ēadwacer, 103 n. 9, see ÔTACHER
Ēadwine, 36 n. 1
Ealhhild, 38, 39 n. 3
East Romans, 18, 42 and n. 4, 43, 80, 103, 113, 147, see also Byzantines
Eckehard I of St. Gall, xvi
— Margrave of Meißen, 35, see ECKEWART
Edeco, 103
Egarð, 29 n. 1, 34, 38, 47, 56, 63, 117, see HARLUNGE
Egill, 141 and nn. 6 and 8, 142 and nn. 7–8.
Eitill, 20, 40, 41 and n. 6, 43, 100 n. 4
Ekka, 29, 33, 34, 44, 65 n. 6, 113, 149 n. 3, see ECKE
Ekkisax, a sword, 4, 29, 33, 34, 95, 113, 152, see ECKESAHS
Ekkivorðr, 35, 60, see ECKEWART
Ellac, 40, 43
Ellind, 20, see KRIEMHILT
Elminrikr, Þetleifr's incognito, 5, 25
Elsa, 36 n. 1
Elso, 36
Elsungr, the father, 25, 36, see ELSE m. (2)
— the son, 6, 29, 36, 76 and n. 9, 84 n. 5, 136 n. 6, see ELSE m. (1)
Embrica, 37, 62, 85, see IMBRECKE
Emelricus, see Ermanaric
Emerca, 38, 39, 47, 62, 63 n. 2, 85, see IMBRECKE
Eormanrīc, 38 and nn. 1 and 4, 52, 56, 62, 65, see ERMENRÎCH
Erckambald, Bishop of Eichstätt, xvi, 36, 49
— Bishop of Straßburg, xvi, 36

Erelieva, 30, 70
Erik Edmund, 21 n. 4
Erka, 29, 40, 42, 66, 67, 70, 100, 103, 110, 111, see HELCHE
Ermanaric (Ermanricus, Hermanaricus, Hermenricus, Emelricus), 6, 21, 28, 31, 37 and n. 9, 38 and n. 3, 39 and n. 6, 41, 46–7, 56 n. 4, 62, 63 n. 3, 103–4, 147, see ERMENRÎCH
Erminfrid, see Hermenfrid
Erminrikr, 25, 29, 37 n. 5, 38, 40, 47, 56, 63, 75 n. 1, 76, 99, 108, 111, 114, 117, 136, 144, 146, 152, see ERMENRÎCH
Ernac, 42, 43
Erpamara, 40 n. 3, 85 n. 1
Erpr, son of Attila and Erka, 24, 40, 43, 66, 67, 100, 146, see ERPFE
— son of Atli and Guðrún, 20, 40, 41 and n. 6, 43, 100 n. 4
— son of Jónakr, 20 and n. 7, 38, 40 and n. 1, 82
Ethele, 28, 41, 67, see ETZEL
Etzelin, 41, see ETZEL

Fáfnir, a dragon, 9, 23, 55, 98 n. 3, 120 and nn. 4–5
Falka, a horse, 29 n. 7, 33, 44, 65, 115, 149 n. 3, 152, see VALKE
Falquor, 20, 45, 60, 111, see VOLKÊR
Fasold, 29, 44, 70, 127, see VÂSOLT
Felectheus, 47, 103, 143
Fenja, 48
Finn, 78 n. 1
Finns, 141 n. 8
Fitela, 123 n. 5, 125 and n. 8
Fjörgyn, 45
Floovant 83, 93, 151
Foglhildr, 38, 39 n. 3, see also Svanhildr
Folker, 45, see VOLKÊR
Folkirus ioculator, 46, see VOLKÊR
Fôre, 35, 87, 92 n. 1, 114
Fortuna, 8, 114, see SÆLDE
Fouchier (Fouchard), 46, 60 n. 8, see VOLKÊR
Franks (Franci), 10, 16, 17, 30, 32, 42, 46, 50, 55, 56, 57 n. 4, 64, 67, 76 n. 11, 77, 82–3, 85, 86 and n. 1, 91, 98 and nn. 1 and 3, 99, 105, 118, 122 and n. 4, 126, 143, 150, see FRANKE
Fredegunda, 16, 21, 122
Frederick I, German Emperor, 80, 110 nn. 5 and 10
— II, German Emperor, 101 n. 1, 154
Frēoþerīc, 38, 47, see FRIDERÎCH (1)
Freyja, 65 n. 1
Fridebrant, 69, 80, 86, 95, 116
Fridericus, son of Felectheus, 30, 47, 103, 143, see FRIDERÎCH (2)
— son of Ermanricus (Ann. Quedl.), 37, 47, see FRIDERÎCH (1)

# INDEX

Fridla, 38, 39, 47, 62, 63 and n. 2, see FRÎTELE
Friðleifr, 48
Fridlevus, 48, 81
Friðrekr, son of Erminrikr, 29 n. 1, 38, 47, 144, see FRIDERÎCH (1)
Friðrik, Osanctrix's incognito, 31, 47, 103
Frigg, 118 n. 4
Frisians, 46, 47, 54, 78 n. 1, 79 n. 2, 86, see FRIESEN
Fritila, 34, 47, 56, 63, see ECKEHART
Fritla, 47, 62, see FRÎTELE
Frōda, 48, see FRUOTE (A)
Fróði, 48, see FRUOTE (I)
Froncas, 83, 151, see Franks
Frotho, son of Fridlevus, 48, 79 n. 3, 81, see FRUOTE (I)
— son of Hadingus, 48, 120 n. 7

Gado, 138, see Wade
Galagrandeiz, 93
Galans (Galant), 142, 143, see WIELANT
Galdra-Heðinn, 72 n. 7
Garibald, 25
Gārulf, 54, 151 n. 8
Gaudon, 52, see GÔDÎÂN
Gautier (Gualter), 137 and n. 2, see WALTHER
Geats, 83, 153
Gebericus, 39
Geisa, 80 n. 2, 105
Gelfrat, 36
Gelimer, 55 n. 11
Genselin, see Kanselin
Gensimund, 77 and n. 6
Gepids, 32, 43, 71
Germer, see Gierlo
Gernoz, 4, 13, 16, 20, 23, 29, 50 and n. 1, 52, 55, 59, 76, 111, 132, see GÊRNÔT (1)
Gero, Margrave of North Thuringia, 49, see GÊRE (1)
Gibica, 17, 51, see GIBECHE (1)
Gierlo (Germer), 50, see GÊRNÔT (1)
Gifica, 16, 51, 52, see GIBECHE (1)
Gilgamesh, 118 n. 4
Gisa, 143
Gislaharius, 17, 52, see GÎSELHÊR
Gíslar, 50, 52, see GÎSELHÊR
Gisler, 4, 9 n. 2, 20, 23, 29, 50, 52, 55, 59, 76, 111, 132, see GÎSELHÊR
Gīslhere, 52, see GÎSELHÊR
Gizurr, 77 n. 6
Gjúki, father of Gunnar, 19, 50, 51, 54, 59, 120, 132, see GIBECHE (1)
— son of Högni, 51
Gjúkungar, 29, 51, 55, 98
Glaumvor, 55 n. 3, 59 n. 3, 60 n. 6
Glomerus, 72
Glomman, 61, 72 and nn. 4–5
Gluna, 60, 121, see also Glaumvor

Godomar, son of King Sigismund of Burgundy, 126
Godomaris, see Gundomaris
Goldbrand, 76
Goldener, 72 n. 7
Gotþormr, see Gutþormr
Gotfrid, a viking, 123
Goths (Gothi), 6 n. 1, 17, 24, 28 n. 4, 30–1, 39, 52, 55, 77, 85 n. 1, 122 n. 5, 147 and n. 1, see also Ostrogoths and Visigoths
Gramr, a sword, 9, 50, 52, 111, 120, 121, 125, 126 and n. 2
Grani, a horse, 15, 44, 120 and nn. 9–10, 121 and n. 2
Greeks, 18, see KRIECHEN, also Byzantines
Grendel, 125, 144 n. 8
Grettir, 144 n. 8
Greutingi, 6, see Ostrogoths
Grímhildr, 132, see UOTE (1)
Grimild, 20, 59 n. 8, 98, 111, see KRIEMHILT
Grimilda, 21 n. 4, see KRIEMHILT
Grimilldr, 4, 15, 20, 23, 29, 42, 52, 55, 58 n. 8, 59–60, 85, 100, 111, 121 and n. 11, 132, 138, see KRIEMHILT
Grímur, a giant, 29, 53, 74, 76, 78, 96, see GRÎME
— a hero, 60, see GUNTHER (1)
Grimylda, 21 n. 1, see KRIEMHILT
Gringalet, Wade's boat, 138 n. 10
Gualchelm, 63
Gualter, see Gautier
Guarnerius, 140, see WERNHÊR (1)
Gudelinda, wife of Roðingeirr, 53, 60, 99–100, 111, see GOTELINT
— wife of Þiðrekr, 30 n. 7, 53
Gūðere, 54, 151 n. 8
Gūðhere, 17, 52, 54, 59, 99 n. 1, 136, see GUNTHER (1)
Guðrún, 13, 15, 19 and n. 6, 20, 21, 22 and n. 5, 29, 38, 39, 40 and n. 1, 41 and nn. 3, 5, and 7, 42 and n. 1, 43, 51, 55, 56, 58 n. 10, 59 and nn. 2–3 and 5, 60 n. 4, 66, 69, 91, 98 n. 3, 100 n. 4, 120 and nn. 12–13, 121 and nn. 1 and 3, 125 n. 7, 132 and n. 3, 137, see KRIEMHILT
Guielandus, 141, see WIELANT
Guillaume, 65 n. 7
Gullbrynja, a byrnie, 9
Gundaharius, 17, 21, 55 and n. 11, 56, see GUNTHER (1)
Gundaric, 55 n. 11
Gundicarius, 55, see Gundaharius
Gundioch I, King of Burgundy, 50
Gundobad I, King of Burgundy, 17, 51 52, 55
— II, King of Burgundy, 50
Gundomaris (Godomaris), 17 and n. 4, 50, see GÊRNÔT (1)
Gunnarr, son of Gjúki (*Edda*), 15, 17, 19 n. 1, 20, 41 and n. 4, 50, 51, 54–5, 56, 59 and n. 3,

158

# INDEX

61, 98 and n. 3, 102, 120 and n. 12, 132 and n. 3, 137, see GUNTHER (1)
— son of Aldrian (Þs), 4, 9 n. 2, 15–16, 20, 23, 42, 50, 52, 55, 59–60, 61, 98, 111, 121, 132, see GUNTHER (1)
— character in *Njálssaga*, 56 n. 1
Günther, Bishop of Bamberg, 28, 41 n. 1
Gunthram, 16 and n. 4, 56, 122
Guthruna, 38, see KRIEMHILT
Gutþormr (Gotþormr), 50, 55, 59, 121, see GÊRNÔT (1)
Gynter, 50, 55 nn. 8 and 10, see GUNTHER (1)

Hacco, 123 n. 3
Haddingjar, 101
Hadingus, 48
Hælsingas, 61, 138 and n. 7
Hagbard, 82 n. 1
Hagena (*Waldere*), 59, 74 n. 1, 136, see HAGEN (1)
— (*Widsith*), 61, 62, 72, 74 and n. 1, 138 and n. 8, see HAGEN (2)
Hagenn, 16, 20, 45, 55 n. 10, 59 n. 8, 60 and n. 4, 121, see HAGEN (1)
Haguenon, 60 and n. 8
*Hāhiwulf, see Achiulf
Haldanus, 76 n. 5
Hálfdan, 48, 57 n. 2
Hāma, 38, 47, 65 and n. 1, 145, 147, see HEIME
Hamðir, 20, 21, 38, 40 and n. 1, 63, 82, see Ammius
Hame, 65, see Hāma
Hamidiecus, 37, see Ammius
Hámundr, 126
Hanale, 66 n. 1, 147
Harelungi, 62, see HARLUNGE
Harelus, 62, see HARLUNG
Harii, 63 n. 3
Harlungi, 47, 62, 69, see HARLUNGE
Hartvin, 63 n. 6, 69, 124, 126
Haymo, 65, see HEIME
Haymon (Aymon), 65, 92, 107, see HEIME
Heaðobeardan, 48
Heaðolāf, 153
Healfdene, 48, 82
Heardrēd, 69
Heðinn, abductor of Hildr, 61, 64, 73 and n. 6, 81, see HETEL
— brother of Helgi, 79
Hēhca, 38, 56, see HÂCHE
Heiðrekr, 6 n. 1
Heimdallr, 65 nn. 1–2
Heimir, brother-in-law of Brynhildr (*Edda*), 15 n. 2, 65, 120 n. 11, 127
— son of Studas (Þs), 7, 29, 38, 44, 65 and nn. 4 and 7, 91, 92, 95, 96, 115, 146, 150, see HEIME
— a dragon (Þs), 65 n. 4
— Þiðrekr's incognito, 65 n. 6

Helgi Hundingsbani, 62, 72 n. 7, 79, 125, 153
— Haddingjaskaði, 70 n. 5
— Hjörvarðzson, 72
Helgunda, 79, 136, 144 n. 6, see HILDEGUNT (1)
Hellespontines, 38, 117
Helm, 153
Hemidus, 37, see Ammius
Henry the Fowler, German Emperor, 66
— V, German Emperor, 90
— the Lion, Duke of Saxony, 90, 110 n. 5, 139
Heoden, 61, 72 and nn. 3–4, 138 and n. 10, see HETEL
Heodeningas, 64, 81, see HEGELINGE
Heorrenda, 64, 81, see HÔRANT
Hephaestos, 143
Herborg, a German princess (*Edda*), 22 and n. 5, 69, see HERIBURG
— wife of Salomon (Þs), 69
— daughter of Salomon (Þs), 69, 82 n. 1, 114
Herbrandr, 57 n. 2, 68 and n. 1, see HEREBRANT (1)
Herburt, 7, 68, 69, 77–8, see HERBORT
Herðegn, the father, 69, see HERDEGEN (1)
— the son, 68–9
Herebrand, 76, see HEREBRANT (1)
Herelingas, 38, 47, 56, 62, see HARLUNGE
Heren, 71, 142, see also Beadohild
Hererīc, 69
Herföðr, cognomen of Óðinn, 63
Heriold, 86, see ÎROLT
Herkja, 20, 21, 29, 66, see HELCHE
Herla, 63
Herlechini, Herlethingi, 63, see HARLUNGE
Herlibo, 62, see HARLUNG
Herman, a count, 63 n. 6, 69, 124, 126, see HERMAN (2) and (5)
— a messenger of King Osanctrix, 69, see HERMAN (1) and (2)
— a knight of King Artus, 69
Hermanaricus (Hermanricus, Hermenricus), see Ermanaric
Hermann Billung, Duke of Saxony, 12
Hermenfrid (Erminfrid), 86, see IRNFRIT
Hermunduri, 32, see Thuringians
Hernidus, see Hemidus
Herod, 27 n. 10, 68, 89, 126
Herodias, 19
Herrað, 29, 66, 70, 76, 136 n. 6, see HERRÂT
Herrant, 81
Hertnið, King of Hólmgarðr, father of Osanctrix, 70, 84, 101 n. 7, 103, 108, 144, see HERTNÎT (1) *and* ORTNÎT (1)
— son of Osanctrix, 25, 44, 70, 84, 103
— son of Ilias, 70, 84
— af Bergara, 29, 34, 70, 86, 101 and n. 7, 150, see ORTNÎT (1)
Heruli, 39, 63 n. 3, 110
Hervor, 141 and n. 8
Hetan (Hetin), 64, 72

159

# INDEX

Hiarno, 48, 81
Hiarrende, 81 n. 6, see Hjarrandi
Hibba (Ibba), 77 and n. 7
Hilda, 62, 72, 73, see HILDE (1)
Hilde, 73, see HILDE (1)
Hildebrand, 76 and n. 1, see HILDEBRANT (1)
Hildeburh, 78 n. 1, 82
Hildegard, wife of Charlemagne, 82
Hildegӯþ, 79, 136, see HILDEGUNT (1)
Hildeprant, Langobard ruler, 77
Hildibrandr, son of Reginballdr (Þs), 6, 9 n. 2, 29, 36, 50, 52, 53, 57, 68, 70, 74 nn. 8 and 10–11, 75 n. 1, 76, 94, 108, 133, 136 n. 6, 146, 153, see HILDEBRANT (1)
— half-brother of Ásmundr (Ásmundar saga), 14, 57, 76 and n. 5, see HILDEBRANT (1)
Hildigerus, 76 n. 5
Hildigrímur, a helmet, 29, 53, 78, 152, see HILDEGRÎN
Hildigunnr læknir, 78 n. 7
— daughter of Sváva, 79
*Hildiko, see Ildico
Hildina, 71, see HILDE (1)
Hildir m., 57 n. 2
Hildisvid, 29 n. 1
Hildr, daughter of Högni, 61, 64, 72 and nn. 2–3, 81, see HILDE (1)
Hilldigundr, 59, 79, 84, 136, see HILDEGUNT (1)
Hilldr, daughter of Artus, 7, 68, 69, 77–8, see HILDEBURC (1)
Hilldur, a giantess, 29, 53, 74, 76, 96, see HILDE (3)
Hillebrandt, 76 n. 8, see HILDEBRANT (1)
Hiluge, 71
Hirðir, 70
Hithinus, 48, 62, 72, see HETEL
Hjaðningar, 64 and n. 1, 72 nn. 4 and 7, 73, see HEGELINGE
Hjalli, 59, 112 n. 2
Hjálprekr, King of Denmark, 67, 120, 124, 126, see HELFERÎCH (1)
Hjalprikr, guardian of the sons of Erka, 67, 84 n. 3, 146, see HELFERÎCH (2) and ILSÂN
Hjarrandi, 72, 81, see HÔRANT
Hjördís, 120, 123 n. 6, 124 and n. 8, 126 and n. 2, see SIGELINT (1)
Hlaðguðr, 141 and n. 8
Hledís, 48
Hliðskjálf, Óðinn's throne, 115
Hljóð, 125, 139
Hlöðr, 6 n. 1, 76 n. 5
Hlöðvér, father of Hervor (Edda), 91, 141 n. 8, see Clovis
Hlodver, father of Konrádur (Þs), 91
Hnæf, 78 n. 1, 82
Hnefi, 82, see Hnæf
Hniflungr (Niflungr), 20 n. 6, 42 n. 1, 59, 98, see also Rancke

Hōc, 78 n. 1, 82, see HÛC
Hōcingas, 82
Hōðbrandr, 57 and n. 2, see HADEBRANT (1)
Hōðr, see Hotherus
Hōginus, 48, 62, 72, see HAGEN (2)
Hogne, 60 and n. 6, 98, 121, see HAGEN (1)
Högni, brother of Gunnarr (Edda), 19 n. 1, 41 and n. 4, 42 n. 1, 50, 51, 55, 56, 58 n. 2, 59 and nn. 1–4 and 7, 61, 74 n. 1, 98 and n. 3, 100, 120–1, 132–3, see HAGEN (1)
— half-brother of Gunnarr (Þs), 4, 16, 20, 27 n. 10, 29 and n. 5, 42, 45, 55, 58 nn. 4, 6 and 8, 59 and n. 9, 60, 61, 79, 85, 98, 100, 111, 121, 132 and n. 3, 136, see HAGEN (1)
— father of Hildr (Edda), 61–2, 64 and n. 3, 72, 73 and n. 6, see HAGEN (2)
— character in Njálssaga, 56 n. 2
Hökingr, 82
Holmrycgas, 61 and n. 6, 74
Hönir, 120 n. 5
Honoria, 42, 67 n. 1
Honorius, Roman Emperor, 17, 67 and n. 1
Horn, 7, 76
Hornbogi, 6, 81, 146, see HORNBOGE (1)
Hotherus, 94, 97 n. 6
Hreiðmarr, 120 n. 5
Hrímnir, 125, 139
Hróðgār, 111 and n. 5
Hróðulf, 111 n. 5
Hrotti, 9, 120 n. 5
Hrunting, a sword, 9 n. 3
Huga, 83
Hūgas, 83
Hugo, 151
Hugon, 82
Hugones, 83
Huguet, 11, 151
Humblum, 6 n. 3, see AMELUNC (2)
Humli, 6 n. 1
Humlungr, 6 n. 1
Hun, ruler of the Huns, 79 n. 3
Húnar, 79, see HIUNEN
Hūnas, 41, 79, see HIUNEN
Hundingr, 120 n. 2, 126
Hungarians (Hungarii, Magyars, Ugri), 40, 80 and nn. 1–2, 105, 110 n. 10, see UNGERN
Huni, see Huns
Hunimundus, 47
Huns (Huni), 6 n. 1, 8, 13, 17, 21 n. 2, 25, 39, 41, 42–3, 55 n. 11, 79 and nn. 2–3, 80 and n. 1, 137, see HIUNEN
Huochingus, 82
Huon de Bordeaux, 101
Hvenild, 20
Hygelāc, 83

Iarmericus, 14, 38 and n. 4, 62, 63, 117, see ERMENRÎCH
Ibba, see Hibba

# INDEX

Ikaros, 142 n. 8
Ildebrand, 76 n. 1, see Hildebrand
Ildico (*Hildiko), 21, 42, see KRIEMHILT
Ilias, 70, 79, 84, 136, see ÎLJAS
Ilja Murometsch, 84 and n. 2, 101, see ÎLJAS
Ingram, Elsungr's man, 76
— a robber, 25
Iring, 85–6, see ÎRINC
Irminfrid, 85–6, see IRNFRIT
Iron, 7, 99, 118 n. 6, see IRAM
Irungr, 13, 20, 60, 85–6, see ÎRINC
Isac, 68, 86, see also Isungr
Isolde, heroine of romance, 62, 86, see ÎSOLDE (1)
Isollde, sister of Þiðrekr, 69, 86
— wife of Iron, 86
— daughter of Iron, 86
— widow of Hertnið af Bergara, 29, 30 n. 7, 86, 101, 150
Isungr, 6, 25, 29 and n. 3, 55, 59, 65, 68, 70, 76, 81, 86, 121, 127, 146
Italians, 16 n. 4, 31, 134–5
Ivarr Ljómi, 62 n. 1

Jarmer, 50, see GÊRNÔT (1)
John I, Pope, 30 and n. 1, 31 n. 1
— Bishop of Ravenna, 103
Jónakr, 20, 21, 38, 40 and n. 1
Jörmunrekr, 20, 37 n. 5, 38 and nn. 2–3, 39, 40, 46, 47, 82, 103 n. 8, 117, 118 n. 1, see ERMENRÎCH
Judas Maccabaeus, 16
Julius Caesar, 16
Justinian, 30, 86
Jutes, 78 n. 1

Kanselin (Genselin), 14, 20, see BLŒDELINCK
Kára, 70 n. 5
Karl, see Charlemagne
Kaupa-Heðinn, 72 n. 7
Kewe, see Chaba
Kjárr af Vallandi, 141 n. 8, see Hlöðvér
Kjartan, 135 n. 2, 136 n. 4
Knefröðr, 137
Konrádur, 6, 22, 76, 91
Kostbera, 59 n. 3
Kreka, 42, 67, see HELCHE
Kremold, 20, 60, see KRIEMHILT
Kumans, 28, 44, see VALWEN

Ladislaus Hermann, Duke of Poland, 70, see HERMAN (4)
Lagulfr, a sword, 74 n. 11
Langben risi (Lanngebeen Redsker), 115, 146 n. 6, 149 n. 3
Langobards, 20 n. 5, 25, 36 and n. 1, 52, 76, 77 and n. 2, 87, 88, 110 and n. 4, see LAMPARTEN
Lanzelet, 93

Lemovii, 72 n. 4
Leo, East Roman Emperor, 30, 43
Liddamus, 112, 152
Liudeger, Duke of Saxony, 90, see LIUDEGÊR (1)
Liutpert, Langobard King, 77
Liutprant, Langobard King, 77 and n. 4
Loðvígr, margrave, 32 n. 2, 91
Lodvígur, father of Konrádur, 91
— Heimir's incognito, 65
Loki, 65 n. 1, 118 n. 4, 120 n. 5
Lorandin, 43
Lothar I, German Emperor, 91, 150 n. 6
Loumer, 20, 41 n. 2, see ETZEL
Lyngvi, 126

Mǣringar, 28 and n. 4
Mǣringas, 28 and n. 4, 38
Magnus, King of Denmark, 21 n. 4
Magyars, see Hungarians
Malek-el-Adel, 92, see MACHOREL
Margaret of Babenberg, 102 n. 2
Maugalie, 93, 151, see MARPALY
Maugis (Amaugis), 66, 92, see MADELGÊR
Maximilian, German Emperor, xv n. 2, 28
Maximinus, 42
Mêland (Ammêland), 141 n. 2, see WIELANT
Menja, 48
Menning, a sword, 95, see MIMMINC
Meranare, 28 n. 4
Merlin, 141
Meroveus, 25 n. 4
Merovingians, 11, 17, 21, 25 n. 4, 56, 76 n. 11, 83, 98, 123 n. 5, 142 n. 1, 150
Miemerinng (Mimering), 94, 96, see MÎME
Mhaček, 99, see NIBELUNGE
Mîlîân, 42 n. 2
Milias, 7, 18, 31, 39 n. 4, 42, 69, 70, 79, 103, 148
Miming, a sword, 94, see Mimming
Mimingh, a sword, 95, 146 n. 10, see Mimungr
Mimingus, 94, 97 n. 6, see MÎME
Mímir, a supernatural being (*Edda*), 94, see MÎME
Mimir, a smith (Þs), 9 n. 2, 34, 94, 101 n. 7, 121, 142, see ECKERÎCH (1) and MÎME
Mimmering, a sword, 95, see MIMMINC
Mimming, a sword, 28 and n. 5, 59, 94 and n. 6, 136, 145, see MIMMINC
Mimo (Mima), 94 n. 1, see Mímir
Mimring, a sword, 95, 142, 146 n. 1, see MIMMINC
Mimungr, a sword, 29, 71, 76, 94–5, 96 n. 1, 121, 142, 146 and n. 10, see MIMMINC
Minos, 143
Mohamet, 91 and n. 2, see MACHMET
Moors, 95, 111, see MŒRE
Mörolf, 81 n. 2, 92, 95, 114
Moses, 96
Mundirosa, 16 n. 8, 19 n. 4, 119 n. 8, 123 n. 1

161

# INDEX

Mundzucus (Mundiucos), 13, 14, 42, see BOTELUNC
Mynning, a sword, 34, 94, see MIMMINC

Nægling, a sword, 96, see NAGELRINC
Naglringr, a sword, 4, 29, 53, 65, 96, see NAGELRINC
Naisier, 91 n. 2
Narcissus, Roman Emperor (*Kaiserchronik*), 31 n. 2
Narses, 30
Nauðungr, 60, 99, 111, 146, see NUODUNC
Nebi, 82, see Hnæf
Nevelon, 98, see NIBELUNGE
Nevelungus (Neuelunchus, Nevelongus, Nivelongus), 76, 98, see NIBELUNGE
Niárar, 70
Nibelungus, 98, see NIBELUNGE
Niðhád, 70, 71, 141 and n. 6, 145, see HERTNÎT (2)
Niding, 20, 98, see NIBELUNGE
Níðuðr, 23, 70 71 and n. 1, 142, see HERTNÎT (2)
Niðungr, ruler of Jutland, 142 and n. 7, 146, see HERTNÎT (2)
— King of Spain, 71, 124, 126
Nielus, 60, see Hagenn
Niflungar (*Edda*), 17, 35, 41, 50, 51, 55, 58 nn. 6 and 9, 59, 97 n. 2, 98, 125 n. 6, 132, see NIBELUNGE
— (Þs), 13, 29, 35, 42, 45, 50, 55, 57, 60, 76, 85, 97 n. 2, 98, 111, 121 n. 11, 133, see NIBELUNGE
Niflungr, see Hniflungr
Nikulús, Abbot of Þverá, 123 n. 7
Nögling, 98, see NIBELUNGE
Nordian, 7, 32, 99, 118 n. 6, 148, see NORDÎÂN
Norðungr, 129
Normans, 15, 23 n. 2, 109
Norpertus, 99, see NORPREHT (1)
Norwegians, 120 n. 11

Obbe Iern, 111, see RÜEDEGÊR
Oda, ancestress of the Saxon imperial dynasty, 133, see Uote (1)
— wife of Biturulfr, 13, 25, 133, see DIETLINT (1)
— wife of Aldrian, 4, 55, 59, 132, see UOTE (1)
— wife of Hildibrandr, 76, 133, see UOTE (2)
— wife of Osanctrix, 7, 18, 70, 103, 133, 148
Oddrún, 55, 102, see ORTRÛN
Odilia, wife of Þetmarr, 25, 29 n. 1
— wife of Sifka, 38, 63, 117
Óðinn, 15 n. 1, 38, 63 and n. 4, 72 n. 7, 81, 82 n. 1, 94, 115, 116, 120 n. 5, 125, 126 and n. 1, 139 and nn. 1 and 5, 144 n. 4, 153 n. 7, see also Woden

Odoacer, 8, 28, 30, 37 and n. 10, 39 n. 6, 47, 103 and nn. 7 and 9, 104, 118, 147 n. 3, 154, see ÔTACHER
Oedipus, 77
Offa, 138
Ogier, 7 n. 6, 65 n. 7, 103 n. 2, 137, 138 n. 6, see also Ædgæir
Oigir, 138, see Ogier
Óláfr Tryggvason, 62 n. 1
Ole, 85 n. 4
Olimpia, 22, 71
Ölrún, 141
Onef, 72
Orco, 100
Orgaie (Orgais), 100
Orkingr, 59 n. 4
Orpheus, 81
Ortvangis, 124 n. 5
Ortvin, 24, 40, 43, 66, 67, 100, 102, 146, see ORTE
Osanctrix, 7, 12, 18, 29, 31, 42, 47, 66, 69, 70, 84, 95, 103 and n. 4, 108, 110, 111, 133, 144 and n. 5, 146, 148, 152, see ÔSERÎCH and ROTHER
Osið, father of Attila (Þs), 42, 70
— nephew of Attila (Þs), 55, 66
Ostacia, 25, 70 and n. 5
Ostrogoths, 6, 16 n. 5, 25, 30, 39 and n. 2, 42, 43, 79, 86, 147 and n. 3
Otnið, 57, 101 n. 8
Otr, 120 n. 5
Otto I, German Emperor, 49, 80 n. 2
— IV, German Emperor, 104
— von Mîssowe, 13 n. 1
Ottokar II, King of Bohemia, 102 n. 2
Otvin, 71
Ougel, 43

Pamige, 78 n. 2
Papagau, Chevalier du, 33, 78 n. 5
Parise la Duchesse, 150
Patzinaks, 105, see PETSCHENÆRE
Pepin I of Landen, 49, 98
— II of Heristal, 7, 98
— III, the Short, 105, see PIPPIN
Peregrinus, Bishop of Aquileia, 105
Pilate, 68, 94
Pilgrim, Bishop of Passau, 105, see PILGERÎN (1)
Pitzia, 114
Placidia, 67 n. 1
Poles, 105, 136 n. 9, see PÔLÂN
Pomeranians (Pomorani), 105, see POMERÂN
Priscus, 21, 42 and nn. 4 and 6, 67, 147 and n. 1
Prussians, 106, see PRIUZEN

Raadengaard, 111 n. 4, see RÜEDEGÊR
Raimond, Duke, 151
Rainoart au tinel, 148

# INDEX

Rancke, 20, 59 n. 8, 60 and n. 4, 98, see also Hniflungr
Randvér, 38 and n. 2, 47, 117, see FRIDERÎCH (1)
Refill, see Riðill
Reginballdr, son of Erminrikr, 29 n. 1, 38
— father of Herbrandr, 68
— father of Hildibrandr, 9, 76 and n. 7
— father of Sintram, 127
Reginn, a smith (*Edda*), 9, 23, 34, 94 n. 4, 120 and nn. 3 and 10, see ECKERÎCH (1)
— a dragon (Þs), 94 and n. 4, 121, see also Fáfnir
Reinaldr, Erminrikr's man, 75 n. 1, 108, 152, see RIENOLT
— Þiðrekr's man, 108
Renaut, 66, 107, 108, see RIENOLT
Rerir, 139
Rhydderich, 141
Richard I, King of England, 104
Riðill (Refill), a sword, 9
Rimenhild, 7
Rimsteinn, 108, 136, see RIMSTEIN
Rinda, 82 n. 1
Ripeu de Ribemont, 107, see RIBESTEIN
Ripuarii, 46, 122 n. 4
Rispa, a horse, 65 and n. 5, 115
Roðgeirr af Salerni, 29 n. 1, 110 n. 2, see Rother
Roðingeirr, 9 n. 2, 29, 42, 50, 52, 53, 55, 60, 66, 99, 108, 111, see RÜEDEGÊR
Roðolfr, 12, 66 and n. 3, 109 n. 7, 110, 111 n. 1
Rodrigo Diaz (El Cid), 111, see RÜEDEGÊR
Roger II, Norman King of Sicily, 109, 110 n. 5, see ROTHER
Rogerius comes, 111, see RÜEDEGÊR
Roland, 113, 137
Rolpho, 111 n. 5
Romans, 3, 17, 24, 32, 36, 42, 55 n. 11, 77 n. 2, 80, 83, 103, 118, 123 and n. 7, 143, 147
Romulus Augustulus, 103
Rosamunda, 20 n. 5
Rosebrant, a sword, 109, see RÔSE
Rosomoni, 39
Rothari, 87, 110, see ROTHER
Rozeleif, 34, 113, see RUOTLIEP
Ruas, 42, 80
Ruczela (Runzela), 112, see RUNZE
Rudegerus marchio, 111 n. 6, see RÜDEGÊR
Ru(d)gerus de Preclara, 111 n. 6, see RÜEDEGÊR
Rûel, 36, 96 n. 2, 109
Rugians, 30, 47, 61 n. 6, 73–4, 103, 143
Rugini, 79 n. 2
Rumanians, 106 and n. 4, 124 n. 2, 134, see WALÂCHEN
Rūmstān, 38, 108, see RIMSTEIN
Runga, 24
Runsa, 112, see RUNZE

Ruska, a hunting-dog
Russians, 84, 108, see RIUZEN
Rustem, 77

Sabinianus, 24, 30, 113–4, see SABENE (1)
Sāēdene, 124 n. 3
Sāēferð, 122 n. 3, see Sigeferð
Salians (Salii), 46, 82–3
Salmân, 23, 81 n. 2, 95, 114, see SALOMÔN
Salme, 81 n. 2, 114
Salomon, father of Herborg (Þs), 69, 114
Samson, biblical figure, 118 n. 4
— father of Þetmarr, 25, 29 n. 1, 36, 38, 114
— son of Erminrikr, 29 n. 1, 38, 114
Saracens, 12, 76, 87, 93, 95, 112, 114–5, 123 and n. 9, 151, see SARRAZÎN
Saraleoz, 34, 39, see Sarus
Sarelo, 37, see Sarus
Sarmatians, 147
Sarus, 37, 39 and n. 3, 63
Säufritz, 120 n. 1, see SÎFRIT (1)
Saxons, 12, 21 n. 4, 42, 46, 79 n. 3, 85, 90, 114, 122, 133, 144, see SAHSEN
Scandinavians, 16 n. 8, 21, 22, 60 n. 4, 64, 74, 77, 99, 120 n. 10, 121 n. 5, 126, 143
Scyld, 48, 116
Scyldingas, 116
Scylfingas, 115
Seafola, 28 n. 3, 38, 113 and n. 4, see SABENE (1)
Secgan (Sycgan), 122 n. 3
Segestes, 126
Segimundus, 126
Segistop, see Sigstaf
Senild, 20, see KRIEMHILT
Serila, 37, see Sarus
Severus, Roman Emperor, 3
Sevill, 113, see SABENE (1)
Seyfrid de Ardemont, 16 n. 8, 19 n. 4, 43, 119 n. 8, 123 n. 1, see SÎFRIT (1)
Siaward, 21 n. 4
Sibicho, Bishop of Speyer, 117
Sibilla, 36 n. 2, 118, see Sybilla
Sienild, 16, 20, 60, 121, see KRIEMHILT
Sifeca, 38, 117, see SIBECHE
Sifian, 126
Sifka m., 37 n. 3, 38, 47, 57, 63, 65, 117 and n. 4, 144, see SIBECHE
— f., 117 n. 4
Sigambri, 118
Sigebert of Metz (†575), 14, 16, 21, 56, 67, 76 n. 11, 122, 123, see SÎFRIT (1)
— King of the Ripuarian Franks († 510), 122 n. 4
Sigeferð, 54, 122 n. 3, 123 n. 5
Sigehere, 124 n. 3
Sigemund, 123 n. 5, 125, 126, 139, see SIGEMUNT (1)
Sigeni, 141
Sigfrid, 60, 121, see SÎFRIT (1)
Sigfrœð, 121 n. 4, see SÎFRIT (1)

163

# INDEX

Siggeirr, 125, 139
Sigi, 139
Sigifrid, a viking, 123, see SÎFRIT (3)
Sigiric, 126
Sigisfroð, 121, see SÎFRIT (1)
Sigismund(us), 126 and n. 7, see SIGEMUNT (1)
Sigmundr, father of Sigurðr (*Edda*), 120 and n. 2, 124, 125 and n. 9, 126 and n. 2, 139; (Þs), 69, 121 and n. 11, 124, 126, see SIGEMUNT (1)
— son of Sigurðr (*Edda*), 19, 56, see GUNTHER (2)
Signe, 82 n. 1
Signelille, 20, see KRIEMHILT
Signý, 125, 139
Sigrdrífa, 15, 120
Sigrlinn, 124 n. 11
Sigrún, 62
Sigstaf (Segistop), 127, 146 n. 3, see SIGESTAP
Sigurðr, son of Sigmundr (*Edda*), 3 n. 2, 9, 15 and n. 1, 19 and n. 6, 20, 23, 34, 39, 50, 55, 56, 59 and nn. 2 and 5, 61, 65, 67, 94 n. 4, 98 n. 3, 120 and nn. 2 and 8–13, 121 and nn. 1–3, 122, 123 nn. 1 and 6, 124 and n. 8, 125 and n. 9, 126, 132, 139; (Þs), 6, 9 and n. 2, 15–16, 20, 29 and n. 2, 34, 42, 44, 50, 52, 55, 59, 60, 94, 95, 101 n. 7, 111, 114, 115, 120 nn. 8–9, 121 and nn. 4–7 and 11, 122, 123 n. 6, 124 and n. 8, 126; (Faroese ballad), 146 n. 1; (Völss), 41 n. 5, see SÎFRIT (1)
— the Greek (Þs), 5, 25 and n. 2, 93
— Roðolfr's incognito (Þs), 66
Sinfjötli, 120 n. 8, 125 and nn. 2 and 8–9, 126 and n. 6, see also Fitela
Sinnelille, see Signelille
Sintarvizzilo, 125 n. 8, see Sinfjötli
Sintram (Sistram), son of Reginballdr, 29 and n. 2, 76 n. 7, 127, see SINTRAM (1)
— Heimir's incognito, 127
Sisibe, 69, 71, 121, 124 and n. 9, see SIGELINT (1)
Sivard, 16, 20, 60, 96, 115 n. 4, 121, see SÎFRIT (1)
Skemmingr (Skeminng, Skjemming, Skimling Gram), a horse, 24, 44, 115 and n. 4, 142, 146, see SCHEMMINC
Skíði, xxi
Skilfingar, 115
Skjöld, 48, 116
Skjöldungar, 116, 137
Slagfiðr, 141 and n. 8
Slavs, 31, 38, 42, 49, 90, 105, 108, 129, 144
Snævarr, 59 n. 4
Sohrab, 77
Sólarr, 59 n. 4
Solomon, 114, see SALOMÔN
Sorbs (Sorabi), 129, see SURBEN
Sörli, 20, 21, 38, 40 and n. 1, 63, 82, see Sarus

St. Ägidius, 51, see GILEGE
St. Brigid, 15, see BRIGIDA
St. Evermar, 123 n. 3
St. Gangolf, 49, 154
St. George, 10, 87–8, 104, 122 n. 7, 148 n. 4, 150, see JÖRGE
St. Gereon, 118 n. 2
St. Gertrude, 49, 98, see GÊRDRÛT
St. Helena, 67
St. John the Apostle, 87, see JÔHAN (1)
— the Baptist, 87, see JÔHAN (2)
St. Liudger, 90
St. Marcellian, 92
St. Mary, the Virgin, 30, 92
St. Michael, 94
St. Pancratius, 104
St. Servatius, 40 n. 5
St. Severinus, 143
St. Sigismund, 126 n. 7, see Sigismundus
St. Victor, 118 n. 2
St. Walpurgis, 134, see WALBURC
St. Zeno, 30 n. 1, 154
Starkad, a Danish champion, 65, 85 n. 4
Starkaðr, character in *Njálssaga*, 78 n. 7
Studas, father of Heimir, 44, 65, 92, 115, see MADELGÊR
— Heimir's original name, 65 n. 4
Studfus (Stodfuss, Stofn(er)), 129, 146 n. 3, see STÛTFUHS
Suanailta, 34, 39, 65, see Sunilda
Sûdân, 94, 116 n. 2, see SCHUDÂN
Sudeli, 22
Suebi, 129
Sunigilda, 39 n. 6, 103
Sunilda, 39 and n. 3
Svanhildr, 19–20, 38, 103 n. 8, 117, see Sunilda
Sváva, 79
Swǣfe, 61, 138
Swanilda, 38, see Svanhildr
Swedes, 13 n. 2, 70, 78
Sybilla, 116, 118, see SIBILLE
Sycgan, see Secgan
Syfred, 96, 150 n. 9, see SÎFRIT (1)
Symmachus, 30 and n. 1, 31 and n. 1
Syrith (Sigred), 22

Tancred of Lecce, 23 n. 2
Tatlar, 25, 29 n. 5, see DIETMÂR (1)
Telegonos, 77
Tell, 142 n. 7
Tervagan(t), 130, see TERFÎANT
Tetricus vetus, 111, see DIETRICH (1)
Teuriohamae, 32
Teutonic Order, 106, 131
Þakkráðr, 23, 142
Theodahad, 24, 86, 147
Theodemer, 25–6, 30, 31, 39, 42, 43, see DIETMÂR (1)
Theodemund, 24, 30, see DIETHÊR (1)
Theodobert, 150

# INDEX

Theodolinda, 25, 110, see DIETLINT (1)
Theodoric of Metz, Frankish King, 30, 46, 83, 85, 86 and n. 1, 150, 151
— the Great, Ostrogothic King, 6, 24, 25–6, 27 n. 11, 28 and nn. 2 and 4, 30 and nn. 1, 3 and 5–7, 32, 37, 39, 41, 43, 47, 70, 77 and n. 3, 86, 102, 103 and n. 9, 104, 113–14, 145 n. 6, 147 and n. 3, 150 and n. 11, 151 n. 7, 154, see DIETRICH (1)
— Strabo, son of Triarius, 30, 31, see DIETRICH (2)
— Visigothic King, 42
Þeodrīc, the Frank, 83, 113, 151 n. 2, see Theodoric of Metz
— the Ostrogoth, 6, 28 and nn. 3 and 5, 38, 39, 94, 113, 140 n. 6, 145, 147, 151 n. 2, see DIETRICH (1)
Þether, 24, 29, 100, 115, 146, 147 n. 2, see DIETHÊR (1)
Þetleifr, 5, 13, 24–5, 29, 70, 84 n. 2, 93, 136, 150, see DIETLEIP
Þetmarr, 25, 29 n. 1, 76, see DIETMÂR (1)
ÞiaurikR, 28 n. 4, see DIETRICH (1)
Þiðrekr, son of Þetmarr, 4, 5, 6, 7, 13, 20, 24, 25, 27 n. 10, 29 and nn. 1–2 and 7, 30, 31, 32 and n. 1, 33, 34 36, 38, 42, 44, 45, 53, 55, 56, 57, 59 and n. 9, 60, 65 and n. 6, 66, 70, 74, 76, 77–8, 81, 86, 89 n. 8, 94–5, 96, 101, 110 n. 2, 111, 115, 117, 121 and n. 7, 127, 133, 136 and n. 6, 140 n. 6, 144, 146 and n. 10, 147 n. 2, 148, 149 n. 3, 150, 152, 153, see DIETRICH (1)
— son of Valldemarr, 29, 31, 33 n. 1, 66, 108, see DIETRICH (2)
— Osanctrix's incognito, 31, 103, see DIETRICH (3)
Þjóðmarr, 25, see DIETMÂR (1)
Þióðrekr, 20, 21, 25, 29, 66, see DIETRICH (1)
Þórgeirr, 78 n. 7
Thrafstila, 32
Thuringians, 32, 46, 85–6, see DÜRINGEN
Thürss, 65
Tídrikur, 25, 29 n. 5, 60, see DIETRICH (1)
Tristan, hero of romance, 95, 149 n. 7
Tristram, brother of Herburt (Þs), 69
Tufa, 30, 147 n. 3

Ugri, see Hungarians
Ulff van Iern, 152, see WOLFHART
Ulfrað, 44, 108, 152, see WOLFHART
Unferð, 9 n. 3
Urajas, 16 n. 5, 122 n. 5
Uriah, 117 n. 2
Uta von Calw, 132 n. 4

Vaði, 133, 138–9, 142, see WATE
Valamer, 25, 30 n. 3, 42, 43
Valdarr, 137
Valdarus, Langobard King, 136
Valentinian III, 42, 67 n. 1

Valldemarr, 29, 31, 33 n. 1, 66, 70, 84, 108, 152, see Vladimir
Valtari, 25, 59, 79, 108, 136 n. 9, 144, see WALTHER
Vandals, 30, 55 and n. 11, 63 n. 3, 85
Velent, 71, 94, 115, 133, 139, 142 and nn. 5 and 8, 143 nn. 3 and 5, 145–6, see WIELANT
Veletabi, see Wilzi
Venedi (Venethi), see Wends
Verland, 142, see WIELANT
Viderick, 95, 115, 142, 146 nn. 5–6 and 13, 149 n. 3, see WITEGE
Viðga, 6, 9, 24, 29, 38, 40, 44, 56, 63, 65, 66, 71, 76, 81, 94, 96 n. 1, 99, 100, 108, 112 n. 1, 115, 121, 126 n. 8, 127, 129, 140 n. 6, 142, 143 and n. 3, 144, 145, 146 nn. 3–5 and 10, 148, 150, see WITEGE
Vidigoia (*Widigōja), 66 n. 1, 146, 147 and n. 1, see WITEGE
Vidimer, 25, 42
Viðolfr, 7, 32, 99, 103, 144, 146, 148 and n. 1, see WITOLT
Vikings, 22, 64 n. 1, 123
Vildimælrikr, Þetleifr's incognito, 5, 25
Vildiver, 32, 44, 103 n. 4, 136 and n. 9, 144 and nn. 3–5 and 7, 146, 148
Vilkus, 146 n. 1
Villcinus, 133, 138, 144, 147
Vingi, 35, 58 n. 9, 137–8
Virga, 145, 146 n. 13, see WITEGE
Virgar, 95, 115 n. 4, 142, 146 nn. 1 and 13, see WITEGE
Visconti, 107 n. 4
Visigoths, 5, 14, 16, 30, 42, 77, 122, 137 n. 5, 147 n. 3
Vitigis, 24, 147
Vizleo, Vildiver's incognito, 144–5, see WISSELAU
Vladimir, Prince of Kiev, 84
Vócaček, 43
Volcae, 135
Völsungar, 9 n. 1, 139, see WELSUNC
Völsungr, 125 and n. 3, 139 and n. 5, see WELSUNC
Völundr, 70–1, 91, 141–2, 143 nn. 3–4, see WIELANT
Vridelo, 47, 62, see FRÎTELE
Vulcan, 143

Wada, 61, 138 and n. 8, 139 n. 1, see WATE
Wade, 76 and n. 1, 138 and n. 10, see WATE
Wæls, 125, 139
Wælsing, 139, see WELSUNC
Walczerz, 79, 136 and n. 9, 144 n. 6, see WALTHER
Waldemar I, King of Denmark, 90
Waldere, 5, 28 n. 5, 41, 54, 59 and n. 1, 79, 94, 136 and n. 3, 141, see WALTHER
Walther, Bishop of Langres, 135 n. 4
— von der Vogelweide, 78, 136

# INDEX

Wasichenstein, 137 n. 3
Wēland (Wēlund), 70, 94, 136, 141 and nn. 4–6, 143, 145, *see* WIELANT
Welsh, 73, 100
Wends (Venedi, Venethi, Winida), 39, 144 and n. 2, *see* WINDISCH
Wenzel I, King of Bohemia, 148, *see* WITZLÂN (1)
— II, King of Bohemia, 140, *see* WENEZLÂN
Werne, 12
Wideke, 30, 95, 133, 146 and nn. 8 and 10, *see* WITEGE
Widia, 28, 70, 94, 141, 145, 146, *see* WITEGE
Widie, 65, *see* WITEGE
*Widigōja, *see* Vidigoia
Wīdsīð, 38, 79
Wilde Jäger, der; Wilde Jagd, 30 n. 1, 33 n. 4, 44, 63 and n. 5, 154 and n. 1
Wilzi (Veletabi, Wilti), 66, 70 and n. 4, 108, 111, 144, *see* WILZEN

Wislaw, 79, 136 and n. 9, 144 n. 6, *see* WISSELAU
Witta, 61, 138, 139 n. 1
Wittelsbach, 36, 102 n. 6
Woden, 26 n. 2, 44 n. 2, 63 and n. 4, 139 n. 1, *see also* Óðinn
Wolfger, Bishop of Passau, 105
Wudga, 38, 47, 65, 145, 146, 147, *see* WITEGE
Wuffingas, 153 n. 5
Wulf, 103 n. 9
Wulfingas, 153
Wuotan, 63 (wuotes heer), 139 n. 1, *see* Woden
Wylfingas, *see* Wulfingas

Ylfingar, 153

Zacharias, Pope, 154
Zekeria, ruler of Tunis, 154
Zeus, 143